S0-AHM-118

GREENE ON GREENS

GREENE ON GREENS

BERT GREENE

ILLUSTRATIONS BY NORMAN GREEN

Workman Publishing, New York

Dedication

This book is for my late parents, Paula and Sam Greene, both of whom would, I suspect, have been proud to lend their name to its title.

More pertinently, it is also for my sister, Myra, the true-bluest of all the Greenes. A very small measure of my appreciation for a lifetime of friendship that would be hard to match, in or out of the family.

Published simultaneously in Canada
by Saunders of Toronto, Inc.

Library of Congress Cataloging in Publication Data

Greene, Bert
Greene on greens.

Includes index.
1. Cookery (Vegetables) I. Title.
TX801.G724 1984 641.6'5 83-40538
ISBN 0-89480-659-9
ISBN 0-89480-758-7 (cl.)

Art director: Paul Hanson
Designer: Julienne McNeer
Cover and book illustrations: Norman Green

Workman Publishing Company, Inc.
1 West 39 Street
New York, NY 10018

Manufactured in the United States of America

CONTENTS

Author's Note

No tome as weighty as this is the result of one person's effort alone. *Greene on Greens* would never have sprouted (or bloomed in earnest) without the constant ministrations of Phillip Stephen Schulz. More than a mere colleague in this three-year project, Phillip was the book's avid recipe collector, historical footnoter, and culinary guru—and I salute all of his efforts in its behalf with extreme gratitude.

Thanks are also in order to Judy Blahnik, my good friend and cooking associate, who tested and retested most of the recipes with unflagging good humor and endless enthusiasm even when her efforts were met with a decidedly down-thrust thumb. Judy's sage wisdom, optimism, and good judgment prevailed in this book and I credit her for sustenance as well.

A special note of gratitude must also be extended to my fine editor, Suzanne Rafer, whose vision and endless perseverance gave each chapter its final form. Also, for their fine work on the book, thanks go to Kathie Ness and Julienne McNeer.

There are many, many attributions in *Greene on Greens* to friends and well-wishers who generously donated recipes, but some special acknowledgment must be made to several favorite old cookbooks that were often a source of inspiration. Notable are Narcissa and Narcisse Chamberlain's *The Flavor of France* and *The Flavor of Italy*, Dagmar Freuchen's *Cookbook of the Seven Seas*, and a lovely collection by Mildred O. Knopf, *Cook My Darling Daughter*.

A GARLAND OF GREENE

This book is actually a love letter to the thirty or so vegetables, green and otherwise, that I prize most in all the world.

More than a recipe collection, it is a garland of Greene's gossip, garden advice, culinary trivia, and shopping wisdom, well tossed with, I hope, a measure of stove-top logic. In fact, it contains all the savvy that I have managed to acquire over several decades of cooking vegetables without foregoing the pleasures of either meat or fish. For while I dearly love vegetables, I am certainly no vegetarian.

Like most of a generation born between the years of boom and crash, I grew up in something of a gastronomic vacuum. Ours was strictly a meat-and-potatoes household. Vegetables came to the table as a matter of course, but mostly as spongy counterfeits of nature: served up straight from the can or else swimming in pools of water. To me, consuming these greens was a penance rather than a pleasure and I ate all garden produce grudgingly, never for a moment convinced that a dreaded forkful of canned spinach would provide me with the requirements of pep, punch, and pluck that Popeye and my elders predicted it would.

Today, from the vantage point of long distance, I have decided that prior to World War II, most cooks in America must have either nurtured grave suspicions about the bacteria inherent in fresh vegetables or just downright hated them. Why else would they have punished the produce with such assiduous overcooking? I realize there were, even then, a few vitamin zealots around who ate their vegetables nearly raw. But by and large, that slim cadre was considered to be part of the lunatic fringe—adjudged almost as quirky as folks who dunked their bodies in the surf in January or (heaven forfend) slept in the nude!

As a tad in the kitchen, I was instructed that cauliflower was to be boiled for one hour, and string beans, broccoli, asparagus, and cabbage not less than half that duration. They were never drained from the kettle until the cooking liquid had turned as green as Tintex dye, while the poor veggie was a heck of a lot paler—not to mention devitaminized—in the process.

I cannot rightly recollect when I learned to cook a vegetable properly, that is to say with respect for its inalienable bite. But I suspect the conversion took place between the summer I planted my first grown-up vegetable garden in the late 1950s and the opening of The Store in Amagansett half a dozen years later. As innovators of what is now called "carry-out cuisine," my partners and I realized early on that what made a cooked-vegetable salad irresistible was its crunch. What caused the crunch was very abbreviated cooking time plus the freshest of ingredients. Working close to the cornucopia of produce that the South Fork of Long Island offers all summer long made it easy to prepare vegetables well—and we did! Almost twenty years later, nothing in the kitchen elicits a more immediate response from this cook than a still life of fresh, crisp greenery. And I cannot wait to get my hands on those glittering spoils as they tumble from a garden basket (or a shopping bag, for that matter) to turn them into a soup, casserole, soufflé, bread, relish, and yes, even a cake or sorbet on occasion.

For a long, long while I wanted to write down a grand accumulation of recipes for the vegetables I love. Every one of them appears in this book—accompanied by tales of my vegetable connections (some thorny as artichokes, others silky as nubile zucchini). They are highly personal memoirs, and inspired, I must admit, by the maxim of yet another vegetable lover, Popeye, who summed up his philosophy in one pithy sentence: "I yam what I yam!" Me too.

With that out of the way, have a big helping of Greene on greens.

ARTICHOKES

Sublime from Leaf to Heart

Artichokes are actually thistle-like stalks nipped in the bud, but sweeter by far with a dab of hollandaise than any purple posies picked in my backyard.

Savants claim that the word "artichoke" itself is a culinary hybrid. The true moniker for this thorny bite of green stuff is said to be cooked up from two Middle English words: *hortus* and *chokt*, literally meaning "a garden strangler." And from the smattering of knowledge that I have picked up about the cultivation of artichokes, there is considerable substance to that description. For the roots of the globe artichoke *(Cynara scolymus)* grow like weeds in the right climate and must be restrained from taking over a garden by some very assiduous surgery.

To tell the truth, I have never attempted to grow an artichoke. They grew wild on a mountainside in Eze (overlooking the Mediterranean) where I lived for a happy autumn, and just attempting to pick them for dinner left my hands bloody and my pot empty; they are well-rooted plants and very prickly into the bargain.

The artichoke, like the oyster, is a food that makes an indelible impression on the untried tongue. Ask me when and where I lost my gastronomic virginity and I will read you chapter and verse.

It was on March 15, 1946. I remember

that date precisely, because the dinner at which I consumed my first artichoke took place six months to the day after the Japanese forces surrendered in the Pacific and World War II came to an end.

The meal was a postponed celebration, given by a well-known writer and his wife in whose company I had observed the original event on a beach at Provincetown. As bells rang out the news and U.S. Coast Guard cutters sent trajectories of orange flares into the summer sky, victory was celebrated, as appropriately as possible in wartime Massachusetts, with warm domestic champagne and even warmer tears. But a valedictory feast, it was agreed, should not be undertaken until the smoke of armistice had truly cleared.

Perhaps the memorable occasion of that delayed celebration still stands out with such clarity because peace seemed a good deal more tenuous that night than it had in September. The Russians, formerly our allies, had in six months' time become our virtual enemies and the world appeared, if anything, less tranquil and more unsettled than ever before.

The meal took place in an elegant dining room high above Central Park. There were perhaps a dozen guests at the table, but I was the youngest by far (barely out of my teens) and little used to the ministrations of uniformed waiters who quietly served and removed plates at the barest summons of the hostess' bell.

What stands out in my memory, almost forty years later, is my utter trepidation at the approach of each successive dish. Though I had been instructed by my parents that a diner begins his meal with the first (farthest) fork on the left and proceeds inward, no memory of this injunction guided my etiquette that day. Instead I sat transfixed at my place, waiting an eternity, it seemed, until my table partners ended their conversation and attacked the first course: *artichokes!*

As the correct utensil for eating an artichoke is the fingers, the shock was mesmerizing. Served my portion with a small bowl of warm hollandaise, I could not perceive (even at close scrutiny) what joy was to be obtained by sloshing a leaf in the liquid and then apparently only wetting one's tongue with it. However, that experience, once tried, altered my culinary perceptions forever.

I must have praised that first course extravagantly, for the table partner on my right raised an eyebrow. Pushing her untouched artichoke in my direction, she exchanged plates so discreetly that neither our hostess nor any other guest was aware of the transaction. But I could not resist a question. Why?

She smiled sweetly at the empty plate before her. "I was born in Castroville," she said. "It's a small town in Northern California that some people call the artichoke capital of the world. My father grew nothing but artichokes on his farm and I ate them every day of my life until I got out of there."

My table companion was a very attractive blond and despite her forthrightness was so soft-spoken no one else heard a word. "I'd rather eat a rattlesnake than an artichoke," she murmured. "And come to think of it, I have!"

Nothing she said cooled my ardor, for I finished her portion as well. I do not remember another dish of the meal. But the first sublimely nutty flavor of that leaf I will not forget until my last breath is taken.

Vegetable Roots

The Greeks had a rather uncomplimentary word for artichokes. Noting a similarity between the plant's petals and a canine's incisor, they dubbed the green *kinara kyon*, or "the tooth of a dog." Greeks boiled their artichokes in a mix-

Artichokes have certainly had their detractors. Supporters, too. Pliny the Elder declared them "the most monstrous production of the earth." However, Catherine de Medici, who introduced this vegetable to France in the sixteenth century, so doted on them that she often fainted from overconsumption.

ture of wine and water and sometimes drank the brew as a restorative after a night on the town—presaging the notion of "hair of the dog" as well! The Romans altered the spelling after they inherited the artichoke as part of their victory spoils at Magnesia in 190 B.C. Insisting that the vegetable was misnamed, they rechristened it *cinara*, "ashes," in honor of its gray-green appearance. To compound the error they also roasted artichokes on open fires, like potatoes, peeling off the outer leaves when they were completely charred and consuming only the smoky hearts. No wonder artichokes went out of style for the next ten centuries!

At the end of the Middle Ages, according to food historian John Evelyn, the artichoke did have a slight revival, but not as a food. One ancient cookbook describes its usage plainly: "If when the pithe and pare be taken away, the roote bee boiled in wine and dronken, it is good against the ranke smell of armeholes."

What to Look For

When selecting an artichoke, look for the brightest, greenest globes you can find. Avoid specimens obviously past their prime, with mottled leaves or shriveled cones that are splayed open. The sweetest artichokes usually have compact heads and bottom leaves that break off with a decided snap between a shopper's thumb and forefinger. Winter is a critical period for artichokes and an unseasonal frost may cause the outer leaves to bronze. These artichokes are known as "Winter Kist" varieties and their outward appearance has nothing to do with their tender hearts, although it does tend to discourage a chef somewhat. Small (baby) artichokes, usually found in summer, are harvested before the prickly choke matures and are sweet and succulent enough to be served raw or barely blanched. Large globes are the best choice for serious artichoke eaters since they have ideal cavities for stuffing.

Artichokes have the special virtue of being rather low in calories. One medium-size cooked artichoke, weighing about ½ pound, usually totals between 10 and 50 calories, depending on its freshness. (Young artichokes have the lowest calorie count.) In addition, artichokes are chock-full of calcium, phosphorus, potassium, and *sodium*. So if you're trying to cut down on salt, you might want to eliminate it altogether in these recipes.

Preparation

For weeks after that fateful dinner I ate artichokes in some form or other at almost every meal. One slight obstacle sullied my passion for this unusual vegetable, however. No one had ever told me how to properly cook an artichoke. More to the point, I had no clue whatsoever that the purplish-yellow fuzz at the base of the inner leaves had to be removed before an artichoke was considered tableworthy. Consequently my dinner guests (with all those artichokes there *had* to be guests, you know) usually coughed or gagged through my entire repertoire, bravely spitting out bits of fiber as they murmured, "*Delicious*, Bert!"

What took me so long to learn I will pass on to you first thing. Some cooks prefer to remove the choke after an artichoke is cooked, but I find that scraping it beforehand lessens any possible damage to the artichoke's delectable heart.

1. Using a sharp knife, trim off the stem so the artichoke rests firmly on its bottom and does not topple over.

2. Using a serrated knife, cut 1 inch off the top of the artichoke. Rub the cut surfaces with half a lemon to prevent discoloration.

3. Pull off any small or coarse leaves at the base. Using a kitchen shears or scissors, trim the sharp pointed tips off the remaining leaves.

4. Hold the trimmed artichoke under cold running water until the leaves separate. Using your fingers, gently pull out the purple-tipped prickly leaves in the center of the artichoke. Then, using a small teaspoon, scrape out the hairy choke. Sprinkle the exposed artichoke bottom with a little lemon juice and press the cone of leaves closed. *Voilà*—the artichoke is ready for the saucepan.

My favored way to cook an artichoke is to poach it in simmering water, but many enthusiasts steam them, in either a steamer or a colander placed over simmering water. Cooking time varies with the size and freshness of the artichoke at hand, but my rule of thumb is about 15 to 20 minutes. You know that an artichoke is done when the leaves pull off easily and the heart is tender when pricked with a knife. (Never use aluminum, iron, or carbon steel to cut or poke an artichoke. These base metals blacken the vegetable's surface and, even worse, leave an unpleasant metallic taste.)

POACHED ARTICHOKES

A classic way to prepare artichokes, followed by two unrivaled accompaniments.

4 medium artichokes, trimmed, chokes removed
Juice of 1 lemon
1½ tablespoons red wine vinegar
10 peppercorns, tied in a cheesecloth bag
½ teaspoon salt

1. Place the artichokes, tips up, in a large saucepan. Add cold water to cover, then the remaining ingredients. Heat to boiling; reduce the heat. Simmer, covered, until tender, 15 to 20 minutes.

2. Remove the artichokes and drain them upside-down in a colander. If you are serving them warm, reheat in a warm oven, loosely covered with aluminum foil. If serving them cold, chill, covered, several hours in the refrigerator.

3. Serve with Mayonnaise or Fail-Safe Hollandaise sauce (see pages 408–409), or one of the sauces below.

Serves 4.

Cold Anchovy Sauce

Here is a variation on the classic mayonnaise sauce for artichokes.

1 egg yolk
1½ teaspoons Dijon mustard
1½ teaspoons anchovy paste
Juice of ½ lemon
1½ cups oil (use 1 cup vegetable and ½ cup olive)
1 teaspoon red wine vinegar

Whisk the egg yolk with the mus-

tard, anchovy paste, and lemon juice in a medium bowl until smooth. Slowly beat in the oil, a few drops at a time, until incorporated. Stir in the vinegar.

Makes about 1½ cups.

Cobbled Crab Dressing

A somewhat richer accessory to a cold artichoke felicitously combines mayonnaise with sour cream and cooked crab.

2 teaspoons minced shallots
½ cup cooked crabmeat
1 cup Mayonnaise (see page 408)
½ cup sour cream
1 teaspoon lime juice
Dash of hot pepper sauce
⅓ cup chopped fresh dill
Salt and freshly ground black pepper

Combine the shallots, crabmeat, mayonnaise, sour cream, lime juice, and hot pepper sauce in a large bowl. Mix well. Add the fresh dill, and salt and pepper to taste. Chill thoroughly before serving.

Makes about 1½ cups.

ARTICHOKE AND COLD MEAT SALAD

A culinary invention (not quite a chef's salad) was composed in my own kitchen recently. It combines artichoke hearts with raw mushrooms, slivers of cheese, and any leftover meat in the refrigerator.

1 package (9 ounces) frozen artichoke hearts
¼ pound mushrooms, sliced (about 1 cup)
¼ pound Monterey jack cheese, cut into thin strips 1½ inches long (about ½ cup)
6 to 7 ounces leftover roast beef, ham, chicken, turkey, or tongue, cut into strips (about 1 cup)
1 large scallion, bulb and green top, minced
1 small clove garlic, minced
¼ teaspoon salt
1 teaspoon Dijon mustard
Juice of ½ lime
⅓ cup olive oil
1 tablespoon sour cream
1 teaspoon red wine vinegar
Salt and freshly ground black pepper

1. Cook the artichoke hearts in boiling salted water until tender, 5 to 8 minutes. Drain. Cool.

2. Combine the artichokes with the mushrooms, cheese, meat, and scallion in a large bowl.

3. Mash the garlic with the ¼ teaspoon salt in a small bowl. Stir in the remaining ingredients. Pour this dressing over the salad and toss well. Add salt and pepper to taste. Serve at room temperature or slightly chilled.

Serves 4.

ALICE B. TOKLAS' ARTICHOKE PUREE

Ms. Toklas served this cold, but I prefer it hot.

4 medium artichokes, trimmed
1 lemon, halved
4 tablespoons (½ stick) unsalted butter
4 cups Chicken Stock (see page 410)
1½ cups water
2 medium potatoes, peeled, thickly sliced
Salt and freshly ground black pepper

1. Wash the artichokes well, and cut each one in quarters vertically. Remove the chokes, rubbing all cut edges with half the lemon.

2. Melt the butter in a medium saucepan over low heat. Add the artichoke quarters; toss well to coat each piece with butter. Add the chicken stock and water. Heat to boiling; reduce the heat. Simmer, covered, 25 minutes.

3. Add the potatoes to the saucepan. Cook, covered, about 20 minutes longer, until the potatoes are tender. With a slotted spoon, remove the artichokes to one bowl and the pieces of potato to another. Strain and reserve the cooking liquid.

4. Using a spoon, scrape all edible parts from each artichoke, including the edible part of each leaf. Add this to the potatoes.

5. Place half the artichoke-potato mixture in a blender or processor; add half the reserved liquid. Purée until smooth. Transfer to a saucepan. Repeat with the remaining artichokes, potatoes, and liquid.

6. Stir the juice from the remaining half lemon into the purée. Cook over low heat, stirring occasionally, until warmed through. Season with salt and pepper to taste.

Serves 6.

CAJUN ARTICHOKES AND SPINACH

In the Cajun country of Louisiana, the artichoke takes an unusual partner, spinach, and an even more exotic seasoning, anise liqueur.

2 pounds spinach, washed, trimmed
1 package (9 ounces) frozen artichoke hearts
4 slices bacon
1 small onion, finely chopped
1 tablespoon all-purpose flour
1 clove garlic, minced
3 whole scallions, bulbs and green tops, finely chopped
½ cup heavy or whipping cream
Dash of hot pepper sauce
Salt and freshly ground black pepper
2 teaspoons Pernod or other anise-base liqueur
2 tablespoons unsalted butter
¼ cup fine fresh bread crumbs

1. Preheat the oven to 400°F. Cook the spinach in boiling salted water until just barely tender, about 2 minutes. Drain thoroughly; roughly chop.

2. Cook the artichoke hearts in boiling salted water for 5 minutes. Drain.

3. Sauté the bacon in a large heavy

skillet until crisp. Drain on paper towels. Crumble and reserve.

4. Pour off all but 1 tablespoon bacon fat from the skillet. Stir in the onion and flour, and cook, stirring constantly, over low heat for 3 minutes. Add the garlic and scallions. Stir in the cream. Cook until the mixture is slightly thickened, about 5 minutes.

5. Add the spinach, artichoke hearts, and bacon to the skillet. Toss well. Add the hot pepper sauce, salt and pepper to taste, and the Pernod. Transfer the mixture to a buttered baking dish.

6. Melt the butter in a small skillet over medium heat. Stir in the bread crumbs. Cook, stirring constantly, until golden. Spoon over the vegetables. Bake until golden brown and bubbly, about 20 minutes.

Serves 6.

ARTICHOKE AND POTATO CASSEROLE

In Spain potatoes, artichokes, and black olives appear in myriad local dishes. The best, a kind of variation on *patatas pobres* ("poor man's potatoes"), finds them baked together in a casserole.

1 package (9 ounces) frozen artichoke hearts
3 tablespoons unsalted butter
2 tablespoons olive oil
1 medium onion, thinly sliced
3 medium potatoes, peeled, thinly sliced
1 clove garlic, bruised
½ cup sliced black olives
Salt and freshly ground black pepper
½ cup freshly grated Parmesan cheese

1. Preheat the oven to 400°F. Cook the artichoke hearts in boiling salted water for 5 minutes. Drain, and cut into thin slices.

2. Heat 1 tablespoon of the butter with the olive oil in a large heavy skillet over medium heat. Sauté the onion slices until golden; reduce the heat.

3. Add the potatoes to the skillet and toss to coat them well. Toss in the artichoke hearts; remove from the heat.

4. Rub a large 2-inch-deep ovenproof baking dish with the bruised garlic. Spread the vegetable mixture over the bottom of the dish. Lay the olive slices over the mixture. Sprinkle with salt and pepper to taste. Dot the top with the remaining 2 tablespoons butter.

5. Bake 15 minutes. Remove from the oven, stir well, and continue to bake until the potatoes are tender, about 15 minutes longer. Sprinkle the top with cheese and bake until golden, an additional 5 to 10 minutes. Let stand a few minutes before serving.

Serves 6.

In Italy, where the artichoke is known as *carciofo*, old women at the market stalls usually rub two together before they make a selection for their shopping bags. If the artichokes make a proper little squeak on contact, they are deemed fresh. If they are *muto* (silent), the ladies simply pass them by.

CARCIOFI ALLA GIUDEA

(Fried Baby Artichokes)

The most famous of all Italian artichoke recipes was discovered in Rome's Jewish ghetto about a hundred years ago. I prefer it when the dish is made with tiny baby artichokes in late summer; but it is equally delicious year round with any size globes, particularly when paired with broiled meats or other vegetable dishes.

12 baby artichokes, or 4 medium
1 lemon, halved
Vegetable oil for frying
4 cloves garlic
Salt

1. If using baby artichokes, cut off the stems, rubbing cut surfaces with lemon. If using larger artichokes, trim off the stems and pull off the tough outer leaves, leaving only the pale interior ones. Remove the chokes, and rub all cut surfaces with lemon.

2. Place the artichokes, one at a time, upside-down on a flat surface. Push down on each artichoke to slightly flatten the tops.

3. Pour oil into a heavy saucepan to a depth of about 1 inch. Heat the oil and add the garlic. When the oil is very hot, add the artichokes, tops down. Using a small lid, press down on the artichokes to flatten the tops. Cook, pressing constantly, until golden, 8 to 10 minutes. Turn the artichokes over and continue to cook until tender, 3 to 4 minutes longer. Baby artichokes will take slightly less time. Drain on paper towels. Sprinkle with salt to taste.

Serves 4.

BRAISED ARTICHOKES WITH PEAS

Peas and artichokes braised together is an old Sicilian peasant dish. They cook it for hours, but I do not.

1 package (9 ounces) frozen artichoke hearts
3 tablespoons unsalted butter
2 tablespoons olive oil
1 small onion, finely chopped
1 small clove garlic, minced
½ cup chopped Black Forest ham or ¼ cup chopped prosciutto
½ cup Chicken Stock (see page 410)
Pinch of sugar
2 cups shelled fresh peas, or 1 package (10 ounces) frozen
Salt and freshly ground black pepper
2 tablespoons minced fresh parsley

1. Cook the artichoke hearts in boiling salted water for 5 minutes. Drain.

2. Heat the butter with the oil in a large heavy skillet over medium-low heat. Stir in the onion and cook 2 minutes. Add the garlic; cook 2 minutes longer. Add the ham and artichoke hearts. Toss to coat well with the butter. Add the chicken stock and sugar. Simmer, covered, 10 minutes. Stir in the peas. Simmer, covered, 5 minutes longer.

3. Raise the heat slightly and remove the cover. Continue to cook, tossing occasionally, until the vegetables are tender and most of the liquid has evaporated. Add salt and pepper to taste. Sprinkle with parsley.

Serves 4.

ARTICHOKE RISOTTO

An unusual vegetable dish from Portugal pairs artichoke hearts, tomatoes, and rice in a sensuous meld of flavorings.

1 package (9 ounces) frozen artichoke hearts
3 tablespoons unsalted butter
2 tablespoons olive oil
1 small onion, finely chopped
1 small clove garlic, minced
2 teaspoons chopped fresh basil, or ½ teaspoon dried
1 large tomato, peeled, seeded, chopped
2 cups hot Chicken Stock (see page 410)
1 cup long-grain rice
½ teaspoon salt
¼ teaspoon freshly ground black pepper
Chopped fresh parsley
Freshly grated Parmesan cheese

1. Cook the artichoke hearts in boiling salted water for 5 minutes. Drain.

2. Heat 1 tablespoon of the butter with the olive oil in a small saucepan over medium-low heat. Stir in the onion; cook 2 minutes. Stir in the garlic, basil, tomato, and ½ cup of the chicken stock. Heat to boiling; reduce the heat. Simmer, uncovered, 10 minutes. Remove from the heat.

3. Heat the remaining 2 tablespoons butter in a heavy 4-quart pot or Dutch oven over medium-low heat. Stir in the rice and cook, stirring constantly, until the rice is transparent. Stir in the tomato mixture, 1 cup of the chicken stock, and the salt and pepper. Heat to boiling; reduce the heat. Simmer, covered, 10 minutes.

4. Stir the artichoke hearts and remaining ½ cup chicken stock into the rice mixture. Continue to cook, covered, until the rice is tender, about 8 minutes longer. If the rice seems too wet, raise the heat slightly and cook uncovered until the liquid is absorbed. Sprinkle with parsley; pass the Parmesan cheese.

Serves 6.

ARTICHOKE PASTA

This pale pasta (perhaps the most delicate ever nibbled) can be used to make lasagne, fettuccine, or any pasta shape desired. It was invented by my friend Jan Weimer. Serve with heavy cream that you have reduced slightly and freshly grated Parmesan cheese, Creamy Tomato Sauce (see page 375), or simply mushrooms sautéed in browned butter.

1 large artichoke, trimmed
½ lemon
2 tablespoons unsalted butter
1 cup Chicken Stock (see page 410)
2 cups all-purpose flour
½ teaspoon salt
2 eggs, lightly beaten

1. Wash the artichoke well. Cut into quarters vertically. Remove the choke, rubbing all cut surfaces with lemon.

2. Melt the butter in a small saucepan over low heat. Add the artichoke pieces; toss well to coat with butter. Add the chicken stock. Heat to boiling; reduce the heat. Simmer, covered, 40 minutes. Drain thoroughly.

3. Using a spoon, scrape all edible parts from the artichoke, including the edible part of each leaf.

4. Place the artichoke pulp, 1¾ cups of the flour, and the salt in the container of a food processor fitted with a steel blade. Purée until the mixture is smooth. With the motor running, add the eggs and process until the mixture begins to form a soft dough.

5. Transfer the dough to a lightly floured board. Knead by hand for 10 minutes, working in more flour as needed to make a smooth dough. Let stand, covered, 20 minutes; then roll to desired shape by hand or with a pasta machine.

Makes about ¾ pound.

HEARTY ARTICHOKE TART

Martha Washington's favorite recipe was said to be a "Harty Choke Pie." The following tart is based on that invention—and crammed with cheese, ham, and artichokes.

Short Crust Pastry (see page 412)
*3 medium artichokes**
1 lemon, halved
1 tablespoon red wine vinegar
5 peppercorns, tied in a cheesecloth bag
½ teaspoon salt
Juice of ½ lemon
1 tablespoon unsalted butter
1 shallot, minced
½ cup finely diced cooked ham
2 teaspoons Madeira
¼ cup freshly grated Parmesan cheese
¼ pound Fontina cheese, diced
¼ pound mozzarella cheese, diced
½ cup heavy or whipping cream
Salt and freshly ground black pepper

1. Make the Short Crust Pastry and set aside.

2. Preheat the oven to 375°F. Cut the stems from the artichokes, rubbing cut surfaces with half a lemon. Pull off the tough outer leaves, leaving only the pale interior ones. Cut the artichokes in half vertically and then in thirds vertically. Remove the chokes. Rub cut surfaces with lemon.

3. Place the artichoke pieces in a medium saucepan with cold water to cover. Add the vinegar, peppercorns, salt, and lemon juice. Heat to boiling; reduce the heat. Simmer, covered, until tender, about 10 minutes. Drain.

4. Melt the butter in a small skillet. Add the shallot and sauté it lightly. Stir in the ham and Madeira. Cook over medium heat until the ham is lightly browned and all liquid has evaporated. Cool.

5. Line a buttered 10-inch loose-bottom tart pan with the pastry. Trim.

Sprinkle the ham over the bottom of the crust, and arrange the artichokes over the ham. Add the cheeses, then pour the cream over the top. Sprinkle with salt and pepper to taste. Bake until golden, about 40 minutes. Let stand 10 minutes before serving.

Serves 6.

*Frozen artichoke hearts may be substituted for fresh. Use one 9-ounce package cooked in ¼ cup boiling salted water until tender, about 5 minutes.

CARCIOFI RIPIENI

(Artichokes Stuffed with Sausage)

This superlative recipe (stuffed artichokes crammed with savory herbs and bits of sausage) was a gift from an Italian acquaintance. Serve it as an appetizer, or as a luncheon dish with buttered pasta on the side.

4 large artichokes, trimmed, chokes removed
4 sweet Italian sausages
1 teaspoon vegetable oil
1 cup fresh bread crumbs
1 clove garlic, minced
3 tablespoons minced fresh parsley
Pinch of dried oregano
Pinch of dried thyme
2 eggs, lightly beaten
¼ cup milk
Salt and freshly ground black pepper
1 can (8 ounces) imported plum tomatoes, drained
1½ tablespoons olive oil
Boiling water
2 whole cloves garlic
2 teaspoons unsalted butter

1. Prepare the artichokes for cooking, but do not press the leaves back together.

2. Remove the sausages from their casing. Rub a heavy skillet with 1 teaspoon oil. Place the skillet over medium heat; add the sausage, breaking up the lumps with a fork. Continue to cook, stirring constantly, until lightly browned. Drain on paper towels, and transfer to a large bowl.

3. Add the bread crumbs, minced garlic, 2 tablespoons of the minced parsley, the oregano, thyme, eggs, and milk to the sausage. Mix thoroughly. Season with salt and pepper to taste.

4. Divide the filling into four equal portions. Stuff the artichokes with filling, starting with the centers, then stuffing between the leaves, pushing the stuffing down as it is added. Press the artichokes closed and tie them around the centers with string.

5. Mash the tomatoes with a fork, and spoon some over the top of each artichoke.

6. Place the artichokes in a large saucepan. Add the oil to the pan with enough boiling water to come 1 inch up the sides of artichokes. Add the whole garlic cloves to the pan. Return to boiling; reduce the heat. Simmer, covered, until tender, 30 to 35 minutes.

7. Remove the artichokes from the liquid. Drain them briefly and transfer to a serving platter. Remove the strings. Dot each artichoke with ½ teaspoon butter and sprinkle with the remaining parsley.

Serves 4.

ITALIAN OMELET WITH ARTICHOKE AND CRAB

This excellent Italian *frittata* (open-faced omelet) combines artichoke hearts and crab in a velvety amalgam that is both irresistible and expeditious. Cooking time: 15 minutes.

*3 medium artichokes**
1 lemon, halved
1 tablespoon red wine vinegar
5 peppercorns, tied in a cheesecloth bag
½ teaspoon salt
Juice of ½ lemon
4 tablespoons (½ stick) unsalted butter
1 teaspoon olive oil
1 small onion, chopped
1 clove garlic, minced
½ red bell pepper, seeded, chopped
½ cup cooked crabmeat
3 tablespoons chopped fresh parsley
5 eggs
2 tablespoons freshly grated Parmesan cheese

1. Cut the stems from the artichokes, rubbing cut surfaces with half a lemon. Pull off the tough outer leaves, leaving only the pale interior ones. Cut the artichokes in half vertically and then in thirds vertically. Remove the chokes. Rub cut surfaces with lemon.

2. Place the artichoke pieces in a medium saucepan with cold water to cover. Add the vinegar, peppercorns, salt, and lemon juice. Heat to boiling; reduce the heat. Simmer, covered, until tender, about 10 minutes. Drain.

3. Heat 2 tablespoons of the butter with the oil in a 10-inch cast-iron skillet. Stir in the onion; cook 2 minutes. Stir in the garlic and red pepper; cook, uncovered, 8 minutes longer. Add the drained artichoke hearts and the crabmeat and parsley. Toss well. Remove from the heat.

4. Beat the eggs in a large bowl until light. Stir in the artichoke-crab mixture.

5. Preheat the broiling unit. Wipe out the skillet and heat the remaining 2 tablespoons butter over medium heat. When the foam subsides, pour in the egg mixture, spreading it evenly in the skillet. Immediately reduce the heat to low. Cook, uncovered, without stirring for 12 minutes. Sprinkle the top with the cheese and place the skillet under the broiler to lightly brown the top, about 1 minute.

Serves 4 to 6.

*Frozen artichoke hearts may be substituted. Use one 9-ounce package cooked in ¼ cup boiling salted water until tender, about 5 minutes.

ARTICHOKE SOUFFLE

In France, *artichaut* was once a derogatory term for a "loose woman"; most probably because artichokes were considered to have aphrodisiac powers. The following is a lovely prescription for an artichoke soufflé that stimulates no other organ than the tongue.

Creamy Tomato Sauce (see page 375)
2 large artichokes, trimmed
1 lemon, halved
6 tablespoons (3/4 stick) plus 1 teaspoon unsalted butter
1 1/2 cups Chicken Stock (see page 410)
2 tablespoons freshly grated Parmesan cheese
1 shallot, minced
3 tablespoons all-purpose flour
3/4 cup milk, hot
4 egg yolks
Pinch of cayenne pepper
1/8 teaspoon freshly grated nutmeg
Salt and freshly ground black pepper
6 egg whites

1. Make Creamy Tomato Sauce. Keep warm.

2. Wash the artichokes well. Cut each artichoke into six pieces vertically. Remove the chokes, rubbing all cut surfaces with lemon.

3. Melt 3 tablespoons of the butter in a medium saucepan over low heat. Add the artichoke pieces; toss well to coat each piece with butter. Add the chicken stock. Heat to boiling; reduce the heat. Simmer, covered, 40 minutes. Drain, reserving the stock.

4. Using a spoon, scrape all edible parts from each artichoke, including the edible part of each leaf. Place this in the container of a food processor or blender with 1/3 cup of the reserved stock. Purée until smooth. Reserve.

5. Preheat the oven to 400°F. Rub a 2-quart soufflé dish with 1 teaspoon butter. Sprinkle with 1 tablespoon of the cheese. Set aside.

6. Melt the remaining 3 tablespoons butter in a medium saucepan over low heat. Stir in the shallot; cook 5 minutes. Stir in the flour, blending it well to form a thick paste. Cook, stirring constantly, 2 minutes. Whisk in the milk all at once. Beat the mixture until smooth and very thick. Remove from the heat.

7. Add the egg yolks, one at a time, beating thoroughly after each addition. Add the cayenne pepper, nutmeg, and salt and pepper to taste. Combine in a bowl with the puréed artichokes.

8. Beat the egg whites until stiff but not dry. Fold them into the artichoke mixture. Pour into the prepared soufflé dish.

9. Place the soufflé in the middle of the oven and bake for 15 minutes. Reduce the heat to 375°F and continue to bake until the soufflé is set and golden brown, about 15 minutes longer. The soufflé is done when a cake tester inserted in the center comes out fairly clean. Serve immediately with Creamy Tomato Sauce.

Serves 6.

ARTICHOKES CROISETTE

(Cold Poached Eggs and Artichokes)

This recipe works for lunch, brunch, or supper. At the heart of the matter is a poached egg, blanketed with a peppery Mediterranean sauce called *rouille*. I inherited the dish from Raymond Sokolov who says it may be served warm or cold, but I prefer the latter version. Try it both ways!

Sauce Rouille (recipe follows)
4 large artichokes
2 lemons, halved
1 tablespoon plus 1 teaspoon red wine vinegar
5 peppercorns, tied in a cheesecloth bag
½ teaspoon salt
4 eggs
1 tablespoon minced fresh parsley

1. Make Sauce Rouille. Chill.

2. Cut the stems from the artichokes, rubbing the cut surfaces with half a lemon. Pull off and discard all the leaves and remove the chokes. Trim the edges of the artichoke bottoms with a sharp knife, again rubbing all cut surfaces with lemon. As they are prepared, place the bottoms in a bowl of cold water to which you have added the juice of ½ lemon.

3. Place the artichoke bottoms in a medium saucepan with fresh cold water to cover. Add the juice of ½ lemon, 1 tablespoon vinegar, the peppercorns, and the salt. Heat to boiling; reduce the heat. Simmer, covered, until tender, 15 to 20 minutes. Drain. Chill.

4. Break each egg into an individual small bowl. Fill a medium saucepan with water; add 1 teaspoon vinegar. Heat to boiling; reduce the heat so that the water barely simmers. Slip the eggs into the water, one at a time. Poach until the whites are firm. Remove them with a slotted spoon, drain well, and transfer to small individual bowls. Cool. Chill, covered, until ready to serve.

5. To serve: Arrange the artichoke bottoms on individual serving plates. Drain off any accumulated water from the cold poached eggs, and slide an egg onto each artichoke bottom. Top each egg with 2 tablespoons Sauce Rouille. Sprinkle each with parsley. Pass the remaining sauce.

Serves 4.

Sauce Rouille

¾ cup Chicken Stock, approximately (see page 410)
1 small potato, peeled, diced
¼ cup seeded, chopped red bell pepper
1 large clove garlic, chopped
1 teaspoon crushed dried hot red peppers
3 to 4 tablespoons olive oil
Salt and freshly ground black pepper

1. Place the chicken stock and the potato in a small saucepan. Heat to boiling; reduce the heat. Simmer, uncovered, over medium-low heat 10 minutes. Add the bell pepper; simmer 5 minutes longer, adding more chicken stock if necessary. The potato and pepper should be just barely covered.

2. Transfer the mixture to a blender container (there should be slightly less than ¼ cup cooking liquid), and add the garlic and crushed peppers. Purée until smooth. Transfer to a small bowl and beat in the oil, a drop at a time, until the mixture is smooth. Cool. Chill, covered, until ready to serve.

3. Just before serving, stir the sauce well and season with salt and pepper to taste.

Makes about 1 cup.

ASPARAGUS

The Harbinger of Spring

For the past ten years I have lived in companionable tranquility with a beautiful redhead named Dinah, whose only real character flaw is an uncontrollable urge for asparagus.

As a matter of fact, Dinah is so affixed on the flavor and crunch of this supple green that she has been known to leap headlong into a sink in April (prime asparagus season, of course) in order to pry a stalk or two from under a flowing tap of cold water. And this extremely fastidious apricot-colored cat is one female who really hates getting her hair wet.

I have been permitted to share Dinah's good graces for the better part of a decade. No small honor, for this feline is extremely choosy about the company she keeps. She loathes dogs; cats are not exactly her dish of tea either. All other quadrupeds (like rabbits, squirrels, and mice) she dismisses with an icy stare and a resolute flick of her tail. Antipathy to the animal kingdom would seem to imply a greater degree of affection for the human race. Not so. Dinah will tolerate the admiration of a few votaries she knows well but, by and large, like the legendary Garbo, *she wants to be alone!*

At a recent party I gave, Dinah disappeared promptly when the first guest arrived at eight and did not surface again until two in the morning (with bursting kidneys) after the last celebrant departed.

However, it is of Dinah's appetite, not her lack of social amenity, that I speak. A delicate, small-boned creature weighing less than eight pounds, she has little interest in nourishment generally and none whatsoever in commercial pet food. What she likes best are bay scallops (sautéed in butter, white wine, and garlic, if you please) and the aforementioned asparagus. Dinah's predilection for the last-named victual is so overwhelming she will even face an alien dinner party if she knows a few asparagus stalks are to be on the menu.

On one notable occasion when I planned to open a meal with a course of this tender vegetable upholstered in mustardy hollandaise, I made a grave error. Busy in the kitchen with the other components of the dinner, I allowed a pound and a half of asparagus (fully peeled and blanched) to rest on the dining room table. When I eventually brought out plates for the asparagus, I discovered that my elegant cat had bitten the green tip from every single spear with the precision of a surgeon's scalpel.

As dinner was less than a half hour off, there was not even time for punishment to fit the crime. Instead the remains were whisked into a blender to become a cool jade soup.

Like the rugged individualist she is, Dinah refused a spoonful when it was proffered her. But she purred all evening long nonetheless!

Vegetable Roots

Egyptians were eating wild asparagus no bigger than a child's forefinger before the second pyramid was constructed at Gizeh, but the delicate stalks firmly resisted all efforts at cultivation along the Nile. It took Roman ingenuity to perform that agrarian miracle several centuries later.

The ancients doted on the flavor of this vernal vegetable. The Greek word *aspharagos* means "as long as one's throat," a label, the pundits tell us, that was conferred on the slender spears because overeager diners often consumed them whole—in one fell swoop—at mealtimes. Soused with dressing, one hopes!

What to Look For

Asparagus is a harbinger of spring.

Or at least it was, before advanced agricultural technology and supersonic transport systems stuck their collective thumbs in the garden. Today fresh green asparagus may be found in metropolitan greengroceries across the country from January to July—with varying levels of flavor and price!

France is home of the famous white asparagus. However, despite the delicacy of this remarkable spear, I must confess that I cling to the American varieties I was raised on, namely the smooth-crowned Mary Washington, and the early-blooming Paradise which, in the words of Alice B. Toklas, "should be no thicker than a darning needle when it is picked!"

To a prejudiced palate like mine, the only true asparagus is marketed from early April, when the southwestern yield is harvested, until late June, when the bumper crops from the Northeast hit the vegetable stands.

When I purchase asparagus for a springtime orgy, I look for spears with straight stalks, uniform green color, and compact, pointed tips. The freshest asparagus will be crisp to the fingernail and usually no thicker than a fat crayon. Buy only the stalks with a scant inch of woody white fiber at the base, since that portion is trimmed off in the kitchen.

This nutritious vegetable is not only super-rich in vitamin A but equally endowed with vitamins B_1, B_2, and C. Asparagus is also a dieter's dream food: less than 35 calories per cup, cooked.

Preparation

Cooked asparagus may be served, hot or cold, as a vegetable first course or as an adjunct to the meal itself. French chefs have been known to substitute it

for a salad course in a pinch, but you eschew *that* practice please! Asparagus is too distinctively flavored to cleanse the palate.

I never wash asparagus until after it is peeled, contrary to the advice you may have read elsewhere. Peeling is a necessity (unless the asparagus is pencil-slim and super-fresh) because the tough outer flesh is hard to digest. Before peeling, break off and discard the bottom of each stalk at the point where it snaps off most easily. I never slice off the bottoms because, as with cut flowers, water enters more freely if the stalk is roughly torn.

Peel the asparagus stalks with a vegetable peeler, removing the scales and stringy skin, but stop at least an inch from the tips. Wash the peeled stalks in a large basin of cold water before they are to be cooked.

I always blanch asparagus, uncovered, in a large flat saucepan or deep skillet half filled with boiling salted water. My technique is to place the stalks loosely in the pan, allow the water to return to the boil, reduce the heat, and simmer 3 to 5 minutes or until just barely tender. Do not overcook! When the asparagus is cooked, place the pan under cold running water until the stalks are cool to the touch. Drain on paper towels before using.

To steam asparagus, place the spears upright, loose or tied in bunches of six to ten, in a deep pot or in the bottom of a double boiler. Add boiling water to a depth of 1 inch, plus salt if desired. Cover with a lid or with the inverted top of the double boiler. Cook over medium heat approximately 10 minutes. By this method, the tougher ends cook in water while the tender tips cook in steam.

A serving note: Most of these asparagus recipes are based on a serving of ½ pound per person. However, if you are serving more than one vegetable with dinner, ⅓ pound probably will suffice.

COLD ASPARAGUS IN MUSTARD CREAM

The following was passed along to me by Ethelyn Maruccia, chef and co-owner of a charming—but no longer extant—Greenwich Village eatery appropriately named The Heavenly Host. Ms. Maruccia's mustard cream is a culinary treasure.

2 pounds asparagus, trimmed, peeled
3 egg yolks
2 tablespoons lemon juice
¼ cup Dijon mustard
½ cup olive oil
Salt and freshly ground black pepper
Chopped fresh parsley

1. Blanch the asparagus and drain it on paper towels. Arrange the asparagus in a shallow serving dish, cover, and chill thoroughly.

2. Meanwhile, in the large bowl of an electric mixer, beat the egg yolks with the lemon juice and mustard for 4 minutes. On low speed, slowly beat in the oil. The mixture will have the consistency of a thin mayonnaise. Add salt and pepper to taste. Chill thoroughly.

3. To serve: Spoon some of the sauce over the asparagus and sprinkle with parsley. Pass the remaining sauce.

Serves 4.

CLASSIC COLD ASPARAGUS VINAIGRETTE

To my tongue, nothing anoints a cold spear of asparagus more felicitously than the combined flavors of lemon and mustard. The first such rendering is for a dish I would nominate as the classic chilled appetizer: Asparagus Vinaigrette.

2 pounds asparagus, trimmed, peeled
1 small shallot, minced
1 small clove garlic, crushed
½ teaspoon coarse (kosher) salt
1½ teaspoons Dijon mustard
Juice of ½ lemon
¾ cup vegetable or olive oil
2 teaspoons red wine vinegar
½ teaspoon freshly ground black pepper
1 hard-cooked egg, yolk and white minced separately
¼ cup chopped fresh parsley

1. Blanch the asparagus and drain it on paper towels. Arrange the spears in a shallow serving dish and sprinkle with the minced shallot.

2. Place the garlic and salt in a small bowl, and mash them together with the back of a spoon until the mixture forms a paste. Stir in the mustard and lemon juice. Whisk in the oil, vinegar, and pepper. Spoon this dressing over the asparagus.

3. Garnish the asparagus with alternating bands of chopped egg white, parsley, and egg yolk. Chill thoroughly before serving.

Serves 4.

ASPARAGUS AND SPINACH SOUP

As a kid raised on pale seas of canned asparagus soup, I find it a decided treat to dip a spoon into the genuine article. The following devise is for such a purée: a melding of green asparagus and even greener spinach leaves steeped in golden chicken stock. Although not the soup I hastily concocted after Dinah made her raid, it is one you certainly should consider when the stalks are plentiful. I always serve it hot, but friends tell me it is equally tonic chilled.

1 pound asparagus, trimmed, peeled
3 cups Chicken Stock (see page 410)
1 cup chopped fresh spinach leaves, washed
2 tablespoons unsalted butter
10 whole scallions, bulbs and green tops, roughly chopped
Pinch of ground cloves
3 tablespoons cornstarch
1 cup heavy or whipping cream
Salt and freshly ground black pepper
Sour cream (optional)

1. Place the asparagus in a medium saucepan and cover with the chicken stock. Heat to boiling over high heat; reduce the heat. Simmer, covered, 3 minutes. Remove the asparagus from the broth and set aside. Add the spinach to the saucepan and cook 3 minutes. Drain; reserve the broth.

2. Cut the tips off the asparagus; reserve. Chop the stems into 1-inch pieces; reserve.

3. Melt the butter in a medium saucepan over low heat. Add the scallions; cook until wilted. Stir in the cloves, cooked spinach, and asparagus stems. Cook, covered, over low heat for 10 minutes. Remove the cover; add the reserved broth.

4. Place the cornstarch in a small bowl. Slowly beat in the cream until the mixture is smooth. Stir this into the vegetable mixture in the saucepan. Heat to boiling; remove from the heat.

5. Cool the mixture slightly and purée it in a blender or processor in two batches (being careful: hot liquid will expand). Return the purée to the saucepan and reheat over low heat. Season with salt and pepper to taste; stir in the asparagus tips. Serve garnished with dabs of sour cream if desired.

Serves 6 to 8.

ASPARAGUS AND SHRIMP SALAD

There is something curiously refreshing about the fearless pairing of two strong flavors in a single pot. Asparagus and shrimp, both ingredients with independent spheres of influence on the taste buds, marry most happily in the following spring-into-summer salad—a dish that my mother would have called "good for what ails you!"

1½ pounds asparagus, trimmed, peeled
½ cup water
1 slice lemon
1 sprig parsley
5 peppercorns
½ teaspoon salt
16 to 20 small shrimp
½ cup Mayonnaise (see page 408)
½ cup sour cream
½ teaspoon lemon juice
¼ teaspoon dry mustard
½ teaspoon prepared horseradish (optional)
1 tablespoon gin
Salt and freshly ground black pepper
Lettuce leaves

1. Blanch the asparagus and drain it on paper towels. Cut off the tips; cut the stems diagonally into 2-inch pieces. Place tips and stem pieces in a large bowl and set aside.

2. Combine the water, lemon slice, parsley, peppercorns, and salt in a medium saucepan. Heat to boiling; reduce the heat. Add the shrimp and simmer, uncovered, until they turn pink, about 4 minutes. Drain; cool slightly, then shell and devein the shrimp and add them to the asparagus.

3. Combine the mayonnaise with the sour cream in a medium bowl. Beat in the lemon juice, mustard, horseradish, gin, and salt and pepper to taste. Spoon this dressing over the asparagus and shrimp, and toss well. Serve on lettuce leaves, at room temperature or slightly chilled.

Serves 4.

FRENCH-FRIED ASPARAGUS

One of the quickest (and most unusual) ways to prepare asparagus is to french-fry it. Time: 3 minutes flat.

1 egg
½ cup milk
Dash of hot pepper sauce
⅛ teaspoon freshly grated nutmeg
1 teaspoon beef bouillon powder
½ teaspoon salt
¼ teaspoon freshly ground black pepper
½ cup all-purpose flour
⅔ cup fresh bread crumbs
1½ pounds asparagus, trimmed, peeled
Vegetable oil for frying

1. Beat the egg with the milk in a medium-size shallow dish. Add the hot pepper sauce, nutmeg, bouillon powder, salt, and pepper. Mix thoroughly.

2. Place the flour and the bread crumbs in separate shallow dishes. Roll each spear of asparagus first in the flour; shake off any excess. Then dip the asparagus into the egg-milk mixture, coating it well, and finally roll it in the bread crumbs.

3. Pour oil into a large heavy skillet to a depth of 1 inch. Heat it until hot but not smoking. Add the asparagus in one layer, in two or more batches as necessary. Cook over medium-high heat until golden, about 3 minutes. Drain each batch on paper towels and keep warm while frying the remaining asparagus.

Serves 4.

ASPARAGUS RISOTTO

Asparagus may be low in calories, but do not delude yourself about the thinning potential of the next dish; borrowed practically intact from a Venetian trattoria, it is clearly meant for overindulgers only!

½ pound asparagus, trimmed (unpeeled)
3½ tablespoons unsalted butter
2 large shallots, minced
Salt and freshly ground black pepper
¼ cup dry white wine
1 cup Italian rice (I prefer Arborio)
2½ to 3 cups Chicken Stock, simmering (see page 410)
⅓ cup freshly grated Parmesan cheese
2 tablespoons chopped fresh parsley

1. Cut the tips from the asparagus; reserve. Chop the stems into ½-inch pieces; set aside.

2. Melt 2½ tablespoons of the butter in a large heavy skillet, and sauté the shallots in it until golden, about 5 minutes. Add the asparagus stems; sprinkle with salt and pepper to taste. Cook 1 minute. Stir in the wine and cook, stirring constantly, until almost all the liquid has evaporated.

3. Stir the rice into the skillet and add 1 cup of the chicken stock. Stir once. Cook, uncovered, over medium-low heat without stirring until the stock is absorbed, about 10 minutes. Reduce the heat if the liquid absorbs at a faster rate.

4. Pour 1 more cup of the stock over the rice. Cook without stirring 10 minutes longer.

5. Stir the reserved asparagus tips into the rice. Add ½ cup of the stock and cook until the liquid is absorbed and the rice is tender, about 8 more minutes. (If rice is not tender at this point, add some more stock. If rice is too wet, raise the heat slightly until liquid is absorbed.) Stir in the cheese, sprinkle with parsley, and serve immediately.

Serves 4 to 6.

Asparagus was a springtime staple of the Roman diet almost two thousand years ago. Even then, chefs knew better than to overcook it. Food snoops tell us that whenever Emperor Augustus wished to terminate some unpleasant business at hand, he would proclaim: "Let it be done quicker than you would cook an asparagus!"

ASPARAGUS A LA PARMIGIANA

This classic from Emilia Romagna (in northern Italy) is served in Italy as an *antipasto*: before the true business of the meal begins. At my table it makes a dandy accompaniment to roast meat or fowl.

2 pounds asparagus, trimmed, peeled
4 tablespoons (½ stick) unsalted butter, melted
Salt and freshly ground black pepper
½ cup freshly grated Parmesan cheese

1. Preheat the oven to 400°F. Blanch the asparagus and drain it on paper towels. Arrange the asparagus in a shallow ovenproof serving dish.

2. Pour the melted butter over the asparagus. Sprinkle with salt and pepper to taste. Spoon the cheese evenly over the top. Bake until lightly browned, about 20 minutes.

Serves 4.

MARGI SMITH'S ASPARAGUS A LA HOLSTEIN

(Asparagus with Fried Egg and Lemon)

Margi Smith, a good friend who is also an intrepid cook, told me about a dish she invented one night after returning home late from the office and discovering only half a bunch of asparagus, some eggs, capers, and a hunk of Parmigiano Reggiano cheese in the refrigerator. It sounded good, so I memorized her formula verbatim. Margi Smith's "fast food" is now one of my favorite light meals during the vernal equinox.

1 pound asparagus, trimmed, peeled
1½ to 2 tablespoons unsalted butter
2 eggs
1 teaspoon lemon juice
½ teaspoon red wine vinegar
2 teaspoons capers
Freshly ground black pepper
1 tablespoon freshly grated Parmesan cheese

1. Preheat the oven to 200°F. Cook the asparagus in boiling salted water, or steam until just tender. Place drained asparagus in a shallow serving dish and keep it warm in the oven. (Asparagus may be blanched ahead of time and reheated in a warm oven, if desired.)

2. Melt ½ to 1 tablespoon of the butter in a medium-size skillet and fry the eggs sunny side up. Place the eggs over the asparagus and return the dish to the oven.

3. Add the remaining 1 tablespoon butter to the skillet and stir in the lemon juice, vinegar, and capers. Cook over medium heat until slightly thickened. Spoon the sauce over the eggs and sprinkle with pepper to taste and the Parmesan cheese. Serve immediately.

Serves 2.

BEDDED ASPARAGUS

1½ to 2 pounds asparagus, trimmed, peeled
4 strips bacon
2 tablespoons unsalted butter
1 small clove garlic, minced
1 shallot, minced
2 hard-cooked eggs, finely chopped
1 cup watercress leaves
1 tablespoon red wine vinegar
Salt and freshly ground black pepper

1. Preheat the oven to 250°F. Cook the asparagus in boiling salted water, or steam, until just tender. Place drained asparagus in a baking dish, and keep it warm in the oven. (Asparagus may be blanched ahead of time and reheated in a warm oven, if desired.)

2. Sauté the bacon strips in a large heavy skillet until crisp. Drain on paper towels, crumble, and reserve.

3. Pour off all but 1 tablespoon bacon drippings from the skillet. Add the butter. Sauté the garlic and shallot over medium-low heat until golden. Stir in the eggs and toss in the watercress. Cook until the watercress is just wilted. Sprinkle with the vinegar, and add salt and pepper to taste.

4. To serve, spread the watercress-egg mixture over the bottom of a serving dish. Lay the asparagus over the top, and sprinkle with the crumbled bacon.

Serves 4.

ASPARAGUS IN MINT CREAM

This dish, plus the two that follow—Asparagus in Whipped Cream and Asparagus Meringue—are all delicate side dishes that make excellent partners to fish and fowl alike; or they can stand alone as a separate course.

2 pounds asparagus, trimmed, peeled
4 sprigs fresh mint
1 sprig fresh tarragon, chopped
1 sprig parsley, chopped
2 shallots, chopped
3 tablespoons dry white wine
3 tablespoons white wine vinegar
¼ cup heavy or whipping cream
1 egg yolk, lightly beaten
¾ cup (1½ sticks) unsalted butter, frozen

1. Preheat the oven to 250°F. Cook the asparagus in boiling salted water, or steam, until just tender. Place the drained asparagus in a shallow serving dish, and keep it warm in the oven. (Asparagus may be blanched ahead of time and reheated in a warm oven, if desired.)

2. Remove the mint leaves from their stems; reserve the stems. Finely chop the leaves; reserve.

3. Combine the mint stems with the tarragon, parsley, shallots, white wine, and vinegar in a small saucepan. Heat to boiling; reduce the heat. Simmer, uncovered, until reduced to 2 tablespoons. Stir in the cream. Return to the boil and again reduce to about 2 tablespoons.

4. Strain the herbed mixture into the top of a double boiler. Beat in the egg yolk. Place over simmering water. Cut the butter into 12 pieces. Using a small wire whisk, beat the butter into the mixture, one piece at a time, stirring well after each addition. When thick, stir in the reserved mint leaves; pour over the asparagus.

Serves 4.

ALICE B. TOKLAS' ASPARAGUS IN WHIPPED CREAM

1½ to 2 pounds asparagus, trimmed, peeled
4 tablespoons (½ stick) unsalted butter
1 cup heavy or whipping cream
½ teaspoon salt
¼ teaspoon freshly ground black pepper

1. Preheat the oven to 250°F. Cook the asparagus in boiling salted water, or steam, until just tender. Place the drained asparagus in a shallow serving dish, and keep it warm in the oven. (Asparagus may be blanched ahead of time and reheated in a warm oven, if desired.)

2. In a small saucepan, melt the butter with ¼ cup heavy cream over low heat. Stir, and pour over the asparagus; return the asparagus to the oven.

3. Beat the remaining ¾ cup cream with the salt and pepper until stiff. Spoon over the hot asparagus. Serve immediately.

Serves 4.

Asparagus is one of a select bunch of garden greens that man has always seemed to invest with aphrodisiac powers. In nineteenth-century France, for instance, convention decreed that a bridegroom's prenuptial dinner contain at least three courses of warm asparagus... Make of that what you will!

ASPARAGUS MERINGUE

2 pounds asparagus, trimmed, peeled
¾ cup Mayonnaise (see page 408)
¼ cup sour cream
1½ teaspoons Dijon mustard
1 teaspoon lemon juice
1½ tablespoons minced chives or scallion tops
4 egg whites
½ teaspoon salt
¼ teaspoon ground white pepper
Pinch of sugar

1. Preheat the oven to 250°F. Cook the asparagus in boiling salted water, or steam, until just tender. Place the drained asparagus in a shallow ovenproof serving dish, and keep it warm in the oven. (Asparagus may be blanched ahead of time and reheated in a warm oven, if desired.)

2. Combine the mayonnaise, sour cream, mustard, lemon juice, and chives in a medium bowl. Mix well.

3. In another bowl, beat the egg whites with the salt and white pepper until soft peaks form. Sprinkle with sugar; beat until stiff. Fold the egg whites into the mayonnaise mixture, and spread evenly over the top of the asparagus. Place the asparagus under the broiler until the top is slightly browned, about 3 minutes.

4. To serve, use a thin spatula to break through the meringue and gently lift out both a piece of meringue and several asparagus spears. Spoon any remaining sauce over the individual portions.

Serves 4.

ASPARAGUS AND SHRIMP PIE

Asparagus' cognomen in early English evolved to a rather neat semi-description: "sparrow's grass." This in turn was altered to "sperage" and eventually "grass" alone, a fact that may account for an ancient British recipe (much written about but undetailed as to ingredients) for a "grass and prawn pie." My stimulated imagination produced the unauthentic rendering that follows.

Short Crust Pastry (see page 412)
¾ pound asparagus, trimmed, peeled
1 tablespoon unsalted butter
1 shallot, minced
1 tablespoon Madeira
½ pound shrimp, shelled, deveined, cut in half crosswise
2 eggs
1 cup heavy or whipping cream
½ cup coarsely grated Jarlsberg cheese
Dash of hot pepper sauce
⅛ teaspoon freshly grated nutmeg
Salt and freshly ground black pepper
1 tablespoon freshly grated Parmesan cheese

1. Make the Short Crust Pastry.

2. Preheat the oven to 375°F. Line a 9-inch loose-bottom tart pan with the pastry. Trim. Line the pastry with aluminum foil weighted down with uncooked rice or dried beans. Bake 10 minutes.

Remove the foil and rice or beans. Prick the bottom of the crust with a fork to allow steam to escape. Bake 3 minutes longer. Cool on a wire rack.

3. Blanch the asparagus and drain it on paper towels.

4. Melt the butter in a medium skillet, and sauté the shallot over medium-low heat until golden, about 5 minutes. Stir in the Madeira and shrimp. Toss 1 minute. Spoon the mixture evenly over the bottom of the prepared crust.

5. Beat the eggs with the cream in a medium-size bowl. Add the Jarlsberg cheese, hot pepper sauce, nutmeg, and salt and pepper to taste. Mix well, and pour over the shrimp. Place the asparagus spears on top in a spoke pattern with the tips facing outward (trim the stalks to fit if necessary). Sprinkle with Parmesan cheese. Bake 30 minutes.

Serves 6 to 8.

CRAVATTA
(Asparagus Ties)

The next asparagus invention springs from Italy. These slim packages of ham wrapped around asparagus and cheese make a perfect lunch, brunch, or supper—just add a loaf of crusty bread and a bottle of dry white wine.

16 medium asparagus spears, trimmed, peeled
½ teaspoon unsalted butter
1 large shallot, minced
1 teaspoon Dijon mustard
2 tablespoons heavy or whipping cream
½ teaspoon lemon juice
½ pound thinly sliced boiled ham (8 slices)
3 tablespoons freshly grated Parmesan cheese
½ pound Fontina cheese, coarsely grated
Freshly ground black pepper

1. Preheat the oven to 400°F. Blanch the asparagus and drain it on paper towels.

2. Melt the butter in a small skillet over medium-low heat. Add the minced shallot and sauté until lightly browned. Remove from the heat. Stir in the mustard, cream, and lemon juice, and blend well.

3. Spread a small amount of the shallot-mustard mixture over each slice of ham. Sprinkle each piece with Parmesan cheese. Divide the Fontina cheese into two portions, and sprinkle one portion evenly over the ham slices.

4. Place two asparagus spears in the center of each ham slice. Fold the ham over the asparagus, and arrange the packages in a lightly greased ovenproof serving dish, seam side down. Sprinkle the remaining Fontina cheese over the top, and add a grating of pepper. Bake until lightly browned and bubbly, 15 to 20 minutes.

Serves 4.

AVOCADOS

A Fruit in Vegetable's Clothing

The avocado was decidedly not a staple of the average American diet when I was growing up. On the East Coast, these leathery-skinned objects were known to consumers as "alligator pears" and were regarded with only a shade less suspicion than might have been accorded the actual reptiles if they had been discovered nesting on a greengrocer's shelf. In that dim culinary time, such comestibles were judged indigestible or, worse yet, immoral, and the middle class gave them a wide berth.

Luckier than most, I was born to high-spirited parents who enjoyed good things and good times. Prior to the Depression our family would go "on the town," as my parents called our weekend outings to Manhattan restaurants. I was something of a finicky eater in those days, but despite that, these outings pleased me as much as my parents. The glitter of crystal, the gleam of silver, and the deferential mien of waiters in tuxedos offered a glimpse of an adult life I longed to inherit.

My parents always ate conventional dishes like shrimp, fruit cocktail, steak, or roast beef for dinner. But not me. Possessed of insatiable fascination for the exotic, I would order items from the à la carte side of the menu: inevitably fare that whetted my imagination if not necessarily my appetite.

Whenever I chose one of these untried dishes, my mother's eyebrows always raised perceptibly. This expression, which my sister Myra called *Mama's*

famous look, implied "You will be sorry you ordered that!" Mama's famous look never stopped me from selecting snails or frogs' legs, but it also never made swallowing these mistakes any easier. One entree I did not even consider ordering was the avocado—for the menu price automatically inhibited even my inquiring taste buds. Luckily time and tide made it more accessible.

Years later when I was a grown man with a substantial position (and an expanded palate), I took my mother to a well-known restaurant in Manhattan. It was French and expensive, situated in the parlor floor of an East Side brownstone long since demolished for a skyscraper. My mother, I knew, was impressed with the surroundings despite her natural reservation about my extravagance. Seated on a banquette across from her, I opened the impressive bill of fare and perused the lefthand side.

"The avocado vinaigrette is particularly good here, Mother."

My parent did not reply to the suggestion but her eyebrows flared wildly. "People do not change" was an opinion she stated often.

"Listen! I've had it before. It's delicious."

I don't think she believed me, but despite her misgiving she allowed me to order two portions. In truth, her dubious expression did not alter until she had tasted the avocado twice.

"You're right," she announced, licking her spoon. "It's not bad at all."

The rest of the dinner was delicious but nothing obviously compared with the appetizer. "You know," my mother shook her head thoughtfully over her coffee cup, "I can't get over that avocado. What I've been missing all these years!"

I never inherited my mother's way with an eyebrow so there would have been little point in elevating mine. Besides, I knew from experience . . . it was love at first bite!

Vegetable Roots

The avocado is an anomaly, a fruit that has been consumed as a vegetable for centuries. Archaeologists digging in the pre-Incan city of Chan Chan, Peru, unearthed a cache of avocado pits along with jars of grain and corn, indicating that it was a diet staple prior to 900 A.D.

Hernando Cortez was probably the first European to ever chomp an avocado in the New World. Happily this conquistador never ventured very far afield without an aide to record his peregrinations, be they combative or gastronomic. The Spanish historian Gonzalo Fernandez Oviedo y Valdes, noting the memorable culinary proceedings for posterity, also gave the first directions for eating a fresh avocado.

> In the center of the greenish-gold oval is a seed resembling a peeled chestnut that must be removed and thrown away because it is both bitter and exceedingly hard to chew. Between this and the tough rind of the skin however is a paste that the Indians consume with great relish. Soft as butter in texture, it is of a very good taste.

Oviedo also observed that the Aztecs ate their avocados directly from the shell, scraping the pulp with their front teeth. Cortez took his with a silver spoon, adding a pinch of salt from time to time because he found the flavor somewhat bland. (That smooth flavor, of course, is what makes the avocado a perfect foil for the accompaniments soon to follow).

What to Look For

The avocado *(Persea americana)* is distantly related to the laurel and shares a common heritage with other nondeciduous evergreens. Over the past hundred years, avocados have migrated from their original home in Mexico to such southerly outposts as Hawaii, Australia, Africa, and Israel and north to California and Florida, where avocado growing has become a major industry.

The most familiar avocado on supermarket shelves in winter is the silky Fuerte, encased in a glossy green rind flecked with gold. The summer avocado is a rough-pebbled globe with much darker skin, known as Hass. Whatever their outer packaging, both have the same creamy texture and subtle nutlike flavor.

The wise buyer purchases an avocado just before it is fully ripe, as the fruit at maturity has a relatively short shelf-life. To test for ripeness, cradle an avocado in the palm of your hand and squeeze it lightly. If fully developed, it will be soft to the touch and will yield to pressure. An underdeveloped one will be quite firm and resistant. Some canny cooks hurry the ripening process by storing avocados in brown paper sacks or wrapping them in layers of tissue paper or foil. This forces the maturation process by concentrating the natural carbon dioxide that the fruit exudes.

I simply store an avocado in a warm, dry place (like an earthenware bowl) until it is obviously ready for slicing. Once ripe, an avocado may be held for a day or so in the refrigerator, but never frozen.

An avocado should be sliced lengthwise, using a sharp stainless-steel knife, and twisted gently to separate the halves. The large center pit is easily removed with the tip of the knife. To prevent darkening, rub the cut surfaces with plenty of fresh lime or lemon juice. I follow the Mexican injunction and always replace the seed when storing a cut half for any length of time; it seems to keep the flesh firmer and greener.

When avocados are served warm, make sure they do not overcook, which will turn the flesh somewhat bitter.

The avocado, which is often thought of as a rich food, produces no serum cholesterol whatsoever and maintains a relatively high protein content despite its immoderate appetite appeal. An average avocado half contains a mere 136 calories, and at least 8 essential vitamins and 5 vital minerals.

Preparation

For many, the classic way to serve an avocado is merely to brush the cut surface with lime or lemon juice and sprinkle with salt and pepper. But that is surely the super-purist approach. Speaking for myself, I would choose an avocado well soused with oil, vinegar, and a mite of chopped onion. And, of course, any of the inspirations that follow.

A word of advice to chary consumers: The avocado ripens best in its own sweet time. According to those Californians (and Floridians) lucky enough to own trees, the fruit is ready to be eaten only when it falls to the ground. Commercial growers pick avocados when they are underripe so the fruit will season on its way to a greengrocer's shelf. An avocado

The avocado pit you're about to toss out may be persuaded to grow into a handsome and hardy houseplant—and with some extra cultivation perhaps, to a full-grown tree.

John Canaday, art and food critic and author of *The Artful Avocado,* is the past master of avocado green-thumbery. He advises that the pit be washed and dried first, then stuck with three or four strong toothpicks to hold it suspended, broad side down, in an ordinary glass filled with tepid (not hot) water.

Keep the seed out of direct sunlight, and it will split and send forth a sprout and roots in about two to six weeks. When it does, plant it, and pray!

that is firm to the touch but appears brownish or discolored inside is the result of refrigerator burn (or too long in cold storage) and, according to the Avocado Information Bureau, should be promptly returned to the seller. For serious queries write: Avocado Information, P.O. Box 19159-MT, Irvine, CA 92713.

AVOCADOS VINAIGRETTE NEW ORLEANS STYLE

1 hard-cooked egg, chopped
1 teaspoon chopped chives or scallion tops
1 teaspoon chopped fresh basil, or ¼ teaspoon dried
1 teaspoon chopped fresh parsley
1 tablespoon red wine vinegar
¼ cup olive oil
2 slices Milano or Genoa salami, cut into thin 1-inch-long strips
2 avocados
Juice of 1 lemon
Freshly ground black pepper

1. Combine the egg, chives, basil, parsley, vinegar, oil, and salami in a small bowl. Toss well.

2. Cut the avocados in half lengthwise, and remove the pits. Sprinkle with lemon juice.

3. Fill each avocado half with the salami-egg mixture. Sprinkle with pepper to taste. Chill well before serving.

Serves 4.

GUACAMOLE

This wondrous hors d'oeuvre, often referred to by food snobs as "the avocado's finest hour," comes from Mexico, where there are as many versions as there are dialects. One rule, however, is unvarying: this dish requires a ripe, mashable avocado, which is seasoned with salt, lime juice, and judicious doses of hot green chile peppers and chopped fresh coriander. The rest is up to the cook's imagination and tolerance for incendiarism.

My favorite guacamole recipe, authentic as a gringo appetite will allow, comes from San Antonio, Texas. With it, have a *damnyankee* warning: A hot pepper's fire is contained in its seeds and pale interior spines. To temper a pepper's pungency, remove both with a sharp knife, but do not touch your face or any other sensitive area of skin until you wash your hands first!

2 tablespoons minced yellow onion
1 small hot green pepper, seeded, minced
4 sprigs fresh coriander leaves (also known as cilantro or Chinese parsley), finely chopped
¼ teaspoon salt
2 medium avocados
¼ cup chopped, seeded tomatoes
2 tablespoons finely chopped red onion
1 tablespoon lemon or lime juice

1. Combine the yellow onion, hot green pepper, half the coriander, and the salt in a small bowl or mortar. Mash until a smooth paste is formed. Set aside.

2. Cut the avocados in half lengthwise; remove the pits and reserve them. Scoop out the flesh of the avocados and mash in a medium bowl until smooth. Add the reserved onion paste. Mix thoroughly. Stir in the tomatoes, red onion, and the remaining coriander. Press the reserved pits into the mixture. Sprinkle with lemon or lime juice. Cover; refrigerate.

3. Just before serving, remove the pits and stir thoroughly. Serve with corn chips, corn tortillas, or flour tortillas.

Makes about 2 cups.

JODY GILLIS' SWEET AND SOUR AVOCADOS

One of the best uses for the "lawyer's pear" is as an appetizer prior to dinner. This recipe for a somewhat radical version comes to me from the treasury of my good cooking friend, Jody Gillis of Santee, California. Jody declares shamelessly, "This dish is so sure fire that when I serve it, I wait for the spoons to hit the lips so the *mmmm*'s can begin!"

8 strips bacon
8 tablespoons (1 stick) unsalted butter
¼ cup sugar
¼ cup ketchup
¼ cup red wine vinegar
1 tablespoon soy sauce
3 avocados
Juice of 1 lemon

1. Sauté the bacon strips in a heavy skillet until crisp. Drain on paper towels, crumble, and reserve.

2. Melt the butter in a small saucepan, and add the sugar, ketchup, vinegar, and soy sauce, stirring over low heat until the sugar dissolves. Keep warm.

3. Cut the avocados in half lengthwise. Remove the pits and sprinkle with the lemon juice.

4. Divide the crumbled bacon into six portions and place some in each avocado cavity. Spoon the warm sauce evenly over the avocados. Serve immediately.

Serves 6.

AVOCADO GRATINE

1 shallot, minced
1 tablespoon minced fresh parsley
3 tablespoons freshly grated Parmesan cheese
2 tablespoons olive oil
1 avocado
Juice of 1 lime
Salt and freshly ground black pepper
Lime wedges

1. Preheat the broiling unit. Combine the shallot, parsley, cheese, and oil in a small bowl. Mix well.

2. Just before serving, cut the avocado in half lengthwise; peel carefully, and remove the pit. Sprinkle well all over with the lime juice.

3. Place the avocado halves on a heatproof dish. Spoon the cheese mixture evenly over the tops and into the cavities. Sprinkle with salt and pepper to taste. Place under the broiler until golden, about 4 minutes. Serve with lime wedges.

Serves 2.

AVOCADO GAZPACHO

Here is a wholly unclassic version of this cold Andalusian soup.

1 cucumber, peeled, seeded, chopped
2 cloves garlic, quartered
2 shallots, quartered
1 green bell pepper, seeded, roughly chopped
1 cup torn lettuce
1 tablespoon plus 1 teaspoon chopped fresh dill
1 tablespoon red wine vinegar
1 cup Chicken Stock (see page 410)
1 avocado
Juice of ½ lemon
2 tablespoons vodka
Salt and ground white pepper

1. Place the cucumber, garlic, shallots, green pepper, lettuce, 1 tablespoon dill, vinegar, and chicken stock (in that order) in the container of a blender or food processor. Blend until smooth.

2. Cut the avocado in half lengthwise. Peel, and remove the pit. Roughly chop half the avocado and add it to the mixture in the blender or processor. Blend until smooth. Transfer to a medium bowl.

3. Finely chop the remaining avocado and sprinkle with the lemon juice. Stir this into the gazpacho; add the vodka, and salt and white pepper to taste. Stir gently, and chill thoroughly before serving. Garnish with the remaining chopped dill.

Serves 4.

HOT AVOCADO SALAD

4 strips bacon
1 green or red bell pepper, seeded, cut into strips
½ small hot green pepper, seeded, minced (see Guacamole headnote, page 37)
1 small yellow onion, finely chopped
1 avocado
Juice of 1 lemon
3 tablespoons red wine vinegar
1 small red onion, thinly sliced
Salt and freshly ground black pepper

1. Sauté the bacon strips in a large skillet over medium heat until crisp. Drain on paper towels, crumble, and reserve.

2. Pour off all but 2 tablespoons bacon drippings from the skillet. Add both peppers and the yellow onion. Cook over medium heat, stirring occasionally, until the onions are golden, about 5 minutes. Reduce the heat to low. Cook, covered, until the peppers are tender, 5 minutes. Remove from the heat; set aside.

3. Cut the avocado in half lengthwise. Peel, and remove the pit. Cut each half into ¼-inch-thick slices crosswise, and sprinkle with the lemon juice.

4. Toss the avocado slices into the onion-pepper mixture. Sprinkle with the vinegar. Toss in the red onion slices and the crumbled bacon. Add salt and pepper to taste.

Serves 2 to 4.

COLD POACHED FISH WITH AVOCADO MAYONNAISE

Avocado mayonnaise is also a perfect partner for raw vegetables or as a fillip for jellied consommés or salads. Be my guest!

Cold Poached Fish:

2½ cups water
½ cup dry white wine
1 small onion stuck with 1 clove
½ rib celery with leaves
1 small bay leaf
½ lemon
6 peppercorns
½ teaspoon salt
1½ to 2 pounds small, firm-fleshed fish filets (such as sole, lemon sole, or flounder), or ¾-inch-thick salmon steaks

Avocado Mayonnaise:

1 cup Mayonnaise (see page 408)
Juice and finely grated peel of 1 large lime
1 avocado
Salt and ground white pepper

1. To poach the fish: Combine all the ingredients except the fish in an enamel skillet or fish poacher. Heat to boiling; reduce the heat. Simmer, uncovered, 5 minutes. Add the fish, a few pieces at a time. Poach gently, uncovered, until the fish flakes easily when pierced with a fork—about 4 minutes for filets, 8 minutes for salmon. Remove the fish from the pan with a spatula and transfer it to a serving platter. Refrigerate, covered, at least 1 hour.

2. To make the Avocado Mayonnaise: Place the mayonnaise and lime juice in the container of a blender or processor. Cut the avocado in half lengthwise; remove the pit. Scoop out the flesh and add it to the blender. Purée until smooth. Transfer the mayonnaise to a bowl, add salt and white pepper to taste, and refrigerate, covered, 1 hour.

3. To serve: Drain off any liquid that has accumulated around the fish. Spoon 2 to 3 tablespoons of avocado mayonnaise over each piece of fish, and sprinkle with the grated lime peel. Pass the remaining mayonnaise.

Serves 4 to 6.

AVOCADO AND SPINACH

1 avocado
Juice of 1 lime
2 tablespoons unsalted butter
1 small onion, finely chopped
10 ounces fresh spinach, washed, trimmed, roughly chopped
1 teaspoon bouillon powder
Dash of hot pepper sauce
Salt and freshly ground black pepper

1. Cut the avocado in half lengthwise. Peel, and remove the pit. Cut each half into a fine dice. Sprinkle with the lime juice, cover, and reserve.

2. Melt the butter in a large heavy skillet over medium-low heat. Stir in the onion; cook 3 minutes.

3. Add the spinach with just the water that clings to the leaves. Sprinkle the bouillon over the leaves. Cook, covered, until the spinach wilts, about 3 minutes.

4. Stir the diced avocado into the spinach mixture. Add the hot pepper sauce, and salt and pepper to taste.

Serves 4.

AVOCADO AND SHRIMP VELVET

According to Diana Kennedy, my sibyl on the subject of Mexican cuisine, the leaves of the avocado tree add a delicate but unmistakable anise flavor to a dish if they are toasted and sprinkled on prior to serving. In the following silken blending of avocado and shrimp, a splash of anise-flavored spirits makes a tasty substitute.

One-Cup Hollandaise (recipe follows)
1 avocado
Juice of 1 lemon
2 tablespoons unsalted butter
Whole scallion, bulb and green top, finely chopped
1 tablespoon chopped fresh tarragon, or ½ teaspoon dried
16 large shrimp, shelled, deveined, split down the backs
¼ cup Pernod, or other anise-based liqueur, warmed
Chopped fresh parsley

1. Make the One-Cup Hollandaise. Keep warm, stirring occasionally, over hot water.

2. Cut the avocado in half lengthwise. Peel, and remove the pit. Cut each half into ¼-inch slices crosswise. Sprinkle the slices with the lemon juice, cover, and reserve.

3. Melt the butter in a large heavy skillet over medium heat. Stir in the scallion; cook 1 minute. Add the tarragon and shrimp. Toss until the shrimp turn pink, 3 to 4 minutes. Toss in the avocado slices. Reduce the heat to low. Add the warmed Pernod. Being very careful, set the Pernod aflame. Shake the pan until the flames subside.

4. Transfer the shrimp mixture to a serving dish. Spoon the hollandaise sauce over the top. Sprinkle with parsley. Toss at the table before serving.

Serves 4.

One-Cup Hollandaise

To make the cook's lot somewhat easier, the essential ingredients of Fail-Safe Hollandaise have been amended here to produce a single cup.

2 egg yolks
2 teaspoons lemon juice
½ teaspoon Dijon mustard
8 tablespoons (1 stick) unsalted butter, frozen
Dash of hot pepper sauce
Pinch of ground white pepper
Salt

1. Beat the egg yolks with the lemon juice in the top of a double boiler. Place over the simmering water; stir in the mustard.

2. Cut the butter into eight pieces. Using a small wire whisk, beat the butter into the egg yolk mixture, one piece at a time, stirring well after each addition. Stir in the hot pepper sauce, white pepper, and salt to taste.

Makes about 1 cup.

Avocado comes from the Aztecs' *ahuacatl*, roughly translated as "green testicles." The Spanish conquistadors, obviously of a somewhat priggish nature, censored that cognomen. They phonetically translated the word as *abogado*, which means "lawyer." Time eventually altered that to *aguacate*, but the damage was done. Both the French and the Germans compounded the misconception. France's *poire d'avocat* and Germany's *advokatbirne* have the same meaning: "lawyer's pears."

CURRIED CHICKEN WITH AVOCADO

Instead of mixing and matching it with astringent flavor contrasts, the French most often cloak the sensual avocado in even more luxuriant upholsteries—to wit: a purely Francophile translation of a curry dish. Serve it for supper, lunch or brunch. Chutney and condiments are optional.

4 tablespoons (½ stick) unsalted butter
1 onion, chopped
1 clove garlic, chopped
1 small apple, peeled, cored, chopped
2 to 3 tablespoons curry powder
⅛ teaspoon ground turmeric
3 tablespoons all-purpose flour
1½ cups Chicken Stock (see page 410)
1 cup heavy or whipping cream
2 cups cooked boned chicken
⅛ teaspoon hot pepper sauce
½ teaspoon salt
2 tablespoons lemon juice
1 avocado
Hot Steamed Rice (see page 412)

1. Melt the butter in a medium saucepan over medium-low heat. Stir in the onion; cook 3 minutes. Stir in the garlic, apple, curry powder, turmeric, and flour. Mix well. Cook over low heat, stirring constantly, 2 minutes. Stir in the chicken stock and cream. Heat to boiling; reduce the heat. Simmer gently, uncovered, 15 minutes. Remove from the heat.

2. Place half the curry mixture in a blender or processor. Purée until smooth (carefully, as hot liquid will expand). Transfer to a medium saucepan. Purée the remaining curry mixture and add it to the saucepan.

3. Place the puréed curry mixture over low heat. Stir in the chicken, hot pepper sauce, salt, and 1 tablespoon of the lemon juice. Cook, uncovered, until warmed through, about 10 minutes.

4. Cut the avocado in half lengthwise; peel, and remove the pit. Cut each half into ¼-inch-thick slices crosswise. Sprinkle with the remaining 1 tablespoon lemon juice.

5. Gently stir the avocado slices into the curry. Heat until just warmed through, about 4 minutes. Do not allow to boil. Serve over rice.

Serves 4.

BRAZILIAN AVOCADO CREAM

This dish, *crema aguascate*, might be considered a dessert, but in Brazil (whence it comes) it is most often consumed for breakfast, with a pot of strong black coffee on the side.

1 avocado
Juice of 2 limes
¼ cup light rum or coconut Amaretto
¼ teaspoon vanilla extract
½ cup plus 2 tablespoons confectioners' sugar
1 cup heavy or whipping cream
2 teaspoons finely slivered lime peel

1. Cut the avocado in half lengthwise; remove the pit. Scoop out the flesh from the avocado and place it in the container of a food processor or blender. Add the lime juice, light rum or coconut Amaretto, vanilla, and ½ cup confectioners' sugar. Purée until smooth. Transfer to a large bowl.

2. In a medium bowl, beat the cream with the remaining confectioners' sugar until stiff. Fold the whipped cream into the avocado mixture. Transfer to a serving bowl and sprinkle with slivered lime peel. Chill thoroughly before serving.

Serves 4 to 6.

BEETS

Robust and Red Blooded

To paraphrase Charles Dickens, the very best meals of my life have always been consumed in the very worst of times.

I grew up in the dark, drear days of the thirties, when necessity smothered invention at our kitchen table. If beets were cheap (and they usually were), we ate beets for better or worse, meal after meal—without complaint, knowing that my mother would change the menu as soon as the corner market altered its current "marked-down" merchandise.

My parent was a fierce shopper who saw the battle for her family's survival in terms of pennies, not dollars. Unfortunately I had no such stout heart and a bad sense of arithmetic into the bargain. So I dreaded being elected as her accomplice on market rounds, a ritual that was embarked upon every Saturday evening when she returned from work.

Paula Greene was a born trader, a gift she inherited from her mother. My grandmother, who was a superb cook, could have achieved detective status on a police force if she'd put her mind to it. That woman could spot a thumb on a butcher's scale at fifty yards and had the kind of shrewd, appraising eye that would turn larcenous shopkeepers ashen whenever she appeared at their counters. Long before she pried open a bin of stale coffee or sniffed into a moldy pickle barrel, her deportment implied the righteous mistrust of a consumerist Carrie Nation.

On the rare occasions when they shopped together, my mother and grandmother would make any small businessman quail. In tandem they would chastise a greengrocer about his puny tomatoes (or strawberries) as if he had planted the crop himself; and then laugh when they heard the price. Laugh, I might add, with such a resounding lack of mirth that the poor man usually lowered the cost immediately to put an end to his harassment.

Like seasoned horse traders they would converge upon some article of grocery (a chine of beef or a bushel of beets) and poke, pinch, and tug at the comestible for so long and with such obvious contempt that the outraged seller would finally snatch it from their reach in order to keep it whole. Only then, when the poor man had been hectored and harangued beyond belief, would my grandmother discreetly lower her eyelids and sigh. "I don't really need this. It's not the quality of merchandise I buy. Actually I had something else in mind when I came into the store. But I feel bad taking up so much of your time." Then, looking the purveyor straight in the eye, her voice would drop an octave.

"How much?"

Whatever she was quoted would be dismissed out of hand, and the eventual price would be negotiated like a peace treaty, with much bowing, bending, and breaking away on both parts before my grandmother handed her daughter the commodious black leather pocketbook she carried at all times.

"Pauline. Pay the man," she would finally command, always managing at the last moment to secure exactly the cut of beef or quality of beet she had wanted for her stockpot in the first place.

The shopkeeper's reward for the terrible ordeal of having my mother and grandmother in his store was the hasty retreat the pair made once a purchase was finally realized.

My reward was somewhat more residual. It came from the amalgam of maligned ingredients—the contested beets and beef—into a revivifying bowl of steaming borscht.

Consuming passion alone kept me steadfast, then and now!

Vegetable Roots

The garden-variety beet is a vegetable with a fairly florid past. Columella, the early Roman agriculturist, noted in the first century A.D. that "this curious plant owes its name, *Beta Vulgaris*, to a physical resemblance to the second letter of the alphabet." That beets grow in clumps is an indisputable fact, but I have rarely uncovered a pair that was impacted end-over-end in my garden. So take that information like the beet itself—with a grain of salt.

Early diners prized beets for the wrong reasons, it seems to me, choosing to consume only the red-veined outer leaves in salads and relegating what Pliny referred to as "the crimson nether parts" to pharmacists, surgeons, and soothsayers. In fact, this habit of picking the leaves created a swollen and juicy root, which was to provide future tables with one of the tenderest comestibles that grows. But it took close to a millennium before some trencherman had the good sense to consume a plateful drenched with butter and a jot of lemon juice.

What to Look For

Beets are a year-round vegetable in most parts of the country, but they are undeniably at their best (read tenderest) when picked fresh any time between late June and early October.

Beet shoppers should look out for smooth, spherical orbs with dark red (unmarred) skins and crisp green (never yellowing) leaves. Beet tops, parenthetically, are a good source of potassium and calcium, besides husbanding 7,400 milligrams of vitamin A per cup.

Preparation

For all their earthly connections, beets require only a scant scrub-up (in cold water) before entry into a saucepan. I use a small nailbrush to remove the loose particles of dirt but am exceedingly careful not to break the skin—which bleeds into the cooking liquid if a beet is bruised. Likewise never, never peel a beet prior to cooking, and leave a good inch or so at the stem and root ends to preserve the vegetable's rosy hue.

There is more than one way to cook a beet, but boiling is the most common method. I also fancy the Italian way of oven-steaming them in aluminum foil, a technique I acquired from Marcella Hazan, cooking teacher and author par excellence, in Bologna several years ago—but more of that anon. The generally accepted practice for boiling beets is to place them in a large heavy-duty saucepan filled with unsalted cold water. Bring the water slowly to a boil and simmer, uncovered, until the beets are barely tender, about 35 to 40 minutes. Then plunge the cooked beets under cold running water to retard the cooking and drain them well before peeling.

Beet tops are best wilted. Cook them quickly in a skillet or sauté pan without any liquid other than the water in which they have been washed. Mature beet tops are too tough for such gentle cookery. Boil large, fibrous leaves in salted water for a few minutes to remove any bitterness.

The classic way to prepare beets (in my prejudiced opinion) was limned in a yellowing cookbook written a hundred years ago. This fragile relic was recently sent to me by the writer's great-great-grandson, who felt I could put his forebear's culinary legacy to good use. The "receipt" for *Grandma Clemon's Beets* reads:

> Cut cooked beets fine. Then make sauce as follows: a little sugar, a little vinegar and a little butter. If you like add a few tablespoons of cream to thicken.

All my best beet recipes are variations on that theme.

FINNISH POLAR BEAR'S EYE

It was in a southern climate that beets first grew and found their way into cultivated gardens, but they certainly thrive best in less temperate zones. Red beets are a much-prized staple in Russian and Scandinavian kitchens all winter long. As a matter of fact, one of the best beet dishes in my lexicon comes from Denmark, where it is most unceremoniously dubbed "The Finnish Polar Bear's Eye."

I must add that no Finn I have ever met has acknowledged knowing or having tasted this savory treat. Who cares? The dish is a must as a warm-weather luncheon dish or a year-round hangover cure, depending upon your physical condition. The original prescription appeared in a long-out-of-print tome, Dagmar Freuchen's *Cookbook of the Seven Seas.*

1 large beet (about ½ pound), trimmed
2 medium potatoes
8 anchovy filets, chopped, with the oil from a 2-ounce can
1 medium onion, diced
4 unbroken egg yolks
Freshly ground black pepper

1. Place the beet in a saucepan; cover with cold unsalted water. Heat slowly to boiling; reduce the heat. Simmer, uncovered, until barely tender, about 35 minutes. Drain under cold water. Remove the skin, dice, and reserve.

2. Meanwhile, cook the potatoes, uncovered, in boiling salted water until barely tender, about 20 minutes. Drain; let stand 5 minutes. Peel and dice.

3. While the potatoes are still warm, combine them with the diced beet, the anchovy filets and oil, and the onion. Toss lightly.

4. To serve, divide the beet mixture into four portions and place each on a separate plate. With the back of a spoon, make a small indentation in each portion. Slide an egg yolk into each little "well" and sprinkle it with pepper. Each person mixes the egg yolk into the beets at the table before eating.

Serves 4.

COLD PINK BORSCHT

To my prejudiced tongue another truly classic beet formula (definitely on a par with the aforementioned Grandma Clemon's) is a very unclassic bowl of borscht.

This version, a shocking pink pottage, is a variation on my mother and grandmother's perennial summer cooler. Both ladies would scoff at the addition of cucumbers and (God forbid) garlic, but that gives this rendering its essential savor in my opinion.

They both served borscht in the best American-Jewish tradition: chilled for hours and hours in a refrigerator and then diluted to lukewarm neutrality by the addition of steaming boiled potatoes at the table. I, however, would never consider an adjunct weightier than chopped chives and parsley in my icy soup bowl!

1 pound beets, trimmed
2 medium cucumbers, peeled, seeded
1 clove garlic, chopped
1 cup milk
16 ounces sour cream
Salt and freshly ground black pepper
Chopped chives or scallion tops
Chopped fresh parsley

1. Place the beets in a saucepan and cover with cold unsalted water. Heat slowly to boiling; reduce the heat and cover. Simmer, uncovered, until barely tender, about 35 minutes. Drain under cold water. Remove the skins and chop the beets fine; reserve.

2. Finely chop 1 cucumber; reserve.

3. Roughly chop the remaining cucumber and place it in the container of a blender or food processor. Add the garlic and milk. Process until smooth.

4. Combine the puréed cucumber mixture with the sour cream in a large bowl. Whisk until smooth. Add the chopped beets and cucumber and add salt and pepper to taste. Chill well before serving garnished with chives and parsley.

Serves 4 to 6.

HOT RED KIEV BORSCHT

The following prescription was acquired in the Ukraine, where the morning borscht is flavored with ham and sausage. Contrary to my prior injunction, you will observe that this calls for peeled raw beets to be grated directly into the stockpot. The reason is simple: rather than being washed away, the beets' color literally hues the brew!

2¾ quarts chicken broth (see page 414)
1 pound leftover cooked ham
2 tablespoons unsalted butter
1 tablespoon oil
1 large onion, finely chopped
1 large clove garlic, minced
1 large carrot, peeled, finely chopped
1 turnip, peeled, finely chopped
1 parsnip, peeled, finely chopped
2 large tomatoes, seeded, chopped
1 pound beets, peeled, roughly grated (about 2½ cups)
1 small cabbage (about 1 pound), shredded
1 pound potatoes, peeled, diced
½ teaspoon freshly ground black pepper
⅛ teaspoon ground ginger
2 tablespoons red wine vinegar
1 pound Kielbasa (Polish sausage), sliced
Salt
1 tablespoon chopped fresh parsley

1. Place the chicken broth and the ham in a large heavy pot. Heat to boiling; reduce the heat. Simmer, uncovered, 25 minutes. Remove the ham and allow it to cool. Reserve the broth. Shred the ham and set aside.

2. Heat the butter with the oil in another large heavy pot over medium-low heat. Add the onion; cook 2 minutes. Add the garlic; cook 1 minute longer. Stir in the carrot, turnip, parsnip, tomatoes, and grated beets. Add 2½ cups of the reserved chicken broth. Heat to boiling; reduce the heat. Simmer, covered, 25 minutes.

3. Add the remaining chicken broth to the vegetable mixture. Add the reserved ham, the cabbage and potatoes. Cook, partially covered, 30 minutes.

4. Stir in the pepper, ginger, and vinegar. Continue to cook, covered, over low heat for 1 hour. (Recipe may be prepared in advance to this point, cooled, and refrigerated until ready to serve. The flavor will improve as it stands.)

5. To serve, reheat the soup if it was made in advance, and add the sliced sausage. Simmer, partially covered, 15 minutes. Add salt to taste, and more vinegar if needed. Sprinkle with chopped parsley.

Serves 8 to 10.

PERSIAN BEETS

One of the most felicitous salads I can name is this one comprised of peeled baby beets anointed with a sauce of heavy sour cream and fresh mint leaves.

1½ pounds small beets, trimmed
2 shallots, minced
1 cup plain yogurt
¼ cup heavy or whipping cream
1 tablespoon strong Chicken Stock, reduced from ⅓ cup (see page 410), or 1 teaspoon bouillon powder
Salt
¼ cup fresh mint leaves

1. Place the beets in a saucepan; cover with cold unsalted water. Heat slowly to boiling; reduce the heat. Simmer, uncovered, until barely tender, about 25 minutes. Drain under cold water. Remove the skins but leave whole.

2. Pat the beets dry with paper towels and place them in a serving dish. Sprinkle with the shallots.

3. Beat the yogurt with the cream in a medium bowl. Beat in the stock or bouillon powder until smooth, adding salt to taste. Spoon the sauce over the beets and decorate with mint leaves.

Serves 4.

OVEN-STEAMED BEETS

Earlier I alluded to the Italian way of oven-steaming beets. This is a must for any vitamin-conscious cook, and the technique is *molto bonario* (very easy). I learned it from Marcella Hazan during a week of her remarkable kitchen wizardry in Bologna, and I never deviate from it a jot.

1. Wash and trim the fresh beets, and wrap each one tightly in aluminum foil. Place them on a rack in a preheated 350°F oven and steam them in their own juices until they sizzle and are tender-crisp, about 1½ hours.

2. Remove the foil, allow the beets to stand until they can be handled, and then proceed with any recipe at hand.

Careful! It's easy to burn your hands when removing the foil, so watch it!

MARCELLA HAZAN'S BAKED BEETS AND ONIONS

After steaming, start dreaming. This makes a simple but heavenly dish.

4 large beets (about 2 pounds), trimmed
1 large Bermuda onion with skin
1½ tablespoons red wine vinegar
½ teaspoon balsamic vinegar (optional; see Notes on Ingredients, page 417)
½ teaspoon salt
⅓ cup olive oil

1. Preheat the oven to 350°F. Wrap each beet tightly in aluminum foil.

2. Cut a ⅛-inch-deep X into the root end of the onion. Place the onion and the beets in a shallow baking pan and bake until barely tender, 1 to 1¼ hours. (To test, pierce the onion and each beet with a wooden skewer.) Remove the foil from the beets; let stand 20 minutes.

3. Remove the skins from the beets and cut into ⅓-inch-wide julienne strips. Peel the onion and cut crosswise into ¼-inch-thick slices, then cut the slices in half. Combine the beets and onions in a medium-size bowl.

4. Combine the vinegars, salt, and oil in a small bowl. Mix well. Pour the dressing over the beets and onion. Let stand at room temperature for 3 hours before serving.

Serves 6.

TANGY MINTED BEETS

In my garden, beets grow in a sunny tract that is otherwise overrun with headstrong mint. The connection is my design. Long ago I discovered that leaf miners (insects that devastate garden greens) abhor the scent of mint and avoid that patch like the plague.

My tender beets are therefore unsullied, and as a reward I season them with lots of fresh mint.

1½ pounds beets, trimmed
2 tablespoons unsalted butter
1 shallot, minced
⅓ cup apple jelly
2 tablespoons chopped fresh mint
2 teaspoons lemon juice
Salt and freshly ground black pepper

1. Place the beets in a saucepan; cover with cold unsalted water. Heat slowly to boiling; reduce the heat. Simmer, uncovered, until barely tender, about 35 minutes. Drain under cold water. Remove the skins and cut the beets into slices; reserve.

2. Melt the butter in a large skillet over medium-low heat. Stir in the shallot; cook 4 minutes. Stir in the beets, apple jelly, mint, and lemon juice. Cook until warmed through. Add salt and pepper to taste.

Serves 4.

BEETS IN HORSERADISH CREAM

1½ pounds beets, trimmed
2 tablespoons unsalted butter
4 slices Canadian bacon, diced
½ cup heavy or whipping cream
2 tablespoons prepared horseradish
3 tablespoons chopped fresh dill
Salt and freshly ground black pepper

1. Place the beets in a saucepan; cover with cold unsalted water. Heat slowly to boiling; reduce the heat. Simmer, uncovered, until barely tender, about 35 minutes. Drain under cold water. Remove the skins and chop the beets; reserve.

2. Melt the butter in a large skillet over medium heat. Sauté the bacon until light brown, about 3 minutes. Stir in the beets, cream, horseradish, and 2 tablespoons of the dill. Reduce the heat to low, and cook 6 minutes. Add salt and pepper to taste and sprinkle with the remaining 1 tablespoon dill.

Serves 4.

BEETS IN MUSTARD SAUCE

1½ pounds beets, trimmed
3 tablespoons unsalted butter
¼ cup minced shallots
1 tablespoon all-purpose flour
½ cup strong Chicken Stock (see page 410)
3 tablespoons Dijon mustard
¼ cup heavy or whipping cream
Salt and freshly ground black pepper
Chopped fresh parsley

1. Place the beets in a saucepan and cover with cold unsalted water. Heat slowly to boiling; reduce the heat. Simmer, uncovered, until barely tender, about 35 minutes. Drain under cold water. Remove the skins and cut into slices; reserve.

2. Melt the butter in a large skillet over medium-low heat. Add the shallots; cook 4 minutes. Stir in the flour and cook, stirring constantly, 2 minutes. Whisk in the stock, then add the mustard and heavy cream. Cook until slightly thickened.

3. Add the beets to the sauce. Cook, stirring often, until warmed through. Add salt and pepper to taste and garnish with chopped parsley.

Serves 4.

GINGERED BEETS

Here's another tasty partnership: beets with a spiking of ginger.

1½ pounds small beets, trimmed
⅓ cup seedless raisins
2 tablespoons unsalted butter
1½ teaspoons minced fresh ginger root
1 tablespoon sugar
1 teaspoon red wine vinegar
1 teaspoon finely slivered lime peel

1. Place the beets in a saucepan; cover with cold unsalted water. Heat slowly to boiling; reduce the heat. Simmer, uncovered, until barely tender, about 25 minutes.

2. Remove just enough beet liquid to cover the raisins in a small bowl. Let them stand 10 minutes. Meanwhile, drain the beets under cold water. Remove the skins and cut the beets into slices; reserve. Drain the raisins; reserve.

3. Melt the butter in a large skillet over medium-low heat. Stir in the ginger; cook 5 minutes. Add the reserved beets and raisins, the sugar, and the vinegar. Cook until warmed through; sprinkle with the lime peel.

Serves 4.

ORANGE-SCENTED BEETS

Beets are fairly hardy in the kitchen, holding their own with any number of otherwise overwhelming flavors. Take, for instance, the next prescription.

1½ pounds small beets, trimmed
2 tablespoons unsalted butter
1 small onion, finely chopped
3 tablespoons sugar
1 tablespoon red wine vinegar
Grated peel of 1 medium orange
Grated peel of 1 small lemon
Juice of 1 medium orange
Pinch of ground cinnamon
Salt and freshly ground black pepper
Chopped fresh parsley

1. Place the beets in a saucepan; cover with cold unsalted water. Heat slowly to boiling; reduce the heat. Simmer, uncovered, until barely tender, about 25 minutes. Drain under cold water. Remove the skins and cut the beets into slices; reserve.

2. Melt the butter in a large skillet over medium heat. Add the onion; cook until golden. Add the sugar, vinegar, orange and lemon peel, orange juice, and the cinnamon. Stir in the beets. Cook, stirring often, 10 minutes. Add salt and pepper to taste, and garnish with chopped parsley.

Serves 4.

IRMA WEHAUSEN'S PICKLED BEETS

When I was a youngster, the same grandmother who made the pink borscht seriously insisted that a small plateful of her pickled beets taken along with meat and vegetables at dinner would ward off "heartache." (She meant heartburn.) Malaprops aside, my grandmother's nostrums were not to be sneezed at: she made a very *tonic* peck of pickled beets, and who knows what magic went into the formula?

A most unlikely successor to my Jewish grandmother is a spare and dignified Lutheran churchgoer from Golden, Colorado, who gave me her own prescription some while back. Mrs. Wehausen's beets may not inhibit heartache, exactly—but they sure taste good enough to give it a whirl.

10 medium beets (about 3 pounds), trimmed
2 cups sugar
2 cups distilled white vinegar
2 teaspoons whole mixed pickling spices
1 medium onion, thinly sliced

1. Place the beets in a saucepan; cover with cold unsalted water. Heat slowly to boiling; reduce the heat. Simmer, uncovered, until barely tender, about 35 minutes. Drain under cold water. Remove the skins and cut into ⅛-inch-thick slices. (You should have about 6 cups.)

2. Combine 2 cups water, the sugar, vinegar, and pickling spices in a large

saucepan. Heat to boiling; add the sliced beets. Return to boiling, reduce the heat, and simmer 10 minutes.

3. With a slotted spoon, transfer the beets to a large mixing bowl. Add the sliced onion and toss well.

4. Return the syrup in the saucepan to boiling; simmer until slightly reduced, about 4 minutes.

5. Place the beet-onion mixture in sterilized jars. Pour enough hot syrup into each jar to cover the beets. Seal, and let stand unrefrigerated at least one week. Chill well before serving.

Makes about 4 pints.

For all its history of culinary restraint, the beet is a most decisive flavor-enhancer to many essentially nonbeet recipes.

For instance: a small beet added to a pan of stewing apples will produce a sweetly roseate sauce; and a mite of grated raw beet (never more than a tablespoon) will give a boost to any lackluster meat loaf, particularly if one amends the drippings with a spoon of heavy cream later.

SOUFFLE ROSE

(Beet Soufflé)

A confession.

In case you hadn't noticed, my American cooking hand is sometimes at war with a European hankering for high-blown nomenclature. Take the next recipe as a case in point: a soufflé with not a drop of *rose* in its architecture; just beets, eggs, and the usual high hopes.

3 tablespoons unsalted butter
1 tablespoon fresh fine bread crumbs
1¼ pounds beets, trimmed, tops reserved
1 teaspoon sugar
3 tablespoons all-purpose flour
1 cup hot milk
⅛ teaspoon freshly grated nutmeg
¼ teaspoon salt
⅛ teaspoon freshly ground black pepper
4 egg yolks
¾ cup grated Swiss cheese
5 egg whites
2 teaspoons cornstarch
¾ cup Beef Stock (see page 409)
3 tablespoons heavy or whipping cream

1. Rub a 1½-quart soufflé dish with 1 teaspoon of the butter. Sprinkle with bread crumbs; set aside.

2. Place the beets in a saucepan; cover with cold unsalted water. Heat slowly to boiling; reduce the heat. Simmer, uncovered, until barely tender, about 35 minutes. Drain under cold water. Remove the skins and roughly grate the beets; reserve.

3. Preheat the oven to 375°F.

4. Remove the veins from the beet tops. Cook the tops for 5 minutes in boiling water to which you have added 1 teaspoon sugar. Drain under cold water. Press lightly to remove excess liquid. Chop and reserve.

5. Melt 2 tablespoons of the butter in a medium saucepan over medium-low heat. Stir in the flour. Cook, stirring constantly, 2 minutes. Whisk in the hot milk all at once. Beat until smooth; continue to cook until very thick. Add the nutmeg, salt and pepper. Remove from the heat and beat in the egg yolks, one at a time, beating well after each addition. Transfer the mixture to a bowl. Stir in the grated beets and cheese.

6. Beat the egg whites until stiff but not dry. Fold them into the beet mixture and spoon into the prepared soufflé dish. Bake until puffed and firm, about 30 minutes.

7. Meanwhile, melt the remaining 2 teaspoons butter in a medium saucepan over medium-low heat. Stir in the cornstarch until smooth. Whisk in the beef stock. Heat to boiling; add the reserved beet tops and the cream. Reduce the heat and simmer until slightly thickened. Taste and add more salt and pepper if needed, and serve the sauce with the soufflé.

Serves 4 to 6.

RED FLANNEL HASH

This recipe is so old-fashioned it hurts. But out of a wealth I have encountered, this is the *most* definitive version, and it's the beet's finest hour. Or maybe the second finest, after the aforementioned borscht!

½ pound beets, trimmed
2 medium potatoes, peeled
3 cups cubed cooked corned beef
2 carrots, peeled, finely chopped
1 small green pepper, seeded, finely chopped
1 large onion, finely chopped
1 small clove garlic, minced
3 tablespoons chopped fresh parsley
2½ tablespoons unsalted butter
1 teaspoon Worcestershire sauce
1 teaspoon hot pepper sauce, or to taste
¼ cup tomato juice, approximately
Salt and freshly ground black pepper
4 to 6 poached eggs

1. Place the beets in a saucepan; cover with cold unsalted water. Heat slowly to boiling; reduce the heat. Simmer, uncovered, until barely tender, about 35 minutes. Drain under cold water. Remove the skins, cube, and place in a large bowl.

2. Cook the potatoes in boiling salted water for 10 minutes. Drain. Cool slightly, cut into cubes, and add to the beets.

3. To the beets and potatoes add the corned beef, carrots, green pepper, onion, garlic, and parsley. Mix well.

4. Melt the butter in a 10-inch ovenproof skillet over medium heat. Press the corned beef mixture into the skillet. Cook, uncovered, 6 minutes. Stir in the Worcestershire sauce, hot pepper sauce, tomato juice, and salt and pepper to taste. Cook over medium-low heat, without stirring, 30 minutes.

5. While the corned beef mixture is cooking, preheat the oven to 350°F.

6. Using two large spatulas, turn the mixture over in the skillet (or flip it over into a second skillet). Place the skillet in the oven and bake until the potatoes are tender and the top is browned, about 30 minutes. Add more tomato juice if the mixture seems too dry. Serve topped with poached eggs.

Serves 4 to 6.

BROCCOLI

The Five Fingers of Jupiter

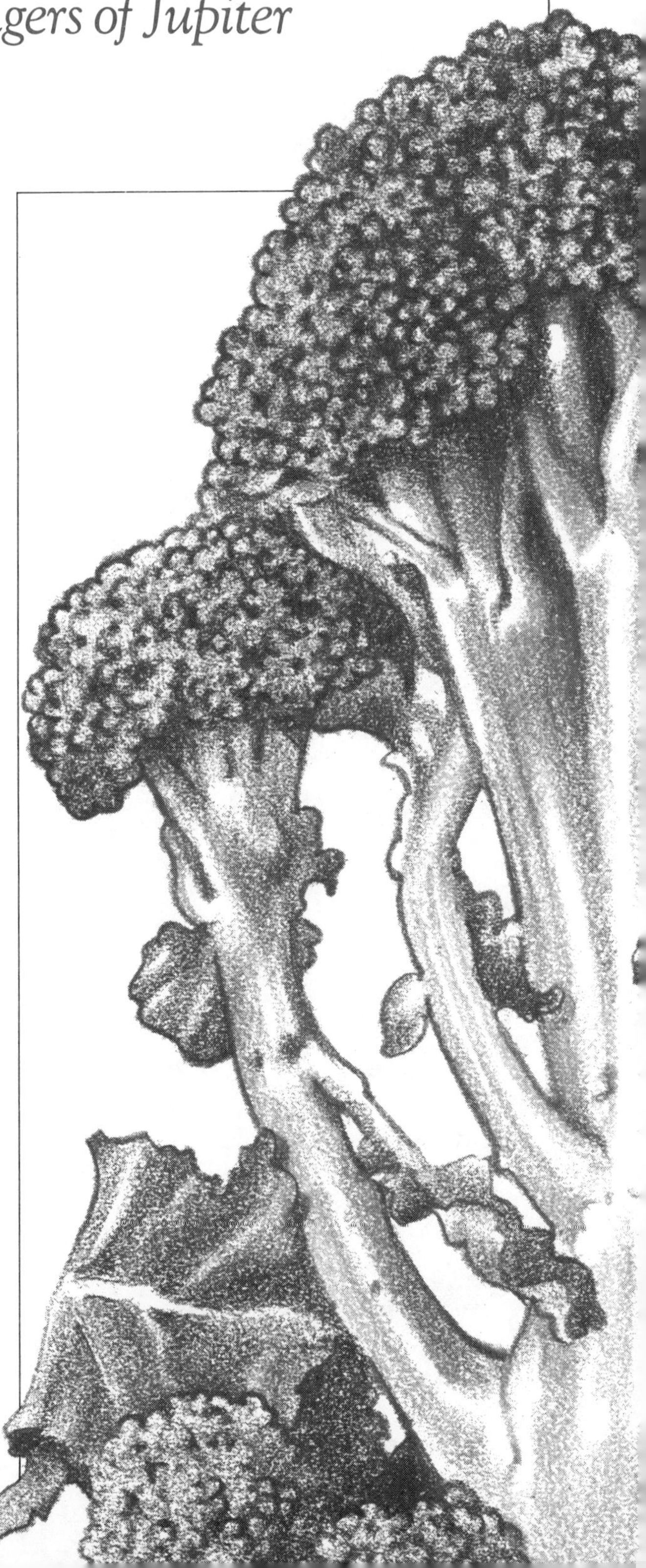

My maternal grandfather was the eldest of five brothers and a paternal type to boot. So it is not surprising that after he emigrated to America he felt compelled to send for his siblings, one by one.

Each successive "greenhorn" brother lived under my grandfather's roof—some for months, others for years—remaining in the familial nest until his patriarchal kinsman had deemed him sufficiently Americanized to fly. And long after these men had advanced to maturity (married and sired progeny of their own) their brother's opinion was inevitably sought on any business matter that concerned their well-being. No one went into business (nor out of it into bankruptcy) without his counsel. And his word, once pronounced, was considered law—except once.

Grandfather's youngest brother, Max, was twenty-five years his junior and of a very different stripe. Sent to this country as a boy (to escape conscription in the Russian army), he was obviously no trailblazer for he remained in my grandparents' home until he was past fifty. Unlike the headstrong brothers who had preceded him, the last arrival never seemed to hunger for independence. He lived most of his life in a bleak room above my grandmother's kitchen, at the top of a steep and exceedingly dark back staircase.

Max's room was like a commercial lodger's, so devoid of belongings or personal stamp it had no smell other than cleansing powder. Besides being anonymous, Max's room was also separated from the body of the house by a hallway bathroom that peremptorily locked him out of the mainstream of the family's life.

Almost a son in age to my grandmother, Max was seemingly unable to elicit from her any form of emotional response other than aloofness. Unquestionably she took pains to see he was well fed and cared for, but nothing else. And though a lifetime has passed, I can still remember how cold her soft eyes would become whenever she spoke to him. Mr grandmother had lost her first born (and only male) child shortly before Max came into her life and while no one in the family ever hinted at any Freudian connection, it seems evident that her public distaste for one stemmed from a private grief about the other.

I never knew my great-uncle when he was young, of course, but he was rumored to have had quite an eye for the ladies. Despite the gossip, Max was hardly a bachelor one might have mistaken for a romantic figure. He had a bad squint for one thing and a hoarse, laryngitic voice for another, plus a touch of deafness. Nor, to put it bluntly, was he much of a *bon vivant*; his thrift was so well marked in the family that my father always referred to him as "your mother's skinflint relative."

Max's single splurge in life was his unexpected courtship of a not-quite-divorced lady. The object of my uncle's affection was a red-haired, boisterous, and extremely well-endowed woman from Cleveland who had come, with a distant cousin of the family, to celebrate Passover in my grandparents' house.

Seder, the holiday dinner at which Jews commemorate the flight of their ancestors, is usually a fairly solemn affair, but not in our family. Both my father and uncles were irreligious types whose attitude inevitably turned the holiday into an unbridled orgy of my grandmother's cooking.

The Ohio guests were rather florid women, speaking in flat accents and laughing louder than necessary at family jokes that were made ritually, year after year. My cousin's friend, who was prettier, laughed loudest and her large bosom shook when she did.

"That lady needs a corset " was my grandmother's only comment after her Passover guest departed. Max did not respond; he had not taken his eyes off her the whole evening.

Family accounts were cloudy (particularly when one was an adolescent whose morals had to be protected at all costs) but from overheard conversations it became increasingly clear that my uncle's passion was full-fledged. And fulfilled.

Less than a month after Passover, Uncle Max made a trip to the Midwest, ostensibly on business. When he returned, he announced to my grandfather that he intended to marry the red-haired Clevelander as soon as she could obtain a divorce.

Prior to World War II, this type of behavior was not common except perhaps in Hollywood—and that was a far cry from Queens. My grandfather heartily disapproved of the match, but my uncle defied him. In due time, leaving his good graces *and* his home, he married the lady in question.

My grandparents were conspicuously absent from the wedding, though to be fair, it was held in Cleveland. My grandmother professed delight to be rid of her brother-in-law, but with a shade of foreboding: "She's too young for him and she dyes her hair. She only married him for one thing—his money. Mark my words, she'll leave him in a year's time," she warned direly, "and he'll want to come back here." That none of her prognostications came about nettled her considerably more than if they had.

To mend the family rift, after Max and his wife returned and established a

home of their own, his wife prepared a long and elaborate dinner to which she invited the entire family. There was much admiration of her china and silver (assembled from the prior marriage), but my grandmother was neither swayed by these artifacts nor mollified by her evident cooking talents. I can still recall her comments on the ride home. My mother, to lighten the mood—for it was funereal, professed mild surprise that her new "aunt" cooked with such apparent proficiency.

"You call that cooking?" my grandmother expostulated with some rancor. "He'll be dead in a year's time . . . mark my words." She shook her head gravely. "Never, never trust a woman who would turn a perfectly respectable vegetable like broccoli into a *casserole* with cheese!"

And that was her last word on the subject.

Vegetable Roots

Broccoli is a legacy we inherited from the Romans. Caesar and all the rest of his crowd loved that leggy green *(Brassica oleracea italica)* with such a passion that it was served up twice and sometimes even three times during a meal—apparently always to the diner's delight although the method of its cookery never varied. Roman chefs simply boiled broccoli "before bruising it" in the manner that Apicius prescribed: "with a mixture of cumin and coriander seeds, chopped onion plus a few drops of oil and sun-made wine."

Drusus, the eldest son of the Emperor Tiberius, was so addicted to this recipe that the poor fellow ate nothing but broccoli for a month. According to Pliny the Elder, Drusus gave up broccoli only when his urine turned bright green, and he was severely upbraided by his father for "living precariously." Let all manic broccoli lovers profit by his example.

The word *broccoli* is a corruption of the Latin *bracchium*, which means a strong arm or branch; Roman farmers referred to this vegetable as "the five green fingers of Jupiter."

What to Look For

Unfortunately most broccoli comes prepackaged these days, but wise shoppers will seek out a supermarket shelf where it is kept cool. You will recognize a fresh bunch by its tight blue-green flowerets and firm stalks. Woody stems and open-cored branches should be avoided; they're hard to chew. Likewise pass by any yellowing or limp buds—always a dead giveaway of an overlong shelf-life. Strong-smelling broccoli will be even stronger-flavored when it is cooked. Skip it, please.

A good method for storing broccoli in the refrigerator comes from Janeen Sarlin, a green-thumbed cooking friend. After breaking the stalks roughly and removing the green leaves, she places the stems of an entire bunch in a 1- to 2-quart pitcher or wide-mouthed jar filled with ice water and covers it with a loose plastic bag. The broccoli stays fresh and tight as a bunch of jonquils for a week.

Preparation

Broccoli is easy to grow and equally easy to prepare. The trick is to cook it quickly, so that each stalk retains a measure of "bite" at the knuckle.

The classic preparation is to blanch (or steam) broccoli quickly in a small amount of boiling salted water in a covered saucepan, never longer than 4 to 5 minutes for a fork-tender floweret and a slightly more resilient stem. If you steam, allow an additional 5 or so minutes.

Different cooks have differing opinions on the steps prior to the pot. One sure-fire way to guarantee that broccoli tops and bottoms cook evenly is to peel the stalks with a vegetable parer, exactly as you would asparagus. Some kitchen pundits claim that a prefatory 30-minute

soaking in cold water with a teaspoon each of sugar and salt will ensure a perfect, crisp branch. Others insist that an X incised in the base of every stem before it hits the boiling water does the trick for them. I eschew all such excess groundwork because my kitchen space and time are both severely limited. More to the point, I can never tell the difference once it's on the fork.

FLAMMIFERO

This most tempting cold hors d'oeuvre comes from Rome and uses broccoli *stalks* only. The raw stalks are whittled to the size of kitchen matches. Hence the moniker: it means "matches." Reserve the flowerets for another recipe.

3 or 4 large, thick broccoli stalks (1½ to 2 pounds)
2 small ripe tomatoes, peeled, seeded, chopped
1 small clove garlic, mashed
¼ teaspoon coarse (kosher) salt
2 teaspoons lemon juice
1 teaspoon red wine vinegar
¼ cup olive oil
3 tablespoons freshly grated Parmesan cheese
Freshly ground black pepper

1. Peel the broccoli stalks and cut them into thin julienne strips, about 2 inches long. Place the strips in a bowl and add the tomatoes. Set aside.

2. Mash the garlic with the salt in a small bowl until a paste is formed. Beat in the lemon juice, vinegar, and oil. Pour the dressing over the broccoli. Add the cheese and pepper to taste. Toss well. Chill at least 1 hour before serving.

Serves 4 to 6.

BROCCOLI HOT POT

Broccoli is an excellent base for soups as it has a remarkable affinity for those things dear to any tureen: chicken broth, potatoes, leeks, and garlic too! My favored broccoli soup prescription actually has a double life. It comes to the table first as a rough-and-tumble hot chowder; then the leftovers make a second appearance, as a pale viridian Broccoli Vichyssoise.

1 pound broccoli
2 leeks
1 tablespoon unsalted butter
1 clove garlic, minced
⅛ teaspoon crushed dried hot red peppers
3 medium potatoes, peeled, diced
3½ cups chicken broth (see page 414)
¼ teaspoon freshly grated nutmeg
Salt and freshly ground black pepper

1. Cut the broccoli tops into flowerets and set them aside.

2. Cut off the top 3 inches of the stems, peel them, and cut them into thin strips, about 1½ inches long. Set them aside.

3. Trim the leeks, leaving about 2 inches of green ends. Wash the leeks thoroughly under cold running water to remove all sand. Pat dry on paper towels. Chop, and set aside.

4. Melt the butter in a large saucepan over medium-low heat. Add the chopped leeks. Cook, stirring occasionally, 4 minutes. Add the garlic and crushed red pepper; cook 3 minutes longer.

5. Add the broccoli flowerets, broccoli stems, and potatoes to the saucepan. Toss lightly. Add the chicken broth and heat to boiling; reduce the heat. Simmer the soup, uncovered, until the broccoli and potatoes are tender, about 25 minutes. Season with the nutmeg, and salt and pepper to taste.

Serves 4 to 6.

BROCCOLI VICHYSSOISE

A long while back, Craig Claiborne started a campaign to instruct Americans how *vichyssoise* should be pronounced. For the record, it's not *veeshy-swah*, but *veeshee-swahze!* The campaign never got very far, but the soup has endured on restaurant menus around the world for almost fifty years. My version, based on the Broccoli Hot Pot above, merely blends the soup (warm) with cream and milk. If you are using leftover soup, just add equal amounts of cream and milk until you come up with a velvety texture. Chill it well before serving.

1 whole recipe Broccoli Hot Pot (see above)
2 cups heavy or whipping cream
2 cups milk, approximately
Salt and freshly ground black pepper
3 tablespoons finely chopped raw broccoli flowerets

1. Make the Broccoli Hot Pot and allow it to cool slightly.

2. Purée the soup in a blender or processor (carefully: warm liquid will expand). Transfer it to a large bowl and add the cream and enough milk for a smooth consistency. Season to taste. Chill thoroughly before serving garnished with chopped broccoli.

Serves 8 or more.

BROCCOLI VALENCIENNE

Two of my best broccoli recipes are summer dividends that may be eaten all year round. Salads (or first courses if you insist), they are amended with the flavors of orange or tomato. The first is a residual of a trip to Spain; the second—Tomato Broccoli—springs full-blown from my catering days at The Store in Amagansett.

1½ to 2 pounds broccoli
2 large shallots, minced
1 small red onion, thinly sliced
1 teaspoon finely slivered orange peel
1 teaspoon Dijon mustard
3 tablespoons tarragon vinegar
1 tablespoon dry sherry
¾ cup olive oil
Salt and freshly ground black pepper
¼ cup toasted slivered almonds

1. Cut the broccoli tops into flowerets. Cut off the top 3 inches of the stems, peel them, and cut into thin strips, about 1½ inches long. Cook flowerets and stems, covered, in 3 inches boiling salted water until just barely tender, 4 to 5 minutes. Rinse under cold running water. Drain.

2. Transfer the drained broccoli to a large bowl. Add the shallots, onion, and orange peel. Toss lightly.

3. Combine the mustard with the vinegar, sherry, and oil in a medium bowl. Pour the dressing over the broccoli and season with salt and pepper to taste. Chill thoroughly before serving sprinkled with almonds.

Serves 4 to 6.

Though broccoli became popular in America in the mid-twentieth century, it arrived here a heck of a long time before that. Most food snoops credit Thomas Jefferson with the distinction of bringing broccoli seeds from Italy to his bountiful gardens at Monticello.

Jefferson's broccoli plants flourished, but the green was never a popular dish at his table. Having done some research on Jeffersonian cuisine lately, I suspect it was because his kitchen staff overcooked it! And as T.J. liked vegetables to have a bite . . . he overlooked it!

TOMATO BROCCOLI

1½ pounds broccoli
2 tablespoons unsalted butter
1 tablespoon vegetable oil
1 medium onion, chopped
1 clove garlic, minced
2 medium tomatoes, chopped
1 teaspoon sugar
1 teaspoon fresh basil, or ½ teaspoon dried
1 teaspoon fresh oregano, or ½ teaspoon dried
½ cup Mayonnaise (see page 408)
Salt and freshly ground black pepper
Halved cherry tomatoes (optional)

1. Cut the broccoli tops into flowerets. Cut off the top 3 inches of the stems, peel them, and cut them into thin strips, about 1½ inches long. Cook flowerets and stems, covered, in 3 inches boiling salted water until just barely tender, 4 to 5 minutes. Rinse under cold water. Drain, and set aside.

2. Heat the butter with the oil in a medium saucepan over medium-low heat. Add the onion; cook 2 minutes. Add the garlic; cook 2 minutes longer. Stir in the tomatoes; sprinkle with the sugar, basil, and oregano. Simmer, uncovered, over medium heat until soft, about 15 minutes. Cool slightly.

3. Transfer the tomato mixture to

the container of a food processor or blender. Process until smooth. In a large bowl, combine the tomato purée with the mayonnaise. Add the broccoli; mix thoroughly. Add salt and pepper to taste. Chill thoroughly before serving garnished with cherry tomato halves.

Serves 4.

BLEU BROCCOLI WITH WALNUTS

An alliance of broccoli sauced with bleu cheese and walnuts that may soon become a classic.

1½ pounds broccoli
¼ pound creamy bleu cheese
¼ cup heavy or whipping cream
2 teaspoons unsalted butter
1 small clove garlic, minced
½ cup roughly chopped walnuts
¼ teaspoon freshly ground black pepper

1. Cut the broccoli tops into flowerets. Cut off the top 3 inches of the stems, peel them, and cut them into thin strips, about 1½ inches long. Cook flowerets and stems, covered, in 3 inches boiling salted water until just barely tender, 4 to 5 minutes. Drain.

2. Mash the bleu cheese with the cream in a small bowl until fairly smooth. Set aside.

3. Melt the butter in a medium-size saucepan over medium heat. Add the garlic and walnuts. Cook, stirring constantly, until lightly browned.

4. Add the broccoli to the walnuts. Add the cheese mixture and pepper. Toss until just warmed through.

Serves 4.

PAPPA D'BROCCOLE

The name of this Venetian dish translates literally as broccoli porridge. But if you would feel better calling it a purée, be my guest.

1½ pounds broccoli
3 tablespoons unsalted butter
2 shallots, chopped
1¼ cups beef broth (see page 414)
⅓ cup chopped sliced prosciutto
½ cup heavy or whipping cream

1. Cut the broccoli tops into flowerets and set them aside.

2. Cut off the top 3 inches of the stems, peel them, and cut them into thin strips, about 1½ inches long. Set them aside.

3. Melt the butter in a medium saucepan over medium-low heat. Add the shallots; cook 2 minutes. Add the broccoli stems and beef broth. Cook, covered, until tender, about 10 minutes.

4. Add the broccoli flowerets, raise

the heat, and cook, uncovered, until almost all liquid has evaporated. Add the prosciutto and continue to cook until all the liquid has evaporated, about 3 minutes. Stir in the cream; cook 3 minutes longer.

5. Transfer the broccoli mixture to a blender or food processor, and process until smooth but not mushy. Reheat slightly before serving.

Serves 4.

CHEVRE'D BROCCOLI

A second broccoli-cum-cheese presentation. This time the vegetable is bedded in a snowy blanket of goat cheese and herbs.

1½ pounds broccoli
2 tablespoons unsalted butter
1 tablespoon olive oil
2 shallots, minced
1 clove garlic, minced
¼ cup Chicken Stock (see page 410)
⅔ cup crumbled chèvre (goat cheese)
1 teaspoon chopped chives
1 teaspoon chopped fresh basil, or ½ teaspoon dried
½ teaspoon chopped fresh tarragon, or a pinch of dried
1 teaspoon chopped fresh parsley
Salt and freshly ground black pepper

1. Cut the broccoli tops into flowerets. Cut off about 3 inches of the stems, peel them, and cut them into thin strips, about 1½ inches long. Set both aside.

2. Heat the butter with the oil in a medium saucepan over medium-low heat. Add the shallots; cook 2 minutes. Add the garlic; cook 1 minute longer. Add the broccoli flowerets and stems and toss to coat each piece. Add the chicken stock. Cover, and cook until just barely tender, 4 to 5 minutes.

3. Raise the heat slightly and cook, uncovered, until all but 1 tablespoon liquid has evaporated. (Do not leave more than that in the pan.) Toss in the chèvre and continue to cook, tossing constantly, until the cheese melts and forms a sauce. Sprinkle with the herbs and add salt and pepper to taste.

Serves 4.

Until the late 1920s virtually no one in America had ever heard of broccoli, let alone tasted it—with the exception of Italian immigrants like our neighbors the Pitellas. I can still recall their garden because it was so unlike everyone else's neatly manicured plot of greenery on the street. No zinnia, gladiolus, or blue flag iris flourished in the sun trap behind their house. Instead, the Pitellas staked tomatoes, peppers, eggplant, and zucchini. Basil bordered their rows and broccoli grew like a weed betwixt the bamboo tethers. It was a windfall of flavors, a veritable *verdura Siciliano*, on the vine. Yet no Greene could be persuaded to try a forkful. Why? Fear of the unknown, I guess. There is a moral here: live and learn—to love broccoli!

BROCCOLI FRITTATA, PARMA STYLE

This is the very best Italian frittata I have ever sampled.

5 tablespoons unsalted butter
1 tablespoon olive oil
1 medium onion, chopped
1 clove garlic, minced
½ cup cooked chopped ham or Canadian bacon
2 cups small broccoli flowerets (from about 1¼ pounds broccoli)
20 strands cooked spaghetti, roughly chopped (leftover is fine)
6 eggs
½ cup freshly grated Parmesan cheese
½ teaspoon crushed dried hot red pepper

1. Heat 3 tablespoons of the butter with the oil in a heavy 10-inch skillet over medium heat. Sauté the onion until golden. Add the garlic and ham; cook 3 minutes. Stir in the broccoli flowerets and spaghetti; toss until well coated with the mixture. Remove from the heat.

2. Beat the eggs in a large bowl until light. Add the broccoli mixture and all but 2 tablespoons of the Parmesan cheese.

3. Melt 1 tablespoon of the butter in the same skillet over medium heat. Pour in the broccoli-egg mixture. Immediately reduce the heat to low; cook, without stirring, 20 minutes.

4. Using a long spatula, carefully loosen the edges of the frittata and run the spatula underneath to loosen the bottom. Place a shallow plate over the skillet and quickly invert the frittata onto it.

5. Melt the remaining 1 tablespoon butter in the same skillet over medium-low heat. Carefully slide the frittata back into the pan. Sprinkle it with the crushed pepper and the remaining Parmesan cheese. Cook 5 minutes longer. Serve from the pan, in wedges—hot, cold, or at room temperature.

Serves 4 to 6.

BROCCOLI MOUSSELINE

In Italy broccoli is sometimes called the "poor man's asparagus," because the ideal rendering for one is so much like the other. Hollandaise sauce is indubitably asparagus' finest upholstery, and you won't go wrong with a spoonful of it on broccoli either. But, in my opinion at least, the rougher texture of the latter green benefits from a silkier and somewhat lightened dressing on occasion. Hence broccoli sluiced with mousseline sauce: hollandaise plus unsweetened whipped cream.

1½ to 2 pounds broccoli
2 egg yolks
2 tablespoons lemon juice
1½ teaspoons Dijon mustard
8 tablespoons (1 stick) unsalted butter, frozen
Dash of hot pepper sauce
Pinch of ground white pepper
Salt
¼ cup heavy or whipping cream

1. Pull apart the large stems of the broccoli bunch. Cut off the bottoms of the stems, leaving about 3½ inches. Peel the stems, and split the large ones in half lengthwise. Cook the broccoli, covered, in 3 inches of boiling salted water until just barely tender, 4 to 5 minutes. Drain. Transfer to a serving platter and keep warm.

2. Beat the egg yolks with the lemon juice in the top of a double boiler. Place it over boiling water, being careful that the bottom of the pan does not touch the water. Stir in the mustard.

3. Divide the butter into eight pieces. Using a fork, stir the butter into the egg yolk mixture, one piece at a time. Stir well after each addition. Stir in the hot pepper sauce, white pepper, and salt to taste. Remove from the heat.

4. Beat the cream until stiff and fold it into the egg yolk mixture. Spoon the sauce over the broccoli.

Serves 4 to 6.

BROCCOLI AND PASTA TIMBALE

Despite my grandmother's pox on the subject, this is the best broccoli casserole formula I have ever encountered. If my forebear were alive, her riposte would be: "Casserole, schmasserole. If it tastes good—that's all that matters!"

1½ pounds broccoli
7 tablespoons unsalted butter
2 tablespoons olive oil
1 shallot, minced
½ cup chopped cooked ham
4 tablespoons all-purpose flour
1 cup hot Chicken Stock (see page 410)
1 cup heavy or whipping cream
¼ teaspoon freshly grated nutmeg
1 tablespoon lemon juice
Dash of hot pepper sauce
1 pound rigatoni (stem pasta) or fusilli (corkscrew pasta)
1 cup ricotta cheese
½ cup freshly grated Parmesan cheese
½ cup cubed Fontina cheese (cut in ¼-inch cubes)
Chopped fresh parsley

1. Cut the broccoli tops into flowerets. Cut off the top 3 inches of the stems, peel them, and cut them into strips, about 1½ inches long. Set both aside.

2. Heat 2 tablespoons of the butter with the oil in a large skillet over medium-low heat. Add the shallot; cook 3 minutes. Add the broccoli flowerets and stems and the ham. Cook, covered, until the broccoli is tender, about 10 minutes. Raise the heat and cook, uncovered, until all moisture has evaporated. Set aside.

3. Melt the remaining 5 tablespoons butter in a medium skillet over low heat. Beat in the flour. Cook, stirring constantly, 2 minutes. Beat in the hot chicken stock all at once. Beat in the cream. Heat to boiling; reduce the heat. Simmer until very thick. Add nutmeg, lemon juice, and hot pepper sauce. Set aside.

4. Meanwhile, cook the pasta in boiling salted water until just barely tender (al dente), about 10 to 12 minutes. Drain.

5. Transfer the pasta to a large bowl. Add the sauce, the ricotta cheese, and the Parmesan cheese. Mix thoroughly.

6. Preheat the oven to 400°F.

7. Butter a 2-quart soufflé dish. Place one third of the pasta mixture in the dish. Add half the broccoli mixture and half the Fontina cheese, pressing down lightly. Add another one third of the pasta, then the remaining broccoli and Fontina cheese. Finish with the remaining pasta.

8. Place in the oven and bake 25 minutes. Let stand for 8 minutes, then run a knife around the edges of the dish. Cover with a serving platter. Gently invert to unmold. Sprinkle with parsley.

Serves 6.

BROCCOLI PESTO

Broccoli is one of the vitamin-high Brassicas (4,500 units vitamin A, 481 milligrams potassium, and 158 milligrams calcium per stalk). It is also happily low in calories (a scant 40 per cupful). This fortuitous happenstance gives a chef some license. Witness the following broccoli pesto sauce to drench over yards and yards of buttered pasta.

2 cups small broccoli flowerets (from about 1½ pounds broccoli)
½ cup coarsely chopped fresh basil leaves
2 large cloves garlic, roughly chopped
¼ cup pine nuts
½ teaspoon coarse (kosher) salt
¼ teaspoon freshly ground black pepper
1 cup olive oil
½ cup freshly grated Parmesan cheese

Place the broccoli in the container of a food processor or blender. Add the basil, garlic, pine nuts, salt, pepper, and oil. Process until smooth. Transfer to a bowl and stir in the cheese. To serve, toss into warm buttered pasta.

Note: Pesto can be kept refrigerated in a tightly covered jar for a week. It may also be frozen, but then it is best not to stir in the cheese until after defrosting.

Makes about 2½ cups, 8 to 10 servings.

BRUSSELS SPROUTS

Belgium's Best Known Ambassadors

Coming from a time unblessed (or unblemished) by modern horticultural technology, I clearly remember when vegetables tasted and looked as Mother Nature intended: flavorful without a doubt, but cosmetically for the birds!

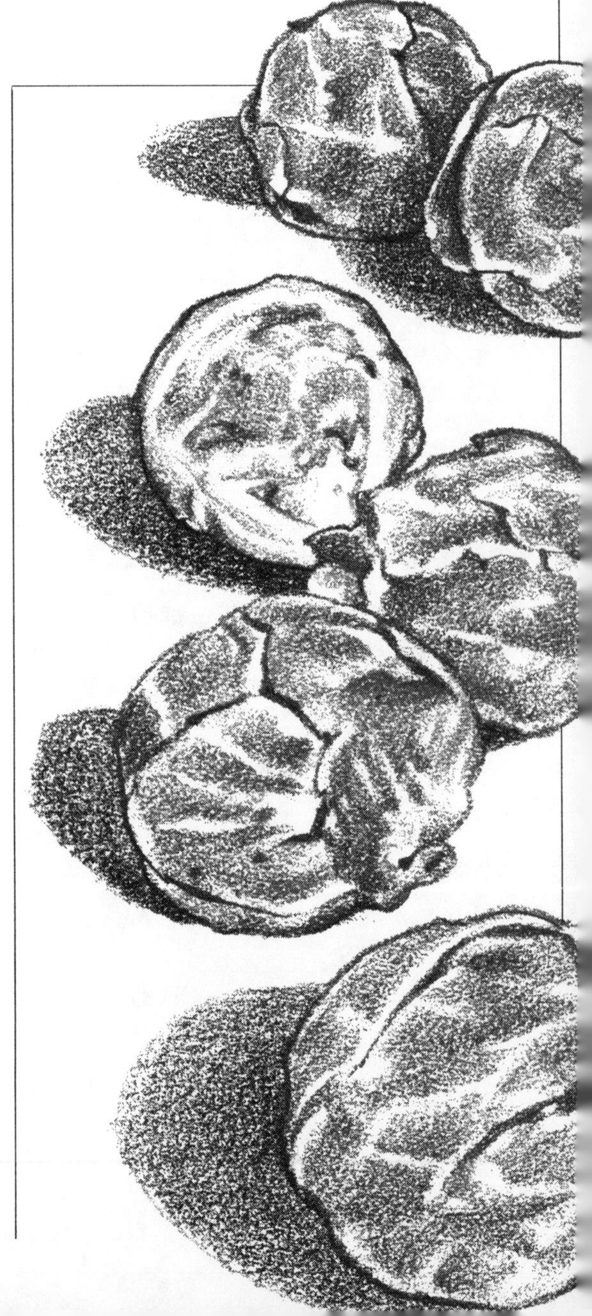

My childhood was spent scrupulously avoiding almost every green gift of the garden that came to the table—not out of dislike but out of panic. For the greenest were inevitably tainted with plant borers, rust, and Lord knows what other form of agricultural scourge.

Skipping the "nightly greens" wasn't easy. My mother, who had once contemplated going to medical school, was not a squeamish person. More pertinently, she did not condone that weakness in either her spouse or her offspring. Her appetite was never dampened by a pinch of sand in the spinach or, worse yet, the discovery of some parboiled alien in the Brussels sprouts, so she could never understand our hue and cry over these indignities. She even had an umbrella maxim to cover any such contingency: "You have to eat a peck of dirt in this life," she would announce airily, pushing any offending object aside on her dinner plate.

She was probably right, but all the earthly contaminations wilted my enthusiasm for second helpings. And I felt victimized by all manner of headed greens for years to come.

Bouts with Brussels sprouts were most painful because I dearly admired the sight of those rosebud cabbages blooming on a single stalk in my grandmother's garden. I also prized the way she cooked them: tossed in brown butter and adorned with chopped nuts or bread crumbs. But then I had spent hours at that good housekeeper's kitchen sink, watching as she scrupulously parted each tiny leaf to make absolutely sure no offending insect ever entered a skillet.

My mother tried that too. But, poor lady, her flesh was weak when it came to what I now recognize as arduous pre-cooking preparation. After unfurling and picking over the first dozen sprouts, she would usually dump the rest into boiling water and let nature take its course.

I will never forget the sensation of utter helplessness when I uncovered a curled denizen of the garden in the center of a partially consumed sprout at our dinner table.

"A worm," I shrieked, throwing my utensils to the floor and kicking my heels. For it was actually *half* a worm I had found. And no amount of supplication or the promise of chocolate cake later could assuage the offense to my wounded sensibilities.

"You let me eat a worm!" I accused.

My mother was sanguine on the subject. "Listen," she said, "I'm sorry. But what happened to you was just part of the balance of nature. Worms have to eat and survive like everybody else, don't they?"

She got no argument from me. Worms' territorial rights were inviolate from that moment on. I simply never ate another Brussels sprout for a decade. Perhaps two.

I also cheered the invention of DDT, which demonstrates how a warped appetite can affect one's sense of survival. But later on, when I had become a gardener myself, I recanted—especially when I read the fine print on the insecticide bottles. And anyway, the cabbage caterpillar is one of the loveliest butterflies in the garden.

Vegetable Roots

Romans called these tender buttons *bullata gemmifera* (diamond-makers) because consumption was rumored to enhance a diner's mental agility. However, Mark Antony is said to have chewed sprouts for days before the battle of Actium—so take that hearsay with a grain of salt.

What was true about these mini-cabbages during antiquity was their rareness. Roman chefs imported them from the seacoasts of western Europe, where they grew wild. Because the cabbage formed a "head," early surgeons assumed sprouts were a natural cure for "drunkenness and the head-ache proceeding from the same," according to Pliny the Elder.

No one knows for certain how or when the Brussels sprout first came to Brussels, but most certainly it is a vegetable that flourishes best in Belgium's particularly rich and loamy soil.

Sprouts have been a source of Flemish national pride for over eight centuries now, gracing palace tablerie and rough peasant boards alike; most often paired with smoky sausages or tender cuts of pink ham. But not until 1820 was the Brussels sprout officially recognized by the king of Belgium's seedsmen as that country's official green.

What to Look For

In Belgium and elsewhere, Brussels sprouts are grown as a fall crop; aficionados claim they are at their best after the first snow falls, for curiously a touch of frost is reputed to sweeten a sprout's flavor.

Shoppers are well advised to search

Anyone who has ever seen a crop of Brussels sprouts in full bloom will understand the kitchen gardener's ambivalence about harvesting them. Like vertical corsages, *Brassica oleracea gemmifera* grow in tight green rosettes on a single stalk that towers over every other leaf vegetable in its immediate vicinity. The furled globes (jammed together on a thick stem) are crowned, moreover, by a full-blown cabbage rose, so top-heavy it appears to dwarf the green treasures in its shadow. But have no fear, Brussels sprouts grow sweeter in the shade!

out the smallest and tightest buds they can find. Garden-fresh sprouts are inevitably crisp to the fingernail and bright green to the eye. Pass by any loose-leafed varieties; Brussels sprouts, like rosebuds, tend to open up after a hiatus on the refrigerator shelf. Likewise avoid yellowing (or rusted) leaves because that is a dead giveaway that the sprout is well past its prime—and usually too strong-tasting to mate with other seasonings.

In Belgium they consider it *déclassé* to serve up a Brussels sprout that is bigger than a child's fingernail. I once watched a large and obviously self-indulgent gentleman consume a whole plateful at one sitting, using nothing but his fingers plus a vast napkin stretched across his chest to catch the overflow. Gastronome or glutton? I cannot say, but he certainly must have had a smattering of nutrition. A cup of cooked Brussels sprouts contains a whopping 810 units of vitamin A, 423 milligrams of potassium, and 112 milligrams of phosphorus with healthy jots of thiamine, riboflavin and ascorbic acid for good measure. Brussels sprouts make choice diet food too, containing a scant 55 calories to every dozen average-size buds. The child's fingernail variety (if ever you could find them) not only taste like velvet but contain less than 2 calories apiece. So bring on the oil and vinegar!

Brussels sprouts are usually packaged in 10-ounce cartons, which yield approximately four servings. Most diners will find that amount sufficient; but for heartier appetites cooks should use their own judgment.

Preparation

The classic way with a Brussels sprout, prior to any other kitchen dress-up, is to either blanch or parboil it, covered, in a large heavy saucepan—preferably one of nonreactive metal such as enameled cast iron or stainless steel. Always pull off any loose outer leaves and trim the stems to a bare minimum. But take care not to slice the stems so close that the sprouts disintegrate in the cooking process. A tiny X cut in the base of each sprout with a sharp knife will hasten the cooking considerably.

To boil sprouts, place them in lightly salted boiling water and cook, covered, for about 12 to 15 minutes, depending upon their size—until they may be easily pierced with a fork. I usually allow 1 cup of boiling water to 1 cup of Brussels sprouts. When they are done, plunge the sprouts under cold running water to retard the cooking. Then proceed with the recipe at hand.

To steam them, place the trimmed sprouts in a steamer tray (or a colander) over a minimum amount of boiling water. Take care that the steamer does not actually touch the water. Cover, and steam until the sprouts are tender-crisp (or *al dente*, as the Italians say), about 10 to 15 minutes. Do not overcook!

BRUSSELS SPROUTS A LA GRECQUE

One of the most enticing openers I know is a melding of Brussels sprouts with herbs and oil, Greek style. This recipe is the brainchild of Roseanne Schlussel, who makes an infinite number of airplane trips between Birmingham, Michigan, and New York City yearly, but never without an interesting recipe tucked up her sleeve.

1 cup water
½ cup olive oil
¼ cup lemon juice
Bouquet garni: 2 parsley sprigs, 1 bay leaf, 2 tarragon sprigs, 6 peppercorns, and ½ teaspoon celery seed, tied in a small cheesecloth bag
1 pound Brussels sprouts, trimmed, an X cut in each stem end
1 teaspoon red wine vinegar
1 teaspoon finely slivered lemon peel
Salt and freshly ground black pepper
1 tablespoon chopped fresh parsley

1. Combine the water, olive oil, lemon juice, and bouquet garni in a medium saucepan. Heat to boiling; reduce the heat. Simmer, uncovered, 10 minutes.

2. Add the Brussels sprouts to the saucepan; return to boiling. Continue to cook, uncovered, until the sprouts are barely tender, about 10 minutes. Remove from the heat; let the sprouts cool in the liquid. Discard the bouquet garni.

3. Transfer the sprouts with their liquid to a serving bowl. Add the vinegar, lemon peel, and salt and pepper to taste. Toss well; chill thoroughly. Serve garnished with parsley.

Serves 4 to 6.

BRUSSELS SPROUTS IN PECAN BUTTER

Another classic rendition of Brussels sprouts is to combine them with crunchy chestnuts—this is the way they are usually eaten in the British Isles. However, my American tongue has a preference for a somewhat more flavorsome nut: pecans.

1 pound Brussels sprouts, trimmed, an X cut in each stem end
3 tablespoons unsalted butter
¼ cup roughly chopped pecans
Freshly ground black pepper

1. Cook the Brussels sprouts, covered, in boiling salted water until tender, about 10 minutes. Drain. Transfer the sprouts to a shallow serving dish and keep warm.

2. Heat the butter in a small saucepan until it begins to turn brown. Add the chopped pecans; toss until they are lightly browned, but do not allow them to burn. Pour the pecans over the Brussels sprouts and sprinkle with pepper to taste.

Serves 4 to 6.

CLASSIC CREAMED BRUSSELS SPROUTS

Probably the most generally accepted upholstery for a Brussels sprout is a mite of butter and a pinch of bread crumbs. My own preference runs to more velvety alliances. For instance, consider this version of creamed Brussels sprouts, which I found scribbled in pencil on the margin of a yellowing recipe book (circa 1918) by an unknown but obviously knowing cook.

1 pound Brussels sprouts, trimmed, an X cut in each stem end
1½ cups milk
1 tablespoon unsalted butter
⅓ cup heavy or whipping cream
Salt and freshly ground black pepper

1. Cook the Brussels sprouts in boiling salted water for 10 minutes. Drain.

2. In a medium saucepan slowly heat the milk to boiling; do not scorch. Stir in the Brussels sprouts. Simmer, uncovered, over medium-low heat until almost all the milk has evaporated, about 30 minutes.

3. Add the butter and cream to the Brussels sprouts. Continue to cook until warmed through, 4 to 5 minutes. Add salt and pepper to taste.

Serves 4 to 6.

MARY BALL'S SPROUT AND FENNEL CHOWDER

A dozen years ago I spent an autumn on a steep and rocky mountainside in Provence where my neighbors were a retired British Navy commander and his wife. As "resident colonials" they kept track of all new arrivals and regularly issued invitations to share a meal and/or the *London Times*.

The Commander's wife was an excellent cook. One of her memorable creations was a stockpot union of very Anglo-Saxon sprouts with a bulb of equally Gallic fennel. The result is no mere soup, I think you'll agree.

4 tablespoons (½ stick) unsalted butter
1 medium onion, chopped
1 small clove garlic, minced
10 ounces Brussels sprouts, trimmed, sliced lengthwise
1 small fennel bulb, trimmed, chopped (about 2 cups)
1 teaspoon anise seed, crushed
3 cups chicken broth (see page 414)
Salt and freshly ground black pepper
4 to 6 slices toasted French bread
4 to 6 teaspoons freshly grated Parmesan cheese

1. Melt the butter in a large saucepan over medium-low heat. Add the onion; cook 2 minutes. Stir in the garlic and sauté until golden, 4 to 5 minutes.

Add the Brussels sprouts, fennel, and anise seed. Cook, covered, 15 minutes.

2. Add the chicken broth to the saucepan. Heat to boiling; reduce the heat. Simmer, covered, 30 minutes. Add salt and pepper to taste.

3. To serve: Preheat the broiler. Ladle the soup into individual heatproof serving bowls. Float a piece of toast in each bowl. Sprinkle each toast with 1 teaspoon cheese and heat under the broiler until golden.

Serves 4 to 6.

BRUSSELS SPROUTS SOUFFLE

Many good cooks rebel at the notion of converting the eminently chewable sprout into a semiliquefied pool of green ooze. You name it: *purée*, *mousse*, or even, God save us, *sorbet*. I too applaud the notion of this vegetable as an honest-to-goodness viand rather than a nouvelle cuisine adjunct, but I must confess that my favored sprout formula is a soufflé so airy it almost floats out of the oven on its own steam. If not actually an art form, this may be Brussels sprouts' finest hour.

Unsalted butter
1 tablespoon freshly grated Parmesan cheese
8 to 10 ounces Brussels sprouts, trimmed
1 medium potato, peeled, cubed
½ cup heavy or whipping cream
3 egg yolks
⅛ teaspoon freshly grated nutmeg
Dash of hot pepper sauce
Salt and freshly ground black pepper
4 egg whites

1. Butter a 1-quart soufflé dish and sprinkle the grated cheese over the bottom and sides. Set aside in a cool place.

2. Cook the Brussels sprouts with the potato, uncovered, in boiling salted water for 15 minutes; drain.

3. Preheat the oven to 400°F.

4. Place half the Brussels sprouts and potato in the container of a food processor or blender. Add ¼ cup cream and process until smooth. Transfer to a medium saucepan and repeat with the remaining sprouts, potato, and cream. Add the second batch to the saucepan.

5. Heat the puréed mixture to boiling; remove from the heat and let stand 1 minute. Beat in the egg yolks, one at a time, beating thoroughly after each addition. Add the nutmeg, hot pepper sauce, and salt and pepper to taste.

6. Beat the egg whites until stiff; fold them into the puréed mixture. Pour the mixture into the prepared soufflé dish. Place the dish in the oven and immediately reduce the heat to 375°F. Bake until puffed up and golden, 30 to 35 minutes.

Serves 6.

Brussels sprouts come with a clutch of odd monikers in other languages. Though the French dub them *chou de Bruxelles* (literally the cabbage of Brussels), Germans disguise them into another plant entirely: *Rosenkohl* (cabbage roses). Italians for some unfathomable reason know them as *cavolina de Brusselle* (the little horses of Brussels).

BLAZING BRUSSELS SPROUTS AND GINGERED SHRIMP

One cuisine that my addled brain could not possibly think of adapting the Brussels sprout to is the Chinese. But curiously, one of the signal dishes in my sprouts repertoire was appropriated from Szechuan cuisine. A fiery compound of shrimp, peppers, ginger, and sprouts, this dish may be whipped up (in a wok) in minutes. But the memory stays a good bit longer on the tongue.

10 ounces Brussels sprouts, trimmed, an X cut into each stem end
¼ cup peanut or vegetable oil
8 whole scallions, bulbs and green tops chopped separately
2 cloves garlic, minced
1½ tablespoons minced fresh ginger root
1 pound shrimp, shelled, deveined
1 teaspoon crushed dried hot red peppers
2 tablespoons chili sauce
1 teaspoon ground mild chiles or chili powder
2 tablespoons sesame oil
2 tablespoons dry sherry
2 tablespoons water
Cooked rice

1. Cook the Brussels sprouts, uncovered, in boiling salted water for 8 minutes. Rinse under cold running water; drain. Cut into ¼-inch-thick slices crosswise; reserve.

2. Heat the oil in a wok or large skillet over medium heat until hot but not smoking. Add the chopped scallion bulbs; cook 1 minute. Stir in the garlic and ginger. Cook until golden, about 3 minutes. Add the shrimp and hot peppers. Cook, tossing constantly, until the shrimp turn pink, 3 to 4 minutes.

3. Combine the chili sauce, ground chiles, sesame oil, sherry, and water in a small bowl. Stir this into the shrimp mixture and cook 1 minute. Add the Brussels sprouts; continue to cook, stirring constantly, until warmed through. Add the chopped scallion tops. Serve over rice.

Serves 4 or 5.

CABBAGE

You Never Have to Ask "What's Cooking"

Raised in what I choose to recollect as simpler times, almost any memory I have of a holiday is indelibly associated with good things to eat.

Thanksgiving, for instance, was never so much a time of benediction in my family as it was an occasion of absolutely unreined feasting. And though the house was filled with an aggregate of odd relatives who spoke in unfamiliar (Midwestern) accents and often wore rather startling clothes, it was the gaudier assemblage of dishes prepared in the kitchen that truly bedazzled me.

To be utterly candid, my parents were curiously matched celebrants. What my mother loved best were all the accoutrements of entertaining. Gleaming silver, snowy damask, and rose-rimmed Limoges (with reassuring bands of eighteen-karat gold on every plate) heartened her far more than the idea of wining and dining the myriad guests who yearly invaded her home. My father, on quite the other hand, preferred the people to the panoply. He simply demanded bounteous and inexhaustible provisions to feed them all.

Even though the wintry economic weather of the 1930s inhibited my father's largess a trifle, the Depression never totally blighted his generous im-

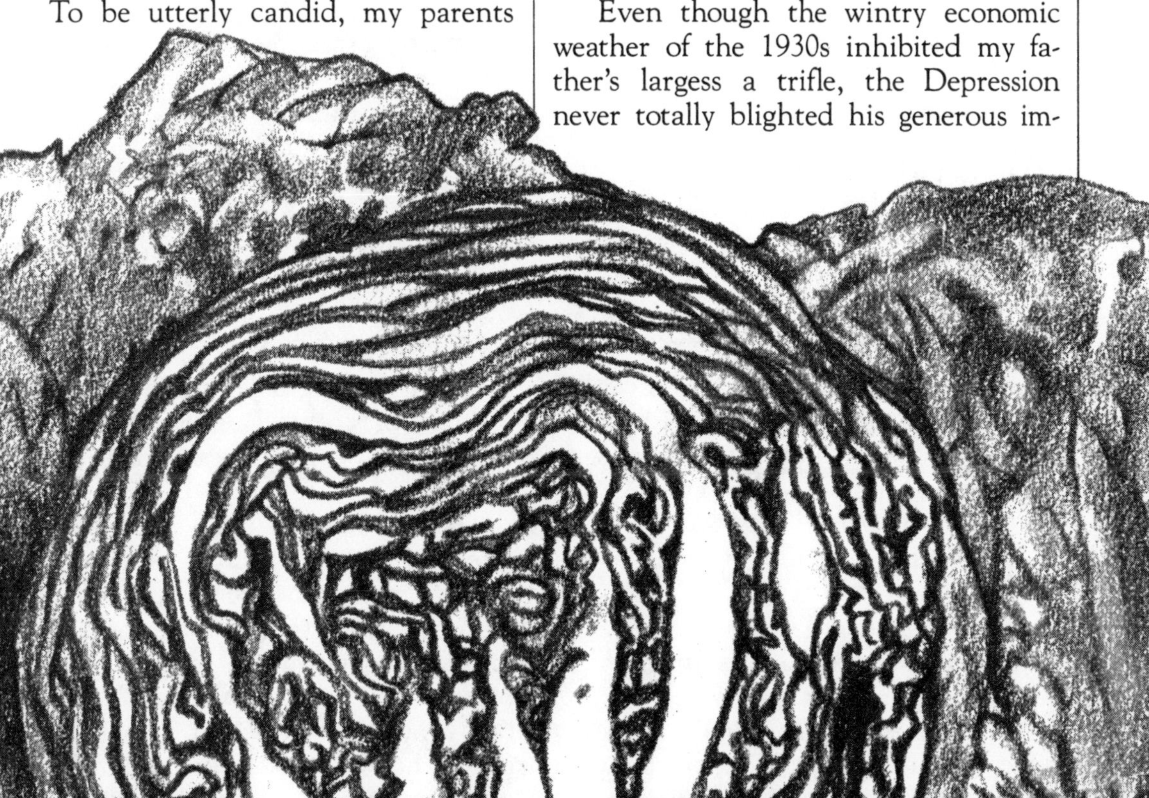

pulses toward company, particularly at the dinner table. In Sam Greene's judgment, holidays were meant to be observed with masses of food and an open liquor cabinet. Indeed these commemorative meals, boasting a prodigious number of courses, went on so long that my mother would take pity on the hired girl in the kitchen and send her home long before dessert and coffee were served. As a consequence my mother would usually wash the dishes herself past midnight (cursing all the while) as my father, the hospitable host, snored in his bed.

If my parent's nature was generous, his tastebuds were frugal as can be. Also, his teeth were faulty and the only foods he actually enjoyed were either boiled, stewed, or fricasseed, so turkey never pleased him in the least. On one occasion, I remember my mother prior to the holiday meal, poring over the kitchen bible she summoned up for culinary ammunition (Fannie Farmer) as her husband ticked off the reasons why the big bird be excluded that year.

"Turkey takes so much time to chew." he complained. "The only thing I ever give thanks for is that I've finally swallowed it!"

My mother kept her temper under control during his diatribe. "Okay," she said at last, "what do you want instead? Duck? Chicken? There's a recipe here for squab under glass."

"No, no, Paulie dear." My father knew how to pointedly ignore her sarcasm. "What I would like for Thanksgiving is something *really* different."

"Like what *really*?"

My father winked before he answered her. "Like corned beef and cabbage."

My mother's reaction is unprintable. But it was a significant riposte.

Oddly enough, his request was duly honored but what transpired between the principals to occasion its happening I cannot tell you. I do know that I will never forget that meal as long as I live. Fully four months prior to Saint Patrick's Day, our house was virtually awash with the eye-stinging perfume of salt beef bubbling away on the stove. And though chrysanthemums were crammed into every vase my mother could muster to counter the scent, cabbage alone was the Greenes' Thanksgiving bouquet.

Vegetable Roots

Historians who have sifted the evidence of man's first serious attempts at cookery conclude it may very well have been a green head of *Brassica oleracea capitata* that occasioned the invention of the cooking pot. When the Paleolithic tongue demanded surcease from an exclusive diet of scorch, pragmatic firetenders fashioned small flat vessels on which to cook meat over live coals rather than tossing it into the fire itself—thus changing the concept of sustenance into something akin to pleasure for the very first time.

With formal cookery came other changes in tribal habits. Meal-taking became a communal ritual, and grasses and grains eventually were added to the meat to stretch it to feed the entire family. Wild cabbage required a larger vessel to fit its ample proportions—and the first cooking pot came into being.

Or so it is bruited about by archeological types.

As I mentioned elsewhere, Brussels sprouts, broccoli, cauliflower—kale and kohlrabi too—are all kissing cousins, descendants of this *true* cabbage. And though it is hard to find a distinct family resemblance, all offshoots of the initial *Brassica* plant do share at least one common characteristic: a strong and unmistakable aroma that is emitted during protracted bouts of cooking. But even that drawback has obviously not diminished the ardor of deep-dyed cabbage lovers from Dublin to Djakarta.

Actually, cabbage has held its own as

Early cabbages grew straight up rather than in the round. The plant's Latin name was *caulia*, which means stem, or more precisely, a very thick stalk. From that etymological evidence one must presume that all inaugural cabbages resembled the Chinese bok choy in shape—if not in subtle flavoring, since *caulia* was a term of slight disparagement among the Romans, implying rudeness!

No one seems to know for sure when cabbages headed up. However, when Caesar invaded Britain, he brought spherical cabbages along as K-rations, and they are noted in his diaries as *capitalae*, "with heads," so evolution or agronomy must have had something to do with its mutation. Fast!

a food staple in Europe and northern Africa for over four thousand years. Until the beginning of the twentieth century, most agronomists assumed that this green-leafed vegetable was native to western soil. However, during the Boxer Rebellion in China, scrolls from 1000 B.C. were uncovered which detail the prescription of white cabbage as the only cure for barrenness in males of advanced age. The Egyptians raised altars to it, and Greeks (and Romans too) believed that cabbage infallibly cured every disease from paralysis to pleurisy. From my own experience, I will tell you that sauerkraut (pickled cabbage) taken in sensible doses prior to a night of heavy drinking will go pretty far to alleviate the *angst* inherent in most hangovers!

What to Look For

The English word "cabbage" is a corruption of the old French word *caboche*, which means "head." Shoppers are advised to take the word to heart. Look for only the headiest (firm, smooth, and tightly circumscribed) oval on your greengrocer's shelf and it will usually be the most flavorsome on the fork.

At the tip of Long Island (where I reside from time to time), hardy cabbage lovers are encouraged to pick their own during the last autumnal blooming before Thanksgiving, when these greens are at their best. A touch of late November chill gives cabbage an extra measure of sweetness, it seems; so the cognoscenti always wait till the air is so bone-chilling that one's hand freezes on contact with the frosty leaf!

Cabbage is really low in calories: a shade under 15 per cupful (and that goes for green, white, and Savoy varieties as well). Red cabbage, slightly sweeter, is slightly higher: 20 calories per cup.

Cabbage is high in potassium (163 milligrams in the average portion), and high in water as well (92 percent per cup), which makes enriching it no hardship—even for a serious dieter.

Preparation

Unlike most of the vegetables in this book, there is no one classic method for preparing cabbage. To my tongue at least, it is equally tonic whether blanched, braised, baked, or even stir-fried.

For years cabbage was considered "immigrant fare" and was usually boiled till it was as limp as the contents of a washing machine. To compound the injury it was then served forth in a puddle of water—which may provide some clue to the dearth of cabbage aficionados prior to World War II.

When I cook cabbage, I always discard the tough outer leaves and quarter the head. Then I core it by cutting out the hard center portions at the base. Cabbage is best when shredded into ¼-inch-wide strips with a long, sharp vegetable knife, so the pieces will be long and

slightly chewy. For my money, processor-chopped cabbage inevitably has too fine a texture and tends to become rather mushy after cooking; so I chop it by hand.

Blanch cabbage by cooking it in a large heavy-duty saucepan (not aluminum as it alters the flavor) with enough boiling salted water to cover. Boil the cabbage, uncovered, for no longer than 5 to 8 minutes; you want it to be *al dente.* After it has boiled, plunge the cut cabbage under cold running water to retard the cooking process. Then season and reheat it as you desire afterward.

SPICY CABBAGE HOT POT WITH PORK

Headed cabbages have been a source of much myth and more mystery in the garden from the very beginning. Babies were said to be found under enveloping cabbage leaves as far back as the third century B.C. And even today, sensible Scots will send their young daughters, blindfolded, out into the cabbage patches on All Hallows Eve. According to lore, they will be able to foretell the nature of their future spouse's physique by the hardiness of the cabbages they stumble upon (if the poor girls do not break their necks doing so). The best part of that ritual is that after the high jinks among the potagerie everyone retires to the kitchen for a hearty meal of (what else?) cabbage soup!

2 pounds pork chops or meaty pork bones, trimmed of excess fat
2 tablespoons minced salt pork
1 medium onion, chopped
2 large shallots, minced
1 large clove garlic, minced
2 pounds green cabbage, trimmed, shredded
6 cups strong Chicken Stock (see page 410)
4 cups water
1½ tablespoons red wine vinegar
⅛ teaspoon ground allspice
⅛ teaspoon ground mace
¼ teaspoon chopped fresh thyme, or a pinch of dried
1 teaspoon salt
¼ teaspoon freshly ground black pepper

For the meatballs:

½ pound ground pork
½ cup fresh bread crumbs
1 egg, lightly beaten
¼ cup milk
1 shallot, minced
½ teaspoon salt
⅛ teaspoon freshly ground black pepper
Pinch of freshly grated nutmeg
2 tablespoons unsalted butter

1. Place the pork chops or bones in a large pot. Cover with cold water; heat to boiling. Remove from the heat and place the pot with chops or bones under cold running water until the water in the pot runs clear. Wipe out the pot; reserve the chops or bones.

2. Sauté the salt pork in the pot over medium-low heat until lightly browned. Add the onion; cook 2 minutes. Add the shallots and garlic; cook 3 minutes. Stir in the cabbage, tossing to coat it well. Add the chicken broth and water. Heat to boiling; reduce the heat. Cook, covered, over medium-low heat for 1½ hours.

3. Add the pork chops or bones to the soup. Continue to cook, covered, another 45 minutes. Add the vinegar, allspice, mace, thyme, salt, and pepper. Remove from the heat and let stand at least 4 hours, or refrigerate overnight.

4. Before serving, combine all the ingredients for the pork meatballs through the nutmeg. Mix thoroughly and form into small meatballs. Melt the butter in a large heavy skillet over medium heat and sauté the meatballs, about a third at a time, until golden brown.

5. Bring the soup to boiling; remove the chops or bones. Shred the meat from the chops and add it to the soup along with the meatballs. Cook, covered, 25 minutes before serving.

Serves 8.

MARY SURINA'S YUGOSLAVIAN SLAW

I have been collecting cole slaw recipes since I was old enough to shred a cabbage and spare a thumb. Out of several hundred renderings, good sense bids me narrow down the list to the quartet that follows.

My dear friend Mary Surina—who adds luster to San Pedro, California, each time she goes near a stove—sent me the first slaw (amended with potatoes, oil, and garlic) with a caveat. "Bert," she wrote, "some people love this dish . . . and some don't!" Count me among the lucky lovers.

1 large potato, peeled, cubed
1 clove garlic, minced
1 teaspoon salt
2½ tablespoons white wine vinegar
⅓ cup olive oil
1½ to 2 pounds green cabbage, trimmed, shredded
Freshly ground black pepper

1. Cook the potato in boiling salted water until tender, about 15 minutes.

2. Meanwhile, with the back of a spoon, mash the garlic in a small bowl with the salt until a paste is formed. Beat in the vinegar and oil.

3. Place the cabbage in a large bowl. Drain the potato and immediately mash the hot potato into the cabbage. The cabbage will wilt slightly. Add the dressing, toss well, and season with pepper to taste. Serve immediately.

Serves 4 to 6.

GERMANTOWN SLAW

This slaw recipe is from a wondrously well-fed section of America (roughly northeast of Cincinnati, Ohio), where the countryside is still lush and largely devoid of tract housing and the creamy cole slaw is often incomparable. Why shouldn't it be good? The Mennonites brought the secret with them!

1½ to 2 pounds green cabbage, trimmed, shredded
1 medium red onion, halved, thinly sliced
1 carrot, peeled, diced
½ green pepper, cored, seeded, finely chopped
1 tablespoon unsalted butter
1 cup cooked ham, cut into strips
1 cup Mayonnaise (see page 408)
½ cup sour cream
2 tablespoons red wine vinegar
1½ tablespoons Dijon mustard
½ teaspoon caraway seeds
Salt and freshly ground black pepper
1 small tomato, seeded, cubed
¾ cup white Cheddar cheese, cut into strips
1½ tablespoons chopped fresh parsley

Germans call cabbage *kohl.* Early Britons dubbed it *cole.* Long before some Francophile English dandy translated *caboche* to cabbage, Saxons had persuaded Angles that there was pleasure in partaking of the chewy noggin raw: hence *cole slaw.* Which actually means "cabbage sliced."

When I was a kid I always spelled it *cold* slaw, which seemed logical as it was my favorite chilled dish after ice cream!

1. Combine the cabbage, onion, carrot, and green pepper in a large bowl.

2. Melt the butter in a small skillet over medium-low heat. Sauté the ham until lightly browned. Transfer the ham, using a slotted spoon, to the vegetable mixture in the bowl.

3. Combine the mayonnaise with the sour cream in a medium bowl. Beat in the vinegar, mustard, caraway seeds, and any ham drippings. Pour this over the cabbage mixture. Mix thoroughly. Add salt and pepper to taste. Add the tomato and cheese, toss lightly, and sprinkle with the parsley. Serve at room temperature.

Serves 6 to 8.

DONALD SACKS' GINGER-DILL SLAW

More geographic slaw. Across the street from the august and protean Dean & DeLuca in New York City's SoHo, there is a tidy little food shop dubbed simply Donald Sacks. Mr. Sacks is an amiable young man who is a kitchen wizard into the bargain. His store sells all manner of good comestibles "to go," with a particular emphasis on green salads, to wit: one of the greenest! The interesting facet of this vaguely Oriental slaw is the mild pickling process, which removes a good bit of the acidity of the raw cabbage and onion.

1½ pounds green cabbage, trimmed, shredded
3 tablespoons coarse (kosher) salt
4 medium red onions, thinly sliced
2-inch piece ginger root, peeled, minced
¾ cup lemon juice
⅓ cup olive oil
1 tablespoon fennel seeds, crushed
¼ teaspoon freshly ground black pepper
1½ cups minced fresh dill

1. Toss the cabbage with 2 tablespoons of the salt in a large bowl; let stand 4 hours. Cover with cold water; let stand 1 hour longer.

2. Meanwhile, combine the onions with the remaining 1 tablespoon salt in a medium bowl; let stand 1 hour. Cover with cold water; let stand 1 hour longer.

3. Rinse the cabbage and the onions separately with cold running water. Drain thoroughly and squeeze dry. Combine the cabbage and the onions in a large bowl.

4. Press the ginger root in a fine-mesh sieve over a small bowl to extract all the juice. Discard the pulp. Whisk the lemon juice, oil, fennel, and pepper into the ginger juice. Pour the dressing over the cabbage mixture; toss well. Add the fresh dill; toss once more. Serve well chilled.

Serves 6 to 8.

SLAW BERNOISE

Berne is a city on the dewlaps of the Jura mountains, which separate Switzerland from France. This local dish combines the best of both sides of the border: good French cabbage and great Swiss Emmenthal cheese.

1½ to 2 pounds green cabbage, trimmed, shredded
1 cup finely chopped celery
¼ pound Emmenthal cheese, cut into strips (1 cup)
1 small clove garlic, minced
4 anchovy filets
1 teaspoon Dijon mustard
1 tablespoon lemon juice
1½ teaspoons white wine vinegar
⅓ cup olive oil
Freshly ground black pepper
2 hard-cooked eggs, quartered

1. Combine the cabbage, celery, and cheese in a large bowl.

2. Mash the garlic with the anchovies in a small bowl until smooth. Stir in the mustard, lemon juice, vinegar, and oil. Pour the sauce over the vegetables and cheese. Mix well. Add pepper to taste. Serve well chilled, garnished with quartered hard-cooked eggs.

Serves 4 to 6.

AMISH SWEET AND SOUR CABBAGE

2½ to 3 pounds green cabbage, trimmed, shredded
½ cup Chicken Stock (see page 410)
1 egg yolk
¼ cup sugar
¼ cup red wine vinegar
2 tablespoons unsalted butter, cut into bits
1 teaspoon Dijon mustard
½ cup heavy or whipping cream
¼ cup chopped fresh dill
Salt and freshly ground black pepper

1. Place the cabbage with the stock in a medium saucepan. Heat to boiling; reduce the heat. Cook, covered, over medium-low heat until the cabbage is tender, about 8 minutes. Drain; keep warm.

2. Meanwhile, combine the egg yolk with the sugar and vinegar in a small heavy saucepan. Cook, stirring constantly, over low heat until the mixture begins to thicken. Do not boil. Stir in the butter, bit by bit. Add the mustard, cream, and dill.

3. Combine the cabbage with the sauce. Add salt and pepper to taste.

Serves 6 to 8.

VENETIAN VERZE SOFEGAE

(Smothered Cabbage)

The following cabbage devise from Venice is a gift from a good cooking companion, Anna Teresa Callen, who also happens to be one of the best teachers of Italian cuisine around. Anna Teresa lives on the same street as me, albeit on the sunnier side. Though our stoves are separated by at least fifty others on the block, I swear I can recognize the good scent of her Abruzzi cooking whenever the wind is right.

3 tablespoons minced pancetta (Italian bacon), fatty prosciutto, or thick bacon
1 clove garlic
Pinch of rosemary
1 tablespoon olive oil
2½ pounds green cabbage, trimmed, shredded
½ cup Chicken Stock (see page 410) or white wine

1. Chop the pancetta with the garlic and rosemary until well minced. This mixture is known as *battuto* in Italy.

2. Heat the oil in a medium saucepan over medum heat. Add the *battuto.* Cook, stirring constantly, until the mixture begins to sizzle. Stir in the cabbage, tossing to coat it well. Cook, covered, over low heat for 1 hour, adding the stock or wine a little at a time.

Serves 6.

FRENCH CHOU CHOU

(Dilled Creamy Cabbage)

One of cabbage's staunchest herbal allies is fresh dill. In this classic cabbage rendering, and also Amish Sweet and Sour, page 79, dill plays a prominent role. Each dish is a peasant bequest: obviously the root of all great cabbage cabala.

1½ to 2 pounds green cabbage, trimmed, finely shredded
4 tablespoons (½ stick) unsalted butter
4 slices Canadian bacon, cut into thin strips
1 teaspoon Dijon mustard
3 tablespoons cognac
1 large onion, finely chopped
1 small package (3 ounces) cream cheese
1 tablespoon heavy or whipping cream
3 tablespoons chopped fresh dill
Pinch of ground cloves
Salt and freshly ground black pepper

1. Cook the cabbage in boiling salted water 5 minutes; drain.

2. Melt 1 tablespoon of the butter in a small saucepan. Add the Canadian bacon and cook over medium-high heat until the strips begin to brown. Reduce the heat to low, stir in the mustard and cognac, and cook 3 minutes. Remove from the heat.

3. Melt the remaining 3 tablespoons butter in a large saucepan. Add the onion and cook over medium-low heat 3 minutes. Stir in the cream cheese and heavy cream. Cook until the cheese melts. Stir in the cabbage, tossing well to coat each piece. Cook 4 minutes. Add the Canadian bacon with the pan juices; continue to cook, tossing frequently, until the cabbage is tender, about 5 minutes longer. Add dill, cloves, and salt and pepper to taste.

Serves 4 to 6.

CABBAGE PANCAKES

Here is the ultimate cabbage dish. If you say it is fit for a king, I will argue. That's a low estimate.

1¼ pounds green cabbage, trimmed, shredded
2 eggs
1 egg yolk
½ cup milk
1 cup all-purpose flour
3 tablespoons unsalted butter, melted
½ teaspoon salt
1½ tablespoons chopped chives or scallion tops
2 to 3 tablespoons unsalted butter

1. Cook the cabbage, uncovered, in boiling salted water for 5 minutes. Rinse under cold running water until cool; drain, pressing out all liquid with your hands. Place the cabbage in a large bowl.

2. Combine the eggs, egg yolk, milk, flour, melted butter, and salt (in that order) in a blender container. Blend until smooth. Combine this mixture with the cabbage in the bowl; stir in the chives or scallions.

3. Melt 1 tablespoon of the butter in a large heavy skillet over medium heat. Spoon the batter, 1 large tablespoon for each pancake, into the skillet. Cook three or four at a time until golden on both sides. Keep warm in a low oven while frying the remaining batter, adding more butter to the skillet as needed.

Serves 4 to 6.

CORNED BEEF AND CABBAGE IN HORSERADISH CREAM

My mother's formula for a cabbage-cum-corned-beef boiled dinner (taught her by my Jewish grandmother) always required the meat to be sliced into rosy quadrangles in the kitchen and served with crisp-cooked carrot sticks and chopped, barely cooked cabbage—which was prepared in a separate pan with a good lump of butter and a *schmecken* of the cooking juices "to ease the pain," as my grandmother said.

The dish, served mostly in mid-March (but on the last Thursday in November on at least one occasion), was inevitably sauced with a snowy alliance of cream, mustard, and freshly grated horseradish—though why I will never know, since my mother's mother had been born into a strictly kosher household in Poland. Obviously she became a freethinker early on. And an even freer cook.

1 corned brisket of beef, about 4 pounds
1 large carrot, peeled, halved
1 white turnip, peeled, halved
1 parsnip, peeled, halved
1 large onion
4 whole cloves
2 tablespoons red wine vinegar
2 sprigs parsley
1 large bay leaf
1 clove garlic
10 whole peppercorns
1 teaspoon mustard seed
Wilted Cabbage (recipe follows)
6 large carrots, peeled, cut into julienne strips
Horseradish Cream (recipe follows)
2 tablespoons chopped fresh dill
2 tablespoons chopped fresh parsley

1. Place the corned beef in a heavy 5-quart pot. Add the ingredients through the mustard seed. Add enough water to cover by 2 inches. Heat to boiling, removing scum as it rises to the top; then reduce the heat to low. Simmer, partially covered, skimming the surface occasionally, until the meat is tender when pierced with a fork, about 3½ hours. Add more water if necessary during the cooking. Remove the beef when tender and place it on a serving dish. Keep it, covered, in the oven on low heat.

2. Remove 1½ cups liquid from the pot. Strain, and reserve. Leave the remaining liquid in the pot.

3. Make the Wilted Cabbage.

4. While the cabbage is cooking, tie the julienned carrots in a cheesecloth bag. Heat the remaining liquid in the pot to boiling. Add the carrots and cook, uncovered, until just tender, about 10 minutes. Remove the carrots, undo the cheesecloth bag, and arrange the carrots around the corned beef. Return the serving dish, covered, to the oven.

5. When the cabbage is done, place it in an ovenproof serving dish and keep it warm in the oven.

6. Make the Horseradish Cream. Remove the serving dishes from the oven and spoon some of the horseradish sauce over the meat. Sprinkle the meat and carrots with dill and parsley. Serve with Wilted Cabbage and mashed potatoes. Pass the remaining sauce.

Serves 8.

Wilted Cabbage

4 tablespoons (½ stick) unsalted butter
1 large shallot, chopped
2 large tomatoes, peeled, seeded, chopped
2½ pounds green cabbage, trimmed, coarsely chopped
½ cup reserved corned-beef liquid
Salt and freshly ground black pepper

Melt the butter in a medium saucepan over medium-low heat. Add the shallot; cook 2 minutes. Add the tomatoes; cook 3 minutes. Add the cabbage and reserved corned-beef liquid, tossing to coat the cabbage well. Cook, partially covered, stirring occasionally, until the cabbage is tender, about 10 minutes. Add salt and pepper to taste.

Serves 6 to 8.

Horseradish Cream

1 tablespoon unsalted butter
2 tablespoons all-purpose flour
1 cup reserved corned-beef liquid
2 tablespoons freshly grated horseradish, or 1½ tablespoons prepared horseradish
1½ tablespoons Dijon mustard
¼ cup sour cream
¼ cup heavy or whipping cream
1 teaspoon lemon juice

1. Melt the butter in a small saucepan over medium-low heat. Whisk in the flour. Cook, stirring constantly, 2 minutes. Whisk in the corned-beef liquid, stirring until smooth. Add the horseradish and mustard. Cook 2 minutes.

2. Remove the sauce from the heat and beat in the sour cream and heavy cream. Stir in the lemon juice. Return it to low heat until warmed through, but do not boil.

Makes about 1½ cups.

CHOU FARCI

Here is stuffed cabbage of a somewhat homelier stripe, in the form of a recipe that came to me via the owner-chef of a boardinghouse I stayed at in Holland a dozen years ago. The lady and I communicated in fractured Franco-Dutch, which is the way I acquired her savory recipe. What puts the savor in a plate of *chou farci*? A mystery ingredient sprinkled on the green envelopes of cabbage just before they gently poach: namely, a little whiff of gin.

2 cups leftover cooked pork, chopped
¼ pound sliced boiled ham, chopped (about 1 cup)
1½ cups cooked rice
1 small onion, finely chopped
1 clove garlic, finely minced
1 tablespoon finely chopped fresh dill
⅛ teaspoon ground allspice
⅛ teaspoon freshly grated nutmeg
¼ teaspoon hot pepper sauce
2 eggs, lightly beaten
Salt and freshly ground black pepper
1½ to 2 pounds green cabbage, leaves separated
2 cups Chicken Stock (see page 410)
1 tablespoon dry gin
2 teaspoons unsalted butter, softened
2 teaspoons all-purpose flour
1½ teaspoons Dijon mustard
1 egg yolk
¼ cup heavy or whipping cream
Dill sprigs

1. Combine all the ingredients through the 2 eggs in a large bowl. Mix well. Add salt and pepper to taste, and set aside.

2. Cook the cabbage leaves in boiling salted water until slightly wilted, about 1 minute. Drain.

3. Place ⅓ to ½ cup filling on each leaf (depending on the size of the leaf) and roll up the leaf, tucking the edges under. Place the rolls in a skillet or heavy saucepan large enough to hold them all in one layer. Add the chicken stock; sprinkle with the gin. Heat to boiling; reduce the heat. Simmer, covered, until tender, about 30 minutes. Remove the cabbage rolls with a slotted spoon. Keep warm, covered, in a low oven.

4. Meanwhile, raise the heat under the cooking liquid and allow it to boil for 3 minutes; reduce the heat to low.

5. Mash the butter with the flour until smooth. Stir this into the cooking liquid. Add the mustard; cook until slightly thickened.

6. Combine the egg yolk with the cream in a small bowl. Whisk this into the sauce. Cook until warmed through, but do not boil. Spoon the sauce over the cabbage and top each roll with a sprig of fresh dill.

Serves 6.

JEFFERSONIAN BAKED CHARTREUSE

One of the most notable fans of *Brassica oleracea capitata* was Thomas Jefferson, who campaigned for this vegetable's acceptance by his fellow Americans his entire food-loving life.

In his incredible gardens at Monticello, Jefferson raised over twenty-two different varieties of cabbage, imported from seedsmen and agronomists all over the world. One of Jefferson's prides was Savoy cabbage: "the wrinkled jade green head with a surface like crackled faience." He brought the seeds back from a trip to Italy and crossbred the plants until they became hardy enough to withstand the coldest Virginia winter. One of the most startling recipes in his voluminous collection was for a monumental loaf called a *Chartreuse*: Savoy cabbage filled with layers of chopped ham and potatoes, carrots, turnips, mushrooms, and veal. A stuffed cabbage like no other before or after! I dread to think how long it took to assemble in Jefferson's time. A processor makes the work load considerably lighter today!

3 pounds firm Savoy cabbage
4 medium potatoes, peeled, quartered
6 tablespoons (¾ stick) unsalted butter
½ cup heavy or whipping cream
2 small onions, finely chopped
¾ pound ground cooked ham
⅛ teaspoon ground mace
1 clove garlic, minced
½ pound mushrooms, minced
Pinch of ground cloves
½ pound ground veal
1 egg, lightly beaten
¼ cup fresh bread crumbs
Pinch of dried thyme
½ teaspoon salt
¼ teaspoon freshly ground black pepper
½ pound carrots, peeled, minced
¼ cup chopped fresh dill
1 teaspoon finely grated lemon peel
½ pound turnips, peeled, minced
1 stalk celery, minced
¼ cup chopped fresh parsley
2 tablespoons minced red bell pepper
⅔ cup dry white wine
1 quart chicken broth (see page 414)
1½ tablespoons all-purpose flour
½ teaspoon Dijon mustard
Dash of hot pepper sauce
1 teaspoon lemon juice

1. Using a sharp knife, slice off the stem end of the cabbage and remove the core. Cook the cabbage, uncovered, in a large pot of boiling salted water 10 minutes, turning once. Drain; cool thoroughly. Separate the cabbage leaves and pat them dry. Reserve.

2. Cook the potatoes in boiling salted water until tender, about 20 minutes. Drain. Mash the potatoes with 1 tablespoon of the butter and ¼ cup of the cream. Cool slightly and combine with 1 chopped onion, the ground ham, and the mace. Mix well; reserve.

3. Melt 2 tablespoons of the butter in a large skillet over medium heat. Add the remaining onion; cook 1 minute. Add the garlic and mushrooms. Cook, stirring constantly, until browned. Remove from the heat and transfer to a bowl. Cool slightly and combine with the cloves, veal, egg, bread crumbs, thyme, salt, and pepper. Mix well; reserve.

4. Combine the carrots, dill, and lemon peel in a bowl. Mix well; reserve.

5. Combine the turnips, celery, parsley, and red pepper in another bowl. Mix well; reserve.

6. To assemble the Chartreuse, lay out a large linen napkin or towel on a flat surface. Arrange the largest cabbage leaves in the center, slightly overlapping with the stems pointing outward, in a circular pattern. (This should look as if the cabbage had been opened upside down.) Spoon half the ham mixture over the leaves. Place the next layer of leaves (overlapping and centered) on top. Spoon half the carrot mixture over the leaves. Continue layering (always stems outward) with half the veal and mushroom filling, and finally, half the turnip filling. Repeat the process in the same order until leaves and fillings are used up. (Stems may be removed on innermost layers of cabbage for easier assembly.) End with the turnip filling. Place 1 tablespoon of the butter in the center of the last layer. Gather the edges of the napkin and pull the corners up and together, returning the cabbage to its original shape. Tie securely with kitchen string.

7. Preheat the oven to 350°F. Place the cabbage in a large ovenproof pot, tied side up. Pour the wine and chicken broth around the cabbage. Heat to boiling. Cover, and cook in the oven for 1¾ hours.

8. Remove the pot from the oven. Carefully move the cabbage to a plate, reserving the cooking liquid. Untie the napkin, place a large shallow ovenproof serving dish over the top, and quickly, but carefully, invert. Remove the napkin. Cook the cabbage in the oven for another 10 minutes.

9. Meanwhile, melt the remaining 2 tablespoons butter in a medium saucepan over medium-low heat. Add the flour. Cook, stirring constantly, 2 minutes. Whisk in 2 cups stock from the pot, the mustard, hot pepper sauce, lemon juice, and the remaining ¼ cup cream. Cook until slightly thickened.

10. To serve, spoon some of the sauce over the cabbage and cut the cabbage into pie-shaped wedges. Pass the remaining sauce.

Serves 8 to 10.

RED CABBAGE ALSATIAN-STYLE

This makes a fine one-dish supper with a plate of tiny boiled potatoes on the side. The recipe came to me on a stained fragment of brown paper after I supplicated long and hard for it after a hearty dinner. It was scribbled in a mixture of French and

German, but as you will see when you have made the dish, nothing whatsoever was lost in the translation!

Incidentally, don't worry that an unlucky dinner guest may chance upon one of the four garlic cloves. The garlic disappears after three hours of cooking and tossing.

4 tablespoons (½ stick) unsalted butter
4 cloves garlic
2½ pounds red cabbage, trimmed, shredded
1 pound smoked pork butt (or smoked shoulder), cut into 1-inch cubes
½ cup dry white wine
½ cup strong Chicken Stock (see page 410), or 1½ cups chicken broth (see page 414) reduced to ½ cup
1 medium onion stuck with 2 whole cloves
Salt and freshly ground black pepper

1. Preheat the oven to 250°F. Melt the butter in a Dutch oven over medium-low heat. Add the garlic; cook 3 minutes. Remove from the heat.

2. Place the cabbage and smoked pork in layers in the Dutch oven. Pour in the wine and the chicken stock. Place the onion in the center, cover, and bake 1 hour.

3. Remove from the oven and toss the mixture. Bake, covered, 1½ hours longer.

4. Raise the oven heat to 350°F. Remove the cover and cook 30 minutes longer. Discard the onion and cloves. Add salt and pepper to taste.

Serves 4 to 6.

CARROTS

Worth Their Weight in Gold

When my grandmother died, the glories of her kitchen expired with her. But her garden, no less glorious, survived for almost seventeen years because my grandfather doggedly took over the task of its cultivation. It was not an easy chore for an old man with a bad leg and no apparent horticultural skills, but clearly he undertook the enterprise as a memorial to his wife.

When she was alive, my indomitable grandmother would have rejected the honor out of hand. To her mind there was a sharp division between the labors permissible to a homemaker and those to a breadwinner. And she would have no more allowed her husband to thin a flower bed than she would have permitted his presence at her stove. Anything to do with house or garden was exclusively her bailiwick and all interlopers were dispatched without ceremony.

But then my grandmother's agricultural act was a hard one to follow. She was blessed with a thumb of pure jade plus a natural instinct for generating life. Any alien cutting that she surreptitiously snipped from a botanical garden or forest woodland immediately took root in her backyard. Even more astonishing, these fragile shoots—wild blue lupine or lady's slipper orchids—did not merely bloom, they grew to awesome proportions, ministered by her constant nagging and massive doses of vitamins, most of which were the detritus of her cooking pots, which she carefully strained before spading into the soil.

"You see what I am doing here, mister?" I recall her quizzing me when I was perhaps eight or nine years old and involved in planning my very first garden.

"This—" indicating the saucepan she held aloft, "—is the water in which last night's vegetables cooked. See how I sprinkle a little on the gladiolas, dahlias, even tulips—the bulbs that need help to send up new shoots. Not roots." She shook her head to emphasize the point. "Soup stock or fish broth is what makes a root grow strong. And as a special treat, maybe a little meat juice once in a while. But be sure to skim off every bit of the fat first. I want you to remember that a slob in the kitchen can be a murderer in the garden!"

Did I heed her advice? My very first vegetable garden was a flag of thick moss behind our garage. The only living thing that ever flourished there was an unpruned and utterly inviolate wild rose bush—a shrub that, like the great god Shiva, sent out a strong-armed threat of new brambles every spring.

In my initial garden, inspired by our Italian neighbors behind the hedge, I planted every glowing packet of vegetable seeds that Burpee and friends provided at our local Woolworth's counter. And though my grandmother duly enjoined me that "crowded gardens are inferior gardens," my enthusiasm for planting knew no bounds. Leaf lettuce, celery, corn, and peppers bisected rows of peas, cucumbers, cabbage, runner beans, and watermelon, with carrots forming a natural border around it all.

I need not have constructed the elaborately staked markers of seed envelopes to identify each seedling. Aside from a feathery line of carrot tops no other trace of green ever appeared in that dark tract. And no matter how many pints of metallic-smelling vegetable juices (accrued from my mother's nightly supply of canned goods) were sluiced on the ground, my only harvest was a clutch of tiny orange fingers poking up—like Mother Nature's reproach for greed.

It might have been worse. The carrots were tasty and plentiful besides. As soon as one was picked, another took its place in the earthly assembly line, seemingly overnight.

After we had dined on produce from my garden for some while, however, my father rebelled.

"This mouthful makes the fortieth carrot I have chewed this week," he declared righteously, laying down his fork and knife. "And enough is enough. What I suggest—request, actually—is that our young gardener here leave the spoils he's still got coming up in the backyard to those who are *needier*."

He paused dramatically for the idea to sink in before winking broadly. "Like rabbits!"

Usually I had some ready answer to my father's jibes, but not that night. Frankly I was so tired of eating carrots myself that I acquiesced at once. With a thin smile.

Of course what neither father nor son realized at that moment was that carrots are a biennial crop. Both Greenes and rabbits dined on those "golden assets" again the following summer. But in moderation. Decidedly in moderation, for I had started planting flowers by then. And compared to a zinnia a carrot is only a carrot, after all. Unless of course it turns out to be a stalk of Queen Anne's lace!

Vegetable Roots

Daucus carota sativa, the benign confederate to stew and pot roast for hundreds of years, has a host of quite unruly relatives beyond the garden gate. Known as the Umbelliferae, this botanical assemblage—whose ranks include anise, caraway, celery, chervil, fennel, parsley, and parsnip as well as Queen Anne's lace—has the odd distinction of being

dubbed a "kitchen mafia" in certain culinary circles, for these strong flavors are known to take over and territorialize the contents of a saucepan!

Queen Anne's lace is obviously the most delicate member of this tribe. In the Balkans, where the plant is cultivated, it is referred to as the "white carrot." American farmers are a bit less generous. They call it "cow's currency," for a herd of cattle has been known to charge through barbed wire for a tasty nibble when the umbels are in bloom.

On the opposite side of the family, carrot's most uncordial relative is the poison hemlock. Now we are talking mafia for real, for this umbellale has a more potent after-dinner effect than all the others put together. It knocks you dead!

Earliest carrot consumption is traced to the hill people of Afghanistan, who were sun-worshipers and believed that eating orange or yellow-colored foods instilled a sense of righteousness.

Greeks and Romans prized this vegetable for somewhat earthier reasons. Sequestered in the Trojan Horse, Athenian foot soldiers subsisted exclusively on a diet of raw carrots, to bind their bowels. On quite the other hand, invad-

As a kid whose first reading material consisted of the *Mother West Wind Stories*, followed in short order by *Peter Rabbit* and the works of Beatrix Potter, I developed early on a solid affection for all the members of his long-eared, cotton-tailed breed.

But not in my garden.

At Amagansett, Long Island, where I have harvested a gilded share of carrots from time to time, the crop may be just a tad sweeter than any other I have known, for the soil is sandy loam and runs deep besides. It certainly produces what I deem "the carrot-lover's carrot"! Why else would a crop of otherwise circumspect rabbits gather daily from May to midsummer to check the growth of my seedlings? These not-so-dumb bunnies sense that something really special is coming up, I can tell you!

Amagansett rabbits are carrot cognoscenti. They even know the difference between a Nantes Half Long, which appears in early spring, and a Coreless Amsterdam, which comes to harvest late every summer. And they await the growth of the latter with the same degree of discrimination that local girl-watchers mark the arrival of a well-filled bikini on the beach.

In the past, I have waged (mild) wars on the rabbit population, using rubber snakes and fences to discourage their attentions. But nothing proved effective in the final analysis. Nowadays we share the yield. I consume whatever the rabbits conspicuously do *not*.

Weeding carrots is probably the most serendipitous experience a gardener can have.

In a well-calculated *potager*, the plants must be thinned so they are far enough apart for healthy growth: a laborious chore, but the gardener can revive his flagging spirit with a little nourishment at the source.

A carrot picked straight from the soil cannot be consumed without a fast brush of any residual loam, but that's what shirttails are for. No matter what time of day the carrot is picked, the temperature will be the same: warm at the skin from its earthly bed but chill as the night wind at the heart, a taste sensation unequaled by any other fresh-dug thing in the universe—up to and including the truffle of Perigord!

ing Roman legions fed their captive females carrots (cooked into a broth) to unloose their stringent morals.

From its obvious erotic design came the carrot's sexual reputation, I suppose. Caligula is purported to have once fed the entire Roman Senate a banquet composed solely of carrot dishes, in one form or another, just to observe these high-minded gentlemen "fornicating like beasts of the field." No account of the proceedings exists but I'll warrant it was more of an ordeal than an orgy for the guests. Since carrots contain more sugar than any other vegetable except the sugar beet, an all-carrot menu could bring on a mass attack of hyperglycemia rather than lust!

Long after the myth of the carrot's aphrodisiac powers waned, physicians in the Middle Ages still prescribed them as an antidote for every imaginable affliction, from syphilis to dog bite. No one ever ate a carrot for pleasure, it seems, until the middle of the Renaissance.

The Dutch actually grew carrots in profusion, having inherited the seeds as a residual of the Saracen invasion centuries earlier. But no Dutchman gave the carrot room on his dinner plate. The lowland dairy farmers reserved the entire crop for their native Holstein cows, which produced the richest, yellowest butter in all of Europe as a consequence.

It was actually a Dutch or Flemish nobleman (history is cloudy on the pedigree) who brought the carrot into our Anglo-Saxon diet. A deputy to the English court, making overtures to Elizabeth I, he presented the queen with two gifts: a tub of native butter and a wreath of tender carrots emblazoned with diamonds, to wear in her hair.

Having better sense than the emissary, good Queen Bess removed the diamonds and sent carrots and butter together to the royal kitchen. And that's how the classic side dish, buttered carrots, entered the menu!

What to Look For

Carrots may be seasonal in a garden but they certainly are permanent residents on greengrocers' shelves these days.

I tend to buy carrots in bunches with their tops intact, because the sprightliness of the greens is always a giveaway of the vegetable's freshness. It is tough for a consumer to judge just how long a topless, plastic-sealed carrot has been around, although there are clues. Old carrots are usually cracked or brittle and send out a rash of tiny white roots. So stay clear of those!

Of late, I have been increasingly aware of the emphasis on "miniature carrots" in supermarkets. The uniform size and pale color of these packaged bantams implies that they have been picked at the prime of garden freshness, so the buyer is expected to pay more for the privilege of adding them to a stew. However, these pale young carrots are decidedly deficient in carotene, the deep rich coloring agent that the human body converts into vitamin A. So my advice is to pass them by. To give the next carrot dish a lighter complexion, use deeply colored carrots and add cream!

Carrots have a curious chemistry. Though they contain more natural sugar than any other vegetable aside from the sugar beet, the calories in a whole average-size carrot amount to less than a package of sugarless gum, about 30. Carrots are also an incredibly high source of vitamin A (7,930 units each) and contain high levels of potassium, calcium, and phosphorus.

Preparation

The classic preparation for any fresh carrot is to peel it first, using a swivel-bladed vegetable peeler that lightly removes the skin. Then, depending upon the recipe, slice, dice, julienne, shred—or leave it whole!

I never peel baby carrots because the tender skin has a particularly appealing sweet flavor, and it is vitamin-high into the bargain, but that option is up to you.

Likewise, out of a purely personal crotchet, I hardly ever steam or boil a carrot until soft, as my mother always did. Instead I blanch them in water, broth, vegetable juices, or a mixture of water and butter, allowing just enough liquid to cover, and cook them over moderate heat, uncovered, until they reach a stage that French chefs call *à point:* barely tender to the fork. I often cook carrots in advance, cool them immediately under cold running water, and reheat them again in a little more butter just before I serve them.

The technique for cooking a carrot à la Greene varies with each one of my recipes, but a small dose of general carrot-cookery wisdom would not be amiss here. To wit: the optimum cooking time for a *sliced* or *diced* carrot is usually 8 minutes flat. Unless of course the slices are on the thick side; then merely increase the cooking time according to your own good judgment. But remember, please: a perfectly prepared carrot is never mushy! *Julienne-cut* carrots (once again depending upon the size of the strips) should cook firm-tender in less time; about 4 minutes. When a recipe calls for *shredded* carrots I actually don't cook them at all, preferring to merely toss them in melted butter over high heat for a few seconds until they warm through. *Whole* carrots, despite whatever other advice you have heard on the subject, are best cooked over low heat in a small amount of liquid in a partially covered saucepan. My timetable? Approximately 20 minutes—but garden-fresh produce will take less.

ELYSIAN BISQUE

This singularly thick and satisfying soup comes from Holland. Its Dutch title translates as "soup of supreme bliss."

5 strips bacon, chopped
1 pound carrots, peeled, chopped
6 whole scallions, bulbs and green tops, chopped
10 mushrooms, chopped (about 1 cup)
3 ribs celery with leaves, chopped (about 1 cup)
1 teaspoon fresh thyme, or 1/4 teaspoon dried
1 small bay leaf, crumbled
4 cups chicken broth (see page 414)
1 cup water
1 cup light cream or half-and-half
Salt and freshly ground black pepper

1. Sauté the bacon in a medium saucepan over medium heat until crisp. Stir in the carrots, scallions, mushrooms, and celery. Cook uncovered, 5 minutes.

2. Add the thyme, bay leaf, chicken broth, and water to the saucepan. Heat to boiling; reduce the heat. Simmer, covered, 50 minutes. Remove from the heat and allow to cool slightly.

3. Place the soup in the container of a food processor or blender. Process until smooth, being very careful as hot liquid will expand. Return it to the saucepan and reheat slowly, adding the cream and salt and pepper to taste.

Serves 6.

COLD CARROTS VICHY

This slaw is a brand-new version of an old (and justly honored) salad I used to make when I ran The Store in Amagansett for a golden decade.

1 pound carrots, peeled, shredded
4 whole scallions, bulbs and green tops minced separately
½ cup minced cooked ham
½ cup Mayonnaise (see page 408)
¼ cup sour cream
¼ cup Chinese duck sauce
½ teaspoon Dijon mustard
Salt and freshly ground black pepper

1. Combine the shredded carrots, minced scallion bulbs, and the ham in a large bowl. Mix well.

2. Beat the mayonnaise with the sour cream in a small bowl until smooth. Beat in the duck sauce and mustard. Pour the sauce over the carrot mixture, toss well, and add salt and pepper to taste. Serve at room temperature or chilled, sprinkled with the minced scallion tops.

Serves 6.

MARILYN HARRIS' BAKED CARROTS AU NATUREL

Before the Second World War, most Americans sliced their carrots the size of poker chips but then perversely boiled them in quarts and quarts of water until the slender rounds acquired the shape and texture of damp powder puffs.

The tide had to turn of course, if only for the sake of vitiated vitamins, and it did in the early 1960s. Since then, mostly in the guise of health food, one is often served carrots so undercooked that cutting them with a fork can cause irremediable damage to heirloom silver.

One of the happiest compromises, a tender yet nutritive carrot dish, follows. I acquired the recipe from Marilyn Harris, director of the cooking school at Pogue's in Cincinnati.

1 pound carrots, peeled
2 tablespoons unsalted butter
Salt and freshly ground black pepper
1 tablespoon chopped fresh parsley

1. Preheat the oven to 325°F. Cut the carrots into strips 2 inches long and ¼ inch thick.

2. Place the butter in a 1½-quart earthenware baking dish or casserole with a cover. Heat the dish in the oven until the butter melts. Then add the carrots, tossing to coat them with the butter. Sprinkle with salt and pepper to taste. Bake, covered, for 1¼ hours. Sprinkle with the parsley before serving.

Serves 6.

ELIZABETHAN BRAISED AND GLAZED CARROTS

To my mind the classic carrot rendition is ultimately the simplest—in this case merely tossed with butter plus an amendment of honey. Since Queen Elizabeth I of England was responsible for the carrot's initial popularity, can one pay greater homage than to name it in her honor?

2 tablespoons unsalted butter
1 shallot, minced
1 pound carrots, peeled, sliced into rounds
½ cup Chicken Stock (see page 410)
1½ tablespoons honey
⅛ teaspoon freshly grated nutmeg
1 tablespoon chopped fresh parsley

1. Melt the butter in a medium saucepan over medium-low heat. Add the shallot; cook 1 minute. Stir in the sliced carrots and the chicken stock. Cook, covered, stirring occasionally, until just tender, about 12 to 15 minutes.

2. Add the honey and nutmeg. Raise the heat slightly, and cook, uncovered, stirring constantly, until the liquid becomes syrupy. Remove from the heat; toss in the chopped parsley.

Serves 4.

PLUM-CRAZY CARROTS

Yet another carrot classic, this one of Polish-Jewish ancestry and said to date back at least 300 years, is a vegetable and fruit amalgam known as *tsimmes*.

A good *tsimmes*, which was meant to be eaten on the sabbath or at a special holiday meal, usually required a full day's cooking time and often depended upon a multitude of odd ingredients (like sweet potatoes, pineapple, apricots, even a cut of brisket on occasion) to flavor the pot. But the mainstays of this dish were always carrots and dried prunes.

Over the years, the word *tsimmes* has acquired a totally different second meaning in Yiddish. These days it generally connotes "an awful fuss."

I offer up my own totally inauthentic rendition of a *tsimmes*, concocted of tender orange carrots and seasonal purple plums. I call it "plum-crazy carrots" and hope that no one feels called upon to make a *tsimmes* about that, please!

1 pound carrots, peeled
2½ tablespoons unsalted butter
2 teaspoons sugar
½ cup chopped pitted fresh blue plums
1 teaspoon finely slivered orange peel
1½ teaspoons brandy
Salt and freshly ground black pepper
Chopped fresh parsley

1. Cut the carrots into strips 3 inches long and about ¼ inch thick. Cook in boiling salted water until just barely tender, about 4 minutes. Rinse under cold running water; drain.

2. Melt 2 tablespoons of the butter in a medium skillet over medium heat. Add the carrots; sprinkle with the sugar.

Cook, tossing gently, until the carrots begin to caramelize.

3. Add the plums and orange peel to the carrots. Cook over medium-low heat until the plums give off their juice and are almost tender, about 5 minutes. Stir in the brandy and remaining ½ tablespoon butter. Raise the heat slightly and cook, tossing gently, until most of the liquid has evaporated. Season with salt and pepper to taste. Serve sprinkled with chopped parsley.

Serves 4.

AMISH CARROT DUMPLINGS

This is a dish of thrifty Pennsylvania Dutch antecedents; it really makes a carrot stretch, and it solves the problem of using up those leftover potatoes!

1¼ cups cold mashed potatoes
1 large carrot, peeled, finely grated
1 small white onion, grated
2 eggs
½ cup finely grated Swiss cheese
⅛ teaspoon freshly grated nutmeg
½ teaspoon salt
¼ teaspoon ground white pepper
1½ cups all-purpose flour, approximately
2 tablespoons unsalted butter
2 tablespoons freshly grated Parmesan cheese (optional)

1. Combine all the ingredients through the pepper in a large bowl; mix thoroughly. Work in the flour with your hands, starting with 1 cup and adding more until a soft dough is formed. Refrigerate, covered, 1 hour.

2. Roll the dough on a well-floured pastry board into ropes about ½ inch thick. Cut each rope into individual dumplings about 1 inch long. Press each end with the tines of a fork. Cook, about ten at a time, in a large pot of boiling salted water just until they float to the surface, about 1 minute or less. Remove with a slotted spoon and drain lightly on paper towels. Transfer to a well-buttered shallow baking dish, and reserve. Continue until all dumplings are cooked. Let them stand, covered, at room temperature until ready to heat.

3. Preheat the oven to 325° F. Dot the dumplings with butter and cook them in the oven until warmed through, 15 to 20 minutes. Sprinkle with Parmesan cheese before serving, if you like.

Serves 6.

PENNSYLVANIA DUTCH BARBECUED CARROTS

This most unusual dish is a souvenir of an absolutely overwhelming feast (half sweets, half sours) enjoyed in the Amish country more years ago than I care to say. The "stickin' sauce," incidentally, will do equal justice to any rib, wing or leg of your choice. The Pennsylvania Dutch, however, splash it on carrots.

1 pound carrots (approximately equal in size), peeled
1 cup Amish Stickin' Sauce (recipe follows)
1 tablespoon chopped fresh parsley

1. Preheat the oven to 350°F. Place the whole carrots in an ovenproof baking dish or casserole. Spoon the sauce over the carrots and toss well.

2. Bake the carrots, covered, 45 minutes. Remove the cover and continue to bake, turning and basting frequently, until crisp and tender, about 45 minutes longer. Sprinkle with the parsley before serving.

Serves 4 to 6.

Amish Stickin' Sauce

2 tablespoons unsalted butter
1 onion, finely chopped
2 cloves garlic, minced
Juice of 1 orange
1 tablespoon raisins
2 tablespoons cider vinegar
2 tablespoons vegetable oil
Grated peel of 1 orange
1 cup molasses
1 cup ketchup
2 teaspoons chili powder
Pinch of ground cloves
1 teaspoon prepared mustard
1 teaspoon Worcestershire sauce
2 teaspoons crushed dried hot red peppers
½ teaspoon salt

1. Melt the butter in a medium saucepan over medium-low heat. Add the onion and garlic. Cook 5 minutes; do not brown.

2. Meanwhile, combine the orange juice with the raisins, vinegar, and oil in the container of a food processor or blender. Process until smooth. Add this mixture, along with the remaining ingredients, to the saucepan. Heat to boiling; reduce the heat. Simmer, uncovered, 15 minutes.

Makes about 3 cups.

CARROT VELVET

To my mind, the tonic thing about such a good-tasting but relatively low-calorie vegetable is that one may enrich it unsparingly, without a speck of guilt.

3½ cups chicken broth (see page 414)
1 pound carrots, peeled, cut in half
3 tablespoons unsalted butter
3 tablespoons all-purpose flour
½ cup heavy or whipping cream
⅛ teaspoon ground allspice
⅛ teaspoon freshly grated nutmeg
Dash of hot pepper sauce
Salt and freshly ground black pepper
¼ cup fresh bread crumbs
2 tablespoons minced fresh parsley
1 tablespoon freshly grated Parmesan cheese

1. Preheat the oven to 350°F. Place the chicken broth in a medium saucepan and bring it to the boil. Add the carrots and reduce the heat. Simmer, uncovered, until the carrots are very soft, about 25 minutes. Drain the carrots, reserving the cooking liquid. Mash the carrots until smooth. Set aside.

2. Melt 2 tablespoons of the butter in a medium saucepan over medium-low heat. Stir in the flour. Cook, stirring constantly, 2 minutes. Whisk in 1 cup of the reserved cooking liquid. Heat to boiling; reduce the heat. Add the cream, allspice, nutmeg, hot pepper sauce, and salt and pepper to taste. Remove from the heat and combine with the mashed carrots. Spoon into a lightly greased shallow baking dish.

3. Melt the remaining 1 tablespoon butter in a small skillet over medium heat. Stir in the bread crumbs and cook until they are golden. Remove from the heat and stir in the minced parsley. Spread the bread crumbs evenly over the carrots. Sprinkle with the Parmesan cheese. Bake until bubbly, about 15 minutes.

Serves 4 to 6.

SAUSAGE AND CARROT PIE

This recipe is a Georgian dividend—from America, not Russia. It is for a luncheon pie, meant to be eaten lukewarm. The formula is over 100 years old and never altered a whit in all that time.

1 recipe Short Crust Pastry (see page 412)
2 tablespoons unsalted butter
1 teaspoon minced shallot
½ pound carrots, peeled, grated
¼ cup Chicken Stock (see page 410)
¼ teaspoon ground mace
¼ teaspoon salt
½ pound mild Italian sausages, sliced
1 ¼ cups heavy or whipping cream
1 egg
1 egg yolk

1. Make the Short Crust Pastry.

2. Preheat the oven to 400°F. Roll out the pastry on a lightly floured board. Line a buttered 10-inch loose-bottom tart pan with the pastry and trim the edges. Line the pastry with aluminum foil; weight with rice or beans. Bake 10 minutes. Remove the foil and beans; bake 5 minutes longer. Cool on a wire rack. Reduce the oven heat to 375°F.

3. Melt the butter in a large skillet over medium heat. Add the shallot; cook until golden. Stir in the carrots, chicken stock, mace, and salt. Cook until the carrots are tender, about 8 minutes. Raise the heat slightly and continue to cook, tossing and stirring, until all liquid has evaporated. Transfer the carrots to a medium bowl and set aside.

4. In the same skillet, sauté the sliced sausages over medium heat until golden brown on both sides. Drain on paper towels.

5. Spoon the carrots evenly over the bottom of the prepared pastry. Arrange the sausage slices on top.

6. Beat the cream with the egg and egg yolk in a medium bowl and pour it over the sausages. Place the tart pan on a foil-lined baking sheet and bake until the pie is puffed and golden, about 30 minutes. Let it stand at least 10 minutes before serving.

Serves 6 to 8.

FINNISH MEATBALLS

Despite (or because of) the carrot's evanescent flavor, its presence may be hard to pinpoint in a dish. For instance in this Scandinavian dish, obviously a first cousin to the Swedish meatball but lighter and more aureate.

1½ pounds ground veal
2 medium carrots, peeled, finely grated
1 egg, lightly beaten
½ cup fresh bread crumbs
¼ teaspoon freshly grated nutmeg
1 cardamom seed, crushed
½ teaspoon salt
⅛ teaspoon freshly ground black pepper
1 medium onion, quartered
½ cup chicken broth (see page 414)
3 tablespoons unsalted butter, approximately
1 tablespoon vegetable oil
1½ cups heavy or whipping cream
½ cup sour cream
⅓ cup chopped fresh dill

1. Combine all the ingredients through the pepper in a large bowl.

2. Place the onion with the chicken broth in the container of a food processor or blender. Process until smooth. Add this to the meat mixture, blend thoroughly, and form into small meatballs.

3. Heat 2 tablespoons of the butter with the oil in a heavy skillet over medium heat. Sauté the meatballs, about ten at a time, until golden on all sides. Transfer to a medium saucepan and keep warm. Add more butter as needed to sauté the remaining meatballs.

4. Place the saucepan over medium-low heat. Add the heavy cream and the sour cream to the meatballs. Simmer gently, uncovered, 20 minutes. Stir in the dill just before serving. Serve with rice, buttered noodles, or boiled potatoes.

Serves 4 to 6.

CARROT-RICE PUDDING

The following nostrum is one that is solid gold, yet lighter than air. A pudding that is definitely *no* dessert.

½ pound carrots, peeled, roughly chopped
1 cup strong Chicken Stock (see page 410)
½ cup heavy or whipping cream
1 tablespoon unsalted butter
2 tablespoons all-purpose flour
½ cup hot milk
Pinch of cayenne pepper
⅛ teaspoon freshly grated nutmeg
Salt and freshly ground black pepper
2 cups cooked rice

1. Preheat the oven to 375°F. Place the carrots with the stock in a medium saucepan. Heat to boiling; reduce the heat. Simmer, uncovered, until the carrots are very tender, about 12 to 15 minutes. Drain, reserving the stock.

2. Place the cooked carrots in the container of a food processor or blender. Add the cream and process until smooth. Reserve.

3. Melt the butter in a medium saucepan over medium-low heat. Stir in the flour. Cook, stirring constantly, 2 minutes. Whisk in the reserved stock and the hot milk. Heat to boiling; reduce the heat. Simmer until thickened, about 5 minutes. Add the cayenne pepper, nutmeg, and salt and pepper to taste. Remove from the heat; stir in the puréed carrots and the rice. Transfer the mixture to a buttered baking dish and bake 15 minutes.

Serves 6 to 8.

CARROT-VANILLA TART

Unfortunately there is no splendid carrot dish of my grandmother's repertoire left to end this memoir of her gorgeously green garden. So you will have to make do with one of my own inventions instead. It is a sweet custard tart of sufficient brilliance to make her proud of her old kitchen acolyte.

1 recipe Orange-Crust Pastry (see page 412)
¼ pound carrots (about 4 medium), peeled, cubed
4 eggs
1 cup sugar
¼ cup orange juice
2 tablespoons vanilla
1 cup heavy or whipping cream
4 tablespoons (½ stick) butter, melted

1. Preheat the oven to 400°F. Roll out the pastry on a lightly floured board. Line a buttered 10-inch loose-bottom tart pan with the pastry and trim the edges. Line the pastry with aluminum foil; weight with rice or beans. Bake 10 minutes. Remove the foil and beans. Bake 5 minutes longer. Cool on a wire rack. Reduce the oven heat to 350°F.

2. Cook the carrots in boiling water to cover until they are very tender, about 20 minutes. Drain. Place the carrots in the container of a food processor and process, using the on/off switch, until smooth.

3. Beat the eggs with the sugar in a large bowl until light and lemon colored. Add the puréed carrots, the orange juice, vanilla, cream, and melted butter. Pour into the prebaked shell and bake 40 minutes. Reduce the heat to 325°F and bake until firm, about 10 minutes longer.

Serves 6 to 8.

CAULIFLOWER

The Cabbage with the College Education

Twenty-five years ago, I became an exurbanite in earnest—without design, however.

There was certainly overpopulation in the area of Manhattan where I lived, and even then the signs of air pollution were unmistakable to anyone with working sinuses. But those were *not* the factors that drove me from city to hinterland. No, it was a deeper need that caused my initial foray to the virtual end of Long Island: love of sea, sand, and most important of all, seclusion.

The place I chose for my retreat would be judged a most unlikely territory for any hermit today, as it is technically part of the very tony Hamptons scene. But a quarter-century ago, Amagansett was so far out of the social swim that it might have been mistaken for East Lynne.

It was a place that real estate agents of stature automatically bypassed when they showed summer rental houses to prospective tenants because the right people did not stop there. I obviously appeared so insubstantial, both socially and financially, that it was the *only* area I was offered.

The small house I eventually rented was known as "the Ely place" (always pronounced *eely* by some odd quirk of the Bonacker tongue) and it was spare

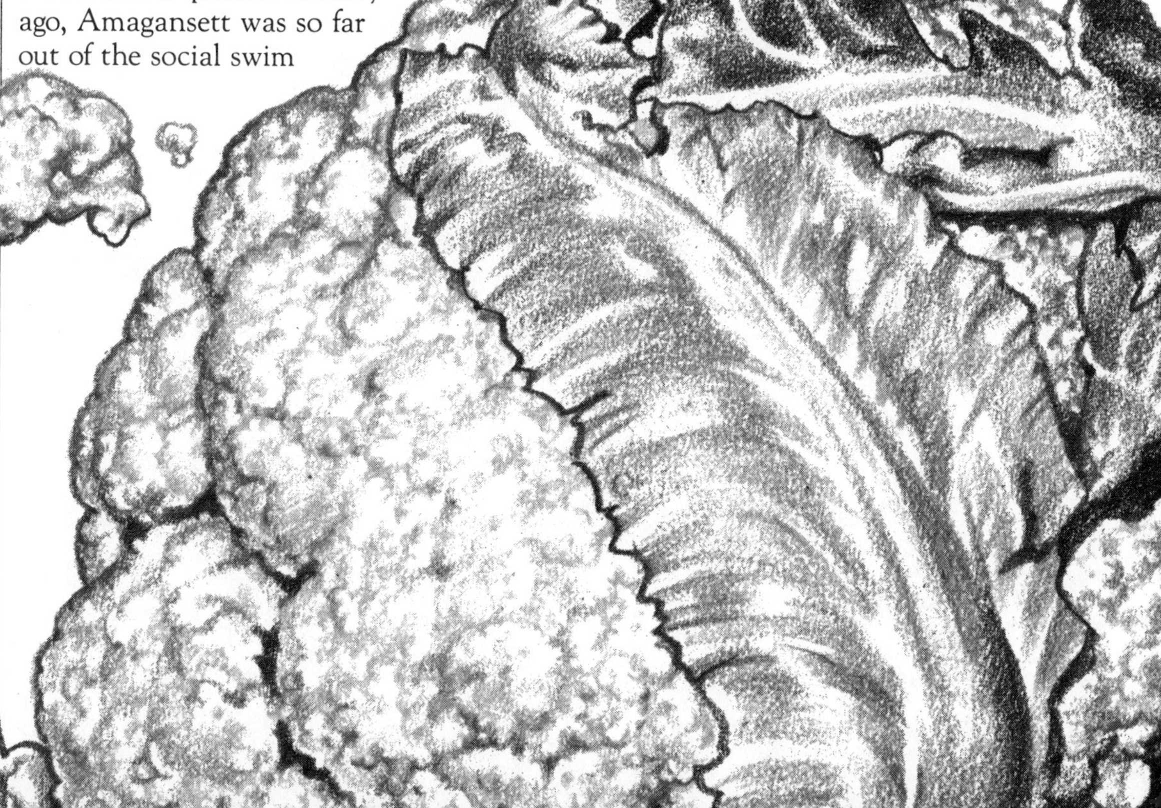

and sparse. But to my eye it was a castle. Set back from the beach road, it faced little other than miles of ocean and a remarkable stretch of sand dunes and gorse where ripe blackberries and beach plums grew in abundance. I settled in this place to rusticate and write a play. Those berries and plums proved too narcotic to resist, however, so I spent half my days gathering them and the rest over a hot stove, sweating the spoils into gleaming jars of jam. How could I not? My private fruit reserve was just across the way, on a tract of overgrown land owned by the federal government that had once been the site of a vital Coast Guard operation housing five hundred young men in regimental whites.

By the late 1950s, the station and barracks had long since been abandoned. A faded sign still proclaimed the property to be "off limits" to civilians but no one in the vicinity took that admonition very seriously. For the blackberry and beach plum would surely have stained the white sand purple and red by summer's end, if willing hands had not come to the rescue and picked them!

At the termination of the first summer's lease, I knew the taste of the wildest berry (not to mention the anodyne of salt in the air) had had an irrevocable effect on my well-being. And shortly thereafter I bought a home of my own in Amagansett.

In those days, like most fellow Hamptonites, I locked the door and turned off the gas and electricity in late fall and did not return to my home in the country again until the following spring.

When I made my vernal reappearance, the signal that the territory had not irremediably altered in my absence was the rash of hand-lettered placards along the highway; signs, crudely crayoned, on farm stands, pickup trucks, and oil-cloth-covered tables along the road announcing: *Strawberries, Pick Your Own, 25¢ a Quart.*

That always meant summer was not far off.

Time does not stand still. Like it or no, a quarter-century wreaks irreparable changes in any landscape. The Coast Guard buildings, for instance, have been razed long since. Blackberry and beach plum likewise vanished, stripped bare by teenage vandals some years back. And rather than the scent of salt in the air these days one smells only high-octane gasoline, for the streets of Amagansett are clogged with trendy summer visitors, most in expensive foreign cars. No canines wander across the dunes any longer, for a town ruling insists that dogs be kept on leashes at all times. Even the once-deserted beaches require an official permit before a resident is allowed to dip his bottom into the sea.

Today, when the signs proclaim *Strawberries, Pick Your Own,* I blush somewhat deeper than the color of the fruit itself at the prices asked. And in summer, I do what all sensible householders have done since the sack of Rome. I rent my home to the invaders and go away!

When I return again in late September, the vital signs are still those hand-lettered placards along the road. But the legend that gives hope in autumn reads somewhat differently: *Cauliflower, 3 Heads for $1.*

I take heart then.

Not only because this greenstuff is the best grown anywhere along the Eastern seaboard (it is, it is) but also because the presence of those jade and white vegetables in the fields is a sure sign that summer is finally over. The earth and the slightly frigid sea are mine again. Without a beach permit.

Vegetable Roots

Cauliflower has been around for a good long time. Brought to Europe when the Moorish armies invaded Spain, this homely plant was promptly dubbed

From time to time in my hot pursuit of vegetable lore, I dip into some fairly esoteric tomes.

A Wyf's Bok of Gardyning, written in 1709, is a good case in point. Consider the following note: "Witches say coleflores eaten reguler by a childeless wyfe alwayes resulten praenansy." The witch's logic, in this case, undoubtedly arose from observation of the cauliflower plant in the garden, which grows to conspicuous proportions, discreetly hidden from any prying eye—a model judged worthy of emulation in the early eighteenth century.

cavoli a fiore (the cabbage that blooms like a flower), and initially its virtues were assumed to be ornamental rather than edible. Indeed, food sleuths tell us that a small, perfect cauliflower was often pressed into the décolletage of an unmarried Spanish maiden to call attention to her natural endowments.

Mark Twain once said, "Cauliflower is just a cabbage with a college education!" He wasn't very far from the mark. Originally known as wild winter cabbage, *Brassica oleracea botrytis* in its purest (uncultivated) state is a tall-growing green flower stalk, slightly on the fibrous side and better loved by goats than gastronomes. Its evolution into one of the staples of the world took place long, long before the birth of Christ, but the changeover was due to man's ingenuity rather than Mother Nature's diligence.

The great snowy head of succulent buds nesting in a wreath of green leaves was the handiwork of an early gardener (most probably a Babylonian) who first cultivated the plant for his dinner table in the Tigris-Euphrates Valley. The technique he used to shape the plant is much the same as the cauliflower growers of eastern Long Island employ two thousand years later.

Shortly after a cauliflower seed is sown in late summer, a stemless green whorl resembling a young cabbage appears. The farmer watches its growth scrupulously, waiting for precisely the right moment to interrupt its cycle. When a small round rosette of green forms in the center of the plant, he gathers the outer leaves and draws them together like a loose pouch. The leaves continue to grow larger while the nourished bud at the heart of the leafy tent increases in size. By harvest time an immense head has formed, tender because it was sheltered from the sun's evaporating rays and pure white because it literally blossomed under wraps.

What to Look For

Use your nose when purchasing cauliflower, in or out of its rightful growing season. Over-the-hill heads of cauliflower smell strong as the dickens and taste worse cooked. A good rule of thumb for freshness is a faint cabbage scent; a reasonably white curd, not turning brown at the leafy ruff; and a texture that retains a measure of crispness after it has been scraped with a fingernail. Avoid excessively crumbly cauliflower in any season: it has usually remained in the field too long after being cut for harvest.

Perhaps the fact that most Long Island cauliflower is permitted to tarry on the vine until the local farmers deem it ready for sale at the roadside accounts for its high proportion of nutritive riches. In addition to the usual complement of *Brassica* vitamin endowments (80 units of vitamin A, 90 milligrams of vitamin C, 339 milligrams of potassium, and 64 grams of phosphorus per cup), the winter vegetable maintains exceedingly high levels of folic acid, prime source of vitamin B in the diet. Since the lack of folic acid is known to cause anemia, this local cauliflower is sometimes described by waggish members of the community as "a roadside vitamin B shot."

Preparation

Cauliflower may be a vegetable for all seasons, but the appropriate method for its cookery varies with those times of the year when it is at its absolutely freshest.

For instance, I do very little preculinary tampering with any head that I pick up from a roadside stand or greengrocer in the fall or winter. I merely cook the cauliflower whole (after it has been trimmed and the core removed) in the largest pot I own—one that can contain at least 3 quarts of water. The simplest way to prepare a whole cauliflower for the pot is to remove the tough outer leaves first, then hollow out the core using a sharp knife. This allows a head to cook evenly. The amount of cooking time depends upon the weight and size of the head, but 8 to 12 minutes usually suffices for blanching. Always cook cauliflower head-down and uncovered.

Once I deem the head to be tender (by poking it with the tip of a sharp knife), I plunge it under cold running water in a colander to retard the cooking. When it is completely cooled I take the recipe from there.

Some culinary savants advise the addition of salt to the boiling water (1 teaspoon salt per quart of water is the rule of thumb), but frankly I do not. I prefer to add salt later when it neither tenderizes nor alters the vegetable's sweetness.

Another crotchet: I never break up a cauliflower into flowerets before I blanch it, as I discovered some while back that a whole cauliflower is more easily divided into segments after it is cooked because then it never disintegrates or crumbles. For flowerets I merely trim the cooked cauliflower with a paring knife to the size that suits my preference.

Less than fresh (cold storage) cauliflower is perfectly acceptable but it demands more attention, for this cold-weather vegetable develops a somewhat stronger flavor as it is stored, even under optimum root-cellar conditions. I always soak out-of-season cauliflower in a bath of cold water for at least half an hour prior to cooking to remove any excessive acidity. Some cooks add a jot of fresh milk or lemon juice to the boiling water to whiten the head as it cooks. I never do, preferring to add a teaspoon or so of white wine vinegar to the cooking water. That's a trick I learned a while back in Italy, and it seems to both bleach and sweeten the head at the same time.

CREME DU BARRY

(Cream of Cauliflower Soup)

Cauliflower soup has been a personal favorite since childhood; my grandmother served it whenever she surmised that a member of her family looked "under the weather." It is a creamy caloric concoction that I always knew as "white soup" until I learned better.

This emollient—most often served warm but quite tonic cold, thinned with milk—is said to be the invention of that French expert in matters both sensual and savory, Madame Du Barry, who started out as a farm girl named Marie-Jeanne Bécu

and ended up as the great and good friend of Louis XV, the last king of France to die a natural death.

The lady may have lost her head over royalty but she retained a sense of delight in simple pleasures (at the table certainly). Just see for yourself.

1½ pounds cauliflower, leaves trimmed, core removed
1 small carrot, peeled, sliced
3 cups chicken broth (see page 414)
⅓ cup unconverted long-grain rice
2 cups milk
1 tablespoon lemon juice
¼ teaspoon freshly grated nutmeg
¼ teaspoon cayenne pepper
½ cup heavy or whipping cream
Salt
Chopped fresh chives or scallion tops

1. Cook the cauliflower in at least 3 quarts of boiling water for 2 minutes. Drain. Cut or break the cauliflower into flowerets. (If using out-of-season cauliflower, soak in cold water for 30 minutes prior to cooking and add 1½ teaspoons white wine vinegar to the cooking water.)

2. Place the cauliflower in a medium saucepan. Add the carrot and the chicken broth. Heat to boiling. Stir in the rice and reduce the heat. Simmer, uncovered, 30 minutes.

3. Place half the cauliflower mixture into the container of a processor or blender with 1 cup of the milk. Process until smooth being very careful, as hot liquid will expand. Transfer the mixture to a medium saucepan. Repeat the process with the remaining cauliflower mixture and milk. Add this to the saucepan. Add the lemon juice, nutmeg, cayenne pepper, cream, and salt to taste. Place over medium-low heat until warmed through. Do not boil. Serve garnished with chives or scallion tops. (Soup may be served cold, thinned with milk after chilling.)

Serves 6.

CAULIFLOWER AND SHRIMP IN A BLANKET OF MAYONNAISE

My most favored cauliflower rendering at the moment (my tastes do change) is a decidedly summer salad in which the pale blanched flowerets are tossed with bright pink shrimp in a snowy mayonnaise.

1½ pounds cauliflower, leaves trimmed, core removed
¾ cup dry vermouth
6 whole peppercorns
3 sprigs fresh parsley, plus 1 tablespoon finely chopped
Pinch of thyme
1 small bay leaf
1 shallot, roughly chopped, plus 2 tablespoons minced
1 whole clove garlic
1 pound raw shrimp
1 cup Mayonnaise (see page 408)
½ cup sour cream
1 tablespoon minced fresh basil
2 teaspoons Dijon mustard
Salt and freshly ground black pepper

1. Cook the cauliflower in at least 3 quarts of boiling water until barely tender, about 10 minutes. Drain. Cut or break the cauliflower into flowerets. Chill. (If using out-of-season cauliflower, soak in cold water for 30 minutes prior to cooking and add 1½ teaspoons white wine vinegar to the cooking water.)

2. Combine the vermouth, peppercorns, sprigs of parsley, thyme, bay leaf, roughly chopped shallot, and garlic in a medium saucepan. Heat to boiling; reduce the heat. Add the shrimp and cook, tossing gently, until the shrimp turn pink, 4 to 5 minutes. Remove the shrimp from the liquid. Strain the cooking liquid and reserve it. When cooled, shell and devein the shrimp and chill them.

3. Beat the mayonnaise with the sour cream in a large bowl until smooth. Beat in the minced shallots, basil, and mustard. Thin the mixture with about ¼ cup of the reserved shrimp broth. Add the cauliflower and shrimp. Toss well; add salt and pepper to taste. Garnish with the finely chopped parsley.

Serves 6.

CARNABEET

(Sephardic Cauliflower)

Carnabeet is a spicy vegetable stew. It is long-cooked over low heat, yet the ingredients retain a remarkable degree of bite and crunch because the vegetables are placed in the pot raw, with only a splash of liquid. It is part of the culinary repertoire of Sephardic cooks, those descendants of the Semitic peoples who settled in Spain, Portugal, Greece, Turkey, North Africa, and in fact most of the countries that form the lush Mediterranean basin. Theirs was a cuisine quite unlike what many uninitiated diners think of as Jewish food, which is usually an amalgam of Russian and Polish cookery that has been altered by a sea change on its way to the New World.

My version of *Carnabeet* has altered over the years with the kitchen ingredients I have had at hand. Orthodox Jews, of course, will omit the butter, but ecumenical food lovers will want to add it to bring out the flavor.

1½ pounds cauliflower, leaves trimmed, core removed
1½ tablespoons vegetable oil
1 small onion, finely chopped
1 rib celery, minced
1 large tomato, seeded, chopped
¼ pound string beans, trimmed
Juice of ½ lemon
⅓ cup strong Chicken Stock, approximately (see page 410)
Salt and freshly ground black pepper
2 tablespoons unsalted butter (optional)

1. Cook the cauliflower in at least 3 quarts of boiling water for 2 minutes. Drain. Cut or break the cauliflower into flowerets. (If using out-of-season cauliflower, soak in cold water for 30 minutes prior to cooking and add 1½ teaspoons white wine vinegar to the cooking water.)

2. Heat the oil in a medium saucepan over medium-low heat. Add the onion; cook 3 minutes. Add the celery, tomato, string beans, cauliflower, lemon

juice, and chicken stock. Cook, covered, until tender, about 30 minutes. Add more chicken stock if the mixture dries out. Add salt and pepper to taste. Toss in the butter just before serving, if desired.

Serves 4.

WHITE-ON-WHITE PUREE

(Cauliflower and Turnip Purée)

There are cauliflower purées and white turnip purées ad infinitum. However, none has the upright character or decided savor of the following partnership.

1 to 1¼ pounds cauliflower, leaves trimmed, core removed
4 tablespoons (½ stick) unsalted butter
½ pound white turnips, peeled, chopped
1 slice lemon
1 small bay leaf
¼ cup heavy or whipping cream
Pinch of ground cloves
Salt and ground white pepper
Dash of hot pepper sauce
1 tablespoon chopped fresh parsley

1. Cook the cauliflower in at least 3 quarts of boiling water until very tender, about 10 minutes. Drain. Break the cauliflower into flowerets. (If using out-of-season cauliflower, soak in cold water for 30 minutes prior to cooking and add 1½ teaspoons white wine vinegar to the cooking water.)

2. Melt 2 tablespoons of the butter in a medium skillet over medium-low heat. Add the turnips; toss to coat them with the butter. Add the lemon slice and bay leaf. Cook, covered, until the turnips are tender, about 12 minutes. Discard the lemon and bay leaf.

3. Place the cauliflower in the container of a food processor. Process until smooth, then transfer the cauliflower to the top of a double boiler. Add the turnips to the processor container and process until smooth. Add them to the cauliflower purée. Stir in the cream, cloves, salt and pepper to taste, and the hot pepper sauce. Reheat over simmering water. Stir in the remaining 2 tablespoons butter and sprinkle with parsley.

Serves 4.

AUSTRO-HUNGARIAN GREEN-TOPPED CAULIFLOWER

This most exquisite combination of cauliflower and bright green peas is a bequest from Austria-Hungary. I first encountered this dish toward the close of World War II in the cooking repertoire of an ex-countess of Hapsburg lineage (or so she claimed), who lived in a tiny suite of rooms at the glossy Sherry-Netherland Hotel with her ten-year-old daughter and an old family servant, while waiting for her husband (the Count) to be mustered out of the RAF in London.

Her recipe was a zealously guarded secret, and I never tried to pry it from her. Instead, I have reconstructed it with a recipe given to me by another enchanting Eastern European lady, Marina Polvay. This version is freely adapted from her book, *All Along the Danube*.

1½- to 2-pound head of cauliflower, leaves trimmed, core removed
5 tablespoons unsalted butter
3 whole scallions, bulbs and green tops, minced
1 package (10 ounces) frozen peas, thawed
Pinch of sugar
1 tablespoon chopped fresh parsley
½ cup heavy or whipping cream

1. Preheat the oven to 275°F. Cook the cauliflower in at least 3 quarts of boiling water until just tender, 10 to 12 minutes. Drain. (If using out-of-season cauliflower, soak in cold water for 30 minutes prior to cooking and add 1½ teaspoons white wine vinegar to the cooking water.)

2. Meanwhile, melt 3 tablespoons of the butter.

3. Place the whole cauliflower in a deep serving dish. Pour the melted butter over and keep it warm in the oven.

4. Melt the remaining 2 tablespoons butter in a medium skillet over medium-low heat. Stir in the scallions; cook until soft, about 5 minutes. Stir in the peas; sprinkle with sugar. Cook 4 minutes. Add the parsley and cream. Transfer the pea mixture to the container of a food processor or blender. Process until smooth. Reheat in a medium saucepan; do not boil. Spoon over the cauliflower and serve.

Serves 4 to 6.

GRATIN OF CAULIFLOWER WITH GINGERED CRUMBS

1½ pounds cauliflower, leaves trimmed, core removed
3 tablespoons unsalted butter
2 tablespoons all-purpose flour
1 cup light cream or half-and-half
1 teaspoon lemon juice
¼ teaspoon freshly grated nutmeg
Dash of hot pepper sauce
¼ cup grated Swiss cheese
¼ cup fresh bread crumbs
⅛ teaspoon ground ginger
2 tablespoons freshly grated Parmesan cheese

1. Preheat the oven to 350°F. Cook the cauliflower in at least 3 quarts of boiling water until just tender, 10 to 12 minutes. Rinse under cold running water. Drain. Cut or break the cauliflower into flowerets. (If using out-of-season cauliflower, soak in cold water for 30 minutes prior to cooking and add 1½ teaspoons white wine vinegar to the cooking water.) Set aside.

2. Melt 2 tablespoons of the butter in a medium saucepan over medium-low heat. Stir in the flour. Cook, stirring constantly, 2 minutes. Whisk in the cream. Raise the heat slightly; cook until thick. Add the lemon juice, nutmeg, hot pepper sauce, and cheese. Remove from the heat and set aside.

3. Place the cauliflower in a well-buttered 1½- to 2-quart soufflé dish or casserole. Spoon the cheese sauce over the top.

4. Melt the remaining 1 tablespoon butter in a small skillet over medium heat. Stir in the bread crumbs and ginger. Cook, stirring constantly, until golden. Spoon the crumbs over the cauliflower and sprinkle with the Parmesan cheese. Bake in the oven until bubbly, 15 to 20 minutes. Let stand 5 minutes before serving.

Serves 4.

BAKED CAULIFLOWER CREAM

To my mind, the most classic versions of pale baked cauliflower (acquired from the kitchens of France, Italy, and Austria) are usually enriched with even paler emollients: cream, sweet butter, or cheese—sometimes all three. As I was raised on cauliflower that was mashed like potatoes, I still retain a childlike affection for the crushed-velvet texture on my tongue. In remembrance of that delectable amalgam, here is the simplest creamed cauliflower dish in my repertoire. It is a splendid adjunct to roasted or broiled meat and may be prepared well in advance of dinner, refrigerated, and then reheated for a scant half hour in a 350°F oven prior to its appearance at the table.

1½ pounds cauliflower, leaves trimmed, core removed
3 tablespoons unsalted butter
1 chicken bouillon cube, crushed
1 medium onion, roughly chopped
1 small clove garlic, chopped
1 cup sour cream
Salt and freshly ground black pepper
Chopped fresh parsley

1. Preheat the oven to 350°F. Cook the cauliflower in at least 3 quarts of boiling water until very tender, 12 to 15 minutes. Drain. Cut or break the cauliflower into flowerets. (If using out-of-season cauliflower, soak in cold water for 30 minutes prior to cooking and add 1½ teaspoons white wine vinegar to the cooking water.)

2. Melt 1 tablespoon of the butter in a medium skillet over medium-low heat. Stir in the bouillon and onion. Cook 1 minute. Add the garlic; cook 4 minutes longer. Remove from the heat.

3. Place the sour cream in the container of a food processor. Add the onion mixture and the cauliflower. Add the remaining 2 tablespoons of butter bit by bit. Process until smooth; the mixture should be the texture of mashed potatoes. Add salt and pepper to taste.

4. Spoon the cauliflower mixture into a lightly buttered 1-quart baking dish. Bake 15 minutes. Garnish with parsley.

Serves 4 to 6.

HEADED CAULIFLOWER

No food writer confers the title "classic" on a recipe without inviting vituperative dissent from the world's culinary arbiters. My tastes (if you haven't noticed already) are all eclectic and I offer no apologies for them. But I do believe, however, that one could not possibly list archetypal cauliflower renditions without including the simplest version I have ever sampled, to wit: the following head, blanched, well buttered, then well cheesed and baked till that upholstery turns a deep golden hue.

1½- to 2-pound head of cauliflower, leaves trimmed, core removed
4 tablespoons (½ stick) unsalted butter, melted
½ cup grated Gruyère or Jarlsberg cheese
⅔ cup freshly grated Parmesan cheese
Freshly ground black pepper

1. Preheat the oven to 400°F. Cook the cauliflower in at least 3 quarts of boiling water until just tender, 10 to 12 minutes. Rinse under cold running water. Drain. (If using out-of-season cauliflower, soak in cold water for 30 minutes prior to cooking and add 1½ teaspoons white wine vinegar to the cooking water.)

2. Very gently pry apart the cauliflower flowerets, but do not detach them from the head. Place the melted butter in a bowl large enough to hold the cauliflower. Place the cauliflower upside-down in the butter. Let it stand 10 minutes.

3. Turn the cauliflower upright and place on a sheet of waxed paper; pour any leftover butter over it. Pat the Gruyère cheese between the flowerets. Dust the whole head with the Parmesan. Sprinkle generously with pepper. Transfer the head to a shallow baking dish and bake 15 minutes. Place under a broiler to brown the top if desired.

Serves 4 to 6.

VENETIAN CAULIFLOWER AND RICE CASSEROLE

This prescription of cauliflower layered over rice with a gilded *besciamella* sauce is unique to the watery landscape of Venice and the provinces of the Po Valley nearby, where Italy's short-grained rice is harvested.

The recipe is a slightly amended version of one in a book I admire enormously and cook from with regularity: *The Cuisine of Venice & Surrounding Northern Regions* by Hedy Giusti-Lanham and Andrea Dodi.

1½ pounds cauliflower, leaves trimmed, core removed
1 cup Italian rice (I prefer Arborio)
6 tablespoons (¾ stick) unsalted butter
1 shallot, minced
¼ cup finely chopped fresh parsley
2 tablespoons all-purpose flour
1 cup chicken broth (see page 414)
⅛ teaspoon freshly grated nutmeg
Salt and freshly ground black pepper
½ cup freshly grated Parmesan cheese

1. Preheat the oven to 400°F. Cook the cauliflower in at least 3 quarts of boiling water until just tender, 10 to 12 minutes. Remove, reserving the cooking liquid, and rinse in a colander under cold running water. Drain. Cut or break the cauliflower into flowerets. (If using out-of-season cauliflower, soak in cold water for 30 minutes prior to cooking and add 1½ teaspoons white wine vinegar to the cooking water.) Set aside.

2. Return the cooking water to the boil. Add the rice, stir once, and cook, uncovered, until just tender, about 12 minutes. Drain, and set aside.

3. Melt 2 tablespoons of the butter in a medium skillet over medium heat. Add the shallot; cook until golden. Stir in the drained rice and 2 more tablespoons of the butter. Stir in the parsley; remove from the heat and set aside.

4. Melt the remaining 2 tablespoons butter in a medium saucepan over medium-low heat. Stir in the flour. Cook, stirring constantly, 2 minutes. Whisk in the chicken broth and cook until thick. Add the nutmeg and salt and pepper to taste. Remove from the heat.

5. Spoon one third of the rice over the bottom of a buttered 2-quart soufflé or deep baking dish. Drizzle with one third of the sauce. Add one third of the cheese and then half the cauliflower. Repeat the layers twice, ending with the cheese. Bake in the oven until bubbly, about 20 minutes. Let stand 5 minutes before serving.

Serves 6.

PARMA-STYLE FRIED CAULIFLOWER

Cauliflower is a truly international vegetable that takes a distinct coloration in each native landscape, and more important, from the natural ingredients of each region where it is prepared.

This batter-fried cauliflower comes from Parma, in the northern bootstrap of Italy. Offhand I cannot think of anything more succulent than those gleaming flowerets forked out of pots of sizzling lard as a ravenous diner waits, salivating, at the prospect of his tongue's immolation.

The secret (no secret at all) is Parmesan cheese in the batter.

1½ to 2 pounds cauliflower, leaves trimmed, core removed
½ cup water
1 teaspoon lemon juice
Dash of hot pepper sauce
6 tablespoons all-purpose flour
6 tablespoons freshly grated Parmesan cheese
1 egg, lightly beaten
1 teaspoon finely grated lemon peel
Vegetable oil for frying
Salt

1. Cook the cauliflower in at least 3 quarts of boiling water until just tender, 10 to 12 minutes. Rinse under cold running water. Drain. Cut or break the cauliflower into small flowerets. (If using out-of-season cauliflower, soak in cold water for 30 minutes prior to cooking and add 1½ teaspoons white wine vinegar to the cooking water.)

2. Combine the water, lemon juice, and hot pepper sauce in a medium bowl. Beat in the flour until smooth. Beat in the cheese, egg, and lemon peel.

3. Heat 2 inches of oil in a medium saucepan until almost smoking. Dip the flowerets into the batter and then fry them, about six at a time, until golden, about 4 to 5 minutes. (Oil should be hot enough that cauliflower will turn dark gold in this time.) Drain on paper towels and keep warm in a low oven while frying the remaining cauliflower. Before serving, sprinkle on salt to taste.

Serves 4 to 6.

CAULIFLOWER AND HAM GRATIN

Gratin is a corruption of the middle-French verb *grater,* which means "to scrape." My best scrapings on the subject include this, which is of French descent, from an old cookbook I found in Burgundy.

1½ to 2 pounds cauliflower, leaves trimmed, core removed
3 tablespoons unsalted butter
1 large shallot, minced
½ pound cooked ham, finely chopped
1 tablespoon Madeira
2 tablespoons all-purpose flour
1 cup hot Chicken Stock (see page 410)
¼ teaspoon freshly grated nutmeg
Salt and freshly ground black pepper
⅔ cup grated Jarlsberg cheese

1. Preheat the oven to 350°F. Cook the cauliflower in at least 3 quarts of boiling water until just tender, 10 to 12 minutes. Rinse under cold running water. Drain. Cut or break the cauliflower into flowerets. (If using out-of-season cauliflower, soak in cold water for 30 minutes prior to cooking and add 1½ teaspoons white wine vinegar to the cooking water.) Set aside.

2. Melt 1 tablespoon of the butter in a medium skillet over medium heat. Add the shallot; cook 1 minute. Add the ham; cook until lightly browned. Sprinkle with the Madeira. Cook, stirring constantly, until all liquid has evaporated. Remove from the heat and set aside.

3. Melt the remaining 2 tablespoons butter in a medium saucepan over medium-low heat. Stir in the flour. Cook, stirring constantly, 2 minutes. Whisk in the hot stock. Cook until thick. Add the nutmeg, and salt and pepper to taste.

4. Place half the cauliflower in a well-buttered 2-quart soufflé dish or casserole. Spoon the ham mixture evenly over the top. Spoon half the sauce over that, and sprinkle with half the cheese. Repeat the layers of cauliflower, sauce, and cheese. Bake in the oven until bubbly, 15 to 20 minutes. Let stand 5 minutes before serving.

Serves 4 to 6.

CAULIFLOWER AND CHEESE WAFFLES

What follows is a recent cauliflower invention: a waffle composed of leftover cauliflower, cheese, eggs, flour, and the usual waffle adjuncts. This dish is ideal for a fast pick-up supper, unexpected luncheon guests, or even a cocktail party nibble in a pinch, when the olive and almond supply is low. Amend the waffle with any topping you desire (creamed chicken, mushrooms, chipped beef) or, here, a splash of shocking-pink tomato sauce.

¾ cup cooked cauliflower, roughly chopped
1 egg
1 cup milk
¼ cup heavy or whipping cream
¾ cup all-purpose flour, sifted
1 teaspoon baking powder
2 tablespoons unsalted butter, melted
½ cup grated mild Cheddar cheese
2 tablespoons freshly grated Parmesan cheese
1 egg white
Creamy Tomato Sauce (see page 375)

1. Place the cauliflower, egg, milk, and cream in the container of a food processor or blender. Process until smooth. Transfer to a medium bowl.

2. Sift the flour with the baking powder. Stir the flour into the cauliflower mixture. Beat until smooth. Add the melted butter and both kinds of cheese.

3. Beat the egg white until stiff. Fold it into the batter. Cook the waffles on a preheated waffle iron according to the manufacturer's directions. Keep the waffles warm on a rack in a low oven while you make the remaining ones. Serve with Creamy Tomato Sauce.

Makes 6 or 7 large waffles.

Note: This batter may be used for pancakes as well.

The French call cauliflower *chou fleur* (cabbage blossom); Germans dub it *Blumenkohl* (blooming cabbage); Italian chefs compromise on *cavolfiore* (cabbage flower).

CELERY AND CELERY ROOT

A Popular Stalk with an Up-and-Coming Root

I never met the celebrated French writer Colette, but she influenced my life as much as anyone I have ever known.

It was in the early 1950s when I first discovered her, during a long summer's bout with the flu. The doctor had prescribed absolute bed rest to combat the fever—so there was nothing to do but read, and I even did that fitfully. Of all the books I skimmed during those torpid days and sleepless nights only Colette's managed to hold my attention. I resolved to write her immediately after I recovered. But good intentions do not often mix with natural timidity and habitual inanition, so I allowed the impulse to pass. When Colette died (at eighty-two) some while after, I deeply regretted that I had not made contact. But our lives did converge (as obviously they were meant to) despite the omission.

A decade later I adapted some stories about her childhood into a theater piece that was performed at The Poetry Center and became the basis for a television play starring Colleen Dewhurst. That my work received praise (and money) gave me considerable gratification, but the fact that it also pleased Maurice Goudeket (Colette's widower) compounded the joy.

"You alone have captured my wife's voice," he wired me from Paris after he had read the script. That compliment became the basis of one of the most satisfying friendships I have ever had. Maurice Goudeket and I became close friends despite the obvious barriers of geography and time. He had been seventeen years younger than Colette and knew how to bridge the differences in our ages with infinite good grace. A tall, extremely elegant man even in his late sixties, Goudeket never chided me for not finishing a play about Colette on which I had fleetingly embarked. Instead he bid me do whatever I really wanted in life. "But Bert... sink your teeth into something real!"

Together we would sit for hours in the afternoon at a table in an empty restaurant overlooking Central Park. Despite the waiter's baleful glances at the clock, Maurice remained completely unperturbed, drinking pot after pot of herbal tea (his choice) and speaking endlessly of his wife's zest for life.

Though I knew much about her already, he filled in all the blanks. Colette's way of making contact in life was utterly sensory. Not content to merely admire a wild plant or herb, she had to sniff and taste it as well. When she entered an unfamiliar garden, he reported, she would kick off her shoes and walk barefoot—crumpling leaves on her tongue and chewing random stalks (even of poisonous berries and deadly toadstools) because, in his words: "She simply had to know every single thing there was to know about life. *Everything!*" When Colette left a garden it was never the same. Nor was she. Her nose would be dusted with more pollen than powder, her hair a wild disarray of twigs and thorns, and her voice breathless with excitement at all she had just discovered. At the end of her life, too!

Colette had a reputation for a voracious appetite. When I asked him once what foods she liked best, her husband laughed out loud.

"Oh my God. That woman loved to sink her teeth into things of substance; crisp roots, ash-roasted potatoes, and chestnuts. Peasant breads with crust so rough it would bruise a normal diner's upper lip. But never hers....

"I will tell you a story of my wife's appetite," he said. "When she had to have her photograph taken with the members of the French Academy for the first time, she went on a rare diet to lose five pounds. For a week she ate nothing but celery. Celery with water. Celery with salt and pepper. But only celery for seven days. Never once complaining even when I was served my normal meals. Later, after she had lost the weight, she confided that one day she had cheated. There had been a small red caterpillar at the heart of a celery stalk, but she was so hungry for meat, she ate it too!" Maurice sighed, "That was Colette."

To someone who had once consumed half a worm, the story made her seem more monumental than ever!

Colette has influenced my life in many ways: her love of rustic things, provincial dishes, and homely furnishings, her love of flowers—all I adopted long, long ago. And I have one more inheritance from this incredible woman: one of her very own paperweights. Maurice gave it to me after our second meeting and it was the basis for my own, not inconsiderable, collection of these baubles. But though I have several dozen on my table always, I never mistake the one that once belonged to Colette with any other. A clear, graceful globe, it holds a crystal bouquet of pale yellow whorls and glass buds; quite perfect but for an infinitesimal flaw of color at the center. Red, like a scarlet surprise in a stalk of celery.

Vegetable Roots

I must admit I treasure celery—in every form except stuffed—almost as much as the Greeks, who awarded great green bunches as prizes to victorious athletes after their games were done. Why not? Celery is composed of 95 percent water, and tastes a heck of a lot better than Gatorade!

Celery is one of those tried and true denizens of the garden whose present discreet mien bears scant resemblance to the wild life it once led, before cultivators brought it into the fold. The original renegade stalk still blossoms in salt marshes along the coastline of southern France. Bees love its tiny white flowers and in fact gave the plant its Latin name, *Apium graveolens*, which means "heavy with bees." All other mammals (man and beast alike) cut a wide swath wherever the wild celery grows, for its bitter flavor marks a lethal dose in every rib.

Wild celery stems from the *Umbelliferae* clan, the same family tree, in fact, that links a parsnip to a carrot to a parsley sprig. But there the resemblance ends. For celery in its wildest guise is a stubby, tough, fibrous weed that holds no possibilities whatsoever for any stockpot.

From wild celery early horticulturists bred two separate and distinct strains of vegetables that have proven the test of palatability for almost four thousand years. *Apium graveolens dulce* (sweet only in comparison with its bitter forebear) is the crunchy green stalk that is every dieter's staff of life. *Apium graveolens rapaceum* (so dubbed because it must be literally ripped from the garden by force) is a bulbous white root that is the indispensable ingredient in one of the world's classiest hors d'oeuvres, *céleri rémoulade.*

Food historians claim that both celery and celery root were developed by the gardeners of the king of Persia around the year 2000 B.C. Cyrus the First was reputedly a vegetarian, and a finicky eater besides. Out of dietary doldrums, he commanded a crew of royal gardeners to come up with something different for his supper. Celery filled the gap—if one can believe the backstairs scuttlebutt after all these years!

One fact about celery may be verified, however: a bunch of this leafy green was sent as a wedding gift to the Empress of China during the T'ang dynasty—which bespeaks a measure of the Persians' high regard for its savor.

It is hard to believe when one brushes past stacks of packaged celery on a supermarket shelf that this leafy stalk was ever so prized, or so rare.

The ancient Egyptians, Greeks, and Romans considered celery a gift from the gods, quite capable of regenerating the human body and mind. Egyptian physicians divided celery's medicinal properties sexually: the strong stalks that grew upward from the ground were judged to be a cure for all masculine dysfunctions from bed-wetting to impotence, while the hairy, tuberous root that swelled beneath the earth's surface was prescribed for female disorders.

Even today in Crete newly married couples are pelted with either celery seeds or barley as they leave the church. Never both. It is claimed that the seed of celery ensures fertility and barley promises a full larder. And obviously both take equal concentration to acquire.

In Rome a stalk of celery was thought to be a cure for both constipation and hangover. Apicius lists at least two surefire remedies for the first ailment and a word of advice for the second: overimbibers are counseled "to wear a wreath of celery 'round the brow to ease the pain."

My own hangover cure seems frankly a jot more effective. The prescription? One large Bloody Mary, well laced with vodka and seasoned generously with lemon juice and Tabasco sauce, served up in a goblet so cold that one's fingers freeze to the surface when it is held aloft. And, oh yes, as anesthetic: a celery stalk in the glass.

Celery

What to Look For

There are celeryphiles and celeryphobes, but even the most unenthusiastic cannot deny this vegetable its due as a pot-flavoring and enhancer of other comestibles.

Celery was once an autumn vegetable, but these days shoppers will find it in plenteous supply year round. Unfortunately the more toothsome stalks (like snowy "White Ice" and self-blanching "Golden") are not a common sight at most greengrocers' except as packaged celery hearts, because the paler varieties have an abbreviated shelf life.

Pascal (the green-ribbed, full-branched, tender-leafed) celery is the hands-down favorite in American households because it is always super-crisp—with a pleasantly astringent flavor that makes it a favored between-meal snack.

Celery shoppers should look for tight heads with compact outer stalks. Never buy browned or cracked bunches of celery; the discoloration is a dead giveaway that the vegetable is less than fresh.

Packaged celery is supposedly prewashed. But, as with garden celery, I always rinse it under cold running water when I get it home. Heeding the advice of the English naturalist John Evelyn, who wrote about celery in 1699:

> For its high and grateful Taste it is ever plac'd in the middle of the Grand Sallet, at our Great Mens Tables, and Praetor Feasts, as the Grace of the whole Board. But *Caution* is to be given of a small red *worm*, often lurking in these stalks.

Happily for dieters, stalk celery is extremely low in calories. A portion averages less than 20 calories per cupful, yet is relatively high in minerals (409 milligrams of potassium) and vitamin A (320 units in each 1 cup serving).

Preparation

Since the dawn of time (or at least dating back to Cyrus the First of Persia), the classic way to consume a stalk of celery has been raw, preferably chilled and stripped of its fibrous strings.

Cooked celery is another kettle of greens entirely. To my captious palate, the only classic method of celery cookery is braising. That is to say, cooking the stalks, covered, with a small amount of liquid until they are barely fork tender.

Though I must confess I rarely bother except when I'm using the celery raw, many culinary savants peel celery prior to cooking it, claiming that it makes the vegetable easier to chew. It's a simple trick. Here's how to do it: With a sharp knife make a small incision at the wide end of a celery stalk without actually cutting through it. Gently loosen the fibers and pull them down the outer layer of the flesh to the narrow end.

Celery Root

Celery root (celeriac) is one vegetable that enjoys enormous popularity at European dinner tables but only the mildest form of approbation over here. The reason, I suspect, is that while this vegetable's flavor is extraordinary, its appearance on a vegetable stand is positively awesome.

Celery root has had other notable drawbacks: it is difficult to peel and to slice. However, rotary-type vegetable peelers and food processors now eliminate those objections.

There are three important reasons for the uninitiated to try celery root immediately: the texture (crisp and rooty even when cooked), the flavor (like superconcentrated celery), and the calories (practically nonexistent—less than 20 in a cupful).

Preparation

Celery root is one vegetable I opt *not* to eat raw. Instead sometimes I boil it unpeeled and then peel and slice it after it has cooled. Or I peel it first, then boil it either whole or in slices.

I most often parboil celery root (to tenderize the tuberous flesh) prior to further cookery. A whole peeled celery root, depending upon its size, takes about 20 to 30 minutes to cook until crisp-tender. Peeled sliced celery root (cut into ¼-inch-thick strips) takes considerably less time, about 8 minutes. Unseasonal celery root (the kind found in late spring and summer) cooks in a shorter time.

The alternative method for cooking celery root (when crunch is not a prerequisite) is to boil it whole, unpeeled, for 40 to 45 minutes. When it is sufficiently tender, remove the root from the saucepan; allow it to cool, peel and slice it, and proceed with the recipe at hand.

CELERY SLAW

No matter where your celery is grown, snip a stalk or two for the most tonic salad you will ever toss.

1 small bunch celery, trimmed
¼ pound mushrooms, sliced
¼ pound Monterey jack cheese, chopped
½ cup olive oil
1 small clove garlic, crushed
3 tablespoons red wine vinegar
¼ teaspoon freshly ground black pepper
Salt
4 strips crisp-fried bacon, crumbled

1. Cut the celery into very thin strips, about 1 inch long; or cut it into paper-thin slices crosswise. Place the celery in a large bowl with the mushrooms and cheese.

2. Combine the olive oil with the garlic, vinegar, and pepper in a small bowl. Pour this dressing over the celery mixture and toss well. Cover and let it stand in a cool place for 1 hour.

3. Add salt to taste, transfer to a serving dish, and sprinkle with the crumbled bacon.

Serves 4 to 6.

COOL, COLLECTED CELERY

In my book, boiling celery is an utter desecration! My mother did it all the time, and I grew up with the notion that all cooked celery was supposed to taste like wet laundry. It is *not*. A prolonged stay in a pan of boiling water may tenderize a bunch of celery on occasion, but it also depletes its natural flavor beyond redemption. For the same reason I do not recommend steaming celery. Even in sophisticated electric steamers, the process takes so long that the nutrients vaporize in the steam, and anyway, steamed celery is uniformly flat-tasting and watery.

My favorite way to cook celery (after braising) is to poach it in broth, with the cooking liquid kept well below the boiling point. This is a version of a small culinary masterpiece offered up by my good friend M. F. K. Fisher in her book *With Bold Knife and Fork*, where it appeared under the imposing title "Celery Victor-Solari-Veneto." After a little adjusting, my amendment carries a far less formal cognomen.

1 large, thick bunch of celery
3½ cups chicken broth, approximately (see page 414)
Simple Vinaigrette Sauce (recipe follows)
1 hard-cooked egg, yolk and white chopped separately
4 anchovy filets
Approximately 8 canned pimiento strips
¼ cup chopped fresh parsley
Freshly ground black pepper

1. Trim the celery of tough outer ribs and trim the top of leaves, leaving the bunch of celery about 8 inches long. Pare the bottom of the celery with a vegetable peeler but do not cut it off. Slice the bunch into 4 quarters lengthwise.

2. Place the celery sections in a large shallow saucepan. Add just enough chicken broth to cover. Heat to boiling; reduce the heat. Cover and cook, barely simmering, until tender, about 25 minutes. Let the celery cool in the broth.

3. Drain the cooled celery and arrange it in a shallow serving dish.

4. Make the Simple Vinaigrette Sauce; pour it over the celery. Chill, turning the celery several times.

5. When well chilled, garnish the celery with alternating bands of chopped egg white, chopped egg yolk, anchovy filets, pimiento strips, and parsley. Season with fresh pepper to taste.

Serves 4.

Simple Vinaigrette Sauce

1 small clove garlic, crushed
½ teaspoon coarse (kosher) salt
1 teaspoon Dijon mustard
Juice of ½ lemon
½ cup olive oil
2 teaspoons red wine vinegar
½ teaspoon freshly ground black pepper

Mash the garlic and the salt together in a small bowl with the back of a spoon. Stir in the mustard and lemon juice. Whisk in the oil, vinegar, and pepper.

Makes about ½ cup.

BOOZY CELERY

This and the recipe that follows—Butter-Crumbed Celery—call for celery stalks that may be peeled or left *au naturel* at your discretion. Both are braise-first, bake-later devises, with cheese as their common topping, but otherwise as unalike as day and night. The first is cloaked in a brandied cream. The second is dusted with fennel seeds and bread crumbs. Each makes an admirable adjunct to a simple dinner where the main course is either broiled or grilled—*sans* sauce.

1 large, thick bunch of celery
½ cup Chicken Stock (see page 410)
½ cup white wine or dry vermouth
1 clove garlic, unpeeled
3 tablespoons unsalted butter
3 tablespoons all-purpose flour
¼ cup heavy or whipping cream
Salt and ground white pepper
1 tablespoon brandy
2 tablespoons freshly grated Parmesan cheese

1. Trim the celery of tough outer ribs and trim the top of the leaves, leaving the bunch of celery about 8 inches long. Pare the bottom of the celery with a vegetable peeler but do not cut it off. Slice the bunch into 4 quarters lengthwise.

2. Place the celery sections in a large shallow saucepan. Add the chicken stock, wine, and garlic. Heat to boiling; reduce the heat. Cook, covered, over medium-low heat until the celery is just tender, about 25 minutes.

3. Meanwhile, preheat the oven to 400°F. Remove the cooked celery from the saucepan with a slotted spoon, reserving the cooking liquid, and transfer it to a shallow baking dish. Set it aside. Discard the garlic.

4. Melt the butter in a medium saucepan over medium-low heat. Stir in the flour. Cook, stirring constantly, 2 minutes. Whisk in 1 cup of the reserved cooking liquid and the cream. Cook until very thick, 3 to 4 minutes. Add salt and pepper to taste. Stir in the brandy.

5. Spoon the sauce over the celery and sprinkle with the cheese. Bake until hot and bubbly, about 15 minutes.

Serves 4.

BUTTER-CRUMBED CELERY

1 large, thick bunch of celery
3 tablespoons unsalted butter
½ cup Chicken Stock (see page 410)
1 tablespoon plus 1 teaspoon Pernod
1 small clove garlic, bruised
½ teaspoon fennel seeds
½ teaspoon salt
¼ teaspoon freshly ground black pepper
½ cup fresh bread crumbs

1. Cut the celery crosswise into ½-inch slices. Combine the celery with 1 tablespoon of the butter, the chicken stock, and 1 tablespoon of the Pernod in a medium saucepan. Heat to boiling; reduce the heat. Cook, covered, over medium-low heat until the celery is crisp-tender, 15 to 20 minutes. Drain.

2. Meanwhile, preheat the oven to

350°F. Rub a shallow baking dish with the bruised garlic. Add the celery and sprinkle it with the fennel seeds, salt, and pepper.

3. Melt the remaining 2 tablespoons butter in a small skillet over medium heat. Stir in the bread crumbs and sauté until golden. Spoon the crumbs over the celery and sprinkle with the remaining 1 teaspoon Pernod. Bake, uncovered, until the celery is tender, about 30 to 35 minutes.

Serves 4.

BRAISED CELERY IN BASIL LEAVES

This recipe is a souvenir from a stay near Nice, where not only celery but also garlic, anchovies, olive oil, and basil are in aromatic profusion year round.

1 large, thick bunch of celery
2 tablespoons unsalted butter
1 tablespoon olive oil
1 onion, finely chopped
1 clove garlic, minced
1 teaspoon anchovy paste
¼ teaspoon chopped fresh thyme, or a pinch of dried
½ cup loosely packed fresh basil leaves, chopped
¼ cup dry white wine
¼ cup strong Chicken Stock (see page 410)
Chopped fresh parsley
Freshly ground black pepper

1. Trim the celery of tough outer ribs and trim the top of leaves, leaving the bunch of celery about 8 inches long. Pare the bottom of the celery with a vegetable peeler but do not cut it off. Slice the bunch into 4 quarters lengthwise. Set aside.

2. Heat the butter with the oil in a large shallow saucepan over medium-low heat. Add the onion; cook 1 minute. Add the garlic; cook 2 minutes longer. Do not brown. Stir in the anchovy paste and thyme. Add the celery sections and turn them several times to coat them with the butter mixture. Add the basil, wine, and chicken stock. Heat to boiling; reduce the heat. Cook, covered, over very low heat until just tender, about 25 minutes.

3. Remove the celery to a shallow serving dish and keep warm. Raise the heat under the saucepan and boil the juices until thick and syrupy. Pour the pan juices over the celery and sprinkle with parsley and fresh pepper.

Serves 4.

Celery is *chin-t'sai* in China, *sedano* in Italy, *céleri* in France, *sellerio* in Germany, and *apio* in Spain—which brings us to the matter of bees.

Celery's flower is a small, compact blossom, creamy in color and shaped like the bell of a lily of the valley. The blooms appear in summer and have a scent that obviously drives the drones wild, for (if you will forgive the pun) they make a beeline to the celery patch like clockwork every August.

CELERY SOUFFLE

My last culinary thought on celery, before attacking its awesome root, is a pale leaf-green soufflé that has been known to inspire diners (even a few celeryphobes). It may be worth noting (before you discover it for yourself) that the celery for the base is boiled—an exception makes all rules unruly.

3 large ribs of celery, chopped
1 inner heart of celery with leaves, chopped
2 baking potatoes, peeled, cut into 1-inch cubes
2 tablespoons strong Chicken Stock (see page 410)
⅓ cup heavy or whipping cream
2 ounces creamy bleu cheese
1 tablespoon unsalted butter
2 egg yolks
Salt and freshly ground black pepper
3 egg whites
1 tablespoon fine fresh bread crumbs

1. Cook the chopped celery, celery heart, and potatoes in boiling salted water until tender, about 20 minutes. Drain.

2. Preheat the oven to 425°F. Place the celery-potato mixture into the container of a food processor (or in batches in a blender). Add the chicken stock, cream, bleu cheese, and butter. Process until smooth but not mushy.

3. Transfer the mixture to a large bowl. Beat in the egg yolks, one at a time. Beat in salt and pepper to taste.

4. Beat the egg whites until stiff but not dry. Fold them into the soufflé mixture.

5. Lightly grease a 1½-quart soufflé dish. Sprinkle it with the bread crumbs. Add the soufflé mixture and place it in the oven. Immediately reduce the heat to 375°F. Bake until fairly firm and dark golden, 35 to 40 minutes. The flavor improves as it cools.

Serves 6.

BROWNSTONE SOUP

(Beef and Celery Soup)

A hearty turn-of-the-century recipe from New York, this soup is composed of both stalk and root and cooked with beef to form a rich and aromatic one-dish meal.

1 tablespoon olive oil
1 to 1¼ pounds flank or skirt steak, trimmed of fat
1 tablespoon unsalted butter
1 large onion, finely chopped
1 clove garlic, minced
2 medium carrots, finely chopped
3 large ribs celery, finely chopped (about 1½ cups)
3 cups beef broth (see page 414)
3 cups water
1 tablespoon chopped fresh parsley, plus extra for garnish

½ teaspoon chopped fresh thyme, or ¼ teaspoon dried
1 small celery root (about ½ pound), trimmed, peeled, cut into thin strips about 1 inch long
Salt and freshly ground black pepper

1. Heat the oil in a large pot or Dutch oven over medium heat. Brown the meat well on both sides. Remove the meat to a plate and discard the cooking fat.

2. Melt the butter in the same pot over medium heat. Add the onion; cook 1 minute. Add the garlic; cook until lightly browned, about 5 minutes. Add the carrots and celery. Cook over medium-low heat 5 minutes. Stir in the beef broth, scraping the sides and bottom of the pot. Return the meat to the pot and add the water. Heat to boiling, removing the scum as it rises to the surface. Reduce the heat and add the 1 tablespoon parsley and the thyme. Cook, covered, over medium-low heat for 1 hour.

3. Add the strips of celery root to the soup. Continue to cook until the meat and celery root are tender, about 30 minutes. Remove from the heat. Allow to cool.

4. Remove the meat from the soup and separate it into chunks with two forks. Return the meat to soup and refrigerate ovenight.

5. Remove any accumulated fat from the surface of the soup and then reheat it over medium-low heat. Add salt and pepper to taste and sprinkle with parsley.

Serves 4 to 6.

CELERY ROOT AND GREEN BEAN SALAD

Celery root makes a sterling stand-in for a potato on occasion, as in this nearly-Niçoise formula. I wanted to dub it "Celery Root Masquerading as Salade Niçoise" until a lack of anchovies in the prescription dictated otherwise.

1 medium celery root (about 1½ pounds)
3 tablespoons dry white wine or dry vermouth
¼ pound thin young string beans, trimmed
1 clove garlic, bruised
2 shallots, minced
½ teaspoon coarse (kosher) salt
1½ tablespoons Dijon mustard
2 tablespoons lemon juice
1 tablespoon white wine vinegar
⅓ cup olive oil
¼ teaspoon chopped fresh thyme, or a pinch of dried
1 teaspoon chopped fresh basil, or ½ teaspoon dried
¼ cup chopped fresh parsley
Salt and freshly ground black pepper
1½ tablespoons slivered black olives

1. Trim and peel the celery root. Cut it into strips about ¼ inch wide, ¼ inch thick, and 1 inch long. Cook in boiling salted water 5 minutes. Rinse under cold running water, drain, and pat dry with paper towels. Place the celery root in a bowl and sprinkle it with the wine.

2. Cook the string beans in boiling salted water until crisp-tender, about 3 minutes. Rinse under cold running water. Drain.

3. Rub a large serving bowl with the bruised garlic. Add the celery root, beans, and shallots. Toss.

4. Crush the garlic and combine it with the salt in a small bowl. Mash until a smooth paste is formed. Stir in the mustard, lemon juice, and vinegar. Beat in the oil. Pour this dressing over the vegetables and add the thyme, basil, and 3 tablespoons of the parsley. Add the salt and pepper to taste. Lightly toss in the olives and sprinkle with the remaining 1 tablespoon parsley. Serve well chilled or at room temperature.

Serves 4 to 6.

CELERY ROOT ABLUSH

There are many wonderful celery root dishes, but the classic rendition is one that a well-seasoned traveler will have encountered on hors d'oeuvre trolleys and at buffet tables all over the western world: *céleri-rave rémoulade*, which means celery root in sharp mustard sauce. My version of this international treasure is, I am afraid, slightly unclassical, since it is not so sharp as it is shocking pink—tinged with the merest dab of rosy tomato.

1 celery root (1¼ to 1½ pounds)
⅓ cup lemon juice
1 egg yolk
2 teaspoons Dijon mustard
1½ teaspoons tomato paste
1 tablespoon red wine vinegar
¼ cup olive oil
½ cup vegetable oil
Salt and freshly ground black pepper
1 tablespoon chopped fresh basil, or ½ teaspoon dried basil chopped with 1 tablespoon fresh parsley

1. Trim and peel the celery root. Cut it into very fine julienne strips about 1 inch long. You should have 3½ to 4 cups. As you cut them, place the strips in a large bowl of ice water to which you have added 3 tablespoons of the lemon juice, to prevent discoloring.

2. Beat the egg yolk with the mustard and the tomato paste in a medium bowl until smooth. Slowly beat in the vinegar and both oils. When smooth and thick, beat in the remaining 3 tablespoons lemon juice, and add salt and pepper to taste.

3. Drain the celery root and pat it dry. Combine it with the dressing and marinate the salad, covered, at least 2 hours in the refrigerator. Sprinkle with the basil before serving.

Serves 6.

CREAMED-AGAIN CELERY ROOT

With such scant calories, it hardly seems amiss to suggest enriching the basic ingredient a jot—with cream and butter in this case. For a change, serve it with a slice of rosy beef in lieu of potatoes.

1 celery root (1 to 1¼ pounds)
3 tablespoons lemon juice
1 tablespoon unsalted butter
1 shallot, minced
2 cups chicken broth (see page 414)
¼ cup heavy or whipping cream
1 egg yolk, lightly beaten
Salt and freshly ground black pepper
Chopped fresh parsley

1. Trim and peel the celery root. Cut it into fine julienne strips about 1 inch long. As you cut them, place the strips in a large bowl of ice water to which you have added the lemon juice, to prevent discoloring.

2. Melt the butter in a large saucepan over medium-low heat. Add the shallot; cook until lightly browned, about 5 minutes. Drain the celery root and add it to the saucepan. Toss the celery root well to coat it with the butter. Add the chicken broth. Heat to boiling; reduce the heat. Simmer, uncovered, until tender, 10 to 15 minutes.

3. Drain the celery root, reserving the broth. Transfer the celery root to a serving dish and keep it warm in a low oven.

4. Return the cooking liquid to the saucepan. Heat to boiling; boil until reduced to ½ cup. Stir in the cream. Return to boiling; remove from the heat.

5. Gradually mix 2 tablespoons of the hot liquid with the egg yolk. Slowly whisk the egg yolk mixture into the remaining hot liquid. Place it over low heat and cook, stirring constantly, until thickened. Do not allow it to boil. Add salt and pepper to taste. Spoon the sauce over the celery root and sprinkle with parsley.

Serves 4.

According to gardening lore (often highly erroneous) the first stalk of celery grew in America a scant sixteen years after the Declaration of Independence was signed. The seedlings, sent for by Thomas Jefferson's gardeners, were meant to grace the herbary at Monticello. However, the plants waned in the torpid Virginia climate, and celery lovers had to go without.

A Dutch immigrant who came to Kalamazoo, Michigan, with a sack of celery seed in his duffel is responsible for celery's full flowering in the U.S. In 1874 the first celery plant was harvested—and a hundred years later it was the third largest agricultural industry in the country (after potatoes and tomatoes).

According to Elizabeth Gordon in *Mother Earth's Children*:

> Said the Endive: I was born in
> France,
> But travel when I get the chance.
> Said the Celery: I travel too,
> But my real home's in Kalamazoo.

SUPER-CRISPY ROAST CHICKEN WITH CELERY ROOT DRESSING

One of my favorite dispositions for a hunk of celery root is to install it inside a chicken. It matters not a whit whether you supplicate a greengrocer for *céleri-rave* (in France), *Knollensellerie* (in Germany), or *apio-nabo* (in Spain)—the pertinent thing is to stuff your very next bird with it!

By the way, this technique of dredging an uncooked fowl with a mixture of buttery crumbs and brandy is old as the hills and eminently worthy of revival, as it produces the most crunchy top crust, without any basting whatsoever.

1 large celery root (about 1¾ pounds)
12 tablespoons (1½ sticks) unsalted butter, softened
1 large shallot, minced
½ cup plus 2 tablespoons heavy or whipping cream
1 tablespoon lemon juice
⅛ teaspoon freshly grated nutmeg
¼ teaspoon freshly ground black pepper
Dash of hot pepper sauce
3 tablespoons chopped fresh parsley
Salt
5½- to 6-pound roasting chicken, interior cavity rinsed and patted dry
1 clove garlic, crushed
½ cup plus 2 tablespoons fresh bread crumbs
2 teaspoons brandy
1 cup Chicken Stock (see page 410)
2 tablespoons all-purpose flour
Freshly ground black pepper

1. Preheat the oven to 425°F. Trim and peel the celery root. Cut it into strips about ¼ inch wide, ¼ inch thick, and 1 inch long. You should have 4½ to 5 cups. Cook in boiling salted water for 2 minutes. Rinse under cold running water and drain. Place the celery root in a large mixing bowl.

2. Melt 2 tablespoons of the butter in a small skillet over medium-low heat. Add the shallot and cook until tender, about 5 minutes. Add this to the celery root.

3. Place ½ cup of the heavy cream in a small saucepan. Slowly heat to boiling; reduce the heat. Simmer until reduced to ¼ cup, about 8 minutes. Add this to the celery root, along with the lemon juice, nutmeg, pepper, hot pepper sauce, parsley, and salt to taste. Mix well.

4. Spoon the celery root mixture into the cavity of the roasting chicken. Sew securely and truss. Pat the chicken dry with paper towels. Place it on a rack in a roasting pan.

5. Mash the garlic with 8 tablespoons of the softened butter. Beat in the bread crumbs until smooth. Slowly beat in the brandy. Spread the butter mixture evenly over the top and sides of the chicken. (Make sure chicken is well coated.)

6. Place the chicken in the oven. Roast 15 minutes. Reduce the heat to 350°F and continue to roast until done, about 2 hours. (Juices will run clear when thigh is pricked with a fork.) Thirty minutes before the chicken is done, add the chicken stock to the juices in the roasting pan.

7. When the chicken is done, transfer it to a platter and let it stand 15 minutes. Remove the trussing strings. Strain the pan juices.

8. Melt the remaining 2 tablespoons butter in a medium saucepan over medium-low heat. Stir in the flour. Cook, stirring constantly, 2 minutes. Whisk in the pan juices and remaining 2 tablespoons cream. Cook until slightly thickened. Add salt and pepper to taste. Serve with the chicken.

Serves 6.

CELERY ROOT AND WILD MUSHROOM HASH

Because it is both smooth in flavor and crisp to the tooth, celery root makes an admirable partner to spicier and softer-textured viands. Consider, for instance, the following lunch (or brunch) hash of shiitake mushrooms, Black Forest ham, and celery root. Obviously a *ménage à trois* made in heaven!

1 small celery root (½ to ¾ pound)
2½ tablespoons unsalted butter
2 tablespoons vegetable oil
1 shallot, finely minced
1 clove garlic, minced
4 ounces shiitake mushrooms (stems removed), cut into ½-inch-wide strips (see Note)
4 ounces Black Forest or smoked ham, cut into ½-inch strips
1 tablespoon lemon juice
Salt and freshly ground black pepper
Chopped fresh parsley

1. Trim and peel the celery root. Cut it into strips about ¼ inch wide and 1 inch long. You should have about 1½ cups. Cook in boiling salted water until just barely tender, 5 to 10 minutes. Drain.

2. Heat 1 tablespoon of the butter with 1 tablespoon of the oil in a large skillet over medium-low heat. Add the shallot; cook 1 minute. Add the garlic; cook 4 minutes.

3. Add the remaining 1½ tablespoons butter and remaining 1 tablespoon oil to the pan. Stir in the mushrooms and cook, tossing frequently, over medium heat until lightly browned. Add the ham and celery root. Continue to cook, tossing frequently, until tender, about 5 minutes. Add the lemon juice and salt and pepper to taste. Sprinkle with parsley.

Serves 4.

Note: See Notes on Ingredients, page 416, for information on shiitake mushrooms.

CORN

The Sooner It's Cooked the Better It Tastes

Gastronomes have different notions of paradise than do mortal men, it seems. The grandest treat for a deep-dyed epicure, I have been reasonably assured, is dining *al fresco* on a freshly dug truffle in Perigord or slurping malossol caviar from a just-caught sterlet along the Volga. My own likes are a darn sight more pedestrian, although the same optimum state of freshness certainly applies. Greene's dream meal? Half a dozen ears of sweet summer corn (preferably picked before sundown) from a cornfield in Iowa. If the geography seems a tad imprecise, I will confess that I have only minimal first-hand knowledge of the Great Plains. I simply chose that territory because it is obviously the "in place" to sample lots and lots of corn—something I have done before, albeit not in Iowa—and therein lies a tale, of course.

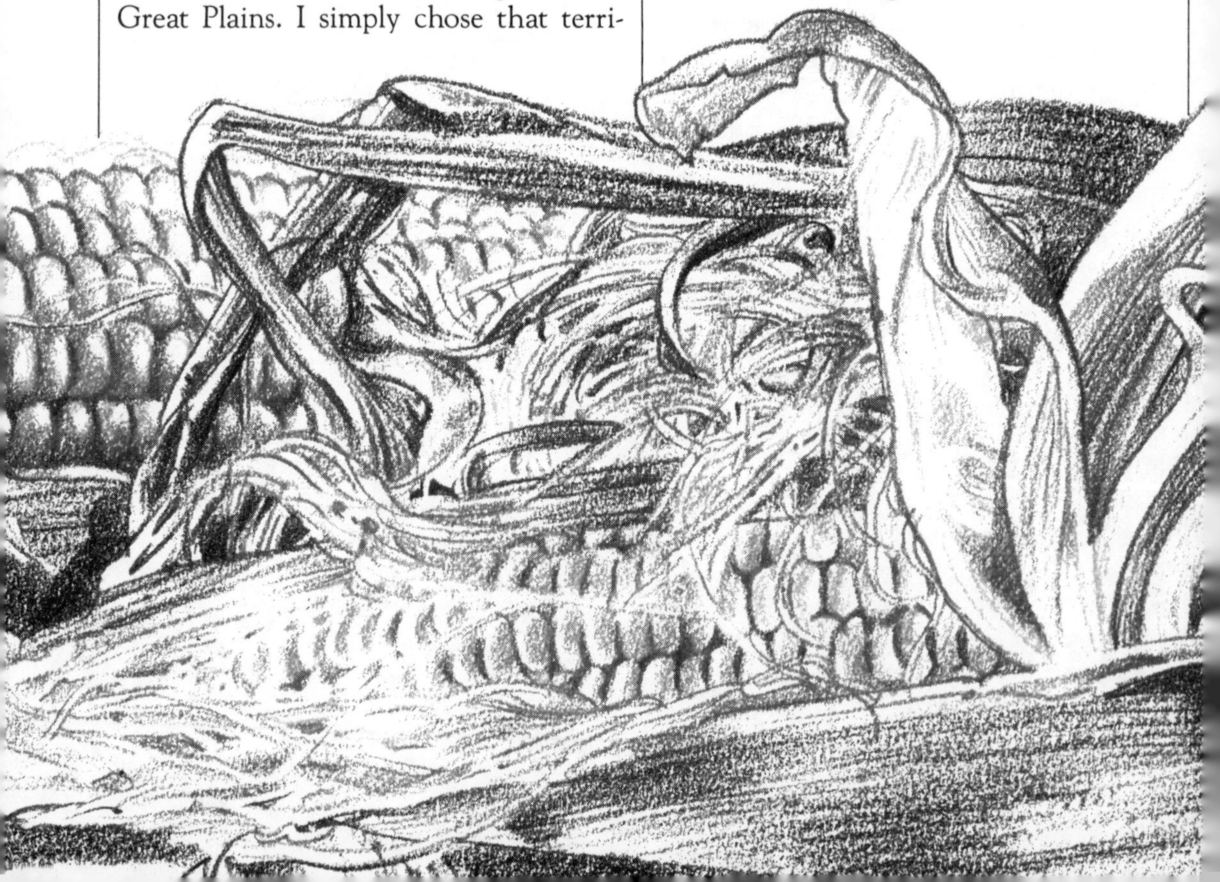

I left home to be completely on my own when I was twenty-two. Many things conspired to arrange my independence. The war ended; my father died unexpectedly; and after a cursory period of mourning, my mother remarried. "For security reasons only," she announced, to ward off any infelicitous hint of romance that might be construed by this rash action. Though she was still exceed-

ingly attractive at forty-eight, my parent seemed openly offended at any sexual implication inherent in her second union. That my stepfather (and her choice for matrimony) turned out to be wildly eccentric seemed beside the point in her view. He was a former suitor who had not only pined after her for thirty years but also managed to accrue some solid assets with which to press his suit.

When my mother announced her plans to marry, I moved. Actually I had been paying rent on an apartment for some time, but put off taking occupancy when my father became ill. No conventional studio, my first home was once the ballroom of a grand mansion off upper Fifth Avenue. From a carved stone balustrade I could even see a stretch of Central Park. Aside from that, and its vast size, this apartment had very few virtues. There was no kitchen or closet, and the bathroom was a mahogany cave equipped with turn-of-the-century fixtures. However, I was young and adventurous, the rent was reasonable, and the building had a private elevator. True, it accommodated only two persons at a time, but it certainly added a touch of class to my bachelor existence.

When I settled into my first apartment I had no furniture whatsoever. In time I acquired a large bed and a bookcase. I had planned to add more household goods before I entertained but natural gregariousness and a new girlfriend, Norma, changed my plans. Norma had recently arrived in New York as well (from a small town in New England), and she lived in a hotel for women where males were forbidden above the lobby floor. Of necessity much of our courtship took place in my quarters.

Norma did not cook. I did, of course, but had nowhere to do it. In the end we spent most of our time like picnickers, roasting our dinner over a log fire in one of the most opulent marble fireplaces ever carved.

Our romance had one other setback. Norma was a vegetarian. We grilled an awful lot of corn (and potatoes) between kisses and I will never forget the flavor of a single singed kernel, though in time my tastebuds rebelled at the diet and I also gained twenty pounds. I enrolled Norma in the best cooking school I knew at the time: Dione Lucas Cordon Bleu, where she shortly gave up her vegetarian principles, and me too, for she married a more aggressive fellow that she met in class. All of which sounds *corny* but is absolutely true!

Norma never heard of it, but there is a tart New England adage that puts down the cooking instructions for corn very concisely. "You may stroll to the garden to cut the corn but you had darn well better run back to the kitchen to cook it!"

That is no exaggeration. As soon as a corn's cob is cut, natural sugar in the kernel's fiber starts to convert to starch. Consequently, the longer the cut corn sits, the mealier each bite will be!

Vegetable Roots

Corn—on the cob and off—antedated Columbus's discovery of America by three thousand years at least—some hint even longer. The first Indian corn, maize *(Zea mays)*, was the chief staple of the Mayan, Aztec, and Incan diets. Corn's origin is traced so far back in Indian history, in fact, that it may date from the very first appearance of man in the western world—when he ate grass seeds to survive.

Food sleuths assert that these precious food seeds, planted along the way of his migration to warmer climes, crossbred; and the result was early corn. Other historians cast a cold eye on that theory, however, insisting that maize, rather than being a wild hybrid, was developed through centuries of cultivation—plus nature's unerring sense of selectivity, of course. Whatever its origin, corn had developed into a tall proud plant long before the first Mayan began to carve his history in stone.

To the early Indian tribes, nature was the only true god. They prayed for fertile fields and strong sons to work them, so it is not surprising that a corn stalk (tall, erect, and capable of reproducing itself *ad infinitum*) was revered as their supreme deity.

Chieftains who considered a maize stalk divine also believed that every kernel off its cob possessed some minor jot of divinity as well. Two or three corn kernels felicitously placed under a brave's marriage blanket was insurance that only strong, worthy (male) offspring would issue from that union.

All Indians held festivals of thanksgiving for a good corn harvest, some of which became bloodbaths of gratitude, since human sacrifices were deemed the ultimate thank-you for a bumper crop. If there was a mite less fervor over corn in the hearts of the early colonists to North America, put it down to dogged puritanism. The first Pilgrims would surely have starved had it not been for the maize they obtained from the local Indians before they had time to plant their own crops.

When the white man added Indian corn to his diet, he added many Indian ways of preparing it too. Hoecake, corn fritters, succotash, and cornbread were all native bequests.

There was one Indian dispensation, however, that early colonists obdurately refused to sample. Dubbed "a soupe," it was a tonic the braves asserted would cure any illness from childbed fever to snakebite. Indians prepared this brew with new corn, boiling ears and husks together for a very long time, then leaving the infusion in the pot for weeks, "until the juices remaining turned sour-sweet and bubbled extensively without the aid of a flame."

The settlers temperately forswore even a drop of this "soupe" because, in the words of Young Spelman, a Virginia homesteader, "Lesse than one pynt consumed causet wild flyinging of arms and legs amng the svges." Worse yet, "wringinge the air with wilde sounds til the spell of this choudier wears off." Corn soup seems a considerably tamer indulgence nowadays. And come to think of it, so does bourbon!

The meal at which the first sweet corn is brought steaming to the table in late July is still a tribal rite for most diners. And the rush of fingers snatching at the ears—ready and willing to be burnt scarlet, it seems, in order to experience the first sensual split of pure gold on the tongue—is a ceremony any Indian would clearly understand.

What to Look For

Corn lovers who do not grow their own should shop early and store the ears (unshucked) in a cold refrigerator until dinner.

When I shop for corn, I look for very grassy green husks with the exposed silk no darker than deep amber in color. A fresh-picked ear of corn will feel gently silken to the thumb, with a slight dampness apparent in the husk.

If your greengrocer has a tolerance for such undertakings, try to peel back the silk to make sure the rows are filled with even, plump kernels. They ought to show a slight ooze when pricked with a fingernail.

The tip-off for old corn is always the stem. After too long a stay on a shelf, the end invariably rusts. So pass those ears by for your next pot of boiling water.

Corn is an uncommonly healthful food—loaded with vitamins (580 units of vitamin A per cupful) and relatively low in calories (a scant 70 for the same amount). Corn also has a large quantity of potassium, phosphorus, and calcium in every ear. Best of all, a single corncob contains less than a trace of salt.

Preparation

Over the years I have developed a wealth of corn wisdom and some very practical advice for its quick cookery. I always bake or roast the ears, depending upon which is more convenient. In my opinion, fresh corn is absolutely at its best when stripped of silk, lightly buttered, then briefly dipped into cold water and rewrapped in the original husks or an ample covering of aluminum foil and then baked or roasted. Twenty minutes in a 350°F oven will usually produce a moist, juicy row of kernels, but more time may be required over an open fire.

Shaker cooks, whose culinary skills I dearly admire, place ears of husked and desilked corn in a large pot of cold water seasoned with the barest pinch of sugar (never salt because it toughens the tender fibers) until the water boils. At that point they cover it and cook it one minute more or as long as it takes to say the Lord's Prayer *fast.* Then they drain and serve the ears as quickly as they can with lots of sweet butter, salt, and pepper on the side.

Another felicitous style of corn cookery comes from Mississippi by way of Evan Jones in his well-versed history, *American Food.* This technique, recommended for less-than-garden-fresh ears and only slightly amended at my New York stovetop, calls for a half-dozen ears of husked and desilked corn to be immersed in a boiling potful of milk and water (one quart each) in which a quarter-pound of sweet butter has been melted. The corn cooks very briefly—5 minutes on my range. What is so special about this method is that the corn tastes as if it had been picked in the garden minutes before. Better yet, each ear is so sweetly succulent that I skip the additional butter entirely. And if, like me, you feel guilty tossing those cooking juices down the drain, simply strain and store the liquid in a covered container in your refrigerator. A cupful will make a head start in most creamed sauces or soups—or sweeten a pan of cornbread in a pinch.

A word or two is probably in order here about "grated corn." There are any number of corn strippers or graters on the market (several in my kitchen cabinet too), but all one needs to be able to scrape corn kernels successfully is a sharp, firm-bladed knife.

To cut kernels, as for Clam and Corn Chowder, stand an ear of corn upright on a plate and carefully slice beneath the rows in a steady downward motion.

To grate kernels, as for the Spicy Texas Corncake, cut off the kernels at about half their depth and then, with the back of the blade, scrape off what is left on the cob, mixing the cut pulp and "milk" with the kernels.

Corn (which rises to heaven as it grows) was believed by Europeans to have otherworldly powers ever since Columbus brought the first samples back to Spain from the Caribbean in 1496.

Early Spanish churchmen, for instance, assumed that the ingestion of raw kernels would cure souls possessed by the devil. Poor martyrs suspected of unearthly connections were often force-fed with a mixture of corn and water (like the geese of Strasbourg) and made to sit naked in the hot sun until the swollen compound either purged them of their sins or they burst. If it sounds terrible, consider the alternative antidote: trial by fire!

MAIS-NOIX
(Corn Nuts)

Old (that is to say, mature) corn has its place in the kitchen from time to time. One of the most addictive cocktail nibbles I know is much dependent upon the texture and bland flavor of aged corn. This is *mais-noix*, a peppery street food that is sold in brown paper sacks on the avenues of Port-au-Prince.

When I visited Haiti for the first time a dozen years ago, my traveling companion was horrified whenever I indulged in the less-than-hygienic snacks the various vendors offered, predicting dire maladies as a consequence of each sampling.

I lived to tell the tale, however, and now happily pass the spoils on to you.

Vegetable oil
1 clove garlic, crushed
1 cup corn kernels (from 2 large mature ears)
1 cup salted dry-roasted peanuts
1 tablespoon mild chili powder or ground fresh sweet chiles

Lightly rub a large cast-iron skillet with oil. Then rub with paper towels. Place the skillet over medium-high heat and add the garlic and corn kernels. Toss, scraping the bottom with a metal spatula, for about 30 seconds. Stir in the peanuts and sprinkle with the chili powder. Toss, continuing to scrape the bottom of the pan, 3 minutes. Transfer to a bowl and serve immediately. (The corn kernels will moisten the peanuts if the mixture sits too long.)

Makes about 2 cups.

TALL-GRASS CORN RELISH

This is one recipe I can never make in sufficient quantity. No matter how many gleaming gilded jars I put up in August, my cupboard is always bare in January. The original formula came from Iowa (where else?) and was rumored to have once taken a blue ribbon at that state's stately fair. Pedigree or no, it is certainly prime piccalilli!

5 cups corn kernels (from 10 large ears)
5 cups finely shredded cabbage
3 cups chopped onions
2½ cups seeded chopped red bell pepper (about 3 medium)
1 cup seeded chopped green bell pepper (about 1 large)
1 quart cider vinegar
1½ cups packed dark brown sugar
¼ cup dry mustard
2 tablespoons salt
1 tablespoon celery seeds

1. Combine all the ingredients in a large heavy pot. Slowly heat to boiling; reduce the heat. Simmer, uncovered, stirring occasionally, 1 hour.

2. Using a slotted spoon, pack the vegetables into sterilized pint jars, leaving 1 inch at the top. Add the hot syrup to each jar to cover. Seal. Process in a hot water bath for 15 minutes.

Makes 5 to 6 pints.

CLAM AND CORN CHOWDER

The early Americans' first original use of corn is rumored to have taken place in a tureen, when the sweet vegetable became a thickener for nourishing chowders. One of the most felicitous reproductions of a Plymouth Rock soup, this was acquired in Truro, at the almost-end of Cape Cod. A velvety mélange of fresh clams, sweet cream, and even fresher, sweeter corn off the cob, it is definitely more than a mere pottage. It is practically poetry.

1½ to 2 quarts clams or quahogs
1½ cups water (or 1 cup clam juice and ½ cup water)
8 tablespoons (1 stick) unsalted butter, at room temperature
2 sprigs parsley, plus chopped parsley for garnish
1 bay leaf
1 small onion stuck with 1 whole clove
4 thick slices bacon, diced
1 large onion, minced
1 large clove garlic, minced
1 rib celery, finely chopped
½ green bell pepper, seeded, minced
6 potatoes, peeled, diced, parboiled 3 minutes
2 cups milk, scalded (just below the boiling point)
2 tablespoons all-purpose flour
2 cups heavy or whipping cream
Dash of hot pepper sauce
Dash of Worcestershire sauce
¼ teaspoon chopped fresh thyme, or a pinch of dried
Salt and freshly ground black pepper
1½ to 2 cups fresh corn kernels (from 3 or 4 large ears)

1. Scrub the clams well and place them in a large pot with the water, 2 tablespoons of the butter, 2 sprigs parsley, the bay leaf, and the onion stuck with a clove. Cover and bring to a boil over high heat. Reduce the heat; simmer 5 minutes. Remove the clams, reserving the liquid, and remove them from their shells; if large, cut them in half. (The clams will be open far enough to pry the shell open with a knife if necessary. Discard any clams that do not open.) Set the clams aside. Strain the liquid and keep it warm.

2. Cook the bacon in 1 quart boiling water for 5 minutes. Drain; pat dry with paper towels. Then fry the bacon in a medium skillet until crisp and golden brown. Drain on paper towels.

3. Remove all but 1 tablespoon bacon fat from the skillet and add 2 tablespoons of the butter. Cook the minced onion over medium heat 1 minute. Add the garlic, celery, and green pepper. Cook 5 minutes.

4. Transfer the onion mixture to a large pot. Add the sautéed bacon, the potatoes, and the milk. Heat to boiling; add the reserved clam liquid.

5. Mix 3 tablespoons of the butter with the flour in a small bowl until smooth. Stir this into the soup. Add the cream and return the soup to boiling; reduce the heat. Simmer 5 minutes. Add the hot pepper sauce, Worcestershire, thyme, and salt and pepper to taste. Stir in the corn. Cook until the chowder is slightly thickened, 5 to 10 minutes. Add the clams and warm through. Stir in the remaining 1 tablespoon butter and sprinkle with parsley.

Serves 6 to 8.

DAUFUSKIE QUILT

The next recipe hails from Daufuskie Island, in the Gullah country of South Carolina—a rural archipelago that one must rent a launch to visit, almost entirely peopled by blacks who have lived and farmed the land there for centuries.

The following dish, as stylized in its own way as the patchwork quilts the "old-timey" island women are famous for, is called *"a lef'over sla."*

I must admit I never acquired a recipe for this salad—Daufuskians are notoriously shy of strangers. But I think my rendering is a fair enough duplication.

2 large ears corn
1½ cups chopped cooked chicken
1 small zucchini, thinly sliced
1 small red tomato, halved and sliced
½ green bell pepper, seeded, finely chopped
2 tablespoons minced red onion
1 clove garlic, crushed
½ teaspoon salt
2 tablespoons red wine vinegar
3 tablespoons olive oil
2 tablespoons chopped fresh parsley
1 tablespoon chopped fresh basil, or ½ teaspoon dried
¼ teaspoon chopped fresh thyme, or a pinch of dried
¼ teaspoon cumin seeds (comino), crushed, or a pinch of ground cumin

1. Cook the ears of corn in boiling water for 3 minutes. Rinse under cold running water; drain. Cut the kernels from the cobs and combine in a large bowl with the chicken, zucchini, tomato, pepper, and onion. Toss lightly.

2. Mash the garlic with the salt in a small bowl to form a paste. Beat in the vinegar, oil, and herbs. Pour this dressing over the salad and toss well. Serve well chilled or at room temperature.

Serves 4.

AMAGANSETT CORN SALAD

Long Island is no slouch as corn-growing territory. This dish is my own invention, a residual of my years as co-proprietor of The Store in Amagansett. Bored with making the same salads day after day, I borrowed a notion from the Shinnecock Indians down the road and put the local harvest to use in a salad bowl.

6 large ears corn
1 large green bell pepper, seeded, minced
1 red onion, finely chopped
2 shallots, sliced thin
4 whole scallions, bulbs and green tops chopped separately
1 large tomato, seeded, cut into ½-inch cubes
¼ cup sour cream
½ cup Mayonnaise (see page 408)
¼ cup strong beef broth (see page 414)
2 tablespoons red wine vinegar
Salt and freshly ground black pepper
Approximately 5 pimiento strips

1. Cook the ears of corn in boiling water for 3 minutes. Rinse under cold running water; drain. Cut the kernels from the cobs and combine them in a large bowl with the pepper, onion, shallots, scallion bulbs, and tomato. Toss lightly.

2. Beat the sour cream with the mayonnaise in a medium bowl. Beat in the broth and vinegar. Pour this dressing over the salad and toss well. Add salt and pepper to taste, and decorate with chopped scallion tops and pimiento strips. Chill well before serving.

Serves 6.

DOROTHY SHANK'S AMISH CORN FRITTERS

I grew up on corn fritters.

They were most often deep-fried and devised by my mother out of the ingredients always found in her kitchen: canned creamed corn, flour, eggs, and a spike of baking soda. I must admit I loved them dearly though they were greasy as the dickens and probably as lethal to one's digestive system as a depth charge. That childhood fritter, however, has absolutely nothing in common with the incredibly airy griddle-sautéed cakes limned below. These fritters virtually melt on the tongue. The recipe came my way by one of those supreme happenstances I generally call "fate."

I was being interviewed on the radio in Niagara Falls a few years ago. The station was a small local outlet and the interviewer was a motherly lady who had obviously faced a thousand authors across the microphone in her time. It was a hot, sultry day and the studio's air conditioning had unpredictably gone awry. The interview began fitfully, she fanning herself with a sheaf of papers and I gulping cold water as the red light that indicated "on the air" flickered ominously. The temperature was probably close to a hundred degrees in the glass booth, but for some reason the show went well. Before either of us knew it we had talked ourselves dry (if not precisely cool), praising the pleasures of American cooking.

At some point during a recorded commercial my interviewer turned to me. "Do you like Amish food?" she asked.

When I assured her I did, she smiled and handed me a small memorandum pad. "I was sure you did," she said happily. "I am of Pennsylvania Dutch stock myself—and heat or no heat, we all love to talk about food in that part of the world. Have you got a pencil? I want to give you a present to remember me by. It's a very special recipe for corn fritters—one that's been in my family for generations. So write fast!"

I did. But it was an easy formula to log—composed of six ingredients and only three sentences of instruction.

Take my word for it: in the end length has nothing to do with magnificence. These are simply the best corn fritters you will ever eat!

4 large ears corn
2 eggs, separated
2 tablespoons all-purpose flour
1 tablespoon sugar
Salt and freshly ground black pepper
Unsalted butter

1. Cut the corn kernels from 2 ears of corn and place them in a medium bowl. With the back of the knife, scrape the cobs over the bowl to extract the juices. Grate the corn from the remaining ears, as described on page 129. Add the grated kernels with their pulp and juice to the whole kernels in the bowl. The mixture will resemble scrambled eggs.

2. Beat the egg yolks in a large bowl until light. Beat in the flour, sugar, and salt and pepper to taste. Stir in the corn.

3. Beat the egg whites in a large bowl until stiff. Fold them into the corn mixture.

4. Heat a heavy skillet or griddle over medium heat and grease it lightly with butter. Drop the batter by small spoonfuls onto the hot griddle and cook until golden, about 30 seconds per side. Transfer the cooked fritters to a lightly buttered serving platter and keep them warm in a low oven while cooking the remaining fritters.

Serves 4.

SPICY TEXAS CORNCAKE

Corn and its natural offspring, cornmeal, are the underpinnings of the Southwestern diet. Where would Tex-Mex cookery be without *masa harina*? Obviously *sans* corn tortillas for starters. My most treasured corn-and-cornmeal prescription (and I have a few at hand) comes from the acknowledged first lady of Tex-Mex cookery, Anne Lindsay Greer, author of *Cuisine of the American Southwest*: a red-hot corncake, meant to be eaten as a brunch, lunch, or picnic adjunct. It is also the single most perfect accompaniment to an egg that I know.

3 large ears corn
1 pound Spanish sausages (chorizos), chopped
1 onion, finely chopped
3 tablespoons unsalted butter, softened
3 eggs
1 cup sour cream
1 can (7 ounces) Mexican "Home Style" or "Green Chile" salsa *(available in most supermarket specialty food sections)*
1 poblano chile, roasted, peeled, seeded, minced (see Note)
1¼ cups very fine yellow cornmeal
½ cup all-purpose flour
1 teaspoon baking soda
1 teaspoon baking powder
1 teaspoon sugar
½ teaspoon salt
1 cup milk
8 ounces Monterey jack cheese, grated

1. Preheat the oven to 350°F. Grate the corn kernels as described on page 129. Set aside.

2. Sauté the chopped chorizos in a large heavy skillet over medium-low heat until they are lightly browned and all grease has exuded. With a slotted spoon, transfer the sausages to a dish and set aside.

3. Pour off all but 1 tablespoon fat from the skillet. Sauté the onion until lightly browned. Set aside.

4. Beat the butter with the eggs in a large mixing bowl until smooth. Beat in the sour cream. Add the onion, *salsa*, and minced poblano chile.

5. Combine the cornmeal, flour, baking soda, baking powder, sugar, and salt in another bowl. Add this to the sour cream mixture. Stir in the milk with a wooden spoon. Stir in the cheese, corn, and sausages.

6. Butter a round baking dish, about 12 inches across and 2 inches deep. Pour the batter into the dish. Bake in the oven until golden, about 45 minutes. Let stand 5 minutes before serving.

Serves 8 to 10.

Note: To roast a poblano chile, hold the chile with a roasting fork over a gas flame. Turn the chile until it is blackened all over. Or place the chile under a broiler until crisp on all sides. Carefully wrap the chile in paper towels and place it in a small paper bag. Let it stand to cool. The peel will easily rub off.

POLENTA PLUS

Corn recipes abound in every cuisine under the sun. This one is a traditional cornmeal porridge of Italian descent. Polenta is served up as a meal in itself or as an accompaniment to meats, depending upon the eater's pocketbook. My version, I must confess, is untraditionally crammed with corn kernels, hence the "plus."

2 large ears corn
2½ cups milk
1 cup chicken broth (see page 414)
1 cup yellow cornmeal
¾ teaspoon salt
1½ tablespoons unsalted butter, melted
1½ tablespoons freshly grated Parmesan cheese

1. Using a sharp knife, grate the corn kernels from the cobs as described on page 129. Set aside.

2. Heat the milk and chicken broth slowly to boiling in a medium saucepan over medium-low heat. (Do not allow to scorch.) Slowly beat in the cornmeal with a wire whisk. Continue to beat until the mixture is smooth and thick. Remove from the heat and stir in the salt and reserved corn. Immediately pour the mixture into a lightly greased shallow 1½-quart baking dish. Place the dish on a rack and keep it, uncovered, in a cool place for at least 1 hour.

3. Before serving, preheat the oven to 375°F. Brush the top of the polenta with the melted butter and sprinkle it with the cheese. Bake 15 minutes. Let stand 10 minutes before serving.

Serves 6.

SOUR-CREAMED CORN

For the record: my idea of the classic way to serve corn is *on the cob* without any embellishment other than a pat of butter and a shaking of salt! Even freshly ground pepper seems a distraction if the corn is good. But there are other less purist renditions. Consider, for instance, the following alignment of barely sautéed corn kernels, scallions, butter, and a dab of sour cream. To be baldly alliterative, it is a dish that is one of corn's consummate collaborations.

4 large ears corn
2 tablespoons unsalted butter
3 whole scallions, bulbs and green tops, chopped
¼ cup sour cream
Dash of hot pepper sauce
Salt and freshly ground black pepper
Chopped fresh parsley

1. Cut the corn kernels from the ears and place them in a bowl. You should have about 2 cups. With the back of the knife, scrape the cobs over the bowl to extract the juices.

2. Melt the butter in a large heavy skillet over medium-low heat. Add the scallions; cook 1 minute. Stir in the corn; cook until barely tender, 4 to 5 minutes. Add the sour cream and hot pepper sauce. Cook until warmed through; do not allow to boil. Add salt and pepper to taste and sprinkle with parsley.

Serves 4.

LOUISIANA MAQUECHOUX

(Sautéed Corn with Vegetables)

Corn, like tomatoes and peppers, is a totally native American vegetable that shows up with stunning frequency in all of our varied culinary geography.

This example stems from the bayou country of Louisiana. A side dish, it is variously known as "*mock shoe*," "*mark show*," and "*maquechoux*," depending upon which strand of the Archafalaya River you travel. The latter spelling means "false cabbage" in the Cajun tongue, but that's not much help because the dish has no relation to any cabbage (or corn) concoction consumed anywhere else in the world. It's a purely local dispensation—and in Louisiana always accompanies turkey to the table at Thanksgiving.

6 ears fresh corn
2 slices bacon
6 whole scallions, bulbs and green tops chopped separately
1 red bell pepper, seeded, chopped
2 ripe tomatoes, seeded, chopped
½ teaspoon sugar
¼ teaspoon fresh thyme, or a pinch of dried
1 teaspoon chopped fresh basil, or ¼ teaspoon dried
½ cup heavy or whipping cream
Salt and freshly ground black pepper

1. Cut the kernels from 2 ears of corn and place them in a medium bowl. Grate the remaining cobs as described on page 129. Add grated corn, pulp, and juice to the kernels in the bowl. Set aside.

2. Sauté the bacon in a large heavy skillet until crisp. Remove the bacon; drain on paper towels. Cook the chopped scallion bulbs with the red pepper in the bacon drippings until soft, about 5 minutes. Add the tomatoes, sugar, thyme, and basil. Cook, uncovered, over medium heat 5 minutes. Add the corn and cream; cook, stirring constantly, until the corn is tender and the mixture is creamy, about 10 minutes. Add salt and pepper to taste. Sprinkle with the scallion tops; crumble the reserved bacon over the top.

Serves 6.

HOT CORN FLAN

The next corn endowment is for a silken vegetable custard—the issue of a mixed marriage between red-hot Texas seasonings and nouvelle cuisine! My father, a man whose wife always cut the corn off a cob to spare his tender gums, would have loved it. It's a corn dish that goes down easy.

1 tablespoon unsalted butter
2 tablespoons minced onion
3 tablespoons minced seeded green bell pepper
3 tablespoons minced canned mild green chiles
1 to 2 tablespoons minced canned hot jalapeño peppers (depending on taste)
1½ cups corn kernels (from 3 large ears)
1½ tablespoons all-purpose flour
½ cup milk
3 eggs
1 cup heavy or whipping cream
1 teaspoon salt
⅛ teaspoon freshly ground black pepper
¼ teaspoon freshly ground nutmeg
Pinch of ground allspice
2 cups grated Monterey jack cheese (about 6 ounces)

1. Preheat the oven to 350°F. Melt the butter in a large skillet over medium-low heat. Add the onion and green bell pepper. Cook 5 minutes. Raise the heat to medium and add the canned chiles, the jalapeño peppers, and 1 cup of the corn kernels. Cook, uncovered, stirring often, 10 minutes. Remove from the heat.

2. Place the remaining ½ cup corn kernels into the container of a blender. Add the flour and milk and blend until smooth.

3. Beat the eggs in a large bowl until light. To the eggs beat in the corn mixture from the blender, the cream, salt, pepper, nutmeg, and allspice. Stir in the corn-pepper mixture and cheese. Pour into a 1½-quart shallow soufflé dish. Place the dish in a roasting pan. Add boiling water to the pan to reach halfway up the sides of the dish. Place the pan in the oven and cook until the mixture is firm, about 1 hour. Let stand 15 minutes before serving. This may also be served chilled.

Serves 6 to 8.

CORN CREPES WITH TWO FILLINGS

In 1515, Thomas Tusser, a British nature-lover, made the following observation on corn's cultivation:

> Sensible seedsmen never sow peas'n corn nor any plant which matures high above the ground—'cept under a rising (waxing) moon.
>
> While rooted stuffs like p'tatoes, parsnips and such are set out during the moon's dark (waning) periods. This is so the moon's light will draw up those seeds which need light and keep safe till they mature, those which need the cover of warm earth.

With that sage advice in mind, I always plant corn when the moon is no larger than a lemon rind and have not had cause to regret the instance yet.

In the kitchen I am somewhat more unorthodox. A while back I invented a corn pancake (crepe if you will) that also waxes and wanes depending upon its filling.

In the first instance, this delicate cover is filled with an amalgam of creamy corn kernels and ham and is rolled conventionally. It makes a refreshing luncheon or supper treat. In the second variation, the thin pancakes are folded into (forgive the pun, please) tiny *corn*ucopias dabbed with creamy corn and whipped egg mixture that makes each turnover rise like a mini soufflé in the oven.

For the Crepes

2 eggs
1 cup milk
½ cup corn kernels (from 1 large ear)
¾ cup all-purpose flour
2 tablespoons vegetable oil
¼ teaspoon salt
¼ teaspoon freshly ground black pepper
⅛ teaspoon ground mace

1. Place the eggs, milk, and corn kernels in the container of a blender and blend until smooth. Add the flour, oil, salt, pepper, and mace. Blend 2 minutes. Scrape down the sides and blend 1 minute longer. Refrigerate, covered, at least 2 hours.

2. Remove the batter from the refrigerator. Line a plate with two sheets of paper towels and set it aside.

3. Lightly rub a crepe or small omelet pan (preferably with a nonstick surface) with a buttered or oiled cloth. Place the pan over medium heat until it is very hot. Remove the pan from the heat and pour about 3 tablespoons of the batter into the center of the pan. Quickly tilt the pan in all directions to cover the bottom evenly, then return the pan to the heat and cook until the edges of the crepe are brown, about 1 minute. Lightly loosen the edges with a spatula. (These crepes are especially tender and limp, so you'll need a flexible spatula to free the edges before inverting.) Holding the towel-lined plate in one hand, quickly invert the pan over the plate with the other hand, so the crepe drops onto the paper towels. Lightly oil the pan once more and continue this process until all the batter is used, placing a double layer of paper towels over each finished crepe.

Makes 12 to 14 7-inch crepes.

Corn and Ham Filling

12 to 14 7-inch crepes
3 tablespoons unsalted butter
1 whole scallion, bulb and green top, minced
2 tablespoons seeded minced red bell pepper
2 tablespoons seeded minced green bell pepper
½ cup diced cooked ham
1 cup corn kernels (from 2 large ears)
2 tablespoons all-purpose flour
¾ cup Chicken Stock (see page 410)
½ cup heavy or whipping cream
Pinch of freshly grated nutmeg
Salt and freshly ground black pepper

1. Preheat the oven to 350°F.

2. Melt 1 tablespoon of the butter in a medium skillet over medium-low heat. Add the scallion, both peppers, and ham. Cook 5 minutes. Add the corn; toss well. Remove from the heat.

3. Melt the remaining 2 tablespoons butter in a small saucepan. Stir in the flour. Cook over medium-low heat, stirring constantly, 2 minutes. Whisk in the stock and cream; cook until thick. Season with the nutmeg, and salt and pep-

per to taste. Stir half the cream mixture into the corn mixture.

4. Invert the crepe stack onto another plate so that all cooked sides are down. Carefully remove the top layers of paper towels. Spoon about 1 tablespoon of the corn filling down the side of the crepe and roll up. Place the crepes on a lightly greased baking dish. When all the crepes are prepared, drizzle the remaining sauce over the top. Bake for 10 minutes before serving.

Makes 12 to 14 filled crepes.

Corn Soufflé Filling

12 to 14 7-inch crepes
1 tablespoon unsalted butter
2 tablespoons all-purpose flour
1 cup milk
2 egg yolks
½ teaspoon salt
¼ teaspoon freshly ground black pepper
Pinch of freshly grated nutmeg
Dash of hot pepper sauce
2 cups corn kernels (from 4 large ears)
3 egg whites

1. Preheat the oven to 350°F.

2. Melt the butter in a medium saucepan over medium-low heat. Stir in the flour; cook, stirring constantly, 2 minutes. Whisk in the milk; cook until thickened, 2 to 3 minutes. Remove from the heat. Beat in the egg yolks, one at a time, beating thoroughly after each addition. Return to low heat, stirring constantly, 1 minute. Do not allow to boil. Add the salt, pepper, nutmeg, and hot pepper sauce. Remove from the heat and stir in the corn.

3. Beat the egg whites until stiff. Fold them into the soufflé base.

4. Invert the crepe stack onto another plate so that all cooked sides are down. Carefully remove the top layers of paper towels. Spoon about 3 level tablespoons of soufflé mixture onto the lower left-hand quarter of each crepe. Gently fold the crepe in half over the soufflé mixture, then fold it in half once more. Place the crepes on a lightly greased baking dish. When all the crepes are prepared, bake until the soufflé centers are cooked and well puffed, 8 to 10 minutes. Serve immediately.

Makes 12 to 14 filled crepes.

NEW MEXICO CORN TART

The Hopi Indians predict weather by the size of a corn row. If the stalks are tall and the leaves grow tight, a hard winter is on the way and they harvest early to prepare for its rigors. If the leaves are full and the ears are heavy, they do not cut the first corn until the full (pumpkin) moon rises in late September or October.

While not exactly a dessert, this Hopi tart makes an excellent breakfast item when topped with a slosh of maple syrup and a dab of sour cream.

8 tablespoons (1 stick) plus 1 teaspoon unsalted butter, softened
¼ cup ground pumpkin seeds ("pepitas"; available in health-food stores)
6 medium ears corn
½ cup heavy or whipping cream
½ cup sugar
3 eggs, separated
1 teaspoon baking powder
⅛ teaspoon ground cinnamon
¼ teaspoon salt
⅛ teaspoon freshly ground black pepper
3 tablespoons dark rum

1. Preheat the oven to 350°F. Rub a round baking dish, 10 inches across and about 2 inches deep, with 1 teaspoon of the butter. Sprinkle with 2 teaspoons of the ground pumpkin seeds. Set aside.

2. Cut the corn kernels from the ears and place them in a bowl. With the back of the knife, scrape the cobs over the bowl to extract the juices. Place half the corn kernels in the container of a blender or food processor. Add the cream and process until fairly smooth. Combine with the corn in the bowl. Reserve.

3. Beat the 8 tablespoons butter with the sugar in a large bowl until light and fluffy. Beat in the egg yolks, one at a time, beating well after each addition. Beat in the baking powder, cinnamon, salt, pepper, and rum. Stir in the corn mixture and the remaining ground pumpkin seeds. Mix well.

4. Beat the egg whites in a large bowl until stiff; fold them into the corn mixture. Pour the mixture into the prepared baking dish. Bake until golden brown and slightly puffed, about 35 minutes. Let stand 10 minutes before serving.

Serves 6 to 8.

CUCUMBERS

The Basis for Success

"Cool as a cucumber" is an expression to which I have never properly related, because most of my experiences with those green gherkins took place in kitchens that were literally hot as hell!

I am thinking specifically of the airless back room of The Store in Amagansett where I toiled for ten summers under a pair of transom windows that could not be opened wider than two inches. In 1966 a misguided workman installed the windows' hinges behind a stainless-steel stove hood, and while The Store's fortunes waxed more than they waned during the next decade, renovation always seemed such a staggering prospect (emotionally as well as financially) that it seemed easier to sweat.

As I said earlier, I came to the town of Amagansett to escape a hectic urban pace. The Store's existence was conceived to prolong my stay near the calming sea, year round. But from the moment this take-out food establishment opened, I knew my serendipitous days were numbered. Almost from the first day the parade of automobiles parked outside caused traffic burdens for miles.

Not just a local success, the venture I co-founded shortly became a national institution. From all over came the rich, the famous, and the hungry through its saffron-colored screen door, eager to partake of the homemade foods prepared daily. It was a period of my life that I tend to think of as "Cucumber Time," because dilled cucumbers, with or without sour cream, were in a salad whose presence was daily made manifest in a chalked scrawl on the blackboard. And I can rarely remember leftovers returning to the kitchen at closing time. Admirers of The Store cucumbers were dogged in their devotion. We must have prepared tons of it every summer and I can remember a notable occasion in midwinter when the wife of a famous TV talk-show host made the hundred-mile trek from Manhattan to Amagansett just to have this dish on the table for her husband's birthday.

What made the cucumbers so memorable? According to my ex-partner, Denis Vaughan, it was the thinness of each slice. Denis was always given to hyperbole, but he claimed that if a cucumber was properly cut for a cucumber salad, one should be able to read the editorials in the *New York Times* through any given slice. Not through my wedges, however. The cutting of these gossamer concentric circles took hours and were the bane of my cooking life at The Store. Very often, I would throw in the towel (or paring knife) before a bowl was even half-filled because the task was not only arduous, it was indigestible as well—at least to a kitchen worker who sampled as he worked. And I always maintained there had to be a better way to do the job.

In the early 1970s I discovered it. On a holiday in France, I observed a curious object that was used for slicing vegetables in most every kitchen I visited. Called a *mandoline*, it was rather like a lethal cross between a miniature slide and a guillotine. Made of wood, this small troughed object was fitted with an adjustable razor-sharp blade and drop slot. The first French housewife I observed using it held a cucumber in the palm of her hand and by dexterously moving it up and down, shaved cucumbers thin enough to read the classified advertisements in *Le Monde*... in seconds! Needless to say, I returned to America with two *mandolines* stashed away in my luggage for The Store's kitchen. There, I regret to say, both hung on the wall collecting dust (like decorative objects) ever after.

No. That is not wholly accurate. One of the *mandolines was* used to cut a cucumber once... by me, as a matter of fact. But after a trial run, the sight of my hand dripping blood on the kitchen floor was so unnerving it discouraged all other takers. We continued to cut our cucumbers as before—and I for one shut up about it!

Vegetable Roots

Most diners tend to think of the cucumber as a raw food or salad ingredient. That, I suspect, is purely a biblical inheritance. The Old Testament tells us that Moses' one regret after the Red Sea parted and his people made their exit from Egypt was that he had neglected to bring a peck of cucumber seeds into the desert. Israelites (and Egyptians too) ate this cylindrical green at every meal, usually dipped into bowls of salted water, for it was believed that the ingestion of three raw *Cucumis* daily protected the human body from the bite of deadly insects and vipers.

Any man with a hoe who has ever staked and poled a cucumber patch will give a nod of credence to that superstition. The area of any garden where cucumbers grow is decidedly off-limits to the red-blooded mosquito and gnat. And I've noticed that garter snakes make detours to avoid that territory as well.

The cucumber, a member of the gourd family, *Cucurbitaceae*, is the distant relative of a host of other vegeteria like pumpkin, squash, melon, and chayote. Like its garden cousins, the cucumber is a native of the region of Pakistan where the overflowing Indus River makes the land muddy and fertile and the warm wind off the Sulaiman mountains blows the tiny seedlets for thousands of miles every spring.

Green-thumbed archeologists tell us

Roman addiction to the cucumber was so marked, according to Pliny, that the Emperor Tiberius consumed at least ten a day, year round. The Romans stole the cucumber from the Greeks after a defeat in the wars with King Pyrrhus of Epirus. The Macedonians (under Alexander the Great's helm) in turn appropriated cucumber plants from the Persian troop ships as spoils of the battle of Granicus. The Persians had filched the cucumber as seed from the Medes, who most probably brought this curiously shaped object back to the Babylonian gardens as a souvenir of some Indian expedition.

The first serious appraisal of cucumbers in Europe occurred in France during the reign of Pepin the Wise at the end of the eighth century. According to his gardener's record books, Pepin ordered that *concombres* be planted in triple rows surrounding his vineyards, to protect the precious grapes from bolls, borers, and cutworms. It took another fifty years before his son finally ate a cucumber for sheer pleasure. It must have tickled his fancy, for Charlemagne decreed at once that the cucumber was a favorite "fruit." He ate them only as dessert, in sweet tarts and custards. Later Frenchmen were also tempted to gild the lily, but good sense turned the cucumber custard from sweet to savory in the nick of time.

that traces of cucumber spore have been unearthed in spirit caves as far off as Burma and Thailand, indicating that thousands of years before formal agriculture existed, this gourd was offered up as appeasement to the gods by the early Asians.

The original Indian species (still found wild from Kumai to Sikkim) had a smooth brownish skin and extremely bitter flesh. Time and tide turned the shell prickly green and the flavor sweeter. Ancient Greeks considered the cucumber so ambrosial that they mixed the pulp with honey and snow, and only dished it up on important occasions (like victory celebrations and royal weddings). The Romans, who prided themselves on their exotic diet, served cucumbers every day of the week when they were in season. But they flavored them so imprudently (with splashes of fish sauces, vinegar and pinches of herbs) that it is doubtful a deep-dyed cucumber-lover would recognize the source from the sauce.

What to Look For

I must declare that I am so long in the tooth, I can perfectly call to mind the days before cucumbers were spray-waxed to give them an extra spate of shelf-life. In that dim past, cucumber eaters ate them skins and all. Today I would not advise such rash consumption, unless you are lucky enough to have a farm stand in the immediate vicinity.

The only unwaxed cucumbers I come upon in urban areas these days (and then only in summer and early fall) are the "kirbies" I use for home pickling. These jade-hued baby gherkins will not add stature to a salad bowl but they make fine eating all the same, since the tiny seeds are tender and easy to digest.

I usually look for a hard cucumber when I shop. Deep viridian is the shade that assures a fairly recent stint on a vine. Skip any large cucumbers that are yellowing, as that is a dead giveaway of a longish stay in the vegetable bin. Likewise cucumbers that are pulpy or pitted to the touch. Soft cucumbers are a residual of an early frost or an over-refrigerated transport truck. Pass 'em by, please!

Cucumber is one vegetable dieters

may consume with a clear conscience. The average size (7-inch variety) tallies at less than 10 calories and is comprised mostly of water. The vitamin content (70 units of vitamin A) vanishes once the peel is removed.

Preparation

My prescription for detoxifying a raw cucumber's bitterness was borrowed intact from the matriarch of a large Swedish family who lived next door to us when I was growing up. Mrs. Johnson's formula was very simple. So is mine.

First, trim the ends from the cucumber. Then carefully peel the outer skin, taking care not to bruise the flesh. The form your raw ingredient takes (either sliced, quartered, or even left whole) is up to you. Merely place the cucumber in an earthenware bowl and add a pinch of salt, a dash of vinegar and a jot of sugar. Allow it to stand for half an hour. That's all. Salt draws out the excess water while vinegar and sugar sweeten the flesh and make it taste more "cucumbery."

The same procedure never hurts a cucumber that is to be cooked. The removal of water is almost critical in any sautéed, stir-fried, or baked cucumber dish since warming inevitably releases the vegetable's juices and can result in a dreadfully waterlogged mess if the cook does not look sharp.

I prefer cooked cucumbers on the *al dente* side—with a measure of resilience to the tooth. Sautéing cut-up cucumbers will usually take about 5 minutes over medium heat. Baked whole cucumbers will take considerably longer: anywhere from 30 to 50 minutes depending upon your addiction to crunch.

Whenever I cook a cucumber I generally seed it first. This job is not as mettlesome as it may appear. After peeling a cucumber, simply halve it lengthwise. Then, using a sharp spoon (like a grapefruit cutter), scoop out all the seeds and any watery flesh that clings to the inside edge. What you will have left is a cucumber "bark" not unlike a slender green canoe—which may be filled, sliced, or cut into chunks.

POUNGIOU
(Cucumber Yogurt Cheese)

Greek farmers today still eat the cucumber just as their great-great-great-grandfathers did—combined with yogurt and herbs into a tangy cheese that is a staple everywhere from the Aegean Sea to the Gulf of Messina. The official name of this dish is *yaourti tou pouggiou*, "yogurt of the pocket," but I never found it in Greece. The estimable Craig Claiborne was my source. Since it is a relatively low-caloried concoction, I serve Poungiou as a diet-minded hors d'oeuvre with lots of fresh vegetables alongside, or spoon a dab over a ripe tomato for lunch.

1 pound unflavored yogurt
2 cucumbers (each about 7 inches long), peeled, seeded, finely chopped
1 tablespoon white wine vinegar
½ teaspoon salt
⅛ teaspoon sugar
1 small clove garlic, minced
2 tablespoons chopped fresh dill
1 tablespoon olive oil
2 teaspoons tarragon vinegar
Salt and ground white pepper

1. Line a colander with cheesecloth. Spoon the yogurt into the cheesecloth; drain. Bring up the edges of the cheesecloth and tie them with a long piece of string. Hang the yogurt in the refrigerator, letting it drip into a bowl, for 24 hours, draining the bowl as necessary.

2. Combine the cucumbers with the wine vinegar, salt, and sugar. Toss well; let stand 1 hour. Drain, pressing out all liquid with your hands.

3. Remove the yogurt "cheese" from the refrigerator and scrape it into a bowl. Add the cucumbers, garlic, dill, olive oil, and tarragon vinegar. Beat until smooth. Add salt and white pepper to taste.

Makes about ¾ cup. Serves 4 as a first course.

CUCUMBER RISOTTO

From the time of its disappearance as a staple of the salad bowl after the sack of Rome until its introduction as a flavoring for the exotic fare conceived during the Renaissance, the *cetriuolo* was frankly in limbo.

Thought to be an unmentionable apothecary ingredient not spoken of in polite society, the cucumber's chief attribute was reputedly aphrodisiac. No one knows how it was disabused of that florid reputation, but let us give thanks that it was.

Better yet, let's add a gramercy for the nameless kitchen worker who first combined a measure of cucumber (chopped) with a saucepan of Italian rice. The result is quite a different renaissance but no less tonic, I assure you.

2 tablespoons unsalted butter
2 shallots, finely chopped
1 small clove garlic, minced
½ cup Italian rice (I use Arborio)
Pinch of crushed dried hot red peppers
2 cucumbers (each about 7 inches long), peeled, seeded, diced
1¾ cups hot chicken broth, approximately (see page 414)
Salt and freshly ground black pepper
Chopped fresh dill

1. Melt 1 tablespoon of the butter in a heavy skillet over medium-low heat. Add the shallots; cook 2 minutes. Add the garlic; cook 1 minute. Stir in the rice, hot peppers, and cucumbers. Mix well.

2. Pour ¾ cup of the hot broth over the rice, and without stirring, let the rice absorb it. This should take about 15 minutes. Reduce the heat to low if the rice is cooking too fast.

3. Stir the rice to mix thoroughly. Pour ½ cup of the remaining hot broth over the rice and again, without stirring, let the rice absorb it, about 15 minutes.

4. Stir the rice once more and pour the remaining ½ cup broth over it. Cook until the rice is creamy and just tender but not mushy, about 10 minutes. (If the rice is not tender when all the liquid has been absorbed, add more broth. The rice should have a bite. If it is too wet when fully cooked, raise the heat slightly. The entire cooking of the rice should take at least 40 minutes.) Stir in the remaining 1 tablespoon butter; add salt and pepper to taste and sprinkle with dill.

Serves 4 as an appetizer.

M.F.K. FISHER'S CUCUMBER SHRIMP SOUP

The cucumber soup of my dreams is one I have swiped from my good friend M.F.K. Fisher. This pottage is a fireless bit of Slavic cookery that Mary Frances claims is "no flimflam." She mixes hers in a pitcher, which takes up less space in the refrigerator than a tureen, and chills it overnight, stirring only when she remembers. I am more compulsive and make it in the morning, so I can stir it every couple of hours.

The secret of this soup is *ease*. The original Fisher formula calls for a can of peeled shrimp, but I am too far gone a gastronome to concur. In my version, the shrimp are freshly poached, then peeled. We do agree on the seasoning, however: it must be yellow (not Dijon) mustard—the mild kind that slathers a stadium hot dog.

1 cup water
½ cup dry white wine
2 parsley sprigs
2 lemon slices
½ pound raw shrimp
1 large cucumber (about 8 inches long), peeled, seeded, chopped
2 tablespoons prepared mustard
1 quart buttermilk
Salt and ground white pepper

1. Combine the water and wine in a heavy (non-aluminum) 10-inch saucepan. Add the parsley sprigs and lemon slices. Heat to boiling; boil until reduced to ½ cup, about 8 minutes. Add the shrimp and cook until pink, about 1½ minutes per side. Remove the shrimp and allow to cool. Strain and cool the cooking liquid.

2. Peel and devein the shrimp. Cut each in half lengthwise, and then cut into ½-inch pieces. Combine the shrimp with the cucumber in a large bowl. Stir in the reserved cooking liquid and the mustard. Mix well; stir in the buttermilk. Cover and chill at least 6 hours. Add salt and white pepper to taste before serving.

Serves 6 to 8.

CUCUMBER AND BAY SCALLOP SLAW

Columbus planted and harvested the first cucumbers sown in the New World, on Hispaniola in 1494. He must have had a remarkably green thumb for it was a bumper crop, and cucumber cultivation spread rapidly to North America.

Hernando de Soto noted cucumber vines growing in profusion in Florida a scant fifty years later, and Jacques Cartier logged row upon row of cucumber plants tended by Iroquois tribesmen in Montreal in 1545.

Although universal in appeal, in the matter of size however, New and Old World cucumber fanciers decidedly do not agree. Americans prefer their cucumbers on the plump and stubby side, never longer than seven or eight inches. Continental cucumbers are usually grown twice that size. When you are cucumber shopping for this delicate salad, however, pass by any that are longer than a man's hand.

2 cups water (see Note)
¾ cup dry white wine
½ lemon
2 parsley sprigs
4 whole peppercorns
1¼ pounds bay scallops
2 cucumbers, each 6 to 7 inches long
3 tablespoons tarragon vinegar
½ teaspoon salt
⅛ teaspoon sugar
½ red bell pepper, seeded, chopped
2 teaspoons finely slivered fresh ginger root
2 teaspoons finely chopped chives or scallion tops
½ teaspoon crushed dried hot red peppers
3 tablespoons lemon juice
1 tablespoon soy sauce
1½ tablespoons olive oil
Salt and freshly ground black pepper
1 tablespoon chopped fresh parsley
Lettuce leaves

1. Combine the water, wine, lemon half, parsley sprigs, and peppercorns in a medium (non-aluminum) saucepan. Heat to boiling; reduce the heat. Simmer 10 minutes. Add the scallops; cook, uncovered, until just tender, 4 or 5 minutes. (Test by cutting a scallop open with a knife.) Drain, and cool the scallops; chill 1 hour.

2. Meanwhile, peel the cucumbers. Cut them in half lengthwise and scoop out the seeds with a spoon. Cut each piece across into thin slices. Place the cucumbers in a bowl with 2 tablespoons of the vinegar, the salt, and the sugar. Let stand 30 minutes. Drain, and chill for 30 minutes.

3. Drain the cucumbers once more if necessary. Combine them with the scallops in a medium bowl. Add the bell pepper, ginger root, chives, and crushed peppers. Toss.

4. Combine the lemon juice, soy sauce, remaining 1 tablespoon vinegar, and olive oil in a small bowl. Pour this dressing over the cucumber-scallop mixture. Toss well and add salt and pepper to taste. Transfer to a serving dish and sprinkle with the chopped parsley. Serve on lettuce leaves.

Serves 4.

Note: 2¼ cups Fish Stock (see page 410) may be substituted for the first five ingredients.

COOL AND CREAMY CUCUMBER SALAD

What I deem the classic method for preparing cold cucumbers is a residual of my long tenure at The Store in Amagansett, an establishment that produced at least a thousand gallons of dill-flecked cucumber salad, to the local gentry's delight, every summer for a decade.

The following devise is the salad that helped make The Store memorable.

2 cucumbers, each about 7 inches long
½ teaspoon salt
2½ tablespoons cider vinegar
1 teaspoon sugar
1 cup sour cream
1 small shallot, minced
½ teaspoon celery seed
1 tablespoon chopped chives
¼ cup chopped fresh dill
Salt and freshly ground black pepper

1. Peel the cucumbers. Cut into thin slices and place them in a large bowl. Sprinkle the cucumber with ½ teaspoon salt, ½ tablespoon vinegar, and ¼ teaspoon sugar. Gently toss. Let stand 30 minutes. Drain, gently pressing out liquid with the back of a spoon. Pat dry with paper towels.

2. Meanwhile, place the sour cream in a medium bowl and whisk until light. Whisk in the shallot, the remaining 2 tablespoons vinegar, the remaining ¾ teaspoon sugar, the celery seed, chives, and salt to taste.

3. Layer one third of the cucumber slices in the bottom of a small shallow serving dish. Spoon one third of the sour cream mixture over the top. Sprinkle with one third of the dill. Continue to layer until all ingredients are used up. Sprinkle the top with pepper to taste. Chill well.

Serves 4.

COOL CUCUMBER SPAGHETTI

The Store cucumbers were prepared two ways: with and without sour cream. This calorie-reduced version has been amended, somewhat, by time and my inability to leave a recipe alone. Instead of being sliced, the green cucumber flesh is finely shredded (with a steel zester) into thin pasta-like strands.

4 cucumbers, each about 7-inches long
⅓ cup plus 1 tablespoon red wine vinegar
½ teaspoon salt
2 teaspoons sugar
1 large shallot, minced
2 tablespoons water
¼ teaspoon freshly ground black pepper
3 tablespoons chopped fresh dill

1. Peel the cucumbers, then scrape the flesh with a vegetable zester lengthwise to form long spaghetti-like strands. Place the strands in a colander; sprinkle them with 1 tablespoon vinegar, the salt, and ½ teaspoon sugar. Let stand 30 minutes.

2. Shake the colander to remove any excess liquid. Do not squeeze the cucumber strands. Transfer them to a bowl and add the shallot.

3. Combine the remaining ⅓ cup vinegar, 1½ teaspoons sugar, and the water. Pour the dressing over the cucumbers; add the pepper and 2 tablespoons dill. Toss lightly with two forks. Refrigerate, covered, 30 minutes. Sprinkle with the remaining 1 tablespoon dill.

Serves 4.

JACK CARNEY'S OUT-OF-THIS-WORLD OUTHOUSE PICKLES

The greatest use for a cucumber is indubitably the pickle, and I have tried lots of impeccable pickle recipes in my time. But this one is special: a bread-and-butter chip with a spicy flavor and, even more important, quintessential crunch.

The prescription is a gift from Jack Carney, Missouri's leading citizen (aside from the governor, of course). Definitely the state's loudest voice, Jack is a talk-show host on a three-hour daily marathon on station KMOX in St. Louis.

Carney conservatively describes his pickles as "simply the greatest in the world." So who am I to disagree? Their firm, inimitable bite is dependent upon a mineral that was once a necessity for every privy user: hydrated lime. Urbanites need not despair, however. This product is sold in hardware stores everywhere—even in Greenwich Village.

3½ pounds small pickling (kirby) cucumbers
1 cup hydrated lime
1 gallon water
1 quart cider vinegar (5% acid content)
4 cups sugar
½ teaspoon salt
½ teaspoon celery seed
½ teaspoon pickling spices
½ teaspoon whole cloves
1 3-inch stick cinnamon

1. Cut the cucumbers, unpeeled, crosswise into ¼-inch-thick slices. Place them in a large crock or heavy enameled pot.

2. Combine the lime and water and pour it over the cucumber slices. Let stand, covered, 24 hours.

3. Rinse the cucumbers at least 8 times under cold running water. Return the cucumber slices to a clean pot. Cover with cold water; let stand, uncovered, 3 hours. Drain. Place the cucumbers in a large pot.

4. Combine the vinegar, sugar, and salt in a large saucepan. Tie the celery seed, spices, cloves, and cinnamon stick in a cheesecloth bag and add this to the pan. Heat to boiling; pour over the cucumbers. Cool, then cover and let stand 24 hours.

5. The next day, drain the cucumbers, transferring the liquid to a saucepan. Heat the liquid to boiling; reduce the heat. Gently simmer (do not boil), uncovered, 35 minutes. Remove the bag of spices. Place the pickles with the juices in sterilized jars while hot. Seal.

Makes about 6 pints.

PACHADI

(Indian Cucumber Salad)

The Indian salad known as *pachadi* is said to soothe the enflamed tongue whenever the curry seasoners run amok along the Ganges.

Pachadi is a mix of chopped vegetables and cucumbers sluiced with vinegar and yogurt to taste. This dish is a happy adjunct to a quickly organized summer picnic (or a beach cookout) when cold meat or an unadorned grilled fish is to be the meal's mainstay.

2 cucumbers, each about 7 inches long
1 tablespoon white wine vinegar
1 teaspoon salt
⅛ teaspoon sugar
1 small red onion, halved, thinly sliced
1 cup sliced red radishes (8 to 10 large radishes)
1 ripe tomato, seeded, chopped
2 small green chile peppers, seeded, minced (see Guacamole headnote, page 37)
½ cup black Greek olives, pitted, sliced
¾ cup unflavored yogurt
2 tablespoons sour cream
Salt and freshly ground black pepper
2 tablespoons chopped fresh mint

1. Peel the cucumbers. Cut each cucumber into quarters lengthwise and scoop out the seeds with a spoon. Cut each piece across into thin slices. Place the slices in a large bowl and sprinkle with the vinegar, salt, and sugar. Toss well. Let stand 30 minutes. Drain, gently pressing out the liquid with the back of a spoon.

2. Place the cucumber slices in a medium bowl. Add the onion, radishes, tomato, chile peppers, and olives. Toss. Stir in the yogurt and sour cream. (Add more sour cream if needed to bind the mixture.) Add salt and pepper to taste just before serving; sprinkle with the mint.

Serves 6.

CUCUMBER RIGADON

This is a Burgundian devise called a *rigadon*, in this instance tempered with sweet cream cheese and flavored with a remarkable fresh green garden herb known as burnet. Why burnet? Because it is a leaf that curiously makes every cucumber taste more cucumbery!

Burnet is easy to grow from seed in a window box or garden. But if you have none at hand, simply skip it.

2 cucumbers, each about 7 inches long
1 tablespoon red wine vinegar
1 teaspoon salt
⅛ teaspoon sugar
1 tablespoon unsalted butter
2 shallots, minced
1 cup milk
3 ounces cream cheese, cubed
4 eggs
1½ tablespoons all-purpose flour
½ cup heavy or whipping cream
½ teaspoon minced fresh burnet (optional)
½ teaspoon chopped fresh dill
Freshly ground black pepper

1. Peel the cucumbers. Cut each in half lengthwise and scoop out the seeds with a spoon. Roughly grate the cucumbers and place them in a large bowl. Sprinkle with the vinegar, salt, and sugar. Let stand 30 minutes.

2. Meanwhile, preheat the oven to 350°F. Melt the butter in a medium saucepan over medium-low heat. Add the shallots and cook until soft but not browned, about 5 minutes. Add the milk and cream cheese; stir until the cheese melts. Remove from the heat.

3. Beat 1 egg with the flour in a large bowl until smooth. Beat in the remaining eggs, heavy cream, milk-cream cheese mixture, burnet, and dill. Strain the cucumbers, pressing out all liquid with your hands. Add them to the egg mixture. Add pepper to taste.

4. Pour the mixture into a 1- to 1½-quart shallow soufflé dish. Place the dish in a roasting pan. Add enough boiling water to the pan to reach halfway up the sides of the dish. Place the pan in the oven and cook until the custard is set, about 1 hour. Let stand 10 minutes before serving.

Serves 6.

BAKED POTATO–STUFFED CUCUMBERS

A variation on the *Backgurcken* described on page 153-154.

2 cucumbers (each about 7 inches long), peeled, halved lengthwise, seeded
2 teaspoons red wine vinegar
1½ cups cold mashed cooked potatoes
1 small egg, beaten
½ teaspoon salt
¼ teaspoon freshly ground black pepper
¼ teaspoon freshly grated nutmeg
1 rounded tablespoon toasted pine nuts, finely chopped
2 tablespoons chopped fresh parsley
1 tablespoon unsalted butter
2 teaspoons minced fresh chives or scallion tops

1. Preheat the oven to 350°F. Cook the cucumber halves in boiling salted water to which you have added the vinegar, 3 minutes. Drain. Place them, hollow side down, on paper towels.

2. Place the potatoes in a large bowl. Add the egg, salt, pepper, nutmeg, pine nuts, and parsley. Mix thoroughly. Fill the cucumber halves with the potato mixture.

3. Rub a shallow baking dish with 1 teaspoon of the butter. Place the cucumbers in the dish. Press the chives into the tops and dot the cucumbers with the remaining butter. Bake 45 minutes.

Serves 4.

BAKED CUCUMBERS IN BASIL CREAM

The following recipe (of French origin) is a minor vegetable classic in my opinion. Cucumbers are baked first, then tossed in a delicate upholstery of reduced cream and fresh green basil. Nothing else!

4 cucumbers, each about 7 inches long
1½ tablespoons red wine vinegar
1 teaspoon salt
¼ teaspoon sugar
2 tablespoons unsalted butter, melted
1 whole scallion, bulb and green top, finely chopped
¼ teaspoon freshly ground black pepper
1 cup heavy or whipping cream
½ cup plus 2 teaspoons chopped fresh basil
Salt and freshly ground black pepper

1. Peel the cucumbers. Cut each in half lengthwise. Scoop out the seeds with a spoon. Cut the cucumbers into ¼-inch-thick strips lengthwise; cut the strips into 2-inch pieces. Place the cucumber strips in a large bowl; sprinkle them with the vinegar, salt, and sugar. Toss; let stand at least 30 minutes. Drain and pat dry on paper towels.

2. Preheat the oven to 375°F. Place the cucumber strips in a shallow baking dish. Add the melted butter, scallion, and pepper. Toss well. Bake, stirring occasionally, until just tender, about 45 minutes. (Cucumbers will color slightly but not burn. Reduce the heat to 350°F if they start to turn brown.)

3. Meanwhile, heat the cream to boiling in a small saucepan. Stir in ½ cup of the basil; reduce the heat. Simmer until the cream has reduced to half, about 10 minutes.

4. Pour the cream sauce over the baked cucumbers. Add salt and pepper to taste and sprinkle with the remaining basil.

Serves 4.

BASQUE CUCUMBERS

This recipe is a most unusual pairing of the prime ingredients of the Basque locale: oranges, onions, bacon, and *pepinos, certiamente.*

3 cucumbers, each about 7 inches long
3 tablespoons red wine vinegar
½ teaspoon salt
½ plus ⅛ teaspoon sugar
3 strips bacon
1 medium red onion, chopped
Juice of 1 small orange or tangerine
Salt and freshly ground black pepper
1 small orange or tangerine, peeled, seeded, cut into thin slices

1. Peel the cucumbers. Cut each cucumber in half crosswise. Scoop the seeds from each piece with a thin knife or a grapefruit spoon. Cut each hollowed-out cucumber into ¼-inch-thick rounds. Place the cucumber slices in a large bowl and sprinkle with 1 tablespoon of the vinegar, the salt, and ⅛ teaspoon of the sugar. Let stand 30 minutes. Drain; pat dry on paper towels.

2. Sauté the bacon in large heavy skillet until crisp. Remove the bacon and drain it on paper towels.

3. Pour off all but 2 tablespoons of the bacon drippings. Sauté the cucumber slices in the pan over medium heat until they just begin to wilt, 3 or 4 minutes. Add the onion; sprinkle with the remaining 2 tablespoons vinegar, ½ teaspoon sugar, and the orange juice. Continue to cook, tossing gently, until all liquid has evaporated. Add salt and pepper to taste. Remove from the heat and stir in the orange slices.

Serves 4.

BROILED TILEFISH WITH GREEN-AND-GOLD SAUCE

The English word for cucumber at one time was *cowcumber.* As the early British naturalist Nicholas Culpepper informs us: "The green tumors grow fullest and fairest when planted upon fields that were once fields of pasturage, enriched by a dominion of cowes dropyngs."

One of the more felicitous sauces in my kitchen repertoire is an English import known as "Green and Gold." I whip up a batch as either upholstery or underpinning for plain-Jane dinners where the entrée is either poached or broiled. Being a British devise, the sauce did come with a culinary caveat. "Always serve a dab over a fillet of fish and under a slice of meat." You take it from there.

4 filets of tile fish (about ½ pound each), skinned
1½ tablespoons olive oil
1 teaspoon red wine vinegar
1 tablespoon finely minced chives
1 teaspoon finely grated lemon peel
1 teaspoon salt
½ teaspoon freshly ground black pepper
1 tablespoon unsalted butter
1 large shallot, minced
1 cucumber (about 7 inches long), peeled, seeded, finely chopped
1 sprig fresh thyme, finely chopped, or a pinch of dried
2 teaspoons lemon juice
⅓ cup sour cream
Salt and freshly ground black pepper

1. Pat the fish dry with paper towels. Combine the oil, vinegar, chives, lemon peel, salt and pepper in a bowl. Spread this mixture over both sides of the fish filets. Let stand at least 30 minutes. (Or longer, covered, in the refrigerator.) Place the fish filets on a broiler tray.

2. Melt the butter in a small saucepan over medium heat. Sauté the shallot until golden.

3. While the shallot is cooking, put the filets under the broiler, to broil about 4 minutes per side.

4. When the shallot is cooked, reduce the heat to medium-low and add the cucumber and thyme. Cook, stirring constantly, 2 minutes. Add the lemon juice and sour cream. Cook over low heat 5 minutes. Do not allow to boil. Add salt and pepper to taste and spoon over the broiled fish.

Serves 4.

BAKED CHICKEN-AND-HAM-CRAMMED CUCUMBERS

If one must lay blame for the cucumber blackout from Rome to Renaissance, put the debit to the account of Attila the Hun. That wild fellow seems to have had extremely limited tastebuds and even more abbreviated sensibilities. But in all fairness one must give his thundering horde a mite of gratitude since one way or another a cucumber seed must have made its way back to the fatherland in time. How else can one explain the next German-inspired prescription: *Backgurcken* (baked cucumbers).

2 cucumbers, each about 7 inches long
Juice of ½ lemon
1 teaspoon salt
1 tablespoon plus 2 teaspoons unsalted butter
1 shallot, minced
1 ¼ cups finely chopped cooked chicken
3 tablespoons finely chopped Black Forest ham or prosciutto
1 tablespoon finely chopped toasted almonds
2 tablespoons fine fresh bread crumbs
¼ teaspoon chopped fresh thyme, or ⅛ teaspoon dried
¼ teaspoon freshly ground black pepper
¾ cup chicken broth, approximately (see page 414)
¼ cup heavy or whipping cream
2 teaspoons all-purpose flour
1 teaspoon Madeira
Salt and freshly ground black pepper
Chopped fresh parsley

1. Peel the cucumbers. Cut each cucumber in half lengthwise and scoop out the seeds with a spoon. Sprinkle the scooped-out cucumbers with the lemon juice and ½ teaspoon of the salt. Place them, hollow sides down, on paper towels. Let stand 30 minutes.

2. Preheat the oven to 350°F. Melt 1 tablespoon of the butter in a small skillet over medium-low heat. Add the shallot; cook until soft but not browned, about 5 minutes.

3. Transfer the shallot with its butter to a medium bowl. Add the chicken, Black Forest ham, almonds, bread crumbs, thyme, remaining ½ teaspoon salt, and the pepper. Mix thoroughly. Add 3 tablespoons of the broth and 3 tablespoons of the cream to moisten. Mix thoroughly. Add more broth if needed for the mixture to hold together.

4. Brush the salt off the cucumber halves and fill them with the meat mixture. Place the stuffed cucumber halves in a Dutch oven just large enough to hold them snugly. Add enough chicken stock to reach halfway up the sides of the cucumbers. Heat the liquid around the cucumbers to boiling and then transfer the pot, uncovered, to the oven and bake until just tender, about 45 minutes.

5. Remove the pot from the oven. Carefully transfer the cucumbers to a shallow baking dish and keep them warm in a low oven. Strain the cooking juices.

6. Melt the 2 teaspoons of butter in a small saucepan over medium-low heat. Stir in the flour. Cook, stirring constantly, 2 minutes. Whisk in the cooking juices. Heat to boiling; reduce the heat. Cook until slightly thickened. Stir in the remaining 1 tablespoon cream and the Madeira. Add salt and pepper to taste. Spoon the sauce over the cucumbers and sprinkle with parsley.

Serves 2 to 4.

EGGPLANT

The One Perfect Health Food

I painted a picture of a purple eggplant long before I ever contemplated cooking one! But then, the artist's *palette* preceded the trencherman's *palate* as the focus of my existence.

As a child I drew constantly. Any scrap of paper I could unearth around the house became a vehicle for my compulsive drawing—which, I realize now, usually consisted of bad line-for-line copies of the baroque Nell Brinkley illustrations that appeared in the Hearst newspaper our family doted upon in the twenties and thirties.

I suspect my parents considered my interest in art questionable to say the least. My father, I knew, held the profession of painter only a small step above the rank of gigolo, or even worse. My mother was somewhat more sanguine in the matter. After realizing that a ban on my artistic animus was impossible to monitor, she eventually framed the best results for her living room, claiming that the talent was probably inherited from her side of the family, since her father was a designer in the fur trade, after all.

I drew night and day, no matter what inhibitory sanctions were placed upon me, for pencil and brush were my only release from a world of painful shyness and introspection.

By the time I was in my last year of grade school, my mother was convinced that I "had the stuff" to study art. In the late 1930s, however, art classes (in high school at least) were joyless exercises. Rather than releasing creative energies, most courses seemed to stunt or downright diminish them. Outfitting the neophyte student for the narrow job market were classes in perspective and mechanical drawing, architectural rendering and block lettering—all studies that required the use of a compass, triangle, and French curve, tools unsuited to the inept hands of a free spirit like me.

When I was fifteen I was summoned to the office of the principal, a command that filled me with trepidation.

"Greene," he said. Never looking up to acknowledge me, he stared hard at my record card as he spoke. "Several of your teachers feel you show a true aptitude for the graphic arts. Now, there is a highly regarded academy [the august Academy of Fine Arts] in New York City that holds a yearly competition for scholarship students. And you. . . ." He coughed discreetly. "Your name has been selected to enter as this school's representative. Of course, you are not obliged to do this, you understand, but it reflects significant honor on this school in passing. . . ." I know he talked on, but I had stopped listening several sentences before. Frankly, I could not believe it. That I had been selected—picked out—over a host of other highly proficient (and, I felt, vastly more talented) classmates was the first real indication of public endorsement I had ever experienced. I liked the emotion enormously. I still do!

The competition for an "actual" art scholarship was the most vivid experience of my young life. What I remember most of this terrible, wonderful ordeal was not the gray stone mansion where it took place, nor the trial by charcoal that came later—but rather the utterly adult lack of condescension to the dozen or so students who had come to compete. I felt more secure on that day than I ever had in the past—even when I discovered I would be faced with the paralyzing prospect of a life-study model who would pose in the nude!

I cannot truly remember the quality of the nude studies I sketched. But the still life—a brace of shiny purple eggplant beside a bowl of green and red peppers, papery onions, and pale gold-flecked zucchini squash—I will never forget as long as I live, for it was a highly impressionistic rendering and unlike any high-school performance I had given prior to that day.

More to the point, I discovered as our paintings were being collected that the entire contents of the composition had been acquired with a dual purpose in mind. Those vegetables were to be the basis of the proctor's dinner later that evening. Though I had never heard of the dish, we competitors had literally painted a ratatouille on the hoof!

I was accepted for the scholarship and studied at the Academy for the next two years, until I went away to college. The people I met there were totally unlike any I had ever known. The ideas exchanged openly about art, politics, dance, theater—and yes, even food—altered my perceptions.

Regretfully I must admit I no longer draw, unless I happen to be in some utterly foreign place. Photography being an alien and terrifying form of expression, I generally sketch the local color instead. At home, my hand is too busy stirring some pot in the kitchen or tapping at my typewriter to miss the vagrant brush or pen. If that seems sad, take my word that it is not, for when I discovered that I could speak, write, and successfully articulate my feelings, I no longer felt the need!

Vegetable Roots

On canvas or in a casserole, the eggplant today is one of the world's most cherished ingredients. But because its appearance was startling to say the least, primitive man eschewed eggplant as an edible entirely.

The Chinese first speculated upon its

possibility as table fare in the third century A.D. It was noted, erroneously, as "stalk of the lotus" in *Erhya*, a dictionary of ancient Chinese terms compiled by the philosopher, Kuo P'u, who formally dubbed it *ch'ieh*—which is the same name Chinese cooks use today, seventeen centuries after the fact.

It took another 300 years for anyone to actually taste an eggplant at the end of his chopstick, however. Chinese diners regarded this victual with the same sense of trepidation that anyone (other than a deep-dyed gastronome) accords rattlesnake or blowfish; the vegetable possessed a reputation for high toxicity in unskilled hands. In the sixth century, in fact, the name *ch'ieh* was officially amended to *ch'ieh-pzu*, which means "medicine" or "poison."

It's not such a stretch of the imagination. Eggplant formally belongs to the Solanaceae, or nightshade, family, which, though it has connections to tomato, potato, and pimiento, also has stronger ties to belladonna, horse nettle, and tobacco—none exactly a source of life-giving nourishment!

The first eggplant grown in China was small, pendant-shaped, and very delicate—presenting a fragile, pearly-hued appearance that many associated with bird's eggs.

Unfortunately, the earliest Occidental to sample one went mad after the first bite. This unlucky diner was an Indian traveler so smitten with the eggplant's appearance that he ate it raw and promptly had a fit. Or more probably a case of acute gastritis.

Sorry for him, but worse luck for the eggplant, as the calamity added yet another blemish to an already spotted reputation. Long, long after the vegetable's migration to the Levant (where it grew larger) and the western Mediterranean (where it developed a deep lustrous color), eggplant was still known as *mala insana*, which means "a bad egg" or "a mad apple," depending upon the latitude of one's Latin! And to this very day the Italian name *melanzana* is a direct descendant of that original slur.

In the late seventeenth century, when Linnaeus, the Swedish naturalist (and codifier of everything that grows in and out of a garden) listed eggplant in his voluminous dossier, he compounded the injury. Designating the vegetable as "a fruited edible" he still called it *Solanum insanum*. But Scandinavian good sense and his own strict conscience must have chafed at the cognomen. Eggplant by that late date was fairly common and exhibited no evidence whatsoever of turning a diner dotty, so Linnaeus renamed it. Compromising (and fracturing the meaning somewhat), he tagged the plant *Solanum melongens*, which means "soothing mad fruit"!

A staple the world was obviously ready for.

What to Look For

Eggplant is one vegetable never out of season, for it seems to bloom anywhere the sun shines and is virtually always available at greengrocers'. Summer, however, brings my favorite crop to the shelf: the small, early variety not much larger than Seckel pears. Equally sweet too!

These mauve-skinned miniatures—sometimes called Italian or Oriental eggplant, since they are inevitably found in those ethnic markets—have many stovetop virtues aside from their blushing hue. Fewer seeds keep them from turning bitter in a skillet for one thing, and thin skins sharply reduce their cooking time for another. No matter what size eggplant you choose, however, make certain to select only spherically shaped globes with firm, taut exteriors and a uniform glossy color. My first cooking teacher (after my grandmother) was the redoubtable Dione Lucas, who claimed somewhat airily that over-the-hill eggplant betrayed its age precisely in the same manner as over-the-hill debutantes: slack skin and slightly puckered posteriors!

It is a good idea for a consumer to press any eggplant of questionable vintage with a judicious thumb. If the slight pressure causes a minor blemish, pass that debutante by, for it obviously sat on the vine too long and will be discolored below the surface. Prime eggplant has a certain weight: a globe should feel substantial to the palm. Lightweight eggplant invariably indicates pulpy or pitted flesh. Likewise, skip an eggplant with a scarred or bruised surface. That is a sure sign of decay in the garden or out. A green cap and stem, if it is truly green, is an emblem of freshness.

In the 1980s, eggplant seems to be enjoying a new vogue among vegetable buyers who choose it for its designer color rather than its flavor. A new summer garden strain, snowy in appearance, is being marketed as "Easter Eggplant," and another pale golden hybrid is on the vine ready to climb, even as we sauté.

No matter what hue eggplant you elect, know that it is a perfect food for dieters: a half cup tabbed at a mere 25 calories. And while relatively low in vitamins, eggplant is extremely mineral-rich and heavy with the amino acids that control essential proteins in the body. Every slice of cooked eggplant affords a diner with megadoses of potassium, phosphorus, calcium, and magnesium.

Preparation

Even avid eggplant growers (like me) are somewhat ambivalent about its kitchen preparation, however. For instance, some cooks never peel the skin; others always do. I play it by ear. If the vegetable is small and appears to be tender (fairly thin-skinned), I skip the amenity entirely. But if the eggplant is large and likely to be fibrous, I zap it with my rotary blade.

Salting eggplant is another matter of mild dissent. I inevitably salt this vegetable prior to cooking. Not only does salt extract the bitterness inherent in most eggplant, I have discovered after myriad bouts of eggplant cookery that a well-salted (drained and dried) slice will absorb fully a third less oil or butter in a skillet than a similar unsalted portion. The result? A healthier and eminently more digestible dish; and somewhat less costly in the final analysis as well. A prudent salting also rids eggplant of its excessive moisture.

My method is routine. I sprinkle coarse salt uniformly on all cut slices and then place them in a colander to drain for at least 30 minutes. Later, I pat the slices free of excessive salt between several layers of paper towels.

Other than salting, another way to avoid bitterness in an eggplant dish is to blanch it first. Boiling the raw vegetable slightly (one minute maximum) flushes away any excessive acidity.

MELITZANOSALATA

(Greek Eggplant Salad)

One eggplant endowment, a cool but tangy salad or first course from Greece, gives the vegetable an entirely unexpected flavor as it is roasted over an open flame first. The recipe came my way from a bright and wildly enthusiastic teacher of her Hellenic kitchen heritage, the estimable Athena Forogolu.

1 medium eggplant (about ¾ pound)
1 large tomato, peeled, seeded, chopped
1 green bell pepper, seeded, finely chopped
1 small onion, grated
1 large clove garlic, crushed
½ teaspoon salt
¼ teaspoon freshly ground black pepper
3 tablespoons red wine vinegar
¼ cup olive oil
Sliced black olives
Chopped fresh parsley

1. Roast the eggplant over a gas flame (or under a broiler) until the skin has blackened and is crisp. Cool.

2. Rub the skin off the eggplant with damp paper towels. Chop the eggplant pulp.

3. Place the eggplant in a bowl and add the tomato, pepper, onion, and garlic.

4. Combine the salt, pepper, vinegar, and oil in a small bowl. Pour this dressing over the vegetables. Toss well. Garnish with olive slices and parsley. Serve well chilled.

Serves 2 to 4.

EGGPLANT AND RED PEPPER POTHER

Delectable as it is, eggplant is habitually bypassed in a soup kettle, for it turns sallow as it cooks—but never when stirred up with a florid pair of tomatoes and a rubescent red pepper, thank goodness!

My next offering, a velvety chowder of British antecedents and pale rosy hue, is unaccountably known as a "pother." Unaccountable (to me) because Webster and friends define that noun as synonymous with "plague," "turmoil," and like emotional disturbances! Nothing could be further from the fact of this pacific brew. Obviously a pother of a different color!

1 large eggplant (about 1½ pounds), peeled, cubed
Salt
1 red bell pepper
1 hot red or green chile pepper (see Guacamole headnote, page 37)
3 tablespoons unsalted butter
1 teaspoon olive oil
1 medium onion, roughly chopped
2 large cloves garlic, chopped
1 medium potato, peeled, cubed
2 medium tomatoes, peeled, seeded, chopped
4 cups chicken broth (see page 414)
Salt and freshly ground black pepper

1. Place the eggplant cubes in a colander. Sprinkle with salt; let stand 30 minutes. Brush the eggplant with paper towels to remove the salt; pat dry.

2. Meanwhile, roast the bell and chile peppers over a gas flame until the skins blacken and are crisp (or place them under a broiler). Carefully wrap them in paper towels, place them in a plastic bag, and let them cool 5 minutes. Rub the skins off with paper towels. Seed and devein. Roughly chop.

3. Heat the butter with the oil in a large heavy saucepan over medium-low heat. Add the onion; cook 1 minute. Add the garlic; cook 3 minutes longer. Add the potato and eggplant, tossing well to coat with the onion mixture. Stir in the peppers and tomatoes; cook 10 minutes. Add the chicken broth. Heat to boiling; reduce the heat. Simmer, uncovered, 30 minutes.

4. Cool the soup for about 15 minutes and then blend it, in batches, in a blender or food processor until smooth. Be careful, as hot liquid will expand. Reheat slightly over medium-low heat before serving. Add salt and pepper to taste. Serve soup warm but not hot.

Serves 6 to 8.

FRIED EGGPLANT SALAD

This is one of the eggplant's finest recipes, and certainly its most egalitarian rendering: it all takes place in one skillet.

1 large, or 2 small, eggplant (about 1½ pounds)
Salt
½ cup olive oil, approximately
1 medium onion, halved, thinly sliced
1 large clove garlic, minced
Juice of 2 lemons
Salt and freshly ground black pepper
Chopped fresh parsley
Lemon wedges

1. Cut the stem from the eggplant and slice it in half lengthwise. Cut each half into ¼-inch-thick slices. Place the slices in a colander, sprinkle them with salt, and let stand 30 minutes. Brush the eggplant with paper towels to remove the salt; pat dry.

2. Heat 2 tablespoons of the oil in a large heavy skillet over medium heat until hot but not smoking. Add enough eggplant slices to cover the bottom. Sprinkle lightly with more oil, and sauté until golden brown on both sides. Drain on paper towels. Continue to sauté the eggplant slices, adding more oil as needed.

3. Pour off all but 2 teaspoons oil from the skillet. Add the onion; cook over medium-low heat 1 minute. Add the garlic; cook until lightly browned, about 5 minutes.

4. Place one fourth of the eggplant in the bottom of a deep, narrow serving bowl. Sprinkle with the juice of ½ lemon. Sprinkle with salt and pepper to taste. Top with one fourth of the onion mixture. Continue to layer, squeezing lemon juice over each successive layer of eggplant, until all ingredients are used up. End with the onion mixture. Chill well. Serve garnished with parsley and lemon wedges.

Serves 4 as an appetizer.

EGGPLANT AU GRATIN

The following dish is French in origin and like most vegetable offerings from France tastes both earthy and ethereal at the same time. No mean trick—whether the chief ingredient is an eggplant or an egg!

1 medium eggplant (about 1 pound), peeled, cut into 1-inch-thick strips about 2 inches long
6 tablespoons (¾ stick) unsalted butter
2 shallots, minced
½ pound mushrooms, sliced
Juice of ½ lemon
1 teaspoon olive oil
1½ tablespoons all-purpose flour
⅓ cup milk
½ cup heavy or whipping cream
¼ teaspoon freshly grated nutmeg
Dash of hot pepper sauce
1 egg, lightly beaten
1 teaspoon minced fresh chives
2 tablespoons minced fresh parsley
Salt and freshly ground black pepper
2 tablespoons fine fresh bread crumbs
1 tablespoon freshly grated Parmesan cheese

1. Cook the eggplant in boiling salted water until tender, 5 to 8 minutes. Drain well, pressing out all liquid with the back of a wooden spoon. Reserve.

2. Melt 2 tablespoons of the butter in a large heavy skillet over medium heat. Stir in the shallots; cook 1 minute. Add the mushrooms and cook, stirring constantly, until lightly browned, about 4 minutes. Sprinkle with lemon juice and continue to cook until all moisture has evaporated. Transfer to a large bowl.

3. Heat 1 tablespoon of the butter with the oil in the same skillet. Add the eggplant strips and sauté over high heat until lightly browned, about 5 minutes. Transfer to the bowl containing the mushroom mixture.

4. Preheat the oven to 375°F. Melt 1½ tablespoons of the butter in a medium saucepan over medium-low heat. Stir in the flour. Cook, stirring constantly, 2 minutes. Whisk in the milk and cream. Heat to boiling; reduce the heat. Cook until thick, about 3 minutes. Add the nutmeg and hot pepper sauce. Stir this into the mushroom-eggplant mixture. Add the egg, chives, parsley, and salt and pepper to taste. Transfer to a shallow baking dish.

5. Melt the remaining 1½ tablespoons butter in a small sauté pan over medium heat. Stir in the bread crumbs; cook until golden. Spoon the crumbs over the eggplant mixture and sprinkle with the cheese. Bake 15 minutes, then place under the broiler to lightly brown the top.

Serves 4.

EGGPLANT ROLLATINI

The following recipe is an Italian-American devise, the gift of a friend who refuses credit for her handiwork since she claims it changes every time she prepares it. Not my rendition . . . nor yours, either, I'll warrant!

1 large eggplant (about 1½ pounds)
Salt
2 eggs, lightly beaten
¾ cup fresh bread crumbs, approximately
4 tablespoons (½ stick) unsalted butter
¼ cup olive oil
1 medium onion, finely chopped
1 clove garlic, minced
½ pound mild Italian sausages, removed from casings, broken up
1½ cups Basic or Creamy Tomato Sauce (see pages 374 and 375)
⅓ pound mozzarella cheese, chopped
Freshly ground black pepper
3 tablespoons freshly grated Parmesan cheese

1. Cut off the stem, then peel the eggplant and cut it lengthwise into ¼-inch-thick slices. Place the slices in a colander, sprinkle with salt, and let stand 30 minutes. Brush the eggplant with paper towels to remove the salt; pat dry.

2. Place the beaten eggs in a shallow bowl. Place the bread crumbs in another shallow bowl.

3. Preheat the oven to 350°F. Melt 2 tablespoons of the butter in 2 tablespoons of the oil in a large heavy skillet over medium heat. Dip each eggplant slice into the beaten egg, then roll it in bread crumbs, and sauté the slices, a few at a time, until golden on both sides. Add more butter and oil as needed. Drain the eggplant on paper towels.

4. Discard the grease and wipe the skillet with paper towels. Heat 1 tablespoon of the butter in the skillet over medium-low heat. Add the onion; cook 1 minute. Stir in the garlic and sausage. Cook over medium heat, breaking up the lumps with a fork, until lightly browned.

5. Spoon about 2 teaspoons of the tomato sauce over each eggplant slice. Sprinkle with the mozzarella cheese and the sausage mixture. Roll each slice (the short way) and place them in a lightly buttered shallow baking dish. Spoon the remaining sauce over the top. Sprinkle with pepper to taste and the Parmesan cheese. Bake 30 minutes.

Serves 4.

MOUSSAKA SOUFFLE

Seven egg whites and a little imagination create a transubstantiation of the great Greek classic dish.

2 medium eggplants (about 2 pounds)
Salt
Olive oil
7½ tablespoons unsalted butter
⅓ cup freshly grated Parmesan cheese
2 large shallots, minced
1 large clove garlic, minced
1¼ cups finely chopped cooked lamb
¼ pound mushrooms, chopped
¼ teaspoon chopped fresh thyme, or ⅛ teaspoon dried
¼ teaspoon chopped fresh rosemary, or ⅛ teaspoon dried
½ teaspoon salt
¼ teaspoon freshly ground black pepper
5 tablespoons all-purpose flour
1½ cups milk, hot
½ cup heavy or whipping cream
¼ teaspoon freshly grated nutmeg
⅛ teaspoon cayenne pepper
6 egg yolks
¼ cup grated Jarlsberg or Gruyère cheese
7 egg whites
Creamy Tomato Sauce (see page 375)

1. Cut the stems from the eggplants and slice each in half lengthwise. Cut lengthwise slashes into the eggplant pulp, but do not pierce the skin. Place the eggplant in a colander skin-side down. Sprinkle with salt; let stand 30 minutes. Brush the eggplant with paper towels to remove the salt; pat dry.

2. Preheat the oven to 350°F. Lightly brush the top of the eggplant halves with oil. Place the eggplant in a shallow baking dish or roasting pan. Add ½ inch of water to the pan. Bake until tender, about 30 minutes. Remove the eggplant and drain upside down on paper towels until cool enough to handle.

3. When cool, trim ¼ inch off the bottom end of each eggplant. Loosen the pulp from the skin with a spoon and pull the pulp away from the skin. Scrape the skins to remove all the pulp. Reserve the skins. Chop the pulp and divide it into two equal parts. Set aside.

4. Rub a 2-quart soufflé dish with ½ tablespoon of the butter. Sprinkle it with 1 tablespoon of the Parmesan cheese. Cut the eggplant skins in half lengthwise. Rub the outside of each piece with butter (about 1 tablespoon). Trim the skins to fit evenly along the sides of the dish. Place any leftover pieces, buttered side down, on the bottom. Press the skins into the side of the dish. Set aside in a cool place.

5. Raise the oven heat to 400°F. Melt 1½ tablespoons of the butter in a large heavy skillet over medium-low heat. Add the shallots; cook 1 minute. Add the garlic; cook 1 minute longer. Raise the heat to medium and stir in the lamb. Cook, stirring constantly, until the meat is heated through. Transfer to a medium bowl.

6. Heat 1 tablespoon of the butter with 1 teaspoon oil in the same skillet over high heat. Add the mushrooms; cook, stirring constantly, until golden. Add the mushrooms to the lamb mixture along with the thyme, rosemary, salt, pepper, and half the chopped eggplant. Mix thoroughly; set aside.

7. To make the base, melt the remaining 3½ tablespoons butter in a medium saucepan over medium-low heat. Stir in the flour. Cook, stirring constantly, 2 minutes. Whisk in the hot milk and the cream. Raise the heat slightly and cook, stirring constantly, until thick, about 3 minutes. Remove from the heat and add the nutmeg, cayenne pepper, and salt and pepper to taste. Stir ½ cup of the base into the eggplant-lamb mixture.

8. Beat the egg yolks, one at a time, into the remaining base. Return it to low heat and cook, stirring constantly, until very thick. Do not allow it to boil. Transfer to a medium-size bowl and cool slightly. Stir in the remaining chopped eggplant, ¼ cup of the Parmesan cheese, and the Jarlsberg cheese.

9. Beat the egg whites until stiff but not dry. Gently fold them into the base.

10. Spoon slightly more than half the eggplant-lamb mixture into the prepared soufflé dish. Spoon half the base over it, then sprinkle with the remaining eggplant-lamb mixture. Top with the remaining base and sprinkle with the remaining Parmesan cheese. Place in the oven and immediately turn down the heat to 375° F. Bake 55 minutes. Let stand a few minutes before serving. Cut into wedges and pass the Creamy Tomato Sauce on the side.

Serves 6.

GOLDEN EGGPLANT CROQUETTES

Eggplant is a vegetable of such protean possibilities that it is very often dubbed the one perfect health food! When I was younger (and so was the vegetarian movement), adherents of meatless meals routinely offered up some mashed or hashed version of eggplant masquerading as "not-for-real veal cutlet" or "mock filet mignon" on their menus. The curious thing about these culinary counterfeits is that, while never precisely on target in either texture or taste, the dishes were not half bad—basically because eggplant is so mutable. For further evidence, note these delicate golden croquettes.

1 medium eggplant (about ¾ to 1 pound), peeled, cubed
1 medium tomato, peeled, seeded, chopped
1 whole scallion, bulb and green top, finely chopped
1 clove garlic, minced
½ cup chopped fresh parsley
2 tablespoons chopped fresh basil, or 1 teaspoon dried
¾ teaspoon salt
⅛ teaspoon freshly ground black pepper
⅛ teaspoon freshly grated nutmeg
1 egg, lightly beaten
2 tablespoons freshly grated Parmesan cheese
½ teaspoon baking powder
½ cup fresh bread crumbs
Oil for frying

1. Cook the eggplant in boiling salted water until tender, 5 to 8 minutes. Drain well, pressing out all liquid with the back of a wooden spoon.

2. Transfer the eggplant to the container of a blender or food processor. Add the tomato and blend until smooth.

3. Transfer the puréed eggplant-tomato mixture to a medium-size bowl. Add the remaining ingredients, except the oil. Mix thoroughly.

4. Heat 2 inches of oil in a heavy skillet over medium-high heat. Form the eggplant mixture into croquettes, about 1 heaping tablespoon at a time, and drop into the hot oil. Cook until very well browned on both sides, 4 to 5 minutes. Drain on paper towels and keep warm while frying the remaining croquettes.

Serves 4.

SHAKLE-MESHI

(Baked Eggplant Boats)

In Middle Eastern countries, some form of eggplant is consumed at all the important meals that mark a man's life: the birth celebration, wedding, and funeral supper. One dish of Jordanian derivation seems highly appropriate for each of the foregoing transitional feeds, since the eggplant in question is trimmed to a boat shape before it is cooked. Actually it's one of the most delectable forms of "Bon Voyage" on record.

1 large eggplant (about 1½ pounds)
Salt
Olive oil
1 tablespoon unsalted butter
1 medium onion, finely chopped
1 clove garlic, minced
2 tablespoons chopped pine nuts
½ pound ground raw lamb
½ teaspoon ground allspice
⅛ teaspoon ground cinnamon
1 tablespoon minced fresh parsley plus additional chopped for garnish
Salt and freshly ground black pepper
1 can (14 ounces) plum tomatoes, drained, crushed

1. Cut the stem from the eggplant, then peel it. Cut the eggplant into four equal quarters lengthwise. Carefully cut a pocket in the top of each piece and gently push the pieces open so that they resemble small boats. Sprinkle with salt and place in a colander; let stand 30 minutes. Brush the eggplant with paper towels to remove the salt; pat dry.

2. Rub each eggplant quarter lightly with oil. Place them on a baking sheet; bake 30 minutes.

3. Preheat the oven to 350°F. Melt the butter in a large heavy skillet over medium-low heat. Add the onion; cook 1 minute. Add the garlic and pine nuts; cook until lightly browned, about 4 minutes. Add the lamb. Cook over medium heat, chopping the meat up with a fork, until the lamb is lightly browned all over. Add the allspice, cinnamon, 1 tablespoon minced parsley, and salt and pepper to taste. Carefully spoon this mixture into the baked eggplant boats.

4. Place the filled eggplant boats in a shallow baking dish and spoon some of the crushed tomatoes over each boat. Bake 45 minutes. Sprinkle with chopped parsley before serving.

Serves 4.

RATATOUILLE AND SHRIMP PIE

Ratatouille is a dish I never savored until I lived in France. For, while I had sampled various recipes on home ground, I never knew what all the shouting was about until I finally managed to sample a forkful in the landscape of its origin. Perhaps, as it is claimed, the hot Midi sun gently ripening each ingredient is responsible for the dish's preeminence, but the stirring arm of the Provençal cook deserves some kudos as well. I once saw a Mediterranean housewife nurse a baby, pluck a chicken, and polish her kitchen floor (with rags tied round her shoes), while she also managed to throw a handful of fresh herbs into her ratatouille pot as it simmered on the stove because the smell did not sufficiently "arouse" her practiced nose. Only when she and her baby had sneezed twice did she deem it ready for the night's dinner!

What follows is not her devise, but indulge in it anyhow. An unexpected version of ratatouille, it nestles between layers of buttery pastry—with fresh shrimp blushing bright pink in the heart of all that largess of eggplant and tomato.

Old-Fashioned Lard and Vinegar Crust (recipe follows)
1 large eggplant (about 1½ pounds)
Salt
½ cup olive oil, approximately
2 small zucchini (about 1 pound), trimmed, sliced
1 tablespoon unsalted butter
1 large onion, halved, thinly sliced
2 large cloves garlic, minced
1 large green pepper, seeded, thinly sliced
2 medium tomatoes, peeled, cut into ½-inch-thick wedges
½ teaspoon salt
¼ teaspoon freshly ground black pepper
⅓ pound shrimp, shelled, deveined, halved
¼ cup chopped fresh parsley
2 cups grated Fontina cheese
½ cup freshly grated Parmesan cheese
1 egg yolk
2 teaspoons water

1. Make the Old-Fashioned Lard and Vinegar Crust.

2. Trim the eggplant and halve it lengthwise. Cut into ¼-inch-thick slices, place them in a colander, and sprinkle with salt. Let stand 30 minutes. Brush the eggplant with paper towels to remove the salt; pat dry.

3. Heat 2 tablespoons of the oil in a heavy skillet over medium heat. Sauté the eggplant slices, a few pieces at a time, until golden on both sides. Add more oil as needed. Drain the slices on paper towels, then transfer to a bowl. In 2 teaspoons oil in the same pan, sauté the zucchini over high heat, tossing constantly, until golden. Reduce heat and cook until soft, about 8 minutes. Drain, and add to the eggplant in the bowl.

4. Wipe out the skillet and melt the butter over medium heat. Add the onion and cook 1 minute. Add the garlic and pepper. Cook, covered, 5 minutes. Stir in the tomatoes, salt, and pepper. Raise the heat and cook, uncovered, until all liquid has evaporated. Stir in the shrimp; cook 1 minute. Add the parsley and the eggplant and zucchini. Mix well.

5. Preheat the oven to 425°F. Roll out half the dough and line a lightly buttered 10-inch glass or ceramic quiche dish with it. Spoon one third of the ratatouille mixture over the bottom of the crust. Sprinkle with one third of each cheese. Continue to layer until all the ingredients are used up, ending with the Parmesan cheese. Roll out the remaining dough, place it over the top, and trim and flute the edges. Cut a slit in the top to allow the steam to escape. Beat the egg yolk with the water; brush over the crust. Bake 10 minutes; reduce the heat to 375°F. Bake 30 minutes longer. Let stand 10 minutes before serving.

Serves 6.

White eggplants were known as "Italian Mad Apples" for centuries. When the color deepened to a ripe purple, however, eggplant's bad name took on an even less virtuous hue. In England in the sixteenth century, eggplants were referred to as "Apples of Sodom." And most diners of any sensibility at all passed them by, no matter what prandial joy seemed inherent in any seedy slice.

Most diners . . . but not all! Enough solid trencherfolk of confirmed taste still indulged in the pleasures that this exotic berry had to offer to cause John Gerard, the pious naturalist who lived in the seventeenth century, to rail against its consumption publicly.

"I wish English men to content themselves with meats and sauce of our owne country," he declared, "than with fruit eaten with apparent perill; for doubtless these Raging Apples have a mischevious qualitie, the use whereof is utterly to be forsaken."

Old-Fashioned Lard and Vinegar Crust

2 cups plus 2 teaspoons all-purpose flour
2 teaspoons sugar
1 teaspoon salt
¾ cup lard
1 egg, beaten
1½ teaspoons red wine vinegar
2 tablespoons cold water

Sift 2 cups of the flour with the sugar and salt into a large bowl. Cut in the lard. Blend with a pastry blender until the mixture is the texture of coarse crumbs. Combine the egg, vinegar, and water in a small bowl. Using a fork, cut the liquid into the flour mixture to form a soft dough. (Do not overwork.) Sprinkle with the remaining 2 teaspoons flour. Chill for 1 hour before using.

Makes enough dough for a 9- to 10-inch double-crust pie.

MIDI-POCHE

(Eggplant Bake)

Hundreds of delectable eggplant dishes have crossed my lips since I have cooked for a living, but the few that remain vividly imprinted on my tastebuds are those I first tasted in the kitchens of Provence. In that area of France, eggplant is a fixed staple at most meals, largely because it grows with such profusion in those clement airs. Frugal housewives there pick the newly sprouted globes before they even have time to purple up. "Less seeds," they claim, "produce sweeter marriages with other vegetables in the pot!" Old wives' tales or no, these ladies know their eggplant to a fare-thee-well. And this is the eggplant's classic rendition. It is a simply wonderful offering—fried first and baked later in a blanket of spicy tomato sauce—served up at least once a week for dinner, supper, and sometimes next morning's breakfast as well.

When pressed for the name of this dish, one cook shrugged at the absurd notion of calling it anything at all. But a wise old chef I met in Nice, who also gave me the general details of its prescription, described it as a *midi-poche.* Literally translated it means a *noon pocket,* which, to my mind at least, implies the optimum time and means of transportation of its ingredients from garden to stove.

2 small eggplants (about ¾ pound), sliced
2 tablespoons lemon juice
1 tablespoon plus ½ teaspoon salt
4 tablespoons (½ stick) unsalted butter
2 tablespoons olive oil
1 shallot, minced
1 small onion, finely chopped
1 clove garlic, minced
3 cups chopped, seeded tomatoes (about 2 pounds)
Pinch of sugar
½ teaspoon chopped fresh thyme, or a pinch of dried
1 tablespoon minced fresh basil, or 1½ teaspoons dried
1 teaspoon crushed allspice
¼ cup all-purpose flour
1 cup cooked rice
¼ cup freshly grated Parmesan cheese

1. Preheat the oven to 350°F. Place the sliced eggplant in a colander. Sprinkle it with the lemon juice and 1 tablespoon salt; let stand 30 minutes.

2. Meanwhile, heat 2 tablespoons of the butter with 1 tablespoon of the oil in a medium saucepan over medium heat. Add the shallot and onion; cook 2 minutes. Stir in the garlic; cook 1 minute longer. Add the tomatoes; sprinkle with sugar. Add the thyme, basil, allspice, and ½ teaspoon salt. Cook, uncovered, over medium-low heat 20 minutes. Set aside.

3. Brush the eggplant with paper towels to remove the salt; pat dry. Dust the eggplant slices lightly with the flour. Heat the remaining butter and oil in a heavy skillet and sauté the eggplant over medium heat until golden on both sides. Drain on paper towels.

4. Spoon one fourth of the tomato sauce over the bottom of an ovenproof baking dish or casserole. Layer half the eggplant over the sauce. Sprinkle the eggplant with half the rice and then spoon half the remaining tomato sauce over the rice. Top with half the grated cheese. Repeat the layers of eggplant, rice, tomato sauce, and cheese. Bake until bubbly, about 15 to 20 minutes. Serve hot or at room temperature.

Serves 4.

LONI KUHN'S BAKED STUFFED EGGPLANT

The next eggplant recipe, while not precisely Italian, is a bequest from Italy-loving Loni Kuhn. A notable American cook and founder of Kuhn's Cook's Tours, one of the first (and best) cooking schools in San Francisco, Loni is one of those wonderful warmhearted, fun-loving, fast-talking women who cook as naturally as they breathe. I have watched her stir a pot, talk on the telephone, and compose a grocery list—and the dish was delectable despite (or because of) the extracurricular kitchen activity. Have one of Loni's best prescriptions. It works equally well for a one-track-minded chef, I promise you.

2 medium eggplants (about ¾ pound each)
¼ cup olive oil
1 large onion, finely chopped
2 large cloves garlic, minced
½ cup drained, seeded canned plum tomatoes
2 teaspoons chopped fresh oregano, or ½ teaspoon dried
¼ cup chopped fresh parsley
¼ teaspoon crushed dried hot red peppers
1½ tablespoons chopped anchovy filets
½ cup cooked rice
⅓ cup plus 1 tablespoon ricotta cheese
½ cup grated mozzarella cheese
2 tablespoons toasted pine nuts
Salt and freshly ground black pepper
2 tablespoons unsalted butter
½ cup fresh bread crumbs
2 tablespoons freshly grated Parmesan cheese

1. Cut the stems from the eggplants and slice each in half lengthwise. Scoop out the flesh with a spoon or grapefruit knife, leaving a shell about ¼ inch thick. Chop the scooped-out flesh.

2. Heat the oil in a large heavy skillet over medium heat. Add the onion; cook 1 minute. Stir in the garlic and chopped eggplant. Reduce the heat to medium-low. Cook the eggplant, tossing constantly, until tender, about 4 minutes. Add the tomatoes, oregano, and parsley. Cook 5 minutes longer. Remove from the heat; cool.

3. Preheat the oven to 350°F. Place the cooled eggplant mixture in a medium bowl. Add the hot peppers, anchovies, rice, both cheeses, and pine nuts. Mix thoroughly. Add salt and pepper to taste. Fill each eggplant half with this mixture.

4. Melt the butter in a small skillet over medium heat. Stir in the bread crumbs. Cook, stirring constantly, until golden, about 2 minutes. Spoon some crumbs over each stuffed eggplant and sprinkle with the Parmesan cheese. Place the eggplants in a shallow baking dish and add ½ inch of water to the dish. Bake 45 minutes.

Serves 4.

EGGPLANT AND SHRIMP SOUFFLE

1 medium eggplant (about ¾ pound)
4 tablespoons (½ stick) unsalted butter
1 tablespoon grated Jarlsberg or Swiss cheese
3 tablespoons all-purpose flour
1½ cups milk, hot
⅓ cup heavy or whipping cream
1 tablespoon cornstarch
1½ tablespoons water
½ teaspoon salt
¼ teaspoon freshly ground black pepper
Pinch of cayenne pepper
⅛ teaspoon freshly grated nutmeg
4 eggs, separated
⅓ cup freshly grated Parmesan cheese
⅓ cup grated Jarlsberg or Gruyère cheese
1 large shallot, minced
1 clove garlic, minced
¼ teaspoon chopped fresh thyme, or a pinch of dried
¼ pound raw shrimp, shelled, deveined, chopped
1½ tablespoons Dijon mustard
Basic or Creamy Tomato Sauce (see pages 374 and 375)

1. Preheat the oven to 400°F. Wrap the eggplant in aluminum foil; bake 40 minutes. Cool; then cut in half and scrape out the pulp. Reserve the pulp.

2. Grease a 1½- to 2-quart soufflé dish with ½ tablespoon of the butter; sprinkle with the Jarlsberg cheese. Chill.

3. Melt 2½ tablespoons of the butter in a saucepan. Stir in the flour; cook, stirring constantly, 2 minutes. Whisk in the milk and half the cream; cook 3 minutes. Combine the cornstarch with the water and stir it into the mixture. Cook until thick. Add the salt, pepper, cayenne pepper, and nutmeg. Remove from the heat. Add the egg yolks, one at a time, beating well after each addition. Stir in the cheeses. This is your soufflé base. Set aside.

4. Melt the remaining butter in a medium skillet. Add the shallot; cook 1 minute. Add the garlic, thyme, and reserved eggplant. Cook, covered, over medium heat, 3 minutes. Stir in the shrimp; cook, covered, 3 minutes longer. Stir in the remaining cream and the mustard. Spoon into the prepared soufflé dish.

5. Beat the egg whites until stiff but not dry, gently fold them into the soufflé base, and pour it over the eggplant. Bake until puffed up and golden, about 40 minutes. Serve with homemade tomato sauce.

Serves 4 to 6.

Greeks call eggplant *melitzano*, an offshoot of the mad Italian apple tree, obviously. In India, this fruit was originally known as *brinjal*; which in time became corrupted to *batinjan* by the Arabians, who acquired a taste for eggplant that was practically deleterious—they ate it at every meal. When the eggplant-loving Arabians invaded Spain, *batinjan* plants went along, to become *berenjena*. Germans call the stuff *Eirfrucht* (egg fruit), while the British stick with the French tag, *aubergine*.

FENNEL

Licorice Flavored and Crunchy, to Boot

As I have said before, my tiny maternal grandmother, Minna Cohn, was an absolutely towering figure at the stove. Yet if you ask me flat out what single dish I associate with her masterful talents, the answer will come as a surprise. For what I remember best (and most lovingly) of all her carefully orchestrated meals is the way they inevitably began: with raw fennel!

A platter of that greenish vegetable, simply trimmed and quartered, was unflaggingly sent to the table—a salt shaker its sole accompaniment—to assuage any vagrant hunger pains before the serious business of dining began.

I cannot know, a century after the fact, how a Polish country girl from a modest farm on the fringes of Warsaw acquired a taste for this exotic Mediterranean stalk. But it was decidedly one of her favored vegetables.

Being a licorice-lover from the time I learned to properly chew, the flavor of this spiky bulb (redolent of Black Crows, gum-drop tar-babies and all the other assorted whips, ropes, and braids that regularly dyed my tongue the color of a full-blooded chow's) became my favorite too.

"Fin-nook" is what my grandmother always called Florence fennel.

"How's your fin-nook today, Joe?" she would demand of the Italian vegetable peddler, whose horse-drawn wagon (literally a pyramid of gleaming produce), she thought nothing of rending asunder to find the single verdant head that gratified her innate sensibilities. "Show me what you got in the way of fin-nook."

"Nice *finocchio*," he would very gently correct her. "You'll like it missus. Very fresh picked."

Truthfully they both knew that my grandmother never liked what she was offered initially, but the interchange never varied. The object she ended up with always seemed to be one that was embedded in the very foundation of his stockpile and had to be extracted with much tugging, and a period of careful reassembly afterward.

Joe started his day before dawn, selecting vegetables and fruit at the old Hunts Point Market in Long Island City, and spent the next twelve or fourteen hours crisscrossing the borough of Queens selling them. Ringing a rope of bells stretched across the front of his horse-drawn wagon, to announce his presence on the tree-lined streets, he never left the bailiwick until his entire supply was depleted.

At my grandmother's stop, he invariably fed his horse (an ignoble gray mare who wore a faded but beribboned straw hat), because she could easily chomp down a bag of oats in the time it took my forebear to make her purchase.

Sometimes Joe would even unwrap his own lunch as well, while my grandmother prowled around the perimeters of his cart, searching for the perfect fennel stalk (rosiest tomato or crispest asparagus by turns) to meet her demanding specifications.

When she found it, she would turn suddenly generous, calling to my maiden Aunt Frances (in the kitchen) to bring out a glass of grape juice and water to help Joe digest his meal on the run.

She was, as you may gather, no easy customer—either in or out of the kitchen! But on later reflection it seems that big family holiday dinners brought out her true iron fist. If a monumental arrangement of the bespoke fennel plus radishes and black olives, prepared by my aunt, displeased her over-captious eye, she would demolish it with an impervious thumb, and then watch critically as it was reconstructed to her exacting standard. Though almost four decades have passed since she died, I can still recall watching her run to the kitchen between courses—while others at her festive table dined happily—to supervise the next awesome round of food.

Approaching the stove, she would don a voluminous apron, toss some meat on a platter, empty a skillet of its perfectly cooked *à point* vegetables, sprinkle a handful of chopped parsley over all, and then, like a proficient strip-tease artist, remove the apron, allowing it to fall to the floor with a shake of her hips as she made her way back into the dining room again, the precious dish held aloft.

I never taste a slice of fresh-cut fennel without the image of that wonderful (impossible) woman returning. I discovered some while back that there is no living up to her precedent, so I no longer try... merely pass the fennel in her honor, instead.

Vegetable Roots

Foeniculum vulgare is a stalk that has been scrunched and munched for millennia. Inhabitants of Mohenjo-Daro (4,000 years before the birth of Christ) believed that knowledge, in the form of fire, was transmitted by the gods to humanity in the lacy branches of fennel. Accordingly, the roots, seeds, and even delicate fronds of this plant were seared and roasted until they turned to fine ash, and the powder used to season most of the foods Mohenjo-Darians consumed. One cannot speculate on the degree of knowledge it brought them, but the flavor obviously tempered their lackluster rations a mite.

Another member of the slightly promiscuous parsley clan, the Umbelliferae (which numbers over 2700 variant species), fennel is somewhat distantly related to all herbs that store essential oils in their seeds—like anise, caraway, coriander, cumin, and dill—as well as being pertinently connected (in a gardening sense) to its carrot, parsnip, and celery-root cousins. But fennel, I must aver, has a taste and odor entirely its own that makes it popular.

What to Look For

To set the record straight, the name fennel covers both the herb and the vegetable. The former is a tall, highly aromatic, but absolutely uncontrollable wayside vagrant—not unlike its cousin-once-removed, Queen Anne's lace. This yellowish umbel flourishes in every warm-tempered quarter of the globe. I myself have tried to weed it from a Provençal garden (impossible) and years later watched with hypnotic fascination as it sprouted from (and eventually ripped apart) some very solid cable car tracks in San Francisco.

Garden fennel is another dish of greens entirely. Not dissimilar to the herb in either appearance or flavor, it is a smaller plant that must be tended carefully to make it "head."

Try to buy fennel with the stalks intact, because it will have more flavor. Test for freshness by lightly pressing the flesh with your thumb. Fresh bulbs will resist the pressure and be on the firm side; skip any that are pulpy or soft.

Fennel is practically a weightless food. A half-pound (raw) totals 56 calories and is high in potassium (784 milligrams) and super-high in vitamin A (7000 units). More importantly for weight-watchers, a large stalk contains at least 94 percent water.

Preparation

There are several accepted methods for cooking a fennel bulb, but only one proper way to prepare it, in my opinion. The optimum procedure is to wash, dry, and trim the stalks so that the bulb itself forms a neat package that may easily be sliced or quartered. (Save any green fronds or thin stalks to enrich a stockpot or garnish a bowl of vegetables at another time.) I usually pare the root end of fennel with a rotary peeler to remove the tough, fibrous portions before I carve it up. Any dry, discolored, or pulpy outer stalks should be removed as well.

Fennel may be blanched (or steamed) first, then sautéed, baked, or fried according to your taste. But to my mind, the classic method for its cookery (like celery) is braising. That is, cooking the slices, covered, on top of the range or in the oven, with a smallish amount of liquid until the fennel is tender and its surface can be easily pierced with a sharp knife or a fork.

FRAGRANT FENNEL SOUP

Because it has been around for so long, fennel is the subject of the best and most curious folklore. Its ingestion has, for instance, been variously credited with restoring sight to the blind, turning the barren fertile, and adding grit to fainthearted soldiers in battle.

A chew or two is also reputed to be a foolproof appetite depressant for dieters. Actually, consuming a little fennel always makes me want to eat more. Speaking of which, here is my recipe for a particularly aromatic and ambrosial brew. It makes me hungry just to write about it.

1 small to medium head fennel (about ½ pound)
2 tablespoons unsalted butter
2 tablespoons vegetable oil
1 large onion, sliced
1 clove garlic, crushed
1 medium potato, peeled, cubed
2 medium tomatoes, peeled, seeded, roughly chopped
Bouquet garni: 1 sprig parsley, 1 bay leaf, pinch of dried thyme, and pinch of dried savory tied in a cheesecloth bag
3 cups chicken broth (see page 414)
2 tablespoons Pernod
1 egg yolk
¼ cup heavy or whipping cream
Salt and ground white pepper

1. Trim the stems from the fennel and peel the bottom. Chop the fronds and reserve. Roughly chop the bulb.

2. Melt the butter in the oil in a medium saucepan over medium-low heat. Add the onion; cook 1 minute. Add the garlic; cook 1 minute longer. Stir in the fennel and the potato. Cook 5 minutes.

3. Add the tomatoes, bouquet garni, and chicken broth to the soup. Heat to boiling; reduce the heat. Cook, covered, over low heat until the fennel is very soft, about 30 minutes. Discard the bouquet garni.

4. Cool the mixture slightly and then purée it (in batches) in a food processor or blender, taking care as hot liquid will expand. Transfer the purée to a clean saucepan. Stir in the Pernod over medium-low heat.

5. Beat the egg yolk with the cream and slowly stir it into the soup. Warm the soup through, but do not allow it to boil. Season with salt and white pepper to taste. Sprinkle with the chopped fennel fronds.

Serves 4 to 6.

FENNEL AND CHICKEN SALAD

More fennel and fowl. A fragrantly crunchy dish which parenthetically would not be harmed a jot by the substitution of leftover Thanksgiving turkey in lieu of an everyday pullet.

2 medium heads fennel (about 1¼ pounds)
2 cups chopped cooked chicken or turkey
1 large shallot, minced
1 cup Mayonnaise (see page 408)
½ teaspoon Dijon mustard
2 tablespoons Pernod
Salt and freshly ground black pepper

1. Trim the stems from the fennel and peel the bottoms. Chop the fronds so you have about 1 tablespoon; reserve. Chop the bulbs and combine with the chicken and shallot in a medium bowl.

2. Beat the mayonnaise with the mustard and Pernod in a large bowl until smooth. Add the fennel and chicken mixture. Mix well. Add salt and pepper to taste and sprinkle with the chopped fennel fronds.

Serves 4 or 5.

SICILIAN COLD BRAISED FENNEL

Since Italians favor fennel in their daily diet, another of my classic braisings (not so curiously) stems from that quarter. It is a Sicilian dish: a first course or salad accompaniment, traditionally served cold. *Molto bene.*

1 large or 2 medium heads fennel (about 1 ¼ pounds)
2 tablespoons unsalted butter
3 tablespoons olive oil
1 medium onion, finely chopped
1 clove garlic, minced
½ teaspoon salt
½ teaspoon freshly ground black pepper
1 ½ teaspoons anise seeds
2 cups chicken broth (see page 414)
½ teaspoon finely grated orange peel
2 tablespoons lemon juice

1. Trim the stems from the fennel and peel the bottoms. Chop the fronds and reserve. Cut each bulb in half from top to bottom. Slice each half lengthwise into four sections.

2. Heat the butter with the oil in a medium saucepan over medium-low heat. Add the onion; cook 1 minute. Add the garlic; cook 1 minute longer. Stir in the fennel, salt, pepper, and anise seeds. Cook, uncovered, 10 minutes, shaking the pan occasionally.

3. Add the chicken broth and orange peel. Cook, covered, over low heat until tender, about 20 minutes. With a slotted spoon, transfer the fennel to a serving dish.

4. Heat the cooking liquid in the saucepan to boiling. Boil until reduced to about ½ cup. Cool slightly and add the lemon juice. Pour this over fennel, cool, and chill for at least 3 hours before serving, sprinkled with chopped fennel fronds.

Serves 4.

BAKED FENNEL WITH CHEESE

No other partner complements a stalk of fennel with more eloquence, in my opinion, than cheese. Not any cheese, but definitely Parmesan and Gruyère. Check out this recipe and the one for Cheese-Fried Fennel, which follows.

1 large or 2 medium heads fennel (about 1 ¼ pounds)
4 tablespoons (½ stick) unsalted butter
1 small onion, chopped
1 medium carrot, diced
1 ½ cups chicken broth (see page 414)
3 tablespoons all-purpose flour
¼ cup heavy or whipping cream
3 minced fresh rosemary leaves, or a pinch of dried
Salt and freshly ground black pepper
½ cup grated Gruyère cheese
3 tablespoons freshly grated Parmesan cheese

1. Preheat the oven to 300° F. Trim

the stems from the fennel and peel the bottoms. Cut the bulbs into ½-inch-thick slices.

2. Melt 1 tablespoon of the butter in a medium saucepan over medium-low heat. Add the onion; cook 3 minutes. Stir in the carrot and sliced fennel. Toss to coat with the butter mixture. Add the chicken broth. Heat to boiling; reduce the heat. Simmer, covered, over medium-low heat until tender, about 15 minutes. Drain, reserving the broth.

3. Transfer the vegetables to a lightly greased shallow baking dish. Keep warm in the oven.

4. Meanwhile, melt the remaining butter in a small saucepan over medium-low heat. Stir in the flour. Cook, stirring constantly, 2 minutes. Whisk in the reserved broth and the cream. Cook until thick, about 3 minutes. Add the rosemary, and salt and pepper to taste. Spoon the sauce over the vegetables in the oven.

In Italy, where fennel is practically a table staple, Italians eat it raw with just a sluice of olive oil and sometimes lemon—and it always tastes absolutely marvelous. I once noticed that Italian housewives only buy fennel when the bulbs are fat as baby rabbits and the tops are deep green and shrubby. They usually break off the smaller stalks and chew the fronds as they make their shopping rounds. You may do the same with utter impunity, since fennel is very, very low in calories.

5. Combine the two cheeses and sprinkle them over the fennel mixture. Place the dish under a broiling unit until the cheese melts and is golden.

Serves 4.

CHEESE-FRIED FENNEL

2 large heads fennel (1½ to 2 pounds)
½ cup all-purpose flour
½ teaspoon salt
2 large eggs
2 tablespoons water
⅔ cup freshly grated Parmesan cheese
⅔ cup fresh bread crumbs
Vegetable oil for frying

1. Trim the stems from the fennel and peel the bottoms. Cut the bulbs lengthwise into ½-inch-wide pieces. Cook in boiling salted water until just tender, about 8 minutes. Drain. Cool slightly and pat dry on paper towels.

2. Combine the flour and salt on a plate. Beat the eggs with the water in a shallow bowl. Combine the Parmesan cheese with the bread crumbs on another plate.

3. Heat about 2 inches of oil in a large saucepan until hot. Roll the fennel pieces lightly in the flour, then dip in the egg mixture, and then roll in the cheese mixture. Fry in hot oil until golden, about 6 minutes. Drain on paper towels. Keep warm in a low oven while frying the remaining pieces.

Serves 6.

GOODWIVES' BRAISED FENNEL

My paradigm example of fennel-braising comes from the South of France. It is a recipe that I reconstructed with a good deal of difficulty because the donor always gave me outrageously misleading clues as to its "secret" ingredient.

A neighbor and friend, who was (as the French say) "a lady of a certain age," drank as she cooked; and it was her penchant for a mid-morning *pastis* (a thimbleful of Pernod in a tumbler of water) that made me realize what made her dish so potently "lickerish" in flavor. She would splash the saucepan with the contents of her glass when she thought no one was watching!

I have been reasonably well informed that the classic French name for such a mixture of cooked fennel, onions, and tomatoes would be *Fenouil Braisé à la Bonne Femme*. But I much prefer the Americanization.

1 large or 2 medium heads fennel (about 1¼ pounds)
2 tablespoons unsalted butter
1 medium onion, finely chopped
2 medium tomatoes, seeded, chopped
Pinch of dried thyme
¼ cup strong beef broth (see page 414)
1½ teaspoons Pernod, Ricard or other anise-based liqueur
Salt and freshly ground black pepper

1. Trim the stems from the fennel and peel the bottoms. Chop the fronds and reserve. Chop the bulb and cook it in boiling salted water 2 minutes. Drain.

2. Melt the butter in a medium saucepan over medium-low heat. Add the onion; cook until lightly golden, about 5 minutes. Add the tomatoes, thyme, beef broth and drained chopped fennel. Cook, covered, over low heat until tender, about 25 minutes.

3. Remove the cover from the saucepan and cook until any excess liquid has evaporated. Add the Pernod, raise the heat slightly, and cook 2 minutes. Add salt and pepper to taste and sprinkle with the chopped fennel fronds.

Serves 4.

MARLENE LEVINSON'S POACHED FENNEL AND PARSLEY

The next fennel recipe is pacific enough to bridge the most troubled familial water. It is an endowment from yet another excellent San Franciscan cook, Marlene Levinson. I met this bright and mettlesome lady some years ago when I was teaching my very first cooking class in California. The class was held in a home in the hills of Sonoma, during the heaviest rainfall to hit northern California in a decade. The kitchen was filled with damp but extremely enthusiastic food lovers from the community, along with a contingent of hardy professionals who had ventured north of the Golden Gate Bridge through the torrent to check out "the man who invented ziti salad." Or so I was told later.

Marlene was one of the hardiest checker-outers. An instant friendship ensued over a bowl of cioppino and one of the residuals of that fraternity is the splendid offering below.

2 medium heads fennel (about 1¼ pounds)
2 cups chopped fresh parsley
4 tablespoons (½ stick) unsalted butter
1 small onion, finely chopped
½ cup heavy or whipping cream
⅛ teaspoon freshly grated nutmeg
Salt and freshly ground black pepper

1. Trim the stems from the fennel and peel the bottoms. Discard any tough outer stems. Separate the bulb into pieces. Cut the large ones in half lengthwise. Chop the fronds and reserve.

2. Place the fennel pieces with the parsley in a medium saucepan. Cover with water. Heat to boiling; boil until tender, 8 to 10 minutes. Drain through a wire sieve.

3. Melt the butter in a large skillet over medium-low heat. Add the onion; cook 5 minutes. Add the cream; cook until fairly thick, about 5 minutes. Toss in the fennel and parsley. Cook until warmed through. Add the nutmeg, and salt and pepper to taste. Sprinkle with the chopped fennel fronds.

Serves 4.

FENNEL PUREE

Fennel's low calorie count makes it an ideal confederate to high-carbohydrate food like potatoes. Two of the very best fennel prescriptions in this log are brightened up with a mite of that snowy tuber.

The first, below, a velvety purée, is yet another *douceur* from the fennel-loving French, while the second—Home-Fried Fennel and Potato Hash, which follows—is as American as a dish can get: a vegetable hash, circa 1900.

2 medium heads fennel (about 1¼ pounds)
2 ribs celery, chopped
2 medium potatoes, peeled, cut into 1-inch cubes
2 to 3 tablespoons strong Chicken Stock (see page 410)
1½ tablespoons unsalted butter
1½ tablespoons Pernod
⅓ cup heavy or whipping cream
Salt and freshly ground black pepper
Chopped fresh parsley

1. Trim the stems from the fennel and peel the bottoms. Chop the fennel bulbs and the fronds and place them in a medium saucepan, along with the celery and potatoes. Add cold water to cover. Heat to boiling; reduce the heat. Simmer, uncovered, until just tender, about 20 minutes. Drain.

2. Place the vegetables in the container of a food processor. Add the chicken stock; process until smooth.

3. Transfer the puréed vegetables to the top of a double boiler. Stir in the butter, Pernod, and cream. Cook, stirring occasionally, over simmering water until warmed through. Add salt and pepper to taste. Transfer to a serving bowl and sprinkle with parsley.

Serves 4 to 5.

HOME-FRIED FENNEL AND POTATO HASH

1 small to medium head fennel (about ½ pound)
2 medium potatoes
2 strips bacon
1 tablespoon unsalted butter
1 small onion, chopped
1 clove garlic, minced
1½ teaspoons fennel seeds
Salt and freshly ground black pepper

1. Trim the stems from the fennel and peel the bottoms. Chop the fronds; reserve.

2. Cook the fennel bulbs with the potatoes in boiling salted water, 12 minutes. Drain and allow to cool. Chop the bulbs and the potatoes, separately, into about 1-inch pieces.

3. Fry the bacon in a large skillet over medium heat until crisp. Drain on paper towels. Add the butter to the skillet. Add the onion; cook 1 minute. Add the garlic; cook 1 minute longer. Add a layer of potatoes to the skillet. Add a layer of fennel pieces. Sprinkle with fennel seeds and salt and pepper to taste. Continue to layer until all the vegetables are used up. End with either potatoes or fennel. Cook over medium heat until the bottom is nicely browned. Turn over in one piece with a large spatula (or flip over into another skillet). Reduce the heat and continue to cook until the vegetables are soft, about 10 minutes.

4. Crumble the reserved bacon and sprinkle it over the fennel-potato mixture. Sprinkle with the chopped fennel fronds.

Serves 4.

FENNEL-STUFFED ROAST TURKEY

One of the stalk's most agreeable appearances takes place within the breast of a capacious bird. Combined with rice, onion, and sausage, it makes a dressing one may truly give thanks for on the last Thursday in November.

Fennel Dressing (recipe follows)
1 fresh turkey (18 to 20 pounds)
2 large cloves garlic, 1 bruised
Salt and freshly ground black pepper
3 strips bacon
⅓ cup dry white wine
1 quart water
1 onion
1 stalk celery, broken
3 sprigs parsley, plus additional for garnish
¼ teaspoon salt
4 peppercorns
1½ tablespoons unsalted butter
1½ tablespoons all-purpose flour
¼ cup heavy or whipping cream

1. Make the Fennel Dressing.

2. Preheat the oven to 325°F. Remove the giblets from the turkey; reserve the giblets, except the liver, for the gravy. You may wish to reserve the liver for another purpose. First wipe the turkey inside and out with a damp cloth, then rub it well, inside and out, with the bruised garlic, salt, and pepper. Stuff the cavity with the dressing, and truss. Place the turkey on a rack in a roasting pan, laying the bacon strips across the breast. Cut a piece of cheesecloth large enough to fit over the turkey. Soak the cheesecloth in the wine and place it over the turkey. Pour any remaining wine over the turkey and roast 30 minutes.

3. Meanwhile, combine the giblets (*not* the liver), water, onion, celery, the remaining garlic clove, 3 sprigs parsley, ¼ teaspoon salt, and the peppercorns in a large saucepan. Heat to boiling, then reduce the heat. Simmer, uncovered, until the liquid is reduced to 2 cups. Strain the giblet stock.

4. Baste the turkey with the giblet stock. Roast, basting with stock every 30 minutes, until the legs move freely and juices run clear when the inner thigh is pierced with a fork, about 5½ to 6 hours total. During the last half hour of roasting, remove the cheesecloth by first wetting the turkey with basting juices. It should lift off easily. Raise the oven heat to 375°F to crisp the skin. Transfer to a carving board; let stand 15 minutes.

5. Meanwhile, strain the turkey drippings, degreasing if necessary. Melt the butter in a medium saucepan over medium-low heat. Whisk in the flour. Cook, stirring constantly, 2 minutes. Whisk in the drippings and cream; simmer 5 minutes. Taste and adjust seasonings. Garnish the turkey with the remaining parsley sprigs. Serve with the gravy and fennel dressing.

Serves 8 to 10 (with leftovers).

When my grandmother spoke of fennel, invariably she called it "fin-nook." Because her command of English was faulty, she would often intersperse a sentence with liberal sprinklings of Yiddish, a language I never understood except by sense meaning. So I was often confused by what I thought she said. The word "fin-nook" for instance, always sounded remarkably like the Yiddish expression *genug* (gen-nook) that emphatically means "enough."

So I grew up—at least until early puberty—believing that all family arguments or heated discussions always ended with a call for *fennel* by my grandmother. Which curiously never arrived!

Fennel Dressing

1 head fennel (about 1 pound)
1 pound sweet Italian sausage, roughly chopped
1 medium onion, chopped
2 tablespoons fennel seeds
2 cups cooked rice
1 teaspoon salt
½ teaspoon freshly ground black pepper
⅛ teaspoon hot pepper sauce

1. Trim the stems from the fennel and peel the bottoms. Cut the bottoms into ½-inch cubes and place them in a large bowl. Chop the fronds and add them to the cubes in the bowl.

2. Place the sausage in a large heavy skillet and sauté over medium heat until lightly browned and rendered of grease. Using a slotted spoon, transfer the sausage to the bowl with the fennel.

3. Remove all but 2 tablespoons grease from the skillet. Add the onion and fennel seeds. Cook, stirring constantly, over medium heat for 3 minutes. Add the onion mixture to the fennel-sausage mixture along with the rice, salt, pepper, and hot pepper sauce. Mix.

Makes enough dressing for an 18- to 20-pound turkey.

FENNEL-POACHED FLOUNDER AND SHRIMP

In France, fennel is unalterably associated with fish. One of the most felicitous dishes to be found in a Mediterranean kitchen is *loup de mer au fenouil,* which is a kind of small sea bass that is grilled and flamed over dried fennel leaves and stalks until the skin is so redolent it perfumes your tongue. I must admit, however, that I have *never* been able to successfully duplicate its wonders on a barbecue pit (or broiler) on home shores. So here is an arresting alternative, also French: a poached fennel, shrimp, and flounder dish that converts the actual poaching liquid (plus cream) into an unusually fragrant blanket for the filets.

1 medium head fennel (about ½ pound)
6 large filets of flounder or sole
Juice of 1½ lemons
18 cooked shrimp, shelled, deveined
½ bottle dry white wine, approximately
1 small onion stuck with 2 cloves
1 slice lemon
Bouquet garni: 1 sprig parsley, 1 bay leaf, and a pinch of dried thyme tied in a cheesecloth bag
3 tablespoons unsalted butter
1 cup heavy or whipping cream
⅛ teaspoon fennel seeds
Salt and freshly ground black pepper
2 egg yolks, lightly beaten

1. Trim the stems from the fennel and peel the bottom. Chop the fennel fronds and reserve. Cook the bulb in boiling salted water until tender, about 20 minutes. Drain, cool slightly, and chop fine.

2. Cut the flounder filets in half crosswise. Arrange them on a plate and sprinkle them with the juice of 1 lemon. Spread a small amount of finely chopped fennel over each piece. Place a cooked shrimp on each. Roll up the filets and place them seam-side down in a large heavy saucepan. Pour in wine to half the depth of the filets. Add the onion, lemon slice, and bouquet garni. Use 1½ teaspoons butter to heavily butter a piece of wax paper. Cover the pan with it. Cook over low heat until the fish flakes easily when pierced with a fork, about 5 minutes. Remove the filets with a slotted spoon to an ovenproof serving dish and keep warm.

3. Preheat the oven broiling unit. Heat the cooking liquid in the saucepan to boiling; boil until reduced by half. Strain the cooking liquid into a medium saucepan and add the juice of ½ lemon, the cream, the remaining butter, and fennel seeds. Heat to boiling; remove from the heat. Add salt and pepper to taste. Stir ¼ cup of the sauce into the egg yolks; slowly beat this mixture back into the sauce. Return to low heat, stirring constantly, until thick. Do not allow to boil.

4. Drain any liquid that has accumulated around the fish filets. Pour the sauce over the filets. Place them under the preheated broiler until lightly browned, 1 to 2 minutes. Garnish with the remaining shrimp and reserved fennel fronds.

Serves 6.

HUNGARIAN FENNEL BREAD

From the Mediterranean area (but from a Hungarian chef), this sensuous white bread is seasoned with a purée of cooked fennel, feathery fronds, and a hailstorm of seeds for good measure.

2 small heads fennel (about 1 pound)
1 small potato, peeled, grated
1 cup Chicken Stock (see page 410)
1 teaspoon salt
1 tablespoon fennel seeds
1 package dry yeast
¼ cup lukewarm water
1 teaspoon sugar
4 cups all-purpose flour, approximately
1 teaspoon unsalted butter, plus 1½ tablespoons melted

1. Trim the stems from the fennel and peel the bottoms. Chop the fennel fronds and reserve. Chop the bulbs and place them in a medium saucepan, along with the potato. Add the chicken stock. Heat to boiling; reduce the heat. Simmer, covered, until tender, about 15 minutes. Drain, reserving ¼ cup of the cooking liquid.

2. Place the vegetables in the container of a food processor or blender. Add the reserved cooking liquid and process until smooth. Transfer to a large bowl. Stir in 1 tablespoon of the chopped fennel fronds, the salt, and the fennel seeds.

3. Combine the yeast with the water and sugar in a small bowl. Let it stand (proof) 10 minutes, then stir it into the fennel purée. Add enough flour to make a fairly stiff dough, about 3 cups.

4. Transfer the dough to a lightly floured board and add the remaining 1 cup flour, kneading for about 10 minutes. Use the 1 teaspoon butter to butter a large bowl. Place the dough in the bowl, turning it to coat it with butter. Cover, and let rise until doubled in volume, about 1½ hours.

5. Punch down the dough; knead briefly. Form it into a loaf and place it in a buttered 9-inch bread pan. Cover with a floured cloth; let stand 1 hour.

6. Preheat the oven to 375°F. With a sharp knife, cut a slash down the center of the risen dough. Brush the top well with the melted butter. Place a roasting pan containing 1 inch of water on the bottom of the oven. Place the bread on a rack in the top third of the oven. Bake until golden brown and hollow-sounding when tapped with your finger, about 45 minutes. Cool on a rack for 10 minutes. Gently loosen the bread from the pan and unmold. Cool completely on the rack. Makes 1 loaf.

Fennel is known as *fenouil* in France, *Fenchel* in Germany, *finocchio* in Italy, and *hinojo* in Spain. The ancient Greeks, however, called it *marathon*, after the verb "to grow thin," and ate it mainly as a diet food. Socrates advised a stalk of fennel and a glass of water as the only cure for a night of culinary excess. I haven't a Greek bone in my body, but I couldn't be in more agreement if I had.

GREENS

The Edible Bouquet

From the reminiscences that stitch this book together a reader might assume that my strongest attachments were reserved for my mother's side of the family, but that is not wholly accurate.

My mother's relatives were certainly closest in proximity—but never quite closest in my heart. It was the Greene descendants who lived miles away—none closer than upper Manhattan and most more distant, in such diverse geography as Passaic, Boston, and Baltimore—for whom that honor was reserved. My father's sisters and their offspring were warm, good-natured people who frankly adored him, and their affection extended to his wife and children too.

Who could help but love this family? Loud, boisterous, and utterly unstinting in their generosity, they turned our infrequent visits into gala holidays. Banquets of usually denied delicatessen foods overloaded the table: steaming frankfurters, glistening porringers of potato salad, pickles, and slabs of rye bread so heavily buttered that a slice usually buckled in the middle before it reached one's lips. These comestibles inevitably led to a mild case of indigestion on the way home, but who cared? From these sporadic get-togethers I managed to glean an image of my father's early life.

If family tales can be believed, my paternal grandmother was a mail-order bride. A very religious girl, speaking nary a word of English, on the advice of a marriage broker she crossed the ocean to wed an itinerant New York blacksmith. Her husband spoke not a word of Russian, and very little Yiddish either. How they communicated is sheer speculation, but somehow this couple managed to produce a dozen children despite the language barrier.

Progeny aside, their union was not a happy one. There were many separations and reconciliations. My grandfather, Michael Greene, was Americanized and not overly religious. He plied his trade—shoeing horses and mending pots and pans in a covered wagon that took him far from New York's lower East Side; clear across the Great Divide, in fact. According to his middle daughter (my aunt Rae, who lived in Boston) he was never home for longer than a month at a time in his entire married life. "Because," she claimed, "the man could abide neither his wife's piety nor her constant accusations."

Grandfather Greene died before he was forty-five, leaving his widow with a houseful of growing children and the nagging rumors of a dozen others born outside the state line.

My grandmother survived him by thirty years. Her children went to work early to support her, but she was never mollified for she strongly disapproved of all of their secular lifestyles. Her youngest son, my father, chose to live in his free-thinking older sister's household when he was barely an adolescent. When he married a young girl whose family was also irreligious, his mother's worst fears were confirmed. She made up for her children's defection with prayer. Resisting any creature comforts pressed upon her, she spent the rest of her life in dark ghetto synagogues. Never having learned to speak English, she mistrusted the world outside the tenements and held in cold contempt all the gaiety and love of life that her children embraced.

My mother was sanguine on the subject of her mother-in-law.

"She was a driven person," she said on more than one occasion. "All she did was pray. She gave any money her children sent her to the poor because she couldn't enjoy it." In point of fact, she expired on her way to a synagogue (where she collected prayer books for Friday night service), with over a thousand dollars in her pocketbook.

I have never seen a photograph of my grandmother Bessie Greene, for it was against her religious principles to permit such an act of vanity, but I am named to honor her memory—so that gives us a common denominator. Her children (my father and aunts) were loving siblings. But, to me at least, the fact that they never spoke of their mother when they gathered as a family meant that her pleasureless life was always manifest—like a pain one has learned to ignore.

My father used to light a candle on the anniversary of his mother's death, but claimed not to be able to remember anything remarkable about her. "She did as well and no better than anyone in her circumstances," he would reply to my questioning. Meaning, I knew, a life of self-denial and little joy. When I asked about the dishes she prepared, he shrugged. "Green soup. She made lots of that."

"Green. What made it green?"

"Beats me. In those days we were so poor we couldn't afford chicken but once a week. My mother used to collect free vegetable tops from markets all over the neighborhood. With a little bit of meat, she made those leaves into a kind of soup-stew." My father shook his head at the recollection. "But y'know, it wasn't half bad."

From my Russian grandmother's pot to her American grandchild's spoon there must be quite a connection, for I do much the same thing. Buying greens at a fancy greengrocer's is of little importance in the final analysis: it's the Greene tradition that counts!

Vegetable Roots

What I call "greens" is a varied crop of leaves, all bearing the same color—some mild, some bitter, some crisp, some crumpled. These plants (all highly nutritious and incredibly tasty) usually act as partners in a saucepan in my kitchen. But in some instances they show up in the salad bowl as well. They are: arugula, chard, collards, dandelion greens, mustard greens, romaine, sorrel, turnip greens, and watercress.

ARUGULA (sometimes known as rocket-salad, ruculo or tiro) is a Cruciferal. The ancients considered that eating it brought good luck.

CHARD, on the other hand, is a beet-top that went wild in the garden. This leaf grew outside when its root *(Beta vulgaris)* shriveled in the cold Swiss soil. The name is a total erratum; early vegetable lovers mistook its splendid foliage for that of the thistlelike cardoon (or *chardon*). They called it Swiss chard and so have greengrocers ever since.

COLLARD is a corruption of the earlier handle *colewort*. It is a member of the cabbage family, but somehow lighter to the tongue and distinctly less weighty in the alimentary canal. Romans and Greeks attributed great therapeutic powers to its consumption. Julius Caesar in fact is rumored to have eaten a plateful after a heavy banquet (much as one would slurp Bromo-Seltzer) to ward off indigestion.

The DANDELION is nothing but a garden desperado gone straight—and tall too! Cousin of the sunflower, marigold, and zinnia (the Compositae tribe), it tastes remarkably better than all three—particularly after a dressing-down with oil and vinegar!

MUSTARD GREENS have a long history. Another member of the populous *Brassicas,* it was growing wild in Asia Minor in the first century, and peoples of the Indus valley ate their barley seasoned with its shoots. Mustard can be found growing wild in the vacant lots of New York City today.

ROMAINE (at times tagged Cos lettuce) is named for the way its long cupped leaves resembled Roman table spoons. Actually romaine was a prandial refinement that Caesar borrowed from the Greeks. Indeed, a persistent rumor in food circles has it that Socrates quaffed his lethal dose of hemlock from just such a "spoon" of fresh romaine.

SORREL is another dish of tea entirely. A pot herb (of the *Rumex* genus and distantly related to buckwheat), sorrel grew wild in Eurasia for centuries without a smidgen of it ever seasoning a pot. For years it was considered a poison because of its slightly astringent flavor. But while its flavor may have been off-putting to humans, sorrel seeds have always been extremely popular with migratory birds. Indeed some food snoops claim that this hardy perennial spread to Europe and the New World on the wing. Henry Cabot, the British explorer, was said to have had a pet bird who doted on sorrel. In most of the world sorrel goes by the pejorative name of sour grass, which is a misnomer; it is merely piquant!

TURNIP GREENS are the curly tops of the garden-variety turnip plant. When the leaves are snipped in May, a fatter, more flavorsome turnip is harvested in July. Of less gastronomic note but equally tonic, the green leaf of this vegetable is said to "awaken slumbering desire in even the most quiescent spouse"—at least according to John Milton's diaries. It must have had some therapeutic effect, for turnip foliage was brewed into potions, restoratives, and pick-me-ups from the sixteenth to the nineteenth century with varying reports of its good pharmacy. Even today in the deep South, a cup of turnip green "pot likker" is still reputed to be the best cure for hangover ever invented.

WATERCRESS can scarcely be dubbed a "garden green" since it requires a babbling brook or a small stream close by to feed its thirsty roots. Watercress thrives best in the shade, a fact that has given it something of a bad name in the past. There was a theory (held by all Puritan diners) that since this plant was grown in the darkness it was a living example of deviltry, "and no consumer of its leaves would profit with good health lest it was mingled with foodstuffs harvested in pure sunlight." Which may explain in part why a stalk of watercress hardly ever arrives on a salad plate without a leaf of lettuce nearby!

What to Look For

Greens have a high water content, so they wilt easily. And once faded they are hard to revive. Search out the bunches at your greengrocer's that have the freshest, greenest leaves. Don't buy yellow or discolored greens; they're a waste of money. I store greens unwashed in the refrigerator, lightly wrapped in damp paper towels inside a plastic bag that has been punctured to allow an even air supply. That way I generally manage to hold greens, with an occasional change of toweling, for up to a week's time.

The green per se is no heavy indulgence. Most are low in the calorie department: a mere 10 calories in a heaping cupful of watercress; less than 65 in a whole one-pound bunch of dandelion and mustard greens. And most are high in potassium (465 milligrams per cupful for turnip, mustard, arugula and watercress) and calcium (125 milligrams in the same quantity). Unfortunately most greens are high in sodium, so low-salt-dieters are advised to consult nutrition charts before going hog-wild in the kitchen. Some greens (like chard, collards, mustard, arugula, and dandelion) contain whopping amounts of vitamin A (7,830 units per cupful).

> If I were to rate greens by "bite," I would start with the mildest: chard, collard, dandelion, and romaine. Arugula, sorrel, and watercress are semi-mild in my opinion, while mustard and turnip greens are the sharpest in flavor. You should experiment with combinations to discover the taste you like best.

Preparation

My view of greens may be influenced by my stint in the South, when I was going to college. Even today, those who live below the Mason-Dixon Line dote on these leaves, slow-cooked in a copious potful of broth or bouillon that is well seasoned with a ham hock or a chunk of fatty bacon and some onions. And I must confess to a predilection for a "mess" of them whenever I am in that geography. However, at my own stove I tend to braise greens in somewhat more abbreviated cooking time, with equally felicitous results.

First I wash the greens well on both sides; hidden dirt often clings to the undersides of the leaves. I believe in three separate washings for all such gardenry, plus a longish stint in the colander to drain them well after the final bath. Then I braise the greens in a covered saucepan with a small amount of liquid plus a jot of butter (or bacon drippings) until the leaves are wilted but not mushy—about 10 to 15 minutes depending upon the toughness of the greens.

Greens may also be blanched first and reheated later. Blanch greens by placing the chopped vegetables in a pot of boiling salted water for a minute or two. Rinse them in a colander under cold running water to retard the cooking. Then drain well, gently pressing out any excess liquid with the back of a spoon. Blanched greens may be prepared early on in the day and then reheated just before serving. Reheat in butter or bacon drippings, tossing them well to warm thoroughly, and season with salt, pepper, and a sluice of vinegar or lemon juice.

Steam greens by placing the chopped vegetables in a steamer basket or colander over a small amount of boiling water for approximately 6 to 10 minutes. Toss gently with a fork and cook a minute or two longer if you prefer them softer (I do not). Be apprised, however, that steaming greens will sometimes intensify the bitter undertaste in the stronger-flavored varieties.

I never cook watercress in advance, as these leaves wilt considerably over heat. Likewise romaine, which is technically a lettuce and will exude moisture, should be cooked over higher heat to dry it. Lettuce is a nice braising partner with sturdier greens (like chard or collards) but will not stand up as well in the pan. Try adding it to greens after half the cooking time has elapsed.

For the record, 2 pounds of large-leafed greens (like chard or collards) will yield 1 pound stemmed chopped leaves. Most raw packed greens will yield approximately one-quarter the amount when long-cooked, more when lightly braised or wilted. A good rule of thumb is to allow ½ cup of cooked greens per serving.

CHARD SHCHAV

I feel certain that my grandmother Greene would have approved of this soup. It is derived from a classic Russian-Polish cold dish named *shchav* or *schav.* The word comes from a local Polish name for sorrel leaves *(szczaw)*, of which most such soups are composed. There is rumored to be a *shchav* recipe for every *shtetl* (Jewish community) that existed in both Poland and Russia at the turn of the century. Mine, however, you will never find recorded among them, for I made it up out of whole cloth a while back. It actually is no *shchav* at all in the generic sense, since the main ingredient in this soup is Swiss chard, not sorrel. Chard makes a very tonic difference to the contents of the soup ladle, for it is both sweeter and blander.

2 pounds Swiss chard
6 whole scallions, bulbs and green tops, chopped
2 quarts Vegetable Stock (see page 411)
4 eggs, lightly beaten
1 pint sour cream
¼ cup lemon juice
⅛ teaspoon hot pepper sauce
Salt and ground white pepper

1. Trim the chard, discarding the stems. Finely chop the leaves.

2. Combine the chard, scallions, and vegetable stock in a medium saucepan. Heat to boiling; reduce the heat. Simmer, uncovered, 12 minutes. Transfer to a heatproof bowl and allow to cool for 10 minutes.

3. Beat the eggs with the sour cream in a medium bowl until smooth. Slowly add the mixture to the chard. Stir in the lemon juice, hot pepper sauce, and salt and white pepper to taste. Serve warm or well chilled.

Serves 6 to 8.

CLARA LESS' ZUPA SZCZAFU

(Polish Sorrel Soup)

Though it is sorrel-based and stems from Poland, this is no *shchav.* My late grandmother would never have allowed a drop to pass her lips, as in the ingredients list there are not only chicken soup and sour cream but salt pork as well. But it comes without any apology, for it is simply one of the best soups I have ever consumed! The prescription is a bequest from a good friend and treasured confidante, Clara B. Less of Dearborn, Michigan.

1 pound fresh sorrel
¼ pound salt pork, finely chopped
1 large onion, finely chopped
2 tablespoons all-purpose flour
2 medium potatoes, peeled, diced
2 cups chicken broth (see page 414)
1 cup water
1 cup sour cream, at room temperature
Salt and freshly ground black pepper
Chopped fresh parsley

1. Trim the sorrel, discarding the stems. Chop the leaves and set aside.

2. Sauté the salt pork in a medium saucepan over medium heat until golden and crisp, about 10 minutes. Stir in the onion; cook until lightly browned, about 5 minutes.

3. Reduce the heat to low and whisk in the flour. Cook, stirring constantly, 2 minutes. Stir in the potatoes, chicken broth, water, and sorrel. Heat to boiling; reduce the heat. Cook, uncovered, over medium-low heat until the potatoes are tender, about 30 minutes.

4. Remove the soup from the heat and slowly stir in the sour cream. Return it to low heat and cook (do not allow to boil) until warmed through. Add salt and pepper to taste and sprinkle with parsley.

Serves 4 to 6.

Greens go by odd appellations in other tongues, some untranslatable. The French call them *légumes verts*, while the Germans dub them *grüne Gemüse.* Italians lump all vegetables together as *verdura*, and though it's a tad imprecise, so do the Spanish. The Swedish call them *grönsaker*, which covers a multitude of garden goods as well.

Red and Green Salad with Melon Vinaigrette

The dressing for my mixed red and green salad is a recent invention: a mixture of sweet and sour made with lime juice, mustard, and surprisingly, a sweet melon liqueur. A simply stunning palliation for the green bounty.

4 or 5 heads mache, or corn salad, separated into leaves (about 1/4 pound)
2 bunches watercress, leaves only
2 small heads bibb lettuce, leaves separated
3 small radicchio (Italian red lettuce) or red-tipped lettuce, leaves separated
4 heads Belgian endive
3 tablespoons green basil leaves
2 tablespoons torn geranium blossoms

For the melon vinaigrette:

1 small clove garlic
1/2 teaspoon coarse (kosher) salt
1/4 teaspoon Dijon mustard
Juice of 1 lime
1 tablespoon melon liqueur
1/2 to 3/4 cup olive oil

1. Wash all the various leaves well, and pat them dry. Make a pile of green lettuce and watercress leaves in a salad bowl. Surround it with the red lettuce leaves. Cut the endives into quarters lengthwise, then into long thin strips, and place them around the edge of the bowl, interspersed with the basil leaves. Sprinkle the top with the geranium blossoms.

2. To make the melon vinaigrette: Mash the garlic with the salt in a small bowl. Stir in the mustard, lime juice, and liqueur. Whisk in the oil. Toss the salad with the dressing at the table.

Serves 6 to 8.

Green Quills

After whipping up many of the dishes in this chapter, I often find myself with a refrigerator residual that gets me down, namely bags and bags of Swiss chard stems. The plan is always to use these vitamin-high end products in a soup or vegetable stock, but in truth I usually toss them out to make room for new comestibles before I get around to that chore. To make use of this accumulation of raw ingredients I devised the following dish. It's simple, eminently satisfying as a side dish, and most important of all, an economic boon for the cook!

3 tablespoons unsalted butter
2 shallots, minced
1 clove garlic, minced
1 pound Swiss chard stems (from approximately 2 pounds Swiss chard), cut into pieces 2 inches long and 1/2 inch wide
1/2 cup chicken broth (see page 414)
3 tablespoons chopped fresh parsley
Salt and freshly ground black pepper

1. Melt the butter in a large skillet over medium-low heat. Stir in the shallots; cook 1 minute. Stir in the garlic;

cook 1 minute longer. Add the chard stems, tossing well to coat with the mixture. Stir in the broth. Cook, covered, until tender, about 15 minutes.

2. Remove the cover and raise the heat. Stir in the parsley. Cook over medium heat, tossing constantly, until all excess liquid has evaporated. Add salt and pepper to taste.

Serves 4.

WILTED DANDELIONS AND POTATOES

My grandmother used to make a dandelion liqueur (not a wine) from time to time when I was a small child. I thought it tasted perfectly horrible. But I thought cognac tasted horrible too! Tastes change but my feelings about the dandelion endure. To this day, I like them best in a pot!

1 pound dandelion greens
3 medium potatoes, peeled, cut into 1½-inch cubes
½ cup Beef Stock (see page 409)
1 tablespoon unsalted butter
½ cup chopped smoked ham (I prefer Black Forest)
1 tablespoon lemon juice
Salt and freshly ground black pepper

1. Trim the dandelion greens and discard the stems. Roughly chop the leaves. Set aside.

2. Place the potatoes with the beef stock and butter in a medium saucepan. Heat to boiling; reduce the heat. Cook, covered, over medium-low heat until the potatoes are not quite tender, 12 to 15 minutes.

3. Stir the dandelion greens into the potatoes. Stir in the ham. Cook, covered, 5 minutes.

4. Remove the cover and stir in the lemon juice. Cook until any excess liquid has evaporated. Add salt and pepper to taste.

Serves 4 to 6.

BRIE ROMAINE

Appropriately enough, the next bequest comes from A New Leaf, a perpetually vernal restaurant at the fabled Shoreham Hotel in Washington, D.C. A new leaf most certainly was turned when this hostelry installed its brilliant young (twenty-three-year-old) chef, Paul Henskens, at the range. Pencil his name on your list of rising cooking stars. Henskens' dish is a first course or possibly a luncheon dish of brie cheese baked in a leafy green for only minutes. Diet food? I seriously doubt it, but delectable without a doubt.

6 large romaine lettuce leaves
¾ pound firm Brie cheese, from a 7-inch Brie
4 tablespoons (½ stick) unsalted butter
3 tablespoons sliced blanched almonds
Quartered cherry tomatoes (optional)

1. Preheat the oven to 450°F. Drop the romaine leaves into boiling salted water and cook until wilted, 45 to 60 seconds. Drain, and pat dry with paper towels. Remove the tough center ribs.

2. Cut the cheese into six equal wedges, each about 3½ inches long. Wrap each wedge in a leaf of romaine. Place them on an ovenproof serving dish and dot with the butter. Sprinkle with the almonds. Bake until the cheese starts to melt, about 5 minutes. Serve immediately, garnished with cherry tomatoes if you like.

Serves 6.

GREENS AND CORNMEAL DUMPLINGS

In the American South, greens are more than a dining prerogative; they are a way of life. Have my version of a classic "Alabama-Tennessee-Georgia-Mississippi" rendering, though I must warn the purists that it is somewhat less long-cooked than it would be in any of those territories. To make up for that lack, I amended it with a Virginia legacy, heavenly cornmeal dumplings. What follows is one *very* filling and fabulous dish. I inevitably make up a batch when I have a larder of leftover greens of varying hues and flavors in the fridge. But you use your own good green judgment in the selection.

1¼ pounds Swiss chard or collard greens
¾ pound mixed greens—mustard, arugula, and watercress
2 tablespoons unsalted butter
1 large onion, chopped
½ pound cooked ham, cut into large bite-size pieces
½ cup chicken broth (see page 414)
½ cup cake flour
½ cup yellow cornmeal
1½ teaspoons baking powder
½ teaspoon salt
1 egg, lightly beaten
⅓ cup milk
1 tablespoon lemon juice
Dash of hot pepper sauce
Chopped fresh parsley

1. Trim the leaves from the chard or collards; chop and reserve. Cut the stems into ½-inch-long pieces; reserve.

2. Trim the leaves from the mustard greens, arugula, and watercress; reserve.

3. Melt the butter in a large heavy skillet over medium-low heat. Stir in the onion; cook 2 minutes. Stir in the ham; cook 4 minutes. Stir in the chard or collard stems and the broth. Cook, covered, 10 minutes. Add the remaining greens; cook, covered, 10 minutes longer.

4. Meanwhile, sift the flour with the cornmeal, baking powder, and salt into a medium bowl. Beat in the egg and milk with a wooden spoon until smooth.

5. Stir the lemon juice and hot pepper sauce into the greens. Drop the cornmeal batter by the tablespoonful over the greens. Cook, covered, until firm, about 18 minutes. Sprinkle with parsley.

Serves 4.

WILTED SUMMER GREENS

My classic way with greens is biblically inspired. The *Pantropheon* tells us that the way the ancient Hebrews ate the fresh leaves that grew in their gardens was "seasoned lightly with herbs and spice and pot roasted till they lay down about a Pascal lamb."

My method is to braise the greens of course, but that roast lamb is not a bad notion as the greens' dinner partner. I make this side dish when the garden (or the greengrocer) has a wide variety of leaves to mix and match in the pot. But it is really a dish for all seasons, despite the summery moniker.

4 tablespoons (½ stick) unsalted butter
1 large onion, minced
1 large clove garlic, minced
2 medium tomatoes, peeled, seeded, roughly chopped
½ cup chopped fresh basil
¼ teaspoon ground ginger
4 to 5 cups (2 to 3 pounds) trimmed, roughly chopped mixed greens, such as chard, collards, turnip, blanched mustard, dandelions, arugula, sorrel
Salt and freshly ground black pepper

Melt the butter in a large saucepan over medium-low heat. Stir in the onion; cook 1 minute. Stir in the garlic; cook until golden, about 5 minutes. Add the tomatoes, basil, and ginger. Cook, uncovered, stirring occasionally, until slightly thickened, about 5 minutes. Stir in the greens and cook, covered, until wilted, 3 to 4 minutes. Add salt and pepper to taste. Serve hot or at room temperature.

Serves 4.

DANDELION GREENS WITH PROSCIUTTO

I first tasted a dandelion leaf when I was thirty and instantly regretted my (till then) misspent appetite, for this is one green that is wondrously trenchant to the tongue. And while I have never joined the forces of those dandelion lovers who hunt the waysides of expressways and thruways with scissors in hand, I do scout the greenest markets (in season) to keep my saucepans and salad bowl amply supplied. Like all greens, dandelion's tangy flavor marries well with the smoky taste of ham, bacon, and the like. For evidence, try this melding of wilted greens and Italian prosciutto. Incidentally, the word "dandelion" is a corruption of the French *dent de lion* ("lion's tooth"), referring to the plant's prominently incised leaves. It's not an odd association, truly, for this green is exceedingly toothsome.

1 to 1¼ pounds dandelion greens
2 tablespoons unsalted butter
1 medium onion, chopped
1 clove garlic, minced
2 tablespoons finely chopped prosciutto
Freshly ground black pepper

1. Wash the dandelions well. Tear the leaves from the stems. Chop the stems.

2. Melt the butter in a large skillet over medium-low heat. Add the onion; cook 1 minute. Stir in the garlic; cook until golden, about 5 minutes. Stir in the prosciutto and dandelion stems. Cook, covered, 4 minutes.

3. Add the dandelion leaves to the skillet. Cook, covered, until the leaves start to wilt, about 30 seconds. Remove the cover and raise the heat to medium. Cook, tossing constantly, until the leaves are tender, about 2 minutes. Add pepper to taste.

Serves 4.

To the gardener, dandelions are something less than splendor in the grass because no matter how hard one weeds them out, they return with a vengeance the following spring. In earlier times, the dandelion was used almost exclusively for medicinal purposes, and American folklore is crammed with notations for its use for malaises as disparate as ptomaine poisoning and water on the knee. Indeed, the dandelion (and its green leaf) was considered so eminently therapeutic that the *United States Pharmacopoeia* listed it as nostrum from 1831 to 1926.

GREEN TIMBALE

(Swiss Chard or Collard Green Custard)

Chard is beet-related, collards are cabbage-connected, and both have seasoned dishes for a millennium. Each is a hardy grower and will withstand a hot summer or a moist one and still remain unruffled in the vegetable patch. In the following prescription for a lofty vegetable custard, an expedient cook might substitute either with a handier green on occasion. Like what? Well, kale or spinach would do—for they are greens too!

4 tablespoons (½ stick) unsalted butter
1 large onion, finely chopped
1 pound Swiss chard or collard greens, stems and leaves chopped separately (about 2 cups leaves, 1½ cups stems)
¼ cup milk
½ cup heavy or whipping cream
½ teaspoon salt
¼ teaspoon freshly ground black pepper
⅔ cup fresh bread crumbs
½ cup grated Jarlsberg cheese
5 eggs, lightly beaten

1. Melt 1 tablespoon of the butter in a large skillet over medium-low heat. Add the onion; cook 2 minutes. Stir in the chard or collard stems; cook, covered, until tender, about 15 minutes. Stir in the chard or collard leaves; cook, covered, until tender, about 3 minutes. Raise the heat to medium-high and remove the cover. Cook, tossing constantly, until all liquid has evaporated. Transfer to a large bowl and set aside to cool.

2. Preheat the oven to 325°F. Melt the remaining 3 tablespoons of the butter and add it along with all the remaining ingredients to the greens mixture in the bowl. Mix well and pour into a buttered 1½-quart soufflé dish. Place the dish in a roasting pan. Pour boiling water in the pan to half the depth of the soufflé dish. Bake until a knife inserted in the center comes out clean, 45 minutes to 1 hour. Remove the dish from the pan; let it stand 10 minutes.

3. Run a sharp knife around the edges of the soufflé dish and very carefully invert it onto a shallow serving platter.

Serves 6.

GREENE'S SOUFFLE

The "bite" that greens can display on the tongue is very noticeable in the next recipe, which combines a spicy variety with the tang of creamy goat cheese. I choose watercress or arugula leaves because those greens are tender enough to mix raw with the other ingredients. And since both watercress and arugula are usually found in salads, their appearance in a soufflé is eminently refreshing.

¼ pound goat cheese
4 egg yolks
½ cup ricotta cheese
1 cup watercress or arugula leaves
Salt
Pinch of cayenne pepper
7 egg whites

1. Preheat the oven to 425°F. Mash the goat cheese with the yolks in a mixing bowl until smooth. Beat in the ricotta cheese. Stir in the watercress or arugula. Add salt to taste and the cayenne pepper.

2. Beat the egg whites until stiff but not dry. Fold them into the mixture. Pour into a lightly buttered 1½- to 2-quart soufflé dish. Bake until puffed, 25 to 30 minutes. Serve immediately.

Serves 4 to 6.

DANDELION FRITTELLA

These greens have always inspired a plethora of lawn-to-stovetop cooking. Here's another: an Italian green quasi-pancake or fritter. Need I add that the little golden "fritterings" are best when the dandelions are fresh and picked at the peak of their seasonal perfection? Romaine lettuce will work well if dandelion is out of season.

1 pound dandelion greens
Coarse (kosher) salt
1 medium onion, minced
1 tablespoon chopped fresh basil
1 tablespoon chopped fresh parsley
½ teaspoon beef bouillon powder
¼ cup freshly grated Parmesan cheese
3 eggs, lightly beaten
1 cup fresh bread crumbs
Salt and freshly ground black pepper
2 tablespoons unsalted butter
Vegetable oil

1. Trim the dandelions, discarding the stems.

2. Place the dandelion leaves in a colander and sprinkle them well with coarse salt. Let stand 1 hour. Rinse under cold running water; drain. Squeeze the leaves dry in a towel. Chop fine.

3. Place the chopped leaves in a medium bowl. Stir in the onion, basil, parsley, bouillon powder, cheese, eggs, bread crumbs, and salt and pepper to taste. Beat with a wooden spoon until mixed.

4. Melt the butter in a 9-inch skillet over medium heat. Add enough oil so that there is ¼ inch of shortening in the pan. Using 1 generous tablespoon of the mixture for each fritter, fry the frittelle a few at a time until deep golden, about 3 minutes per side. Drain on paper towels. Keep warm in a low oven while frying the remaining ones.

Serves 4.

POACHED GREEN SAUSAGE

The next "greens-and" devise is a dish that is made in Provence, France, with regularity whenever there is a fresh crop of green leaves showing in the kitchen garden. Needless to say, in that precinct there is always some leftover meat in the kitchen. These sausages are skinless of course but freeze remarkably well after the light poaching period. Chard or collard greens (the mild ones in my spectrum) meld best with all the provincial flavorings.

1½ cups chopped Swiss chard or collard leaves (from about 1 pound)
1½ tablespoons unsalted butter
3 large shallots, minced
½ pound lean ground round of beef, raw
6 ounces sweet Italian sausages, removed from casings
1½ cups ground cooked beef (from pot roast)
2 cloves garlic, crushed
1 teaspoon salt
¼ teaspoon freshly ground black pepper
¼ teaspoon ground allspice
¼ teaspoon ground mace
¼ teaspoon oregano
¼ teaspoon hot pepper sauce
3 tablespoons Madeira
½ cup freshly grated Parmesan cheese
2 eggs, lightly beaten
½ cup all-purpose flour, approximately
1 cup homemade Basic or Creamy Tomato Sauce (see pages 374 and 375)

1. Cook the greens in boiling water until tender, about 1 minute. Rinse under cold running water and drain, pressing out all liquid with the back of a spoon. Place in a large bowl.

2. Melt the butter in a small skillet over medium-low heat. Add the shallots; cook until tender, about 5 minutes. Transfer the shallots to the bowl with the greens, and add all the ingredients through the eggs. Mix well. Form into sausage shapes, about 2 inches long.

3. Preheat the oven to 375°F. Roll the sausages lightly in the flour. Poach, about six at a time, in boiling salted water until firm, about 30 seconds. Remove with a slotted spoon, drain lightly on paper towels, and transfer to a well-buttered shallow baking dish. When all are poached, spoon the tomato sauce over them and bake for 20 minutes.

Serves 6.

CRUSTLESS GREENS PIE

For centuries, greens were more beloved by peasants than by princes. With good reason too, for the populace most often used what was closest at hand for their dinner table. One such devise is a great personal favorite. I found it in Eze, but I suspect its genesis is closer to the Italian border. It is a crustless pie made up of all the greens, onions, peppers, and zucchini a farm wife can carry from a garden in her apron. No cousin to either quiche or pizza, it could substitute admirably for each without a second thought. And more to the point, perhaps, it is the quintessential one-dish vegetarian meal.

1½ pounds Swiss chard
½ pound arugula
¾ pound dandelion greens
3 tablespoons unsalted butter
1 tablespoon olive oil
1 onion, finely chopped
2 cloves garlic, minced
½ small yellow pepper, seeded, finely chopped (about ½ cup)
2 small zucchini (about ½ pound), grated
⅓ cup chopped fresh basil
¼ cup chopped fresh parsley
½ teaspoon salt
¼ teaspoon freshly ground black pepper
3 extra-large eggs, lightly beaten
¼ cup freshly grated Parmesan cheese
¼ cup grated Jarlsberg cheese
¼ cup fresh bread crumbs

1. Trim the chard, arugula, and dandelion greens. Discard the stems and chop the leaves.

2. Preheat the oven to 375°F. Heat 1 tablespoon of the butter with the oil in a medium saucepan. Add the onion; cook 1 minute. Add the garlic; cook 1 minute longer. Stir in the pepper, chard, arugula, dandelions, zucchini, basil, parsley, salt, and pepper. Cook, covered, over medium heat until very tender, about 15 minutes. Remove the cover and cook, stirring frequently, until all liquid has evaporated, about 25 minutes. Transfer to a large mixing bowl.

3. Beat the eggs into the greens and pour the mixture into a buttered 9-inch glass or ceramic quiche pan. Sprinkle with the Parmesan and Jarlsberg cheeses.

4. Melt the remaining 2 tablespoons butter in a small skillet over medium heat. Stir in the bread crumbs and sauté until golden. Spoon them over the pie. Bake 25 minutes. Let stand at least 10 minutes before serving.

Serves 6.

GREENS-STUFFED PORK CHOPS

An unusual green and meat partnership follows. It is a dish I first tasted in the South: pork crammed with wilted and vinegar-seasoned greens. It is a match made in heaven for a deep-dyed pork chop lover like me. The mix of greens is fairly arbitrary; use whatever is freshest in your market.

1 pound Swiss chard or ¾ pound collard, turnip, or dandelion greens
4 tablespoons (½ stick) unsalted butter
1 small onion, finely chopped
1 clove garlic, minced
¼ cup heavy or whipping cream
2 tablespoons red wine vinegar
1¼ cup stale bread cubes
Salt and freshly ground black pepper
4 double pork chops with pockets for stuffing
1 cup dry white wine
2 teaspoons cornstarch
2 teaspoons water
Chopped fresh parsley

1. Trim the chard or other greens and discard the stems. Chop the leaves; you should have about 1 cup.

2. Preheat the oven to 350°F. Melt 3 tablespoons of the butter in a medium saucepan over medium heat. Add the onion; cook 1 minute. Add the garlic; cook 2 minutes. Stir in the chard or other greens and cook, covered, tossing occasionally, over medium-low heat until tender, about 15 minutes. Remove the cover; stir in the cream and vinegar. Cook until thickened, about 5 minutes. Stir in the bread cubes, and salt and pepper to taste. Mix well. Remove from the heat.

3. Stuff the pork chop pockets with the greens mixture. Close the pockets with wooden toothpicks.

4. Melt the remaining 1 tablespoon butter in a Dutch oven over medium heat. Sauté the pork chops until well browned on both sides. Pour the wine over the chops. Bake, covered, turning once, 1 hour.

5. Remove the chops to a platter and keep warm. Mix the cornstarch with the water in a small bowl until smooth. Stir the cornstarch into the cooking juices. Heat to boiling; reduce the heat. Cook until slightly thickened. Spoon over the pork chops. Sprinkle with parsley.

Serves 4.

BUTTERFLIED FLANK STEAK WITH GREENS

My father always preferred his greens cooked with meat, so the flavor of one would enhance the other. I obviously inherited his taste for all such greenly combinations, as you will observe from the recipe that follows: a rolled flank steak, filled with a compound of greens and ground veal, pot-roasted on top of the stove. It is a very satisfying dinner entrée hot and also makes the best cold dinner-party fare I know.

½ pound Swiss chard or collard greens
½ pound arugula
3½ tablespoons unsalted butter
3 onions: 1 large, finely chopped, and 2 medium, sliced
1 pound ground veal
2 eggs, lightly beaten
1 tablespoon chopped fresh parsley, plus extra for garnish
¾ teaspoon chopped fresh thyme, or ⅛ teaspoon dried
Salt and freshly ground black pepper
1½- to 2-pound flank steak, butterflied
1 carrot, peeled, chopped
½ cup Beef Stock (see page 409)
½ cup red wine
½ teaspoon tomato paste

1. Trim the chard or collard greens and the arugula, discarding the stems. Chop the leaves.

2. Melt 1 tablespoon of the butter in a large skillet over medium-low heat. Add the chopped onion; cook until soft, about 8 minutes. Stir in the chard or collard greens and the arugula. Cook, covered, until soft, about 15 minutes. Raise the heat and remove the cover. Cook, tossing constantly, until all the liquid has evaporated. Transfer to a mixing bowl and allow to cool.

3. Mix the veal with the greens. Add the eggs, the 1 tablespoon parsley, the thyme, and salt and pepper to taste. Mix well.

4. Spread the veal mixture over the flank steak and roll it up. Use household string to tie the meat in various places, to keep it from unrolling.

5. Melt 1 tablespoon of the butter in a large Dutch oven over medium heat. Sauté the tied meat roll on all sides until well browned. Place the sliced onions and the carrot around the meat and stir them slightly. Add the beef stock and wine. Heat to boiling; reduce the heat. Cook, covered, over medium-low heat until tender, about 1¼ hours.

6. Remove the meat to a serving platter and keep it warm. Strain the meat juices into a small saucepan. Stir in the tomato paste, and cook over medium heat until slightly thickened. Stir in the remaining 1½ tablespoons butter. Spoon some sauce over the meat and sprinkle with parsley. Pass the remaining sauce.

Serves 6 to 8.

Greens often show up in my salad bowl as a nightly digestive. I eat salad like a trencherman but always *after* a meat course—and usually in place of dessert. These days, I often tear up the most unusual varieties of lettuce (and/or greens) that I can find for tossing—notably corn salad (which the French export under the name *mache*, but which my friends in the Midwest always called lamb's lettuce) or radicchio (red Italian lettuce), which seems to be everywhere I look on the greengrocers' shelves these days. But any combination of bitter and mild leaves will do. Ever since I lived in the South of France, I have come to like the flavor of tangy geranium blossoms torn into my salad too. If you are not a daring soul, you can skip that amenity. But be assured, this is not just some cookbook writer's crotchet: the tiny scarlet or pink petals give a salad a very special tang.

WATERCRESS AND MUSHROOM CREPES

My favorite indulgence at the moment is a watercress-and-mushroom crepe much reduced in flour and milk from conventional crepes and absolutely smashing for the alteration.

This crepe (which may be made in advance and frozen, then thawed and filled before reheating) makes a very winning dish for lunch, brunch, or supper.

For the crepes:

2 tablespoons unsalted butter
1 medium shallot, chopped
½ cup sliced mushrooms (about 7 small mushrooms)
1 egg
¾ cup milk
2 tablespoons water
¼ cup watercress leaves
2 tablespoons vegetable oil
⅓ cup all-purpose flour
¼ teaspoon salt
¼ teaspoon freshly ground black pepper
Pinch of ground allspice

For the filling:

1 cup sour cream, plus extra for garnish
1 tablespoon lemon juice
1 cup sliced mushrooms
½ cup watercress leaves
Salt and freshly ground black pepper
6 slices bacon, fried crisp and crumbled

1. To make the crepe batter: Melt the butter in a small skillet over medium-high heat. Add the shallot and mushrooms. Cook, tossing the mixture constantly, until the mushrooms are deep golden. Cool slightly. Place the egg, milk, water, watercress, and mushroom mixture in the container of a blender. Blend until smooth. Add the oil, flour, salt, pepper, and allspice. Blend at high speed, 2 minutes. Scrape down the sides and blend 1 minute longer. Let stand 15 minutes.

2. To make the crepes: Place the crepe mixture in a bowl. Line a plate with two sheets of paper towels and set it aside. Lightly rub a crepe or omelet pan (preferably with a nonstick surface) with a buttered cloth. Place the pan over medium heat until hot. Remove the pan from the heat and pour about 3 tablespoons of the batter into the center of the pan. Quickly tilt the pan in all directions to coat the bottom evenly. Return the pan to the heat and cook until the edges of the crepe are brown, about 1 minute. Turn the crepe with your fingers; cook the second side 15 seconds. Flip out onto the paper-towel-lined plate. Cover the crepe with another paper towel. Lightly grease the pan once more and continue the process until all the batter is used up, placing paper towels between the finished crepes.

3. To make the filling: Beat the sour cream with the lemon juice until light. Add the mushrooms, watercress leaves, salt and pepper to taste, and the crumbled bacon. Mix well.

4. Spoon about 1 tablespoon of the mixture down one side of each crepe and roll it up. Place the rolled crepes in a lightly buttered shallow baking dish.

5. Before serving, heat the crepes in a preheated 350°F oven for 10 minutes. Place a dab of sour cream on top of each.

Makes about 12 crepes.

WATERCRESS AND GOAT CHEESE SCRAMBLE

6 eggs
¼ cup heavy or whipping cream
2 tablespoons unsalted butter
2 ounces goat cheese, crumbled or chopped
½ cup watercress leaves
Salt and freshly ground black pepper
Hot cooked spaghetti (optional)

1. Beat the eggs with the cream.

2. Melt the butter in a large heavy skillet over low heat. Pour in the eggs and cook, uncovered, whisking frequently, until they are velvety, about 25 minutes. (Eggs can be removed from the heat to hold, or to keep from cooking too quickly.) Stir in the cheese and watercress. Add salt and pepper to taste. Serve immediately over spaghetti or as a brunch dish.

Serves 2 or 3.

WATERCRESS-PINEAPPLE SNOW

Watercress' finest hour (in my prejudiced opinion) is also its chilliest. The devise is something the French call a sorbet, but in my lexicon it's a *snow*. Have my favorite all-year blizzard—green of course!

1½ cups sugar
1 cup water
¼ cup watercress leaves, plus extra for garnish
Pulp of 2 large or 3 small limes, seeds removed
2½ cups chopped fresh pineapple (about 1 medium pineapple)

1. Combine the sugar with the water in a medium saucepan over medium heat. Stir to dissolve the sugar. Remove from the heat and allow to cool.

2. Combine the watercress, lime pulp, and pineapple in the container of a food processor or blender. Purée until smooth. Combine with the cooled sugar syrup.

3. Pour the mixture into the canister of an ice cream maker and proceed according to manufacturer's directions.

4. To serve, spoon the sorbet into dessert glass dishes and garnish each with a watercress leaf.

Makes about 1½ quarts.

KALE

A Survivor of the Dinosaur Age

As I have mentioned, before her marriage my mother had been trained as a concert pianist. Highly praised after her first recital, she was denied the opportunity of pursuing a musical career or even accompanying other performers in concert (if they were male) by her strict father—something she never entirely forgave him for, even when she was middle-aged. She claimed it showed a lack of confidence in her ability, but in all candor, I suspect my grandfather's misgivings had more to do with his eldest daughter's passionate nature than with her talent at the keyboard.

"Play for pleasure," he reputedly counseled, "or teach if you must." Being a dutiful girl she did the latter until she married, but never with the pleasure or patience needed to become an inspired instructor. Yet when our family finances faltered, my mother turned to her piano.

With a small accumulation of savings and the halfhearted support of her sister Muriel, who had studied the violin, she rented the top floor above our local movie theater. There she installed a very large mirror, a ballet barre, and a rented piano. Then she had a sign painted, which announced in bold script: *Home of the Paula School of Arts & Crafts*.

How artistic this school truly was, I cannot verify, but it certainly appeared

to be a crafty venture. Instruction took place in a large "studio" that overlooked the lights of the theater marquee.

The ground floor of the building was shared by an open-air vegetable market and a Greek luncheonette, and the way in was often strewn with green vegetables (frozen in bushel baskets) that would be bought up cheaply by the Greek, who converted them into all manner of spicy soups and stews. My memory of the Paula School of Arts & Crafts is still, in fact, indelibly printed with the scent of those aromas *and* the sound of endless music exercises.

My mother and my aunt gave private lessons in the studio's front rooms, which faced a major thoroughfare with a trolley line that offered up a counterpoint of clanging bells during each student's crucial trill and cadenza. My aunt's friend, an artist named Kay Quinn, was persuaded to instruct classes in portraiture, clay sculpture, and *nature morte* (as my mother referred to still-life painting) in a small bleak room at the rear where the required north light was almost completely obscured by a looming elevated structure.

Besides teaching desultory piano students, my mother also instructed a few culture seekers in Voice and Elocution and provided accompaniment for the dance classes (Ballet, Eurythmics, and Modern Tap) presided over by a birdlike Frenchwoman, Mademoiselle Ginsburg (pronounced Gans-bourg), who always dressed in a severe black leotard and ballet slippers and demonstrated every *plié*, *jeté*, and *entrechat* with a cigarette dangling from her lips.

I do not know where my mother acquired this foreign adjunct to her faculty but they never maintained a very amicable business relationship—the dance mistress mistrusted the school's fiscal surety and insisted on being paid in cash daily. After every class, in fact.

I came to know Mademoiselle G (as she was addressed by the school body) when I was importuned to attend the Saturday morning "Beginners Ballet Class." This offer of dancing lessons had been made by my mother not so much to add poise to my sluggard comportment as to flesh out the scanty student enrollment. But that cut no ice with Mademoiselle. And being a "shill" neither protected me from her sarcasm nor her cigarette ashes, which fell in constant flurries as she forced me to repeat the dreaded first, second, third, fourth, and fifth dance positions over and over again for hours. The repetitions were asked of me not to improve my elevation, but as an object lesson to all the other maladroit in the class. I only appeared for several weeks of dance instruction before my involvement was summarily interrupted—whether as a result of Mademoiselle G's jeremiads or my own diffidence, I will never know.

It was of little matter, in the final analysis, as the children's class was disbanded, for want of takers, soon after, and agile artist Kay Quinn, who had been waiting in the wings—metaphorically—observing Mademoiselle's measured movements, took over all other dance classes shortly thereafter.

Eventually lack of students and funds sent my mother to other forms of employment, but there was some residual for us all in the blighted enterprise: I learned to know (and in time, cook) the wintery blue-green leaves of a vegetable that was regularly displayed in the market located downstairs from my mother's school. If you are thinking that arctic leaf was *kale*, you are absolutely correct!

If the discovery of kale as something good to eat is a remnant of my mother's Depression-era venture into the arts, some of the ways I learned to prepare it are no less indebted to that enterprise. After a period over the picture palace, the Paula School of Arts & Crafts moved from the noisy Junction Boulevard movie house to the Greene residence. That was when I first found myself pressed into domestic service: preparing our family's nightly dinner in the kitchen, while Aunt Muriel fiddled and my mother pounded the ivories.

I was a frightfully excessive child-chef, and only strongly scented dishes seemed to enflame my culinary sensibilities. When I cooked kale, for instance, it was spiced with garlic and curry powders, plus oregano to give it sufficient savor to meet my demanding tastebuds. The dish passed muster, I guess; everyone but my less-than-stoic father consumed it with apparent grace. But the house reeked for days afterward.

Not willing to kill the goose that had laid the golden eggs, so to speak, my mother said nothing about my incautious seasoning. She merely lit incense and sprayed the light bulbs with cologne before a class began.

Her sister, my feisty Aunt Muriel, was not so sanguine, however. "Listen, kiddo," she rebuked me sharply the morning after one of my headier undertakings at the stove, "you have to learn to cook with judgment—so it doesn't smell like an opium den crossed with a hash-house in here! Otherwise we lose this ball game altogether!"

Mindful of the value of a dollar, I learned to cook with more discretion. That the music-and-dancing academy bit the dust was probably a foregone conclusion. The residual of its existence was my burgeoning recipe collection.

Vegetable Roots

Kale (or *Brassica oleracea acephala*, formally) is sometimes known as a cabbage that will not grow up, but that is hardly an apt description, for this plant with neither head nor heart—which grows resolutely flat in every season—is actually a worthy survivor. Some scientists claim that a wild grass not unlike this one covered the earth billions of years ago, transplanted to dry ground from the sea where it had once flourished. Leaf impressions discovered in the remains of eluvial ooze where dinosaurs once lumbered are in fact almost line-for-line copies of the same vegetable I batter-fry or chop into a skillet whenever the yearning for honest winter greens assails my tongue.

I usually choose to dine on kale in its true season, which begins in late November and barely lasts until March. The ancient Egyptians had a shorter growing season and believed that the lack of this green in their diet was a punishment

---

Kale's moniker in other languages is highly descriptive, to say the least. French call it *chou frisé* ("curly cabbage"), while Germans tag it *Krauskohl* ("crispy cabbage") and Italians know it as *cavolo arricciato* ("curled cabbage"). The Spanish *col rizada* ("cabbage waves") is no less graphic. But leave it to the sensible Dutch to come up with the perfect cognomen. Knowing a good bucolic viand when they grew it, Netherlanders christened kale *boerenkool* ("farm cabbage").

In the British isles, kale is considered to be a plant with mystical powers. For example, the Irish say fairies ride kale stalks in the dark of the moon. When an Irish farmer finds the curly leaves in disarray at sunup, it means his crops will all flourish and grow tall.

My own experience growing kale has been less positive, however. When I find the leaves splayed horizontally in my vegetable patch, it most often augurs an invasion of aphids on the underside of every stalk. Go fight legends, as my mother would say!

from the gods. Serious wine-bibbers considered kale a prophylactic against hangovers; when the stalks withered, headaches flourished, including the pharaoh's, it appears. In Akhenaton's tomb, the sarcophagus was paved with kale leaves carved of jade so they would never shrivel.

What to Look For

Do yourself a favor when you shop for kale: buy it fresh! Frozen kale has an anonymous texture that makes it interchangeable with kelp or khas-khas and has a taste as flavorsome as antic hay.

Kale is a winter vegetable, which means that farmers by and large do not harvest it until after the first (killing) frost—which seems to intensify its flavor. As kale is mostly water anyway (and does not store particularly well once it is cut), sensible gardeners usually leave it in the ground until the first snowfall as well. Look for dark bluish-green bunches with a jot of curl to the stalk ends. Skip yellowed leaves or any foliage that appears wilted or shopworn. Kale that sits overlong on a greengrocer's shelf develops a bite that has nothing in common with succor.

Inordinately high in vitamin A (over 9,000 units per cup), kale is also a veritable windfall of calcium (206 grams) and potassium (243 milligrams), which helps to build strong bones and enrich the blood supply.

Preparation

As kale is basically a peasant food with no pretension to *haute cuisine*, its optimum classic rendering is a homely braising—covered with only a minimal amount of liquid.

Not actually as harsh-tasting as some of the greens already discussed, kale does not require an obligatory blanching prior to cooking, in my opinion. Wash it well, however. I usually separate the leaves first and soak them in tepid water for about ten minutes before moving on to any advance preparation. This helps to remove the loose soil that often accumulates in the folds. After bathing the leaves I rinse them under cold running water, then simply remove the tough center ribs before I start the cooking.

DANISH KALE SOUP

My favored soup dispensation comes from Denmark. More than a menu starter, this hearty quaff is actually a meal unto itself, as each jade bowlful is enriched with a perfect poached egg at the heart. Serve it with salad, cheese, bread, wine, and a roaring fire if possible.

2 tablespoons unsalted butter
1 onion, minced
1 clove garlic, minced
1/8 teaspoon ground cinnamon
3/4 pound kale, stems removed, finely chopped
4 cups strong Beef Stock (see page 409)
4 eggs
1 teaspoon red wine vinegar
Salt and freshly ground black pepper
Chopped chives or scallion tops

1. Melt the butter in a large saucepan over medium-low heat. Add the onion; cook 5 minutes. Do not brown. Add the garlic; cook 2 minutes longer.

2. Stir the cinnamon into the onion mixture. Add the kale, tossing to coat it well. Add the stock. Heat to boiling; reduce the heat. Simmer, covered, 20 minutes.

3. Break each egg into an individual small bowl. Fill a medium-size skillet with water; add the vinegar. Heat to boiling; reduce the heat so the water barely simmers. Poach the eggs, two at a time. Remove with a slotted spoon and place in individual serving bowls. Spoon the hot soup over the eggs. Sprinkle with salt and pepper to taste and chopped chives. Serve immediately.

Serves 4.

KALE SLAW

These next two kale devises—this one raw and crunchy, the other, Batter-Fried Kale, crispy golden—are both long on taste, short on smell.

3 strips bacon
1 pound young, tender kale, stems removed, leaves chopped
½ small cabbage, shredded (1 to 1½ cups)
1 small red onion, sliced thin
1 medium tomato, seeded, cubed
½ green bell pepper, seeded, finely chopped
½ red bell pepper, seeded, finely chopped
1 cup Mayonnaise (see page 408)
½ cup sour cream
1 teaspoon Dijon mustard
½ teaspoon curry powder
2 tablespoons milk
1 tablespoon white wine vinegar
Salt and freshly ground black pepper
2 tablespoons chopped fresh parsley

1. Sauté the bacon in a medium skillet until crisp. Drain on paper towels. Crumble and reserve. Reserve the bacon drippings.

2. Combine the kale with the cabbage, red onion, tomato, green pepper, and red pepper in a large bowl. Lightly toss.

3. Combine the mayonnaise with the sour cream in a medium bowl. Beat in the reserved bacon drippings, the mustard, curry powder, milk, vinegar, and salt and pepper to taste. Pour the dressing over the salad. Toss until well mixed. Sprinkle with the reserved bacon and the chopped parsley. Serve at room temperature.

Serves 4 to 6.

BATTER-FRIED KALE

½ cup all-purpose flour
1 teaspoon dry English mustard
½ teaspoon freshly grated nutmeg
¼ teaspoon salt
2 eggs, separated
1 teaspoon Dijon mustard
½ cup beer
1 pound young, tender kale, stems trimmed but leaves left intact
Vegetable oil for frying
Salt

1. Combine the flour, dry mustard, nutmeg, and salt in a medium bowl. Combine the egg yolks, Dijon mustard, and beer in another bowl. Whisk the egg mixture into the flour mixture until smooth. Refrigerate, covered, 8 hours.

2. Wash the kale well and pat it dry with paper towels.

3. Beat the egg whites until stiff; fold them into the chilled batter.

4. Heat 2 inches of oil in a heavy saucepan until hot but not smoking. Dip the kale leaves into the batter. Shake off excess batter, and fry, a few at a time, until golden on both sides. Drain on paper towels. Sprinkle with salt to taste, and serve immediately; or reheat in a preheated 400°F oven for 5 minutes.

Serves 4 to 6.

KALE PUDD'

Scotland is a place where kale flourishes in prophesy as well as pot!

It is a favored pastime of marriageable maidens in the Highlands to strip the leaves from kale as we would from a daisy, calling out the name of every eligible male in town as each leaf is tossed into a casserole. The name assigned to the very last leaf is reputedly the spouse-to-be!

Scottish lassies may alter the prognostication, however—by simply refusing to eat the dish concocted of those leaves. If a girl skipped the following Scottish baked pudding out of such high-handedness, she would certainly not have my sympathy. For it is *verra verra* special!

¾ pound kale, stems removed
½ cup Chicken or Beef Stock (see page 410 or 409)
½ cup water
2 tablespoons unsalted butter
3 tablespoons all-purpose flour
1 cup milk, hot
½ cup heavy or whipping cream, hot
Dash of hot pepper sauce
Pinch of ground allspice
¼ teaspoon freshly grated nutmeg
¼ teaspoon freshly ground black pepper
Salt
2 cups cooked rice
½ cup cubed white cheese (I like mozzarella)
2 tablespoons freshly grated Parmesan cheese

1. Preheat the oven to 350°F. Combine the kale with the stock and water in a medium saucepan. Heat to boiling; reduce the heat. Simmer, covered, until tender, about 15 minutes. Drain, reserving the cooking liquid.

2. Transfer the drained kale to the container of a food processor or blender. Add ¼ cup of the cooking liquid; process until smooth. Reserve.

3. Melt the butter in a medium saucepan over low heat. Stir in the flour. Cook, stirring constantly, 2 minutes. Whisk in the milk and cream. Raise the heat slightly and cook until thick, about 5 minutes. Add the hot pepper sauce, allspice, nutmeg, pepper, and salt to taste. Stir in the puréed kale.

4. Transfer the mixture to a large bowl. Add the rice and white cheese, and mix well. Transfer to a buttered baking dish and sprinkle with the Parmesan cheese. Bake until bubbly, about 20 minutes.

Serves 4 to 6.

COUNTY KERRY KALE

The Irish donation to my collection of kale recipes may appear, at first glance, to be a reprise of the first farmhouse braising. It's not. While the vegetable is sautéed in bacon drippings first and seasoned with vinegar later, the Irish potato that joins the green gives a very different flavor to the dish. It is a confederation every denizen of Eire may be rightfully proud to claim, but I picked up the recipe from a Dubliner.

6 strips bacon
2 tablespoons unsalted butter
1 clove garlic, minced
¼ cup Chicken Stock (see page 410)
1 pound kale, stems removed, roughly chopped
3 medium potatoes, peeled, diced
1 tablespoon red wine vinegar
Salt and freshly ground black pepper
Chopped fresh parsley

1. Sauté the bacon in a large saucepan until crisp. Drain on paper towels. Crumble and reserve.

2. Remove all but 1 tablespoon bacon drippings from the saucepan. Add the butter and garlic. Cook over medium-low heat until golden, about 3 minutes. Add the stock and kale. Heat to boiling; reduce the heat. Cook, covered, 5 minutes. Stir in the potatoes. Cook, uncovered, stirring occasionally, until the potatoes are tender and almost all the liquid has evaporated, about 15 minutes. Sprinkle with the vinegar and add salt and pepper to taste. Sprinkle with the crumbled bacon and chopped parsley.

Serves 4 to 6.

KALE FRIBBLE

I have decided to add a second offering to my classic nominations. A version of baked kale at its very best, this is one dish I truly pine for whenever the green is out of season—which is practically half the year. Some might consider the following mixture of chopped kale, cream, and cheese in a shell of buttery crumbs a "crustless pie." But not I. The recipe was given to me by a British cook who announced, "It's a fribble but delicious anyway!" According to Webster and friends, a fribble seems to be a lightweight affair—so I let the name stand, unaltered.

2½ pounds kale, stems removed
4½ tablespoons unsalted butter
2½ tablespoons all-purpose flour
1 cup Chicken Stock, hot (see page 410)
½ cup grated Gruyère or Jarlsberg cheese
½ teaspoon salt
½ teaspoon freshly ground black pepper
¼ teaspoon freshly grated nutmeg
Dash of hot pepper sauce
½ cup fresh bread crumbs

1. Preheat the oven to 425°F. Cook the kale, covered, in boiling salted water until very tender, about 15 minutes. Rinse under cold running water; drain, pressing out all liquid with the back of a

spoon. Chop fine.

2. Melt 2½ tablespoons of the butter in a medium saucepan over low heat. Stir in the flour. Cook, stirring constantly, 2 minutes. Whisk in the hot chicken stock. Cook until very thick, about 2 minutes. Add ¼ cup of the cheese, the salt, pepper, nutmeg, and hot pepper sauce. Stir in the kale. Transfer to a buttered shallow baking dish.

3. Melt the remaining 2 tablespoons butter in a small skillet over medium heat. Stir in the bread crumbs. Cook, stirring constantly, until golden. Spoon over the kale mixture. Sprinkle with the remaining ¼ cup cheese. Bake until bubbly, 15 to 20 minutes.

Serves 6 to 8.

FARM-STYLE BRAISED KALE

My prototypical kale recipe is borrowed from a farm kitchen. Not just one, however, for I have uncovered the very same recipe performance with ever so slight variations at homespun stoves everywhere from Caen to Kansas City. And inevitably dined well on each offering.

Serve this dish hot off the stove with any main dish you have up your sleeve and gather the hurrahs with confidence!

2 strips bacon
1 tablespoon unsalted butter
1 small onion, finely chopped
1 pound kale, stems removed, roughly chopped
Salt and freshly ground black pepper
Pinch of ground allspice
1 tablespoon red wine vinegar
1 lemon, sliced thin

1. Sauté the bacon strips in a large skillet until crisp. Drain on paper towels. Crumble and reserve.

2. Add the butter to the bacon drippings in the skillet. Cook the onion over medium-low heat until golden, about 5 minutes.

3. Meanwhile, rinse the kale in cold water.

4. Add the kale to the skillet, with just the water that clings to the leaves. Cook, covered, stirring occasionally, until tender, 15 to 20 minutes. Add salt and pepper to taste, the allspice, and the vinegar. Sprinkle with the reserved bacon and garnish with lemon slices.

Serves 4.

TURKISH MEATBALLS WITH KALE AND BARLEY

Turks have a saying about kale that roughly translates as "Every leaf you chew adds another branch to the tree of your life!" To make the point greener, Turkish

housewives serve kale in a multitude of different ways with stunning regularity—often three times a day.

Here's the best version I know. It is nutritious as the dickens; it is also wonderful into the bargain.

½ cup barley
1½ pounds ground raw lamb
1 onion, minced
3 tablespoons finely chopped parsley
½ cup fresh bread crumbs
1 egg, lightly beaten
1½ cups chicken broth, approximately (see page 414)
Pinch of ground allspice
⅛ teaspoon freshly grated nutmeg
¾ teaspoon salt
¼ teaspoon freshly ground black pepper
2 teaspoons olive oil
1 tablespoon unsalted butter
¾ pound kale, stems removed, roughly chopped
2 cloves garlic, crushed
1 teaspoon ground coriander
1 cup sour cream

1. Cook the barley in a large pot of boiling salted water, partially covered, until tender, about 20 minutes. Drain; reserve.

2. Meanwhile, combine the ground lamb with the onion, parsley, bread crumbs, egg, ½ cup of the chicken broth, the allspice, nutmeg, ½ teaspoon of the salt, and the pepper in a large bowl. Mix well. Form into small meatballs.

3. Rub a heavy skillet with 1 teaspoon of the oil. Sauté the meatballs, a few at a time, over medium-high heat, until lightly browned on all sides. Set aside.

4. Melt the butter in a large pot or Dutch oven over medium-low heat. Add the kale and ½ cup of the chicken broth. Simmer, covered, 20 minutes.

5. Mash the garlic with the coriander and the remaining ¼ teaspoon salt until a paste is formed. Heat the remaining 1 teaspoon oil in a small skillet over medium heat. Add the garlic mixture and sauté until golden, about 3 minutes.

6. Stir the garlic mixture into the kale. Add the barley, meatballs, and remaining ½ cup chicken broth. Mix well, being careful not to damage the meatballs. Simmer, covered, 30 minutes, adding more chicken broth if the mixture seems too dry. (This dish may be made in advance to this point and reheated.)

7. Just before serving, stir the sour cream into the meatball mixture. Cook until warmed through; do not allow to boil.

Serves 6.

NETHERLANDERS' BAKED KALE

This dish makes an eminently serviceable meatless main course. If you wish to serve it as an adjunct to a full-course meal, eliminate the butter sauce and simply use drippings or gravy in its place. The batter increases in flavor as it bakes, so do not be tempted toward overseasoning.

For the sauce:

8 tablespoons (1 stick) unsalted butter
1 shallot, minced
½ teaspoon minced fresh tarragon, or ¼ teaspoon dried
Pinch of dried thyme
1 teaspoon tarragon vinegar

For the kale:

1 pound kale, stems removed
4 medium potatoes, peeled, cubed
4 tablespoons (½ stick) unsalted butter
1 cup heavy or whipping cream
3 egg yolks, lightly beaten
1½ cups grated Edam cheese
⅛ teaspoon freshly grated nutmeg
¼ teaspoon ground white pepper
Salt
4 egg whites

1. To make the herbed butter sauce: Melt the 8 tablespoons butter in a small heavy saucepan over very low heat. Add the shallot, tarragon, and thyme. Cook, uncovered, stirring occasionally, 1 hour. Do not allow the butter to brown.

2. Meanwhile, preheat the oven to 400°F. Cook the kale, covered, in boiling salted water until very tender, about 15 minutes. Drain well. Chop fine.

3. Cook the potatoes in boiling salted water until tender, about 15 minutes. Drain. Rice or mash the potatoes until smooth. Stir in the 4 tablespoons butter and the cream. Beat in the egg yolks, chopped kale, 1¼ cups of the cheese, the nutmeg, pepper, and salt to taste.

4. Beat the egg whites until stiff but not dry. Fold them into the potato-kale mixture.

5. Lightly butter a 2-quart soufflé dish. Sprinkle the bottom and sides with the remaining ¼ cup cheese. Spoon the potato-kale mixture into the dish. Bake 30 minutes.

6. Just before serving, stir the vinegar into the herbed butter sauce. It is traditional to have each person make a well in their potatoes to hold the butter sauce, which is passed on the side.

Serves 6 to 8.

KOHLRABI

Its Ugliness Is Only Skin Deep

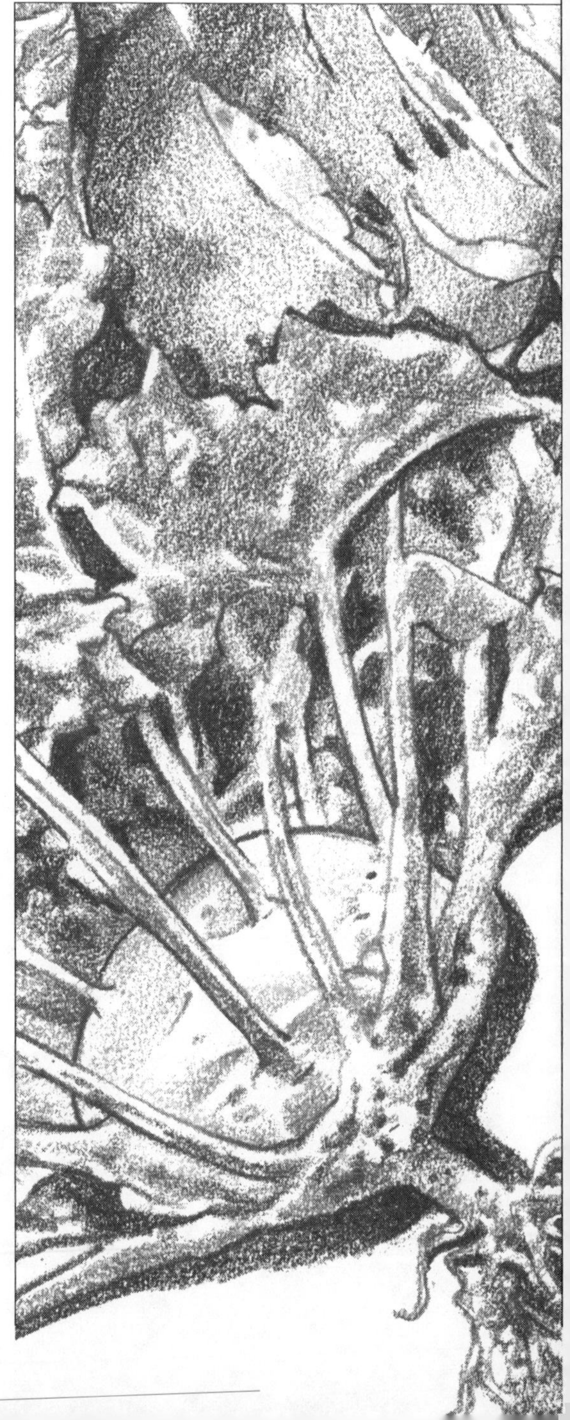

Back when I was young, the term "Public Enemy" was in common usage around the nation—at our house as well, but for a somewhat more personal reason.

True, it was an era when Bonnie and Clyde, Dillinger and Capone made headlines daily, and movies like *Scarface* or radio shows like *Gang Busters* held most of the U.S. in thrall. But the public enemy list I logged had nothing to do with run-of-the-mill gangsters. It was instead a hand-scrawled sheet, thumbtacked to our kitchen cupboard (by me), that listed all the vegetables I hated and absolutely refused to ever eat!

If my action seems like strong stuff, it was not. Because when push came to shove, I usually consumed whatever was placed before me, just like every other American kid during the Depression. I was just a tad more vocal about my prejudices.

My list of enemy vegetables was long and labored. It changed with the seasons and the somewhat lacklustre seasonings in our kitchen. But one name inevitably led all the rest. *Kohlrabi!* For reasons not exclusively based on taste.

When I was young, scholarship was not my strong point. I read haltingly. My handwriting was illegible. More to the point, I could neither add, subtract, multiply, or (Oh God!) face a fraction without the use of every outside appendage I possessed.

Athletics were no better, and forget my manual skills entirely! It took two terms of weekly "shop" classes for me to construct a very rudimentary birdhouse.

A hapless if not hopeless student, I did have one small aptitude, however: spelling. My mother claimed I inherited this gift from her. As a young girl she had been an accomplished winner of spelling contests and never lost her zeal for the ABC's. Her favorite litanies "*i* before *e* unless after *c*" and "it always takes four *s*'s to possess" are still the very maxims I dredge up when in doubt at the typewriter today.

My mother's pride at knowing how to spell was infectious, and I would often study the dictionary for hours, trying to uncover really big words (of four or five syllables at the very least) that would stump her. I never succeeded. But the training and my pleasure in these words (though often mispronounced) managed to impress one of my teachers, who determined that I would make an eminently worthy team captain at the fourth grade spelling bee.

This contest, if won, usually led to an interschool, then a borough-wide tournament that in turn presaged a city, state, and (with any luck at all) national handicap. I knew well—from the rotogravure section of the Sunday newspapers—the image of a small serious child (hair slicked down and bandbox-neat) standing on tiptoe to receive a solid gold medal plus a kiss from Eleanor Roosevelt. The new spelling champion of the United States. And I dearly coveted that hour of glory.

I studied for weeks before the event, drilled by my mother. *Ostensible*, *science*, *languish*, and even *rendezvous* were all words I could unfurl at the tongue's end—long before the day of the fateful meet arrived.

Where did all this confluence of verbiage end? In disaster, I regret to say. For while he lasted through rounds of jawbreakers like *carousel* and *homogenized* and *piety*, Greene the speller was felled in the very last round by *kohlrabi*, the green. It was one word I had never come across in my nightly perusal of Webster, and I assumed that since it tasted not unlike cauliflower, it was probably spelled the same way.

"C-A-U-L-R . . ." I began, and went down to defeat in ignominy.

Kohlrabi entered my public enemy list that very night and stayed there, if not forever, far too long.

Obviously I was the loser in more ways than one. It's a delicious vegetable.

Vegetable Roots

Not just another pretty face in the garden, kohlrabi is one of the least-consumed vegetables that grow, because its appearance is frankly so off-putting to most cooks.

Yet another *Brassica* cousin, this member of the cabbage tribe is long on stem and short on stern, with rather formidable bulbs that rise like pale green tennis balls just above the earth's surface. The plant is topped with a network of spiky dark leaves that are extremely tender on the fork when newly sprouted, and will, in a pinch, perform admirably as a stand-in for some of the more rugged greens already limned in this book.

Grace notes about kohlrabi's antecedents are rather sketchy. The name itself is Teutonic in origin and literally means "a cabbage turnip," which may be technically correct but more than a tad imprecise if one is describing the flavor. The eclectic Alice B. Toklas once particularized kohlrabi's taste as "having the pungency of a high-born radish bred to a low-brow cucumber." That's somewhat closer to the mark.

Rumor has it that kohlrabi came to Western Europe from Asia along with Attila the Hun. Its earliest notation in manuscripts (as wild head cabbage) dates back to the fourth century, when that barbarian was making the first of his "cultural missions" abroad. Attila was repulsed half a century later, but kohl-

If the kohlrabi we dine on has a decidedly German name, so does the vegetable that "cabbage-turnip" lovers conspicuously consume in the rest of the world, for it is almost always a literal translation: *chou rave* in France; *col rabáno* in Spain; *cavolo rapa* in Italy; *kohlrabee* in Russia; *kaalrabi* in Denmark, and *couve rábano* in Portugal.

Greeks, however, give it a slightly different tag. As they consider this wild cabbage to be a vegetable that "sprang from the sweat of Jupiter," they dub it *agrio lahano,* which in its classic sense means "wild heat."

rabi stayed on to flavor the stew pots of the Holy Roman Empire. But not Charlemagne's. He fed "caulo-rapa" exclusively to grazing cows because his court physicians asserted that digestion of this "wintry root" turned fighting men bovine. No mention is made of its effect on the cows.

The initial botanical record of kohlrabi's other therapeutic properties (compiled by Matthiolus in 1554) states that "immeasurable amounts" taken as part of the diet will cure dropsy, arrest rising wind, and retard temporary deafness as well. There is, of course, no mention in his pharmacy of just what would constitute an "immeasurable amount."

For what it is worth, Doctor Greene's advice is more specific: keep your kohlrabi out of the medicine chest. Its health-giving attributes are decidedly more pronounced in a saucepan!

What to Look For

Kohlrabi is harvested in home gardens from mid to late summer but never makes its appearance on greengrocers' shelves till the tan is on the pumpkin and frost covers everything else. Look for relatively small, well-rounded, uniform globes when you shop, though in all honesty I must tell you that a standard-size kohlrabi is hard to find. Pass on any that are larger than three inches in diameter, however, as they have obviously stayed in the garden patch too long and will be slightly "woody" in texture if not woebegone in taste. Likewise avoid cracked or split kohlrabi. The leaves of this vegetable are generally a clue to its tenderness. Choose the foliage of brightest hue and crispest character if there is an option.

I judge a pound of raw kohlrabi (with leaves) to yield approximately twelve ounces cooked—about two to three generous servings.

A highly nutritive green, kohlrabi is a dieter's dream dish since it contains a scant 29 calories per ⅔ cup. This vegetable is also sky-high in potassium (372 milligrams) and, like other *Brassicas*, filled with healthy jolts of calcium (42 milligrams), magnesium (37 milligrams) and phosphorus (51 milligrams). Not as vitamin-enriched, kohlrabi still contains a healthy dose of ascorbic acid (66 milligrams) per 100 grams.

Preparation

Many reputable authorities declare that this vegetable should be cooked first and peeled later (because the more flavorsome flesh is closest to the skin.) I do not agree for a multitude of reasons. Frankly it is a nuisance to peel hot vegetables, and as kohlrabi is a particularly dense root, it does not cook evenly. If a recipe calls for the cooked kohlrabi to be diced or cut into julienne strips, I discover that while the center may indeed be firm, the outer portion is often disconcertingly mushy and soft. As a consequence, I inevitably attack this vegetable with a rotary blade prior to its cookery.

Peeling a kohlrabi can be tricky. It is best to trim off the green stems with a sharp knife first. Make sure to remove all veins as you peel the skin, as there is nothing more unpleasant than discovering a hint of this fibrous matter in a finished dish. A well-peeled, uncooked kohlrabi is almost white.

KALARABELEVES

(Hungarian Kohlrabi Soup)

According to my best source of Hungarian information (the quick-witted, bright-eyed, and super-sensuously-tongued George Lang), "the secret of good Hungarian string instrumentalists is that they have a well-developed *sound sense* just as Hungarian housewives and cooks are either born with or develop a keen *soup sense*."

In Hungary, according to George, thickened soups are with limited logic called either "white soup" or "brown soup." The following rendering (though not Lang's) is what one might safely adjudge to be a tawny (tangy) compromise.

2 strips bacon, chopped
2½ tablespoons unsalted butter
1 large onion, halved, sliced
1 clove garlic, chopped
2 large ribs celery, chopped
1 large carrot, chopped
1 tablespoon chopped fresh parsley
3½ cups chicken broth (see page 414)
1 large chicken (3½ to 4 pounds), cut into serving pieces
1 cup water
1 pound kohlrabi with leaves (2 to 3 bulbs)
1 tablespoon all-purpose flour
1½ tablespoons lemon juice
Salt and freshly ground black pepper

1. Sauté the bacon in a medium-size saucepan over medium heat until crisp. Add 1 tablespoon of the butter and the sliced onion; cook 1 minute. Add the garlic, celery, carrot, and parsley. Cook, covered, 5 minutes. Add 1 cup of the chicken broth and continue to cook, covered, until the vegetables are tender, about 10 minutes.

2. Transfer the mixture to the container of a blender or food processor. Process until smooth (being careful: hot liquid will expand). Strain the mixture into a large saucepan. Heat to boiling. Add the remaining chicken broth, the chicken pieces, and the water. Return to boiling; reduce the heat. Simmer, covered, skimming the surface occasionally to remove fat, until the chicken is tender, about 50 minutes.

3. Meanwhile, trim, peel, and dice the kohlrabi bulbs. Wash the leaves and cook them in boiling water 1 minute. Rinse the leaves under cold running water, drain, and chop. Set aside.

4. Remove the chicken from the soup. Add the diced kohlrabi bulbs to the soup. Cook, uncovered, until the kohlrabi is tender, about 15 minutes.

5. Meanwhile, remove the meat from the chicken; keep warm.

6. Melt the remaining 1½ tablespoons butter in a medium saucepan. Stir in the flour. Cook, stirring constantly, 2 minutes. Whisk in 1 cup hot soup. Stir this mixture back into the soup; cook until slightly thickened, about 10 minutes. Add the cooked chicken and the chopped kohlrabi leaves; cook 5 minutes. Add the lemon juice, and salt and pepper to taste.

Serves 6 to 8.

KOHLRABI AND CARROT SLAW

Add carrots, peppers, and onions to kohlrabi for a crunchy salad, then add up the vitamins, and count your culinary blessings.

1 1/4 pounds kohlrabi, trimmed, peeled, shredded
2 large carrots, shredded
1/2 red bell pepper, seeded, diced
1/2 cup chopped whole scallions, bulbs and green tops
1 teaspoon chopped fresh dill
1 egg
1/3 cup olive oil
1/3 cup tarragon wine vinegar
1/3 cup sour cream
1 teaspoon ground mild chiles
1/2 teaspoon ground cumin
1/2 teaspoon salt
1/4 teaspoon freshly ground black pepper

1. Combine the kohlrabi, carrots, bell pepper, scallions, and dill in a large bowl. Toss lightly.

2. Beat the egg in a medium bowl. Slowly add the oil, vinegar, sour cream, chiles, cumin, salt, and pepper. Pour this dressing over the vegetables and toss well. Refrigerate, covered, for 2 hours before serving.

Serves 4 to 6.

KOHLRABI BENNE SALAD

Farmers in the South first planted kohlrabi as a rotation crop with cotton—not for sale, but as "vittles" for the slave quarters in the hard-pressed Southern winter. One remnant of the black cooks' inventions still remains. It is a North Carolina formula: a salad of raw kohlrabi pickled in vinegar, onion, and ginger and seasoned with benne (sesame) seeds to bring the diner good luck.

2 large kohlrabi bulbs (about 2 1/2 pounds), trimmed, peeled
2 small white onions, sliced thin
1/2 cup tarragon wine vinegar
1/4 cup sugar
2 teaspoons benne (sesame) seeds
1/2 teaspoon minced fresh ginger root
1/2 teaspoon crushed dried hot red peppers
1 teaspoon salt
1/2 teaspoon freshly ground black pepper

1. Cut the kohlrabi bulbs into strips about 1/4 inch thick and 2 inches long. Cook them in boiling salted water for 1 minute. Rinse under cold running water and drain. Transfer the kohlrabi to a bowl, add the onions, and toss lightly.

2. Combine the vinegar and sugar in a small bowl. Add the benne (sesame) seeds, ginger root, hot peppers, salt, and pepper. Pour this dressing over the kohlrabi and onions and toss well. Chill, covered, for 2 hours before serving.

Serves 4 to 6.

WARM KOHLRABI AND SMOKED SAUSAGE SALAD

One place kohlrabi is popular is in the provincial kitchens of France. Devotees of *haute* and *nouvelle cuisine* usually give it a wide berth, but less rarefied appetites seem to dote on its astringency, particularly in winter when other pickings are slim.

The best *chou rave* I ever tasted in France grew in Alsace-Lorraine, not far from the German border, where kohlrabi first took root in Europe. A dish I am extremely fond of owes its genesis to that locale. It is borrowed almost intact from the French dish known as *pommes de terre à l'huile avec saucisse* (sliced potatoes in oil and vinegar dressing with smoked sausage). Kohlrabi does not exactly take the place of a potato, mind you, but it makes an arresting proxy. Less than half the calories too!

6 medium kohlrabi bulbs (about 2½ pounds), trimmed, peeled
3 tablespoons dry vermouth
2 tablespoons red wine vinegar
2 teaspoons Dijon mustard
¼ teaspoon salt
⅓ cup olive oil
2 tablespoons unsalted butter
1 pound smoked sausage (I use a soft beef variety), sliced about 1 inch thick, on the diagonal
2 whole scallions, bulbs and green tops, trimmed, chopped
1 tablespoon chopped fresh parsley

1. Cook the peeled kohlrabi bulbs in boiling salted water, uncovered, until tender, about 40 minutes. Drain.

2. Meanwhile, in a small bowl, combine the vermouth, vinegar, mustard, salt, and oil. Set aside.

3. Melt the butter in a large skillet over medium-low heat. Sauté the sausage slices until golden brown on all sides, about 8 minutes. If the slices are excessively fatty, drain on paper towels.

4. Meanwhile, cut the kohlrabi into ¼-inch-thick slices and place them in a medium bowl. Whisk the vermouth dressing and pour it over the kohlrabi. Add the sliced sausage and scallions. Toss lightly and serve sprinkled with fresh parsley.

Serves 4 to 6.

KOHLRABI IN AVGOLEMONO SAUCE

The next rendering, Greek of course, is a toss of cooked kohlrabi roots and leaves together in a golden lemon sauce.

4 medium kohlrabi (about 2 pounds) with leaves
2 cups chicken broth (see page 414)
1 tablespoon unsalted butter
1 tablespoon all-purpose flour
2 eggs
Juice of 2½ lemons
Salt and ground white pepper

1. Trim and peel the kohlrabi bulbs.

Reserve the leaves. Cut each bulb into ¼-inch-thick slices. Place the slices in a medium saucepan, add the chicken broth, and heat to boiling; reduce the heat. Simmer, covered, until tender, about 20 minutes. Drain, reserving 1 cup of the cooking liquid. Keep the kohlrabi slices warm.

2. Trim the leaves of any tough stems. (You should have about 1 cup of leaves.) Cook the leaves in boiling salted water, uncovered, until very tender, about 10 minutes. Drain, pressing out the liquid with the back of a spoon. Chop the leaves.

3. Melt the butter in a medium saucepan over medium-low heat. Stir in the flour. Cook, stirring constantly, 2 minutes. Whisk in the reserved cooking liquid. Cook 2 minutes.

4. Beat the eggs in a small bowl. Slowly beat ½ cup of the hot sauce into the eggs. Beat this mixture back into the sauce. Add the lemon juice. Cook, stirring constantly, over low heat until thickened, about 10 minutes. Do not boil. Add the chopped kohlrabi leaves, and salt and white pepper to taste. Spoon the sauce over the kohlrabi slices.

Serves 4.

Note: The sauce for the kohlrabi can be held for at least 30 minutes in the top of a double boiler over hot water.

> In the garden, kohlrabi grows a foot tall. Twice as wide too, if the tender blossoms are dutifully pinched back before the growing season. Mine never are. Not just because I like the flowers (these creamy yellow petals are particularly graceful), but for an ulterior motive as well: fragrant kohlrabi blooms discourage more garden pests than a pint of malathion!

BRAISED KOHLRABI WITH TARRAGON

The ultimate rendering of kohlrabi would appear to depend entirely on the taste buds of the diner. To my mind, however, its most classic rendering is a fast braise (in a covered pot) with only the most elemental seasonings as its amendment—in the following case, a sluice of strong chicken stock and a sprinkling of tarragon leaves, which seem to enhance the kohlrabi's quintessential crunch.

1½ to 2 pounds kohlrabi, trimmed, peeled
2 tablespoons unsalted butter
¼ cup strong Chicken Stock (see page 410)
1 teaspoon fresh tarragon, minced
Salt and freshly ground black pepper
Chopped fresh parsley

1. Cut the peeled kohlrabi bulbs into strips about 3 inches long and ¼ inch thick.

2. Melt the butter in a large heavy skillet over medium-low heat. Add the kohlrabi strips, tossing well to coat them. Add the stock and tarragon. Cook, covered, until just tender, about 15 minutes. Remove the cover and raise the heat slightly. Cook until golden. Add salt and pepper to taste. Sprinkle with parsley before serving.

Serves 4 to 6.

KOHLRABI MORVANDELLE

This is kohlrabi's finest hour—standing in for potatoes again, this time in a sea of cream. I'd rather eat this dish than win a spelling bee, any day!

3 tablespoons unsalted butter
1 small onion, minced
1 small clove garlic, minced
¼ cup chopped cooked ham
1 tablespoon chopped fresh parsley
2 eggs
3 tablespoons heavy or whipping cream
½ cup grated Jarlsberg cheese
1½ to 2 pounds kohlrabi, trimmed, peeled, coarsely grated
Salt and freshly ground black pepper

1. Preheat the oven to 375°F. Melt 1 tablespoon of the butter in a small skillet over medium-low heat. Add the onion; cook 1 minute. Stir in the garlic and ham, raise the heat slightly, and cook 2 minutes. Remove from the heat. Stir in the parsley.

2. Beat the eggs with the cream in a medium bowl until light. Stir in the ham-onion mixture and the grated cheese.

3. Squeeze all liquid out of the grated kohlrabi with your hands. Add the kohlrabi to the ham-cheese mixture. Add salt and pepper to taste.

4. Place the remaining 2 tablespoons butter in a shallow ovenproof baking dish and heat it in the oven until the butter foams. Spoon the kohlrabi mixture into the dish. Bake 25 minutes.

Serves 4.

COMFORTED KOHLRABI

A less established kohlrabi prototype is my own invention. It is a style of creamed vegetable cookery, I must add, that is rapidly becoming a classic in its own right since the briefly blanched ingredient cooks in seasoned cream alone, just until the sauce thickens and turns velvety. No flour added, no stirring necessary, and only one pot to wash up afterward! I call this technique "comforting."

6 small kohlrabi bulbs (1½ to 2 pounds), trimmed, peeled
2 tablespoons unsalted butter
1 cup heavy or whipping cream
1½ tablespoons lemon juice
Dash of hot pepper sauce
Salt and freshly ground black pepper
1½ tablespoons chopped fresh dill

1. Cut the peeled kohlrabi bulbs into ⅛-inch-thick slices. Cook in boiling salted water, 5 minutes. Drain.

2. Melt the butter in a large skillet over medium-low heat. Add the kohlrabi slices, tossing well to coat with butter. Add the cream. Heat to boiling; reduce the heat. Simmer, uncovered, until the kohlrabi is tender and the cream is thick, about 10 minutes.

3. Stir in the lemon juice, hot pepper sauce, and salt and pepper to taste. Sprinkle with the fresh dill.

Serves 4 to 6.

KOHLRABI BAKE

Of Magyar extraction, this is a reworking of one of Marina Polvay's prescriptions pairing kohlrabi with ham in a paradigm casserole.

2 pounds kohlrabi, trimmed, peeled
4 tablespoons (½ stick) unsalted butter
Salt and freshly ground black pepper
½ to ¾ pound cooked ham, cut into 1-inch strips
¼ cup chopped fresh parsley
2 tablespoons all-purpose flour
1½ cups heavy or whipping cream
⅛ teaspoon freshly grated nutmeg
4 egg yolks

1. Preheat the oven to 350°F. Cut the kohlrabi bulbs into ⅛-inch-thick slices.

2. Melt the butter in a large saucepan. Toss in the kohlrabi slices. Cook, covered, over medium-low heat, tossing occasionally, about 15 minutes.

3. With a slotted spoon transfer one third of the kohlrabi to a 1½- to 2-quart baking dish. Sprinkle with salt and pepper to taste. Add half the ham. Sprinkle with half the parsley. Continue to layer, finishing with a layer of kohlrabi. Reserve the pan liquids.

4. Add the flour to the cooking juices in the saucepan and whisk until smooth. Cook over medium-low heat, stirring constantly, 2 minutes. Add the cream. Continue to cook until slightly thickened, about 3 minutes. Add the nutmeg, and salt and pepper to taste.

5. Beat the egg yolks in a small bowl. Add ½ cup of the hot sauce. Stir this mixture back into the sauce. Pour the sauce over the kohlrabi and bake until bubbly, about 30 minutes. Let stand 5 minutes before serving.

Serves 4 to 6.

VEAL-STUFFED KOHLRABI

This Germanic dish is stuffed first and then stewed—a pouch of kohlrabi crammed to the hilt with subtly herbed ground veal.

8 medium kohlrabi bulbs (of equal size if possible), trimmed, peeled
2 tablespoons unsalted butter
1 small onion, minced
1 small clove garlic, minced
¾ pound ground veal
1 egg, lightly beaten
½ teaspoon chopped fresh tarragon, or a pinch of dried
1 teaspoon chopped fresh parsley plus additional for garnish
½ cup fresh bread crumbs
¼ cup heavy or whipping cream
½ teaspoon salt
¼ teaspoon freshly ground black pepper
1½ cups chicken broth (see page 414)
2 tablespoons all-purpose flour

1. Slice the bottoms off the kohlrabi bulbs so they will stand upright. With a small spoon scoop out the centers, leaving a shell about ¼-inch thick. Finely

chop enough scooped-out kohlrabi to make ¼ cup. (Reserve remaining centers for salads or stock.)

2. Cook the prepared kohlrabi bulbs in boiling salted water until almost tender, about 20 minutes. Drain. Preheat the oven to 350°F.

3. Melt 1 tablespoon of the butter in a small skillet over medium-low heat. Add the onion; cook 2 minutes. Add the garlic and raise the heat slightly; cook until golden, about 3 minutes.

4. Place the veal in a medium bowl. Add the onion mixture, egg, tarragon, 1 teaspoon parsley, bread crumbs, cream, salt, and pepper. Mix thoroughly.

5. Fill the prepared kohlrabi bulbs with the meat mixture. Place them snugly in a baking dish or Dutch oven. Pour the broth around, not over, the kohlrabi. Cover, and bake 30 minutes.

6. Transfer the kohlrabi bulbs to a shallow platter and keep warm. Reserve the cooking juices. Melt the remaining 1 tablespoon butter in a medium saucepan over medium-low heat. Stir in the flour. Cook, stirring constantly, 2 minutes. Whisk in the cooking juices. Heat to boiling; cook until slightly thickened, about 5 minutes. Spoon the sauce over the kohlrabi and sprinkle with the remaining chopped parsley.

Serves 4.

KOHLRABI GOUGERE

I crossed kohlrabi off my public enemy list years ago when I discovered how compatible this vegetable could be when paired with other viands of equally strong flavors. The next recipe proves the root's versatility more eloquently than any prose. A Burgundian loaf (perfect for lunch or hors d'oeuvres), it is seasoned with kohlrabi plus a smattering of prosciutto and Swiss cheese.

7 tablespoons unsalted butter
¾ pound kohlrabi, trimmed, peeled, diced (about 1¼ cups)
1 cup milk, scalded
1 teaspoon salt
⅛ teaspoon freshly ground black pepper
1 cup all-purpose flour, sifted
4 eggs
¾ cup diced Swiss or Jarlsberg cheese
¼ cup chopped prosciutto
1 teaspoon chopped fresh chives or scallion tops
1 tablespoon cold milk

1. Melt 3 tablespoons of the butter in a medium skillet over medium-low heat. Stir in the diced kohlrabi, tossing well to coat it with butter. Cook, covered, until tender, about 10 minutes.

2. Strain the scalded milk into a large saucepan; add the remaining 4 tablespoons butter, the salt, and the pepper. Heat to boiling; reduce the heat. Add the flour all at once. Cook over low heat, beating briskly with a wooden spoon, until the mixture forms a ball and cleans the sides of the pan.

3. Remove the pan from the heat. Beat in the eggs, one at a time, with a wooden spoon, making sure that each egg is well blended into the mixture. When the mixture is shiny and smooth, stir in slightly more than ½ cup of the cheese, the kohlrabi, prosciutto, and chives. Cool.

4. Preheat the oven to 375°F. Using a stick of butter, trace or loosely draw a

7-inch circle on a baking sheet. Divide the dough in half. From the first half of the dough, shape rounds with a large serving spoon and arrange them on the circle, using a rubber spatula to scrape the dough from the spoon. Smooth the tops of the rounds with the back of a spoon to connect them into a ring. With a teaspoon, shape smaller rounds from the second half of the dough, and arrange them on top of the ring. (Dough should resemble a bumpy coffee ring.)

5. Brush the dough with the cold milk and sprinkle the remaining cheese over the top. Bake until the gougère is puffed and golden brown, 45 to 50 minutes. Cut into wedges to serve.

Serve 6 to 8.

Note: Gougère can be prepared in advance, formed into a ring, and frozen uncooked. Before serving, bake it in a preheated 350°F oven until done, about 1 hour and 10 minutes.

OKRA

There's More to It Than Gumbo

I was printed by the flavor of okra early. And though it was a vegetable alien to most Northern households at the time, I came to know it through expedience rather than choice. I can date my first bite to a period during the Depression when the demise of my mother's "dancing school" (as my father always called the Paula School of Arts & Crafts) sent that intrepid lady out to work to keep our family finances alive.

My mother's term of employment was long and varied, but the single trauma for me was not the matter of an absent parent or coming home from school to an empty house. Truly, I never minded being alone. But I actively dreaded the idea of eating a cold lunch.

As soon as I developed sufficient manual skills to properly use a can opener, I banished all the packages of cold cuts and the icy cartons of potato salad that my mother had left in our refrigerator for my noonday meal—and heated a bowl of soup instead.

Being a compulsive type even as a small boy, I would go to the corner grocer's long shelf of tinned soups and select a new flavor daily, until I had worked my way through the entire Campbell's *oeuvre*.

In retrospect most of those soups—aside from some miscalculations, like sludgy Mock Turtle or blistering Pepper Pot—were highly edible. Waiting for the liquid to bubble up in the pan, I would scrupulously study the serving instructions on the back of each can, though more out of affection for the kewpie-doll cooks (in chef's hats and aprons) on the label than any culinary wisdom they imparted.

How does all this relate to okra? Circuitously.

You see, my favorite Campbell's offering was Chicken Gumbo. I adored that soup so much and consumed it so often that I sometimes depleted our grocer's entire stock in a mere week's time. I realized, as I sipped each delectable spoonful, that the ingredient that gave the gumbo its elusive savor was the spoke-shaped flecks of green that floated on the surface like miniature life preservers. Okra.

I would like to be able to report that I promptly learned to make an okra-thickened chicken gumbo from scratch, but that would be a lie. It took nearly forty years until I successfully duplicated that wondrous dish—after I had been instructed in the homely art by a generous Cajun cook in southwestern Louisiana. But my tastebuds had been primed for it practically from the day my mother first went off to work.

Vegetable Roots

In the Deep South, slender green okra is sometimes referred to as "slave fruit" without a mite of disparagement. For this vegetable came to the New World out of Africa along with the first black Americans. The earliest records in the Carolina House of Burgesses (dated 1627) list sales of *nkruman* seed (the original Tshi name; it is a Gold Coast word) to arriving English colonists at twelve shillings per twelve-pound sack. Which apparently was a bargain no settler could resist, since okra crops flourished like wildflowers thereafter.

It's not as offhand a simile as one would imagine. While most vegetables we grow are relatively closely connected (potato being cousin to tomato and eggplant, and cabbage not only father to sprout but titular head of the entire Brassica family as well), okra stands alone. For this viand is technically not a vegetable at all but the edible pod of the mallow, *Hibiscus esculentus*.

The blossom of *Hibiscus esculentus* (which precedes the pod) is exceedingly showy. Pale yellow at dawn, this flower turns golden as the sun rises, its petals flaring wider and wider until it reveals a slash of crimson at the heart—usually at the moment the sun sets. For this reason, ancient Arab physicians called okra pods "sun vessels." They believed the ripening seeds contained therapeutic properties that, once consumed, floated through a man's body forever. This notion, shared by many primitive peoples, caused okra to be highly prized in their diet.

There are even tales of bloody *ngombo* (an Angolan word for okra) raids in the folklore of Angola. Lootings would occur periodically when one tribe, covetous of another's thriving *ngombo* crop, would make "sharp-knife" raids in the dark of the moon to lay hands on their neighbor's fields, often killing any man, woman, or child who offered resistance.

The taking of this okra probably caused them little joy, however. According to old gardener's lore, no mallow can be rudely plucked from the ground without leaving a stigma of retribution on the hands of the plunderer. Just touching the green leaves, in fact, will cause a scarlet rash that takes days and sometimes even weeks of calamine lotion to palliate. Wise pickers therefore wear long sleeves and a pair of stout gloves before entering an okra patch!

What to Look For

Okra is a vegetable that comes with a caveat. Although I would never consider using a pod that was not fresh, frozen okra is a possibility in a gumbo or a long-steeped stew where texture is not of prime importance. But do not, even for a moment, consider the idea of substituting frozen for fresh in a dish where

crispness is a major prerequisite.

At the greengrocer's, the brightest, sprightliest pods are usually the ones that came to market last, so search them out. Smaller pods are most often tenderer and worth the nuisance of sifting through the pile. Test a pod for elasticity; the crunchiest will bend slightly without oozing. Old pods that darken or are spotty should be passed by.

Dieters may consume okra with utter impunity as there are less than 36 calories in every handful, figuring 10 pods per hand. This vegetable is likewise high in amino acids and minerals—the same handful scoring a rousing 520 units of vitamin A and over 249 milligrams of potassium. This applies to okra that is barely blanched or raw. The health quotient (though not the calories) lessen as the pods are cooked—which is the best reason in the world for eating it practically off the vine.

Preparation

For centuries okra has had more detractors than admirers in the kitchen, largely because of the way it was traditionally served up. Okra changes as it is cooked. From being extremely crisp and firm-textured in its raw state, it becomes thick, gooey, and almost mucilaginous after a long stint in a saucepan. This viscous quality is the result of a high sugar-carbohydrate content, which releases a thickening agent when heated. It took a strong stirring arm plus a litany of handed-down family recipes to turn *ngombo* into the dish with which it has become synonymous: Southern Gumbo. But truly there is more than one way to cook up a mess of okra.

My method is to cook okra as little as possible. I leave the pod practically uncut, simply shaving off the tip of the stem as it enters the pot. The tenderest okra is never more than 2 inches long and is as thin as a child's pinky. More mature pods (2½ to 3 inches in length) may require a jot more surgery at the tip and even the complete removal of a tough stem, but never, never cut into the body of the pod unless it is to be sliced into rounds.

This unorthodox way of preparing okra is its most classic rendition, to my mind at least: merely blanch the okra whole for less than a minute (no matter what its size), plunge it into icy cold water to retard the cooking, and then reheat it briefly in a warm oven before it is to be served.

Never cook okra in an iron, copper, or brass utensil. The metal will turn the pod a grayish hue which, while harmless enough, may occasion a qualm in the finicky. I always use glass or enamel-over-cast-iron pots for okra.

SNAPPY PICKLED OKRA

The crunchiest pickle ever to cross my lips—truly!

½ pound tender young okra, stems lightly trimmed
2 hot green peppers (see Guacamole headnote, page 37)
2 cloves garlic
2 cups distilled white vinegar
¼ cup water
¼ cup salt
1 teaspoon celery seed
1 teaspoon mustard seed

1. Wash the okra and pack it into two sterilized pint jars. Add 1 hot pepper and 1 clove garlic to each jar.

2. Combine the remaining ingredients in a medium saucepan. Heat to boiling; remove from the heat. Pour this over the okra in the jars. Seal. Let stand 2 weeks, turning occasionally. Chill well before serving.

Makes 2 pints.

OPTIMIST'S SALAD

(Okra and Tomato Salad)

This okra and tomato salad is reputed to cure a hangover! I believe it, but then I am a confirmed optimist.

¼ cup olive oil
1 tablespoon red wine vinegar
1 tablespoon lemon juice
½ teaspoon salt
¼ teaspoon freshly ground black pepper
1 small clove garlic
1 tablespoon sour cream
¼ pound tender young okra, stems lightly trimmed, cut in half lengthwise
1 large ripe tomato, cut into ½-inch-thick wedges
Lettuce leaves
Chopped fresh parsley

1. Combine the oil, vinegar, lemon juice, salt, pepper, and garlic in a small jar. Seal the jar and shake well. Let it stand 30 minutes. Remove the garlic clove. Add the sour cream. Seal and shake well again.

2. Place the okra halves and tomato wedges in a medium bowl. Pour the dressing over, mix gently, and let stand 15 minutes.

3. Line a small salad bowl with lettuce leaves. Spoon the tomato and okra mixture into the center; sprinkle with parsley.

Serves 2 or 3.

OKRA WITH RUMMED MUSTARD SAUCE

This *al dente* rendition is crisp as the dickens, and eminently receptive to its unctuous sauce.

1½ pounds okra, stems lightly trimmed
2 egg yolks
2 teaspoons Dijon mustard
2 teaspoons lemon juice
¼ teaspoon finely grated lemon peel
1 tablespoon dark rum
8 tablespoons (1 stick) unsalted butter, frozen, cut into 8 pieces
Salt and ground white pepper

1. Cook the okra in boiling salted water 45 seconds; drain. Keep warm in a low oven. (If blanching in advance of cooking time, rinse the blanched okra under cold running water until cool, and then drain. Reheat in a 350°F oven for 8 to 10 minutes.)

2. Combine the egg yolks, mustard, lemon juice, lemon peel, and rum in the top of a double boiler. Place over simmering water and stir constantly until slightly thickened. Add the frozen butter, one piece at a time, until the sauce is smooth and thick. (If the sauce should curdle, beat in a few drops of boiling water until it is smooth again.) Add salt and white pepper to taste. Spoon the sauce over the okra.

Serves 4.

Unlike the Southern blacks, who depended on okra as a staple, the Arabs deemed it a rare delicacy and prepared it only for special occasions like weddings and baptisms. The Arab name for okra, *uëhka*, means "a gift."

LIMPING SUSAN
(Okra with Bacon and Rice)

"Limping Susan" came my way from Jean Hewitt, a brilliant editor and good friend. Jean's "Sue" (a slightly backwoodsy version of risotto) is slightly different from the one I dug up in Savannah, but she pointed me in the right direction.

4 thick strips bacon, diced
½ pound okra, cut into ½-inch-thick rounds
1 cup long-grain rice
1 tablespoon chopped fresh basil, or 1½ teaspoons dried
2 cups Beef Stock (see page 409)
⅛ teaspoon hot pepper sauce
Salt and freshly ground black pepper

Sauté the diced bacon in a medium saucepan over medium heat until crisp. Stir in the okra; cook 1 minute. Stir in the rice, basil, stock, hot pepper sauce, and salt and pepper to taste. Heat to boiling; reduce the heat. Cook, covered, over medium-low heat until the rice is tender, about 25 minutes. Remove the cover and continue to cook until the mixture is fairly dry.

Serves 4 to 6.

MEDITERRANEAN STEWED OKRA WITH TOMATOES

There are probably as many recipes for stewed tomatoes and okra in the South as there are spatterware enamel skillets in which the dish is traditionally made. Most versions are thick, anonymous in hue, and frankly less than felicitous to my Northern tongue. The genesis of okra cooked with tomato, however, is old as the hills. Paula Wolfert, in *Couscous and Other Good Food From Morocco*, reports that in Tetuan, cooks who make okra and tomato *tagines* and do not wish the sauce to be inordinately thick, string the pods together with a needle and thread. The okra "necklace" is poached in the sauce but lifted up every time the tomatoes need stirring. The okra cooks yet remains ornamental in the dish. I haven't the patience or the threading-eye for such hijinks myself, so I borrow my okra-tomato stew from the good housewives of Provence. They cook the tomatoes with olives and garlic early in the day, and later toss the okra into the pot, for only as long as it takes a bottle of wine to breathe—10 minutes in my kitchen!

1 pound okra, stems lightly trimmed
½ cup red wine vinegar
2 tablespoons salt
½ cup olive oil
2 medium onions, coarsely chopped
2 cloves garlic, minced
2 large tomatoes, peeled, seeded, chopped
1 can (14 ounces) imported Italian plum tomatoes
Pinch of sugar
2 tablespoons chopped fresh basil, or 2 teaspoons dried
Pinch of thyme
¼ cup sliced Greek or Italian olives
2 anchovy filets, chopped
1 tablespoon unsalted butter
Freshly ground black pepper

1. Combine the okra, vinegar, and salt in a medium bowl. Let stand 30 minutes. Rinse under cold running water; drain.

2. Heat the oil in a medium saucepan over medium heat. Add the onions; cook 1 minute. Add the garlic; cook until golden, about 3 minutes. Add the fresh and canned tomatoes, sugar, basil, thyme, olives, and anchovies. Cook, uncovered, over medium-low heat until thick, about 40 minutes. Add the butter, okra, and pepper to taste. Cook 10 minutes longer.

Serves 4 to 6.

"OLE MISS" OKRA FRITTERS

I have a friend in Jackson, Mississippi, who sends me long missives and short homey recipes from time to time. I have promised never to divulge this donor's identity as she has a considerable reputation in another field. However, I am permitted to pass on her recipes to the grateful world.

½ cup all-purpose flour
1 teaspoon dry mustard
½ teaspoon freshly grated nutmeg
¼ teaspoon salt
2 eggs, separated
1 teaspoon Dijon mustard
½ cup beer
¼ cup chopped fresh basil, or 1 tablespoon dried chopped with 3 tablespoons fresh parsley
Vegetable oil for frying
1 pound tender young okra, stems lightly trimmed
Salt

1. Combine the flour with the dry mustard, nutmeg, and ¼ teaspoon salt in a small bowl.

2. Combine the egg yolks with the Dijon mustard and beer. Add this to the flour mixture and whisk until smooth. Refrigerate, covered, 8 hours.

3. Stir the chopped basil into the batter. Beat the egg whites until stiff but not dry; fold them into the batter.

4. Heat 2 inches of oil in a large heavy saucepan until hot but not smoking.

5. Dip the okra into the batter, letting the excess batter run off. Fry the okra in the hot oil, about ten pieces at a time, until golden, about 4 minutes. Drain on paper towels. Sprinkle with salt to taste. Keep warm in a low oven while frying the remaining okra.

Serves 4 to 6.

BAMIYA

(Stewed Okra and Apricots)

The first record of okra as an ingredient in a formal recipe was made by Abul-Abbas el Nebáti, a Spanish Moor from Seville, in the thirteenth century. An eminent botanist (and obviously a food lover), he first tasted this vegetable in a stew in Egypt in 1216 and noted in his diary that its qualities seemed eminently medicinal, "but reviving to the body without being repulsive to the tongue." Which is more than could be said for most other health foods of his day!

In his notes, Abul-Abbas calls okra *bamiyah*, which is curiously akin to *bamiya*, the tag for this vegetable in Armenian. It also happens to be the name for an utterly beatific ragout of stewed okra and apricots—Armenian as well.

1 tablespoon unsalted butter
1 medium onion, halved, sliced
¾ cup Beef Stock (see page 409)
2 tablespoons tomato paste
Juice of ½ lemon
¼ teaspoon ground allspice
½ pound okra, stems lightly trimmed
8 dried apricots, halved
Salt and freshly ground black pepper
Chopped fresh parsley

Melt the butter in a medium saucepan over medium heat. Add the onion; sauté until golden, about 4 minutes. Add the stock, tomato paste, lemon juice, and allspice. Mix thoroughly. Stir in the okra. Arrange the apricots over the top. Heat to boiling; reduce the heat. Simmer, covered, over medium-low heat for 45 minutes. Add salt and pepper to taste, and sprinkle with chopped parsley. Serve over rice or barley.

Serves 4.

CROSS CREEK SHRIMP AND OKRA

One of my favorite cookbooks was written by a woman who claimed never to measure an ingredient—Marjorie Kinnan Rawlings, denizen of Cross Creek, Florida, where she wrote both her Pulitzer Prize–winning novel *The Yearling* and *South Moon Under.* Mrs. Rawlings's last book, *Cross Creek Cookery,* was the genesis of the following okra and shrimp fry, a dish I urge you to pair with an equally Southern dish, a hominy pudding called Awendaw Bread, which you will find in the chapter on Peppers.

4 tablespoons (1/2 stick) unsalted butter
2 whole scallions, bulbs and green tops, chopped
1 clove garlic, minced
1 pound raw shrimp, shelled, deveined
1/2 pound okra, cut into 1/2-inch-thick rounds
Salt and freshly ground black pepper

1. Melt 2 tablespoons of the butter in a large heavy skillet over medium-low heat. Add the scallions; cook until slightly wilted, about 3 minutes. Add the garlic; cook 2 minutes longer.

2. Add the remaining 2 tablespoons butter to the skillet. Add the shrimp and cook, tossing constantly, 3 minutes. Add the okra and cook, tossing constantly, 3 minutes longer. Add salt and pepper to taste.

Serves 4.

ROUMANIAN SHEPHERD'S SUMMER STEW

After first flowering in tropical Africa, okra became transplanted to the Arab countries, where it flourished. The Arabs, who were great wanderers, added it to the pack of other exotic vegeteria, like eggplant, peppers, and cucumbers, that they traded with the rest of the world. Consequently okra grew wherever the European sun was brightest. A nice example of its transmigration is the gift that follows. A Roumanian dish, it has a name that translates into *Shepherd's Summer Stew.*

1/4 cup all-purpose flour
1/2 teaspoon salt
1/4 teaspoon freshly ground black pepper
2 pounds boneless lamb, cut into 1-inch cubes
3 tablespoons unsalted butter, approximately
3 tablespoons vegetable oil, approximately
1 large onion, finely chopped
1 clove garlic, minced
3 large tomatoes, peeled, seeded, chopped
2 teaspoons dark brown sugar
1/2 cup dry white wine
1 cup Chicken Stock (see page 410)
3/4 pound tender young okra
2 tablespoons Scotch whisky or cognac
Chopped fresh parsley

1. Preheat the oven to 350°F. Combine the flour with the salt and pepper in a shallow bowl. Roll the meat in the flour mixture, shaking off any excess. Reserve the excess flour mixture.

2. Heat 2 tablespoons of the butter with 2 tablespoons of the oil in a Dutch oven over medium heat. Sauté the meat, a few pieces at a time, until well browned on all sides. Transfer each batch to a plate as you continue to sauté. Add more butter and oil as needed.

3. Add the onion to the Dutch oven. Cook over medium-low heat, 1 minute. Add the garlic; cook 3 minutes. Return the meat to the Dutch oven and sprinkle

with 1 teaspoon of the remaining flour mixture. Stir in the tomatoes; sprinkle with the brown sugar. Add the wine and chicken stock. Heat to boiling. Transfer to the oven and cook, covered, 1 hour.

4. Remove the stew from the oven and stir in the okra and whisky or cognac. Place the Dutch oven over medium heat and simmer, stirring constantly, 3 minutes. Sprinkle with parsley, and serve with rice or boiled potatoes.

Serves 6.

SEAFOOD AND OKRA GUMBO

Seafood gumbo is a fairly free-form dish. Flavor it with whatever catch of the day is at hand (or affordable to the pocket). Okra gives it territorial authority.

¼ cup vegetable oil
¼ cup all-purpose flour
5 tablespoons unsalted butter
2 large onions, chopped
1 pound okra, coarsely chopped
3 large tomatoes, peeled, seeded, chopped
2 large green bell peppers, seeded, chopped
3 large cloves garlic, minced
1 pound raw shrimp, shelled, deveined
1 quart Fish Stock (see page 410)
1 quart water
2 tablespoons crushed dried hot red peppers
1½ teaspoons salt
2 bay leaves
2 teaspoons Worcestershire sauce
1 teaspoon ground allspice
¼ teaspoon dried thyme
1 pound red fish or red snapper, cut into pieces
1 pound cleaned crabmeat
16 small oysters, shucked
Freshly ground black pepper
4 cups Hot Steamed Rice (see page 412)
Filé powder (see Note)
Hot pepper sauce

1. Whisk the oil with the flour in a large heavy skillet (preferably cast iron) until smooth. Cook, stirring frequently, over medium-low heat until the roux turns a dark mahogany brown, about 1 hour. Do not allow it to burn. Set aside.

2. Melt 3 tablespoons of the butter

Gumbo is my favorite okra soup—but it is hardly a soup at all in most diner's lexicons, as it is actually a meal in a soup plate.

The dish is best, I think, when prepared in the manner of the Cajun country folk of southwest Louisiana, where the Acadiens stir the flour for the roux an hour or longer, until it is deemed sufficiently colored to marry the other ingredients in the pot.

In this part of the world, gumbo is composed of any ingredients a cook may have on hand. What gives a gumbo its gumption, however, is the African ingredient (okra) that thickens the pottage, and the Choctaw seasoning (filé powder) that gives it dimension. The last-named ingredient is a mixture of dried, crushed sassafras that imparts a truly distinctive bite (faintly like the tang of pine needles) to the finished dish. No Cajun ever adds filé powder to the cooking pot, however, as it turns stringy as it cooks.

in a large heavy pot over medium-low heat. Add the onions; cook 3 minutes. Stir in the okra; cook 3 minutes. Stir in the tomatoes, and cook, uncovered, 30 minutes.

3. Meanwhile, melt the remaining 2 tablespoons butter in a large skillet. Add the peppers and garlic; cook 5 minutes. Stir in the shrimp and continue to cook, tossing constantly, until the shrimp turn pink, about 3 minutes.

4. Transfer the shrimp mixture to the pot containing the tomato mixture. Stir in the roux. Add the fish stock, water, hot red peppers, salt, bay leaves, Worcestershire sauce, allspice, and thyme. Heat to boiling; reduce the heat. Cook, covered, over medium-low heat for 1½ hours. Remove the bay leaves.

5. Add the fish, crabmeat, and oysters to the gumbo. Return to boiling; reduce the heat. Cook over medium-low heat, 15 minutes. Add pepper to taste. Serve in shallow soup bowls. Pass the rice, filé powder, and hot pepper sauce.

Serves 8.

Note: A little filé powder goes a long way for most folks, so if you have never had filé before, I suggest you start with just a sprinkle and go from there.

True gumbophiles share an idiosyncrasy. They never combine okra and filé powder in the same pot, claiming the two make one superfluous thickening agent. Nonpurists I encountered in the environs of New Iberia and Abbeville do add a pinch of the greenish powder to their soup bowls even when okra is part of the dish, but say it goes for "seasonin'" only.

OKRA, SAUSAGE AND GAME-HEN GUMBO

In Cajun country, the hens in the following dish are often wild game bagged in the field. Mine are Cornish, from the supermarket, bagged at the checkout counter.

2 Cornish hens (about 2½ pounds total weight), cut into serving pieces
1½ teaspoons salt
¼ teaspoon freshly ground black pepper
3 tablespoons unsalted butter
2 tablespoons vegetable oil
3 tablespoons all-purpose flour
¾ pound okra, coarsely chopped
2 medium onions, finely chopped
1 small green pepper, seeded, finely chopped
1 medium rib celery, finely chopped
2 cloves garlic, minced
1 quart Chicken Stock (see page 410)
1 cup water
1 teaspoon cayenne pepper
1 pound smoked sausage, cut into ¾-inch-thick slices
3 cups Hot Steamed Rice (see page 412)
Filé powder (see Note, above)

1. Sprinkle the Cornish hen pieces with ½ teaspoon of the salt and the pepper.

2. Heat 2 tablespoons of the butter with 1 tablespoon of the oil in a large heavy pot over medium heat. Sauté the hen pieces until golden brown on both sides, about 15 minutes. Transfer to a plate.

3. Add the remaining 1 tablespoon butter to the pot. Whisk in the flour. Cook, stirring frequently, over medium-low heat until the roux turns a dark mahogany brown, about 1 hour. Do not allow it to burn.

4. Meanwhile, heat the remaining 1 tablespoon oil in a medium skillet over medium-low heat. Add the okra, onions, green pepper, celery, and garlic. Cook, stirring occasionally, 25 minutes.

5. Stir the okra mixture into the roux (after it has cooked for an hour). Add the chicken stock, water, remaining 1 teaspoon salt, and cayenne pepper. Heat to boiling; reduce the heat. Stir in the Cornish hen pieces, along with any juices. Cook, covered, over medium-low heat for 1 hour. Stir in the sausage. Cook, covered, 40 minutes longer, skimming any fat that rises to the surface. Serve in shallow soup bowls, and pass the rice and the filé powder.

Serves 6.

CHICKEN, HAM, AND OKRA GUMBO

¼ cup plus 1 tablespoon vegetable oil
¼ cup all-purpose flour
1 large chicken (3½ to 4 pounds), cut into 12 pieces
Salt and freshly ground black pepper
4 tablespoons (½ stick) unsalted butter
1¼-pound ham steak, cut into strips ¼ inch wide and about 2½ inches long
2 medium onions, chopped
2 cloves garlic, minced
2 ribs celery, chopped
1 green pepper, seeded, chopped
2 cups peeled, seeded, chopped tomatoes (about 3 medium)
6 cups Chicken Stock (see page 410)
1 tablespoon Worcestershire sauce
1 bay leaf
½ teaspoon chopped fresh thyme, or ¼ teaspoon dried
¼ teaspoon dried oregano
¼ teaspoon ground allspice
⅛ teaspoon ground cloves
¾ pound okra, trimmed, cut into ½-inch rounds (about 2 cups)
2 scallion tops, chopped
2 tablespoons chopped fresh parsley
3 cups Hot Steamed Rice (see page 412)
Filé powder (see Note, Seafood and Okra Gumbo)

1. Whisk the ¼ cup oil with the flour in a large heavy skillet (preferably cast iron) until smooth. Cook, stirring frequently, over medium-low heat until the roux turns a dark mahogany brown, about 1 hour. Do not allow it to burn. Set aside.

Roux is the backbone of Cajun cookery. A properly made, long-stirred roux becomes dark in color and deep in taste. Its rich, earthy flavor melds a rather highly seasoned cuisine; and according to Louisiana cooks it tickles the tastebuds, makes food easier to digest, and for some mysterious reason inhibits spoilage, important in a hot climate.

2. Sprinkle the chicken with salt and pepper to taste.

3. Heat 2 tablespoons of the butter with the remaining 1 tablespoon oil in a large heavy pot over medium heat. Sauté the chicken pieces, about half at a time, until dark golden, 8 to 10 minutes per side. Transfer to a plate.

4. Remove all but 1 tablespoon fat from the pot. Sauté the ham strips over medium-high heat until lightly browned, about 4 minutes. Transfer them to the plate with the chicken, along with any juices.

5. Melt the remaining 2 tablespoons butter in the pot over medium-low heat. Add the onions; cook 3 minutes. Add the garlic; cook 1 minute. Add the celery, green pepper, and tomatoes. Cook 5 minutes. Stir in the roux; mix well. Add the chicken stock, Worcestershire sauce, bay leaf, thyme, oregano, allspice, and cloves. Heat to boiling and stir in the sautéed chicken and ham, including any accumulated juices. Return the gumbo to boiling; reduce the heat. Cook, covered, over medium-low heat for 1 hour. Add the okra and cook, uncovered, 30 minutes longer. Discard the bay leaf. Sprinkle with the scallion tops and parsley. Serve in shallow soup bowls, and pass the rice and filé powder.

Serves 6.

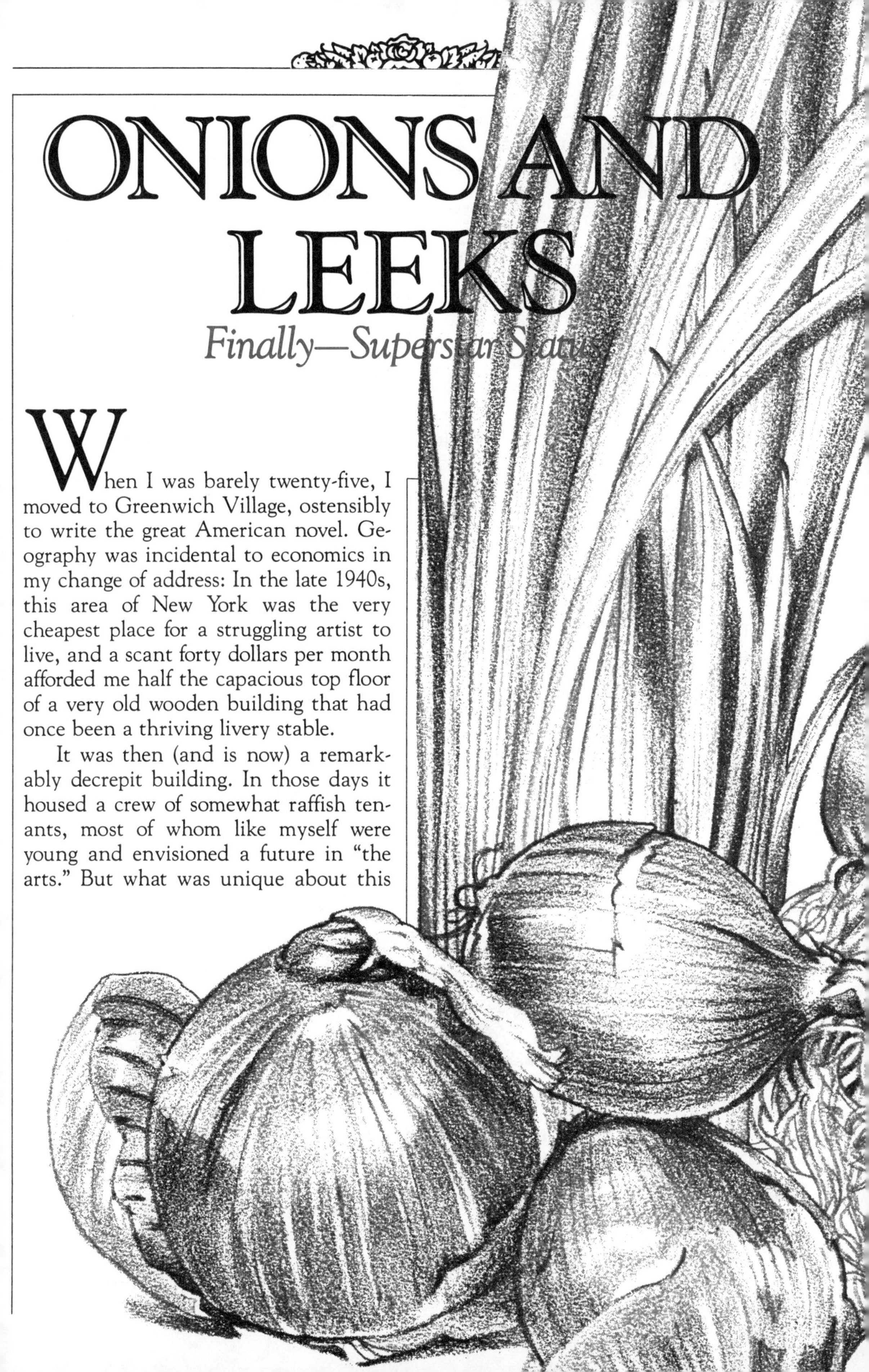

ONIONS AND LEEKS

Finally—Superstar Status

When I was barely twenty-five, I moved to Greenwich Village, ostensibly to write the great American novel. Geography was incidental to economics in my change of address: In the late 1940s, this area of New York was the very cheapest place for a struggling artist to live, and a scant forty dollars per month afforded me half the capacious top floor of a very old wooden building that had once been a thriving livery stable.

It was then (and is now) a remarkably decrepit building. In those days it housed a crew of somewhat raffish tenants, most of whom like myself were young and envisioned a future in "the arts." But what was unique about this dwelling was not its current inhabitants' aspirations, but rather its former occupants' effloresence. Every time it rained, the entire edifice reeked of horses!

My neighbor from the front half of the top floor was Helen. Recently shed of a husband, this pretty young woman announced her intention to quit a dreary job and audition for the Actors Studio, one morning when we met at the mailbox. It was surprising news, yet not as wholly capricious as it sounded. I knew she had come to New York from a small town some years before with dreams of becoming an actress. More pertinently, there was an aura about her that caused absolute strangers to stop and stare whenever she walked down a street. But it was not star quality that attracted me to Helen. On the contrary, it was her cooking ability.

Born on a farm, this girl was an absolute whiz at the stove. After she confessed her theatrical ambitions, I would often find myself knocking at Helen's door at dinner time to discuss her upcoming audition. Together we would eat first, then read plays together the whole evening, searching for a scene that would display her talents to the fullest. After a week of exemplary dining, we came upon one. It was a brief love scene from a highly romantic drama called "Lilliom," in which the part of unworldly Julie complemented Helen's lissome good looks.

The leading man in the scene was a carnival barker, a handsome rogue no woman could resist. It was a hard part to fill. All of Helen's actor friends were either "engaged" or frankly unwilling to commit the amount of time she demanded to polish her performance. As a consequence she and I (as stand-in) would rehearse the scene together, night after night.

One evening after we had both memorized the lines, Helen turned to me and broke her concentration.

"You know... you *were* Lilliom just now," she said. "No other actor could play that part better. Why don't you do the audition with me?"

I had known this would happen, even as I demurred and deprecated, for though I was certainly not the physical type of this dashing *macho* man, I had begun to sense his presence between the lines, and had dredged up almost alien feelings to fit the specifications.

What I remember most of those endless rehearsal sessions is the weather. In late spring it rained incessantly, and the former stable smelled so strongly of horses that one could hardly breathe. As we practiced the scene (with windows wide open to the storm), Helen would sauté huge pans of onions to dispel the equine aroma. But to my consternation, I often would find myself thinking more of food (and what dish Helen would whip up from those slow-frying onions) than the infatuation Lilliom was supposed to feel for the young girl beside him. After our rehearsals ended, we would consume onions in every conceivable guise that resourceful Helen could invent (tarts, soup, croquettes), with a ravenous kind of gluttony.

The onions (and Helen too) kept me in a state of emotional and digestive turmoil. For little by little, and not entirely against my will, I began to see the audition as *my* entrance into the world of the theater, not Helen's. I was so certain that the Actors Studio would choose me instead (as the chunkier Brando, Dean, or Newman) that I began to devise ways to make amends to Helen for the bypass. I need not have bothered.

On the day of our audition, my feet turned to clay. The lines I had rehearsed for a month fled from my tongue; instead of speaking, I choked, losing all sense of Lilliom (as well as the scene) in the throes of a paralyzing attack of stage fright. Helen, on quite the other hand, was a vision. She bloomed under the footlights, and was so assured that she rose at the scene's end and walked across the stage with a grace I could never have imagined she possessed. I watched her transfixed, knowing full well that our onion-eating days were over.

Of course she was accepted at the Studio. I went back to ignominy—and my novel, which was almost as bad. Realizing that the stage was decidedly not my metier was a hard pill to swallow. As for Helen, our paths which had become so inexplicably entwined came apart like a raveled string. We never ate together again for she never had the time. Some while afterward she moved, and the only memory of our nightly sessions (when I dreamed of a life on the stage) are random scraps of paper: recipes, all onion dishes too!

The onion has provoked many snippets of *pro* and tatters of *con* in its time.

In his seventeenth-century *Herbal* John Gerard, for instance, noted: "The juice of an onion annointed upon a bald head in the sun bringeth the haire again very speedily." However, the same gentleman was less than praiseful about its culinary bequests. "Though it be boyled, the onion causeth head ache, hurteth the eyes and make a man dim-sighted and . . . dull!"

George Washington, no slouch at pronouncements himself, never heard Gerard's theory, for a hundred years after Gerard he wrote in his journals: "The onion is the most favored food that grows!" And he vowed that he would eat one any way that it was prepared, "even cored, baked and stuffed with mincemeat like an apple!"—then and now a curious conceit at best.

Robert Louis Stevenson, obviously another *Allium*-lover, called the globe onion "the poetic soul of a capacious salad bowl."

Vegetable Roots

In every other chapter of this book, from artichokes to zucchini, the onion acts as an architectural underpinning or seasoning to make other vegetables more flavorsome. Not here. Now the onion stands alone.

In spite of its strong flavor and frankly tear-making complexion, the onion is probably the noblest vegetable that grows. The name itself bears testament to the high esteem in which the plant was held by earlier civilizations. *Onion* stems from the Latin *unus*, which means "one" and was conferred on that single-bulbed stalk because its spherical shape was equated with a symbol of the universe. The fact that it sprouted from the same family tree as the sacred lily *(Allium)* invested the onion with its official touch of reverence, perhaps, but thousands of years before the first Christian celebrated Easter, early man had anointed his body as well as his cookpots with onion juices. Hardly for its aromatic incense: the scent of onions kept his predators at bay!

Onion history goes farther back in time than most food chroniclers care to delve. It's a very pungent subject. In Central Asia, where anthropologists place the site of its first cultivation, the onion (and its siblings: garlic, leek, chive, and shallot) was invested with absolute divinity. Where an onion bloomed, a temple was erected. Where an onion withered, the land was considered fallow and not even beasts of the field were permitted to graze. Yet, though they tended onions assiduously, no resident seems to have ever chomped or sautéed a slice. For in the Eastern view, the golden fruit with its myriad layered skins was regarded as a symbol of eternity, a globe to be held close to the heart when invoking a solemn oath, perhaps, but far too celestial for mere human consumption.

The ancient Egyptians transplanted the same preconceptions about the onion along with the green seedlings they planted on the banks of the Nile. Egyptian high priests considered the onion to be sacred, like the lotus, a dispensation from Ra, the sun god. Instead of eating onions or using them to season their barley, these holy fellows wore them. Entwining ropes of onions like phylacteries around their naked bodies, they said their daily prayers. They most probably were weeping as well, for the onions that bloom on Egyptian soil have always been particularly thin-skinned!

Happily this custom was short-lived. By the time the great pyramid was under construction in Gizeh, the onion had achieved a place at the Egyptian table. It is often bruited about (among onion lovers of course) that the workmen who performed the arduous task of building the pyramids would never have had the energy to lift the first stone if nutritious onions had not been part of their daily fare. In fact, onions were so firmly entrenched in the Egyptians' culture that the one regret voiced by the Israelites leaving for the Promised Land, once the Red Sea had precipitously closed behind them, was the absence of onion in their desert diet. Then God performed yet another miracle. After a hundred days, chives were said to be found blossoming in Canaan.

According to Herodotus, Greek males preparing for the Olympic races were advised to consume one onion the size of a fist upon arising and one onion the size of a thumb before retiring, "to lighten the balance of the blood." Roman physicians must have concurred with that nostrum. In Caesar's time, athletes were fed a breakfast of nothing but onions before they entered any competitive games. A hundred years later, during Nero's reign, gladiators were massaged with the juice of onions before entering the arena of the Forum, to keep their bodies firm and in passing to deplete the lions' appetite somewhat.

In the Middle Ages, ingestion of a raw onion was deemed "the only sure cure for dog or adder bites—besides being helpful to the bladder and a curative for the stings of certain venomous worms." Later still, in the Shaker colo-

Though onion and leek are close garden relatives, their names have decidedly varying antecedents. Leek is a corruption of *loch*, a word Romans used to describe any medicine that could be licked to cure a sore throat. Nero (who sang as well as or better than he fiddled) had a partiality to keeping a leek in his mouth, the way other males chomp cigars—to add timbre to his vocal chords. Eventually Roman *loch* became early English *leác* and German *lauch*. Leek in French is *poireau*, however, which like the Italian *porro* and the Spanish *puerro* means "pear-shaped." Which may be an oblique reference to Nero's golden tenor. Who knows?

Onion's cognomen, on quite the other hand, translates into some numerical configuration. French dub it *oignon*, a derivation of *unum*, which means "first." German *Zweibel* is "more than once," obviously referring to the onion's two-season stay in the ground before it blooms. Italian *cipolla* and Spanish *cebolla* are less concise. Some etymologists claim they mean "singularity" or "uniqueness" whereas others insist they refer to "blessings."

nies of America in the early nineteenth century, onions were adjudged to cure heart disease, diabetes, falling hair, and rheumatism. The patient with any or all of those diseases was merely spooned an extract of roasted onions daily to ensure complete recovery.

Americans have always loved onions. Some food historians claim they are even indigenous to this continent, as traces of wild garlic and *ramps* (a strong clumping chive) have been found in shards of the earliest Indian cooking artifacts. Be that as it may, the yellow onion positively entered American saucepans courtesy of the *Mayflower* contingent at Plymouth Rock. According to colonists' diaries, onion seeds were planted as soon as the Pilgrim fathers could clear the land. But sad to say, no harvested onion made it to the first Thanksgiving. For onions are notorious slowpokes in the garden!

What to Look For

The onion is a year-round vegetable, one of the handful that grows with equal felicity in northern and southern climates. When buying onions, I look for orbs with papery dry skins and no scent whatsoever. A strong-smelling onion is usually bruised beneath its bland exterior. In supermarkets, I search out flat white Bermudas and dusky gold Spanish giants that are firm to the touch, or red-purple Italian onions that are slightly supple to the palm. Always avoid onions that have begun to sprout or that are wet-skinned: that is a sure sign they are on their way to spoilage.

I store my onions in a wire egg basket so they receive the benefit of air circulation, which keeps them compact. However, a basket lined with paper towels in the refrigerator will do equally well.

The one onion available year round is the *yellow* or *golden globe* variety known by its dry and tawny skin. A yellow onion varies in size depending upon its grower. It may weigh in at an ounce or a pound. Size has little to do with its flavor, however, which while pungent raw is extremely palliative in all cooking alliances. *White* or *pearl* onions are smaller, firmer, and sweeter. These may be successfully substituted in recipes calling for medium yellow onions but since their size is so dainty (one truly makes a mouthful), they are most often served up whole in stews or casseroles. *Baby pearls* are the tiniest pick of the white crop and usually end up in a cocktail glass, converting a dry martini into a drier Gibson. *Spanish* onions are not from Spain at all. Though they originated in Europe, these large brown or yellow spheres have been one of the prime southwestern vegetable crops for the past fifty years. Spanish onions require a bit of culinary concern. Reputedly the mildest onion of all, they often have a bitter undertaste when raw that must be ameliorated by slow cooking and judicious seasoning. *Bermuda* onions, which truly do come from Bermuda, are ivory-colored, flat-topped and

Being a biennial, onion plants require two years' growth. During the first summer, however, when the scallions bloom, an onion field is at its prettiest. By mid-June, each bears a ruff of tiny white flowers that eventually becomes round as a small peach. These blossoms are known as puffballs, for the wind demolishes them like puffs of smoke.

In Ireland there is a superstition that the Little People (the leprechauns) choose the farmhouse with the largest puffballs for their summer revels. As a reward for leaving his scallions intact, the farmer's chickens are made to lay twice as many eggs the rest of the year.

sweet as can be. Consider a wedge on your next hamburger or on a slice of freshly baked, lavishly buttered bread! Bermudas have a brief shelf life. April to June are the months to buy them most economically. *Red Italian* onions, also grown in the U.S., are mildest of all. This is a sweet onion variety that takes kindly to salad greens and vegetables in creamy dressings. Unfortunately, red onions are seasonal as well. Look for them in spring and summer—and buy them on a rope you can hang. Air retards their spoilage considerably.

A word or two about SCALLIONS, sometimes called green onions. Onions are slow bloomers, so farmers plant more seeds than they actually require. When these seeds germinate (usually in late spring or early summer) and the base of the onion stalks are no larger than a child's forefinger, they are dug up, then pulled and bunched. These green onions are known as scallions.

The name is a bastardization of *ascalonia caepa*, which means onion of Ascalon, where, according to food lorists, chives first bloomed in Canaan.

The scallions you purchase should be unscarred (and clean of soil at the root ends) and possessed of long sturdy green stems that will not collapse in a refrigerator crisper for at least a week's time. I store scallions, wiped well, in lightly moistened paper towels inside plastic bags.

SHALLOTS (somewhat sweeter than the mildest onion) have a tenuous shelf life. It is a good idea to buy them in small quantities and store them in some cool, dry place. Many cooks keep shallots wrapped loosely in paper towels on the lowest shelf of the refrigerator. As a heavy user, I keep mine in a wire basket where fresh air can freely circulate about them. Shallots keep for about 3 weeks at a normal kitchen temperature.

CHIVES are usually sold in clay pots from early spring to late fall. To keep chives thriving it is a good idea to transplant the clump to a larger pot after several weeks of snipping. A good light window will keep a pot of chives lively for a year with a little prudent removal of the withered stems from time to time.

The LEEK *(Allium porrum)* has no bulb like the onion's and no slender shoot like the scallion's, but only a tall thick stalk of shaded green layerings closely wrapped one over the other.

The base and the white part of the leaves are the parts of the leek that are eaten, and no onion, not even the delicate purple shallot, has a comparable flavor.

The best leeks to buy are never more than 1½ to 2 inches in diameter. Slender leeks cook quickly, while larger leeks become tougher and more pronounced in flavor over extended periods on the stove. A fat leek is fine for soup but less than felicitous in a vinaigrette or a wine-basted casserole. I usually trim a leek lengthwise, never allowing more than 2 inches of green to remain above the white base.

Onions, and leeks too, are super-healthful, totally therapeutic vegetables that provide an immeasurable quantity of minerals and acids for the body's daily requirements. An average onion (only 38 calories) contains over 157 milligrams of potassium and 36 milligrams of bone-building phosphorus. Yellow varieties of onion are endowed with high jots of vitamin D as well. Leeks are equally low in calories; three or four large stems contain a scant 52, plus 347 milligrams of potassium. Leeks are also rich in calcium (52 milligrams) and phosphorus (50 milligrams), and each individual stalk is further blessed with 40 units of vitamin A into the bargain.

Preparation

During my cooking lifetime I have been offered many sure-fire methods for peeling and slicing onions. Holding a crust of dry bread between the teeth is a noteworthy scheme; it is supposed to absorb the onion's acid spray. But what happens is that I get hungry and eat the crunchy morsel before the first batch of onions is even halved. So the deluge of tears comes. A different trick calls for the onion to be peeled and sliced under running water. The hydrogen in water reputedly washes out a measure of the onion's oils so that any mincing that follows may be accomplished with a clear cool eye. I tried that too; and almost amputated a finger for my effort and wailed like a banshee, though whether from the loss of blood or the redolent onion I am still uncertain.

I must confess I peel onions wearing my reading glasses, which seem to protect the tear ducts a bit. If you have better vision, a scuba-diver's mask will work just as well, but try answering the doorbell in that getup—even in Greenwich Village! The best method for peeling an onion is to cut a shallow slice from each end, place it on a firm surface, and then quickly slit and remove the skin. To slice, I halve peeled onions vertically from tip to root without absolutely penetrating the root end, which holds the onion in place as I turn it around and slice it horizontally as well. The root attachments are always severed in the final mincing that follows. But to my mind "roughly chopped" means exactly that; I leave well enough alone.

Before attempting to skin a passel of tiny white onions for a stewpot, I first drop them into a saucepan of boiling water for approximately half a minute; then immediately plunge them under cold running water. While not cooking long enough to blanch the onions, the hot water bath certainly loosens their skins so they may be easily removed without damage to the snowy underlayers. Use the sharpest vegetable knife you can muster to peel them, and always cut a shallow X at the root end of each onion to ensure even cooking.

Washing leeks can be sheer hell. But persist and you will be amply rewarded, for the end result is decidedly worth the bother. I fill a sink half full of lukewarm water first and plunge the stalks in until a healthy collection of grit is washed out. Then I empty the water, fan out the leaves with my fingers, and hold the stalks under cold running water as long as I possibly can. I have a friend who washes leeks in her dishwasher (on the rinse cycle) three times before holding them under cold running water, but even after all that one can never be sure all sand is removed until a grain hits your tongue at the dinner table.

PICKLED ONIONS AND FISH

My grandmother always made a dish of pickled onions and fish whenever one of her brood developed a case of quinsy or croup. She swore that "once the onion smell got through the kids' stuffed noses, throats opened like magic!"

No such bona fide cure is claimed for the next recipe. A pickled onion and fish dish of another color, it is the handiwork of Ray deNardo, chef of the prestigious Pear Tree Restaurant in Rumson, New Jersey. His hors d'oeuvre, while utterly delectable, is guaranteed to open nothing but taste buds. But that's saying a lot.

2 pounds boned, cut-up fish: salmon, swordfish, and lemon sole or halibut, in equal parts
2 cups red or white Burgundy
2 cups red or white wine vinegar
1 cup vegetable oil
1 small carrot, cut into thin julienne strips
1 cucumber, peeled, seeded, sliced thin
2 large red onions, halved, sliced thin
¼ cup chopped fresh dill (fresh is a prerequisite here)
2 bay leaves
1 tablespoon whole black peppercorns
1 tablespoon green peppercorns
1 teaspoon fresh thyme, or ½ teaspoon dried
Salt

1. Combine all the ingredients in a large crock or glass jar. Refrigerate, tightly covered, for at least three days. (This dish can be held for about 1 week.)

2. Before serving, let the crock stand at room temperature for 30 minutes, as the oil will have congealed. Remove the bay leaves and toss lightly before serving.

Serves 10 to 12.

KAREN CHEWNING'S REMARKABLE ONION SOUP

One of the best—if least traditional—onion soups I have ever slurped requires a scant four onions. But I warn you: they must be very, very finely sliced.

This wonderful pottage is a bequest from a smashingly attractive young lady named Karen Chewning, whom I was lucky enough to meet when I gave some cooking classes at elegant Sea Pines Island in South Carolina a while back. Luckier than most, I was also invited to dine at the Chewning home afterward and permitted to guess at the components of Karen's unusual brew. Like other admirers of this velvety concoction, I failed of course. But Karen's handsome husband, George, insisted she pass along her culinary secret. This privy information describes a priceless soup. George Chewning reputedly proposed marriage after the first sip.

2 tablespoons unsalted butter, plus 1 tablespoon melted
4 medium yellow onions, peeled, sliced thin
1 tablespoon all-purpose flour
4 cups beef broth (see page 414)
1 beef bouillon cube
¼ cup boiled milk
½ cup sour cream
½ cup grated mozzarella cheese
Salt and freshly ground black pepper
4 thin slices dry French bread

1. Melt the 2 tablespoons butter in a medium saucepan over medium heat. Add the onions; cook until golden, about 5 minutes. Reduce the heat.

2. Sprinkle the onions with the flour. Cook, stirring constantly, over low heat for 2 minutes. Stir in the beef broth and bouillon cube. Heat to boiling, stirring constantly with a wooden spoon; reduce the heat. Simmer, uncovered, 20 minutes. Stir in the boiled milk.

3. Preheat the broiling unit. Combine the sour cream with ½ cup of the soup mixture. Stir this mixture back into the soup. Add ¼ cup of the grated cheese. Cook, stirring constantly, over low heat until the cheese melts. Do not allow the soup to boil. Add salt and pepper to taste.

4. Pour the soup into an ovenproof serving dish. Place the sliced bread on the top. Sprinkle the bread with the remaining ¼ cup grated cheese and the melted butter. Place under the broiler until golden, about 1 minute.

Serves 4.

CHILLED TANGERINE AND ONION SLAW

The onion and orange are longtime culinary confederates. Tangerines, however, give the salad a bright new tang!

8 tangerines, well chilled
1 medium red onion, thinly sliced, rings separated
Peel of 1 lemon, finely slivered
1 clove garlic, minced
½ teaspoon coarse (kosher) salt
1 teaspoon Dijon mustard
Juice of 1 lemon
½ cup olive oil
Juice of 1 orange (about ¼ cup)
Freshly ground black pepper
1 teaspoon chopped fresh tarragon
1 bunch watercress, leaves only

1. Peel the tangerines. Using a sharp knife, remove the pith and slice off the inner edges to remove any seeds. Place the sections in a serving dish. (You should have about 3 cups.) Place the onion slices over the tangerine slices. Sprinkle with the lemon peel.

2. In a medium bowl mash the garlic with the salt, using the back of a spoon. Stir in the mustard and lemon juice. Very slowly whisk in the oil. The mixture will be quite thick. Thin with the orange juice. Pour this dressing over the tangerine-onion mixture. Sprinkle with pepper to taste. Chill until ready to serve.

3. Just before serving, sprinkle the top of the salad with the chopped tarragon and garnish with watercress leaves. Toss the salad at the table.

Serves 4 to 6.

ONION MARMALADE

Indubitably one of the great inventions to come out of the kitchen of Michel Guérard, this rich, dark conserve was originally meant to enrich the somewhat bland fare of his Cuisine Minceur regimen.

With a deep bow to the master plus a mite of literary license, I have adapted his formula into an equally intense marmalade that while far too heady for any slice of toast will produce a roast of unbelievable savor. Try a dab or two on a raw steak prior to the barbecue pit, or a hamburger before it hits the skillet, for true culinary derring-do. A speck of onion marmalade will also do wonders for unbuttered vegetables or a baked potato. And it stores well—up to six months in a sterilized jar in the fridge.

8 tablespoons (1 stick) unsalted butter
2 pounds yellow or white onions, halved, sliced ½ inch thick
1 teaspoon salt
½ teaspoon freshly ground black pepper
⅔ cup sugar
2 tablespoons dry sherry
2 tablespoons red wine vinegar
1 cup red wine
¼ cup honey
½ cup chopped dried pitted prunes

1. Melt the butter in a large skillet over medium heat until bubbly. Stir in the onion slices, tossing well to coat them with the butter. Sprinkle with the salt and pepper; reduce the heat to low. Cook, covered, 30 minutes.

2. Remove the cover from the skillet, add the remaining ingredients, and cook, uncovered, over medium heat until very dark in color and thickened, about 2 hours. Take care, as the marmalade will burn easily toward the end of the cooking time. Reduce the heat if it is cooking too fast. Cool and store, tightly covered, in the refrigerator.

Makes about 2 pints.

ONION PROSCIUTTO BREAD

For the following onion and prosciutto bread, put all the hybrids out of your mind. Only red Italian onions give the loaf its definitive bite.

1 package dry yeast
¼ teaspoon sugar
1⅔ cups warm water
3½ cups all-purpose flour
2 teaspoons salt
2 tablespoons olive oil
1 large red onion (about ½ pound), finely chopped
1 clove garlic, minced
¼ pound thinly sliced prosciutto, chopped
Cornmeal
1 egg yolk
2 teaspoons water

1. In a medium-size bowl, dissolve the yeast and sugar in ⅓ cup of the water. Whisk in 2 tablespoons of the flour and let the mixture stand until bubbly, about 10 minutes.

2. Add the remaining water to the yeast mixture. Stir in the salt, and enough flour to make a soft dough, about 3 cups. Turn the dough onto a well-floured surface; let it rest 3 minutes. Knead the dough until it is smooth and elastic, adding more flour if needed, about 10 minutes. Let it rest 3 minutes. Knead 1 minute longer and transfer to a lightly greased bowl. Cover and let rise until tripled in volume, about 2½ hours.

3. Meanwhile, heat the oil in a large skillet over medium-low heat. Add the red onion; cook 1 minute. Add the garlic; cook 3 minutes. Stir in the prosciutto; set aside.

4. Turn the dough out onto a lightly floured board; punch it down and roll it out into a circle about ½-inch thick. Spread the onion-prosciutto mixture over the dough. Fold the left third over the center; cover with the right third. Fold the top third over the center; cover with the bottom third. Turn the dough over and place it in a greased bowl. Cover and let it rise 1 hour.

5. Turn the dough out onto a floured board; let it rest 3 minutes. Knead briefly, roll out, and repeat the folding steps listed above. Place the dough on a baking sheet sprinkled with cornmeal. Form a long loaf. Cover the dough with a flour-rubbed towel and let it rise until doubled in volume, about 1 hour.

6. Preheat the oven to 400°F. Make three slashes across the top of the bread. Combine the egg yolk and 2 teaspoons water; brush this over the loaf. Place a roasting pan half-filled with water in the bottom of the oven. Place the bread, still on the baking sheet, in the top third of the oven. Bake 30 minutes. Remove the pan of water from the oven; continue to bake 25 minutes longer.

Makes 1 large loaf.

Chopping onions in a food processor can be a tricky business if you are not particularly adept with the on-off switch. Overprocessing turns even a crisp onion mushy, so a measure of care should be exercised. Frankly I do not think it is worth the bother of a cleanup operation to chop a single onion in a food processor. Large batches should be done in relays—with a word of caution. Always quarter the onions prior to processing!

GOLDEN ONION LOAF CAKE

One of the onion dishes I give thanks for is solely American. Known as Onion Loaf, but no bread at all, this is a collection of batter-dipped onion rings loosely crammed into an oblong wire basket and fried till golden.

My version (sans basket and French-fryer) is a trifle simplistic. The onions are fried first, baked later; then turned out like a cake, which in turn is cut into thick crusty wedges. Different—but not a jot less addictive, I promise.

Beer Batter (recipe follows)
2 large Bermuda onions (about 2 pounds)
Vegetable oil for frying
1¼ cups grated Monterey jack cheese, regular or with jalapeño peppers
Salt and freshly ground black pepper

1. Make the Beer Batter.

2. Cut the onions into ¼-inch-thick slices. Place the sliced onions in a large bowl, cover with ice water, and let stand 30 minutes.

3. Heat 2 inches of oil in a large heavy saucepan until hot but not smoking. Drain the onions, divide into rings, and lightly pat them dry.

4. Dip the onions into the batter, shaking off any excess. Fry them in the hot oil, about four or five at a time, until golden brown. Drain on paper towels.

5. Preheat the oven to 400°F. Generously butter an 8- or 9-inch springform pan. Line the sides with onion rings. Place one third of the remaining onion rings over the bottom. Sprinkle with ½ cup of the grated cheese. Add another layer of onion rings and sprinkle with ½ cup of the cheese. Top with the remaining onion rings and sprinkle with the remaining ¼ cup cheese. Bake 15 minutes.

6. To remove from the springform pan, first run a knife around the edges. Remove the sides of the pan, then gently flip the onion loaf over onto a serving platter. Carefully remove the bottom of the pan. Sprinkle with salt and pepper to taste.

Serves 6 to 8.

Beer Batter

1 cup all-purpose flour
2 teaspoons dry mustard
1 teaspoon freshly grated nutmeg
½ teaspoon salt
4 eggs, separated
2 teaspoons Dijon mustard
1 cup beer

Sydney Smith was a nineteenth-century English clergyman and poetaster. Have his "Recipe for Salad Dressing":

> Let onion atoms dwell within the bowl
> And scarce suspected, animate the whole.

1. Combine the flour with the dry mustard, nutmeg, and salt in a medium bowl.

2. Combine the egg yolks with the Dijon mustard and beer. Add this to the flour mixture and stir until smooth. Refrigerate, covered, 8 hours.

3. Just before using the batter, beat the egg whites until stiff; fold them into the batter.

Makes about 3½ cups.

GREEN-CRESTED ONIONS

Another baked onion partnership, this one clearly demonstrating the incredible savor an onion adds in combination with creamy mounds of green spinach blended with potatoes. I serve this as an adjunct to turkey on Thanksgiving.

4 large yellow onions
½ cup chopped fresh spinach leaves, washed
2 medium potatoes
2 tablespoons unsalted butter, softened
¼ cup heavy or whipping cream
¼ teaspoon freshly grated nutmeg
Salt and ground white pepper
2 tablespoons freshly grated Parmesan cheese

1. Peel the onions and cut an X in the root end of each one. Cook the onions in boiling salted water for 8 minutes; drain. When cool enough to handle, slice off the onion tops, and with your fingers carefully remove the insides, leaving a double layer of onion to be filled. (Reserve leftover onions for use at another time.)

2. Cook the spinach in boiling salted water until tender, about 3 minutes. Drain, pressing out all liquid with the back of a wooden spoon. Set aside.

3. Preheat the oven to 400°F. Peel

the potatoes; cut them into eighths. Cook the potatoes in boiling salted water until tender, about 18 minutes. Drain, and mash or rice until smooth. Beat in the butter, cream, nutmeg, and spinach. Mix well; add salt and white pepper to taste. (Add more cream if the mixture seems too heavy.) Spoon the potato mixture into the onion shells, mounding the filling high. Place the onions in an ovenproof baking dish; sprinkle them with the cheese. Bake until the tops are lightly browned, about 20 minutes.

Serves 4.

BAKED GLAZED ONIONS

My favored method for cooking onions is simply to bake them in a glaze of very down-to-earth ingredients (honey, mustard, paprika, and vinegar), a confluence that produces a crunchy orb that is neither sweet nor sour yet perfectly suited to any other dish, be it fish, fowl, or fine red meat.

4 medium yellow onions, peeled
1 tablespoon unsalted butter, softened
¼ cup honey
2 teaspoons Dijon mustard
1 tablespoon red wine vinegar
½ teaspoon ground paprika
Pinch of ground cloves
½ teaspoon salt
⅛ teaspoon freshly ground black pepper
¼ cup water

1. Preheat the oven to 350°F. With a sharp knife, score the top of each onion about ½ inch deep. Using your fingers, slightly open each onion.

2. Combine the butter, honey, mustard, and vinegar in a small bowl. Whisk until smooth. Add the paprika, cloves, salt, and pepper and mix well.

3. Place the onions in an ovenproof dish so that they fit fairly snugly. Pour the water around the onions. Spoon about 2 teaspoons of the glaze over each onion. Bake for 1 hour, basting with the remaining sauce every 10 minutes.

Serves 4.

BAKED WHITE ONIONS

One of my best baked onion confederations, this would make a splendid adjunct to any meal. It combines white onions with crescents of fresh, aromatic *shiitake* (Golden Oak) mushrooms.

¾ pound medium white onions, unpeeled
1½ tablespoons unsalted butter
¼ pound shiitake mushroom caps, sliced
¼ cup olive oil
2 cloves garlic, minced
1½ teaspoons finely chopped fresh parsley
Salt and freshly ground black pepper

1. Preheat the oven to 300°F. Place the onions in a medium saucepan and cover with cold water. Heat to boiling; reduce the heat. Simmer, uncovered, 12 minutes. Drain, and allow to cool slightly. Peel the onions and place them, whole, in a lightly buttered baking dish.

2. Melt the butter in a medium skillet over medium heat. Add the sliced mushrooms and sauté until lightly browned.

3. Add the mushrooms to the onions in the baking dish. Sprinkle with the olive oil, garlic, parsley, and salt and pepper to taste. Bake, covered, until tender, about 1 hour. Remove the cover during the last 20 minutes of baking if necessary to reduce the juices.

Serves 4 to 6.

PRASSA

(Leeks)

The first leek recipe is a Jewish bequest. It stems from a small but fascinating recipe book, *The Sephardic Cooks*, compiled and published by Congregation OR VeShalom Sisterhood, in Atlanta, Georgia. It's a slim volume, but eminently collectible.

2 tablespoons olive oil
6 leeks, trimmed of green tops, washed, cut into 1-inch pieces
1 large onion, chopped
1 clove garlic, minced
1 can (14 ounces) plum tomatoes, drained
1 cup chicken broth (see page 414)
½ teaspoon salt
1 teaspoon sugar
Juice of 1 lemon
1 medium potato, peeled, cubed
1 tablespoon chopped fresh basil or parsley

1. Heat the oil in a medium saucepan over medium-low heat. Add the leeks and onion. Cook, stirring constantly, 4 minutes. Add the garlic; cook 2 minutes longer.

2. Add the tomatoes to the onion mixture. Stir in the chicken broth, salt, sugar, and lemon juice. Simmer, covered, 40 minutes.

3. Add the potato to the vegetable mixture. Continue to cook, covered, until the potato is tender, about 20 minutes longer. If the mixture seems too wet, remove the cover, raise the heat, and cook until thickened. Sprinkle with the basil or parsley before serving.

Serves 4 to 6.

POIREAUX NICOISE

(Stewed Leeks and Tomatoes)

The next devise, leeks stewed in olive oil with tomatoes, is frankly a borrowing from the estimable Elizabeth David's *Provincial French Cooking*. But I must admit I have been fiddling and fussing with this recipe for so long, I don't think Mrs. David would care to own up to it any longer.

¼ cup olive oil
2 pounds leeks, trimmed of green tops, washed (about 6 to 8 leeks)
½ teaspoon salt
¼ teaspoon cayenne pepper
2 medium tomatoes, peeled, seeded, chopped
2 cloves garlic, minced
¼ teaspoon ground allspice
1 tablespoon chopped fresh basil
Juice of ½ lemon
2 tablespoons chopped fresh parsley

1. Heat the oil in a large heavy skillet over medium heat. Add the leeks in one layer. As the oil starts to bubble, turn the leeks over. Sprinkle with the salt and cayenne pepper. Cook for 1 minute; reduce the heat to medium-low. Cook, covered, until the leeks are tender, 12 to 15 minutes.

2. Transfer the leeks to a serving dish. Keep warm.

3. Add the tomatoes to the skillet and cook over high heat 1 minute. Add the garlic, allspice, and basil. Cook 1 minute longer. Add the lemon juice and 1 tablespoon of the parsley. Stir to mix, and spoon over the leeks. Sprinkle with the remaining parsley. Serve hot or cold.

Serves 4 to 6.

Leeks are long garden survivors. Seeds of this plant were carried to Britain by Roman invaders as an indispensable medicinal safeguard against the inclement dampness and rainwashed air. The herb must have worked. For though the Romans eventually decamped, most of them survived, and the leeks flourished like daisies on British soil. To this very day, every proper Welshman wears a leek in his hat on Saint David's Day to commemorate its unwonted arrival.

DRUNKEN LEEKS IN RED WINE

This heavenly first course is a Francophile offering: green leek stalks soused with butter, garlic, and good red wine, baked, and eaten either hot or cold as you wish. My choice? Room temperature.

3 tablespoons unsalted butter
6 to 8 small leeks, trimmed of green tops, washed
1 large clove garlic
¼ teaspoon salt
½ cup red wine
1 teaspoon red wine vinegar
Freshly ground black pepper
2 tablespoons chopped fresh parsley

1. Melt the butter in a large heavy skillet over medium heat. Add the leeks and garlic. Cook 3 minutes. Turn the leeks over and sprinkle with the salt and red wine. Cook, covered, 10 minutes. Remove the cover and cook until the leeks are tender, about 5 minutes longer. Discard the garlic. Transfer the leeks to a serving dish and keep warm.

2. Add the vinegar to the sauce in the skillet. Mix well, and pour over the leeks. Sprinkle with pepper to taste and the chopped parsley.

Serves 4.

LEEKS VINAIGRETTE A LA LUCAS

As learned years ago from an expert—Dione Lucas, who certainly knew her onions.

1 quart water
½ cup dry white wine
½ lemon
2 whole cloves
½ teaspoon salt
10 whole peppercorns
2 sprigs parsley
10 to 12 small leeks, trimmed of green tops, washed
1 small clove garlic, minced
½ teaspoon coarse (kosher) salt
4 teaspoons Dijon mustard
1 teaspoon lemon juice
3 tablespoons red wine vinegar
½ cup olive oil
¼ cup vegetable oil
Chopped chives

1. Combine the ingredients through the parsley in a large saucepan. Heat to boiling; reduce the heat. Simmer 5 minutes. Add the leeks; return to boiling; reduce the heat. Simmer, covered, until tender, about 10 minutes. Drain the leeks and transfer them to a shallow serving dish.

2. In a medium bowl mash the garlic with the coarse salt, using the back of a spoon. Stir in the mustard, lemon juice, and vinegar. Whisk in both oils. Pour the dressing over the leeks. Serve chilled or at room temperature, sprinkled with chopped chives.

Serves 4 to 6.

FRITTERRA

My favorite scallion chomp (after raw) is the following tender-hearted patty, Israeli in heritage. It was a gift from a taxi driver, who related it in pieces—each time we stopped for a light.

12 whole scallions, bulbs and green tops
2 eggs, lightly beaten
¼ teaspoon freshly grated nutmeg
½ teaspoon salt
Freshly ground black pepper
¼ cup fresh bread crumbs
1½ cups cold mashed potatoes
1 tablespoon olive oil
2 tablespoons vegetable oil

1. Wash and trim the scallions, leaving about 2 inches of green stems. Cook in boiling water until tender, about 5 minutes. Drain and chop.

2. Place the scallions in a medium-size bowl. Add the eggs, nutmeg, salt, pepper to taste, bread crumbs, and mashed potatoes. Mix well.

3. Heat the oils in a large skillet until hot but not smoking. Shape the onion-potato mixture into patties, using 2 rounded tablespoons of the mixture for each patty. Sauté, about six at a time, until golden brown on both sides, 2 or 3 minutes per side. Keep warm while sautéing the remaining patties.

Serves 4.

KERRY CHICKEN WITH SCALLIONS

3½-pound chicken, cut into 10 pieces
1 clove garlic, bruised
½ cup all-purpose flour
½ teaspoon salt
¼ teaspoon freshly ground black pepper
⅛ teaspoon ground allspice
4 tablespoons (½ stick) unsalted butter
1 tablespoon vegetable oil
¼ cup chopped scallions, bulbs and green tops
¼ cup dry white wine
1½ cups Chicken Stock (see page 410)
16 scallions, trimmed, leaving 1½ inches green tops
1 egg yolk
½ cup heavy or whipping cream
Pinch of ground cloves
Salt and freshly ground black pepper
¼ cup chopped fresh parsley

1. Rub the chicken pieces well with the bruised garlic. Discard the garlic. Combine the flour, salt, pepper, and allspice in a medium paper bag. Add the chicken pieces. Shake well to coat; reserve the excess flour.

2. Heat 3 tablespoons of the butter with the oil in a 12-inch heavy skillet over medium heat. Sauté the chicken pieces until deep golden on all sides, about 12 minutes. Transfer to a Dutch oven.

3. Remove all but 1 tablespoon grease from the skillet. Add the remaining 1 tablespoon butter and the chopped scallions. Cook over medium-low heat 2 minutes. Stir in 2 tablespoons of the reserved flour mixture; cook over low heat, stirring constantly, 2 minutes. Whisk in the wine and chicken stock. Heat to boiling; pour over the chicken in the Dutch oven.

4. Heat the mixture in the Dutch oven to boiling; reduce the heat. Cook, covered, over medium-low heat 15 minutes. Add the whole scallions, sticking the bulbs down into the stock. Cook, covered, until the chicken is tender, about 10 minutes. The scallions should still be slightly crunchy.

5. Transfer the chicken pieces to a serving dish and arrange the scallions around the chicken. Keep warm. Meanwhile, strain the sauce if desired. Heat to boiling. Boil until slightly thickened, about 5 minutes. Remove from the heat.

6. Combine the egg yolk with the cream in a small bowl. Slowly stir it into the hot sauce. Return the sauce to medium-low heat; cook 2 minutes. Do not allow it to boil. Add the cloves, and salt and pepper to taste. Pour the sauce over the chicken and sprinkle with the chopped parsley.

Serves 4.

All of the onion kith and kin that grow in a garden—Spanish Golds, Pearl Whites, Italian Reds, slender scallions—have a common denominator. Each is an amazing stimulator, able to invigorate even an anesthetized tongue. Why, you ask? Sheer biological impulse. Because the onion, like the hot pepper, is possessed of astringent oils which irritate the membranes of the mouth, forcing the taste buds to react positively to flavor. More important perhaps, it is also capable of carrying that flavor to the seat of all taste, the wondrous sensual barometer known as the nose.

FLAMICHE
(Onion and Cheese Tart)

This Alsatian tart is tender-crusted, meltingly rich, and onion-bedezined beyond description. The name means "spark," and it will excite even a tired appetite.

Short Crust Pastry (see page 412)
2 tablespoons unsalted butter
2 tablespoons olive oil
¾ pound yellow onions, finely chopped
¾ pound white onions, finely chopped
1 teaspoon sugar
2 cloves garlic, minced
⅛ teaspoon ground cloves
1 tablespoon all-purpose flour
Salt and freshly ground black pepper
3 eggs
½ cup heavy or whipping cream
4 ounces Roquefort cheese, crumbled (about ½ cup)
2 tablespoons freshly grated Parmesan cheese

1. Preheat the oven to 400°F. Roll out the pastry and line a 9-inch pie plate. Trim and flute the edges. Line the pastry with aluminum foil; weight with rice or beans. Bake 10 minutes. Remove the foil and rice or beans; bake 5 minutes longer. Cool. Reduce the oven heat to 375°F.

2. Heat 1 tablespoon of the butter with the oil in a large skillet over medium-low heat. Stir in both the onions; cook, stirring frequently, until the onions lose their color, about 8 minutes. Sprinkle with the sugar. Add the garlic and cloves. Cook, uncovered, over low heat, stirring occasionally, until the onions are tender, about 40 minutes. Stir in the flour and add salt and pepper to taste. Remove from the heat.

3. Beat the eggs with the cream in a large bowl. Slowly add the onion mixture. Add the Roquefort cheese. Pour this mixture into the prepared pastry shell. Sprinkle the top with the Parmesan cheese. Dot with the remaining tablespoon of butter cut into bits. Bake until golden, about 30 minutes. Allow to stand 5 minutes before serving.

Serves 6 to 8.

To the roll of yellow onions, there probably should be an amendment to include some succulent new hybrids that have recently hit the American marketplace—notably the Vidalias from Georgia, the Walla Wallas from Oregon, and the Mauis from Hawaii.

All of these relatively new onions have in common a remarkable sweetness to the tongue and a low acid threshold that will *not* bring tears to the eye. However, each bears an uncomfortably high price tag that is sure to bring a howl to most shoppers' lips. Why? Because of demand and no supply. All these hybrids require a nine-month growing cycle that culminates in a very abbreviated harvest, which in turn means little or no shelf life.

The reason for the new onions' popularity is indubitably their flavor, which stems from an extremely loamy soil that is low in sulphur in the first two instances and high in volcanic ash in the third. Onion cognoscenti who will insist on a bite no matter what the tariff can take heart: Mail-order sources are listed in the Notes on Ingredients at the back of the book.

LEEK CUSTARD

The next is an Alpine offering. And why not—since no people on earth make a custard dish better than the Swiss. Particularly when the foamy eggs and cream are commingled round nubbins of pink ham and green leek. Consume it for lunch, supper, or picnic fare. It chills to perfection.

4 large leeks, trimmed of green tops, washed
2 teaspoons unsalted butter
1 shallot, minced
¼ cup diced cooked ham
1 tablespoon Madeira
1 cup heavy or whipping cream
2 eggs
Salt and freshly ground black pepper
⅓ cup grated Jarlsberg cheese
2 tablespoons freshly grated Parmesan cheese
⅛ teaspoon freshly grated nutmeg

1. Preheat the oven to 350°F. Cook the leeks in boiling salted water until very tender, about 15 minutes. Drain; cut in half lengthwise; reserve.

2. Melt the butter in a small skillet over medium-low heat. Add the shallot and ham; cook 3 minutes. Stir in the Madeira; cook, stirring constantly, until all liquid has evaporated. Remove from the heat.

3. Lightly grease a 2-inch-deep baking dish, about 1¼ quarts in capacity. Layer the leeks in the bottom. Spoon the ham mixture between the leeks.

4. Beat the cream with the eggs in a large bowl until smooth. Add salt and pepper to taste, the Jarlsberg, 1 tablespoon of the Parmesan, and the nutmeg. Pour this over the leek mixture. Sprinkle the remaining 1 tablespoon Parmesan over the top. Bake until puffed and golden, about 30 minutes.

Serves 4.

PARSNIPS

A Chequered Career

Curiously, I have spent both the early and the late summers of my life in houses by the sea, watching parsnips grow.

The first was a small bungalow my parents owned on the South Shore of Long Island. It was a trim shingle cottage, shaded front and back by screened porches and set, without a foundation, in a row of absolutely uniform dwellings on a treeless, unpaved street. Slatted wooden footpaths were the only sidewalks.

In those days only Long Beach's main avenues were hard-topped. Streets were dusty arteries that began at the railway station and ended abruptly at either the Atlantic Ocean or the Sound, depending upon which side of the tracks you lived on.

Thc oceanside we inhabited was the territory most residents chose to swim in during the day and to promenade along most of the night, for it was the site of Long Beach's legendary boardwalk. What I remember most clearly from the months spent "at the shore" are the remarkable attractions that wooden thoroughfare offered. There were hotels, theaters, swimming pools, Turkish and Russian bathhouses, penny arcades, plus popcorn and hot dog vendors at every crosswalk. My favorite enterprise of all was the salt water taffy factory.

My father spent only weekends at the

shore, so the hard work of running this second household was inherited by my mother. And she detested it.

"Too much sun," she would complain. "Too much rain," she would rail. "And sand underfoot no matter the weather. Get me out of here before I go nuts."

My father brought visitors to cheer her up, but was hardly thanked for his efforts. "If I wanted to run a boarding house, I'd put a sign in the window!"

My mother's parents and her unmarried sisters were frequent sojourners at our summer quarters. But the air of *pater familias* did nothing to mollify my mother's discontent. Indeed her parents' presence, and her younger sister Sally's constant stream of suitors, only seemed to worsen her temper. When my grandmother took over most of the kitchen chores and her sisters "straightened" the house, she acted as if her housewifely abilities were a subject of censure. And the air of strife in our bungalow was manifest as the film of salt, outside. I will never forget my mother's mute irritation one summer when her garden-loving mother and sister (my Aunt Frances), challenged by the unused sun trap behind our back porch, planted rows of seedlings in the sandy soil.

She observed their action with raised eyebrows but no comment, and scrupulously avoided watering this garden once they left for home. "It's simply not worth bothering about" was her rationale. "My mother has a green thumb so she thinks anything she puts in the ground will grow. But not in *this* desert."

Despite her tacit dismissal, at summer's end some of the vegetables they planted had actually managed to survive the gritty soil. They were woody and overgrown, but my thrifty parent managed to pick a clump of ivory parsnips from the bed. She cooked them for our supper—swallowing, with grim asperity, more than her actual share, as I recall.

The story has a coda.

Thirty-odd years later, my mother and I shared another meal of beach-grown parsnips. This supper took place in my first rented house in Amagansett, also on Long Island's South Shore but practically at its outermost point.

It was end of summer and the friends with whom I had shared the tenancy of this dwelling had all decamped for autumnal pursuits. My mother surveyed the quarters critically, for she never had liked houses by the sea. This one, the antithesis of a bungalow, was gray clapboard, a turn-of-the-century farmhouse with a trellised porch covered with climbing morning glories and runner beans.

My mother inspected the old-fashioned kitchen and the remnants of my first vegetable garden on the table with some amused tolerance. "You really inherited my mother's thumb," she said as she pushed a pale cooked parsnip to the edge of her plate. "More than that. You got her whole *gesheft*."

In Yiddish that word literally means "a store." Figuratively it implies a treasury, however, and that was quite a compliment coming from my mother. But I was not permitted to bask in the glow of her observation for very long.

"Unfortunately," she continued, "you don't know a hill of beans about parsnips. Look!" She made a circle of her thumb and forefinger. "You don't pick them when they get bigger than this. No. You leave them in the ground till the following spring when they either soften up—or you feed 'em to horses!" My mother smiled. "Now that's a piece of advice you inherited from me. Remember it!"

I remember.

Vegetable Roots

Parsnips grew wild in the northern, windswept territories of Eastern Europe for thousands of years. Food pundits assert they would be there still if some mettlesome Visigoth raiding party had not brought them to Rome to season their spearheads: wild parsnip roots are exceedingly lethal.

The barbarians were repulsed without a contest, but their ammunition apparently took root and was cultivated, the sandy banks of the Tiber providing an ideal setting.

Cultivated parsnips are a mild lot, so sweet that nursing mothers in the Middle Ages weaned their babies by giving them this root to suck. Wild parsnips (then and now) are lethal bulbs that even intrepid weed-eaters like cows avoid.

The word "parsnip" itself is an appropriation, albeit a horticultural one. Early Roman farmers furrowed their vegetable fields with a long tapering tool known as a *pastinum* that made deep, even holes in the ground for easy planting. Because the equally tapering parsnip resembled that tool, they dubbed it a *pastinaca.*

That cognomen remained unaltered for almost five hundred years, until the fifteenth century when a loyal English farmer demonstrating his support of Henry VIII's break with the Church of Rome altered the Latin names of all the vegetables that grew in his garden. *Pastinaca* became *pastinepe,* which in time was corrupted to *pasnepe.* Some early Virginia housewife, who obviously could not spell, is credited with the name's final evolution. Among the Roanoke Colony farm records is a listing: "Two mere bushels parnips picked. Half a hundred other snips left in the ground to winter." Taxonomists, scientists unswayed by political and religious feelings, have retained *Pastinaca sativa* for the official label.

The parsnip has had a chequered career at the dining room table. When they were first consumed in Rome, the aristocracy alone dined on them—usually as a sweetmeat, preserved in honey or grated with fruits and frothed up into little cakes.

In the Middle Ages, parsnips began to be eaten by the masses as well, but not for dessert. All extant *moyen age* recipes couple parsnips with salted cod, pickled eel, or smoked herring.

From the Renaissance to the late eighteenth century, the parsnip decidedly moved to the center of the table. Before the potato entered the European diet (courtesy of Sir Walter Raleigh), this vegetable was considered the only fitting accompaniment to the roasted birds, sides of beef, broiled swans, and other fanciful dishes that made groaning boards groan. When the potato arrived, the little p's popularity in the Old World waned a jot—but the unsinkable root acquired twice as many admirers among the colonists in the New one!

In Virginia and Massachusetts (the two earliest outposts in America) there is overwhelming evidence of parsnip popularity; this vegetable came to the table as wine, whipped into puddings, baked into bread, mashed into casseroles, and even fried with fish. There is even an actual recording of a parsnip wedding cake (composed of dried parsnip flour) that was served in Jamestown, unfortunately *sans* recipe.

What to Look For

The reason why parsnips flourished near the beach is quite simple: the burrowing taproot of this vegetable likes a loose and sandy soil for *lebensraum.* And little other attention. When I have mulched and fertilized them to a fare-thee-well, the pickings are inevitably slimmer and a lot less tasty.

Like their cousin the carrot, parsnips are slow bloomers. When they do appear, the young shoots are extremely delicate and lacy, much affected by changes of weather. The wise noncoastal agrarian often plants radishes in the same vegetable furrow since those more vigorous shoots, pushing upward with almost

gravitational force, loosen the soil and provide the frailer parsnip with a healthy head start. Of course by the time the parsnips are sufficiently hardy to fend for themselves, the radishes have long since hit the road, or more precisely, the alimentary canal.

A truly ripe parsnip takes a growing season of almost six months to mature, never developing to the required size (4 inches long and 1½ to 2 inches in diameter) until late September or October.

To compensate for their slow growth, parsnips are exceedingly hardy and will overwinter in most climates underground. I have a friend in Vermont who digs them up from under a blanket of snow whenever the irresistible urge for a parsnip comes upon him—most often around St. Patrick's Day, for this sweet root turns the alliance of mere corned beef and cabbage into a celestial culinary confederation (see page 82).

When parsnip shopping—even for those that come in plastic wrappers—keep a weather eye out for smooth roots and plump, shaded members that are free of nicks or deep pits. Pass on any bags of disproportionate sizes as well, for they are difficult to time in cookery. Likewise skip "waxed" parsnips or any produce with shriveled roots or, perish the thought, soft, flabby skins.

Besides flavor, parsnips have an added virtue for our daily meals: they are literally diet food. An 8-ounce cupful, or half a large cooked parsnip, contains a scant 76 calories. The same amount, however, provides over 50 units of vitamin A plus 541 milligrams of potassium and 16 milligrams of vitamin C, as well as healthy increments of phosphorus and iron.

Preparation

My first precept about cooking parsnips is to choose only those of equal size for your pot. Surprisingly, the best are not easily found at greengrocers', unless one has the time to sift through the pile and match the root ends. I must confess I usually buy mine at a supermarket, choosing the prepackaged, plastic-wrapped variety that are graded as to size. My preference in a parsnip is a short, squat root, which has less core and more flesh.

To prepare parsnips for cooking, merely wash off any residual dirt and peel them. Although many recipe manuals advise cooking parsnips whole before they are peeled, I do not. The vegetable is much easier to handle raw. In most of the recipes that follow, the parsnips are peeled, parboiled, and then cooked or sauced. Steamed parsnips, however, are always left unpeeled, as the skins slip off easily once they cool.

I have discovered that halving (or quartering in the case of super-size roots) will allow the parsnip's central core to cook to the perfect degree of tenderness and save time into the bargain. I never cook a halved parsnip longer than 5 to 8 minutes. A whole parsnip, on the other hand, may take anywhere from 12 to 15 minutes until it is tender.

Really monster parsnips (the kind that have stayed in the ground for almost a year's time) may require removal of the core with a sharp knife after precooking. Large cores will become tender but the texture is always slightly woody. Use your judgment and your tongue—taste it first.

PIKE'S PEAK SOUFFLE

One of the most unusual guises a parsnip has ever taken is indubitably the following dish: a pale ivory soufflé, the title resurrected from a menu found in Colorado's Central City and the dish reconstructed in my small apartment kitchen in New York. On my honor, it will hit your tongue like a steaming blizzard.

3 tablespoons plus 1 teaspoon unsalted butter
1 pound medium parsnips, peeled, quartered
1 small onion, minced
3 tablespoons all-purpose flour
1 cup milk, boiling
4 egg yolks
¼ teaspoon cayenne pepper
½ teaspoon salt
½ teaspoon ground mace
¼ teaspoon freshly ground black pepper
3 tablespoons dark rum
6 egg whites

1. Preheat the oven to 400°F. Lightly butter a 1½-quart soufflé dish with the 1 teaspoon butter. Set aside.

2. Cook the parsnips in boiling salted water until very tender, about 8 minutes; drain. Remove the cores.

3. Chop the cored parsnips and transfer them to the container of a food processor. Process until smooth. (You should have about 1¼ cups.) Set aside.

4. Melt the remaining 3 tablespoons butter in a large heavy saucepan over medium-low heat. Add the onion and cook, stirring occasionally, until tender, about 5 minutes. Do not allow it to brown. Stir in the flour. Cook, stirring constantly, 2 minutes. Whisk in the milk. Return to boiling; boil 1 minute. Remove from the heat. The mixture will be quite thick.

5. Beat the egg yolks, one at a time, into the soufflé base. Add the cayenne pepper, salt, mace, black pepper, and rum. Stir in the puréed parsnips.

6. In a medium bowl, beat the egg whites until stiff but not dry. Stir one quarter of the egg whites into the parsnip mixture. Fold in the remaining egg whites. Spoon the mixture into the prepared soufflé dish.

7. Place the soufflé in the oven and immediately reduce the heat to 375°F. Bake until puffed and golden, about 30 minutes.

Serves 4 to 6.

PALE FRIED PARSNIPS

To my mind, the classic rendering of a parsnip always takes place in a skillet. One such felicitous fry that I have loved since I was a young kid is a reconstruction of a recipe described in Laura Ingalls Wilder's *Little House on the Prairie*. According to the author, no Christmas dinner was ever official without this dish on hand.

1 pound medium parsnips, peeled, halved lengthwise
2 tablespoons unsalted butter
2 tablespoons dark brown sugar
2 tablespoons red wine vinegar
Salt and freshly ground black pepper
Chopped fresh parsley

1. Cook the parsnips in boiling salted water until just tender, about 5 to 8 minutes. Drain. Cut each parsnip lengthwise into ¼-inch-thick slices.

2. Melt the butter in a large skillet over medium heat. Add the parsnips; cook until lightly browned, about 4 minutes. Sprinkle with the brown sugar. Turn the parsnips over; continue to cook until very tender, about 4 minutes longer.

3. Transfer the parsnips to a serving platter. Sprinkle with the vinegar, salt and pepper to taste, and chopped fresh parsley.

Serves 4.

UNPARALLELED PARSNIP CREAM

Parsnips have a wonderful fragrance that has endeared them to man's palate for centuries. In no rendering of this vegetable is that elusive scent more manifest than in a soup bowl. Consider inclusion of a whole parsnip in any chicken, beef, or vegetable chowder in your kitchen repertoire. It will add body to each brew.

Or merely try your hand at the following pale creamy eminence. Actually, this recipe is a variation of a classic vichyssoise, unclassically seasoned and spiced to make it seem newly minted. It is the handiwork of a brilliant young chef, Felipe Rojas-Lombardi of The Ballroom restaurant in New York City.

1½ tablespoons unsalted butter
1 large onion, chopped
1 small leek, white part only, washed, chopped
1 small green chile pepper (see Guacamole headnote, page 37), or canned jalapeño, seeded, chopped
½ teaspoon sugar
½ teaspoon minced fresh ginger root
⅛ teaspoon ground turmeric
⅛ teaspoon freshly grated nutmeg
1 pound parsnips, peeled, chopped
1 medium potato, peeled, chopped
3 cups chicken broth (see page 414)
4 cups water
Salt and ground white pepper
⅓ cup sour cream
Chopped fresh parsley

1. Melt the butter in a large saucepan over medium-low heat. Add the on-

Parsnip has a very flexible moniker. The original Latin was translated into French as *panais.* Hidebound Italians still call it by a generic tag, *pastinaca,* while the Spanish dub it with an entirely improbable sound, *chirivia,* and a most logical meaning: a "dug-up"! The Germans, who probably brought the parsnip to Rome in the first place, are a tad ambivalent about its sobriquet: they call it *Pastinak, Pastinake,* or *Pastinakwurzel,* depending upon their geography.

ion, leek, chile pepper, sugar, ginger root, turmeric, and nutmeg. Cook, stirring constantly, 5 minutes. Add the parsnips and potato; cook, stirring occasionally, 5 minutes.

2. Add the chicken broth and water to the vegetable mixture. Heat to boiling; reduce the heat. Simmer, uncovered, until the vegetables are tender, about 20 minutes. Add salt and white pepper to taste. Cool.

3. Purée the soup, in batches, in a food processor or blender. To serve the soup hot: reheat over medium-low heat without boiling, and serve with a dab of sour cream in each bowl, sprinkled with parsley. To serve the soup cold: chill well, and just before serving stir in the sour cream, then sprinkle with parsley.

Serves 6 to 8.

PARSNIPS IN MELTING MUSTARD SAUCE

This dish is a purely personal invention. The parsnips are sluiced with mustard, honey, and bourbon. Definitely worth writing home about!

1 pound medium parsnips, peeled, halved lengthwise
3 tablespoons unsalted butter
2 tablespoons Dijon mustard
1 teaspoon honey
3 tablespoons bourbon
Salt and freshly ground black pepper
Chopped fresh parsley

1. Preheat the oven to 375°F. Cook the parsnips in boiling salted water until just tender, about 5 to 8 minutes. Drain. Cut each parsnip lengthwise into ¼-inch-thick slices. Place them in a buttered shallow baking dish in a single layer. Bake 10 minutes.

2. Melt the butter in a small saucepan over low heat. Slowly add the mustard, honey, and bourbon. Cook 5 minutes. Brush this sauce evenly over the baked parsnips. Sprinkle with salt and pepper to taste. Place the parsnips under a preheated broiler to lightly brown, about 1 minute, before serving sprinkled with parsley.

Serves 4.

PARSNIPS IN GINGERY CREAM

From the American South, a dish of sautéed parsnips cloaked in a delicately gingered warm sour cream—perfect with fried chicken or ham.

1 pound parsnips, peeled
1 tablespoon unsalted butter
½ cup sour cream
Pinch of ground mace
1 teaspoon roughly chopped candied ginger
Salt and freshly ground black pepper

1. Cook the parsnips in boiling salted water until barely tender, about 10 minutes. Drain. Cut into ¼-inch-thick rounds.

2. Melt the butter in a large skillet over medium heat. Add the parsnips. Sauté until lightly browned, about 4 minutes. Reduce the heat to low.

3. Slowly stir the sour cream into the parsnips. Add the mace and cook until warmed through. Do not allow to boil. Add the candied ginger, and salt and pepper to taste.

Serves 4.

LULLWORTH CROQUETTES

To mix a metaphor totally, parsnips are decidedly not everyone's cup of tea! The French, for instance, will not touch this vegetable with a ten-foot *cuillère.* They may slip one into pot au feu but would never consider the prospect of attacking one with a knife or fork.

The English have better sense. They add parsnips to all manner of stews. On occasion they even stir them into fritters and croquettes as well. *Par example* the next devise, from Devonshire.

1½ pounds parsnips, peeled, quartered
1 teaspoon salt
2 tablespoons dark brown sugar
2 eggs, lightly beaten
1½ teaspoons finely slivered orange peel
¼ teaspoon freshly grated nutmeg
¼ cup all-purpose flour
2 tablespoons unsalted butter

1. Cook the parsnips in boiling salted water until very tender, about 10 minutes. Drain and mash.

2. In a medium-size bowl combine the mashed parsnips with the salt, sugar, eggs, orange peel, and nutmeg. Shape into small patties and roll them in the flour.

3. Melt the butter in a large skillet over medium heat. Sauté the parsnip croquettes until golden on both sides, about 2 minutes per side. Keep warm in a low oven until ready to serve.

Serves 4 to 6.

APPLE 'N' PARSNIP SAUCE

A sensational variation on applesauce. Serve it with roast pork or duckling for a real tastemaker. Or put it out on Thanksgiving in lieu of cranberries.

1 pound medium parsnips, peeled, quartered
Salt
1 pound tart green apples (about 3 medium), peeled, cored, sliced
1 cup apple juice or cider
½ cup packed dark brown sugar
1 tablespoon slivered orange peel
3 tablespoons apple brandy or apple schnapps

1. Cook the parsnips in boiling salted water until barely tender, about 5 minutes. Drain. Remove the cores and roughly chop the parsnips.

2. Combine the parsnips, apples, apple juice, and brown sugar in a medium saucepan. Slowly heat to boiling; reduce the heat. Cook, uncovered, over medium heat until the apples and parsnips are soft, about 15 minutes. Remove from the heat.

3. Lightly mash the parsnips and apples in the saucepan. Stir in the slivered orange peel and apple brandy or apple schnapps. Allow to cool.

Makes about 2½ cups.

OLD-FASHIONED PARSNIP MARMALADE

This recipe has its heritage in the Midwest. Its period: the early nineteenth century, when winters were hard, fruit was scarce, and farmers' children were sweet-toothed.

1 pound parsnips, peeled, grated (about 3½ cups)
Finely slivered peel of 1 lemon
Juice of 1 lemon
Finely slivered peel of 3 small oranges
Pulp and juice of 3 small oranges
2 cups sugar
Pinch of ground cinnamon
¼ cup orange liqueur

Combine all the ingredients except the liqueur in a medium saucepan. Slowly heat to boiling, then reduce the heat. Simmer, uncovered, stirring occasionally, 25 minutes. Stir in the orange liqueur and cook 5 minutes longer. Pour into sterilized jars and seal. Process in a hot water bath for 12 minutes.

Makes 3 cups.

CARAMEL CHICKEN WITH PARSNIPS

Have the following dish of glistening golden chicken sautéed with parsnips. It is the closest thing I know to sublimity at the dinner table.

1 teaspoon ground cinnamon
1 teaspoon salt
¼ teaspoon freshly ground black pepper
1 large chicken (about 3½ to 4 pounds), cut into 10 pieces
2 tablespoons unsalted butter
1 tablespoon vegetable oil
1 pound medium parsnips, peeled, halved lengthwise
¼ cup sugar
¼ cup water
2 tablespoons tarragon wine vinegar
2 tablespoons chopped fresh parsley

1. Preheat the oven to 325°F. Combine the cinnamon, salt and pepper in a small bowl. Rub the mixture into the chicken pieces.

2. Heat the butter with the oil in a large skillet over medium heat. Sauté the chicken pieces until golden brown on both sides, about 15 minutes. Transfer the chicken to a shallow baking dish, reserving the drippings in the skillet. Place the chicken in the oven.

3. Cook the parsnips in boiling salted water for 5 minutes. Drain, and cut them lengthwise into ¼-inch-thick slices. Cut each slice into pieces about 3 inches long and 1 inch wide.

4. Heat 3 tablespoons of the reserved drippings in the skillet used for sautéing the chicken. Add the parsnips; cook over medium-low heat until tender, 12 to 15 minutes. Place the parsnips around the chicken and return to the oven.

5. Lightly wipe out the skillet and add the sugar. Heat, stirring constantly, over medium heat until the sugar melts and begins to caramelize. Carefully stir in the water and vinegar. Stir until smooth. Spoon this sauce over the chicken and parsnips and bake 10 minutes longer. Serve sprinkled with parsley.

Serves 4.

PURITAN PIE

A parsnip conceit that marries the old-fashioned American marmalade and a wondrous, strictly Viennese linzer torte. The issue should probably be dubbed a *Pastinakwurzel* torte, but I prefer to think of it as . . . Puritan Pie. I am no purist but since I use the processor to make almond paste for this recipe, I advise its use for the other steps as well.

For the Pastry:

6¾ ounces blanched almonds
1½ cups all-purpose flour
¾ cup sugar
Finely grated peel of 2 lemons
¼ teaspoon ground cinnamon
½ teaspoon ground allspice
8 tablespoons (1 stick) unsalted butter, cut into bits
3 egg yolks
2 teaspoons water, approximately

For the Almond Paste:

5 ounces blanched almonds
½ cup sugar
1 egg, lightly beaten

For the Final Assembly:

1¾ cups Old-Fashioned Parsnip Marmalade (see preceding recipe)
1 egg yolk
2 teaspoons water

1. To make the pastry: Place the almonds in the container of a food processor fitted with a steel blade. Process until finely ground. Add the flour, sugar, lemon peel, cinnamon, and allspice. Process briefly. Add the butter and process until well mixed. Add the egg yolks and water. Process until a soft dough is formed, adding more water if needed. Scoop out the dough onto a lightly floured board. Knead briefly.

2. Remove slightly more than half the dough. Place the smaller half, wrapped, in the freezer. Line a 10-inch loose-bottom tart pan with the remaining dough, pressing the dough over the sides and bottom with your fingers.

3. Preheat the oven to 375°F. Wipe out the processor container; put back the steel blade. To make the almond paste: combine the almonds and sugar in the container of the processor. Process until finely ground. Add the beaten egg, and process until a smooth paste is formed. Carefully spread the paste over the bottom of the prepared tart pan.

4. Spoon the Old-Fashioned Parsnip Marmalade over the almond paste in the shell.

5. Remove the chilled dough from the freezer. Roll it out between layers of waxed paper until thin. Remove the top layer of waxed paper. With scissors, cut the dough into strips about 1 inch wide, cutting right through the bottom paper with the scissors. Pick up the strips, one at a time, and flip them over onto the top of the tart to form a lattice pattern. Carefully pull off the waxed paper. Press the edges into the shell.

6. Combine the egg yolk with the water in a small bowl. Brush this over the pastry. Bake 10 minutes. Reduce the heat to 350°F and bake 20 minutes longer. Cool on a wire rack. Remove the outside ring from the pan before the pie has completely cooled.

Serves 8 to 10.

PEAS

From Marble Size to Petits Pois

My older sister, Myra, brought culture into my life after my parents gave up trying. A worldly type even as an adolescent, she permitted me to join her (whether as acolyte or accomplice I am not certain) in the sophisticated pursuit of grace and style. Most of our education was acquired from the movies we attended three or four times a week; our role models were the movie stars, whose elegant manners and modish dress we attempted to emulate whenever our parents were out of earshot.

When I was still very young, we would play elaborate games of "let's pretend," sometimes imagining that the airy upstairs bedroom we shared was the

cabin of a luxury zeppelin gliding across the Atlantic or the suite of a chic European hotel, where breakfast served on trays (prepared earlier by my sister) would be consumed sybaritically in bed on Sunday mornings.

Myra also kept a collection of scrapbooks stocked with pictures of elegant homes and all manner of tony furnishings, which she clipped from a pile of magazines on my mother's subscription list. With shears in hand, Myra would study a color photo thoughtfully before she decided whether or not to paste it into her "Dream House" book. Her favored color scheme in those days was "old rose and pearl gray," so any advertisement of a household object (be it limousine or lingerie case) in either shade would instantly be removed to her bulging file. When I asked her once why she collected such a multitude, her answer was vague, if optimistic.

"One never knows when Dame Fortune will smile," said Myra. "I may need lots and lots of options."

As the Depression grew ever more pronounced in our lives, she banished the mundane present with prospects of a rosier future. She knew that one day we would both be dining on lamb chops in frilled white paper millinery and *petits pois* along with our vintage champagne.

My sister's sole food fixation was tiny green peas—the littler the better. Even during the depths of the Depression, whenever she assisted my mother on shopping expeditions, a can always ended up in the family grocery bag, usually bearing the legend *Product of France.*

For my own part I was never particularly impressed with these underdeveloped legumes. They were too soft and olive drab to satisfy either my tongue or my eye. But Myra doted on them. And *petits pois* (as she always referred to them) inevitably became a part of all celebratory meals. I recall her favorite birthday dish well. It was creamed chicken studded with those tiny greenish seed pearls, served up in brittle and unfailingly soggy-bottomed patty shells.

Myra considered that meal to be the height of prandial elegance, and once spent the better part of a Saturday morning showing me how to consume the contents of a patty shell without causing a hailstorm of pastry at a table setting. It was a valuable lesson, like all of my sister's cultural bequests.

I haven't tasted creamed chicken and peas (with or without patty shells) in years, but if my sister made the request I would gratefully whip up a batch tomorrow.

Vegetable Roots

A truly wild pea is almost impossible to find these days, although *Pisum sativum* has been part of man's diet since the Bronze Age, when sticks and stones were his only tablerie. Traces of early peas have in fact been carbon-dated in the prehistoric lake dwellings at Herzogenbuchsee, Switzerland: roughly 9,750 years before the birth of Christ. A record for any vegetable that is still consumed with a measure of relish!

The peas favored by cavemen, however, were far from the kind that migratory birds (or even Birdseye) would opt for today. The earliest peas were as large as marbles and probably as tasty. Archeologists believe they were always roasted and peeled (like chestnuts) before they were deemed fit for a tribe's digestion. Uncultivated peas grew in bogs and rambled rather than climbed, which made picking them a considerable chore for the lady of the cave. But they must have been worth the trouble because in time they were planted and tended as crops.

From Switzerland to India is decidedly no short hop, but pea seeds migrated there and flowered in the cool climate of Himachal Pradesh. However,

In 1602 the Mayflower Colony log book records that peas planted by Captain Bartholomew Gosnold bloomed and bore fruit on the island of Cuttyhunk. Soon peas flourished and were tossed into skillets with every other ingredient that was harvested on the island: beans, barley, sweet potatoes, and corn.

the cultivated peas that were eaten in India and later in Greece and Rome were inevitably dried and involved lengthy cooking.

For centuries a tender pea, straight from its green pod, was regarded to be a near-lethal pellet and was dried to cure it of its "noxious and stomach-destroying canker." Farmers in Rome often left green peas on the vine in their fields to kill foraging rabbits, who, having better sense than the agrarians, flourished instead.

The standard dish of dried peas that Apicius describes as a household staple was cooked for hours until it became a thick gruel, then splashed with a mite of oil and vinegar and eaten for breakfast. If it brings to mind *pease porridge* rumored to stay in the pot until nine days old, it is no coincidence. That recipe stuck to the ribs of western Europe in one form or another for over 500 years.

It took a Frenchman, of course, a gardener named Michaux, to convince the world that green peas were not only edible but, more pertinently, delectable. In the sixteenth century he developed a hybrid pod that climbed on trellises and grew sweeter and tenderer with each foot of elevation. These legumes, at first known as *miches* (small lumps) in honor of their grower, eventually received a more generic tag, *vert pois* (green or garden peas), and became the rage of France. In one of her letters, dated 1696, Madame de Maintenon warmed to the subject of the pea at the court of Louis XIV: "The impatience to eat them, the pleasure of having eaten them, the joy of eating them again, are the three questions that have occupied our princes for the last four days!"

A sharp observer of the pea's effect on court life, she also wrote: "There are ladies here, who having supped with the King and supped well, retire to the privacy of their chambers; there to feast in secret on dishes of petits pois." She concluded, "*C'est une mode et une fureur!*" (This is both a fashion and a madness!) Pea-preoccupation to say the least, and it never abated until the French Revolution, when the vegetable entered the diet of the proletariat with no less partiality.

What to Look For

As a pea fancier, I am highly prejudiced on the subject of what is offered for sale these days. The most tender—and that implies a desirable jot of moisture under the skin—must be grown in a backyard or window box, I regret to say. The varieties I opt for in seed catalogues (in order of preference) are "Laxton's Progress," "Little Marvels," and "Dwarf Telephones," with "Mammoth Melting Sugars" the runner-up.

Shopping for a passel of peas at the greengrocer's or on a supermarket shelf, I pick whatever seems perkiest. One should try to buy pods that will snap rather than bend under slight pressure from the thumb; likewise those with the brightest color. One can tell the old-timers: they are usually frayed at the edges or bedraggled-looking.

Like most vegetables, raw peas are somewhat higher in nutrients than cooked. Three quarters of a cup of blanched shelled peas represents about 84 calories with an extremely high ratio of amino acids and minerals; notably 316 milligrams of potassium, 27 units of vitamin C, and a whopping 640 units of vitamin A. So eat them with surety. They are making you healthy and satisfied at one and the same time.

Preparation

Unlike my sister, Myra, I judge a pea to be prime *only* when it is served up near-raw. My grandmother, who never ate between meals, was so addicted to the flavor of fresh-from-the-pod peas that she could never shell a handful without popping at least one out of every four into her mouth "for energy!"

Peas, like corn, are rich in natural sugar which turns to starch within hours after picking, so wise gardeners usually cook them minutes after they are harvested. Without the lucky option of a pea patch at your back door, try blanching them first and reheating them later. My technique is to drop the peas into boiling salted water for a scant minute—less if they are particularly small. Without waiting for the water to return to the boil, I immediately plunge them under cold running water. Once cool, I drain and store them for later use. To my mind, steaming peas is slightly dispiriting since the color fades appreciably. If you admire a bright-eyed pea as much as I do, pass on that cooking technique.

I must admit in all candor, however, that when peas are either over the hill or overpriced, I make do with the commercially frozen kind. I look for the variety that are labeled "Baby Peas," but never boil them first as the directions on the package suggest. Instead I merely defrost and use them thawed in the same manner I would a batch of blanched—with no appreciable loss of taste though the texture is a far cry from fresh.

GREEN AND GOLD CREAM OF PEA SOUP TOKLAS

Although Alice Toklas spent much of her life cooking on French soil, this dish is characteristically American in style, as the peas in it are neither puréed nor mashed but allowed to float gently on its surface like polka dots.

One caveat: This soup most definitely depends upon a good strong chicken stock for its base. Canned broth will produce an anemic approximation of its goodness.

1 tablespoon unsalted butter, plus 4 tablespoons (½ stick), cut into bits
1 tablespoon olive oil
½ cup ¼-inch bread cubes
3 cups Chicken Stock (see page 410)
1 small onion, peeled
1 small clove garlic, peeled
1 sprig parsley
1 pound fresh peas, shelled (about 1 cup), blanched 1 minute, or ½ (10-ounce) package frozen peas, thawed
1 extra large egg yolk
3 tablespoons heavy or whipping cream

1. Heat the 1 tablespoon butter with the oil in a medium skillet over medium-high heat. Add the bread cubes; sauté until golden, about 4 minutes. These are now croutons. Drain on paper towels; reserve.

2. Heat the stock to boiling in a medium saucepan. Tie the onion, garlic, and parsley in a cheesecloth bag. Add this to the stock; reduce the heat. Simmer, uncovered, over medium-low heat 15 minutes. Add the peas; cook 2 minutes longer. Remove the soup from the heat and discard the cheesecloth bag.

3. Dot the surface of the soup with the butter bits. Allow the butter to melt over the surface of the soup without stirring.

4. Beat the egg yolk with the cream in a serving bowl or tureen. Pour the soup over the yolk-cream mixture. Serve immediately with croutons.

Serves 4.

NEWLY MINTED PEAS

This is a cold salad devised of fresh peas and fresh mint in a creamy golden dressing. I first made it years ago at The Store in Amagansett, but it always tastes newly minted.

½ cup Mayonnaise (see page 408)
¼ cup sour cream
1 small onion, minced
¼ cup coarsely chopped fresh mint
¼ teaspoon Dijon mustard
3 pounds fresh peas, shelled, blanched 1 minute
Salt and freshly ground black pepper
Pimiento strips

Combine the mayonnaise with the sour cream in a medium bowl. Add the onion, mint, and mustard. Stir in the peas, and season with salt and pepper to taste. Transfer to a serving dish and garnish with pimiento strips. Serve chilled.

Serves 4 to 6.

PEAS AND KNEPP

The German word for pea is *Erbse*, which according to some keen etymologist friends is a corruption of an earlier Saxon noun, *erbe*, which means an inheritance. The pea is a bequest wherever it is found in my book, but in the following instance it makes a particularly felicitous gift. In this formula, highly prized by the Pennsylvania Dutch, short golden swirls of dough poach as the bright green peas cook.

4 tablespoons (½ stick) unsalted butter
6 tablespoons all-purpose flour
¼ teaspoon salt
Pinch of cayenne pepper
⅛ teaspoon freshly grated nutmeg
½ teaspoon chopped chives
¼ cup water
½ cup chicken broth (see page 414)
2 pounds fresh peas, shelled (about 2 cups), blanched 1 minute, or 1 package (10 ounces) frozen peas, thawed

1. Combine 2 tablespoons of the butter with the flour in a small bowl. Mix well. With a wooden spoon, work in the salt, cayenne pepper, nutmeg, chives, and water. Beat until thick and smooth. Set aside.

2. Heat the remaining 2 tablespoons butter with the chicken broth in a medium skillet. When it starts to boil, add the peas; cook 1 minute. Reduce the heat.

3. Add the dumpling mixture (knepp) by teaspoonfuls. Cook, covered, over medium-low heat, until the knepp are firm, about 6 minutes.

Serves 4.

SAUTEED PEAS WITH WALNUTS

While peas did not cause the French Revolution (pearls did), they most certainly brought an end to the reign of King John of England. He, poor addictive soul, was reputedly so affixed on the flavor of these green goods that he died from an attack of overindulgence at dinner—after consuming seven bowls of peas!

You be more circumspect with the following pea sauté livened by the addition of toasted walnuts and honey.

1 tablespoon unsalted butter
1 large shallot, minced
¼ cup Chicken Stock (see page 410)
2 teaspoons honey
2 pounds fresh peas, shelled (about 2 cups), blanched 1 minute, or 1 package (10 ounces) frozen peas, thawed
⅛ to ¼ teaspoon hot pepper sauce (depending on taste)
Salt and freshly ground black pepper
½ cup roughly chopped walnuts, toasted in a 400°F oven for 5 to 8 minutes

Melt the butter in a large skillet over medium-low heat. Add the shallot; cook 3 minutes. Add the chicken stock and honey. Raise the heat to medium-high; stir in the peas. Cook, stirring constantly, until the liquid has evaporated and the peas are tender, about 3 minutes. Add hot pepper sauce, salt, and pepper to taste. Stir in the walnuts.

Serves 4.

WILTED PEAS AND LETTUCE

For the classic alignment of peas and lettuce, which the French have made into a national side dish, I choose a purely American version. Its kitchen architect was no less than the estimable Thomas Jefferson. This devise is from his daughter Martha's kitchen notebook and is not much altered from the original, written in a mercurial downhill scrawl, now in the Jefferson collection at the University of Virginia.

1½ cups Chicken Stock (see page 410)
1¼ pounds fresh young peas, shelled
1 cup heavy or whipping cream
1 cup torn lettuce (bibb, Boston, or romaine)
2 tablespoons finely chopped chives or scallion tops
Salt and freshly ground black pepper

1. Heat the chicken stock to boiling in a medium saucepan. Add the peas, cook 1 minute, and drain. (Reserve the stock to use at another time.)

2. Heat the cream to boiling in a medium skillet; reduce the heat. Simmer until the cream has reduced to half, about 12 minutes. Stir in the peas and lettuce. Toss until the lettuce is just wilted, about 3 minutes. Add the chives and the salt and pepper to taste.

Serves 4.

GREEN AND GOLD SPOONBREAD

A rendering of the pea in its greenest and most original form: as spoonbread. This is a culinary invention for which I can take no credit, for it is solely the bright work of my collaborator, co-worker, and closest friend, Phillip Stephen Schulz. Phillip's fine hand is in evidence on every page of this book, but this is one of his finest gifts.

2 pounds fresh peas, shelled (about 2 cups), blanched 1 minute, or 1 package (10 ounces) frozen peas, thawed
¼ cup heavy or whipping cream
2 cups light cream or half-and-half
4 tablespoons (½ stick) unsalted butter
1 tablespoon honey
1 cup white cornmeal
4 eggs, separated
1 teaspoon baking powder
⅛ teaspoon hot pepper sauce
Salt and freshly ground black pepper

1. Preheat the oven to 375°F. Place the peas in the container of a food processor and add the heavy cream. Process, using the on/off switch, until finely chopped but not mushy. Set aside.

2. Combine the light cream, butter, and honey in a medium saucepan. Cook over low heat, without boiling, until the butter melts. Stir in the cornmeal. Continue to cook, stirring constantly and without boiling, until thick, about 4 minutes. Transfer to a large bowl.

3. Beat the egg yolks, one at a time, into the cornmeal mixture. Beat in the processed peas, baking powder, hot pepper sauce, and salt and pepper to taste.

4. Beat the egg whites until stiff but not dry, and fold them into the spoonbread mixture. Pour into a buttered 2-quart soufflé dish. Bake until puffed and golden, about 35 minutes.

Serves 6 to 8.

A pea crop set down by the colonists of Jamestown, Virginia, was so abundant that Captain John Smith wrote in his diaries in 1614: "Pease dry everywhere for nxt winter's fodder but stille the green seedkins are so bounteous we eat of them at evry meale in some forme or t'other. Namely on porridges, in pigeon pots and over puddings too!"

MUSTARDY PEAS WITH HAM

Peas aligned with snippets of frizzled ham.

2 tablespoons unsalted butter
1 small onion, finely chopped
½ cup chopped cooked ham
¼ cup dry white wine
1 teaspoon Dijon mustard
¼ cup chicken broth (see page 414)
2 pounds fresh peas, shelled (about 2 cups), blanched 1 minute, or 1 package (10 ounces) frozen peas, thawed
1 teaspoon finely slivered orange peel
Salt and freshly ground black pepper

1. Melt the butter in a large skillet over medium-low heat. Add the onion; cook 1 minute. Stir in the ham; raise the heat slightly. Cook until the ham is lightly browned, about 2 minutes. Add the wine and cook over medium heat, stirring constantly, until the liquid is syrupy, about 5 minutes.

2. Stir the mustard into the ham mixture. Add the broth and peas. Cook, stirring constantly, until the liquid has evaporated and the peas are tender, about 3 minutes. Add the orange peel and salt and pepper to taste.

Serves 4.

CLOAKED CHICKEN AND PEAS IN CREAM

A Virginia recipe, this aromatic casserole pairs homegrown peas with fowl in a minty cream gravy—tasty enough to cause even my sister to forswear any other version of creamed chicken. Though, I never asked her up till now.

¼ cup all-purpose flour
½ teaspoon salt
¼ teaspoon freshly ground black pepper
1 chicken, cut into serving pieces
3 tablespoons unsalted butter
1 tablespoon vegetable oil
¼ cup chicken broth (see page 414)
2 pounds fresh peas, shelled (about 2 cups), blanched 1 minute, or 1 package (10 ounces) frozen peas, thawed
½ cup heavy or whipping cream
1 egg yolk
¼ teaspoon ground white pepper
Pinch of cayenne pepper
2 tablespoons chopped fresh mint
Salt
1 tablespoon cognac
Chopped fresh parsley

1. Preheat the oven to 325°F. Combine the flour, salt, and pepper in a paper bag. Add the chicken pieces; shake well to coat with the flour.

2. Heat the butter with the oil in a large heavy skillet over medium heat. Sauté the chicken pieces until golden brown on all sides, about 12 minutes. Transfer the chicken to a shallow baking dish. Bake 30 minutes.

3. Remove all but 1 tablespoon fat from the skillet. Add the chicken broth; heat to boiling. Stir in the peas; cook 2 minutes. Remove from the heat.

4. Combine the cream with the egg yolk in a small bowl. Slowly stir this into the peas. Place over low heat; cook until slightly thickened, about 5 minutes. Do not allow to boil. Add the white pepper, cayenne pepper, mint, and salt to taste. Stir in the cognac. Pour this sauce over the chicken; sprinkle with parsley.

Serves 4.

FETTUCCINE CON FETTI

Keep a store of Pea-Green Pasta in the freezer, and with only some pink smoked ham bits, purple shallots, and red pepper flakes in a blanket of cream, you will have an incredibly festive party dish. Best of all, it takes less than fifteen minutes to prepare. I timed it!

5 tablespoons unsalted butter
2 shallots, minced
¾ cup finely chopped smoked ham
1 cup heavy or whipping cream
¼ teaspoon hot pepper sauce
1 teaspoon lemon juice
Salt and freshly ground black pepper
1 pound homemade Pea-Green Pasta (recipe follows), cut into fettuccine noodles
Freshly grated Parmesan cheese

1. Melt 2 tablespoons of the butter in a medium saucepan over medium heat. Add the shallots; cook 1 minute. Stir in the ham; cook 3 minutes longer. Add the cream, hot pepper sauce, and lemon juice. Heat to boiling; reduce the heat. Simmer until slightly thickened, about 5 minutes. Add salt and pepper to taste.

2. Meanwhile, cook the pasta in boiling salted water until just tender, about 2 minutes, longer if frozen. Drain, and wipe out the pot the pasta was cooked in. Add the remaining 3 tablespoons butter and place over low heat. Return the pasta to the pot. Toss well. Pour the ham-cream mixture over the pasta. Toss lightly and serve with Parmesan cheese.

Serves 4 to 6.

Pea-Green Pasta

A light green pea-dappled pasta also devised by *confrère* Schulz.

½ cup shelled peas (about ½ pound fresh unshelled peas)
¼ cup water (for processing peas)
2 cups all-purpose flour, approximately
1 egg, lightly beaten
1 tablespoon vegetable oil

1. Cook the peas in boiling salted water until very tender—about 5 minutes for frozen peas, longer for fresh. Drain.

2. Place the peas in the container of a blender or processor. Add ¼ cup water. Blend until smooth. (You will end up with tiny flecks of peas, but don't worry about that. If you use a processor, keep scraping down the sides until the mixture is fairly smooth.)

3. Place the flour in a large bowl. Make a well in the center. Add the beaten egg, the oil, and the puréed pea mixture. Using a fork or your fingers, incorporate the mixture into the flour until a fairly stiff dough is formed. Scoop the mixture out onto a lightly floured board. Knead, keeping the board lightly floured, for 10 minutes. Allow the dough to rest, covered, 30 minutes.

4. Roll the pasta dough out by hand or by machine until 1/16 inch thick. Cut into desired shape.

Makes about 1 pound.

Note: Because of the fresh vegetable ingredient, it is not a good idea to dry the pasta. It can be frozen successfully, however.

FETTUCCINE DUE VERDI

A toss of pea pasta with smoked salmon, vodka, butter, and more peas of course. This dish may be whipped up in a mere ten minutes!

4 tablespoons (½ stick) unsalted butter
2 whole scallions, bulbs and green tops, minced
½ pound smoked salmon, cut into strips
⅓ cup vodka
½ pound fresh peas, shelled (about ½ cup), blanched 1 minute, or 1 package (10 ounces) frozen peas, thawed
Salt and freshly ground black pepper
1 pound Pea-Green Pasta (see page 271), cut into fettuccine noodles
Chopped fresh parsley

1. Melt 2 tablespoons of the butter in a large skillet over medium-low heat. Add the scallions and salmon. Cook, tossing gently, 4 minutes. Add the vodka and peas; cook 2 minutes. Add salt and pepper to taste.

2. Meanwhile, cook the pasta in boiling salted water until just tender, about 2 minutes, longer if frozen. Drain, and toss with the remaining 2 tablespoons butter. Combine the pasta with the salmon-pea mixture and sprinkle with parsley.

Serves 4 to 6.

GREEN PEA PASTA SOUFFLE

The final pea creation is my own bright idea, presented with a deep bow to two ladies I am extremely fond of, Jo Bettoja and Anna Maria Cornetto. Jo is an American from Georgia; Anna Maria stems from Rome. Together they run a remarkable school for cooks near the Fontana di Trevi, called *Lo Scaldavivande*, which means "the covered dish." They had the original notion of a pasta soufflé. With a little luck, Greene turned it upside down and coincidentally green.

5 tablespoons unsalted butter
1 cup plus 3 tablespoons freshly grated Parmesan cheese
1 clove garlic, minced
2 tablespoons all-purpose flour
1⅓ cups milk, boiling
4 egg yolks
¼ pound fresh fettuccine noodles (Pea-Green Pasta, page 271, may be used)
1 cup plus 3 tablespoons grated Jarlsberg or Gruyère cheese
½ cup finely chopped cooked ham
2 teaspoons chopped fresh basil, or ½ teaspoon dried
1 pound fresh peas, shelled (about 1 cup), blanched 1 minute, or half a 10-ounce package frozen peas, thawed
6 egg whites

1. Preheat the oven to 400°F. Rub a 1½-quart soufflé dish with 1 tablespoon of the butter; sprinkle it with 3 tablespoons of the Parmesan cheese. Set aside in a cool place.

2. Melt the remaining 4 tablespoons butter in a medium saucepan over medium-low heat. Add the garlic; cook 1 minute. Stir in the flour. Cook, stirring constantly, 2 minutes. Whisk in the milk. Heat to boiling; boil until thick and smooth, about 1 minute. Remove from the heat. Beat in the egg yolks, one at a time. Set aside.

3. Cook the fettuccine noodles in boiling salted water for 2 minutes, longer if frozen. Rinse under cold running water; drain. Add the noodles to the soufflé base. Stir in the remaining 1 cup Parmesan cheese, the Jarlsberg cheese, ham, basil, and peas. Mix well.

4. Beat the egg whites until stiff but not dry. Stir one fourth of the egg whites into the soufflé mixture. Fold in the remaining whites. Pour into the prepared soufflé dish, place it in the oven, and immediately reduce the heat to 375°F. Bake until puffed and golden, about 45 minutes.

Serves 6.

Though cultivated in India, non-dried peas were first eaten by the early Chinese who called them dō or dōū, depending upon the season of their flowering.

That is a far cry (phonetically) from the Latin *pisum* or the Anglo-Saxon *pisu*, which eventually became *pois* in French and *pease* in English. The abbreviation took place (or so it is reported) on our native shores. Two were *pease* but one was a pea.

Pea translations are a mite abstract. The Spanish *guisante* means health-making. *Pisello* ("pea" in Italy), on the other hand, means "little tiny seed."

PEPPERS

Another of Columbus' Discoveries

In December of the year I turned sixteen (and was already well over six feet in height), my father secured temporary employment for me for the holidays. Through one of his cronies at the Democratic Club, I was offered a job at the post office for the princely sum of two and half dollars an hour: incredible pay for an unskilled worker when average salaries were less than thirty-five a week.

It was, needless to say, not an opportunity to be dismissed lightly. Still, I was reluctant.

"What will I have to do?" I asked my father charily.

"Clerking. Sorting mail. Selling stamps . . . whatever they ask you to do!"

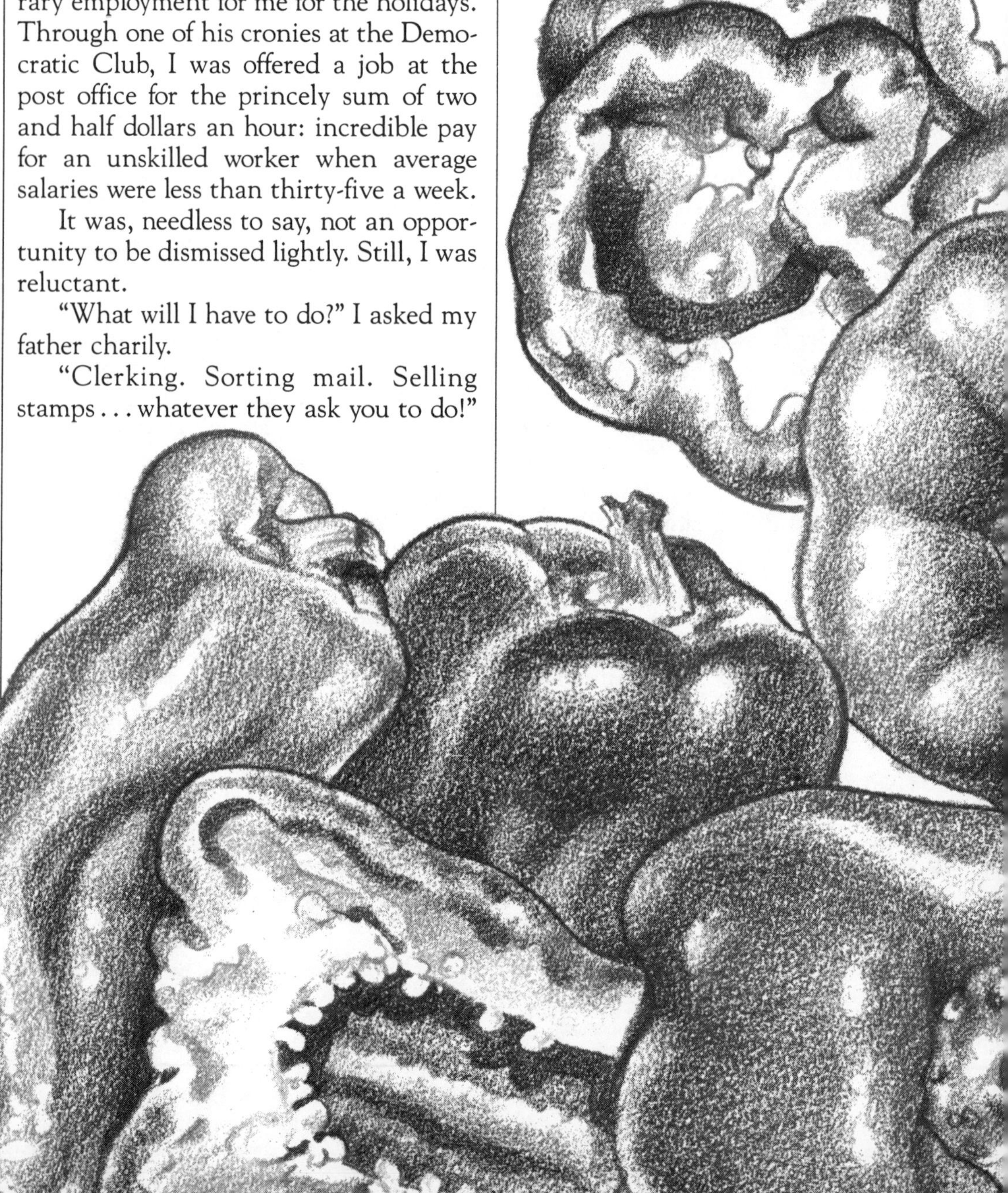

"Not carrying the mail, Sam!" my mother interjected, her voice rising tremulously.

"Of course not," my father replied. "I told them he's just a kid!"

Next morning, in the freezing cold and when it was still dark outside, I reported to the post office to begin my tenure. At the cavernous entry I was inspected briefly by a white-haired deputy, given a badge, and handed a bulging leather bag.

"I thought I was supposed to have an inside job," I protested weakly.

"That's work for women and cripples only," said the veteran with a curl of his lip. "You're a big, strapping fella. You can handle it!"

My father's injunction as I left home still rang in my ears. "Don't give 'em any guff," he had said. "There's fifty other guys waitin' for the job."

So I agreed to carry the mail.

In those dim days, there were no carts to share the heavy burden of Christmas packages and endless brightly colored envelopes. Instead the load was slung across your shoulder like an ammunition belt.

In the unheated mail truck that took me and the other raw recruits to our assigned territories, we were advised of our rights and responsibilities as government employees, albeit temporary ones.

"No smoking on the job. No loafing. No secret meetings with friends. And what is more, no coffee break or lunch until the bag is completely empty."

Along with our back-breaking freight, we were supplied huge sets of master keys on rings, maybe a hundred icy metal stipes that clanged at the hip as one walked to announce an arrival more overwrought than Marley's ghost.

As we temporary mail carriers started on our appointed rounds, another young red-faced "temp" examined my key ring.

"Jeez." He whistled. "So they gave you *the stuffed peppers!*"

"Stuffed peppers?" I brightened instantly. It was barely eight o'clock in the morning but my stomach was rumbling.

"That's what they call the big housing development in Woodside. There are three and four tenants in every apartment, so you have to read the names on each box carefully or else you mix up the mail. It's a helluva place, dark in the halls and stray dogs in the courtyard."

I was slightly afraid of dogs. But hungry enough to pursue this subject further. "Do a lot of people *make* stuffed peppers there?" I asked him, innocently.

"A lot of people *are* the stuffed peppers."

I did not arrive at the housing project until almost noon. With chapped hands and frost-bitten ears I had pounded the pavements of Queens, squeezing large envelopes into narrow slots and pressing down packages in order to slip them under doorways. Still my leather bag bulged ominously. I had to go to the bathroom, but was so imtimidated by my role as a surrogate member of the postal system, I did not dare. My bladder was held tight by sheer willpower by the time I reached the large, looming brick edifices. As predicted, the hallways were dim and the names on the mailboxes barely discernible. Instead of the warm homey aroma of braised meat nestling in peppers, the vestibules smelled of insecticide and cat urine. Worse yet, every building in this vast complex had its own set of keys that needed to be extricated from the big ring I carried, and the boxes unlocked before the mail could be sorted.

I had completed a scant third of the delivery when from behind me a huge vulpine creature appeared. It was the largest dog I had ever seen, with a black tongue and reddish eyes that betrayed it was part Chow. Its remaining pedigree was anyone's guess, but it was not a friendly canine. Instantly it lunged for my pants leg, snarling and shaking its head.

"Good boy. Down!" I quaked as it came closer, all the while stuffing letters into the open mailboxes wholesale, with no regard for matching up correct names or addresses. The dog was openly snapping by this time and I tossed letters into slots like confetti.

As soon as I left that building, I found a corner mailbox and shamelessly emptied the contents of my bag into it.

Then I went home, never to return to the P.O.

One good thing came out of this misadventure. I got the flu and my father never berated me for defection in the line of duty. After I recovered, I looked up a recipe for stuffed peppers and learned to make them—very, very well. But see for yourself.

Vegetable Roots

It may give a diner pause, as he is about to swallow a mouthful of green pepper, stuffed or otherwise, to learn that this aromatic vegetable was discovered in America by Columbus.

Some deep-dyed pepper lovers, who are to be sure a tad prejudiced in their behalf, adjudge the former act on a par with his more celebrated uncovering. For the *Capsicum frustescens* is a flavoring few kitchen practitioners can do without.

To set the pepper story straight, the captain of the *Santa Maria*, *Nina*, and *Pinta* observed sweet green and red peppers growing on the vine almost immediately after his convoy landed in the West Indies in 1492. Since his commission from the queen of Spain had been to find a more efficacious route to the Indies in order to corner the spice market, Columbus knew he was on to something big.

What his eye noticed his nose and tongue confirmed. Once Columbus had sampled cooked peppers in dishes that the local Indians hospitably offered his crew, he had the hold of one entire ship stocked with this produce for a return voyage to Spain. Though he had actually been seeking the berries of *Piper nigrum*, the spicy seasoning we crush in our pepper grinders, Columbus, with his fine Italian palate, knew Europeans would flip over his tangy cargo. And they did.

Peppers made Columbus a hero. The vegetable was instantly named "Spanish Pepper" and reports of its culinary wonders spread all over the continent—even to England. In 1493 a British courier to the king wrote that Columbus had brought back to Isabella "a pepper more pungent than any fruit from the Caucasus." Pepper plants were at once cultivated in royal Spanish gardens and a brisk trade in the vegetable was shortly in operation. More important (to me at least), the green and red bell pepper entered the world's cooking pots!

What to Look For

All vegetable peppers, sweet and hot alike, are members of the *Capsicum* family tree. The sweets are often referred to as "bells" by virtue of their shape. The hots are known as chile peppers or *chiles* and grow in a multitude of sizes and shapes, from long and skinny to conical and round, with varying degrees of heat. Red bell peppers are no hotter than greens, merely riper.

What makes a chile pepper hot is the amount of sheer warmth (known as capsaicin) lodged within its innocent-looking seeds and pale interior spines. Remove both with a sharp knife and you considerably defuse a hot pepper's pungency. But I am not speaking of peppers as seasoners here, only as vegetables; and they are uniformly mild.

Bell peppers turn a tad sweeter as they redden. They also require more care on the vine, so consumers inevitably pay an increment for ripeness. However, many deep green bells, jade Cubanelles, light yellow-green Italians, and even

bright yellow banana varieties have exactly the right degree of "bite" to give a dish its desired stimulating flavor.

When pepper shopping, scout for firm globes that are bright in color. Anemic-shaded skin indicates that a bell tolled too early for this pepper; it was picked before it had a chance to ripen and develop flavor.

Dehydrated peppers are the wallflowers of the patch: they were picked after their prime. You can usually tell a less than juicy pepper by its feel; lacking water content, they are less weighty than they appear.

Peppers store well in the refrigerator. I keep mine a week or longer in a ventilated plastic bag, away from excessive moisture. However, red (riper) peppers will not have the same degree of shelf-life. Use them sooner.

Pepper is a healthy indulgence for your diet. One large bell pepper (either green or red) tallies less than 22 calories. Better yet, this glistening harbinger of good living is high in amino acids with a relatively good jot of minerals as well. Each average globe contains 213 milligrams of potassium and is rich in vitamin A (420 units) and vitamin C (120 units).

Preparation

There are no hard and fast rules on pepper cookery. They are delicious raw, fried, roasted, or blanched first and then sautéed or braised, depending upon the recipe at hand. Charring a raw pepper over a gas flame (or close up to a broiler unit) until the skin blisters and blackens gives a peeled pepper still another totally different taste and texture. Positive pepper-lovers will try each method with (forgive the pun) relish!

BURRO ROSSO

One of my best friends, in or out of a kitchen, is Cornelius O'Donnell. Neal is a slightly cherubic charmer, whose form and face you are bound to recognize from his cookbook, billed simply as *Cooking with Cornelius*. I for one have cooked with this man—and he's unbeatable. More pertinently, Neal is one of the most generous and good-natured cooking teachers in the business. His bequest to this collection is called *Burro Rosso* (Red Butter). It is a sauce he teaches his students to splash over curly pasta or use as a basting sauce for roast chicken or pork. Coming from Neal, it is pure and wonderful. Coming from Bert, it is less pure (I added a red pepper for extra bite) but just as wonderful. Even Cornelius agrees.

1 small red bell pepper
2 cloves garlic
¼ cup heavy or whipping cream
8 tablespoons (1 stick) unsalted butter
2 tablespoons tomato paste
½ teaspoon chopped fresh sage, or ¼ teaspoon dried, crumbled
1 teaspoon ground paprika (preferably Hungarian)
Salt
⅓ cup freshly grated Parmesan cheese
½ pound cooked spiral-shaped pasta

1. Roast the bell pepper over a gas flame, turning until charred all over (or place under a broiler until charred). Carefully wrap the pepper in paper towels and place it in a plastic bag. Let it stand until cool. Rub the charred skin from the pepper with paper towels. Core the pepper; roughly chop.

2. Place the pepper, garlic, and cream in the container of a food processor or blender. Process until smooth.

3. Melt the butter in a medium saucepan over medium-low heat. Whisk in the tomato paste and the pepper-garlic purée. Add the sage, paprika, and salt to taste. Cook, without boiling, until hot. Stir in the cheese and hot cooked pasta. Serve immediately.

Serves 4 as a first course.

POTTED PEPPER CHOWDER

The best soup in my pepper repertoire is *not* Pepper Pot. That is a pottage dependent upon tripe as well as peppers, and frankly more work than it is worth in my opinion. And I will take my lumps gladly when the Pepper Pot lovers (all from Philadelphia, if rumormongers are to be believed) send their letters of protest.

Until then, have this next brew. It's a breeze to make, peppery but still a beatitude in the soup spoon!

2 large potatoes, peeled, cubed
4 tablespoons (½ stick) unsalted butter
1 medium onion, finely chopped
1 clove garlic, minced
1 cup cubed cooked ham
½ cup chopped celery
1 medium green bell pepper, seeded, chopped
1 medium red bell pepper, seeded, chopped
1 teaspoon crushed dried hot red peppers
1 can (4 ounces) jalapeño peppers, finely chopped
1 quart milk
1½ teaspoons salt
12 allspice berries, crushed, or ½ teaspoon ground
¼ teaspoon cumin seeds (comino)
¼ cup chopped fresh parsley
1 teaspoon chopped chives or scallion tops

1. Cover the potatoes with cold water in a medium saucepan. Heat to boiling; drain.

2. Melt 3 tablespoons of the butter in a large heavy saucepan over medium-low heat. Add the onion; cook 1 minute. Add the garlic; cook 1 minute longer. Stir in the ham, celery, green pepper, red pepper, dried red peppers, and jalapeño peppers. Cook, stirring constantly, 3 minutes.

3. Stir the potatoes into the pepper mixture. Add the milk. Slowly heat, stirring constantly, to boiling; reduce the heat. Add the salt, allspice, and cumin seeds. Cook, stirring occasionally, until the potatoes are very tender and the soup is slightly thickened, about 30 minutes. Stir in the remaining 1 tablespoon butter, and sprinkle with the parsley and chives.

Serves 6.

HOT TUNA AND PEPPER SALAD

This is a provincial recipe, easy to do and economical besides. Also great to eat. A salad, but a hot one!

2 tablespoons olive oil
1 small shallot, minced
1 clove garlic, minced
1 red bell pepper, seeded, cut into thin strips
1 green bell pepper, seeded, cut into thin strips
3 anchovy filets, chopped
1 can (7 ounces) tuna, drained
½ teaspoon crushed dried hot red peppers
Salt

1. Heat the oil in a large skillet over medium heat. Add the shallot; cook 1 minute. Add the garlic, both bell peppers, and the chopped anchovies. Reduce the heat to medium-low. Cook, covered, 5 minutes.

2. Add the tuna and dried red peppers to the mixture in the skillet. Cook, stirring constantly, until the peppers are just barely tender, about 4 minutes. Add salt to taste. Serve as a warm salad or over cooked spaghetti.

Serves 2 or 3.

COLD LAMB AND PEPPER SALAD

Add peppers to a salad dish next time the vinaigrette is dark and mustardy. The one below, composed of leftover roast lamb and roasted peppers, can be served cool or at room temperature. In this instance, the peppers are baked (blanched first to give them a measure of tenderness) rather than charred.

4 green bell peppers
4 red bell peppers
¼ cup chopped shallots
1½ to 2 cups cold cooked lamb, cut into strips
2 tablespoons Dijon mustard
2 tablespoons red wine vinegar
2 teaspoons soy sauce
⅓ to ½ cup olive oil
Salt and freshly ground black pepper
¼ cup chopped fresh parsley

1. Preheat the oven to 350°F. Cook the peppers in boiling salted water 1 minute; drain. Place the peppers on a foil-lined baking sheet. Bake until they are lightly browned and the skins peel off easily, about 50 minutes.

2. Cool the peppers slightly; peel, core and seed them. Cut the peppers into thin strips, and combine them with the shallots and lamb in a large bowl.

3. Combine the mustard, vinegar, and soy sauce in a medium bowl. Slowly beat in the oil, a few drops at a time. Add salt and pepper to taste. Pour this dressing over the lamb and pepper mixture. Sprinkle with the parsley. Serve chilled or at room temperature.

Serves 4.

BARBECUED SWEET PEPPERS

One of the most original pepper notions I know is a relish (or condiment, you name it) of charred, scraped peppers in a spicy Texas-inspired emollient. Select thick, firm-skinned peppers for this. Otherwise you will find yourself with more sauce than substance.

4 green bell peppers
4 red bell peppers
1 recipe Dynamite Barbecue Sauce

1. Roast the peppers over a gas flame, turning until charred all over (or place under a broiler until charred). Carefully wrap the peppers in paper towels and place them in plastic bags. Let them stand until cool. Rub the charred skin from the pepper with paper towels.

2. Meanwhile, make the Dynamite Barbecue Sauce.

3. Core and seed the peppers; cut them into 2-inch-long strips, about ¼ inch wide. Place the pepper strips in sterilized pint jars (about 1¼ cups peppers per jar). Fill each jar with sauce (¾ to 1 cup sauce per jar). Seal.

Makes about 2½ pints.

Dynamite Barbecue Sauce

1 tablespoon vegetable oil
3 small onions, finely chopped
2 cloves garlic, minced
1¼ cups ketchup
¼ cup Worcestershire sauce
3 tablespoons A-1 steak sauce
1½ tablespoons dark brown sugar
6 tablespoons water
⅛ teaspoon hot pepper sauce

Heat the oil in a medium saucepan over medium-low heat. Add the onions; cook 1 minute. Add the garlic; cook 4 minutes. Add the remaining ingredients. Heat to boiling, reduce the heat, and simmer, uncovered, 20 minutes.

Makes about 3 cups.

RED PEPPER CHEESE BREAD

The red bell pepper's sweet alliance in meat and vegetable dishes is not particularly surprising. However, its appearance in the three totally unalike breads that follow is a good deal less predictable. No coincidence, each is indescribably good. Peppery too!

1 large red bell pepper
1 package dry yeast
1¼ cups lukewarm water
1 teaspoon light brown sugar
2 teaspoons salt
⅛ teaspoon cayenne pepper
1 teaspoon crushed dried hot red peppers
1 teaspoon sesame seeds
1 teaspoon fennel seeds
1 teaspoon anise seeds
½ cup lukewarm milk
1½ cups stone-ground whole-wheat flour
1 cup grated Monterey jack cheese
3 cups all-purpose flour, approximately
1 tablespoon unsalted butter, melted

1. Roast the bell pepper over a gas flame, turning, until charred all over (or place under a broiler until charred). Carefully wrap the pepper in paper towels and place it in a plastic bag. Let it stand until cool. Rub the charred skin from the pepper with paper towels. Core and seed the pepper; chop fine.

2. Place the yeast in a large bowl and sprinkle it with ¼ cup of the water. Let stand a few minutes to soften; then stir in the sugar, salt, cayenne pepper, dried red peppers, chopped bell pepper, sesame seeds, fennel seeds, anise seeds, and milk. Stir in the whole-wheat flour, alternating with the remaining 1 cup water. Beat in the grated cheese.

3. Slowly beat in 2 cups of the all-purpose flour with a heavy wooden spoon. Transfer the dough to a lightly floured board. Knead the dough for 15 minutes, incorporating the remaining 1 cup all-purpose flour. Add more flour as needed. When the dough is elastic, let it stand 5 minutes.

4. Divide the dough in half; roll each half into long French- or Italian-style loaves. Place the dough in French bread pans. Cover with a flour-rubbed tea towel. Let stand until doubled in volume, 1½ to 2 hours.

5. Preheat the oven to 400°F. Gently slash the top of each loaf lengthwise with a sharp knife. Brush the tops with the melted butter. Place a roasting pan half-filled with water in the bottom of the oven. Place the bread in the top third; bake 12 minutes. Reduce the heat to 325°F and continue to bake 35 minutes longer. Cool on racks.

Makes 2 loaves.

In my garden years ago, I observed a fascinating aspect of the pepper's adaptive nature. When its vines are filled with tiny green fruit (usually in midsummer), a pepper bush will unpredictably drop its blossoms, leaving a faint trail of delicate petals on the ground to confound an anxious gardener, who will spray and spade it to absolutely no avail. Only when the bush turns so feeble its yield is plucked out of desperation, will the plant come back to life again. Once its heavy load is harvested, a pepper bush will even sprout blossoms again and allow the growing cycle to continue.

The moral of this earthly sensibility? Peppers are an example of good economy in the garden.

RUTH SUGAR BERESH'S SWEET RED PEPPER CORNBREAD

The next bread 'n' pepper confederation is a sweet one. It came to me from a student in a cooking class in Michigan a while back. A wonderful dish, it arrived with the following pedigree:

"I prepare this with our Thanksgiving dinner. I don't know its actual origin but the source I received it from said her source said that her sources said that . . . *it's old!*"

I hope you enjoy this, for it is most unusual.

2 medium red bell peppers
1½ cups cornmeal
½ cup all-purpose flour
2 tablespoons sugar
1 teaspoon baking powder
1 teaspoon baking soda
1 teaspoon salt
2 eggs, lightly beaten
1 cup buttermilk
2 cups sweetened condensed milk
3 tablespoons unsalted butter, melted

1. Preheat the oven to 400°F. Cook the peppers in boiling salted water for 1 minute. Drain. Core, seed, and finely chop.

2. Sift the dry ingredients together into a large bowl. Combine the eggs, buttermilk, and 1 cup of the condensed milk in another bowl. Stir the liquid into the dry ingredients. Stir in the chopped peppers and melted butter.

3. Pour the mixture into a lightly buttered 9-by-13-inch cake pan (or any 8-cup casserole about 2 inches deep). Drizzle the remaining condensed milk over the top of the batter, taking care not to allow the milk to build up in the corners. Do not tip the pan. Bake until set and golden brown, 25 to 30 minutes.

Serves 10.

AWENDAW BREAD

The last pepper bread association comes from the Gullah people, who live along the windswept Atlantic coastline of South Carolina. Awendaw (pronounced ow! endow) is part of the black grandmotherly tradition of dropping everything and baking a batter bread when someone unexpectedly stops in around dinnertime. It is made of grits, cornmeal, and peppers mainly—all the other ingredients are improvised depending upon "what's in the icebox!" Or so I was told.

4 tablespoons (½ stick) unsalted butter
½ red bell pepper, cut into thin strips about 1 inch long
½ green bell pepper, cut into thin strips about 1 inch long
1 small hot green pepper, seeded, minced (see Guacamole headnote, page 37)
2 cups milk
2 cups water
1 teaspoon salt
1 cup hominy grits
1½ cups milk, boiling
½ cup cornmeal
2 eggs, lightly beaten
1 cup grated Monterey jack cheese with jalapeño peppers

1. Preheat the oven to 375°F. Melt 2 tablespoons of the butter in a small skillet over medium-low heat. Stir in the bell peppers and the hot pepper. Toss well to coat the pieces with butter. Cook, covered, until tender, about 8 minutes. Remove from the heat.

2. Combine the 2 cups milk with the water in a medium saucepan. Heat to boiling; reduce the heat. Stir in the salt and hominy grits. Cook, stirring constantly, over low heat until very thick, about 8 minutes. Stir in the remaining 2 tablespoons butter.

3. Transfer the grits mixture to a large bowl. Slowly stir in the 1½ cups boiling milk, the cornmeal, beaten eggs, and cheese. Pour into a well-buttered 2-quart soufflé dish or casserole. Bake until firm and golden brown, 45 to 50 minutes.

Serves 6 to 8.

MISS TOKLAS' BRAISED STUFFED PEPPERS

Stuffing a pepper is my favorite way to cook this vegetable. This classic version is yet another borrowing, only slightly altered, from the kitchen mentor I never met, Alice B. Toklas. I keep her slim cookbook always within hand's reach on the shelf and her yellowed obituary inside the volume as a bookmark. She would, I know, approve of the notion enormously.

2 bell peppers, preferably 1 red and 1 yellow
4 tablespoons (½ stick) unsalted butter
¼ cup chopped mushrooms
1 cup lean ground veal (about ½ pound)
½ cup ground cooked ham
1 egg yolk, lightly beaten
1 tablespoon chopped fresh basil, or 1 teaspoon dried
1 tablespoon chopped fresh parsley
1 tablespoon dry white wine
Juice of ½ lemon
1½ tablespoons freshly grated Parmesan cheese
¼ teaspoon ground cumin
⅛ teaspoon crushed saffron
Salt and freshly ground black pepper
½ cup chicken broth (see page 414)
2 medium tomatoes, peeled, seeded, chopped
Chopped fresh parsley

1. Cut the peppers in half lengthwise; remove the core and seeds. Cook in boiling salted water 2 minutes; drain and pat dry.

2. Melt 1 tablespoon of the butter in a medium skillet over medium heat. Add the mushrooms; sauté until golden, about 4 minutes. Remove from the heat.

3. Place the veal and ham in a large bowl. Mix lightly. Add the mushrooms, egg yolk, basil, parsley, wine, lemon juice, Parmesan cheese, cumin, saffron, and salt and pepper to taste. Mix well.

4. Fill the blanched pepper halves with the meat filling.

5. Melt the remaining 3 tablespoons butter in a medium saucepan over medium-low heat. Add the peppers, filled side up. Pour the chicken broth around the peppers. Sprinkle the tomatoes over and around the peppers. Heat the sauce to boiling; reduce the heat. Simmer, covered, over medium heat 20 minutes. Transfer the peppers to a serving platter with a slotted spoon and keep warm. Raise the heat under the saucepan and boil the liquid until slightly thickened, about 4 minutes. Pour this over the peppers and sprinkle with chopped parsley.

Serves 2 to 4.

The French, somewhat more sophisticated about food than we, adjust pepper's name topically. What comes out of a shaker may be *poivre*, but what is sautéed with onion and garlic is inevitably *pimenton doux*. In Germany a pepper is a sweet pepper always *(Ziegenpfeffer)*, while in Italy it is a little or diminutive one *(peperone)* whether it is hot or not. The Spanish dub all sweet peppers *pimiento*, which is such a good idea the British and Americans borrowed it—but only for cooked sweet peppers in little jars.

TAMALE-PIE STUFFED PEPPERS

The second stuffed pepper amalgam is my invention—a swipe of one of my best recipes (for Southwestern Tamale Pie) crammed into green pepper shells rather than a pie plate. The change of venue makes for even more flavor and twice the bite.

3 tablespoons cornmeal
¼ cup cold water
½ cup plus 1 tablespoon boiling water
1 tablespoon unsalted butter
¼ pound sausage meat
¾ cup finely chopped onion
1 large clove garlic, minced
1 tablespoon chili powder
⅛ teaspoon ground cumin
½ pound ground beef
⅛ teaspoon hot pepper sauce
¼ cup finely chopped celery
1½ teaspoons seeded, minced hot green peppers (see Guacamole headnote, page 37)
1 large tomato, peeled, seeded, chopped
1 ear fresh corn
Salt
4 green bell peppers
5 pitted black olives, sliced
¼ cup grated Monterey jack cheese
⅓ cup grated mild Cheddar cheese

1. Gradually stir the cornmeal into the cold water in a small bowl. Stir this mixture into the boiling water in a small saucepan. Heat, stirring constantly, to boiling; reduce the heat to medium-low. Stir in the butter. Cook, covered, stirring occasionally, 35 minutes. Remove from the heat.

2. While the cornmeal is cooking, sauté the sausage meat in a large heavy skillet over medium heat, breaking up the lumps with a fork, until it begins to lose its pink color. Add the onion and garlic; cook 5 minutes. Stir in the chili powder and cumin. Add the ground beef and continue to cook, breaking up the lumps with a fork, until the beef loses its color, about 5 minutes. Add the hot pepper sauce, celery, and hot green pepper. Cook 5 minutes. Stir in the tomato; cook 5 minutes longer.

3. With a sharp knife, cut the corn kernels off the cob, slicing about halfway through the kernels. Using the back of the knife, scrape the cob to remove the remaining kernel bits and milky residue. Add the corn to the tomato-meat mixture. Cook 10 minutes longer. Add salt to taste; remove from the heat.

4. Preheat the oven to 350°F. Cook the peppers in boiling salted water 2 minutes. Trim off the tops with a sharp knife. Core, and remove the seeds.

5. Fill each pepper with the meat mixture, packing it down firmly with the back of a spoon. Leave about ½ inch of space at the top of each pepper. Cover the top of each pepper with olive slices. Sprinkle with Monterey jack and cheddar cheese. Spread a thin layer of the cornmeal mixture over the top, using about 2 teaspoons per pepper. Place the peppers in a baking dish. Bake 50 minutes. Let stand 5 minutes before serving.

Serves 2 to 4.

PEPPERED MEAT LOAF

See how wondrously a little bit of peppers stretch (and give style to) a lowly dish like meat loaf. Because of its coloration, this loaf will nicely grace a buffet.

1 ¼ pounds lean beef, ground
½ pound veal shoulder, ground
¼ pound pork shoulder, ground
1 medium onion, finely chopped
2 small shallots, minced
¼ cup minced green bell pepper
¼ cup minced red bell pepper
1 can (10 ounces) mixed tomatoes and jalapeño peppers, roughly chopped
1 teaspoon chopped fresh basil, or ½ teaspoon dried
1 teaspoon chopped fresh parsley
⅛ teaspoon thyme
½ teaspoon salt
½ teaspoon freshly ground black pepper
1 egg, lightly beaten
½ cup fresh bread crumbs
2 teaspoons Dijon mustard
2 teaspoons chili sauce
1 teaspoon chili powder

1. Preheat the oven to 375°F. Place the three ground meats in a large bowl and mix thoroughly. Add the remaining ingredients through the bread crumbs and again mix thoroughly. Form into a loaf in a shallow baking dish.

2. Combine the mustard, chili sauce, and chili powder in a small bowl. Mix well and spread over the meat loaf. Bake 15 minutes. Reduce the heat to 350°F and bake 1 hour longer.

Serves 6 to 8.

SMOKED TONGUE WITH RED PEPPER SAUCE

In this instance, blazing red pepper is the basis of a crimson sauce to amend a slice of smoked tongue. Even if you have always shunned this meat, this is a dish you will not care to miss.

4 pounds smoked tongue
1 large carrot, peeled, halved
1 white turnip, peeled, halved
1 parsnip, peeled, halved
1 large onion, unpeeled, halved
4 whole cloves
2 tablespoons red wine vinegar
2 sprigs fresh parsley
1 large bay leaf
1 clove garlic
1 teaspoon mustard seeds
2 red bell peppers
2 tablespoons unsalted butter
2 tablespoons all-purpose flour
2 tablespoons prepared horseradish
1 teaspoon Dijon mustard
¼ cup heavy or whipping cream

1. Place the tongue in a 5-quart pot or Dutch oven. Add the carrot through the mustard seeds, plus enough water to cover the meat by two inches. Heat to boiling; reduce the heat. Cook, partially covered, over medium-low heat 45 minutes per pound, or about 3 hours.

2. Half an hour before the meat is done, add the bell peppers to the pot. Simmer, covered, 20 minutes, then remove them from the broth. Peel, core, seed, and roughly chop the peppers.

3. Place the peppers in the container of a food processor or blender. Add ¼ cup of the meat liquid. Process until smooth.

4. Melt the butter in a medium saucepan over medium-low heat. Stir in the flour. Cook, stirring constantly, 2 minutes. Whisk in 1¼ cups of the meat liquid and the puréed peppers. Heat to boiling; reduce the heat. Stir in the horseradish and Dijon mustard; continue to cook until the mixture is slightly thickened, about 5 minutes. Stir in the cream. Cook another 2 minutes.

5. Remove the tongue from the cooking liquid. Remove the skin, and slice on the diagonal. Spoon some of the sauce over the meat. Pass the remaining sauce on the side.

Serves 6 to 8.

ALL-AMERICAN PEPPER JAMBALAYA

First tasted by Columbus in the Caribbean, peppers were simmered and stewed by the Indians over low fires until they became so thick that a handful could be lifted out of the barely steaming pot with two fingers, blown upon, and then swallowed without burning hand or mouth! This kind of dish was known as *abalay.*

Without any evidence to support the theory except a good nose for a story, I suggest that when pepper *abalay* was seasoned with *jambon*, the cured ham that French colonists brought to Louisiana, and stirred up by the strong slave arms that sprinkled African scallions and herbs into the pot as well, the dish suffered a name change—to *jambalaya.*

You don't agree? Well, I said it was only my notion.

The dish that inspired the reverie is something closer to gospel, however, leastwise among jambalaya aficionados. It is a mixture of ham, shrimp, apricots, and (bless them all) five separate and distinct varieties of pepper.

½ cup chopped dried apricots
⅓ cup apricot brandy
3 tablespoons unsalted butter
1 tablespoon vegetable oil
1 cup thinly sliced whole scallions, bulbs and green tops
1 clove garlic, minced
¾ cup ¼-inch-wide strips of cooked ham
1 large green bell pepper, cut lengthwise into ⅛-inch-wide strips
1 large red bell pepper, cut lengthwise into ⅛-inch-wide strips
1 pound raw shrimp, shelled, deveined
1 tablespoon lemon juice
1 tablespoon soy sauce
2 teaspoons cornstarch
⅛ teaspoon crushed dried hot red peppers
1½ tablespoons chili powder
⅓ cup roughly chopped pimiento
¼ cup slivered almonds, toasted
Hot Steamed Rice *(see page 412)*

1. Combine the apricots and apricot brandy in a small bowl; let stand, covered, at least 15 minutes.

2. Heat the butter with the oil in a large heavy skillet over medium heat. Add the scallions; cook 1 minute. Add the garlic, ham, and the green pepper and red pepper strips. Cook, stirring constantly, until the peppers are almost tender, about 5 minutes. Stir in the shrimp; cook, stirring constantly, 3 minutes. Add the apricot mixture; cook 3 minutes longer.

3. Combine the lemon juice, soy sauce, cornstarch, and dried red pepper in a small bowl. Stir this into the shrimp-pepper mixture. Add the chili powder and pimiento. Continue to stir until the chili powder is well incorporated and the mixture is slightly thickened, about 4 minutes. Sprinkle with the toasted almonds. Serve over rice.

Serves 4.

POTATOES

Apples of Love

I have dwelled long on my love for the Atlantic shore. But how I moved from an early infatuation with suburban Long Beach to a more mature passion for countrified Amagansett is worth a speck more sandy amplification.

The emotional distance, you see, was traveled with a stopover: Fire Island.

Much has been written of this curiously raffish resort and the denizens of sun-and-fun seekers who invade its isolated ten-mile boundaries every summer. But no one's view of the place is quite like my own, for I was an unassessed homeowner there one fateful summer—living on a semi-deserted dune. A strip of beach property that had been occupied (illegally) by squatters for years before me, my home was known simply as "The Dump."

Actually the place where I summered was not a garbage disposal area at all but more of a landfill constructed of the

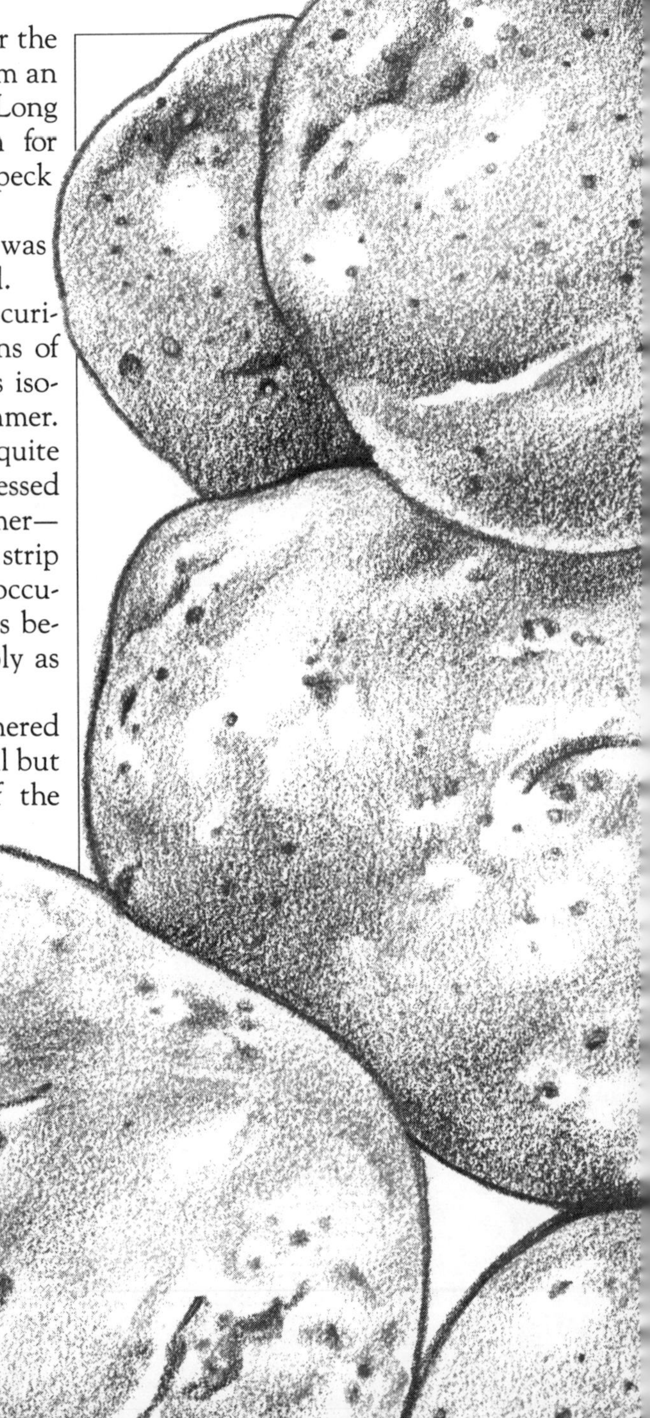

island's detritus in order to preserve the natural character of the dunes. But "The Dump" is what residents called it, and its mountainous confines held a veritable treasure trove of goodies: abandoned jeeps lurked there along with sun-dried bricks, deck chairs, refrigerators, and Thonet rockers, plus piles of lumber and pipe, mostly the remains of over fifty island households blown thither by a devastating hurricane in 1938.

I came upon this sequestered beach during a Sunday excursion to Fire Island with some acquaintances who claimed to be house-hunting. The time was the mid-1950s. They had a car. I didn't drive and so literally came along for the ride. Then as now, one parked vehicles in a black-topped lot across the water from Fire Island, for no cars other than beach-buggy taxis are permitted on its shores. A ferry is the only way in or out.

As I recall, we looked at dreary houses for sale without any real incentive or enthusiasm until the real estate agent left, and then we ventured out of the rabbit warren of cedar shingle cottages. Trudging in the sand past sleek modern houses on the far perimeter of the town, we discovered an utterly deserted stretch of dune and beach (albeit flanked by the bespoke "dump") that was so inviting not one of us could resist tearing off our clothes and swimming in the surf, naked as water babies. Later, drying in the warm sun, we resolved to come back to this place and "camp out" the following weekend. Or at least I did.

Fire Island and that incredible baptism in its wild surf forced me to buy my first automobile. It was a postwar Chevy convertible, precisely the color of beach sand, and cost one hundred dollars, third-hand. A car owner but unable to drive, I persuaded first one friend then another to chauffeur the camping trips. Once a driver was established at the helm, however, the old coupe was so crammed with passengers and assorted gear that it rarely exceeded forty miles per hour on the highway.

We would leave Manhattan at dawn on Saturday mornings to avoid beach traffic. No breakfast was ever taken prior to the ride. Not even a cup of coffee was consumed until we had arrived at our point of destination: a supermarket near the ferry where we shopped like demons for the weekend. Since there is little for sale on the island itself, all comestibles must be hauled and tugged by hand. Our initial meal (after we arrived on land and rented a jeep and driver to convey us to "The Dump") was always the same: Danish pastries oozing butter and washed down with Bloody Marys. The first of many odd repasts to come.

Members of the camping team expanded and altered during the course of the summer. More friends and more cars were invited, and the "commune at the dump," as we were known to anxious householders nearby, often harbored as many as a dozen adults plus one small child and two dogs per weekend.

It was the most carefree summer of my life, though we never stopped working from the moment of arrival until the hired beach buggy appeared to carry its weary band back to the boat on Sunday night. After spending the first night out-of-doors in makeshift sleeping bags, we built a house (of sorts) to protect our motley crew from the elements. It was made of found lumber and fitted with a heavy-duty clear plastic roof and walls. Like a glass house it shimmered in the sunlight and could be seen for miles along the surf. More important, this shelter withstood all manner of seasonal catastrophes (like windstorms and wasps) and remained intact even after a troop of hiking boys impounded it for a midweek hostel. Though to be truthful, the walls, much ventilated by cigarette burns, did have to be replaced the following week.

Besides sleeping quarters, we also

built a long trestle table and benches for dining, an ice house, a latrine (well secluded in a bluff of dwarf pine), *and* a pit where we barbecued and cooked. This outdoor stove was actually a deep-dug trench, lined with rocks and covered with a steel grate under a hinged Volkswagen trunk lid (yet another prize resurrected from our dump), where potatoes roasted nightly for dinner.

Fire Island potatoes were usually barbecued, slow-cooked over embers and sluiced with tomatoey glop that turned the skins to bronze and fissured them like Chinese gongs. No potato anywhere has ever tasted so good. A small lifetime has passed but I can still recall the cries of ravenous diners in bathing suits (returning from a fourth or fifth dip in the surf), demanding that the potatoes be served before the moon rose.

At summer's end, I traded in my old jalopy for a newer-model Chevy and eventually pressed eastward to Long Island. All I brought from Fire Island to Amagansett were memories—and a great potato recipe.

Vegetable Roots

Over a beach fire or in a boiling pan of water, what a wonder is the potato!

Eaten by mankind for subsistence for almost three thousand years, the starchy appendage of the *Solanum tuberosum* has been under fire by its detractors almost as long as it has been over fire as a source of nourishment. In the fifteenth century, the Pope denounced this "apple of love" as the "root of man's licentious and depraved moral behavior," and righteous churchgoers were warned to avoid its aphrodisiac taint for their very salvation. One hundred years after, *pommes de terre* were still in jeopardy. Believed to be the cause of leprosy, potatoes were burned in great Burgundian conflagrations ignited by order of the crown to protect the citizenry from "its base addiction and craving." According to one report, the bonfires served only to whet appetites, for the scent of potatoes roasting proved utterly irresistible to the peasants. Snatching them from the burning embers, many ate them on the spot, blackened skins and all. Lived to tell the tale, too.

The potato, like the pepper and the tomato, is native to the Americas. It grew and was eaten (mostly raw) in Peru as far back as 3000 B.C. The cooked potato was brought to European kitchens courtesy of the Spanish explorer Gonzalo Jiménez de Quesada, whose scouting parties discovered a strain of small potatoes blooming under crowns of brilliant blue flowers, sixteen thousand feet up in the Andes. Being somewhat short-rationed and cold (besides faint from the high altitude), these resourceful fellows dug up the plum-size tubers of these blue blossoms to stoke their campfires. Anyone who has ever sniffed the perfume of a potato roasting in the wild will understand at once why they not only sampled the burnt offerings but became positive aficionados after the first steamy bite.

Potatoes came to Spain on the next boat.

Within fifty years this tender-hearted vegetable had achieved such a toehold in European larders that (detractors aside) it was adjudged to be a prime necessity for the colonists in the New World. And by reverse logic, the potato crossed the Atlantic to be planted on its native soil once again.

Another distant relative of deadly nightshade, the potato is its least virulent cousin. Neither a fruit nor a root, it is a portion of the underground stem of the plant. According to potato farmers at the eastern end of Long Island, a potato "peeps" (or is ready for the plucking) only when the earth has been at a base temperature of 55 degrees or more for at least one month's time. Potatoes may take a long time to ripen but they grow sweeter and more toothsome every day spent undercover. Ancient Incas believed they flourished best when fertilized with human blood and held gory sports on potato fields to guarantee a hearty crop, but spring rain usually does just as well in my part of the country!

What to Look For

Shoppers might be advised that there are over 400 varieties of potatoes grown at the moment, but ask for any one of 396 at your supermarket and you will be met with a rude comment or, even worse, a vacant stare. Most greengrocers codify the potato by geography alone: Maine, Long Island, California, and Idaho. Wholesalers are not much better, classifying them as round whites, round reds, russets, and long whites with no amend. If you wish to know the difference between a Red Pontiac Chippewa, Norgold Russet, and a Mohawk, you'll have to dip into a seed catalogue, I expect.

Farmers know potatoes by their growing cycles. New potatoes are fresh-dug. Old potatoes have lingered longer in the ground and as a consequence have grown starchier for their hiatus. New (low-starch) potatoes have firm textures and thin skins and are your best bet for boiling, roasting, casserole dishes, and potato salad. Old (high-starch) potatoes are mealier and more substantial—prime nominees for the french-fryer, the skillet, and the baking rack.

In the supermarket, choose weighty potatoes that are firm, relatively clean—if that is possible—and smooth to the touch. Avoid a tuber that is sprouting, for that indicates a long stay on the shelf. Likewise pass on any potato that is bruised, soft, or patched with green. A pale, mottled-green potato is not merely underripe—it is bitter, containing a high proportion of solanine, a mildly toxic substance that will (in large doses) cause skin irritations.

I store potatoes in a ventilated cabinet, or on the lowest shelf in the refrigerator. Cool air retards spoilage; warm, confined, moist environments (like plastic bags) increase it.

Contrary to specious rumor, the potato is not fattening in the least. Butter and cream *are*, however, but let's skip that for the moment. A naked medium-

Though the Irish are generally credited as being Europe's prime potato eaters, the Germans got there first. *Ein Neu Kochbuch (A New Cookbook)*, compiled and printed on Gutenberg's press in 1581, contains the first annotated German recipes; and there are a dozen potato dishes listed among them. One, surprisingly enough, is a very tasty baked tart. A hundred years after its publication, however, no more potatoes were being eaten than before. Those that were, were consumed mainly by noblemen who imported them from France or the Lowlands. Frederick Wilhelm, sensing that the potato could prove a windfall for his country's laggard economy (and feed the peasantry into the bargain), issued what is sometimes referred to as "The Brandenberg Potato Paper." An edict, it ordered Prussian farmers to plant potatoes or risk the pain of having their ears (and noses) cut off! Will it come as a shock to discover that the potato shortly became a staple in the German diet? Frederick was soon after dubbed "Frederick the Great," and great potato dishes proliferated all along the Rhine—and westward, in time, as well.

size baked potato is tabbed at less than 100 calories, and boiling will reduce the calories to a scant 80. As you may have surmised (if you have ever grated a potato for a potato pancake), the reason they are low in calories is that potatoes are mostly water: 77 to 80 percent of their total composition, in fact. In terms of dry weight, a potato consists of an average of 66 percent starch, 9 percent protein, and 4 percent sugars, with about 0.5 percent assorted potassium, phosphorus, fats, vitamins, and random minerals. High in vitamin B (including niacin, thiamine, riboflavin, and pyridoxine), the potato is really good for you—as well as being good to eat.

Preparation

In my opinion, nothing beats a new potato boiled tender and served up neat—with salt and pepper on the side and butter as a caloric elective. Whether you cook a potato peeled or unpeeled is up to personal preference. However, what you choose to boil is not. Low-starch or waxy new varieties are to my mind the most felicitous choices for boiling, particularly if you plan to mash the potatoes. Avoid using baking potatoes; they tend to remain lumpy no matter how long one flails at them, and old high-starch potatoes turn gluey and thick. I always boil potatoes uncovered, in cold water, salting the water only after it has boiled. Cooking times vary with potato sizes but the average spud will take approximately 20 to 25 minutes, after the water has come to the boil, to become fork-tender.

The optimum mashed potato is put through a ricer, then beaten hard with a wooden spoon as the butter and cream are added. My generous rule of thumb: 1 to 1½ tablespoons butter per cupful of potatoes, plus 2 to 4 tablespoons of heavy cream, depending upon the texture you prefer. I like mine to drift heavy on the plate (Illinois-blizzard style)!

No baking potato is ever foil-wrapped in my oven, as this steams rather than bakes the contents. But I very often grease the skins with a smidgen of vegetable oil, as I admire a chewy exterior. In a baked potato, I skip any amendment other than unsalted butter—but sour cream, chives, crumbled bacon, and a splash of red wine vinegar all make very acceptable gildings of this lily.

I rarely fry a potato these days, because I am watching my waistlinc assiduously. That is a shame because a good French fry is as hard to find as a slice of homemade apple pie. The optimum method for frying potatoes requires either an electric deep-fat fryer or a large pot that will comfortably hold a metal strainer. The size of a fried potato is important: first, I slice mine lengthwise, never thicker than ¼ inch. These slices are then cut into ¼-inch-wide strips. It is a good idea to soak the cut potatoes in ice water for at least an hour prior to frying, and then drain them thoroughly on paper towels before placing them in the pot. I fry potatoes in hot (375°F) Crisco in two stages. First, I fry them for 2 to 3 minutes until lightly golden but not crisp, then drain them on brown paper (or in a paper bag) until they cool. Before serving, I refry the potatoes for 2 to 3 minutes until all the moisture in the potato evaporates. The fries will be *really* crisp. While they drain on paper towels or more brown paper, I get busy with the salt and pepper, and serve them up immediately.

Fried-potato buffs insist that a minimal amount of meat fat (lard, suet, bacon, etc.) when added to the hot grease will produce a sublimely flavored shoestring. I do not disagree, but never reserve that grease to use a second time, as the flavor intensifies as it cools.

CRIMPED POTATO SKINS

When I was a kid, I would watch dumbfounded at the table as my father carefully removed the snowy contents of a baked potato. He would always butter and mash the stuffing, then push the crunchy (and infinitely more delectable) potato skins to the side of his plate. I expect he meant them for the garbage pail but they never got that far, thanks to my sister's and my own watchful eye. Much affixed on the crackling texture of buttered skins, we would ask his permission to spear the detritus once his napkin was laid upon the table.

These days my potato skins are toasted and broiled, a trick I learned from the kitchen wisdom of James Beard. They make a great hors d'oeuvre, if you have the self-control to husband a batch after you have made those Heavenly Mashed Potatoes.

4 medium baking potatoes
Vegetable oil
3 tablespoons unsalted butter
Salt and freshly ground black pepper

1. Preheat the oven to 375°F. Prick the potatoes with a fork, and lightly rub them with oil. Bake the potatoes on a rack until tender, about 1 hour. Allow them to cool slightly.

2. Cut the potatoes in half lengthwise and scoop out the interiors. (Reserve the interiors for hash, or use for Heavenly Mashed Potatoes.) With scissors, cut the skins lengthwise into strips. Rub the skins well with the butter, and sprinkle with salt and pepper to taste. Place them under a preheated broiling unit until crisp on both sides.

Serves 2 or 3.

SOPA DE APATZINGAN

(Potato and Cantaloupe Soup)

I have two favored potato soup nominations, neither of which is vichyssoise. Not out of animus—merely overexposure, for I made that velvety brew twice a day for ten summers of my life when I ran The Store in Amagansett and now cannot face a spoonful.

This cold potato soup comes from Mexico. It is a fabled confederation of cooked potato and raw melon fused in a blender—brought to my attention by the doyenne of Latin American cuisine, Diana Kennedy.

1 pound potatoes, peeled, cubed
2 cups cubed cantaloupe (about 1 medium melon)
2 cups milk
4 tablespoons (½ stick) unsalted butter
Juice of 1 large lime
4 egg yolks
Salt and freshly ground black pepper
Ground cinnamon
1 cup unsweetened whipped cream

1. Cook the potatoes in boiling

salted water until tender, 15 to 20 minutes. Drain.

2. Place the potatoes and cantaloupe in the container of a food processor. Add 1 cup of the milk and process until smooth.

3. Melt the butter in a large saucepan over medium-low heat. Add the puréed potato mixture and remaining 1 cup milk. Stir in the lime juice. Cook over low heat 5 minutes.

4. Beat the egg yolks until light and lemon-colored. Stir the egg yolks into the soup. Remove the soup from the heat. Add salt and pepper to taste. Cool.

5. Chill the soup for at least 4 hours. Serve in individual soup bowls, sprinkled with cinnamon. Add a dab of whipped cream to each bowl.

Serves 6.

PO' POTTAGE

(Potato-Ham Soup)

This hot soup stems from the potato fields of Tennessee. It is a farmer's supper (only slightly enriched in my kitchen) and still one of the best one-dish meals around.

2 tablespoons unsalted butter
1 medium onion, chopped
1 small clove garlic, minced
⅓ cup diced cooked ham
2 ribs celery, finely chopped (about ½ cup)
⅛ teaspoon dried thyme
1 small bay leaf
2 medium baking potatoes (about ¾ pound), peeled, cubed
3 cups chicken broth (see page 414)
Salt and freshly ground black pepper
¼ cup chopped fresh parsley
2 tablespoons sour cream

1. Melt the butter in a medium saucepan over medium heat. Add the onion; cook 1 minute. Add the garlic and ham; cook until lightly browned, about 5 minutes. Reduce the heat. Add the celery, thyme and bay leaf; cook, covered, over medium-low heat for 5 minutes.

2. Remove the cover and add the potatoes; toss well. Add the chicken broth. Heat to boiling; reduce the heat. Simmer, uncovered, until the potatoes are tender, about 20 minutes. Add salt and pepper to taste.

3. Remove the soup from the heat; stir in the parsley. Combine the sour cream with ½ cup of the soup in a small bowl. Whisk this mixture back into the soup. Serve immediately.

Serves 2 as a main course, 4 as a first course.

FRENCH PROVINCIAL POTATO SALAD

Dedicated potato salad fanciers are a very special breed—prejudiced about mayonnaise versus oil and vinegar, or hot opposed to cool, and (more importantly) what or what not to slice up as the main ingredient.

Speaking for the French and not myself, they always opt for a mealy (high-starch) tuber like a White Rose or Mohawk, which often goes by the generic family tag Idaho though in fact they are merely deep-dug denizens of any ashy western soil.

Other potato salad heads of my acquaintance hold equally strong opinions about round reds (medium starch) in their salads. Pontiacs, La Sodas, La Rouges, and McClures are all red-skinned members I have chewed with equal relish.

In the final analysis, the only criteria for a potato salad potato are its crispness and flavor. Try your favorite tuber (if you have one) in either of the next two alliances.

This version is a full century old. It springs from France—Provence to be exact, where there are as many potato salad variations as there are garlic buds.

8 medium potatoes
1 large clove garlic, bruised
⅓ cup dry white wine
½ cup plus 1 tablespoon olive oil
1 tablespoon white wine vinegar
2 thick slices stale French bread
1 tablespoon unsalted butter
2 large shallots, minced
3 tablespoons chopped fresh parsley
Salt and freshly ground black pepper

1. Cook the potatoes in boiling salted water until just tender, about 18 minutes. (Centers should not be thoroughly cooked.) Drain. Cool, peel, and cut into ¼-inch-thick slices.

2. Rub a large bowl with the garlic. (Do not discard the garlic.) Add the potatoes; sprinkle with the wine, ½ cup oil, and vinegar. Toss gently. Let stand, covered, 1 hour.

3. Meanwhile, rub the French bread on both sides with the garlic. Cut the bread into croutons. Heat the remaining 1 tablespoon oil and the butter in a medium skillet over medium-high heat. Add the croutons. Sauté, stirring constantly, until golden. Drain on paper towels; reserve.

4. Add the shallots, parsley, and salt and pepper to taste to the potato salad. Fold in the croutons just before serving.

Serves 6.

SPECK'S FAMED POTATO SALAD

Another nifty potato salad, this one is of German descent. Only *half* a century old, it springs from a vanished restaurant, Speck's, once a St. Louis hostelry of deserved repute. The formulation for this salad (yellowing with age) was copied and sent by a loyal friend from that admirable precinct along the broad Mississippi. Ricky Duhart amended the copy with three brief words: "Old but good."

That says it all.

3 pounds potatoes
¼ cup finely chopped bacon
1 small onion, finely chopped
2 tablespoons all-purpose flour
1 teaspoon salt
4 teaspoons sugar
¼ teaspoon freshly ground black pepper
⅔ cup cider vinegar
⅓ cup water
½ teaspoon celery seed
3 tablespoons chopped fresh parsley
1 egg white, lightly beaten (optional)

1. Cook the potatoes in boiling

salted water until just tender, about 18 minutes. Centers should be slightly firm. Drain, peel, and slice thin. Place in a large bowl.

2. Sauté the bacon in a large heavy skillet over medium heat until crisp. Add the onion; cook 1 minute. Stir in the flour, salt, sugar, and pepper. Cook, stirring constantly, 1 minute. Add the vinegar and water. Cook, stirring frequently, 10 minutes. Pour over the potatoes.

3. Sprinkle the potato mixture with the celery seed and parsley. Toss gently until thoroughly mixed. If you are using it, pour the egg white over the top. Serve while still warm.

Serves 6 to 8.

Potatoes have names in other lands that are as diverse as the ways in which they are cooked at home. If, for instance, you are forking into a *patata*, it's either Spain or Italy; a *peruna*, Finland; a *papa*, Colombia; and a *pomme de terre*, France. Roumanians dub their potatoes *cartofi*, the Russians and Germans call them *Kartoffel*, and the Czechs tag them *brambors*—all of which may prove a bit unsettling to a traveling potato lover.

NEW POTATOES IN LEMON

This recipe is a gift from Elaine Light, a gracious and extraordinarily good cook, author of *The New Gourmets and Groundhogs*, which is published in Punxsutawney, Pennsylvania—where the groundhog and Elaine are both to be found.

1 1/4 pounds small new potatoes, red or white
6 tablespoons (3/4 stick) unsalted butter
1 teaspoon grated lemon peel
1 1/2 teaspoons lemon juice
1 tablespoon minced chives
Salt and freshly ground black pepper

1. Cook the potatoes in boiling salted water until tender, 10 to 12 minutes. Drain. Allow to cool slightly, then remove the skins with your fingers or a sharp knife.

2. Melt the butter in a large heavy skillet over medium-low heat. Stir in the lemon peel, lemon juice, and chives. Add the potatoes; roll until well coated with the mixture. Sprinkle with salt and pepper to taste.

Serves 4.

NEW POTATOES IN MUSTARD

Number two new-potato recipe is a dispensation from San Francisco—from friend Marlene Levinson, in fact.

1 1/4 pounds small new potatoes, red or white
4 tablespoons (1/2 stick) unsalted butter
1 1/2 tablespoons Dijon mustard
1/3 cup chopped fresh parsley
1 teaspoon chopped fresh chervil, or 1/2 teaspoon dried
Salt and freshly ground black pepper

1. Cook the potatoes in boiling salted water until tender, 10 to 12 minutes. Drain. Allow to cool slightly, then remove the skins with your fingers or a sharp knife.

2. Melt the butter in a large heavy skillet over medium-low heat. Stir in the mustard, parsley, and chervil. Add the potatoes; roll until well coated with the mixture. Sprinkle with salt and pepper to taste.

Serves 4.

NEW POTATOES IN WHITE WINE

Number three is a slightly less conventional mating: the tuber is poached in good white wine. From Cincinnati's Marilyn Harris.

1 1/4 pounds small new potatoes, red or white
4 tablespoons (1/2 stick) unsalted butter
2/3 cup dry white wine
Salt and freshly ground black pepper
3 tablespoons chopped fresh parsley
1 tablespoon chopped fresh dill

1. Cut away a small strip of peel around each potato with a vegetable peeler. The potatoes should look candy-striped. Cook the potatoes in boiling salted water until barely tender, 8 to 10 minutes. Drain.

2. Melt 2 tablespoons of the butter in a large skillet over medium heat. Add the potatoes and roll them in the skillet until a light crust forms, but do not let them brown. Add the wine; raise the heat and cook, stirring constantly, until the wine is reduced and the sauce is fairly thick, about 5 minutes. Sprinkle with salt and pepper to taste, the parsley and the dill. Stir gently to coat the potatoes with the herbs.

Serves 4.

NEW POTATOES SLICED IN TARRAGON CREAM

Number four is the end of all that potato name-dropping. I invented it myself.

2 tablespoons unsalted butter
1 large shallot, minced
1/2 teaspoon chopped fresh tarragon, or 1/4 teaspoon dried
1/2 pound new potatoes, red or white, sliced 1/8 inch thick
1 cup heavy or whipping cream
Salt and freshly ground black pepper

1. Melt the butter in a large heavy skillet over medium-low heat. Add the shallot; cook 2 minutes. Add the tarragon and potatoes. Toss to coat the potatoes with butter.

2. Pour the cream over the potatoes. Heat to boiling; reduce the heat. Simmer, stirring occasionally, until just tender, 18 to 20 minutes. Add salt and pepper to taste.

Serves 4.

ALSATIAN POTATO TART

This recipe is a residual of my stay in France in the early 1970s. A devise of obviously mixed heritage (part French, part German), it is one culinary instance in which potatoes dabbed with bacon and frothed in egg do not a breakfast make. Serve it instead with roast chicken or turkey!

3 strips bacon
1/4 cup heavy or whipping cream
2 eggs, at room temperature
3 tablespoons finely grated onion
2 tablespoons all-purpose flour
1 teaspoon salt
1/4 teaspoon freshly ground black pepper
2 allspice berries, crushed, or a pinch ground
6 medium potatoes

1. Preheat the oven to 400°F. Sauté the bacon in a 9- or 10-inch cast-iron skillet until crisp. Drain on paper towels, crumble, and reserve. Reserve the bacon drippings in the skillet.

2. Beat the cream with the eggs until light. Stir in the onion, flour, salt, pepper, and allspice. (If possible, use dried, crushed berries. They are more potent.)

3. Peel the potatoes and grate them directly into the cream-egg mixture. Mix well. Stir in the reserved bacon.

4. Place the bacon skillet with its drippings in the oven for 5 minutes. Swirl the drippings over the bottom and sides of the skillet, then pour the potato mixture into the hot skillet. Bake until puffed and lightly browned, 30 to 35 minutes. Cut into wedges to serve.

Serves 6 to 8.

POTATO PUNTS

A year ago, I stumbled onto yet another tonic use for the potato skin: as a hangover cure. Or perhaps a preventive; you be the judge. I am not at all certain of the efficacy of potato therapy, but this medicine is inspired stuff. The dish was created as a late-night snack at a New York restaurant called Simon's. Instead of a plate of crunchy skins with a drink, this hostelry serves up the shell as a slender skiff, packed with a precious cargo of sautéed, herbed potato balls. A wonderful idea for your very next steak!

2 large baking potatoes
Vegetable oil
4 teaspoons unsalted butter
Dried rosemary
Salt and freshly ground black pepper

1. Preheat the oven to 375°F. Prick the potatoes with a fork, and lightly rub them with oil. Bake the potatoes on a rack until tender, about 1¼ hours. Let cool for 30 minutes.

2. Cut the potatoes in half lengthwise and scoop out the interiors with a melon scoop. Set aside.

3. Heat ½ inch of vegetable oil in a medium skillet until hot but not smoking. Fry the potato skins until crisp on all sides. Rub each interior with 1 teaspoon of the butter and sprinkle with rosemary to taste.

4. Add the potato balls to the hot oil. Fry until crisp and golden. Drain quickly on paper towels. Fill each potato boat with potato balls, sprinkle with salt and pepper to taste, and serve immediately.

Serves 4.

Potatoes have had their share of roasting, mainly at the hands of church fathers.

Ever since the Pope's pronouncement about these brown orbs' erotic potential, Catholic priests in Rome sprinkle holy water on potato patches, religiously, at the close of Lent.

In Scotland, the Presbyterian clergy in 1770 declared the potato unsafe to eat—not for moral reasons, but simply because it was one food *not* mentioned in the Bible.

A hundred years later, an American minister in Boston cited the potato as the start of moral decay among city dwellers. Far from being an aphrodisiac, Reverend Richard Sewell declared that potato cookery led to wantonness in housewives because it required far too little kitchen preparation and left hands idle!

CRUNCHY BAKED POTATOES

Another baked potato of remarkable savor is roasted in salt and darn little else. The formula was sent me by a friend, Janet Cook Wilmoth, an American writer who lives in England. Janet and I became pen pals some while back and became recipe exchangers shortly afterward. Her spuds are very special—but they're not a good choice for those on low-sodium diets.

4 medium baking potatoes
Vegetable oil
Salt

Preheat the oven to 425°F. Pierce each potato with a fork. Pour about 1½ tablespoons oil in your hands and rub each potato thoroughly. Pour an equal amount of salt (or more if desired) into your hands. Rub into each potato. Place the potatoes on a rack and roast them in the oven until tender and crisp, about 45 minutes. (Reduce the heat if the potatoes begin to get too dark.)

Serves 4.

BARBECUED BAKED POTATOES

The potato cookery that requires the least possible amount of energy is roasting. My favorite version (brought back from Fire Island) is splashed with barbecue sauce as it bakes. Use whatever sluice pleases you most, but one will not go wrong with the spicy stuff teamed with barbecued peppers in the previous chapter.

4 medium baking potatoes
½ cup Dynamite Barbecue Sauce (see page 280)

Preheat the oven to 350°F. Lightly prick the surface of the potatoes with a fork and place them on a roasting rack set in an oven pan. Brush each potato with barbecue sauce. Bake in the oven 1¼ hours, basting and turning the potatoes every 10 minutes.

Serves 4.

TATER 'N' TOMATER PIE

Glowing orange as a Texas sunrise, this recipe was passed on to me by a rawboned lady who sat through three of my cooking demonstrations at a department store in San Antonio. As the lights at Foley's winked a closing notice, she pressed the formula for this dish in my palm. "It's good. It has no name. It's old and it's made outta unpeeled taters and tomaters."

4 tablespoons (½ stick) unsalted butter
1 medium onion, finely chopped
1 clove garlic, minced
2 medium tomatoes, seeded, roughly chopped
½ teaspoon thyme
1½ teaspoons chopped fresh basil, or ½ teaspoon dried
¼ teaspoon sugar
1 beef bouillon cube, mashed
2 large baking potatoes, unpeeled, cut into ⅛-inch-thick slices
Salt and freshly ground black pepper
Chopped fresh parsley

1. Preheat the oven to 350°F. Melt 2 tablespoons of the butter in a large ovenproof skillet over medium heat. Add the onion; cook 1 minute. Add the garlic; cook 1 minute. Add the tomatoes, thyme, basil, sugar, and bouillon cube. Cook, uncovered, over medium heat, stirring occasionally, until thickened, about 20 minutes. Transfer the mixture to a bowl.

2. Melt 1 tablespoon of the butter in the same skillet over medium heat. Spread one third of the sauce over the bottom of the skillet. Add one third of the potato slices. Repeat the layers twice, ending with the potato slices, and dot with the remaining 1 tablespoon butter. Bake 30 minutes.

3. Run a knife around the edges of the potato pie and loosen the bottom with a spatula. Invert onto a serving platter. Sprinkle with salt and pepper to taste and chopped fresh parsley. Cut into wedges to serve.

Serves 4.

HEAVENLY MASHED POTATOES

My classic mashed potato franchise is unorthodox to be sure, since the potato is not boiled but baked first, then scooped out of its shell, creamed, seasoned, and buttered last of all. However, it is a treasure of a recipe—a slightly amended version of one my friend Miss Toklas invented.

2 pounds baking potatoes
Vegetable oil
1 teaspoon salt
¼ teaspoon freshly ground black pepper
¼ teaspoon freshly grated nutmeg
12 tablespoons (1½ sticks) unsalted butter, softened, plus 2 tablespoons melted
4 egg yolks
½ cup whipped cream

1. Preheat the oven to 350°F. Prick the potatoes with a fork and rub them lightly with oil. Bake them, on a rack, until tender, about 1 hour. Cut the potatoes in half lengthwise and scoop out the interiors. Reserve the skins for Crimped Potato Skins (see page 293), if desired. Rice the potatoes or mash them through a strainer.

2. Place the potatoes in a large bowl. Add the salt, pepper, nutmeg, and softened butter. Beat until smooth. Beat in the egg yolks, one at a time, beating thoroughly after each addition. Stir in the whipped cream.

3. Transfer the mixture to a baking dish. Bake 15 minutes. Drizzle the melted butter over the top, raise the heat to 450°F, and bake 5 minutes longer.

Serves 6.

KAREN'S MASHED POTATO ROLLS

Let's let the potato fatten us up, pleasurably. My choice of decadence? The sticky bun! This is the best version and a half you will ever sample, upon my honor. The donor is a food writer for the San Antonio *Express-News*, Karen Haram. Karen forfeited this treasured family recipe for mashed potato rolls with variations when she heard me bemoaning the loss of homey good things to eat. Her formula is old as the hills—from the Midwest, as was Karen originally—but it suffers no alteration whatsoever in either the dry airs of the Lone Star or the damp ones of the Empire State. Save up the calorie allowance for this one!

1 cup milk
½ cup sugar
2 teaspoons salt
1 package dry yeast
2 large eggs, lightly beaten
1 cup mashed potatoes
5½ cups all-purpose flour, approximately
8 tablespoons (1 stick) unsalted butter, melted

1. Scald the milk; cool it to lukewarm and pour it into a large bowl.

2. Add the sugar and salt to the lukewarm milk and stir well. Then, stir in the yeast; let stand 2 minutes. Beat in the eggs, mashed potatoes, and 1½ cups of the flour. Do not overbeat; some lumps will remain. Let stand until bubbly, about 5 minutes.

3. Add the melted butter to the flour-yeast mixture. Stir in the remaining flour, 1 cup at a time, until smooth and not sticky. Transfer to a floured board and knead 2 minutes, adding more flour if necessary.

4. Place the dough in a well-buttered large bowl. Turn the dough to coat it with butter. Cover the dough and let it rise until tripled in volume, about 2 hours. Proceed with the variations that follow.

Although Jiménez de Quesada brought potatoes from Peru to Spain, it was Sir Francis Drake who hustled them to England. The last of a longish line of Elizabethan explorers, Drake's reputation was based as much on his amatory pursuits as his naval intelligence. When he came upon the bespoke potato blooming in the Andes and heard of its prandial wonders, Drake simply took a shipload home as a souvenir for the Queen.

On the way back, however, a rampant case of scurvy broke out aboard ship. Against Drake's injunction, the captain-at-arms fed the crew the Queen's potatoes, raw, which saved their lives. How he knew that valuable vitamin C lay beneath the potato's umber cover is anyone's guess.

Queen Elizabeth received a single potato plant as booty. But the story has a bitter end. The Queen's cook, unaccustomed to foreign ingredients, threw all the potatoes away and served Her Majesty the green leaves instead.

The Queen was *not* amused.

Karen's Parker House Rolls

1 recipe Mashed Potato Rolls
Flour for dusting
3 tablespoons unsalted butter, plus 2 tablespoons melted

1. To make Parker House–type rolls, pull off pieces of dough slightly larger than a Ping-Pong ball. Flatten each with your hands. Then, using a floured knife, make a crease down the middle of each. Lightly butter one half and fold it over, pressing the edges securely with your fingers. Place the rolls, seam side up, about 1 inch apart on a greased baking sheet. Brush with melted butter. Cover loosely and let rise 40 minutes.

2. Preheat the oven to 400°F. Bake the rolls until lightly browned, about 15 to 18 minutes.

Makes 18 rolls.

Karen's Caramel Rolls

1 recipe Mashed Potato Rolls
½ cup granulated sugar
2½ teaspoons ground cinnamon
8 tablespoons (1 stick) unsalted butter, softened
1 cup firmly packed dark brown sugar
1 cup heavy or whipping cream

1. Divide the risen mashed potato dough in half. Roll each half into a rectangle, ¼ inch thick.

2. Combine the granulated sugar with the cinnamon and softened butter. Beat until smooth and spread over each rectangle. Roll up like a jelly roll and slice into 1-inch pieces. You should get nine pieces per roll.

3. Combine the brown sugar with

the heavy cream. Pour into two buttered 8-inch-square cake pans. Place the rolls, flat-side down, on top of the sugar mixture, nine rolls in each pan. Cover and let rise until doubled in volume, about 1 hour.

4. Preheat the oven to 350°F. Bake the rolls until golden brown, 25 to 30 minutes. When done, cover with a serving platter and invert. Remove the pan after 1 minute, allowing the caramel to run down over the rolls.

Makes 18 rolls.

Karen's Butter Pecan Rolls

1 recipe Mashed Potato Rolls
8 tablespoons (1 stick) unsalted butter, melted, plus 12 tablespoons (1½ sticks)
2½ cups firmly packed dark brown sugar
2 teaspoons ground cinnamon
1½ cups chopped pecans

1. Divide the risen mashed potato dough in half. Roll each half into a rectangle, ¼ inch thick.

2. Brush each rectangle with the melted butter. Combine ½ cup of the brown sugar with the cinnamon and sprinkle this over the dough. Roll up like a jelly roll and slice into 1-inch pieces. You should get nine pieces per roll.

3. Melt the 12 tablespoons butter with the remaining 2 cups brown sugar over medium heat. Divide the mixture between two buttered 8-inch-square cake pans. Sprinkle the nuts evenly over the sugar mixture. Place the rolls, flat side down, on top of the nuts, nine rolls in each pan. Cover and let rise until doubled in volume, about 1 hour.

4. Preheat the oven to 350°F. Bake the rolls until golden brown, 25 to 30 minutes. When done, cover with a serving platter and invert. Remove the pan after 1 minute, allowing the caramel to run down over rolls.

Makes 18 rolls.

MYRA'S POTATO LATKES

Let me state at once that I am very much in favor of these weighty ovals. I was raised on *latkes* that were not only light but greaseless and highly digestible, which is not a common occurrence in every Jewish-American home. The lightness was due to a speck of baking powder; the lack of grease related to a minimum of shortening (always Crisco) in the pan; and the digestibility was reinforced by quick cookery.

The recipe came from my grandmother, who passed it on to my mother, who passed it on to my sister. I could never get the hang of the darn things. My sister grates her potatoes by hand, using the finest blade. Quite by accident I grated them roughly once and had to process them afterward. The trick worked, so I recommend it to all but hard-nosed latke makers.

In our house the potato pancake was always served with a rich meaty gravy, plus applesauce on the side. Never, never with sour cream!

1½ pounds baking potatoes
Juice of 1 lemon
1 small onion, finely grated
1 large egg, lightly beaten
2 tablespoons all-purpose flour
2 teaspoons baking powder
Salt and freshly ground black pepper
Crisco shortening
Mechana (recipe follows)
Applesauce

1. Preheat the oven to 250°F. Peel the potatoes and roughly grate them into a large bowl of cold water to which you have added the lemon juice. Let stand 30 minutes.

2. After the potatoes have soaked in the water, drain them and squeeze them dry with your hands. Place the potatoes in the container of a food processor. Process, using the on/off switch, until fairly smooth but not wet. Transfer to a large bowl. Add the onion, egg, flour, baking powder, and salt and pepper to taste. Stir until smooth.

3. Place a large cast-iron skillet over medium heat. Film the bottom of the skillet with the shortening. Using about 1 large tablespoon for each, add four latkes to the skillet. Cook until golden brown and puffed, about 1 minute. Turn over and brown the other side. Place on a rack and keep warm in the oven while sautéing the remaining latkes. Film the bottom of the skillet after each batch. Serve with *mechana* and applesauce.

Serves 4.

Mechana
(Meat Sauce)

1 large yellow onion, thinly sliced
4 pounds beef brisket
1 to 3 bay leaves (optional)
1½ cups beef broth (see page 414)

1. Preheat the oven to 350°F. Place the onions over the bottom of a large Dutch oven. Add the beef, and the bay leaves if desired. Cook, covered, in the oven for 1 hour.

2. Continue to cook, adding beef broth to the pot as needed, until the meat is very tender and shreds easily, about 2½ hours longer. Lightly shred the meat into its cooking juices before serving.

Serves 6 to 8.

SPINACH

The Chinese Flower

If I were faced with the onerous chore of selecting a last meal on earth, one of the dishes would have to include spinach. I'd choose a salad of tender greens with a healthy tinge of grit between the leaves to remind me of the transitory retribution mortality imposes. But, come to think of it, I have already consumed that repast. Memorably.

The meal was taken at the Broadmoor Hotel in Colorado Springs, in the shadow of Pike's Peak, and it was a belated birthday celebration I would just as lief have skipped. My host and tour guide to Colorado was Phillip Schulz, a young man raised in that rustic state who has since become my collaborator, advisor, and truest friend in and out of the kitchen. On this occasion, after a month of successful, if wearying, cooking classes in Denver and parts west, we were playing hookey. Phillip proposed a day off "to see the mountains" before we flew on to Chicago to resume teaching, and I agreed with alacrity.

Our sortie began early because a Schulz family gathering was planned to honor the prodigal son at his parents' home later that evening. I knew those fabulous dinners well, having had the good luck to be included among the clan on more than one occasion and would not have missed it for the world. That I almost did is the sand in this spinach story, for the Broadmoor's bowlful was flawless.

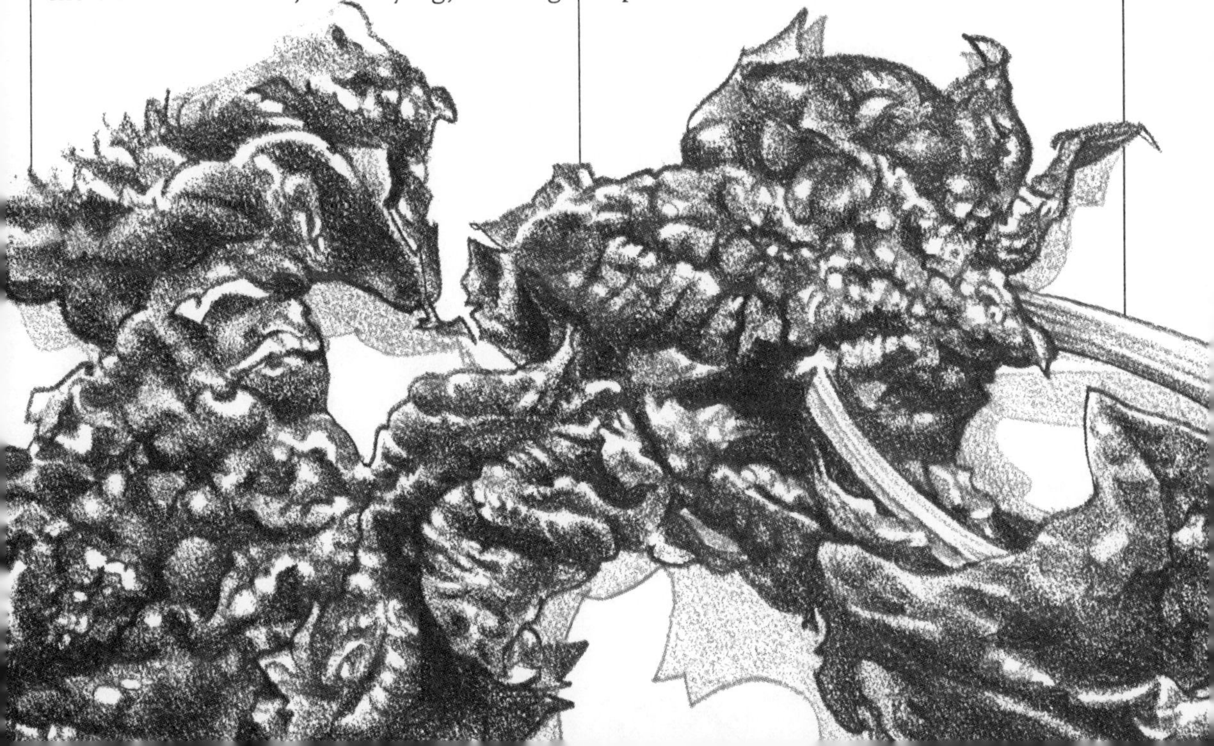

Like a Victorian castle preserved in amber, this old hotel nestles among tall aspen trees and taller mountains scarred with ski trails. We had come there via a superhighway dotted with tract homes and shopping centers, and the alteration of the virgin landscape was dispiriting to both of us. Phillip had done a stint of army duty at Fort Carson nearby and knew every conceivable route back to his parents' home in Golden, so when he proposed a return through the Cheyenne Mountain pass and Cripple Creek, I jumped at the opportunity. The names alone were a whiff of the Old West I had come here expressly to inhale. The moment I agreed, Phillip seemed a tad reluctant.

"It *is* a longer way back of course," he announced soberly, settling into the driver's seat of our rented car. "And the mountain roads can be dangerous."

"On a day like this?"

It was mid-October but so warm we had both divested ourselves of our jackets after lunch. Phillip scanned the mountainside with a native's eye. "It doesn't seem likely. But there is a touch of snow along the ridges."

"Phillip! Let's go."

We did, and with pleasure for the first few miles, for the road up Cheyenne Mountain was relatively untraveled and the twisting single lane of macadam that took us high above the town made driving easy. Then, quite abruptly, the pavement ended—or more specifically, became a dirt road that in time turned to icy mud as we traveled higher, past the timberline. Worse than the loss of road was the absence of sunlight; what had been a golden day minutes before became gray, patchy fog, and the light snow observed from below was now a treacherous embankment that made the car swerve precipitously as we inched along.

"How far is it to Cripple Creek?" I asked charily after a terrible quarter-hour of silence.

"I don't know. Twenty or thirty miles. Think we should go back?"

The question was rhetorical, for clearly there was no way. We drove at a virtual snail's pace now, taking each new twisting curve with bated breath. The road had diminished to a trail barely wider than the car and we hugged the cliff side so tightly that loose rocks and snow often covered the windshield. The alternative was a sheer glacial descent of perhaps two thousand feet.

"Phillip! What happens if another car comes along this road?"

He looked straight ahead before answering, his fingers never leaving the wheel. "Technically, the car going uphill has the right of way. If we are on a downside, we would have to drive in reverse until we reached a stretch that's passable. But I will tell you right now, I have no intention of testing the principle. If one comes, we simply abandon ship!"

"Then what?"

"I don't know. Hike, or hitch a ride!"

Thankfully none came, but the drive was an endless torment nevertheless. After several hours of hairpin turns, I pressed my friend for a judgment on how much farther we would have to travel. It was the only time he ever lost his composure, for Phillip Schulz is a most proficient driver.

"How the hell do I know? I can't remember. I was younger when I did this last. I was probably drunk too! If you can't face it, go to sleep."

I tried, but without much success. So to calm my nerves, I worked on thinking about pleasanter things. It had grown dark in the car and at one point I must have been murmuring, for my friend turned to me and asked, "Are you saying your prayers?"

"No. Recipes. How do you think spinach salad would taste with bits of bacon and a warm goat cheese dressing?"

"Good. But then, anything would," said Schulz the pragmatist. "I'm hungry."

Truthfully, so was I. And with that

heartening life sign intact, we eventually crossed the mountain—but not until I had had the time to work on a few more culinary notions, my most calming topic of thought!

We arrived for dinner late and unkempt, but starving and glad to be alive. I wish I could report that we ate spinach in some guise but we did not; it was roast pork and absolutely mouth-watering. In the Schulz family, no meal is ever begun without a grace. Never was a benediction spoken with more fervor or gratitude than by the mountain climbers that night. And the last meal on earth was postponed once more.

Vegetable Roots

The ancient Medes prescribed twelve washings for every leaf of spinach that went into a pot—eleven of which (in water) were meant to free the vegetable of its dark, earthly associations. The twelfth (in human tears) was supposed to season it with God's wisdom.

Tears probably came easily after all that laundering; it will come as no real shock to discover that few Medes ever consumed a forkful!

A late bloomer, *Spinacia oleracea* was originally noted growing wild near the desert lands of Dasht-e-Kavir and was transplanted to Persian gardens, where it was cultivated mainly to satisfy the appetites of much-prized Persian cats. The absence of a proper Sanskrit name for this vegetable suggests that the first seeds were planted well after the death of Christ. In Persia, spinach was (and still is) known as *isfānākh*, which means a green hand.

From Persia fingers of that hand traveled east to China in the sixth century. Whether Chinese cats appreciated its peppery flavor is not recorded, but spinach certainly made its way into the population's soup bowls, as "Persian herbs."

The Chinese raised spinach extensively along the outer fringes of their rice fields, where the soil is sandiest; and in time they transported the green to India and Nepal as well, where it bore the designation "China flower."

The invading Moors introduced spinach to Spain in the twelfth century—along with beheadings, circumcisions, and several other cultural gratuities. Only spinach took root. Within a hundred years this therapeutic leaf was known all over Western Europe as *spanacha*, or Spanish greens.

Some say Columbus brought spinach to the New World. Others claim it was part of the *Mayflower* cargo. True or false, it matters not a whit for this vegetable was resolutely unpopular with settlers and natives alike. An early Pilgrim child's prayer invokes the Good Lord's protection from fire, famine, flood, and *unclean foreign leaves*; read, sandy spinach. And it took another five hundred years (along with the invention of spin-dry vegetable laundering machines) to convince American kids that a random portion of green on a plate does not necessarily indicate a deposit of grit between the molars!

What to Look For

I must confess I am something of a Tartar when I buy spinach, always poking about the packages on the supermarket shelf to uncover the freshest bundle. Less than prime spinach develops an acrid, unpalatable taste, so it is wise to sniff as well as scrutinize the produce you plan to purchase. Freshly picked spinach has a fine green earthy scent; sour cabbage-smelling leaves mean the stuff is definitely over the hill.

Fresh (unpacked) leaf spinach is a shopper's best buy. Prepackaged bunches tend to yield a high proportion of stems, not to mention bruised leaves, under their plastic covers; these bruised leaves must be removed prior to refrigerating or they will rot the rest. Fresh spinach, on the other hand, is sandy; so you pays your money and takes your choice in the matter!

When I buy fresh spinach, I search for the crispest, greenest leaf. When plastic is the option, the bundle should retain a measure of spring when it is pinched. Avoid all spinach, in or out of a wrapper, that is yellowing, moldy, or wet.

As a kid I believed (doubtless out of devotion to Popeye) that regular dinner doses of spinach built muscles of cast iron or maybe even steel. There is indeed some basis for that assumption, since spinach is famous for its iron content. Unfortunately the iron in spinach is not in a readily assimilated form, so weight lifting is still the answer for the muscle-bound. However, do not get me wrong. A single cup of cooked spinach is exceptionally rich in vitamins (14,580 units of A alone), and contains 583 milligrams of potassium and 167 grams of calcium to boot. The best spinach news of all is the calorie count: less than 15 calories in a cup of raw spinach and a scant 40 in a cup of cooked.

Preparation

As recently as fifty years ago, cookbooks dictated seven washings for all leaf spinach prior to cooking. I usually settle for a longish stint under a running faucet while I remove the fibrous stems—even when the content of my colander is plastic-packaged spinach. Newly picked leaves take a good deal longer. After an initial shower under the tap, I place garden spinach in a basin of cool water for fifteen minutes; then I change the water and keep changing it until no trace of sand is left in the bottom of the bowl.

Cooking spinach is a somewhat more personal matter. On occasion I wilt it briefly in boiling water (no longer than five minutes) and then plunge it under cold running water to retard the cooking; then I drain it well before proceeding with my recipe. At other times I will add the (cleaned, chopped) raw spinach directly to the dish I am making. However, my basic cooking approach—recommended for general use—is what I call pot-steaming. I place the cleaned spinach in a heavy-duty (non-aluminum) saucepan with a tight-fitting lid. I add no water other than the drops that cling to the leaves after rinsing, and cook the spinach over low heat. Time? About five minutes per pound, or until the leaves crumple and soften. Then I drain the spinach thoroughly in a colander (saving any juices for my soup-stock collection) and proceed with the recipe.

It might be a good idea to note in passing that 2 to 3 pounds of fresh spinach yields 2 cups of cooked, and ½ cup cooked spinach is the average amount most diners will usually consume.

BRUMMAGEMS

(Spinach Rolls)

In my formula for Viennese vegetable rolls, the filling is homemade tomato purée and diced mushrooms, and the roll (100 percent spinach) is anointed with oil and vinegar. It makes a fine first course, salad dish, or hors d'oeuvre, garnished with a slice of the reddest onion you can find.

1 tablespoon olive oil, plus extra to taste
1 onion, finely chopped
2 cloves garlic, minced
3 pounds ripe tomatoes, peeled, seeded, diced
Sprig of marjoram, chopped, or a pinch of dried
Pinch of ground allspice
Salt and freshly ground black pepper
⅓ pound mushrooms, finely chopped
10 ounces fresh spinach, washed, stems trimmed
Red wine vinegar
½ red onion, sliced very thin

1. Heat the oil in a large saucepan over medium-low heat. Add the onion; cook 1 minute. Add the garlic; cook 4 minutes. Stir in the tomatoes, the marjoram, and allspice. Heat to boiling; reduce the heat. Simmer, uncovered, stirring frequently, until the sauce is as thick as a paste, about 1 hour. Season to taste with salt and pepper. Set aside.

2. Cook the mushrooms in a medium skillet over medium heat (without oil or butter) until all liquid has evaporated, stirring occasionally. Set aside.

3. Preheat the oven to 350°F. Cook the spinach in boiling salted water until just wilted, about 30 seconds. Drain immediately under cold running water. Unfold the leaves and pat them dry with paper towels.

4. On a work surface, place 3 or 4 spinach leaves, overlapping, to form a crepe shape, about 4 inches across. Spread with 2 tablespoons of the tomato mixture and 1 tablespoon of the mushrooms. Roll up and place on a lightly greased baking sheet. Continue until all ingredients are used up. Bake for 15 minutes.

5. Cool and refrigerate, covered, overnight. Sprinkle with vinegar and oil to taste before serving. Garnish with red onion slices.

Makes about 12.

SLOW-BAKED SPINACH TART

This borrowing from M.F.K. Fisher is a heavenly cracker-wafer-toast fabrication. A most unusual canape or accompaniment to cold or hot dishes, it is a recipe well worth notching on your culinary belt. But you must make sure to bake it for the required time: four hours! It may look done before that time, Mrs. Fisher cautions, but it is not!

10-ounce package frozen spinach, or 10 ounces fresh, washed, stems trimmed, cooked until tender
½ cup spinach liquid (see step 1)
1 medium onion, roughly chopped
1 clove garlic
2 large ribs celery, chopped
⅓ cup roughly chopped fresh parsley
8 to 10 fresh basil leaves
2 sprigs fresh thyme, or ¼ teaspoon dried
¾ cup olive oil
2 eggs
1 cup grated Jarlsberg cheese
Salt and freshly ground black pepper
⅛ teaspoon freshly grated nutmeg
1 cup fresh bread crumbs
¼ cup freshly grated Parmesan cheese

1. Thaw the spinach over a strainer if using frozen; reserve ½ cup of the liquid. If using fresh, press the liquid from the cooked spinach to get ½ cup. Add water if necessary.

2. Preheat the oven to 275°F. In the container of a blender or food processor, combine the spinach with the juice, onion, garlic, celery, parsley, basil, thyme, and ½ cup of the oil. Blend until smooth. Add the eggs; blend 30 seconds longer. Transfer to a bowl and stir in the Jarlsberg cheese. Add salt and pepper to taste and the nutmeg. Spread this mixture evenly over the bottom of a lightly oiled 10-by-15-inch baking sheet. Sprinkle the top with the bread crumbs and Parmesan cheese. Drizzle the remaining oil over the top. Bake until dry and crisp, about 4 hours. Serve hot or cold, sliced into squares. (The spinach squares can be stored in an airtight container or in the freezer.)

Makes 2½ to 3 dozen.

POTAGE VERT

(Spinach and Vegetable Soup)

French workers and farmers enjoy a *bonne soupe* as their midday meal; the contents change with the topography and local produce. I have eaten cabbage soups in Alsace Lorraine and bean versions in Burgundy, always with a goodly measure of green vegetables in proportion to the other weighty endowments in the pot. The following *bonne soupe* comes from the Alpes-Maritimes, where the spinach grows thick as poppies—maybe thicker. The dish (bright green with uncooked spinach) is a perfect way to begin a winter's dinner or—more likely—serves excellently as a meal in itself. To the local formula for a *bonne soupe* I have added another French amendment: my friend Julia Child's dipping sauce for the chicken and beef that turns any *soupe* super.

1 tablespoon unsalted butter
1 teaspoon vegetable oil
2 to 2½ pounds beef chuck roast
1 beef bone (leftover bones are fine)
2 onions, finely chopped
1 clove garlic, minced
2 large carrots, chopped
1 stalk celery with leaves, chopped
2 leeks, well cleaned, trimmed, sliced
2½-pound chicken
4 parsley sprigs, tied together with string
5 cups chicken broth (see page 414)
3 cups water
1 tomato, peeled, seeded, chopped
2 tablespoons lemon juice
½ cup broken thin spaghetti
8 to 10 ounces fresh spinach, washed, stems trimmed, shredded
Salt and freshly ground black pepper
Sauce de Sorges (recipe follows)

1. Heat the butter with the oil in a large heavy pot or Dutch oven over medium heat. Add the beef and beef bone. Sauté until browned; remove from the pot and set aside.

2. Add the onions to the pot; cook 1 minute. Add the garlic, carrots, celery, and leeks; cook 5 minutes. Add the chicken, browned beef and bone, parsley sprigs, chicken broth, and water. Heat to boiling, skimming the surface as necessary; reduce the heat. Simmer, covered, 1 hour. Remove the chicken when tender; set aside and cover with aluminum foil. Continue to cook the soup until the beef is tender, about 1 hour longer.

3. Remove the beef, bone, and parsley from the soup. Set aside.

4. Add the tomato and lemon juice to the soup; simmer, uncovered, 10 minutes. Add the spaghetti. Continue to cook until the spaghetti is tender, about 12 minutes longer.

5. Meanwhile, cut the beef into slices; remove the meat from the beef bone; and remove the meat from the chicken, discarding the skin and bones.

6. When the spaghetti is tender, add the beef, chicken, and spinach to the soup. Cook 5 minutes longer. Add salt and pepper to taste. Serve with Sauce de Sorges.

Serves 6 to 8 as a main course.

The spinach plant is a rather aggressive member of the goosefoot family, whose other members include Swiss chard and beets. Spinach grows on spines which resemble a webbed biped—or at least they did to some unnamed naturalist's eye. Out of that association the veg's moniker might have been "goose-green," and in fact the British called it that for a time in the twelfth century to show their distaste for the rash of Frenchifications that had entered their language. Somewhat later they relented and allowed the Francophile *épinard* to become the Anglo-Saxon *spynoches*, which in time was trimmed to mere spinach—which is a blessing for a man who makes his grocery list on his shirt cuff.

Armenians call spinach *spanax*. Germans dub it *Spinat*. But it's really best abbreviated: *spnch!*

Sauce de Sorges
(Herbal Mayonnaise)

1 egg
1 teaspoon Dijon mustard
Pinch of salt
1 tablespoon white wine vinegar
¾ cup olive or vegetable oil
1 tablespoon heavy or whipping cream
2 small shallots, minced
2 teaspoons capers
2 to 3 tablespoons chopped fresh dill

1. Boil the egg for 3 minutes. Shell the egg, and carefully scoop the soft yolk into a small bowl. Chop the white and set it aside.

2. To the egg yolk, add the mustard, salt, and vinegar. Slowly beat in the oil, then thin with the cream. The sauce should be the texture of a thin mayonnaise. Stir in the egg white, shallots, capers, and dill.

Makes about 1 cup.

WARM GOAT CHEESE AND SPINACH SALAD

On any occasion, a spinach salad is the better for a thorough washing of the greens first. Though its invention is definitely a result of that treacherous trip through Colorado's mountains, this dish also owes a debt to the green cuisine of my Californian friend, Wolfgang Puck, owner and chef at the restaurant Spago.

½ pound fresh goat cheese (chèvre)
¾ cup olive oil
1 teaspoon chopped fresh thyme, or ⅛ teaspoon dried
1 pound fresh spinach
1 teaspoon Dijon mustard
1 teaspoon chopped fresh tarragon, or ¼ teaspoon dried
1 tablespoon hazelnut liqueur
2 teaspoons tarragon vinegar
1 egg yolk
¼ teaspoon salt
Freshly ground black pepper
3 strips crisp-fried bacon, crumbled

1. Cut the goat cheese into eight equal pieces. Place them in a shallow bowl, and drizzle with ¼ cup of the oil. Sprinkle with the thyme. Cover, and refrigerate overnight.

2. Remove the goat cheese from the refrigerator 1 hour before serving.

3. Trim the stems from the spinach, wash the leaves well, and tear them into bite-size pieces. With paper towels, gently squeeze out the excess liquid. Place the spinach in a large bowl.

4. In a medium bowl, whisk the mustard with the tarragon, liqueur, vinegar, egg yolk, and salt. Slowly whisk in the remaining ½ cup oil. Add pepper to taste. Pour this dressing over the salad and toss well.

5. Place 2 tablespoons of the oil marinade from the cheese in a large heavy skillet over medium heat. When hot but not smoking, add the cheese pieces, lifting them out of the remaining marinade with a slotted spoon. Sauté 30 seconds per side. Add the cheese to the salad, and sprinkle with the bacon.

Serves 4.

SPINACH WITH SESAME SEED DRESSING

One diet food I dearly dote upon is a spinach salad. Everyone knows the bacon, egg, and Parmesan cheese version, but few are acquainted with an equally brilliant spinach salad that is a Japanese invention: spinach cooked and then sluiced with soy sauce and sesame seeds. The recipe is one given to me by Elizabeth Andoh, author of *At Home with Japanese Cooking*. It's terrific.

1 pound fresh spinach, washed, stems trimmed
3 tablespoons sesame seeds
2 tablespoons superfine sugar
2½ tablespoons soy sauce

1. Cook the spinach leaves in boiling water until just wilted, about 30 seconds. Rinse under cold running water, drain well, and chop coarsely.

2. Heat a large heavy skillet over medium-high heat. Add the sesame seeds and cook, shaking the pan constantly, until they are lightly browned. Transfer the seeds to a small bowl or mortar and crush them with a heavy wooden spoon or pestle until finely ground. Add the sugar and continue to grind. Stir in the soy sauce.

3. Toss the spinach with the dressing in a serving bowl. Serve chilled or at room temperature.

Serves 2 to 4.

FOUR-DAY SPINACH

This spinach out-take is of Russian descent, and a number worthy of some czar's kitchen. It is a curious but fabled rendition: spinach that is seasoned with only butter and vodka and cooked, then set aside, then enriched and cooked again, over a period of ninety-six hours. The recipe is from Phillip Schulz's excellently spirited cookbook, *Vodka 'n Vittles*.

2 pounds fresh spinach, washed, stems trimmed
1 cup (2 sticks) unsalted butter
5 teaspoons vodka
2 teaspoons lemon juice
1/8 teaspoon freshly grated nutmeg
Salt and freshly ground black pepper

1. Heat 4 quarts of salted water to boiling. Turn off the heat and stir in the spinach. Let it stand 2 minutes, then rinse under cold running water and drain. Gently squeeze the spinach to remove excess liquid. Roughly chop.

2. Melt 4 tablespoons of the butter in a medium saucepan over low heat. Add the spinach. Cook, stirring constantly, until all the butter has been absorbed into the spinach and the spinach is warmed through. Sprinkle with 1 teaspoon of the vodka. Transfer the spinach to a bowl and allow it to cool. Cover, and chill 24 hours.

3. The next day, heat the spinach in another 4 tablespoons of the butter. Cook, stirring constantly, until all the butter has been absorbed and the spinach is warmed through. Sprinkle with another 1 teaspoon of the vodka. Transfer to a bowl, cool, cover, and chill 24 hours.

4. Repeat this process again on the third day.

5. On the fourth day, repeat the process once more. When the spinach is warmed through, add the remaining 2 teaspoons vodka, the lemon juice, nutmeg, and salt and pepper to taste. Serve immediately.

Serves 4.

SPINACH AND COCONUT MORUGA

One of the most unusual spinach devises in my file stems from the Caribbean island of Trinidad, where it is most often served up with hard-cooked eggs after a long church service. Not a lunch or dinner dish, it might be considered something between a snack and a repast. At my table it accompanies broiled chicken or a grilled chop.

One point worth noting: in the recipe I acquired, coconut milk was the sole liquid. Since fresh coconuts often are hard to come by outside of an island paradise, I modified the ingredients and made a "milk" all my own. It's delicious and a jot more practical.

1 can (3½ ounces) sweetened coconut
1 cup milk
3 tablespoons unsalted butter
¼ teaspoon crushed dried hot red peppers
¼ teaspoon salt
⅓ cup chopped macadamia nuts
10 ounces fresh spinach, washed, stems trimmed, roughly chopped

1. Combine the coconut with the milk in the container of a blender or processor. Blend until fairly smooth. Strain the coconut into a small bowl. Skim the surface of the milk, reserving ½ cup milk.

2. Melt 2 tablespoons of the butter in a small skillet over medium heat. Stir in the peppers, salt, and macadamia nuts. Cook, stirring constantly, until the nuts are lightly browned, about 4 minutes. Stir in the strained coconut. Continue to cook, stirring constantly, 3 minutes. Remove from the heat.

3. Melt the remaining 1 tablespoon butter in a medium saucepan over medium heat. Add the spinach and reserved ½ cup coconut milk. Cook, tossing constantly, until the spinach is wilted, about 5 minutes. Raise the heat slightly and continue to cook until almost all liquid has evaporated. Stir in the coconut–macadamia nut mixture.

Serves 4.

GNOCCHI TICINESE

This version of gnocchi stems from the Swiss Italian Alps—the canton of Ticino, to be exact. It is a province far to the north of Milan, where cheese making is the way of life. Not surprising to discover, then, that there gnocchi are a mixture of nothing but spinach and ricotta cheese. An unbelievably delicate devise, this recipe was passed on to me by a wonderfully talented writer and cook from Elmira, New York: Mary Cassetti.

10 ounces fresh spinach, washed, trimmed of stems
1 pound ricotta cheese
1 large egg, beaten
¼ teaspoon freshly grated nutmeg
¾ cup grated Jarlsberg cheese
¼ cup freshly grated Romano cheese
½ cup all-purpose flour
1 cup heavy or whipping cream
¼ cup freshly grated Parmesan cheese

1. Cook the spinach in boiling water for 4 minutes. Drain, and gently squeeze out the excess liquid. Place the spinach in the container of a food processor and add the ricotta cheese. Process 10 seconds. Add the egg, nutmeg, Jarlsberg cheese, Romano cheese, and flour. Process until mixed.

2. With floured hands form the dough into small balls or ovals and place them on a plate. Cover, and chill for 24 hours.

3. The next day, drop the gnocchi, about 6 at a time, into boiling salted water until they rise to the top. Remove with a slotted spoon and drain lightly on paper towels. Transfer to a well-buttered baking dish. When all the gnocchi are done, reheat in a 300°F oven for 12 minutes.

4. Meanwhile, heat the cream to boiling in a small saucepan. Simmer until thickened, about 5 minutes. Pour the cream over the gnocchi and sprinkle with the Parmesan cheese.

Serves 8.

GNOCCHI SPINACIO

(Spinach Dumplings)

In Italy dishes that are dappled green with spinach are usually dubbed Florentine this or Florentine that on menus. I never knew why until I drove to this Renaissance city on the Arno and saw the mountainsides nearby covered with a delicate plant, which I took to be myrtle but was actually spinach. *Spinacio* grows like a weed in Florence in the springtime.

Naturally enough the vegetable is shipped to other areas of the boot and flavors varied Italian dishes. These Roman *gnocchi* are potato dumplings fused with spinach. Each forkful is as light as a cloud.

6 ounces fresh spinach, washed, trimmed of stems, chopped
2 eggs
½ cup all-purpose flour
1¼ cups cold cooked mashed potatoes
¼ teaspoon freshly grated nutmeg
½ teaspoon salt
3 tablespoons freshly grated Parmesan cheese
Ground white pepper

1. Place the spinach with just the water that clings to the leaves in a medium saucepan. Cover, and cook over medium-low heat until very tender, about 10 minutes. Remove from the heat, drain, gently squeeze out the excess liquid, and cool.

2. Beat the eggs in a large bowl until light. Beat in the spinach, flour, mashed potatoes, nutmeg, salt, and Parmesan cheese. Mix thoroughly. Add white pepper to taste.

3. Scoop up the dough with a spoon, 1 tablespoon at a time, and drop into boiling salted water. Do no more than 6 gnocchi at one time. Let simmer until firm, about 1½ minutes. Remove with a slotted spoon and drain lightly on paper towels. Transfer to a well-buttered baking dish. When all the gnocchi are done, reheat in a 300°F oven for about 12 minutes. Serve with extra Parmesan cheese if desired.

Serves 4.

GREEN CREAMED RICE

To my mind, the classic spinach rendering is always enveloped in cream and delicately scented with nutmeg. My favorite such alliance is also fortified with cooked rice. The originator is a good cook named Gail Firestone, though I doubt she would now recognize her creation. Things have a way of changing at my stove.

⅔ cup long-grain rice
1 pound fresh spinach, washed, stems trimmed
¼ teaspoon crushed dried hot red peppers
1 cup hot milk
4 tablespoons (½ stick) unsalted butter
2 tablespoons all-purpose flour
½ cup heavy or whipping cream
1 teaspoon honey
⅛ teaspoon freshly grated nutmeg
Salt and freshly ground black pepper

1. Add the rice to a large pot of boiling salted water; stir once while the water returns to boiling. Simmer over medium heat until the rice is just tender, about 12 minutes. Drain in a colander. Place the colander over simmering water and cover with a layer of paper towels. Let the rice steam for 15 minutes or longer.

2. Place the spinach with just the water that clings to the leaves in a large skillet. Sprinkle with the crushed red peppers. Cover, and cook over medium-low heat until the spinach is wilted, about 5 minutes. Place the spinach in the container of a blender or food processor; add ¼ cup of the milk. Blend until smooth. Set aside.

3. Melt 2 tablespoons of the butter in a medium saucepan over medium-low heat. Stir in the flour. Cook, stirring constantly, 2 minutes. Whisk in the remaining ¾ cup milk and the cream. Add the honey and nutmeg. Heat to boiling; reduce the heat. Simmer until slightly thickened, about 5 minutes. Add the spinach; cook 3 minutes.

4. Combine the spinach mixture with the cooked rice. Mix well. Add salt and pepper to taste, and cut in the remaining 2 tablespoons butter.

Serves 4.

SANTA FE SPINACH AND BEAN BAKE

Because of its Mideastern heritage, spinach is largely aligned to exotic dishes and dark, long-cooked brews. However, it is an ingredient that has adapted itself to other environments. Here, for example, is a "Tex-Mex" casserole of beans and peppers out of Sante Fe.

½ pound dried pinto beans
3 strips bacon, chopped
1 large onion, finely chopped
1 clove garlic, minced
1 small hot red pepper, seeded, deveined, minced (see Guacamole headnote, page 37)
10 ounces fresh spinach, washed, stems trimmed, chopped
2 tablespoons mild ground chiles
1 teaspoon salt
¼ pound Monterey jack cheese with jalapeño peppers
¼ cup beef broth (see page 414)

1. Cook the beans in boiling salted water until tender, 1½ to 2 hours. Drain.

2. Preheat the oven to 400°F. Sauté the bacon in a medium skillet over medium heat until crisp. Add the onion; cook 1 minute. Add the garlic and hot pepper; cook 3 minutes. Stir in the spinach and continue to cook, stirring constantly, until the spinach is wilted, about 5 minutes. Stir in the ground chiles, salt, the cooked beans, cheese, and beef broth. Pour into a baking dish. Bake 20 minutes.

Serves 6.

LONG ISLAND BANK ROLL

This is a recent creation of mine: spinach-and-shrimp-stuffed fish filets, named in memory of palmy days at The Store in Amagansett.

1 cup clam juice
1 cup dry white wine
1 slice lemon
1 teaspoon fennel seeds, tied in a cheesecloth bag
6 raw shrimp, shelled and deveined
1 cup roughly chopped fresh spinach, washed and trimmed first
2 shallots, minced
1 tablespoon chopped fresh basil, or 1 teaspoon dried
4 flounder filets, about ¼ pound each
1 tablespoon unsalted butter
1 medium cucumber, peeled, seeded, finely chopped
1 sprig fresh thyme, chopped, or a pinch of dried
2 teaspoons lemon juice
⅓ cup sour cream
Salt and freshly ground black pepper

1. Heat the clam juice, wine, lemon slice, and fennel seeds to boiling in a heavy enameled skillet; reduce the heat. Simmer 5 minutes.

2. Chop 2 of the shrimp and place them in a medium-size bowl. Add the spinach, half of the minced shallots, and the basil. Mix well and spread over the fish filets. Roll the filets up lengthwise. Place the filets in the skillet and poach, covered, in the liquid for 3 minutes. Turn the fish over and add the whole shrimp to the pan. Cook, uncovered, until the fish flakes easily and the shrimp are pink, about 4 minutes. Transfer the fish to a serving platter and keep warm in a low oven. Reserve the shrimp.

3. Melt the butter in a small saucepan over medium-low heat. Add the remaining minced shallot; cook 2 minutes. Add all the remaining ingredients; cook without boiling for 4 minutes. Spoon this sauce over the fish and decorate with the whole shrimp.

Serves 2 to 4.

SPINACH-AND-RICE-STUFFED CHICKEN

3- to 3½-pound roasting chicken
Salt and freshly ground black pepper
2 tablespoons unsalted butter, plus 1 tablespoon softened
1 shallot, minced
2 tablespoons all-purpose flour
½ cup hot chicken broth (see page 414)
½ cup heavy or whipping cream
½ cup chopped cooked ham
1 cup cooked rice
10 ounces fresh spinach, washed, stems trimmed, chopped
½ teaspoon freshly grated nutmeg
1 teaspoon lemon juice
1 clove garlic, bruised

1. Preheat the oven to 375°F. Rinse the chicken and pat it dry with paper towels. Sprinkle the chicken inside and out with salt and pepper to taste.

2. Melt the 2 tablespoons butter in a medium saucepan over medium-low heat. Add the shallot; cook 3 minutes. Add the flour; cook, stirring constantly, 2 minutes. Whisk in the broth and cream. Heat the mixture to boiling, stirring constantly until very thick. Remove from the heat and stir in the ham, rice, spinach, nutmeg, and lemon juice. Mix thoroughly.

3. Stuff the chicken with the spinach-rice mixture. Sew up the cavity securely so the stuffing will not leak out. Truss.

4. Rub the chicken with the garlic and softened butter. Roast on a rack for 20 minutes. Reduce the heat to 350°F and continue to roast, basting occasionally with pan juices, until juices run yellow when pricked with a fork, about 1 hour longer.

Serves 2 to 4.

ISFANAKH FATIRA

(Spinach Pancake)

Speaking, as I was, of things Mideastern—here's the real thing: a wondrous pale green spinach-and-egg pancake. Neither *frittata*, *piperade*, nor *crêpe*, it is a reminder of all three on the tongue. I serve it for brunch sluiced with sour cream; Persians choose yogurt, so you be the judge. It is easy as the dickens to make and (unlike its Arabic forebears) permits a slice of bacon alongside.

4 tablespoons (½ stick) unsalted butter
4 scallions, bulbs and green tops, chopped
¼ cup chopped fresh parsley
½ pound spinach, washed, trimmed of stems, chopped
3 eggs
Salt and freshly ground black pepper
Sour cream or yogurt

1. Melt 3 tablespoons of the butter in a medium skillet over medium-low heat. Add the scallions and chopped parsley. Cook, stirring constantly, 2 minutes. Add the spinach and cook, covered, until the spinach starts to wilt, about 5 minutes. Remove the cover and continue to cook, stirring occasionally, 20 minutes.

2. Beat the eggs in a large bowl until light. Beat in the spinach mixture. Add salt and pepper to taste.

3. Melt the remaining 1 tablespoon butter in a 10-inch heavy skillet over medium heat. Pour in the spinach mixture. Cook, covered, 10 minutes.

4. Loosen the edges of the pancake with a spatula and turn it out onto a serving platter. Serve with sour cream or yogurt.

Serves 2 to 4.

SQUASH
A True American Original

Neither my mother nor my father was an animal lover, which probably explains why both my sister and I are.

To be fair, Father was something of a pushover for puppies, and from time to time he would manage to sneak some small furry orphan into our home. Unerringly not housebroken, this stray creature would be allowed a limited tenancy (the back steps or the cellar) until my mother declared it had gotten under foot too often. Then it would disappear, either under its own steam or by way of my mother's "open door" policy.

Her attitude toward animals not in her possession was exceedingly tolerant. She loved our four-footed friends, or so she claimed, but felt that enforced domesticity was a burden that robbed an animal of its right to pursue happiness where and with whom it chose.

"Animals should be free!" Mother would discourse airily. What she really meant was that humans should be freed of the obligation of caring for them.

When I became an adult and collected first a cat, then a dog and eventually two more in quick succession, my mother professed amazement.

"I never knew you were such a Saint Francis," she remarked pointedly after a car ride with my menagerie. "You certainly never showed any such inclination when you were a kid!"

Mother had a short memory. Mine is longer.

I recall a snub-nosed terrier pup that was a gift from my father when he felt such responsibility would be character-building for his son. My mother dismissed that theory as cant.

"You can't learn anything from a nervous dog," she announced at breakfast one morning, "and that dog is *neurasthenic.* It cried all night long! I say when he gets to know us better, he'll bark all day as well!"

She was right. Fluffy yelped constantly. To keep his high-pitched cries out of my mother's earshot, I attached him to a long rope which gave him access to our yard but kept him tethered to the cellar doorknob, away from the areas of the house where my mother held her bridge games or played the piano.

Neurotic or no, Fluffy hated the restraint and neither his barking nor his crying diminished. One afternoon when I returned from school, the rope was still attached to the doorknob but Fluffy was decidedly *not* at the opposite end.

When I rushed inside to inform my mother he had gotten loose, she was utterly insentient.

"The dog did not seem to be happy here," she explained. "So I gave him a test and loosened the rope. If Fluffy hung around, we'd have known he wanted to be with us. Right?"

The first family dog I can remember was called Tootsie. She was a poodle with bad breath and a mane of dun- to rust-colored ringlets that obscured her vision considerably. Tootsie was not lovable: she too barked a good deal, and she pushed her face into one's lap at awkward moments, but I loved her dearly.

Tootsie's end was tragic. Allowed to roam loose (by my mother, of course) she was hit by a passing vehicle not far from our house. Discretion led my family to shield me from this scene of carnage but I made my way there despite them.

Tootsie had been so flattened by the impact that a policeman was forced to shoot her—as I watched. It was my first encounter with the inevitable and horrifying. I returned home in hysterics, screaming, "Squashed. Tootsie was squashed!"

My mother, who had been sitting at the kitchen table composing a grocery list for dinner, attended to my grief solicitously, drying my tears between each new outburst as I screamed, "Squashed! She was squashed!"

My mother's patience must have been tried by these ear-splitting wails, for she rose at last and went back to the table.

"Now, that's enough," she stated with finality. "Tootsie may have been squashed on earth but she is whole again in heaven. And there is absolutely nothing else we can do for her."

Her tone silenced me at last and I watched through reddened eyes as she picked up her grocery list again, penciling in an addition to her inventory.

I could read the word upside down: ɥsɐnbS. My mother was a lady who made fast word associations, you see.

Vegetable Roots

The word *squash* is actually a "cut down," abbreviated by the Pilgrims who had a difficult time with the tongue-twisting Indian name for this gourd. The Narragansetts called it *askutasquash*, the Iroquois, *isquoutersquash* and the Algonquins, *askoot*. All of which have precisely the same meaning: "something that is eaten raw." Curiously, it was the first dish the Indians taught the settlers how to cook!

Squash is decidedly a native American food, and an old one to boot. Stems, rinds, and seeds found in the Ocampo Caves in Mexico's Tamaulipas mountains date this gourd's appearance in a local pot to about 3000 B.C. Ancient Indian peoples called squash "the apple of God," since its seeds were believed to increase fertility when planted in close proximity. Braves with large squash crops inevitably produced large families, which in turn led to larger crops.

The earliest American colonists obviously had small knowledge of squash's potential fruitfulness for they never cultivated the plant at all, considering its size "uncivilized to contemplate." Evidently they did not appreciate the vegetable's flavor either, as few recipes for its preparation (aside from "pompion pie") survive. However, a dubious beauty tip does: the following advice from a bride's book written by Elisabeth Skinner in Roanoke, Virginia, dated 1611.

> The seeds [of certain squash] pounded with meale and their own sweet iuyces . . . doth beautifie the face, for it taketh away freckles and al spottes . . . if the place be well rubbed with it—in the sonne's light.

All squash are Cucurbitaceae but there are two distinct branches to the family tree. *Cucurbita pepo* (yellow crookneck and straightneck, patty pan, zucchini, and pumpkin too) are known as summer squash, though in point of fact most supermarkets carry these varieties year round. *Cucurbita maxima* (acorn, butternut, chayote, Hubbard, spaghetti squash, and turban) are winter squash. They too are available much of the year.

Summer Squash

What to Look For

Summer squash have different names and assorted shapes, but when you come right down to it, most are very similar in flavor and may be used interchangeably in a recipe without any noticeable alteration to the finished dish. Zucchini, a stand-out summer variety, has its own chapter in this book, but you might want to check those recipes, too, for further interchanges.

Among *yellow squash*, there are two familiar types: crookneck and straightneck. The pear-shaped crookneck has a long furled throat and creamy yellow pulp. Straightneck is somewhat plumper and grainier in texture, with whiter pulp. When buying either, look for the smallest and firmest available. Fresh yellow squash bruises easily. A sure way to judge its state of vitality is to scrape the surface with a fingernail. If there is resistance, pass it by. *Patty pan*, also known as cymling, is a disk-shaped squash with a pretty scalloped edge. Patty pan are best picked young and no wider in circumference than an English muffin. Look for this variety to be a light apple-green shade; patty pans whiten as they mature, so a chalky-looking one will usually have a pulpy interior, not to mention a decided lack of flavor.

Preparation

Summer squash requires very little kitchen "prep" prior to the stove. I never peel a yellow squash because I always bring home the tiniest I can find and they don't require it. I never wash them either. Unless a squash is really dirty, a fast wipe with a dampened paper towel will usually suffice. Farm-picked squash may require a sluice of cold water but do *not* presoak this vegetable please; too much liquid breaks down the cell structure. I hardly ever salt a summer squash before I cook it. Salting releases a measure of the vegetable's excessive moisture and some cooks claim that this facilitates even cooking, but unfortunately it also wilts the flesh in the process, turning crisp slices sodden in no time at all. There is one exception to my no-salt rule. When I shred squash I find that a very light salting (plus a stint in the colander) will shorten the cooking time. I never blanch or parboil summer squash, as it is watery to begin with. I most often braise or sauté this vegetable in its own juices with only a pat of butter or a speck of bacon drippings to temper the saucepan. Quick cooking over moderately high heat just prior to serving dispels the excess liquid nicely. With few exceptions, the aim in cooking summer squash is to achieve a crisp *al dente* texture. At least when Greene is at the stove.

Pumpkin

What to Look For

Pumpkin, although botanically listed as summer squash, is available only in the fall. Since it has a texture and physiognomy in common with winter squash, I tend to think of it as a "pre-winter" variety.

Although it has something of an abbreviated season in the marketplace, pumpkin lasts much, much longer than one would suspect, particularly if the globe is unsullied and the storage temperature low enough. Pumpkin pundits claim this squash will stay best on a bed of straw or hung in a mesh bag to allow air to freely circulate about its girth. Do not take that as gospel, however. I have had a pumpkin sitting in the cool hallway of my house for the past five months, without any sign of wear or tear yet.

Preparation

The biggest problem with pumpkin is getting at the tender flesh inside. The prospect of carving and cooking a pumpkin is so overwhelming that most kitchen practitioners reach for a can instead of a carving knife. But don't!

The easiest way to cut up a pumpkin (according to my friend Sandra Silfven of the *Detroit News*) is to pretend it's an orange. First, Sandy sets a pumpkin on its side on a cutting board and slices straight across the stem end. Then she cuts straight across the bottom end too, so the darn thing will sit upright. Following the curve of the globe, she slides her knife under the skin and pares it from top to bottom before cutting it in half and scooping out the strings (and saving the seeds for roasting later). Once she has a peeled pumpkin, she steams, boils, or bakes it until the flesh is tender.

For pumpkin purée my trick is a jot less surgical. After cutting the unpeeled pumpkin in half and scraping out the seeds and strings, I place the halves in a buttered pan, shell sides up, and simply bake it in a 325°F oven. The baking time depends upon a pumpkin's size of course, but an hour usually will do the trick. When it is done the pumpkin shell begins to fall in and the pulp is very tender. After it cools, I scrape out the pulp and process or blend it until it is very smooth. For the record: a medium-size pumpkin (2 to 2½ pounds) will yield enough pulp for one pie (1½ cups).

Winter Squash

Winter squash, to many Americans, is an unknown quantity. While hundreds of varieties are grown, most never

make their way beyond the farm stand or specialty greengrocer because chary product managers at supermarkets give shelf space only to those with proven track records at the check-out counter.

The winter squash's common denominator is a rough-silk texture within—after it is cooked—and a hard protective shell without. Unlike their summer counterparts, winter squash have very separate and distinct flavors. And while a cooked acorn squash might conceivably stand in for pumpkin in a pie shell at Thanksgiving dinner, there would be a discernible difference on the tongue.

What to Look For

When buying winter squash, large size is never a deterrent; in the matter of the gigantic Hubbard squash, bulk indicates a long stay on the vine and the squash will inevitably be sweeter for it.

Happily for the consumer, winter varieties like green *acorn* squash, tan *butternut* squash, and gaily striped *turban* squash all *keep*. That is to say, any one may be stored in a cool dry area for months or even a year without fear of spoilage. Sharp-eyed shoppers will look for winter squash that are smooth to the touch and brightly complexioned. A deep exterior shade (even when the skin is naturally mottled) is usually an indication that the interior flesh will be dry and sweet. *Spaghetti* squash is the sole exception to this rule: the sweetest of those are always a very pale yellow. Winter squash should be weighty. A light acorn squash will not be more tender, merely dehydrated. So go for the heavyweights every time!

Preparation

Essentially I cook winter squash three basic ways: I bake it, braise it, or boil it (sometimes stuffing it as well). Baked halved squash is rather a plus for the cook as it goes straight from the oven to the table, eliminating the problem of serving dishes. It's good besides! I halve squash either lengthwise or at the midriff depending upon its size, and scoop out any stringy fiber and seeds. Squash seeds (like pumpkin seeds) should be saved. They are really quite tasty seasoned and/or salted and dry-roasted in a low oven for several hours.

If I am serving baked acorn squash, I slice a small section from the rounded bottom so it will sit felicitously in my baking pan. Seasoning is optional, but butter is a necessity to an acorn squash. I place mine in a pan and add an inch of water to keep the vegetable moist. Then I bake it, cut side up of course, in a preheated 350°F oven for about 45 minutes to an hour.

The one *Cucurbita maxima* I always boil is spaghetti squash. This hybrid is a relative newcomer to the kitchen. A so-called winter squash (it actually blooms from early October to mid-December), spaghetti squash came originally from Italy. It was hybridized in Japan but then developed in America during the past century and grows best in a semi-dry climate. This squash has a hard shell and considerable girth; the average size is between two and three pounds. Its football shape makes it appear to be more of a candidate for the Super Bowl than the serving dish, but nothing could be further from the truth.

The special virtue of spaghetti squash is its delectable fleshy interior. When boiled (30 to 45 minutes depending upon its size), halved, and seeded, the squash unravels into an enormous quantity of pasta-like strands that are the exact circumference and translucent shade of *capelli d'angelo* (angel-hair noodles) but a hundred times less caloric on a fork end.

However, spaghetti squash is *not* pasta. Strong tomato sauce or garlic overwhelms its tenuous flavor.

NATIVE AMERICAN BOUILLABAISSE

(Summer Squash and Seafood Soup)

According to food historians, one of the first foods that the Narragansett Indians shared with the Pilgrims of Plymouth Rock was a chowder composed of seafood and squash. However, those starchy folk (as narrow in their dining habits as in their morals) refused to sample a spoonful. After the Indians left, they fed the soup to their pigs, dubbing it "the meanest of God's blessings."

My version of the pottage comes with a brand-new name and an age-old benediction: "Praise the Lord for he is good and his mercy endureth forever."

¼ cup olive oil
1 leek, trimmed, washed, chopped
2 whole scallions, bulbs and green tops, trimmed, chopped
2 cloves garlic, minced
2 ribs celery, finely chopped
1 small green bell pepper, finely chopped
1¼ pounds summer squash, trimmed, grated
1 teaspoon chopped fresh thyme, or ¼ teaspoon dried
¼ cup chopped fresh basil, or 2 tablespoons dried (chop with the parsley)
¼ cup chopped fresh parsley
1 teaspoon fennel seeds
Pinch of saffron
6 cups Fish Stock (see page 410)
Salt and freshly ground black pepper
1½ pounds mussels
¼ teaspoon cornstarch
1 large red snapper, cleaned
1 pound flounder filets
½ pound bay scallops
1 pound shrimp, shelled, deveined (use shells in stock)
Aioli (recipe follows)

1. Heat the oil in a large heavy saucepan over medium-low heat. Add the leek and scallions; cook 2 minutes. Add the garlic, celery, and green pepper. Cook, uncovered, 5 minutes. Stir in the squash, thyme, basil, parsley, fennel seeds, saffron, and fish stock. Heat to boiling; reduce the heat. Simmer, uncovered, 30 minutes. Add salt and pepper to taste.

2. Meanwhile, scrub the mussels and place them in a large pot of cold water with the cornstarch (this will cause the mussels to effectively clean themselves). Let stand 15 minutes, then wash under cold running water and set aside. Cut the snapper into 1-inch-wide pieces. Cut the flounder into pieces.

3. Add all the seafood to the bouillabaisse. Cook, covered, until the fish flakes and the mussels are open, 5 to 8 minutes.

4. To serve: spoon some of the soup liquid into serving bowls; add seafood to each bowl. Add about 1 teaspoon aioli to each bowl as well, and pass the remaining aioli.

Serves 6.

Aioli

(Garlic Mayonnaise)

1 slice stale homemade white bread, or 2 slices French bread, ½ inch thick
3 tablespoons milk
6 cloves garlic, crushed
1 egg yolk, at room temperature
¼ teaspoon salt
1 cup vegetable oil
½ cup olive oil
3 tablespoons boiling water
2 to 3 tablespoons lemon juice

1. Trim the crusts from the bread and break the bread into pieces in a small bowl. Add the milk; let stand 10 minutes. Place the milk-soaked bread in the corner of a clean tea towel and squeeze it dry. Transfer the bread to a large bowl.

2. Add the garlic to the bread and pound them together with the back of a heavy spoon or a pestle until very smooth. Pound in the egg yolk and salt.

3. Whisk in the oils, a drop at a time, until the mixture thickens; then slowly whisk in the remaining oil, 3 tablespoons at a time, until smooth. Whisk in the boiling water, and lemon juice to taste. Refrigerate, tightly covered, until ready to use.

Makes 2 cups.

The American Indians of colonial times lived on a fairly spartan diet—squash, beans, and corn—which they supplemented in summer with berries and greens and in winter with wild fowl or fish. Unfortunately the winged and finned denizens were not always eaten fresh, so the Indians developed worms from the change of diet. As a worm expellant, they chewed squash seeds. And while there is only folklore and hearsay to document the cure, the high degree of potassium and ascorbic acid in a summer squash might just have done the trick!

KATE'S PAN-FRIED SUMMER SQUASH

Kate's pan-fried squash is a dispensation from Nathalie Dupree's Southern kitchen. Kate Almand is her factotum wherever Nathalie teaches—and in her own right one of the best down-home cooks below the Mason-Dixon line. Or above it for that matter. Kate's summer squash, despite my earlier injunction about fast cookery, is "sweated" in a skillet for over half an hour. But remarkable for every second on the fire.

1½ pounds yellow summer squash, trimmed, sliced
1 cup chicken broth (see page 414)
1 medium onion, thinly sliced
½ teaspoon salt
¼ teaspoon freshly ground black pepper
3 tablespoons fatback or fatty bacon drippings
3 tablespoons unsalted butter

1. Combine the squash, chicken broth, onion, salt, and pepper in a large skillet. Heat to boiling; reduce the heat to medium. Cook, uncovered, stirring frequently, until all liquid has evaporated, about 10 minutes.

2. Add the fatback or bacon drippings and the butter to the squash. Cook, uncovered, stirring occasionally, over low heat, 30 minutes longer.

Serves 4 to 6.

SUMMER SQUASH IN TARRAGON CREAM

Summer squash is what I deem a mutable vegetable. Pair it with a stronger flavor and rather than losing its own identity, it becomes fortified (and enriched) by the alliance.

3 tablespoons unsalted butter
1 large shallot, minced
1 pound summer squash, trimmed, sliced
⅔ cup heavy or whipping cream
1 teaspoon chopped fresh tarragon
Salt and freshly ground black pepper
Chopped fresh parsley

Melt the butter in a large heavy skillet over medium-low heat. Add the shallot; cook 1 minute. Add the squash and cook, uncovered, tossing constantly, 3 minutes. Add the cream. Heat to boiling; reduce the heat. Simmer over medium heat, 5 minutes. Stir in the tarragon; cook 5 minutes longer. Add salt and pepper to taste and sprinkle with the parsley.

Serves 4.

MUCVER
(Turkish Squash Cakes)

From the Pilgrims on, summer squash has had its detractors. When this vegetable crossed the Atlantic to England in the late seventeenth century it was known as "harrow marrow," for only cattle would eat it. The French were no better; when the famed geese of Strasbourg choked on summer squash seeds, they gave the entire vegetable a bad name, calling it *malmain* ("bad hand").

Only the Turks consumed summer squash with any relish. They reputedly acquired a taste for it when a ship bound for Russia with a cargo of fodder in the hold sank in the harbor at Constantinople. All hands were lost but the squash floated across the isthmus and took root. Fact or fiction is utterly beside the point: squash certainly became part of the Middle Eastern diet shortly afterward. For further evidence, try these delicate squash and cheese fritters.

½ pound crookneck squash (about 2 small), trimmed, grated
2 tablespoons crumbled feta cheese
2 tablespoons ricotta cheese
2 tablespoons finely chopped fresh dill
2 tablespoons finely chopped fresh mint
1 tablespoon finely chopped fresh parsley
¼ teaspoon salt, plus extra to taste
⅛ teaspoon freshly ground black pepper
1 egg, lightly beaten
½ cup all-purpose flour
Oil for frying

1. Combine the squash, cheeses, dill, mint, parsley, salt, and pepper in a bowl. Add the egg and flour; mix thoroughly.

2. Heat ¾ inch of oil in a heavy skillet until hot but not smoking. Drop rounded tablespoons of the mixture, a few at a time, into the oil. Fry until golden, about 2 minutes per side. Drain on paper towels. Sprinkle with salt to taste before serving.

Makes 8 to 10; serves 4.

SQUASH AND SAUSAGE RATATOUILLE

Though summer squash is as American as you can get, my classic rendering for this vegetable is totally European. It is a devise for a provincial *ratatouille* minus the traditional ingredients and the slow cooking process. Unorthodox? Unchauvinistic? Certainly. Delectable? You bet. Serve it with a good crusty loaf to soak up the juices.

2 tablespoons olive oil
1 small onion, chopped
1 clove garlic, minced
¾ pound sweet Italian sausage, sliced into ⅛-inch-thick rounds
1 pound yellow summer squash, trimmed, sliced into ⅛-inch-thick rounds
1 medium green Italian frying pepper, seeded, cut into thin rounds
1 tablespoon red wine vinegar
Salt and freshly ground black pepper

1. Heat the oil in a large heavy skillet over medium-low heat. Add the onion; cook 1 minute. Add the garlic; cook 4 minutes longer. Stir in the sausage slices. Cook, stirring frequently, until well browned, about 12 minutes. Using a slotted spoon, transfer the mixture to a plate.

2. Pour off all but 3 tablespoons fat from the skillet. (If there is not enough fat, add butter to compensate.) Add the squash and Italian pepper. Cook, tossing frequently, until tender, about 10 minutes.

3. Return the sausage mixture to the skillet, stirring well. Cook, covered, over medium-high heat for 5 minutes. Remove the cover and sprinkle the mixture with the vinegar. Cook, uncovered, stirring constantly, 3 minutes longer. Add salt and pepper to taste.

Serves 4.

MARILYN HARRIS' SUMMER SQUASH CASSEROLE

Another summer squash endowment (baked) is a gift from a great Midwestern kitchen, Marilyn Harris's to be specific. This wonderful cook teams the ingredient with cream, white wine, and cheese. The result is a delight!

4½ tablespoons unsalted butter
1 small onion, finely chopped
1 pound summer squash, trimmed, sliced ⅛ inch thick
½ cup grated Monterey jack cheese
1 egg, lightly beaten
½ cup sour cream
2 tablespoons dry white wine or vermouth
½ teaspoon salt
½ teaspoon sugar
Dash hot pepper sauce
½ cup fresh bread crumbs
1 tablespoon chopped fresh parsley

1. Preheat the oven to 350°F. Melt 1 tablespoon of the butter in a large skillet over medium-low heat. Add the onion; cook until tender, about 5 minutes. Transfer to a bowl.

2. Add 2 tablespoons of the butter to the pan over medium heat. Stir in the squash. Cook, tossing frequently, until all moisture has evaporated and the squash is tender, about 10 minutes. Transfer to the container of a food processor and process, using the on/off switch, until fairly smooth.

3. Transfer the puréed squash to a large mixing bowl. Add the cheese, egg, sour cream, wine, salt, sugar, hot pepper sauce, and sautéed onions. Mix well. Pour into a buttered baking dish.

4. Melt the remaining 1½ tablespoons butter in a small skillet over medium-high heat. Stir in the bread crumbs; sauté until golden, about 2 minutes. Sprinkle the crumbs over the squash mixture. Bake until lightly golden, about 30 minutes. Sprinkle with the parsley before serving.

Serves 4.

SWEET SUMMER SQUASH BUNDT

Summer squash has a multitude of kitchen uses but to my mind its finest guise is undubitably the sweetest. Take, for example, the bundt below. Golden in color and texture, this elegant cake is the best thing to hit a tea tray (or brunch table) in years. Serve it all year round—with the amendment of sweetened whipped cream at your own discretion.

For the cake:

¼ pound yellow summer squash, trimmed, grated (about 1 cup)
1 teaspoon finely slivered orange peel
½ cup chopped dried dates
½ cup chopped pecans
2 cups plus 1 tablespoon all-purpose flour
1 teaspoon baking powder
1 teaspoon baking soda
¼ teaspoon salt
3 eggs
1 teaspoon vanilla extract
1¼ cups granulated sugar
1 cup sour cream

For the glaze:

2 tablespoons orange juice
2 tablespoons lemon juice
2 tablespoons superfine sugar

For the icing:

1 cup confectioners' sugar
1 teaspoon ground cinnamon
2 tablespoons orange juice
1 teaspoon heavy or whipping cream

1. Preheat the oven to 350°F. Combine the squash, orange peel, dates, and pecans in a small bowl. Toss thoroughly

with the 1 tablespoon flour. Set aside.

2. Sift the remaining flour with the baking powder, baking soda, and salt. Set aside.

3. Beat the eggs in a large bowl until frothy. Add the vanilla and granulated sugar; beat until light and lemony. Beat in the sour cream. Add the sifted ingredients and beat until smooth. Add the squash mixture and mix well.

4. Pour the batter into a lightly buttered and floured 1½- to 2-quart bundt cake pan. Bake until a toothpick inserted in the center comes out clean, about 1 hour. Cool on a rack for 10 minutes. Unmold. Prick the top and sides of the cake with a toothpick.

5. Meanwhile, make the glaze: Combine the orange juice, lemon juice, and superfine sugar in a small bowl. Spoon this over the cake, allowing it to soak in until the cake is moist but not wet. Cool completely.

6. Before serving, make the icing: Combine all the ingredients in a small bowl. Beat until smooth, and drizzle over the cake.

Serves 8 to 10.

PUMPKIN ROLLS

Pumpkin rolls are the best dinner companions I know. This recipe comes from New Hampshire, from a Methodist church bulletin printed around the turn of the century, when most everything in America still had natural savor.

1½ teaspoons dry yeast
1 teaspoon granulated sugar
¼ cup lukewarm water
3 cups all-purpose flour, approximately
3½ tablespoons unsalted butter
2 tablespoons light brown sugar
¼ teaspoon salt
1 cup puréed cooked pumpkin (see page 322)
1 egg, lightly beaten
¼ cup maple syrup
¼ teaspoon ground cinnamon
1 cup stone-ground whole-wheat flour

1. Combine the yeast, granulated sugar, and water in a large bowl; let stand 5 minutes. Stir in ½ cup of the all-purpose flour. Cover, and let rise for 1 hour.

2. Melt 2 tablespoons of the butter and pour it in a medium bowl. Beat in the brown sugar, salt, pumpkin, egg, maple syrup, and cinnamon. Add this mixture to the risen roll base. Beat until smooth. Add the whole-wheat flour and enough all-purpose flour, about 2½ cups, to make a firm dough. Knead it briefly in the bowl. Cover, and let rise for 2 hours.

3. Punch the dough down and transfer it to a floured board. Knead briefly and roll out until about ½ inch thick. Cut into 1-inch circles. Place them on flour-rubbed baking sheets, cover with flour-rubbed tea towels, and let rise for 1 hour.

4. Preheat the oven to 425°F. Melt the remaining 1½ tablespoons butter and brush the rolls with it. Bake 15 minutes.

Makes about 2 dozen rolls.

PUMPKIN PROSCIUTTO GNOCCHI

1 cup puréed cooked pumpkin (see page 322)
1 egg, lightly beaten
¼ cup freshly grated Parmesan cheese, plus extra for garnish (optional)
¾ cup finely chopped prosciutto (or any smoked ham)
1¾ cups all-purpose flour
¼ teaspoon freshly grated nutmeg
¼ teaspoon salt

1. Whisk the pumpkin with the egg in a large mixing bowl. Stir in the cheese and prosciutto. Slowly stir in the flour and beat with a wooden spoon until fairly elastic, about 4 minutes. Add the nutmeg and salt; beat 1 minute longer.

2. Using two demitasse spoons, form small ovals of dough and drop them into a large pot of boiling salted water. When the gnocchi rise to the surface, remove them with a slotted spoon and drain them lightly on paper towels. Transfer to a buttered baking dish. Continue until all batter is used up.

3. Before serving, reheat for 15 minutes in a 350°F oven. Serve with more Parmesan cheese on the side if desired.

Serves 4.

POT-ROASTED BEEF WITH PUMPKIN

In the pumpkin recipe department, consider a wholly untraditional burnished pot roast enriched with amber chunks of this squash in lieu of potatoes. It's not a new idea. A seventeenth-century Oneida recipe specified that pumpkin "be boiled with meat till it achieves the consistency of potato soup." This is not that formula, however—this is better!

2½- to 3-pound boneless chuck roast
1 large clove garlic, bruised
2 tablespoons unsalted butter
1½ teaspoons vegetable oil
1 medium onion, finely chopped
3 peeled carrots, 1 chopped and 2 quartered
1 small tomato, peeled, seeded, chopped
½ teaspoon chopped fresh thyme, or a pinch of dried
1 teaspoon chopped fresh basil, or ¼ teaspoon dried
1 teaspoon chopped fresh parsley, plus extra for garnish
1½ cups strong beef broth (see page 414)
4 small potatoes, peeled, halved
1 pound fresh pumpkin, peeled, cut into 1½-inch cubes

1. Preheat the oven to 350°F. Rub the roast well with the bruised garlic. Mince the garlic and reserve.

2. Heat 1 tablespoon of the butter with half the oil in a large heavy skillet over medium heat. Brown the meat on all sides. Transfer to a Dutch oven.

3. Add the remaining butter and oil to the skillet. Add the onion; cook 1 minute. Add the reserved garlic and the chopped carrot and tomato. Cook 3 min-

utes. Sprinkle with the thyme, basil, and parsley. Stir in the beef broth. Heat to boiling, scraping the sides and bottom of the pan with a wooden spoon. Pour over the meat. Bake, covered, until the meat is not quite tender, about 2½ hours. Add the potatoes, quartered carrots, and pumpkin. Continue to cook, covered, until the vegetables and meat are very tender, about 45 minutes longer. Sprinkle with parsley.

Serves 4 to 6.

PUMPKIN MOUSSE

Simply a pale orange blizzard trying to pass itself off as a pumpkin mousse. Calorie counters beware: there is rum and ruination in every spoonful.

3 eggs, separated
⅓ cup granulated sugar
1½ tablespoons cornstarch
¼ teaspoon vanilla extract
¾ cup milk, scalded
2 tablespoons golden rum
1 cup puréed cooked pumpkin (see page 322)
⅛ teaspoon ground cinnamon
⅛ teaspoon ground cloves
⅛ teaspoon freshly grated nutmeg
⅛ teaspoon ground ginger
¼ cup orange juice
1 tablespoon unflavored gelatin
2 cups heavy or whipping cream
3 tablespoons confectioners' sugar
Slivered candied ginger

1. Beat the egg yolks in a medium bowl until light. Slowly beat in the granulated sugar. Whisk in the cornstarch and vanilla until smooth. Whisk in the scalded milk. Transfer to the top of a double boiler and cook, stirring constantly, over boiling water until thick enough to coat a wooden spoon, about 10 minutes. Remove from the heat; stir in the rum. Cool, then stir in the puréed pumpkin and spices.

2. Combine the orange juice with the gelatin in a small bowl. Let stand 5 minutes. Place the bowl over hot water and stir until the gelatin dissolves. Cool.

3. Combine the custard and gelatin mixtures in a medium bowl. Place the bowl in a larger bowl filled halfway with ice. Stir the custard with a wooden spoon until the mixture begins to thicken.

4. Beat 1 cup of the cream with 2 tablespoons of the confectioners' sugar until thick. Fold into the pumpkin mixture.

5. Beat the egg whites until stiff but not dry. Fold them into the mixture and pour it into a 6-cup soufflé dish or serving bowl. Refrigerate, covered, at least 6 hours or overnight.

6. About 1 hour before serving, beat the remaining 1 cup cream with the remaining 1 tablespoon confectioners' sugar. Fill a pastry bag with the whipped cream and pipe a decorative pattern over the mousse. Garnish with slivered candied ginger.

Serves 8.

PUMPKIN FRUITCAKE

This pumpkin fruitcake is designed for those who eschew fruitcake in any form. It is tender, nutty, and only vaguely scented with rum and spice. Parenthetically, it keeps wonderfully well—if you can keep your hands off it. I cannot!

1 cup seedless raisins
¼ cup plus 3 tablespoons dark rum
1 cup pitted dates, roughly chopped
3½ cups all-purpose flour
1 cup (2 sticks) unsalted butter, softened
3 cups granulated sugar
4 eggs
1 cup puréed cooked pumpkin (see page 322)
1 teaspoon ground cinnamon
1 teaspoon ground ginger
1 teaspoon baking powder
½ teaspoon salt
1 teaspoon baking soda
1¼ cups buttermilk
1 cup walnuts, chopped, lightly toasted
Finely slivered peel of 1 orange
Finely slivered peel of 1 lemon
½ cup orange juice
Confectioners' sugar

1. Place the raisins in a bowl and add the ¼ cup rum. Cover and let stand several hours or overnight.

2. Preheat the oven to 325°F. Butter and flour a 9-cup bundt or tube pan. Set it aside. Sprinkle the dates with 1 tablespoon of the flour. Set that aside.

3. Beat the butter in the large bowl of an electric mixer until light. Slowly beat in 2 cups of the granulated sugar. Add the eggs, one at a time, beating thoroughly after each addition. Beat in the pumpkin, cinnamon, and ginger.

4. Sift the remaining flour with the baking powder and salt. Combine the baking soda and buttermilk. Using a wooden spoon, stir the flour mixture into the pumpkin mixture in three parts, alternating with thirds of the buttermilk mixture. Stir in the reserved raisins and rum. Stir in the dates, walnuts, orange peel, and lemon peel. Spoon the batter into the prepared cake pan. Bake until a toothpick inserted in the center comes out clean, about 1¼ hours. Cool on a rack for 10 minutes. Unmold.

5. Meanwhile, combine the remaining 1 cup granulated sugar with the remaining 3 tablespoons rum and the orange juice. Brush this over the cake until it is moist but not wet. Sprinkle with confectioners' sugar before serving.

Serves 8 to 10.

THE ULTIMATE PUMPKIN PIE

I do not think lovers of that American treasure, pumpkin pie, would forgive its omission here. The recipe is the best I have ever tasted in forty-eight states (never made it to Alaska or Hawaii), and that's a strong statement. It is borrowed from my earlier book, *Bert Greene's Kitchen Bouquets*, with no apology whatsoever.

Short Crust Pastry for a 10-inch pie (see page 412)
1½ cups puréed cooked pumpkin (see page 322)
3 tablespoons unsalted butter, melted
½ cup sugar
¼ cup maple syrup
1 teaspoon ground cinnamon
½ teaspoon freshly grated nutmeg
¼ teaspoon ground cloves
3 eggs, separated
½ cup milk
¼ cup heavy or whipping cream
Sweetened whipped cream

1. Make the pie pastry. Roll it out and line a 10-inch pie plate. Trim and flute the edges.

2. Preheat the oven to 350°F. Combine all the ingredients except the egg whites and sweetened whipped cream. Mix thoroughly.

3. Beat the egg whites until stiff but not dry. Fold them into the pie mixture. Pour the mixture into the pie shell and bake until a toothpick inserted in the center comes out clean, about 50 minutes. Cool. Serve with sweetened whipped cream.

Serves 8.

The name *pumpkin* was bestowed on that grand and glorious globe by a misguided scholar in the late seventeenth century. Actually the moniker was an amalgam lifted from the Indian word *pompom* (which means round) and the classic Greek *sikuous pepon* (which indicates a weighty proportion). Early colonists called pumpkins by many names—pompions, pommions, pumpions—and in the case of Captain John Smith, never spelt the word the same way twice, so a formal appellation obviously helped.

ACORN SQUASH FLAN

This squash flan is *not* a dessert. Though it is delicately caramelized, the taste is decidedly vegetable! Serve it as a first course or as a prime luncheon dish with cold meat and a salad.

1 medium acorn squash
½ cup sugar
¼ teaspoon ground cinnamon
2 tablespoons unsalted butter, melted
½ teaspoon ground ginger
¼ teaspoon freshly grated nutmeg
⅛ teaspoon ground cloves
⅛ teaspoon crushed dried hot red pepper
½ teaspoon salt
1½ cups milk
1 cup heavy or whipping cream
3 eggs
3 egg yolks
1 tablespoon brandy

1. Preheat the oven to 350°F. Cut the squash in half lengthwise; scoop out the seeds. Place the squash, cut sides down, on a lightly buttered baking sheet. Bake in the oven until very tender, about 45 minutes. Cool, then scoop out the pulp.

2. Place a 1-quart soufflé dish in the oven for 5 to 6 minutes to warm.

3. Meanwhile, heat the sugar with the cinnamon in a small saucepan over high heat until the sugar starts to melt. Continue to cook, stirring constantly, until the sugar has melted and the caramel turns a deep golden color. Remove the soufflé dish from the oven and carefully pour the caramel into the dish, turning the dish to coat the bottom and sides. Invert the soufflé dish on a buttered sheet of foil (to prevent drippings from hardening on any work surfaces). Let stand.

4. Place the squash pulp in the container of a food processor or blender. Add the melted butter, ginger, nutmeg, cloves, red pepper, and salt. Process until smooth.

5. Meanwhile, combine the milk and cream in a saucepan and place over medium-low heat until hot. Do not allow to boil.

6. Beat the eggs with the egg yolks in a large bowl. Beat in the puréed squash mixture. Slowly stir in the hot milk and cream. Add the brandy.

7. Pour the custard mixture into the prepared soufflé dish and place the dish in a roasting pan. Pour boiling water into the pan to come halfway up the side of the soufflé dish. Bake until a knife inserted in the center comes out clean, about 1 hour. Remove the dish from the pan and let it stand 10 minutes.

8. Run a sharp knife around the edge of the soufflé dish and very carefully invert it onto a shallow serving platter. Serve the flan warm or well chilled.

Serves 8.

CURRIED WINTER SQUASH BISQUE

The most silken winter squash soup I know is a delicate blending of curried butternut squash combined with winter's best plum tomatoes, onions, garlic, and a mite of ham. A soup for all seasons, perhaps this brew is best of all in late winter when the supper table is set early. Consume yours with bread, cheese, and salad as the only other courses, for this soup is filling.

2 tablespoons unsalted butter
6 whole scallions, bulbs and green tops, finely chopped
1 clove garlic, minced
1 small green pepper, seeded, finely chopped
¼ cup chopped fresh parsley, plus extra for garnish
2 teaspoons chopped fresh basil, or 1 teaspoon dried
2-pound butternut squash, peeled, seeded, cubed (see Note)
1 ham bone, or ½-pound chunk of smoked ham
1 can (14 ounces) plum tomatoes
4 cups chicken broth (see page 414)
½ teaspoon ground allspice
¼ teaspoon ground mace
Pinch of freshly grated nutmeg
2 teaspoons curry powder
Salt and freshly ground black pepper

1. Melt the butter in a large saucepan over medium-low heat. Add the scallions; cook 2 minutes. Add the garlic, green pepper, ¼ cup chopped parsley, and basil. Cook, stirring occasionally, 5 minutes.

2. Add the squash to the saucepan. Toss to coat it with the scallion mixture. Add the ham bone or meat, tomatoes, broth, allspice, mace, and nutmeg. Heat to boiling; reduce the heat. Simmer, covered, until the squash is very tender, about 1 hour. Remove the ham bone. (If ham meat was used, remove and save for use at another time.)

3. Purée the soup in batches in a blender, being careful as hot liquid will expand. Transfer it to another large saucepan and stir in the curry powder. Heat to boiling; reduce the heat. Simmer 10 minutes, stirring frequently. Add salt and pepper to taste and sprinkle with parsley.

Serves 6 to 8.

Note: You may use an acorn squash for this recipe. If you do, bake it cut-side down, on a lightly buttered baking dish, in a 350°F oven for 45 minutes. Skip the water bath.

ZUCOTTE

(Braised Garlicky Winter Squash)

To braise winter squash it must be peeled first, then uniformly sliced or diced to ensure even cooking. I always braise squash in the Italian manner—in a covered saucepan with a small amount of butter, white wine, or chicken broth as flavoring. In the following instance, another Italian notion, the butter is literally loaded with garlic—and the dish is breathtaking!

3 tablespoons unsalted butter
2 tablespoons white wine
10 cloves garlic, peeled
1¼ pounds butternut or other winter squash, peeled, seeded, diced
Salt and freshly ground black pepper
3 tablespoons chopped fresh parsley

1. Melt 1 tablespoon of the butter in a large heavy skillet over low heat. Add the wine and garlic. Cook, covered, stirring occasionally, 20 minutes. The garlic will brown slightly but should not burn.

2. Mash the garlic with a fork. Stir in the remaining 2 tablespoons butter and the squash. Toss thoroughly to coat. Cook, covered, stirring occasionally, until the squash is tender, about 20 minutes. Add salt and pepper to taste and sprinkle with the parsley.

Serves 4.

Summer and winter squash may bear the same family name but they have practically nothing else in common. Not flavor, not texture, not even nutrition! Summer squash is diet food: low in sodium and calories and high in vitamins C, A, and niacin. Winter squash is comfort food: higher in calories and lower in vitamin C, though it does contain over 8,600 milligrams of vitamin A per cupful and is a prime source of riboflavin and iron to boot. Luckily there's room for both—in the garden and at the stove.

CRANBERRIED SQUASH PUREE

The classic winter squash recipe in my collection is also rather untraditional: a purée of acorn squash combined with other chill-factor ingredients like red wine, fresh cranberries, and zippy spices. The result is a most elegant and different side dish. But try it for yourself.

2 medium acorn squash
4 teaspoons unsalted butter, plus 2 tablespoons softened
1 cup water
2 tablespoons dark brown sugar
2 tablespoons red wine
1/8 teaspoon ground allspice
1/4 cup fresh cranberries, rinsed, finely chopped
Salt and freshly ground black pepper

1. Preheat the oven to 400°F. Cut each squash in half; scrape out the seeds. Place the squash in a shallow roasting pan, cut side up. Place 1 teaspoon of the butter in each cavity. Pour the water around the squash, and bake until tender, about 1 hour.

2. Remove the squash from the oven; cool slightly. Scrape out the cooked flesh and process it in the container of a food processor or blender until smooth. Transfer it to the top of a double boiler.

3. Add the brown sugar, red wine, softened butter, and allspice to the puréed squash. Cook over boiling water 5 minutes. Add the cranberries; cook 10 minutes longer. Add salt and pepper to taste.

Serves 4 to 6.

SPAGHETTI SQUASH TETRAZZINI

Spaghetti squash's finest culinary hour may be at hand—the vegetable's presence in a plate of fabled Chicken Tetrazzini has to be some kind of milestone!

1 medium spaghetti squash (about 2½ pounds)
1 clove garlic
1 small onion stuck with a clove
3 sprigs parsley
Pinch of dried basil
1½ cups chicken broth (see page 414)
1 whole chicken breast, skinned, boned, halved
4 tablespoons (½ stick) unsalted butter
2 tablespoons minced shallots or scallion bulbs
1 cup sliced mushrooms
2 tablespoons all-purpose flour
3/4 cup heavy or whipping cream
2 teaspoons dry vermouth
1/4 teaspoon freshly grated nutmeg
Dash of hot pepper sauce
1 teaspoon lemon juice
Salt and freshly ground black pepper
1/4 cup freshly grated Parmesan cheese

1. Place the whole squash in a large pot; cover with cold water. Heat to boiling; reduce the heat. Simmer, covered, until fork-tender, turning once, about 45

minutes. Drain and allow to cool slightly. Cut the squash in half lengthwise. Scrape out the seeds with a fork. Scrape the remaining squash with the fork, carefully separating the vegetable into pasta-like strands. Set the strands aside.

2. Meanwhile, preheat the oven to 375°F. Combine the garlic, onion with clove, parsley, basil, and chicken broth in a large skillet. Heat to boiling; reduce the heat. Add the pieces of chicken breast; cook, covered, until tender, about 4 minutes per side. Remove the chicken to a plate. Reduce the broth to 1 cup; strain. Cut the chicken into strips and reserve.

3. Melt 2 tablespoons of the butter in a skillet over medium-low heat. Add the shallots or scallions; cook 3 minutes. Add the mushrooms; cook over medium heat until golden. Set aside.

4. Melt the remaining 2 tablespoons butter in a large saucepan over low heat. Stir in the flour; cook, stirring constantly, 2 minutes. Stir in the cream, vermouth, nutmeg, hot pepper sauce, lemon juice, and salt and pepper to taste. Cook until thick, about 4 minutes. Stir in the chicken, squash, and mushrooms. Transfer to a buttered baking dish. Sprinkle with the cheese. Bake until golden and bubbly, about 20 minutes.

Serves 4.

SPAGHETTI SQUASH PRIMAVERA

"Spaghetti squash is best served with a light and delicate pasta sauce," according to James Beard. To second the master's notion, I came up with several exceedingly delicate variations. Consider the following velvety upholstery for starters.

1 medium spaghetti squash (about 2½ pounds)
1 cup heavy or whipping cream
5 tablespoons unsalted butter
1 shallot, minced
¼ cup minced cooked ham
1 carrot, minced
1 tablespoon Madeira
Dash of hot pepper sauce
Pinch of freshly grated nutmeg
⅓ cup lightly blanched peas
Salt and freshly ground black pepper
3 tablespoons freshly grated Parmesan cheese, plus extra for serving

1. Place the whole squash in a large pot; cover with cold water. Heat to boiling; reduce the heat. Simmer, covered, until fork-tender, turning once, about 45 minutes. Drain and allow to cool slightly. Cut the squash in half lengthwise. Scrape out the seeds with a fork. Scrape the remaining squash with the fork, carefully separating the vegetables into pasta-like strands. Set the strands aside.

2. In a small saucepan heat the cream to boiling; reduce the heat. Simmer until reduced by half. Stir in 4 tablespoons of the butter; remove from the heat.

3. Melt the remaining 1 tablespoon butter in a large saucepan over medium-low heat. Add the shallot, ham, and carrot. Cook 3 minutes. Raise the heat slightly and add the Madeira. Cook until most of the liquid has evaporated.

4. Stir the reduced cream mixture into the vegetable mixture over low heat. Add the hot pepper sauce, nutmeg, peas, and salt and pepper to taste. Toss in the cooked spaghetti squash. Toss over low heat until warmed through. Stir in 3 tablespoons Parmesan cheese. Pass more cheese on the side.

Serves 4.

SQUASH BOATS

In pre-Columbian times, the cave dwellers in the Tamaulipas mountains used dried winter squash shells for carrying water and goat's milk. Three thousand years later this vegetable still takes well to odd culinary cargo. To be specific, consider the one-dish meal below. Any meaty squash will do as a boat, but the delicately flavored varieties are most compatible: consider acorn, turban, buttercup, or even green chayote. Butternut squash is perfect from the standpoint of flavor, but be forewarned: the skin is thin and the cavity small, so it must be carefully enlarged prior to stuffing.

2 medium winter squash
5½ tablespoons unsalted butter
1 small onion, minced
1 clove garlic, minced
½ cup chopped cooked ham
1 tablespoon bourbon
1 small tomato, peeled, seeded, chopped
1 whole scallion, bulb and green top, finely chopped
½ cup diced cooked chicken
2 tablespoons all-purpose flour
½ cup hot chicken broth (see page 414)
3 tablespoons heavy or whipping cream
½ teaspoon ground allspice
Dash of hot pepper sauce
2 tablespoons chopped fresh parsley
Salt and freshly ground black pepper
¼ cup dry bread crumbs

1. Preheat the oven to 350°F. Cut the squash in half lengthwise and scoop out the seeds. Place the squash shell side up in a lightly buttered baking dish. Bake until tender, about 45 minutes to 1 hour, depending on the squash you use. Remove from the oven. Cool, then scoop out the pulp, leaving about ½ inch of pulp inside the shells. Chop the scooped-out pulp and reserve. Place the shells on a lightly buttered ovenproof serving dish.

2. Reduce the oven temperature to 325°F. Melt 2 tablespoons of the butter in a large skillet over medium-low heat. Add the onion; cook 1 minute. Add the garlic; cook 4 minutes longer. Stir in the ham, bourbon, tomato, scallion, chicken, and reserved pulp. Cook 1 minute. Remove from the heat and set aside.

3. Melt 2 more tablespoons of butter in a small saucepan; whisk in the flour. Cook, stirring constantly, until the mixture is golden, about 15 minutes. Whisk in the broth and cream. Heat to boiling; cook until very thick, about 3 minutes. Add the cream mixture to the chicken and ham mixture. Add the allspice, hot pepper sauce, parsley, and salt and pepper to taste, and stuff the shells.

4. Melt the remaining 1½ tablespoons butter in a small skillet. Sauté the bread crumbs over medium heat until golden, about 4 minutes. Spoon them over the squash. Bake 25 minutes.

Serves 4.

WINTER SQUASH CREME BRULEE

An aureate *crème brulée* compounded of winter squash and more deviltry than a deep-dyed Puritan could shake a stick at—and crusted to the nines with burnt sugar.

3 cups heavy or whipping cream
½ cup granulated sugar
6 egg yolks
⅓ cup puréed cooked winter squash
¼ teaspoon ground cinnamon
⅛ teaspoon ground ginger
Pinch of ground cloves
1 tablespoon dark rum
⅓ cup packed light brown sugar

1. Preheat the oven to 325°F. Heat the cream and granulated sugar in the top of a double boiler over hot water until the sugar has dissolved. Remove from the heat.

2. Beat the egg yolks in a medium bowl until light. Add the squash, cinnamon, ginger, and cloves. Whisk in the hot cream mixture. Stir in the rum.

3. Pour the squash mixture into a 1½-quart soufflé dish. Place the dish in a roasting pan and add boiling water to the pan to come halfway up the sides of the dish. Bake until the center is fairly firm, about 1½ hours. Remove from the water and allow to cool. Refrigerate overnight.

4. About 15 minutes before serving, preheat the broiling unit. Sprinkle the brown sugar over the custard. Place the dish in a pan and surround it with ice cubes. Heat it under the broiler, gently shaking the pan, until the sugar melts. Serve immediately.

Serves 6 to 8.

STRING BEANS

-With No More Strings Attached

When I was a youngster, one of the unalloyed joys of my life was being sent to spend the afternoon at my father's place of business. Or better yet, to sit in the back of his grubby automobile amid the assorted nippers, wrenches, pliers, and coils of shiny wire while he visited "The Job" to inspect the status of the houses he had under construction.

There among the skeletal wooden dwellings I would play solitary games while my father checked the naked uprights with tape measure and spirit level before he allowed his men to lay the thick ropes of insulated cable in place. My father's job sites were almost always treeless, muddy quarries where cement foundations surrounded blank holes smelling of sewage and other earthly entrails, and whose yawning darkness was terrifying.

But if I skinned an elbow or cut a finger, I always knew that one of the burly fellows in my father's employ would bandage the spot with a handkerchief that I would be bidden to spit into first. My favorite among these helpers was a red-haired fellow named Herman who always gave me a stick of chewing gum or a cough drop as an anodyne. "Does it hurt bad, Stringbean?" he would ask. I always shook my head, no. Even if it did I would never have admitted the suffering, for I liked being thought a stoic. I also liked being called "Stringbean."

I received that appellation when I was about seven or eight years old and started to grow tall, almost overnight. My father's secretary, a tall blond young woman who used to let me draw on the triplicate pages of billheads while she typed envelopes, started that nickname.

"You grew so tall over the summer," she announced when I returned from my first year at summer camp, "I can't tell you apart from a stringbean!"

"I'm tougher," I replied.

"No," said Ruth. "You're just fresher!" But the name stuck.

As I said before, I loved to spend the afternoon at my father's business. Aside from the permissiveness of easy-going Ruth there was so much to see and smell there. I can still summon up the crackling hiss of copper wire as it was unwound and the faintly dangerous scent of live electric current in the air.

As my father's finances fluctuated from bad to worse during the Depression, he would attempt to cut back on his monthly overhead. First one man, then another (all good companions of mine), was laid off. Good-hearted Ruth was forced to look for another job, and finally the shop itself was shuttered, the contents auctioned to satisfy creditors.

My father's business went on, however, albeit spiritlessly. My mother claimed that he ran it out of his hat. Indeed, the brim of the soiled gray fedora he wore was always crammed with business cards and folded bits of paper, where other men fancied feathers or Tyrolean brushes.

Once when I was in my last year at grammar school, I accompanied my father to "The Job" once again. The marshy landscape had not altered a whit and the frame underpinnings of architecture were still raw and sere. This time, almost an adolescent, I no longer played along the sidings nor allowed my knees and wrists to be scraped. I sat in the car alone, reading a book.

After my father had been gone for what seemed hours but was probably fifteen minutes, I heard a knock on the car window and immediately recognized my old friend, Herman.

"Is that really you, Stringbean?" he asked through the glass. "You got so big I almost didn't recognize you."

"I am over five feet, seven inches tall," I said eagerly. "I'll show you." And clambering out of the car, I stood against the hood so he could observe my increased height.

"You really grew up." Herman whistled, wiping his hands on his overalls. "All around. Can't rightly call you Stringbean any more." He laughed. "Broad bean'd be a better name now."

It was true of course. I had become increasingly chunky with each added inch of height. But I hated to have the matter aired in public. By the time I had returned to the car and rolled up the window, I resolved never to go to my father's job again. And I do not think I ever did.

Sic transit glorious stringbeans.

Vegetable Roots

Despite my pique at having outgrown its sobriquet, the green bean (stringless or otherwise) is a vegetable that has never suffered alienation of my affections. A plateful appears at my dinner table at least three or four times a week. For to my mind, nothing in the garden (or on the greengrocer's shelf) can be prepared as easily and yet remain so eminently toothsome.

Phaseolus vulgaris was another bequest to European kitchens from the New World, where they grew wild. It is hard to believe, but the green bean was originally brought back to Spain by the conquistadors as a flowering plant, not as a food. Adjudged too intractable for civilized tongues (or teeth), bean pods were grown only ornamentally. These red-to-pink blossoms known as *pincel* ("paintbrush") glorified Spanish gardens for over half a century and would be there still if not for a happy accident. According to vegetable lore, a bunch of green pods fell into a pot of soup one day. Since it was too close to dinner to start the dish anew, the soup was served up without amend and pronounced "*perfecto!*" Who the enterprising cook was is anyone's guess, but let bean lovers everywhere give thanks for the culinary stratagem.

Once the Spanish cooked string beans, the rest of Europe followed suit. As they were easy to grow and simpler to harvest, beans shortly became a kitchen staple, eaten fresh in summer and dried during the rest of the year. In France, where they prized a stew of meat and vegetables known as a *hericoq*, beans were added to the dish and consumed with such apparent relish that the single legume soon replaced all other ingredients. When the bean took over the stew, it appropriated its name as well. Frenchmen have called beans *haricots* ever since, making the distinction between dried and fresh by dubbing the latter *haricot vert*, "green bean." String beans are now grown the world over. There are a hundred varieties in seed catalogues, but to give the Gallic original its due, none is tenderer, more delicately flavored, or thinner (often no wider than a darning needle) than the *haricot vert*. To honor it, cooks everywhere slice less svelte string beans vertically and call them "Frenched."

Though string beans have been consumed in the Americas for thousands of years, they have been raised commercially in the U.S. only since 1836. The very first string bean crop was harvested by an enterprising truck farmer outside Utica, New York, who reportedly mortgaged his family home to import the seeds from France. Ten years later, they say, he was so filthy rich that he moved his family to the Riviera. One thing is certain, however: his initial product made good. In the latter half of the nineteenth century string beans were so fashionable that they were marketed by vegetable distributors as "The Ninth Wonder of the World." Eventually lawyers for P. T. Barnum, who had coined the phrase, threatened legal action and the legend was amended to read: "The Wonder of the World [and in smaller type] of Food!"

Despite all the flim-flam, the string bean was truly popular, and it never lost favor at the dining table. A couple of decades ago the string bean (though stringless since 1894) was ranked the fifth-best-liked vegetable in America. And while it came in well after the potato and the pea, it still outdistanced the cucumber!

What to Look For

String beans come to the table year round these days. However, we pay for the privilege of out-of-season consumption with largely lackluster produce. I can remember the days prior to World War II when the only string beans eaten between September and June sprang from a formidable Del Monte can; and one literally went crazy for fresh by spring. Women who gardened (like my grandmother) would mark off the days on a calendar, waiting for the bean runners to send out sufficient pods for the first meal of the year. Young diners (like me) were always instructed to make a wish before sampling the first slender pod. In our family we often ate new string beans slightly before they were deemed pickable according to the Burpee catalogue—but who cared? Starved for the taste of fresh, we simply could not wait a day longer.

At the supermarket, look for packages of string beans of evenly matched lengths; they will cook more uniformly. If a greengrocer allows you to select your own, try for beans that are unblemished, relatively crisp, and endowed with small seeds. Fresher beans have slightly fuzzier skins. I do not recommend the practice, but my mother always snapped a bean in half to ascertain how long it had been in circulation. Fresh beans will snap with dispatch and reveal a generous spurt of juice at the seam. Buy them immediately. Avoid limp, soggy-looking pods or any that appear to be swollen with seeds. Those beans stayed on the vine too long!

If the label "string bean" is merely a vestigial cognomen these days, since most beans are stringless, it still conjures up a nice thin image for me. No surprise, I guess, since the green bean is composed of 92 percent water and there are less than 30 calories in a cooked cupful. The bean is at its optimum state when fresh—literally loaded with potassium (180 milligrams), calcium (63 milligrams), and phosphorus (46 milligrams) in every eight ounces. Plus a whopping shot of vitamin A (680 units) per 125-gram serving, which averages out to a scant cup.

Preparation

If I am lucky enough to acquire produce that is freshly picked (and luckier still, pencil slim), I leave the beans whole. Mature, thick-waisted beans I usually run through a small hand-held device known variously as a "Beanex" or a "Krisk Bean Stringer & Slicer," which will halve even a huge pod admirably.

My sole crotchet in the matter of cooking string beans is to blanch them first and then reheat them later.

To blanch string beans: Bring a large pot of salted water to a rolling boil. My rule of thumb for salt is light these days: a scant half teaspoon per quart of water. But I do go heavy on the water because the more water you use, the faster it will return to the boil once the beans are added. I always cook beans uncovered and boil them only long enough to ensure a crisp-tender texture, about 1½ to 2 minutes after the water returns to the boil. If you like your string beans more tender, add a minute or two to the cooking time. Drain the cooked beans in a colander and rinse under cold running water until they are cool. The icy bath not only guarantees a bright green color, it retards the cooking process as well. When the beans are cool to the touch, drain them dry and either proceed with the recipe at hand or refrigerate. Chilled beans may be stored in an airtight plastic bag and held in the refrigerator up to 24 hours.

MARY SURINA'S BEAN AND BARLEY SOUP

One of the heartiest soups I know is compounded of two kinds of beans, dried and green, as well as a multitude of old-fashioned ingredients like a ham hock, spareribs, and barley. This might intimidate the untried soup maker, but dismiss that notion at once. The soup is easy to make and all its components can be found at any supermarket. I know, I bought them there! This stick-to-the-ribs pottage is of Yugoslavian extraction by way of San Pedro, California. It was given to me by my friend Mary Surina, who is without challenge one of the finest cooks in San Pedro.

8 ounces dried pinto beans
1 pound spareribs, trimmed of fat, cut into 2-inch sections
1 tablespoon unsalted butter
1 onion, chopped
2 cloves garlic, minced
2 carrots, finely chopped
2 ribs celery, finely chopped
1 ham hock (about 1 pound)
1 quart chicken broth (see page 414)
2 quarts vegetable broth or water (see page 414)
1 cup barley
½ pound string beans, trimmed, cut French-style, halved
Salt and freshly ground black pepper
1 tablespoon chopped fresh parsley

1. Cover the pinto beans with water in a large pot. Heat to boiling; boil 2 minutes. Remove from the heat and let stand, covered, 1 hour. Drain.

2. Preheat the oven to 350°F. Cover the spareribs with cold water in a large pot. Heat to boiling; drain immediately under cold running water until cool. Pat dry with paper towels.

3. Melt the butter in a 5-quart Dutch oven over medium-low heat. Stir in the onion; cook 1 minute. Add the garlic, carrots, and celery. Cook 4 minutes. Add the pinto beans, spareribs, ham hock, chicken broth, and 1 quart of the vegetable broth or water. Heat to boiling; remove from the heat. Cook, covered, in the oven for 1 hour.

4. Remove the Dutch oven and stir in the remaining 1 quart vegetable broth or water. Stir in the barley and string beans. Return the soup to the oven and continue to bake, covered, until barley is tender, about 1 hour longer.

5. Remove the soup from the oven. Remove the spareribs and ham hock. Cut the meat off the bones and return the meat to the soup. Add salt and pepper to taste. Serve sprinkled with the parsley.

Serves 6 to 8.

VAGUELY CHINESE STRING BEAN SALAD

This is the handiwork of Donald Sacks, who runs a charming food shop in New York. Donald has one caveat about his slaw: the beans must be crunchy or all is lost.

1 pound tender young string beans, trimmed
1½-inch piece fresh ginger root, minced
¼ cup vegetable oil
1½ tablespoons sherry vinegar
¼ teaspoon sesame oil
¼ teaspoon coarse (kosher) salt
Pinch of sugar
⅛ teaspoon ground white pepper
1½ to 2 tablespoons toasted sesame seeds

1. Cook the beans in boiling salted water until crisp-tender, about 1½ to 2 minutes. Rinse under cold running water; drain. Cover, and chill 1 hour.

2. Press the ginger root in a fine-mesh sieve over a large bowl to extract the juice; discard the pulp. Whisk in the vegetable oil, vinegar, sesame oil, coarse salt, sugar, and white pepper. Add the beans; toss to coat them with the dressing. Cover, and chill 4 hours, tossing every hour.

3. Just before serving, sprinkle with the sesame seeds.

Serves 4.

ROMAN GREEN BEANS WITH FONTINA CHEESE

My favorite time to eat string beans is in summer. Besides being at their tenderest when in season, nothing makes a more spectacular salad. For further evidence, see this dispensation from Efrem Funghi Calingaert and Jacquelyn Days Serwer, from their excellent book *Pasta and Rice, Italian Style.* A mix of green beans with Fontina cheese, it is atypical *antipasto* but devilishly good eating.

1 pound string beans, trimmed
½ pound Fontina cheese, cut into strips about 3 inches long and ¼ inch wide
1 clove garlic, minced
½ teaspoon Dijon mustard
¼ cup lemon juice
½ cup olive oil
Salt and freshly ground black pepper

1. Cook the beans in boiling salted water until crisp-tender, about 1½ to 2 minutes. Rinse under cold running water; drain. Combine with the cheese in a large bowl.

2. Mash the garlic with the mustard in a small bowl. Stir in the lemon juice. Slowly whisk in the oil. Pour this dressing over the beans and cheese. Toss well and add salt and pepper to taste. Serve at room temperature or slightly chilled.

Serves 4.

HOT WAX BEAN CHEF'S SALAD

Another unusual wax bean rendering, this is a warm salad that combines the pods with strips of chicken, ham, and herbs in a delicate mustardy vinaigrette. Yes . . . you read it right, warm! And wonderful too. Serve it for lunch or dinner with a good loaf of crusty bread.

For the mustard vinaigrette:

2 tablespoons Dijon mustard
1 tablespoon red wine vinegar
1 tablespoon lemon juice
6 tablespoons olive oil
1 tablespoon vodka

For the salad:

½ pound wax beans, trimmed, cut French-style
1 small red bell pepper, seeded, cut into thin strips
1 tablespoon unsalted butter
1 scallion, bulb and green top, minced
1 clove garlic, minced
¼ pound thinly sliced cooked smoked ham, cut into strips
1 tablespoon chopped fresh basil
2 cups roughly chopped cooked chicken

1. To make the mustard vinaigrette: Whisk the mustard with the vinegar and lemon juice in a small bowl until smooth. Slowly whisk in the oil, then the vodka. Cover and refrigerate at least 1 hour.

2. Cook the wax beans and red pepper in boiling salted water until crisp-tender, about 3 minutes. Drain.

3. Melt the butter in a large skillet over medium heat. Add the scallion; cook 1 minute. Add the garlic; cook 3 minutes. Add the wax beans and red pepper, the ham, basil, and chicken. Cook, tossing constantly, until warmed through.

4. Transfer the warm salad to a serving dish. Pour the chilled vinaigrette over the top and toss at the table.

Serves 4.

The wax or yellow bean is nothing more than a string bean that has been cultivated for its lightened (and some consider more appealing) color. In the process of hybridization a jot of folic acid (source of vitamin B) is lost, but the flavor and texture are otherwise indistinguishable. In France, wax beans are known as *mange-tout,* which roughly translates as wholly edible—and they are!

MILDRED SCHULZ'S STRING BEANS AND POTATOES

*T*he next delectable string bean formula in this volume is my own personal talisman. It is a donation from Mildred Schulz of Golden, Colorado, who is not only a good friend but also a kind of benefactor. Mildred has contributed a recipe to every book I have written, and just seeing her name in the index again brings me a sense of inner security and personal joy. That all of her offerings have been wonderful is almost beside the point. They are lodestars.

2 medium potatoes (about ½ pound), unpeeled
½ pound string beans, trimmed
3 strips bacon
1 medium onion, halved, sliced
¼ cup red wine vinegar
2 tablespoons water
1 tablespoon unsalted butter
Salt and freshly ground black pepper

1. Cook the potatoes in boiling salted water until just barely tender, about 15 minutes. Drain. Cut into ¼-inch-thick slices.

2. Meanwhile, cook the beans in boiling salted water until crisp-tender, 1½ to 2 minutes. Rinse under cold running water; drain.

3. Sauté the bacon in a heavy skillet until crisp. Remove and drain on paper towels. Crumble and reserve.

4. Cook the onion in the bacon drippings over medium heat until golden. Stir in the vinegar and water. Cook, stirring constantly, until slightly thickened, about 3 minutes. Reduce the heat to medium-low and toss in the potatoes and string beans. Cook, tossing gently, for 5 minutes. Stir in the butter and add salt and pepper to taste. Sprinkle with the reserved bacon.

Serves 4.

GREEN AND GOLD

(Sautéed Spinach and Wax Beans)

The name of this side dish of golden wax beans and bright green leaf spinach is borrowed from my alma mater's school colors. In honor of William and Mary.

2 tablespoons plus 1 teaspoon unsalted butter
½ cup Chicken Stock (see page 410)
1 pound wax beans, trimmed, cut on the diagonal into 2-inch pieces
4 ounces fresh spinach, chopped (about 1¼ cups)
1 tablespoon chopped fresh parsley
⅛ teaspoon crushed dried hot red peppers
¼ teaspoon freshly grated nutmeg
Salt and freshly ground black pepper

1. Melt the 2 tablespoons butter in a medium saucepan over medium heat. Add the chicken stock and heat to boiling. Add the beans and cook, covered, over medium heat until the beans are barely tender, about 8 minutes. Remove the cover and cook until half the liquid has evaporated.

2. Add the spinach and parsley to the beans. Cook, uncovered, tossing constantly, until the spinach wilts, about 3 minutes. If the mixture seems too wet, raise the heat and cook some more, until fairly dry. Stir in the remaining 1 teaspoon butter, the crushed peppers, the nutmeg, and salt and pepper to taste.

Serves 4.

GREENE'S OUT-OF-SEASON BEANS

Of late I have been able to buy thin and extremely tender imported *haricots verts* at the greengrocer's, albeit at astronomical prices. In summer, I often purchase similar domestic pods at farm stands or greenmarkets. These baby green beans are not cheap either, but they are excellently toothsome, so I pay gladly. When neither is available and thick-skinned, relatively flavorless supermarket varieties are the only option, I "fudge" the issue with the following recipe. It is unorthodox but tasty, I assure you.

1 pound string beans, trimmed, cut French-style
2 tablespoons unsalted butter
1 large shallot, minced
½ teaspoon beef bouillon powder
1 small tomato, peeled, seeded, chopped
Salt and freshly ground black pepper
Chopped fresh parsley

1. Cook the beans in boiling salted water until almost tender, about 3 minutes. Rinse under cold running water. Drain.

2. Melt the butter in a large saucepan over medium-low heat. Add the shallot; cook 3 minutes. Toss in the beans, bouillon powder, and tomato. Cook, tossing constantly, over medium heat until warmed through. Add salt and pepper to taste, and sprinkle with parsley.

Serves 4.

EZE

(String Beans Sautéed with Chartreuse)

When I lived in the South of France, the women who ran the local outdoor vegetable market always referred to a green bean as a *nigaud*. Not exactly a pejorative, it is no compliment either, meaning a fool or a noodle. Take your pick! Neither describes the next green bean recipe, though I did invent it in France one day when I had a basket of perfect *haricots verts* at hand and a bottle of fine Chartreuse in the cupboard.

1 pound tender young string beans, trimmed (larger ones cut French-style)
2 strips bacon
3 tablespoons unsalted butter
3 shallots, minced
2 tablespoons chopped fresh basil, or 1 teaspoon dried
3 tablespoons Chartreuse liqueur
Freshly ground black pepper

1. Cook the beans in boiling salted water 1 minute. Rinse under cold running water. Drain.

2. Sauté the bacon in a large heavy skillet until crisp. Remove with a slotted spoon and drain on paper towels. Crumble and reserve.

3. Pour off all the drippings in the skillet. Add 2 tablespoons of the butter and the shallots. Cook over medium-low heat 3 minutes. Add the beans, basil, and Chartreuse. Continue to cook, stirring frequently, 5 minutes. Stir in the remaining 1 tablespoon butter and sprinkle with pepper to taste. Sprinkle with the reserved bacon.

Serves 4.

LEMON STRINGS

According to legume savants, the Incas cultivated the string bean not so much for flavor as for theology. They were sun worshipers, and so (apparently) was the bean. A green bean will climb any vertical surface, notably a pole, twisting and turning in its search for the light. For the Incas, chewing the pods was seen as an act of sacrament. But those poor folks missed the point entirely, since string beans are delicious into the bargain. One of the sun-loving bean's more felicitous matings is with another golden globe, the fragrant lemon. Though it may seem immodest to brag about my recipes, one bite of this could turn an Inca (or any other non-bean-lover) into a deep-dyed fan.

1 pound string beans, trimmed
¼ cup Chicken Stock (see page 410)
Juice of 1 lemon
4 tablespoons (½ stick) unsalted butter
Finely slivered peel of 1 lemon
Salt and freshly ground black pepper
1 teaspoon chopped fresh parsley

1. Cook the string beans in boiling salted water until crisp-tender, about 1½ to 2 minutes. Rinse under cold running water until cool. Drain.

2. Combine the chicken stock and lemon juice in a large skillet over medium heat. Heat to boiling; boil until reduced by half, about 4 minutes. Add the butter and stir until smooth. Add the beans and lemon peel. Toss until warmed through, about 2 minutes. Add salt and pepper to taste, and sprinkle with the parsley.

Serves 4.

String bean is no aphorism. This variety of green bean once had a tough strand of green filament down its back side that a poor housewife had to diligently remove with a sharp knife prior to cooking. But no longer. Agrogeneticists have bred a new and virtually stringless pod that requires a mere snip at the top and tail ends before it is popped into boiling water.

SNAP BEAN PUREE

The first *haricot vert* was introduced to England by a band of French immigrants, Huguenots, who made a gift of this vegetable to Queen Elizabeth I as a gratuity for allowing them religious freedom in her land. Good Queen Bess found the bequest of green beans "much engaging to the royal taste." So much so, in fact, that green beans were planted in the garden at Hampton Court and shortly thereafter in greenswards all over the island. English farmers became so attached to the green bean that they even, chauvinistically, renamed it the *Elizabeth Bean.* But that cognomen never stuck. When Elizabeth died and James took over, the beans were once again dubbed simply "Frenchies." What follows is a purely Francophile rendering—a velvety purée, which, parenthetically, can be prepared with wax beans as well.

1 large potato, peeled, diced
¾ cup Chicken Stock, approximately (see page 410)
2 pounds green or wax string beans, trimmed
Salt and freshly ground black pepper
1 tablespoon unsalted butter

1. Cook the potato, covered, in the chicken stock until tender, about 12 minutes. Drain, reserving the stock. Mash or rice the potato. Set aside.

2. Cook the beans in boiling salted water until very tender—4 to 5 minutes for green, about 10 for wax. Drain.

3. Place the beans in the container of a food processor. Process, using the on/off switch, until smooth, adding just enough reserved chicken stock to make a smooth mixture. Combine the beans with the potato and transfer to the top of a double boiler.

4. Just before serving, reheat the purée in the top of a double boiler over simmering water. Add salt and pepper to taste, and stir in the butter.

Serves 4 to 6.

BRAISED GARLIC AND STRING BEANS

To my way of thinking, the ultimate way to prepare a string bean is with the fewest ingredients and the least amount of fuss. With those parameters established, have my nomination for a classic rendering. The ingredients are mainly beans, butter, and garlic, but never was a legume sauced more eloquently. Or in less time!

1 pound tender young string beans, trimmed (cut larger beans French-style)
3 tablespoons unsalted butter
4 to 5 large cloves garlic
1 teaspoon chopped fresh sage, or a pinch of dried
1 tablespoon chopped fresh parsley
Salt and freshly ground black pepper

1. Cook the string beans in boiling salted water until crisp-tender, about 1½ to 2 minutes. Rinse under cold running water until cool. Drain.

2. Melt the butter in a large skillet over low heat. Add the garlic cloves; cook, covered, until lightly golden and soft, 20 to 25 minutes. Do not let the butter burn. Remove the cover and mash the garlic with a fork until well mixed with the butter.

3. Add the beans to the skillet; toss over medium heat until warmed through. Add the sage, parsley, and salt and pepper to taste.

Serves 4.

SWEET GREEN BEAN PICKLES

With such a healthy dose of vitamins per bean, one can be a bit frivolous in this recipe for a sweet pickle.

1½ to 2 pounds string beans, trimmed
2 cups cider vinegar
⅓ cup sugar
1½ tablespoons mixed pickling spices, tied in a cheesecloth bag
1 tablespoon whole black peppercorns
1 bay leaf
1 clove garlic
1 large onion, chopped
1 small red bell pepper, seeded, chopped
3 large sprigs dill

1. Cook the beans in boiling salted water for 1 minute. Rinse under cold running water; drain.

2. Place the vinegar, sugar, pickling spices, peppercorns, bay leaf, and garlic clove in a medium saucepan. Heat to boiling; reduce the heat. Simmer, uncovered, 10 minutes. Discard the spice bag. Add the onion and bell pepper; simmer 10 minutes longer. Discard the bay leaf and garlic.

3. Pack the beans upright in sterilized jars (up to 1 inch from the top). With a slotted spoon, divide the onions and red peppers evenly among the jars. Place a dill sprig in each jar and pour in hot syrup up to ½ inch from the top. Seal the jars. Process in a hot water bath for 15 minutes.

Makes 3 pints.

FASULYE VE KUZU

(Turkish String Beans and Lamb Cakes)

I have never traveled to the Bosphorus, but I know the Turks have a way with string beans. A friend who has been to that country and back several times brought me the following recipe, somewhat stained with thumbprints of oil and redolent with garlic, from an encounter in Istanbul. And while the name of this dish is virtually unpronounceable (and the spelling suspect), the taste is one you will not soon forget.

1½ pounds ground lamb
½ pound ground beef
1 medium onion, finely chopped
2 cloves garlic, minced
½ cup fresh bread crumbs
¼ teaspoon ground allspice
Pinch of ground cinnamon
2 tablespoons chopped fresh parsley
Dash of hot pepper sauce
1 egg, lightly beaten
¼ cup water
½ teaspoon salt
¼ teaspoon freshly ground black pepper
2 tablespoons unsalted butter
1 tablespoon olive oil
1 medium onion, thinly sliced
1 pound string beans, trimmed, cut French-style
8 ripe Italian plum tomatoes, peeled, or 1 can (28 ounces) plum tomatoes, drained
¼ teaspoon sugar
¼ cup chopped fresh basil
Finely slivered peel of 1 large orange
¼ cup chopped fresh parsley

1. Preheat the oven to 350°F. Combine all the ingredients through the pepper in a large bowl. Mix thoroughly, and form into small meatballs.

2. Heat the butter with the oil in a large heavy skillet over medium heat. Sauté the meatballs, about six at a time, until golden brown on all sides, about 5 minutes. Transfer them to a Dutch oven.

3. Add the onion to the skillet. Cook, scraping the sides and bottom of the pan, over medium heat 3 minutes. Add the onions to the meatballs in the Dutch oven, along with the string beans, tomatoes, sugar, and basil. Stir gently to mix. Bake, uncovered, 1 hour. Stir in the orange peel and sprinkle with the parsley.

Serves 6.

Though the green bean was discovered in South America, food historians assert that varieties migrated to the more temperate climes of North America long, long before Columbus made his first crossing. In 1524, Giovanni Verrazano, the Florentine explorer who first traveled the Atlantic seacoast, wrote to his wife from the New World describing the foods that native Indians ate: "They grow slender pods born on bushes with bright green leaves. These have the virtue of a good flavor but require long and careful chewing even after a long stay in the cook pot"—probably so noted because the natives generally dried their beans prior to cooking or ate them when very mature.

SAUTEED STRING BEANS AND BAY SCALLOPS

After the summer tenants depart my Amagansett house, anything left on the vine I claim. And the scallops? They are never sweeter than in September when Gardiner's Bay has a harvest all its own.

½ pound string beans, trimmed, cut French-style
1 red bell pepper, seeded, cut into thin strips
1 pound bay scallops, or sea scallops, quartered
Juice of ½ lemon
½ cup all-purpose flour
4 tablespoons (½ stick) unsalted butter, approximately
2 tablespoons olive oil
2 shallots, minced
2 cloves garlic, minced
½ cup dry white wine
Salt and freshly ground black pepper
1 tablespoon chopped fresh basil, or ½ teaspoon dried
1 tablespoon chopped fresh parsley
Hot Steamed Rice (see page 412)

1. Preheat the oven to 350°F. Cook the beans in boiling salted water for 2 minutes. Rinse under cold running water; drain.

2. Cook the pepper in another pot of boiling salted water for 2 minutes. Rinse under cold running water; drain.

3. Sprinkle the scallops with the lemon juice and dust them lightly with the flour.

4. Melt 2 tablespoons of the butter in 1 tablespoon of the oil in a large skillet over medium-high heat. Add half the scallops and cook, stirring constantly, until golden, about 3 minutes. Add half the shallots and half the garlic. Toss thoroughly. Transfer to a baking dish.

5. Add the remaining butter and oil. Sauté the remaining scallops until golden; add the remaining shallots and garlic. Transfer to the baking dish. Toss in the beans and pepper and mix thoroughly.

6. Pour the wine into the same skillet and cook over medium-high heat, scraping the sides and bottom of the pan, until thick and syrupy, about 4 minutes. Pour this sauce over the scallop-vegetable mixture and add salt and pepper to taste. Bake, uncovered, 20 minutes. Sprinkle with the basil and parsley. Serve over Hot Steamed Rice.

Serves 4.

String beans grow two ways: as pole beans and as bush beans. The Omaha Indians had better names for both varieties. They called them "walking beans" and "beans not walking." To keep the horticultural notes succinct, the bush bean is a stay-at-home. While the plant grows thick as a dwarf pine, the bean picker never has to stretch for a handful of pods. Pole beans, being somewhat less constricted, wander all over the garden. Never a pleasure to pick, pole beans are (in my opinion at least) sweeter for their nomadic tendencies.

NORMAN BEANS WITH EGGS

My friend Paul Milikin is an actor. I rarely get to see him perform because he is most often on the road, but I do hear from him with unerring regularity. His missives are usually postcards from cities with notable repertory companies and include some good recipe that he managed to acquire locally. For besides being a fine actor, Milikin is also a notable cook. The following string bean dish is his. It was sent from France a while back and rates a critical rave in my book, for either lunch or brunch, and particularly if one's guests happen to be vegetarian.

1 pound string beans, trimmed
2 tablespoons unsalted butter, melted
½ teaspoon lemon juice
1 teaspoon chopped fresh chives
1 teaspoon chopped fresh parsley
½ teaspoon salt
¼ teaspoon freshly ground black pepper
4 eggs, lightly beaten

1. Preheat the oven to 400°F. Cook the beans in boiling salted water until crisp-tender, about 1½ to 2 minutes. Drain.

2. Place the warm beans in a bowl and add the remaining ingredients. Toss well and pour into a buttered shallow baking dish. Bake until set, about 10 minutes. Cut into wedges to serve.

Serves 4.

SWEET POTATOES

I Yam What I Yam

I suspect I can pinpoint the development of my taste buds to the moment when I left home for college. The school I had elected, William and Mary in Williamsburg, Virginia, was too far away for weekend excursions, and even long-distance phone calls—except in case of dire emergency—had been discouraged in advance by my ever-thrifty mother. So the snowy day when I boarded the Pennsylvania Railroad for geographic parts unknown was in actuality the beginning of a much longer journey: to a life *on my own.*

The startling revelation of utter freedom came upon me when I realized that my grandfather, unexpectedly appearing at the frosty station to say goodbye, had pressed a crisp hundred-dollar bill into my palm as we gravely shook hands.

My mother had already given me some injunctions about money. "Never give big tips," she cautioned. "People don't expect 'em from kids anyway." After noting there was a night's layover en route, she had been most specific about where and how I spend this respite. "Find a clean *second-class* hotel," she advised. "Ask a cab driver to take you to one where salesmen stay! And be sure to skip fancy restaurants. Only eat at lunch counters or cafeterias. They're generally cleaner!"

With a hundred dollars in my wallet, I dismissed all these admonitions out of hand. The first act of independence: a solo reservation in the train's dining car.

What a glory it was! A caravan of polished mahogany with shaded windows and shell-like sconces that shone day and night. White damask covered the tables where salt cellars and water goblets danced like marionettes at each reverberation of the train's wheels.

As I had never dined alone in a restaurant, even on solid ground, the prospect of eating in one on the move seemed doubly intimidating. The black headwaiter at the door was obviously one of a vanishing breed of amiable men who took pleasure in their work. White-coated and benign as a preacher, he settled me at an empty table next to a window. Then, recognizing my awe at the multitude of options, he pointed out the specialties on the menu.

When I announced my decision—a meal of terrapin followed by roast pheasant under glass and sweet potato pone—he shook his head gravely.

"You sure don' want that, son," he confided. "Terrapin is snapping turtle no matter what you call it, and the pheasant . . . well!" He whistled. "That's been on the tracks for some time now. Why don' you let me bring you a nice cup of crab bisque instead, followed by a club sandwich and pie à la mode."

I acquiesced to his superior judgment about the first choices, but balked severely at giving up the pone. I had never tasted this sweet dish but the name itself, so mouth-watering, conjured up all manner of images: Scarlett O'Hara, Rhett, Tara. I insisted he bring me a slice.

Reluctantly he agreed. But midway between Trenton and Camden, he reappeared, empty-handed. "Son," he whispered, "I do not tell this to most folks who ride the Pullmans but you seem to be a young man who really enjoys his vittles. If so, don't eat no Northern pone served here!" Handing me a slip of folded paper, he continued, "You got a mouth for sweet potato? Take note of this place in Richmond. It's the best you will ever find!"

The name scrawled on the sheet was *Blue Milton on Main St.* Just that. I gave him a large tip for his good offices and promised faithfully to heed the advice.

I did so the very next week. Blue Milton was most definitely "a place" and not a restaurant. Situated at the end of Richmond's Main Street in an area that, I later discovered, housed all the city's fancy houses, it was actually a wooden shack next to a closed service station. It bore no name and was papered outside and in with Coca Cola and Dr. Pepper posters faded by time. "The Mill," as most denizens called it, was run by a black couple and was remarkable in 1941 for the fact that it was totally integrated. White and black patrons stood on line together waiting for a slice of pone or a plateful of ribs and a fried ham bun, without a measure of discontent. First come was first served. And royally, I might add, for it was probably the best food in the city at the time—certainly the best I had ever tasted, and I returned often.

Blue Milton is long since gone, but the memory of its luscious golden pone, sweeter than youth itself, will never be erased from my tongue!

Vegetable Roots

Actually no potato at all, the sweet potato is a rooted tuber that is first cousin to the morning glory. I have never seen one in full bloom, but the rose-purple trumpets are reputedly so dazzling that on occasion a sweet potato crop has been seriously threatened by overacquisitive posy pickers.

A New World native (albeit in the less temperate of its zones), *Ipomoea batatas* has been in culinary currency for over a thousand years. When Columbus made his second appearance on this side of the Atlantic in 1493, he noted in his diaries that the native Indians (in Hispaniola, where he landed) subsisted exclusively on a diet of fish, coconut, and sweet potato, a root he variously called *b-aje*, *āge*, or *baāge*. Columbus probably had misheard the word. Scholars assume it was actually *ba-hich*, and it meant "tongue burn." With good reason. The Taino Indians there ate boiled sweet potatoes out of a communal pot. Reaching into the center of the cauldron with bare hands, they would toss the steaming chunks into the air to cool, but invariably scorched their lips swallowing them.

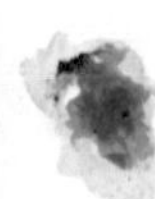

According to one of Columbus's Spanish crewmen who passed this intelligence on to his brother years later, the method of consuming *baage* was torturous but its flavor so intriguing that one went through the oral immolation willingly. The taste he compared to the commingling of ripe oranges and roasted chestnuts.

No wonder the Spanish court eagerly awaited its first bite of this new "root fruit." From all accounts no one was displeased, though they considered its name utterly unpronounceable. In time, *baage* underwent a change to *batata*, which was remarkably like the existing Spanish word for potato, *patata*, and caused these dissimilar tubers to be linked ever since!

The sweet potato did not come to European tables from Spain voluntarily. On the contrary, Spanish gardeners zealously husbanded the secret of its growth. Henry VIII, whose first wife, Catherine of Aragon, was Spanish, received the sweet potato as part of her dowry and admired the flavor so much that he insisted that Spain export the tubers to England, which they did with some reluctance. Henry VIII adored the sweet potato and was noted for his ability to digest two dozen per sitting. His palate was so devoted to what he called "the Spanish potato" that after his divorce from Catherine, he gave a prize of land and gold to the gardener who could grow one in Britain. The incentive proved felicitous, and by the mid-sixteenth century sweet potatoes bloomed all over the British Isles. The rage was brief, however, most likely because the sweet potato needs a warmer climate to survive. All plants withered in a typically cool English summer, and never grew there again.

The sweet potato is an unusual vegetable in that it is not grown from seed. Instead, plants are started from sprouts—cut from the roots or from the vines of a prior crop. The unorthodox progeny in time gave rise to yet another name. When *batatas* were cultivated in Jamestown in 1648, the farmers who planted the slips called them "bastards"—a moniker that clung for some years, until righteous members of the community had it expunged, and the "bastard" became the legitimate "Virginia potato."

What to Look For

There are two general kinds of sweet potatoes at our table. Growers (dependent upon matters of climate and geography) variously dub a sweet potato as either "moist" or "dry." Neither tag has a jot to do with its water content. Moist types, often called yams, have somewhat reddish brown skins and deep orange flesh, with a high starch content that converts to sugar as it cooks, and may be deemed a sweeter sweet potato. Dry types have tan or fawn shaded skins and yellow-to-gold flesh that converts less starch to sugar—and are decidedly less sweet on a fork!

It may be worth noting that the moist, sweet yam that happily ends up as pone or pie has absolutely no kinship with a true yam *(Dioscorea bulbifera)*, a tropical vine whose globes are a hundred times sweeter and mealier. American yams got the wrong name by association. The first slaves, who had lived on the yams in their native land, called them by the African word "to eat" (variously the Gullah *njam*, the Senegar *nyami*, or the Vai *djambi*), and the appellation obviously stuck.

Shopping for sweet potatoes, the sharp-eyed consumer will ferret out the smoothest-skinned specimens. Look for medium sizes that taper at the end. Most sweet potatoes on the market are precured and have had some stint in storage prior to the supermarket shelf. So choose members that are not bruised, blemished, or, worse yet, sprouting. Sweet potato harvests begin in late summer, and by Thanksgiving it is virtually impossible to find any that are uncured.

Curing is a process that allows sweet potatoes to keep. Once they are dug, tubers are held in controlled high-heat, high-humidity environments for about a week to allow the conversion of starch to dextrins and sugars to begin before they are stored. So, a sweet potato that is boiled and then mashed into a velvety chowder will taste a heck of a lot sweeter in winter and spring (after curing) than in August when it is straight from the vine.

The sweet potato is nutritious, make no mistake about it. One medium sweet (boiled, then peeled) provides more than twice the recommended daily allowance of vitamin A (11,940 units), along with healthy increments of potassium, calcium, and ascorbic acid. On the debit side, a boiled sweet potato adds about 172 calories to your diet (though somewhat less when baked.)

Preparation

I am very catholic, culinarily speaking, in the matter of sweet potato cookery. I boil, bake, or fry them, and even on occasion make ice cream out of them. The surest way to retain a sweet potato's nutrients (and parenthetically to prevent the natural sugar from leaching out) is to boil it in its jacket and peel it afterward.

I usually bake sweet potatoes quickly in a fairly warm oven (400°F), and I never grease the skins. An 8-ounce sweet will bake in 40 to 45 minutes. One may place a sweet potato directly on the oven rack, but I do not for they often have infinitesimal fissures in the skin and leave a sticky residue that requires a scrub-up later. Most often I bake them on a shallow baking dish or tray and turn them once during the oven stint. When you can insert a fork into the flesh with ease, the sweet potato is definitely ready to go to the table.

Once a sweet potato has been cooked, it keeps. I store mine (cooled) in the refrigerator for up to a week's time. You may leave them in their skins, or if you wish, scrape the pulp into a covered container prior to storage. A sweet potato's sweetness increases in repose.

SWEET 'TATER POTTAGE

My ultimate sweet potato soup is called a pottage out of loose Biblical connection: in my opinion, Esau would have sold his birthright for a single slurp.

1 tablespoon unsalted butter
1 medium onion, chopped
1 large rib celery, chopped
½ pound sweet potatoes, peeled, sliced
1½ cups chicken broth (see page 414)
1 cup V-8 or spicy tomato juice
¼ cup heavy or whipping cream
1 tablespoon bourbon
⅛ teaspoon ground cinnamon
⅛ teaspoon freshly grated nutmeg
Salt and freshly ground black pepper

1. Melt the butter in a medium saucepan over medium-low heat. Stir in the onion; cook 1 minute. Stir in the celery and potatoes; cook 5 minutes. Add the broth and the tomato juice; cook, uncovered, until tender, about 25 minutes. Cool.

2. Place the soup, in batches, in the container of a blender or food processor. Blend until smooth.

3. Pour the soup into a medium saucepan. Stir in the cream, bourbon, cinnamon, and nutmeg. Heat over low heat until warmed through. Do not boil. Add salt and pepper to taste. Serve hot, or chill and serve cold.

Serves 4.

COLD CURRIED YAMS

On the subject of curry, try a less authentic sweet potato rendering. If one were bold (as I am not) it would be dubbed sweet potato salad. In my bailiwick it teams remarkably with fried chicken and baked ham on a picnic table.

4 large yams (about 1¾ pounds)
1 medium red onion, finely chopped
½ green bell pepper, seeded, finely chopped
½ cup Mayonnaise (see page 408)
½ cup sour cream
¼ cup strong Beef Stock, cooled (see page 409)
1 tablespoon curry powder
Salt and freshly ground black pepper
2 tablespoons chopped fresh parsley

1. Cook the yams in their jackets in boiling salted water until just barely tender, 20 to 25 minutes. Drain. Cool, peel, and cut into ⅛-inch-thick slices.

2. Combine the sliced yams, red onion, and green pepper in a large bowl.

3. In a medium bowl, whisk the mayonnaise with the sour cream. Whisk in the stock, curry powder, and salt and pepper to taste. Pour this dressing over the yam mixture. Toss lightly to combine, and serve sprinkled with the parsley.

Serves 4.

SCALLOPED SWEETS

In North America, the term "sweet potato" did not become official until about 1740, and then only to distinguish it from the white potato, thought to be Irish and brought over about twenty years earlier.

Here's my version of what most Irish potato lovers consider their own preserve: scalloped potatoes, turned exotically different with a "bastard-Spanish-Virginia-Chinese-Japanese" member as its main ingredient.

4 large sweet potatoes (about 2 pounds)
3½ cups heavy or whipping cream
¾ teaspoon salt
½ teaspoon ground ginger
1 tablespoon lime juice
Finely grated peel of 1 lime
¾ teaspoon ground white pepper
2 teaspoons unsalted butter, cut into bits

1. Preheat the oven to 350°F. Peel the potatoes and cut them into ⅛-inch-thick slices.

2. Combine the potatoes, cream, salt, ginger, lime juice, lime peel, and white pepper in a large saucepan. Heat to boiling, stirring constantly.

3. Pour the potato mixture into a well-buttered shallow baking dish. Dot the surface with the butter. Bake until lightly browned, about 1 hour.

Serves 6 to 8.

BAKED YAMS

On most American tables, sweet potatoes have always maintained an aura of a "Sunday special"—their appearance assured only on major holidays like Thanksgiving. However, since it is a ubiquitous vegetable in the Deep South, the sweet potato was a mainstay of most sharecroppers' diets. Some of its most original table guises, in fact, demonstrate necessity mothering invention. To wit: this easy, economical, extremely tasty rendering.

2 strips bacon
2 medium yams
1 teaspoon dark brown sugar
Freshly ground black pepper

1. Preheat the oven to 375°F. Sauté the bacon strips in a heavy skillet until crisp. Drain on paper towels, reserving the drippings. Crumble and reserve the bacon.

2. Cut the yams in half lengthwise. Score the top of each half in a lattice pattern, about ¼ inch deep. Do not cut through the skins. Brush the top of each with bacon drippings, squeezing the yams lightly to open them up. Sprinkle each half with ¼ teaspoon of the brown sugar.

3. Bake the potatoes 1 hour. Sprinkle them with the crumbled bacon and bake 2 minutes longer. Sprinkle with pepper to taste.

Serves 2.

MASHED SWEETS

Henry VIII laced his sweet potato with rum and Demerara sugar. I dote on them flavored with butter, cream, and bourbon.

4 large sweet potatoes (about 2 pounds)
3 tablespoons unsalted butter
3 tablespoons heavy or whipping cream
2 tablespoons bourbon
Salt and freshly ground black pepper

1. Cook the potatoes in their jackets in boiling salted water until tender, 45 to 50 minutes. Drain.

2. Carefully peel the potatoes and place them in a medium saucepan. Mash, over very low heat, with a potato masher until smooth. Beat in the butter, cream, bourbon, and salt and pepper to taste. Cook, stirring constantly, until warmed through.

Serves 4.

SWEET POTATO PONE

To my prejudiced tongue, the definitive pone is one that is not too sweet. I acquired this recipe from a beguiling book of regional Southern fare (sadly out of print): *Damnyankee in a Southern Kitchen* by Helen Worth.

2 large eggs
2 cups milk
1½ tablespoons vanilla extract
1 cup sugar
¼ teaspoon freshly grated nutmeg
½ teaspoon grated orange peel
3 medium sweet potatoes (about 1 pound), peeled, grated
6 tablespoons (¾ stick) unsalted butter, melted

Preheat the oven to 350°F. Beat the eggs in a large mixing bowl. Beat in the remaining ingredients and pour into a buttered 2-quart soufflé or baking dish. Bake until firm and golden brown, about 2 hours. Let stand 20 minutes before serving. The flavor intensifies as it stands.

Serves 8.

There is a rumor that early Spanish explorers (like Balboa) may have carried the sweet potato as far as the Philippines, where it also took root. Later Portuguese voyagers (like Magellan) may have transported it even farther—to India, China, and Malaya. At any event, its entry into Eastern cuisine was so unobtrusive that its point of origin has been largely overlooked for centuries. In southern regions of Japan, for instance, it is called *kara-imo* ("the Chinese potato"), but it is known as *satsuma-imo* ("the Japanese potato") in the rest of the country.

FRIED SWEET POTATO CRISPS

3 medium sweet potatoes (about 1 pound)
2 tablespoons salt
Oil for frying
Salt and freshly ground black pepper

1. Peel the potatoes and cut them into ⅛-inch-thick round slices. Place the slices in a large bowl. Cover with cold water; stir in the salt. Let stand 10 minutes.

2. Heat ¼ inch of oil in a heavy skillet until hot but not smoking. Drain the potatoes; pat them dry with paper towels. Fry, a few slices at a time, until lightly brown on both sides, about 4 minutes per side. Drain on paper towels and sprinkle with salt and pepper to taste. Keep warm in a low oven while frying the remaining potatoes.

Serves 4 to 6.

MADRASI KARI

(Sweet Potatoes, Beef, and Pork, Madras-style)

One of the most unusual sweet potato recipes in my collection is Indian. From southerly Madras, it is a curry that teams this vegetable with beef and pork. I often improvise the heartier components with whatever leftovers I have on hand. Naturally the dish varies, but it is the sweet potato that gives it its essential savor.

1 large sweet potato (about ½ pound), peeled, cubed
2 tablespoons unsalted butter
3 tablespoons vegetable oil
1 medium onion, finely chopped
1 clove garlic, minced
½ pound cooked beef, cut into 2-by-½-inch strips
½ pound cooked pork, cut into 2-by-½-inch strips
1 tablespoon curry powder
⅛ teaspoon ground cloves
⅛ teaspoon ground cinnamon
⅛ teaspoon ground cardamom
Juice of ½ lime
Salt and freshly ground black pepper
⅛ teaspoon crushed dried hot red peppers
½ cup light cream or half-and-half

1. Cook the potato in boiling salted water for 5 minutes. Drain.

2. Melt 1 tablespoon of the butter in 2 tablespoons of the oil in a large heavy skillet over medium heat. Stir in the potato; cook 3 minutes. Add the remaining 1 tablespoon butter and oil. Stir in the onion; cook 1 minute. Stir in the garlic; cook 1 minute longer.

3. Add the beef and pork to the skillet. Sprinkle with the curry, cloves, cinnamon, and cardamom. Mix well. Stir in the lime juice. Cook, covered, over medium-low heat until the potatoes are tender, about 30 minutes.

4. When the potato is tender, add salt and pepper to taste, sprinkle with the crushed peppers, and stir in the light cream. Cook until warmed through.

Serves 4.

SWEET POTATO BEIGNETS

If you are not worried about calorie content, walk, do not run, to your kitchen and try out the silkiest rendering you will ever set your tongue to: an elegant, lightly crusted beignet (half cruller, half fritter). It is the most wholly seductive breakfast food (or even dessert in a pinch) that I know.

2 medium sweet potatoes (about 2/3 pound)
1 egg yolk, lightly beaten
1/4 cup packed dark brown sugar
1/2 cup all-purpose flour
1/8 teaspoon ground allspice
1/8 teaspoon ground cinnamon
1/8 teaspoon ground cloves
1/4 teaspoon freshly grated nutmeg
2 egg whites
Oil for frying
1 cup finely ground pecans
1/2 cup granulated sugar

1. Cook the potatoes in their jackets in boiling water until very tender, about 45 minutes. Drain. Cool, peel, and mash until smooth.

2. Place the mashed potatoes in a large bowl. Beat in the egg yolk, brown sugar, flour, allspice, cinnamon, cloves, and nutmeg.

3. Beat the egg whites until stiff but not dry. Fold them into the potato mixture.

4. Heat 1½ inches of oil in a medium saucepan until hot but not smoking.

5. Place the ground pecans in a shallow bowl. Drop a teaspoonful of potato batter into the pecans. Roll it gently with your fingertips to coat. Cook the potato balls in the hot oil, a few at a time, until golden brown, about 2 minutes per side. Drain on paper towels and sprinkle lightly with granulated sugar. Keep warm in a low oven while frying the remaining beignets.

Makes about 18 beignets.

YAMMYCAKES

In Virginia, where sweet potatoes first flourished among the colonists, they were usually whipped up as a dessert in pie, pudding, or "panniquakes." Witness an old, old pancake recipe—not authentically prerevolutionary, to be sure, but of certain long lineage. And Southern to boot!

1¾ to 2 pounds yams (4 or 5 large)
1 cup all-purpose flour
1 teaspoon baking powder
1/4 teaspoon salt
1/2 teaspoon ground cinnamon
1/4 teaspoon ground ginger
1/8 teaspoon ground allspice
Pinch of ground cloves
2 eggs, lightly beaten
1/2 cup heavy or whipping cream
1/3 cup orange juice
1/4 cup vodka
Confectioners' sugar

1. Cook the potatoes in their jackets in boiling salted water until tender, about 45 minutes. Drain.

2. Carefully peel the potatoes and either mash or purée them in a food processor. Transfer 2 cups of the potato purée to a large mixing bowl. Add the remaining ingredients except the confectioner's sugar. Mix well.

3. Heat a large griddle or nonstick skillet over medium heat. Grease it lightly, and spoon about ¼ cup of the batter onto the hot surface. Turn the pancake over when small bubbles appear on the surface. Cook 1 minute on the second side. Keep warm on a rack in a low oven while making the rest of the pancakes. Dust with confectioners' sugar before serving.

Serves 6 to 8.

YAM ICE CREAM

The great black botanist George Washington Carver is reputed to have devised five hundred uses for this wondrous tuber. I am adding the five hundred and first. It's an ice cream, whipped up in any conventional ice cream freezer, but totally unlike any you have ever sampled. Carver would be proud of me. So would the owners of the Blue Milton!

3 medium yams (about 1 pound)
1 cup sugar
2 tablespoons dark rum
1 teaspoon vanilla extract
1 egg yolk
1 cup milk
3 cups heavy or whipping cream

1. Cook the yams in their jackets in boiling water until very tender, 35 to 40 minutes. Drain. Cool, peel, and quarter.

2. Place the yams in the container of a food processor or blender. Add the sugar, rum, vanilla, egg yolk, and milk. Process until smooth.

3. Transfer the yam mixture to a large bowl. Whisk in the cream. Pour the mixture into the canister of an ice cream maker and proceed according to the manufacturer's directions. It's best when solidly frozen.

Makes about 1½ quarts.

TOMATOES

A Summer Garden Classic

When I was not quite seven years old and far too unformed for the regimen, my ill-advised parents sent me off to summer camp. Why not? My sister had been an ebullient camper for two summers and when I tagged along on a "Parents' Day" in midsummer, I had been so overwhelmed by all the wonders of athletic outdoor life that I spontaneously evinced a desire to participate in these bucolic revels myself.

It was one of my most misguided judgments. The camp my father and mother selected for my induction was called Pawnee. It was known as a brother-sister institution, though why I will never understand, since male and female campers had little or no contact except at meals and some other segregated activities. A large chilly lake kept the sexual barriers firmly enforced.

My cabin, on the brother side of the water, was ruled by a tall, handsome, and unfeeling counselor whom I and my five bunkmates were bidden to address as "Uncle Sid." Always needing a shave, this young man seemed alternately so preoccupied or punitive that I rarely spoke to him at all, except at dinner, or "mess" as it was aptly known.

It was Uncle Sid's theory (and he was probably twenty at the time) that children compliantly eat whatever is set before them—*sans* cavil. Finicky at best, I always ate less than the prescribed portion and supplemented my diet with Hershey bars (sent by my grandmother and stashed away in a footlocker). Uncle Sid discovered this cache after one of my particularly bad showings at lunch and confiscated the chocolate permanently—which provoked my first insurrection. I wrote about this to my grandmother and was punished for recalcitrance when the letter was censored by, who else, Uncle Sid.

My next infraction occurred soon after, when tomatoes ripened and I refused to admit a scant forkful between my lips. "No! Never," I shouted, causing several tables of young campers to turn in my direction.

"If you do not eat what is on your plate," Uncle Sid stated in a firm voice, "you will go to your bunk immediately and stay there off-limits without supper or camp privileges!"

Missing supper was no blow. But camp privileges encompassed the week's movie, the only respite from seven days of torturous immoderation in the hot sun and cold water. I wailed my disappointment. In fact I screamed so loudly that my sister heard the hullabaloo clear across the segregated dining room.

Myra rushed to my defense with a filial affection I had never witnessed before. "What have you done to my brother?" she upbraided my counselor.

Uncle Sid was plainly disconcerted by her tone. "He refused to eat his tomatoes," he replied. "That's against regulations, so he is being restricted to his bunk. Let him go!"

"I won't," cried my sister passionately—much influenced, I suspect, by the enforced parting of Evangeline and Basil in the movies. Two other counselors had to drag her away.

"Have you never heard of the bill of rights?" she snarled at my tormentors. "It is his inalienable right to refuse a tomato. As an American!"

She was right. But neither the flag-waving nor any other argument cut ice with Uncle Sid. I was remanded to my cabin and missed the movie. But in passing I developed a healthy admiration for my sister's sense of outrage. My love of tomatoes came in time as well.

Vegetable Roots

Despite any misgivings I may have harbored about the tomato, it is now the most eagerly awaited vegetable that grows in my garden. Other food lovers must agree, as it is the third-most-popular fresh vegetable (after potatoes and peas) in the United States. However, tomatoes were not always appreciated.

A native American plant, the first tomato was considered a weed. It was discovered sprouting wild in among the maize and bean fields of the early Incas. They (and the Mayas and Aztecs too) successfully cultivated its seeds. The Aztecs gave the tomato its name *(tomatl)* and considered its sun-swollen fruit to be a symbol of good fortune from the gods. Despite the augury, the tomato's history is a good deal more crimson than one would suspect. For centuries after they had been brought by caravel to Spain, tomatoes were admired—at a distance. Thought to be a highly potent aphrodisiac, they bloomed but went unconsumed, except by hard-core sybarites. For lesser men feared that even a forkful would cause moral decay or downright doom!

The notion that eating a tomato was synonymous with living dangerously stemmed in part from its family connections: *Lycopersicon esculentum* is a cousin twice removed of deadly nightshade. In the sixteenth century, Pierandrea Mattioli, the Italian herbalist, included tomato in the narcotic bouquet of lethal *Solanumae.* In his *Commentaries on the Six Books of Discorides,* Mattioli dubbed the tomato *mala insana* (or "bad egg"), since all those grown in his time were of a decidedly sulphurous hue. Worse yet, he lumped it together with belladonna, henbane, mandrake root, and arsenic—none of which even an intrepid kitchen practitioner would choose to season a pot of spaghetti sauce.

Throughout its checkered past, the tomato has been the target of much curious legend—and lore galore. Up until the twentieth century the rubicund orb was known as a "love apple." Theories vary, but the one I subscribe to blames this on the Spanish. It seems that when the first conquistador clapped eyes on a tomato, he called it *manzana,* or apple, because that's what he thought it was. As apples do not flourish in Spain, it was a natural enough mistake I sup-

A good crop of scarlet tomatoes is any gardener's joy, even those whose vegetable patch happens to be a window box. Since I love growing tomatoes almost as much as I enjoy eating them, I will offer some twice-told wisdom for their Where and Care.

Early in March, well before planting time, sensible seedsmen will turn the soil and add a spot of humus (and quicklime if needed). I like to poke a little jot of well-seasoned manure and compost into the soil as well. But don't overdo the fertilizers; a quart to every ten square yards of garden is more than enough.

Tomato seedlings raised indoors in peat pots are the surest way to have plants that will bear fruit in season. Never put them out (plant them, that is) until all fear of frost may be dismissed. Water them well before and after they are planted to make the transition less traumatic. When you plant tomato seedlings (or seeds for that matter), make sure to mound the earth high around each plant. A well-made tomato garden should look like molehills (not mountains) with staked tomato plants in the centers.

Not all tomatoes require stakes, but I never take chances with lank vines. I tie the stems to poles with the flexible strips you find in packages of plastic bags, but string or twine will do equally well. A good tomato gardener is a fearless soul who will pinch back the top of his plant as soon as it sprouts an inch or two above the initial greenery. Don't be timid about cutting new growth—it will allow the plant's energies to be concentrated on a healthy yield rather than conspicuous foliage. Remember, it's a tomato you're growing, not a palm—so be bold.

Tomatoes require lots of watering, on a window ledge or in the garden, so be generous with the H_2O. Proceed with pesticides and fumigants at your own sensibility. I choose not to spray home-grown tomatoes at all, preferring the occasional cutworm or patch of rust to any further chemical warfare in my life.

Having said all this, pick your tomatoes from early July to late September with the knowledge that the best things in life are still relatively freely given—and righteously enjoyed.

pose, but *manzana* did not tempt the Hispanic palate. After several poor showings in a pastry shell it was banished to the Spanish garden, rather than the kitchen, where it was cultivated for purely decorative purposes till the middle of the sixteenth century. A traveling Italian chef reputedly reclaimed the tomato's reputation. He brought the plant to Florence, and flavored a sauce of *pomo d'oro* ("apple of gold") there shortly afterward for the Borgias. If it seems a far-fetched translation of *manzana*, keep in mind, all early tomatoes were yellow. According to tittle-tattle, when the Borgias' chef started serving tomatoes (fearing a negative reaction as they had developed a rather wayward culinary reputation by this time), the name was altered to *pomo dei Mori*, or "Moor's apple," to emphasize the fruit's Spanish connection. Needless to say, the tomato's flavor caught on.

When a French dignitary visited Italy and sampled tomato sauce for the first time, he misunderstood the name of the chief ingredient and assumed *pomo d'Moro* was *pomme d'amour*, or "apple of love." The story is probably apocryphal, for the notion that tomatoes were sexually stimulating antedates the Renaissance.

The tomato's revenge on Mattioli's countrymen was sweet. It turned rosy for one thing and became inseparably linked with Italian cooking for another. Since the early 1800s, when the vegetable's status as a deadly poison was officially rescinded, more tomatoes have been consumed in southern Italy (in confederation with pasta and cheese) than anywhere else on the face of the globe! And no slackening of the national appetite is in sight.

What to Look For

Tomatoes come in many shapes and sizes. Big, burly beefsteaks are usually stolidly scarlet and smell faintly minty when picked. They are unexcelled first choices for my salad bowl, broiler tray, or BLT. Smaller, deeper-shaded globes (with more conventional tomato physiognomies) grow quickly, have a higher ratio of juice to flesh, and will cross over from tuna surprise to tomato juice (and/or gazpacho for that matter) with equal felicity. Plums, the elongated egg-shaped tomatoes whose annual appearance pinpoints midsummer for me, may seem less than toothsome raw (they are pulpy) but cook up into remarkably dense sauces and velvety chowders. The tiny cherry tomato, besides making a splendid addition to an hors d'oeuvre tray, will also outperform less flavorsome varieties in a tangy salsa or stewpot. Yellow tomatoes (with a higher pH factor that indicates less acid) may seem pale in partnership with spaghetti but are the basis for a tomato jam included in this chapter that is the best you will ever sample.

When shopping for a seasonal tomato, choose the ones that have the deepest color. Look for a firm (but not baseball-hard) texture and a bright complexion. Optimally a ripe tomato is neither squashy nor blemished. But frankly, I will settle for one streaked with green on the stem or with a blemish on the stern rather than a plastic specimen with perfectly inedible flesh below the surface. Tomatophiles tell us to select fruit that is heavy to the hand, but the only real test in my book is to slice into one. Good tomato color is really red—a shade between a fire engine and a field of poppies.

When a fresh tomato is at its ripest and reddest (in August and September on my vine), its classic rendering requires little or no preparation aside from pepper and salt and a sprinkling of fragrant basil leaves. However, heavy-duty doctoring or canned substitutions may be required for tomato cookery during the rest of the year, classic or otherwise!

Speaking for myself, I hate to buy out-of-season produce. But I do often in the case of tomatoes, choosing Mexican, Israeli, Belgian, or Chilean fresh imports (even at exorbitant prices) over the tasteless and rock-hard orbs that are the only consumer alternative. Most U.S. tomato strains in common currency at supermarkets are picked green and forced to redden (if never properly ripen) in ethylene gas chambers. More pertinently, these commercial varieties have also been bred to such a state of flat-ended, straight-sided, thick-skinned conformity that every wan globe survives the rigors of a long-distance shipping trek without a solitary bruise. And, sad to say, without a scintilla of natural flavor intact.

If I am unwilling to expend the cash required for unseasonal imports, I usually elect cherry tomatoes instead. If you keep these miniatures covered in a paper (not plastic) bag for several days, the natural ethylene gas inherent in all acidic vegetables will intensify the flavor and they will approximate the taste of more seasonal varieties.

I grow my own tomatoes every summer for the same reason I diet then: it makes me feel righteous! Another benefit is therapeutic, since there are only a scant 35 calories to a medium-size tomato. A tomato (even if you pronounce it *tomah-toe*) provides a healthy supply of potassium (300 milligrams) to the diet and a whopping jolt of vitamin A (1,110 units). In the matter of vitamin C, the tomato takes a back seat to the orange, I am afraid. It requires 8 ounces of tomato juice to equal the amount of C in 4 ounces of orange juice. Even more dispiriting for green tomato lovers, the amount of vitamins is slashed virtually in half when the tomato is firmly unripe.

Preparation

In the matter of preparing a fresh tomato for cooking, there is a maxim of Mrs. Beeton's that I heartily endorse: "Peel with discretion. Seed by rote!" If you suspect that is a vestigial culinary nicety left over from the Victorians, you are mistaken. Tomato skins fissure and split during periods of extended cookery and the resulting fragments are not only unattractive to the eye, but unpleasant to the tongue as well. There are a few exceptions to the rule. If a cooked tomato is to be puréed and sieved later, the skin may be left on for the jot of flavor it will impart. Likewise in baking, when the skin acts as a shell to hold the tomato together, there is no need to peel it. But at all other times, strip it bare! I peel a tomato by immersing it, impaled on a fork, into a saucepan of boiling water for half a minute. Then, after it has cooled slightly, I run a sharp knife under the skin and peel the sections with my fingers. Seeding is something else. In my opinion, a tomato's seeds turn astringent if not downright bitter the moment they are heated, so I always expunge them prior to the stove. My technique came from my grandmother. She halved a tomato in two at the midriff and squeezed out the seeds—just as she would juice an orange—with a small strainer placed over a bowl to catch any residual pink juices, which she added to the dish she was cooking.

American Indians claim that a cut ripe tomato is an unbeatable room deodorant. Moreover, they assert that the acid in a tomato, when well rubbed onto the skin, will remove the scent of garlic, wild onion, skunk, and any other noxious bouquet you can name.

MARY CASSETTI'S DOUBLE-ZAPPED TOMATO SHELLS

This recipe is more handiwork from that talented cook from Elmira, New York: Mary Cassetti. Mrs. Cassetti's dish is highly unusual, employing both ripe fresh tomatoes and sun-dried tomatoes in the pasta's embroidery. Sources for Italian sun-dried tomatoes are listed in Notes on Ingredients, page 417. However, spirited do-it-yourselfers with a spare bushel or two of tomatoes at hand might wish to peruse the instructions for making their own (see box).

½ pound pasta shells
2 tablespoons unsalted butter
3 sun-dried tomatoes, cut into thin slivers
1 large fresh tomato, peeled, seeded, diced
3 tablespoons plain yogurt
2 tablespoons freshly grated Parmesan cheese
Salt and freshly ground black pepper

1. Cook the shells in boiling salted water until tender, 3 minutes for fresh, longer for packaged. Drain.

2. Melt the butter in a medium saucepan over low heat. Stir in the pasta, dried tomatoes, fresh tomato, yogurt, and Parmesan cheese. Add salt and pepper to taste. Serve immediately.

Serves 4 as a first course.

There are two ways to dry a tomato. The first (baked) method requires any conventional home oven with a thermometer setting of 150°F and a nylon screen drying tray. That's all. A drying tray may be improvised of nylon window screening stretched and stapled over a picture frame. Never use metal screening, however. The combined acids in the tomatoes and the metal's surface could cause the dried tomatoes to become toxic.

Tomatoes to be dried should be sliced thin (vertically), laid on the tray, and placed in the 150°F oven initially for 3 hours. Then the heat should be lowered to 130°F until the tomatoes are dry (approximately 2 to 3 hours longer). Dried tomatoes will be tough-to-crisp in texture. Note that super-acidic tomatoes should be steam-blanched whole for approximately 3 minutes prior to slicing.

The second (old-fashioned) method is to dry tomatoes in the sun. This cannot be done except on a very hot day. Slice (and/or steam-blanch) the tomatoes as directed above. Place the thin slices on a large unpainted board (plywood will do nicely). Care should be taken to slant the board slightly so any surplus tomato juices will run off. Salt the tomatoes well. Prop the board against the side of a wall (or a back porch step) so the surface will reflect heat onto the tomatoes. Place a layer of cheesecloth or mosquito netting over the drying tomatoes to keep insects off. When the tomatoes shrivel completely and are firm to the touch, they are sun-dried. Brush off excess salt before storage.

Store both oven-dried and sun-dried tomatoes in sterile dry jars and seal for keeping. Dried tomatoes may also be kept in olive oil, as the Italians do.

TOMATO FISH BISQUE

The compound of rosy-ripe orbs and snowy fish filets makes the following soup a tomato's manifest destiny. It is for all seasons, but is best in late summer.

2 tablespoons unsalted butter
1 small onion, finely chopped
1 small clove garlic, minced
Pinch of ground allspice
¼ teaspoon ground mace
Pinch of ground cloves
2 tablespoons all-purpose flour
3 cups Fish Stock (see page 410)
3 medium tomatoes, quartered (about ¾ pound)
1 can (14 ounces) plum tomatoes, drained
1¼ teaspoons salt
1 teaspoon sugar
1 tablespoon chopped fresh basil, or 1 teaspoon dried
¼ cup long-grain rice
1 pound flounder or sole filets, cut into 1-inch pieces
½ cup heavy or whipping cream
Salt and freshly ground black pepper
1 tablespoon cognac
Chopped fresh parsley

1. Melt the butter in a medium saucepan over medium-low heat. Stir in the onion; cook 1 minute. Stir in the garlic; cook 4 minutes. Add the allspice, mace, and cloves. Whisk in the flour. Cook, stirring constantly, 2 minutes. Whisk in the fish stock. Heat to boiling; reduce the heat. Simmer, uncovered, 5 minutes.

2. Place the quartered and plum tomatoes in the container of a food processor or blender and process until smooth. Strain the mixture into the soup. Add the salt, sugar, and basil. Return to boiling; reduce the heat. Simmer, uncovered, 30 minutes. Stir in the rice; continue to simmer, uncovered, until the rice is tender, about 12 minutes.

3. Add the fish to the bisque and poach (do not boil) for 5 minutes. Stir in the cream; heat to warm through. Add salt and pepper to taste. Stir in the cognac and sprinkle with parsley.

Serves 6.

CUBAN TOMATOES

This first course came to me from a Cuban friend and is comprised of nothing but ripe tomatoes freely strewn with freshly grated coconut. It is sauced with a vinaigrette concocted with coconut rum liqueur—or you can substitute light rum mixed with fresh coconut milk (or grated coconut), blended and strained.

4 sliced tomatoes
¼ cup shredded fresh coconut
1 teaspoon chopped chives
1 tablespoon coconut rum liqueur or white rum (see above)
1 tablespoon Dijon mustard
½ cup olive oil
Juice of 1 lime
Salt and freshly ground black pepper

1. Arrange the sliced tomatoes on a serving platter. Sprinkle with the fresh coconut and chives.

2. Whisk the coconut rum liqueur with the mustard in a medium bowl. Slowly whisk in the oil until thick. Whisk in the lime juice, and salt and pepper to taste. Spoon this over the tomatoes and let stand at least 30 minutes before serving.

Serves 4 to 6.

FRIED GREEN TOMATOES

One of my favorite late September–early October tomato bonuses for the cook is Fried Green Tomatoes. They are a simply unforgettable vegetable, made in Greene's kitchen whenever the hint of frost turns the gardener panicky and he picks whatever is still on the vine—fast!

3 medium-size firm green tomatoes
1 egg
2 teaspoons heavy or whipping cream
¼ cup V-8 juice or Bloody Mary mix
Dash of hot pepper sauce
½ cup fresh bread crumbs
⅛ teaspoon ground allspice
4 tablespoons (½ stick) unsalted butter, approximately
1 teaspoon chopped fresh chives

1. Cut the tomatoes crosswise into ½-inch-thick slices.

2. Beat the egg with the cream, V-8, and hot pepper sauce in a shallow bowl. Combine the crumbs and allspice in another shallow bowl.

3. Melt 2 tablespoons of the butter in a heavy skillet over medium heat. Dip the tomato slices in the egg mixture, shaking off any excess. Then lightly coat with the bread crumbs. Fry, a few slices at a time, until golden on both sides, about 4 minutes. Keep warm in a low oven. Continue to fry tomato slices, adding more butter as needed. Sprinkle with the chives before serving.

Serves 4.

RISOTTO TOMATO

After the Borgias endorsed the tomato (in cooked form) and their dinner guests lived to tell the tale, other Italian noblemen followed suit. Indeed, by the mid-sixteenth century when Catherine de Medici came to France to marry Henry II, this vegetable had achieved such rarified culinary status that Catherine's detractors claimed that her only assets as Queen were Italian charm, cheese, and tomatoes!

I can't vouch for the first but the other two ingredients were nothing to sneeze at—then or now! Tomatoes and cheese are connected to many of the best Italian dishes in my lexicon. For a spectacular example, I call your attention to the following.

3½ tablespoons unsalted butter
2 large shallots, minced
½ teaspoon salt
¼ teaspoon freshly ground black pepper
¼ cup dry white wine
1 cup Italian rice (I prefer Arborio brand)
3 cups Chicken Stock, simmering (see page 410)
2 medium tomatoes (about ⅔ pound), peeled, seeded, chopped
⅓ cup freshly grated Parmesan cheese (optional)

1. Melt 2½ tablespoons of the butter in a large heavy skillet over medium heat. Stir in the shallots; cook 1 minute. Sprinkle with the salt and pepper; stir in the wine. Cook until almost all liquid has evaporated. Add the rice, and stir until well coated with the shallot mixture. Reduce the heat to medium-low.

2. Stir 1 cup of the stock into the rice mixture. Gently simmer until the rice has absorbed the stock, about 15 minutes. Stir in the tomatoes and another 1 cup of the stock. Gently simmer until the rice has absorbed the stock, another 15 minutes. Stir in the remaining 1 cup stock and continue to simmer until the rice is just tender (not mushy), about 12 minutes longer. Raise the heat if the rice is too wet—it should be creamy but not wet. Stir in the remaining 1 tablespoon butter. Stir in the Parmesan cheese if you are serving the risotto with a bland main course. Omit the cheese with strong-flavored entrées.

Serves 4.

BAKED HERBED TOMATOES

The classic tomato renderings in my kitchen (there are two) both come as souvenirs from a longish stay in Eze, France, over a dozen years ago. Tomatoes in the Mediterranean region are the reddest and most glorious in all the world—with the possible exception of Mexico. This version is crumbed and herbed and ever so slightly scented with garlic and anchovy, Provence's prime flavors.

4 medium tomatoes (about 1 pound)
Salt
1 large shallot, minced
1 large clove garlic, minced
½ teaspoon anchovy paste
2 tablespoons unsalted butter, melted
2 tablespoons finely chopped fresh parsley
2 tablespoons finely chopped fresh basil
1 teaspoon chopped fresh thyme, or ¼ teaspoon dried
1 cup fresh bread crumbs
Freshly ground black pepper

1. Cut the tomatoes in half crosswise. Gently squeeze out the seeds. Sprinkle each half with salt and turn upside down on paper towels. Let stand 30 minutes.

2. Preheat the oven to 400°F. Mash the shallot with the garlic and anchovy paste in a medium bowl. Stir in the butter, the herbs, and the bread crumbs. Mix well.

3. Spoon the crumb mixture onto each tomato half, packing the mixture down with the back of the spoon. Sprinkle with pepper to taste. Bake 10 minutes, then place under a broiler until lightly browned. Serve hot, or cold sprinkled with vinegar and oil.

Serves 4.

MUSHROOM-STUFFED TOMATOES

The other Eze specialty is simply crammed with fresh moist mushrooms—best when the fungus has a wild flavor. I use shiitakes, but any will do in a pinch.

2 medium tomatoes (about ½ pound)
Salt
2 large fresh shiitake mushrooms, chopped (about 1 cup)
1½ teaspoons lemon juice
1 tablespoon unsalted butter
1 shallot, minced
1 tablespoon chopped fresh basil
1 teaspoon chopped fresh parsley
½ teaspoon sugar
4 teaspoons heavy or whipping cream
1 egg yolk
Salt and freshly ground black pepper
2 tablespoons freshly grated Parmesan cheese

1. Cut the tomatoes in half crosswise. Gently squeeze out the seeds. Scoop out the pulp with a spoon; chop it and reserve. Sprinkle each half with salt and turn them upside down on paper towels. Let stand 30 minutes.

2. Preheat the oven to 400°F. Sprinkle the mushrooms with the lemon juice. Melt the butter in a medium skillet over medium heat. Stir in the mushrooms; sauté 1 minute. Add the shallot; sauté until golden, about 5 minutes longer. Stir in the tomato pulp, herbs, and sugar. Continue to cook until the mixture thickens, about 10 minutes. Reduce the heat to low.

3. Lightly beat the cream with the egg yolk. Stir this into the mushroom mixture. Cook until warmed through; do not boil. Add salt and pepper to taste.

4. Place the tomato halves in a shallow baking dish. Fill each with some of the mushroom mixture and sprinkle with the Parmesan cheese. Bake until lightly browned, about 20 minutes.

Serves 4.

JILL GARDNER'S TOMATO SHORTCAKES

This very American tomato rendering was passed on to me by an extremely gifted food writer, who is also a whiz at the oven.

2 cups all-purpose flour
1 teaspoon salt
2½ teaspoons baking powder
6 tablespoons (¾ stick) cold unsalted butter, cut into pieces
1½ cups heavy or whipping cream
3 tablespoons red wine vinegar (I prefer Italian balsamic for this)
½ teaspoon sugar (optional, depending on sweetness of tomatoes)
2 teaspoons finely chopped chives
2 teaspoons finely chopped fresh basil
Salt and freshly ground black pepper
4 large ripe tomatoes (1½ to 2 pounds), peeled, seeded, roughly chopped

1. Preheat the oven to 400°F. Sift the flour with the salt and baking powder into a large bowl. Cut in the butter with a knife. Blend the mixture with a pastry blender until it is the texture of coarse crumbs. Stir in ¾ cup of the cream to make a soft dough.

2. Transfer the dough to a floured board; knead briefly. Pat the dough into a circle about ¾ inch thick. Cut out 6 rounds with a 3-inch biscuit cutter. Place the rounds on a lightly buttered baking sheet and bake until golden brown, about 20 minutes. Split each in half while still hot. Reserve.

3. Beat the remaining ¾ cup cream until soft peaks form. Beat in the vinegar, and the sugar if you are using it. Beat until stiff. Fold in the herbs; add salt and pepper to taste.

4. To serve: Spread the chopped tomatoes evenly over the bottom halves of the biscuits. Top each with some of the whipped cream dressing and cover with a biscuit top. Serve immediately.

Serves 6.

There is a less traditional method for growing a tomato—if one may still call a globe weighing two pounds a tomato.

According to an old farmers' wives' tale, one digs a deep, narrow hole for each seedling to be planted. Twenty inches is the required depth. At the bottom, the gardener places a layer of cracked corn cobs. Over that, 3 inches of manure. (In the formula I have in hand, chicken or cow manure is requested.) Never commercial fertilizers. Over the second layer place 4 inches of soil. Then set the tomato plant in the hole, leaving only the main branches atop, and mounding the soil around them. Supposedly the cobs hold moisture and cause the manure to heat up, warming the soil and creating a condition the reverse of hothouse agriculture. As the roots press downward, growth is increased thricefold. Or so the tale goes. Someday I will try it out and grow cherry tomatoes the size of oranges.

BASIC TOMATO SAUCE

I have two remarkable tomato sauces in my repertoire and both are used in dishes throughout the book. This one is dense and highly aromatic—perfect for pasta.

4 tablespoons (½ stick) unsalted butter
1 medium onion, finely chopped
1 clove garlic, minced
1 rib celery, finely chopped
4 large ripe tomatoes, peeled, seeded, chopped
1 teaspoon chopped fresh basil, or ½ teaspoon dried
1 teaspoon chopped fresh oregano, or ¼ teaspoon dried
Pinch of thyme
2 teaspoons sugar
¼ teaspoon grated orange peel
Salt and freshly ground black pepper

Melt the butter in a medium saucepan over medium-low heat. Add the onion; cook 1 minute. Add the garlic and celery; cook 4 minutes. Stir in the tomatoes, basil, oregano, thyme, sugar, and orange peel. Cook, uncovered, stirring occasionally, until thick, about 45 minutes. Add salt and pepper to taste.

Makes about 1½ cups.

CREAMY TOMATO SAUCE

Splashed with cream and less insistent in flavor than my Basic Tomato Sauce, this tomato cream makes a marvelous upholstery for all manner of subtle or simple dishes.

2 tablespoons unsalted butter
1 small onion, chopped
1 small clove garlic, chopped
½ rib celery, chopped
2 large tomatoes, peeled, seeded, chopped
1 teaspoon chopped fresh basil, or ½ teaspoon dried
½ teaspoon chopped fresh oregano, or a pinch of dried
Pinch of thyme
Pinch of ground cloves
½ teaspoon sugar
⅓ cup heavy or whipping cream
Salt and freshly ground black pepper

1. Melt the butter in a medium saucepan over medium-low heat. Add the onion; cook 1 minute. Add the garlic and celery; cook 4 minutes. Stir in the tomatoes, basil, oregano, thyme, cloves, and sugar. Cook, uncovered, stirring occasionally, until soft, about 20 minutes.

2. Transfer the mixture to the container of a blender or food processor. Blend until smooth, being careful as hot foods will expand. Return it to the saucepan and stir in the cream. Cook over low heat, without boiling, until warmed through. Add salt and pepper to taste.

Makes about 1 cup.

TOMATO SOUFFLE

Germans once called the tomato *Paradies Apfel* ("apple of paradise"). They had got their wires crossed and believed the Turks brought it from the Holy Land, the original location of Biblical paradise.

My own view is somewhat narrower. I think the tomato is a heavenly foodstuff because it gilds all other ingredients with which it is paired. Consider this tomato-suffused cheese soufflé for instance. It comes with a cavil, however: if fresh tomatoes are not rosy and ripe, use canned. My preference? The intensely flavored San Marsano brand imported from Italy.

6 tablespoons (¾ stick) plus 1 teaspoon unsalted butter
2 tablespoons freshly grated Parmesan cheese
5 tablespoons grated Fontina cheese
1 onion, chopped
1 clove garlic, chopped
2 large tomatoes (about 1 pound), peeled, seeded, chopped
1 teaspoon chopped fresh basil, or ¼ teaspoon dried
1 teaspoon chopped fresh parsley
Pinch of sugar
Pinch of ground allspice
¼ teaspoon tomato paste
3 tablespoons all-purpose flour
1 cup milk, boiling
4 egg yolks
Salt and freshly ground black pepper
5 egg whites

1. Rub a 1½-quart soufflé dish with the 1 teaspoon butter. Sprinkle with 1 tablespoon of the Parmesan cheese and 1 tablespoon of the Fontina cheese. Set aside.

2. Melt 4 tablespoons of the butter in a medium saucepan over medium-low heat. Add the onion; cook 1 minute. Add the garlic, tomatoes, basil, parsley, sugar, and allspice. Cook, uncovered, stirring occasionally, until the tomatoes are soft and fairly thick, about 20 minutes. Stir in the tomato paste; cook 5 minutes longer. Cool slightly. Transfer the mixture to the container of a blender or food processor. Blend until smooth, being careful as hot food will expand. Set aside.

3. Preheat the oven to 400°F. Melt the remaining 2 tablespoons butter in another medium saucepan over medium-low heat. Whisk in the flour. Cook, stirring constantly, 2 minutes. Whisk in the milk all at once. Whisk until smooth and very thick, 2 to 3 minutes. Remove from the heat and beat in the egg yolks, one at a time, beating thoroughly after each addition. Transfer the mixture to a large bowl. Stir in the blended tomato mixture, the remaining 4 tablespoons Fontina cheese, and salt and pepper to taste.

4. Beat the egg whites until stiff but not dry. Fold them into the tomato mixture. Spoon the mixture into the prepared soufflé dish and sprinkle with the remaining 1 tablespoon Parmesan cheese. Place the dish in the oven and immediately reduce the heat to 375°F. Bake until puffed and firm, 25 to 30 minutes.

Serves 4 to 6.

YELLOW TOMATO JAM

Thomas Jefferson raised yellow tomatoes in his garden at Monticello in 1782 and noted that the pale fruit made a preserve not unlike the flavor of a tart apricot.

I make yellow tomato jam whenever I find a batch harvested and waiting. But I must confess I never grow them, for the low acidity makes them popular with *bees!*

1 pound yellow cherry tomatoes
¼ cup lemon juice
1 teaspoon finely slivered lemon peel
3 cups sugar
⅛ teaspoon ground cinnamon

1. Cut the tomatoes in half lengthwise and place in a medium-size heavy saucepan. Add the lemon juice and slowly heat to boiling. Simmer 10 minutes.

2. Add the lemon peel, sugar, and

cinnamon to the tomatoes. Continue to simmer until the jam will set when a teaspoonful is placed on a cold plate, about 20 to 30 minutes. Pour into sterilized jars and seal. Place in a hot water bath for 20 minutes. Store in a cool place.

Makes 2 pints.

BUBBLING TOMATO CHICKEN

The dish that follows is a slightly revised version of a family tomato and chicken dish that was my sister Myra's favorite food when she was growing up. My mother named it "Bubbling Chicken" and made it with a can of Campbell's Cream of Mushroom Soup. I opt for homemade béchamel sauce and fresh mushrooms, but it still bubbles bounteously.

1 large chicken (about 4 pounds)
1 carrot, peeled, chopped
2 ribs celery, broken
1 unpeeled onion stuck with 2 cloves
1 large clove garlic
12 whole peppercorns
3 cups chicken broth (see page 414)
¼ cup dry white wine
1 teaspoon lemon juice
7 tablespoons unsalted butter
4 large mushrooms, sliced
¼ cup all-purpose flour
¾ cup heavy or whipping cream
1 can (28 ounces) Italian plum tomatoes, drained, chopped
¼ cup chopped fresh parsley
1 tablespoon chopped fresh basil
6 tablespoons fine fresh bread crumbs
2 tablespoons freshly grated Parmesan cheese

1. Combine all ingredients through the lemon juice in a large pot. Add water to cover. Heat to boiling; reduce the heat. Simmer, partially covered, until the chicken is tender, about 1 hour.

2. Remove the chicken from the stock and remove the meat from the bones in large pieces. Cover and reserve. Return the bones and skin to the pot. Simmer the stock, uncovered, until reduced to about 2 cups, about 30 minutes. Strain, and set aside.

3. Preheat the oven to 350°F. Melt 2 tablespoons of the butter in a medium skillet over medium heat. Quickly sauté the mushrooms until golden; set aside.

4. Melt 3 tablespoons of the butter in a medium saucepan over medium-low heat. Whisk in the flour. Cook, stirring constantly, 2 minutes. Whisk in the strained chicken stock and the cream. Heat to boiling; reduce the heat. Simmer until thickened, about 15 minutes. Stir in the reserved mushrooms.

5. Spread one third of the tomatoes over the bottom of a lightly greased casserole. Sprinkle with one third of the parsley and one third of the basil. Add one third of the cooked chicken pieces. Spoon one third of the sauce over the top. Repeat the layers two more times.

6. Melt the remaining 2 tablespoons butter in a small skillet over medium heat and sauté the bread crumbs until golden. Spoon the crumbs over the chicken mixture. Sprinkle with the cheese. Bake until golden and bubbly, about 20 minutes.

Serves 4 to 6.

PASTA A LA CAPRESE

(Pasta Shells with Marinated Tomatoes)

If the derivation of the next recipe is vague, forgive it please. I simply cannot remember who pressed the typewritten 3-by-5 card in my hand, containing four words to describe this dish of hot pasta and cold sauce. "It's Italian. It's good!" said the donor. Whoever it was, was right!

6 plum tomatoes, chopped
2 cloves garlic, minced
½ yellow or red sweet pepper, seeded, diced
2 tablespoons roughly chopped fresh basil
½ cup olive oil
1 teaspoon salt
¼ teaspoon freshly ground black pepper
1 pound pasta shells (penne or rigatoni)
8 ounces mozzarella cheese, grated
Freshly grated Parmesan cheese

1. Combine the tomatoes, garlic, sweet pepper, basil, oil, salt, and black pepper in a bowl. Mix well; let stand at room temperature for 1½ hours.

2. Just before serving, cook the pasta in boiling salted water until just tender, about 3 minutes for fresh, longer for packaged. Drain, and place in a large serving bowl. Stir in the mozzarella cheese and the marinated vegetables. Toss and serve immediately with Parmesan cheese on the side.

Serves 4 to 6.

ITALIAN FLAG

(Green Fettuccine with Tomatoes, Chicken, and Prosciutto)

The Italian flag is green, red, and white. So is the following dish, devised of spinach fettuccine, red tomatoes, and chunks of snowy chicken breasts. I came upon the recipe in Darien, Connecticut, however. The hostess, admitting its obvious ethnic antecedents, claimed to have found it in an old copy of *Gourmet*. No matter. It's a wonderfully satisfying dish to honor any flag at all.

1 whole chicken breast (about 1¼ pounds)
1½ cups chicken broth, approximately (see page 414)
¼ cup olive oil
1 small onion, halved, thinly sliced
½ cup sliced mushrooms (about 6 mushrooms)
9 tablespoons unsalted butter
¼ pound thinly sliced prosciutto, cut into strips
2 medium tomatoes (about ½ pound), peeled, seeded, chopped
½ cup heavy or whipping cream
⅛ teaspoon freshly grated nutmeg
Salt and freshly ground black pepper
½ pound green fettuccine noodles
Freshly grated Parmesan cheese

1. Place the chicken breast in a medium saucepan and add enough chicken broth to cover. Heat to boiling; reduce the heat. Simmer, covered, until tender, about 12 minutes. Remove the chicken breast and allow it to cool. Cut it into strips and set aside. Reserve broth for use at another time.

2. Heat the oil in a large saucepan over medium heat. Add the onion; sauté until golden. Add the mushrooms; cook, tossing gently, 2 minutes. Stir in 8 tablespoons of the butter, the prosciutto, and the tomatoes. Cook 6 minutes. Stir in the chicken and cream. Heat to boiling; reduce the heat to low. Add the nutmeg, and salt and pepper to taste. Keep warm over low heat.

3. Meanwhile, cook the fettuccine in boiling salted water until just tender, about 2 minutes for fresh, longer for packaged. Drain. Return the noodles to the saucepan and toss with the remaining 1 tablespoon butter.

4. Toss the fettuccine into the chicken-prosciutto mixture. Serve with Parmesan cheese on the side.

Serves 4.

TOMATO APPLE TARTIN

Strictly speaking, the tomato is a fruit (a berry if we are speaking even stricter), but we consume it as a vegetable and they are so classified. However, the tomato also has a curious power in a dessert dish. To prove my point, consider the love apple in confederation with one of the loveless variety (like a Granny Smith or a Greening). In my oven, this combo is the basis for one of the best French desserts ever invented: a tartin (an upside-down pie), baked first, then reversed and drizzled with caramel. This is possibly the best public image the rosy fruit will ever have.

Short Crust Pastry (see page 412)
10 tablespoons unsalted butter
2 large tomatoes (about 1 pound), peeled, seeded, chopped
¼ cup orange juice
2⅔ cups granulated sugar
½ teaspoon finely slivered lemon peel
½ teaspoon finely slivered orange peel
¼ cup packed dark brown sugar
½ cup fresh bread crumbs
4 large green tart apples
Juice of 1 lemon
Sweetened whipped cream

1. Make the Short Crust Pastry.

2. Melt 2 tablespoons of the butter in a medium saucepan over medium-low heat. Stir in the tomatoes, orange juice, 1½ cups of the granulated sugar, lemon peel, and orange peel. Heat to boiling; reduce the heat. Simmer, uncovered, until very thick, about 40 minutes. Remove from the heat.

3. Preheat the oven to 425°F. Melt the remaining 8 tablespoons butter and combine it with ⅔ cup of the granulated sugar and the brown sugar in a medium bowl. Stir in the bread crumbs. Mix thoroughly. Spread the mixture over the sides and bottom of a deep 10-inch pie plate. Refrigerate until ready to use.

4. Peel, core and cut the apples into ¼-inch slices. Place them in a large bowl and sprinkle with lemon juice as you cut them to keep them from turning brown. Pour the tomato mixture over the apples. Mix well. Spoon into the prepared pie plate.

5. Roll out the short crust pastry on a floured board. Place it over the apples and trim and seal the edges. Cut a hole in the center of the crust to allow steam to escape. Bake 30 minutes. Raise the oven heat to 500°F and bake 10 minutes longer.

6. Loosen the tartin by running a knife around the edge of the crust. Very carefully, place a heatproof 10-inch shallow serving dish over the tartin; invert the tartin onto the dish. Carefully remove the pie plate. Cool on a rack.

7. Just before serving, heat the remaining ½ cup of granulated sugar in a saucepan over high heat until the sugar starts to melt; cook, stirring constantly with a wooden spoon, until the sugar liquifies. Reduce the heat; cook, stirring constantly, until the caramel turns deep golden. Drizzle over the top of the tartin. Serve with sweetened whipped cream.

Serves 8.

TOMATO DEVIL'S FOOD WITH TOMATO BUTTER CREAM FROSTING

The tomato's name has not evolved much since the first Inca plucked and dubbed one a *tomatl*. Though Italians retain the Borgia inheritance of *pomodoro*, Frenchmen, Germans, and the Spanish still call it *tomate*. If you think a tomato is the same in any language, how mistaken you are! The most unusual tomato rendering in my collection is a dense and wonderfully sensuous cake of rich chocolate seasoned with fresh tomatoes—a love potion with its aphrodisiac powers compounded by a heavenly gilded butter cream, flavored with even more tomato.

Make this recipe only when tomatoes are in season. Winter varieties will not do.

For the cake:

2 large ripe tomatoes (about 1 pound)
4 ounces sweet chocolate
1 cup packed dark brown sugar
¼ cup milk
3 egg yolks
2 cups sifted cake flour
1 teaspoon baking soda
½ teaspoon salt
8 tablespoons (1 stick) unsalted butter, softened
1 cup granulated sugar
1 teaspoon vanilla extract
2 egg whites

For the frosting:

1 medium ripe tomato (about ¼ pound)
1½ cups (3 sticks) unsalted butter, softened
4 extra-large egg yolks
1 tablespoon cognac
¾ cup confectioners' sugar

1. Preheat the oven to 350°F.

2. To make the cake: Peel and seed the tomatoes. Place them in a blender container; blend until smooth. Measure off 1¼ cups tomato purée; reserve.

3. Place the chocolate, brown sugar, milk, and 1 of the egg yolks in the top of a double boiler. Cook, stirring occasionally, over hot water until smooth and slightly thickened. Set aside.

4. Sift the flour with the baking soda and salt.

5. Beat the butter in a large mixing bowl until light. Slowly beat in the granulated sugar. Add the remaining 2 egg

yolks, one at a time, beating thoroughly after each addition. Add the tomato purée, the vanilla, and the chocolate mixture. Beat thoroughly. Slowly stir in the flour mixture.

6. Beat the egg whites until stiff but not dry. Fold them into the cake batter. Pour the batter into two buttered and floured 9-inch cake pans. Bake until a toothpick inserted in the center of the cake comes out fairly clean, 25 to 30 minutes. Do not overcook. Cool on a wire rack. Unmold.

7. To make the frosting: Cut the tomato in half and place it in the container of a blender. Blend until smooth. Strain through a sieve. Measure off 4½ tablespoons of the sieved purée; reserve.

8. Beat the butter in a large bowl until light. Add the egg yolks, one at a time, beating thoroughly after each addition. Add the strained tomato purée and the cognac. Slowly beat in the confectioners' sugar. Spread the icing over the bottom layer, sides, and top of the cake. Keep the cake in a cool place until serving, but do not refrigerate.

Serves 8 to 10.

TURNIPS AND RUTABAGAS

Hearty Roots for Warming Dishes

When I was young, kitchen odors—even felicitous ones—were considered *déclassé.*

The late 1930s and early '40s may have been hard times, but they were also hidebound by convention and provincialism. If you were respectable (a word my mother summoned up with righteousness all her life), no one was ever supposed to know what was really cooking in your pots!

Being a first-generation American dictated that one's mores be as puritan as possible, likewise one's cooking habits—so anonymous that a Greene could pass for a Smith, a Jones, or any other born-and-bred Yankee.

Even my grandmother, who dearly loved the lusty evidence of good aromas in her kitchen, concurred in the matter of odorous decorum. She would always leave a curl of orange peel near the pilot light of her stove so that the oils, released as it dried, masked any "foreign" smell emanating from her saucepan.

My mother, having neither the patience nor the domestic stripe to allow orange rind to turn into fine white ash on her shiny porcelain gas range, would light sticks of incense around the house

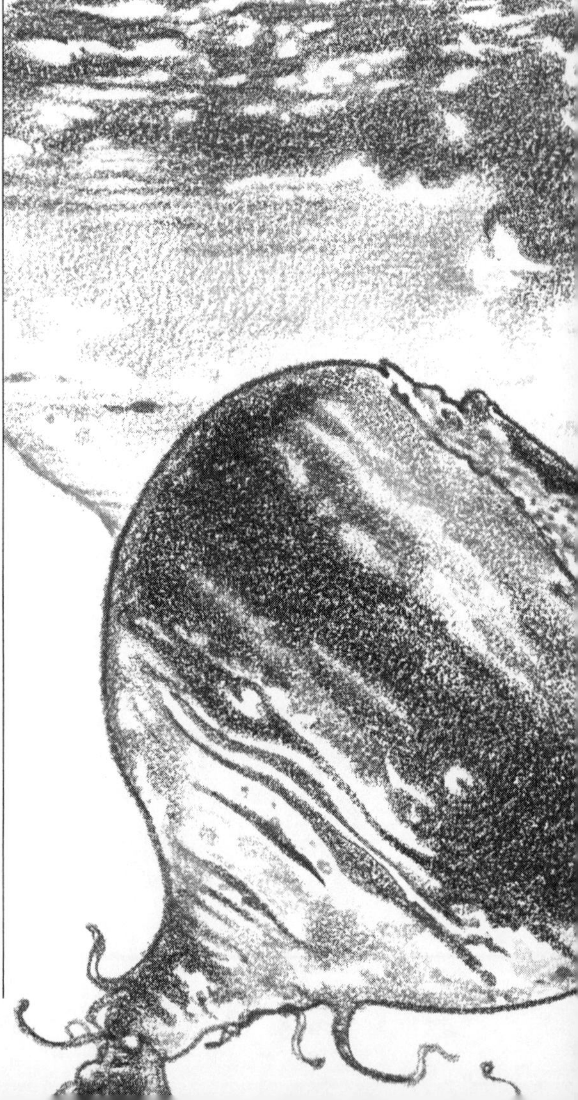

instead. Or worse yet, rub a drop or two of perfumed oil on the electric light bulbs after she had cooked something that was particularly flavorful. So after dinner, the house would usually reek with the overpowering scent of musk rather than any homelier scents, like boiled turnips.

When I was in my late teens and began to take a serious interest in the opposite sex, my mother laid out what she considered to be the qualifications of respectability in a girl friend.

"Pick someone who comes from a good home," she intoned, "not a family of *shickers* [drunkards] or loose-livers. Remember, background means more than physical beauty, which fades."

Always attracted to exquisite creatures, I resented all of my mother's sage wisdom out of hand. "How in the world do you expect me to know any of that?" I remonstrated with some heat. "Most people do not advertise their pedigrees!"

"Aha!" said my mother. "You are wrong there. Just keep your eyes, ears, and nose open. Empty beer and whiskey bottles all over the place are not a good sign. But—" and here my mother shook her finger triumphantly "—books on the shelves *are!*"

"Really? Well, how about incense?" I asked sarcastically. "What kind of sign is that?"

"Sensitivity," replied my mother. "And a lot better than the smell of yesterday's dinner!"

I was not convinced.

To be honest, the first time I was invited to dine with the family of a girl I was deeply smitten with, I could not for the life of me get my mother's precepts out of my head or my nose. For the entire apartment (it was in a stately old building overlooking Central Park) was suffused with the most intoxicating perfume I think I have ever inhaled: rutabaga braising to a dull tarnished gold in a bath that would give any alchemist joy—onions, red wine, and bits of bacon. Open liquor bottles crowded a small table that also served as a bar. I, who barely drank, counted Scotch, brandy, bourbon, and gin beside a bucket that held a magnum of champagne on ice.

All of this added up to a bad sign, according to my mother. But the floor-to-ceiling bookshelves were also crammed to capacity with volumes in three languages. So I breathed in the scent of those burnishing roots without compunction.

I wish I could report that some serious alliance was the result of that first memorable dinner. All that ensued was a deep friendship with the family and a great recipe or two for my collection. With the turnip (and its cousin, rutabaga) I have maintained a less transient love affair.

Vegetable Roots

Probably the oldest vegetable known, the turnip was there when early man stopped thrashing about in eluvial ooze long enough to think of his stomach—which was always empty. Turnips filled the void, and when dipped in salt water were not entirely unpleasant to his tongue.

Then and now, the white and yellow turnip *(Brassica rapa)* is a fleshy root that grows fast, requires little care, and is high in nutrients. By the time the first caveman took a wife and made a communal fire, he discovered that his family could not only subsist on this high-fiber food but they grew stronger with every bite. According to evidence uncovered in the caves at Choukoutien, near Peking, turnip was not merely eaten raw by its first consumers; it was roasted with meat (on flat stones in the fire) or wrapped up with fern ends or wild onions and steamed in flat wet leaves. One thing about the turnip is fairly self-evident: it was eaten because it was available. If a hunter did not always return home with a slab of sabre-toothed tiger under his arm for dinner, his mate knew where to "root around" in the bog for supplementary rations—and they survived!

Several millennia later (as the cave paintings near the village of Aurignac, France, show), these very same roots were still on the fire! But by then they were boiled in watertight pots of clay, which was quite a way up the prandial ladder. When the ancient Greeks and Romans finally inherited the turnip, its kitchen status was so elevated that devotees literally held forums to theorize on the ideal culinary fabrication. In Rome (according to the *Pantropheon*) the optimum cookery took several hours and the roots were steamed successively with cumin, rue, and benzoin; then pounded in a mortar with honey, vinegar, gravy, boiled grapes, and a little oil; and then simmered well before they were served. Frankly, I would rather eat a turnip neat!

Rutabaga is a turnip's younger sibling. Or to be more accurate, it is a turnip mutation. This curious yellow globe whose stem swells underground rather than above (as conventional turnips do) is technically *Brassica napobrassica*, even though it came to our tables through the crossbreeding of a cabbage with a turnip by Swiss botanist Gaspard Bauhin in the seventeenth century. The birth was neither heralded nor honored, but it should have been. For half the northern countries of the world live on rutabagas half of every year, and this vegetable, thriving in cool air, keeps the denizens of Scandinavian countries a heck of a lot healthier than they would be without its mineral-high presence in saucepans every winter. In fact, for centuries the rutabaga has been variously known in vegetable circles as Russian turnip, Canadian turnip, Bulgarian turnip, and Swedish turnip or swede. Only the last name stuck, however, because this root, with its penchant for cool, glacial soil, flourishes best and is eaten most in Sweden.

According to food pundits, who disagree violently about almost everything that appears in a saucepan, the rutabaga did not arrive in the United States until 1806. How it came here no one seems to know for sure, but despite its northerly association in the Old World, its first official appearance in the new one was in a seed catalogue that advertised it as "South of the Border Turnip"!

What to Look For

Whether shopping for turnips or for rutabagas, the market imperatives are the same. Fresh vegetables will be firm and quite smooth to the hand. A wrinkled turnip is a sure sign that the root has lost its moisture and that the texture beneath the skin will be spongy. I pass on large turnips as a matter of course, as the small ones (dappled with an edge of purple at the soil level) are by far the sweeter. If you have the option, select turnips with fresh green leaves, for that is a clear indication the vegetable is not long out of the garden. Rutabagas should always feel weighty. Search for a globe that is streaked with purple and fairly free of large bruises or hoe marks. The heavy waxy coating (on all but farmstand produce) is sprayed on the rutabaga to prevent dehydration. Peel it off with a vegetable parer prior to a kitchen wash-up.

Turnips and rutabagas, though genetically connected, have one major culinary difference. Turnips are fragile; they will last only a week in a refrigerator. Rutabagas keep for a month or even longer. As a matter of fact, when I was a kid, farmers used to "hold" rutabagas in root cellars for almost a year, packed in sawdust or sand.

Turnips and rutabagas both are high in nutrients, low in calories, and yet tonic enough to please even the most jaded appetite.

An average ¾ cup portion of turnips, for instance, holds a scant 30 calories yet is exceedingly high in minerals (39 milligrams calcium, 30 milligrams phosphorus, and a bounteous 268 milligrams of potassium). Turnips are not high in vitamins, but rutabagas are. The same quantity of rutabagas contains 46 calories but is super-streaked with minerals (239 milligrams potassium, 66 milligrams calcium, and 39 milligrams phosphorus), with traces of all essential vitamins plus 43 units of vitamin C and a towering 580 units of vitamin A.

Preparation

Since both the turnip and rutabaga are tough roots, always use a sharp knife to slice them. Work on a wooden surface and insert the blade carefully at a point midway between the root and the stem, going directly into the heart of the root before you slice it in two. Peel the halves at that point. Then, with the cut sides down, slice first vertically, then horizontally, until the entire vegetable is cubed.

Both turnips and rutabagas profit by the standard cooking instructions for all root vegetables: braising, boiling, and steaming; and in that order of preference at my stove top.

To braise: Cut either vegetable into uniform shapes and place them in a covered skillet along with a modicum of butter and enough liquid (broth or vegetable juices) to generously cover the bottom. My average braising time for these root vegetables is 10 to 12 minutes for turnips, 15 to 20 minutes for rutabagas.

To boil: Fill a saucepan halfway with cold salted water. When the water is at a rolling boil, add the cut vegetables and cook them till fork-tender, about 15 minutes for a whole turnip and 20 to 25 minutes for a 2½-inch cube of rutabaga. Young vegetables may require less cooking time.

To steam: Bring approximately 1 inch of water to a boil in a steamer or saucepan. Place the turnips or rutabagas in a steamer basket or colander, bearing in mind that cooking times may only be approximated since the sizes of the vegetables vary. However, an average-size turnip will steam crisp-tender in about 10 to 12 minutes. A rutabaga (2½-inch-size cubes) will require twice that long, about 25 to 30 minutes.

In passing let me state that there are two schools of thought on all turnip and rutabaga cookery: those who cook them first and peel them later, and those like me who want the job over and done with and say: to heck with the vitamin dividend I just tossed down the drain!

TURNIP SAVARIN WITH GRUYERE SAUCE

With so much sheer health in every portion, I thought it might be pleasantly perverse to indulge in a splurge of sheer, unabashed dietary largess. It is a turnip savarin, white-gold in color and silken to the tongue, particularly when dappled with the accompanying sauce of melting Gruyère cheese. I serve this as a first course to a dinner that is fairly spartan (broiled chicken or grilled chops), but it will make a spectacular brunch offering as well if strips of crisp bacon, ham, and sausages are crammed into the inner circle of the mold.

Incidentally, the recipe comes from the same collection that afforded me the Gingered Rutabaga. It's a borrowing, without a doubt, but what magazine was its original source beats me!

2 pounds turnips, peeled, cut into ½-inch cubes
2 cups chicken broth (see page 414)
4 tablespoons (½ stick) unsalted butter
3 tablespoons all-purpose flour
1 cup hot milk
3 eggs
4 egg yolks
¼ teaspoon freshly grated nutmeg
Salt and freshly ground black pepper
Gruyère Sauce (recipe follows)

1. Combine the turnips and chicken broth in a medium saucepan. Heat to boiling; reduce the heat. Cook, covered, until tender, about 20 minutes. Drain, reserving the broth.

2. Preheat the oven to 375°F. Place the cooked turnips in the container of a food processor and process until smooth. Transfer the mixture to a saucepan. Cook over medium heat, stirring frequently, until any excess liquid has evaporated. Remove from the heat.

3. Melt the butter in a medium saucepan over medium-low heat. Whisk in the flour. Cook, stirring constantly, 3 minutes. Whisk in the milk. Cook until thick. Slowly add the turnip purée; remove from the heat.

4. Beat the eggs and egg yolks in a large bowl. Slowly beat in the turnip mixture. Add the nutmeg, and salt and pepper to taste. Pour into a buttered 6-cup savarin ring mold. Place the mold in a roasting pan and add boiling water to come halfway up the sides of the mold. Bake until firm, about 45 minutes. Let stand 5 minutes before unmolding onto a serving platter. Spoon some of the Gruyère Sauce over the turnip savarin. Pass the remaining sauce.

Serves 8 to 10.

Gruyère Sauce

3 tablespoons unsalted butter
2 tablespoons all-purpose flour
1½ cups warm reserved turnip broth, or chicken broth (see page 414)
½ cup heavy or whipping cream
½ cup grated Gruyère cheese
⅛ teaspoon freshly grated nutmeg
Salt and cayenne pepper

Melt the butter in a medium saucepan over medium-low heat. Whisk in the flour. Cook, stirring constantly, 2 minutes. Whisk in the turnip broth and cream. Cook, stirring constantly, until fairly thick, about 3 minutes. Stir in the cheese and allow it to melt. Do not boil. Add the nutmeg, and salt and cayenne pepper to taste. Serve with the turnip savarin.

Makes about 2½ cups.

To the ancients, the turnip was adjudged to possess medicinal balms for the body's outer ills. Case in point: Discorides reported that a fresh white turnip (cooked) applied on a sore foot would "renounce" the pain of that ailment immediately. Likewise, Apicius counseled women of approaching middle age to make a thick paste of cooked turnip, cream, and smashed rosebuds. This unguent, he advised, when rubbed thoroughly into all crevices and hollows of the face, neck, and shoulders will make those surfaces smooth as a baby's thigh after two applications.

MIXED TURNIP CHOWDER

One of the best soups I have ever tasted in my life is a compound of turnips, rutabagas, and potatoes. It was invented in my kitchen on a winter's day when the air of gloom outside was as impenetrable as fog. One sip of this golden chowder and the sun shone bright. I wish you the same good fortune.

2 tablespoons unsalted butter
1 large onion, finely chopped
1 large rib celery, finely chopped
1 pound turnips, peeled, diced
1½ pounds rutabagas, peeled, diced
2 medium potatoes, peeled, diced
1 quart chicken or vegetable broth (see page 414)
Salt and freshly ground black pepper
⅛ teaspoon ground mace

1. Melt the butter in a medium saucepan over medium-low heat. Add the onion; cook 2 minutes. Add the celery; cook 2 minutes longer. Stir in the turnips, rutabagas, potatoes, and broth. Heat to boiling; reduce the heat. Simmer, uncovered, until vegetables are tender, about 20 minutes.

2. Remove one half of the vegetables and place them in the container of a blender or food processor. Add 1 cup of the broth. Blend until smooth, being careful as hot liquid will expand. Return the puréed mixture to the soup. Add salt and pepper to taste and stir in the mace. Simmer 5 minutes before serving.

Serves 8.

FARMHOUSE TURNIPS

My classic turnip and rutabaga renderings follow. The first is a devise I acquired from a country gentlewoman in Ohio some years back. She told me that her great-grandmother had written this recipe down over a hundred years ago and she had never seen fit to alter it a jot. Such endorsement is good enough for me. I never altered it either, for it is very, very special.

3 tablespoons unsalted butter
1 small onion, minced
1 pound turnips, peeled, cut into strips 2 inches long by ½ inch wide
1 medium tomato, peeled, seeded, roughly chopped
¼ teaspoon sugar
¼ teaspoon ground allspice
1 teaspoon salt
½ teaspoon freshly ground black pepper
1 tablespoon chopped fresh parsley

Melt the butter in a medium saucepan over medium-low heat. Stir in the onion; cook 5 minutes. Stir in the turnips, tomato, sugar, and allspice. Mix well. Cook, covered, stirring occasionally, until tender, about 15 minutes. Add the salt and pepper, and sprinkle with the parsley.

Serves 4.

BRAISED RUTABAGA

The second classic is a version of a memorable Burgundian way with root vegetables (either turnip or rutabaga will do here). It was culled originally from Julia Child and her friends Mesdames Bertholle and Beck, in *Mastering the Art of French Cooking*. This formula I suspect may have changed over the years, for I first made it when I was a storekeeper in Amagansett (as a Thanksgiving adjunct to turkey), but the genesis is unmistakable. Still superb too!

2½ pounds rutabagas, peeled, cut into 2-inch cubes
⅔ cup finely diced slab bacon
1 tablespoon unsalted butter
1 large onion, finely chopped
1 tablespoon all-purpose flour
¾ cup beef broth or stock (see page 414)
¼ teaspoon sugar
Salt and freshly ground black pepper
1 teaspoon chopped fresh sage, or ¼ teaspoon dried
Chopped fresh parsley

1. Cook the rutabagas in boiling salted water for 4 minutes. Rinse under cold running water; drain. Reserve.

2. Cook the diced bacon in boiling water 10 minutes. Drain. Pat dry with paper towels.

3. Melt the butter in a heavy saucepan over medium-low heat. Add the bacon; sauté until lightly browned. Stir in the onion; cook, covered, 5 minutes. Stir in the flour. Cook, stirring constantly, 2 minutes. Whisk in the broth, sugar, salt and pepper to taste, and sage. Cook 3 minutes. Add the rutabagas, tossing well to coat with the mixture. Cook, covered, until tender, 20 to 25 minutes.

4. When the rutabagas are tender, remove the cover and raise the heat. Cook, stirring constantly, until the liquid is thick and syrupy. Sprinkle with parsley.

Serves 6.

MASHED SWEDES

Ever since the first *rottebagge* (or "baggy root") was harvested in Sweden, it has been consumed with equal relish by the bourgeoisie and the bovines of that country—giving rise to an unusual proliferation of deep golden butter and unearthly scented cream that the self-indulgent Swedish regularly mash into their rutabagas.

1 pound rutabagas, peeled, cut into cubes
½ teaspoon beef bouillon powder
1 tablespoon unsalted butter
2 tablespoons heavy or whipping cream
Salt and freshly ground black pepper

1. Cook the rutabagas in boiling salted water until tender. Drain.

2. Place the rutabagas in a medium saucepan over low heat. Mash them with the bouillon powder and butter until smooth. Beat in the cream and add salt and pepper to taste.

Serves 4.

BASHED NEEPS

(Mashed Rutabagas and Potatoes)

The French call rutabaga *navet de Suede*, while the English dub them *swedes*, Italians know them as *rapa svedese*, and the Spanish tag them *nabo sueco*—which are all variations of the same moniker when you come down to it. But not the Scottish handle, for a rutabaga is referred to as a "neep" from Edinburgh to the Orkneys. Scots have a way with this vegetable: they *bash* them with a mix of white potatoes, lots of butter, and nutmeg—and they are the best thing I have ever tasted in Scotland or anywhere else a rutabaga is rooted.

1 pound rutabagas, peeled, cut into cubes
½ pound potatoes, peeled, cut into cubes
2 tablespoons unsalted butter
¼ teaspoon freshly grated nutmeg
Salt and freshly ground black pepper

1. Cook the rutabagas in boiling salted water for 10 minutes. Add the potatoes; cook until both vegetables are tender, about 15 minutes longer. Drain.

2. Mash the rutabagas and potatoes with the butter until smooth. Add the nutmeg, and salt and pepper to taste. Place over low heat to warm through.

Serves 4.

APPLE-SAUCED RUTABAGA

This is the result of a Thanksgiving prepared in a good friend's house in Vermont. My host forgot the cranberries, but he had a turnip in the cellar and old apple tree in the meadow, so I made apple-sauced rutabaga instead.

2½ pounds rutabagas, peeled, cut into ½-inch cubes
2 tablespoons unsalted butter, softened
½ cup heavy or whipping cream
¾ cup Lemon-Rum Applesauce (recipe follows)
Salt and freshly ground black pepper

1. Cook the rutabagas in boiling salted water until very tender, about 30 minutes. Drain.

2. Preheat the oven to 350°F. Mash the rutabagas in a large bowl or pot until fairly smooth. Mash in the butter and cream until as smooth as possible. Beat in the applesauce. Add salt and pepper to taste.

3. Transfer the mixture to a baking dish. Bake for 15 minutes before serving.

Serves 6 to 8.

Lemon-Rum Applesauce

The secret of the elegant and savory vegetable dish above is a good, really good, portion of homemade applesauce. I don't like to brag but I doubt you will ever taste one better than the sensuous stuff that follows. It may be prepared in larger batches at your disposition and discretion, of course.

2 large green apples, peeled, cored, sliced
½ teaspoon finely slivered lemon peel
¼ cup packed dark brown sugar
⅛ teaspoon ground cinnamon
1 tablespoon dark rum
1 tablespoon unsalted butter

Place the apple slices with the lemon peel, brown sugar, and cinnamon in a medium saucepan. Cook, covered, over low heat, stirring occasionally, until tender, about 30 minutes. Mash until smooth. Stir in the rum and butter.

Makes about ¾ cup.

HONEY-PEPPERED TURNIPS

The following recipe is reputedly a transcript from *De Re Coquinaria*, the earliest cookbook to be formally compiled. It is a tribute to Roman ingenuity and my high school Latin, for I made the translation with the aid of what we once called "a trot." Accurate? I have no idea, but delicious without question.

1 tablespoon unsalted butter
2 tablespoons honey
1 pound turnips, peeled, cut into ¼-inch cubes
½ teaspoon freshly ground black pepper
Salt
Chopped fresh parsley

Melt the butter with the honey in a medium saucepan over medium-low heat. Stir in the turnips and pepper. Cook, covered, until tender, about 12 minutes. Add salt to taste and sprinkle with parsley.

Serves 4 to 6.

ROOTS IN ESCABECHE

Navet, Rübe, rapa, nabo—all mean nothing more or less than "root," which is succinct if not terribly tantalizing. The turnip's finest appearance in my repertoire is as co-star with rutabagas in a highly seasoned Cajun dish (from New Iberia, Louisiana) called, equally succinctly, roots in escabèche.

1 pound carrots, peeled, cut into julienne strips
1 pound turnips, peeled, cut into julienne strips
1 pound rutabagas, peeled, cut into julienne strips
2 cups olive oil
1 cup distilled white vinegar
½ cup minced pitted green olives
½ cup minced pimiento
1 clove garlic, minced
¼ teaspoon freshly ground black pepper
2 small onions, thinly sliced

1. Cook the carrots in boiling salted water until just tender, about 8 minutes. Drain; reserve.

2. Cook the turnips in boiling salted water until just tender, about 8 minutes. Drain; reserve.

3. Cook the rutabagas in boiling salted water until just tender, about 10 to 12 minutes. Drain; reserve.

4. Heat the oil, vinegar, olives, pimiento, garlic, and pepper in a medium saucepan to boiling; reduce the heat. Simmer, uncovered, 5 minutes.

5. Combine the carrots, turnips, rutabagas, and onions in a heatproof bowl. Pour the dressing over the vegetables and cool to room temperature. Refrigerate, covered, 4 hours or overnight.

Serves 6 to 8.

GINGERED RUTABAGA

A favorite devise, in which rutabagas are sluiced with ginger ale and fresh ginger too. Uncovered in a huge box of ancient clippings (all recipes), this was bequeathed to me by a reader of my newspaper column some while back when she moved to Florida. The recipes were tattered and yellowing, but this one caught my eye and my culinary fancy as well.

2 pounds rutabagas, peeled, cut into ½-inch cubes
½ teaspoon salt
6 whole cloves, tied in a cheesecloth bag
2 cups ginger ale
4 teaspoons grated fresh ginger
¼ cup dark rum
2 tablespoons unsalted butter

1. Combine the rutabagas, salt, cloves, and ginger ale in a medium saucepan. Heat to boiling; reduce the heat. Cook, covered, over medium-low heat until tender, about 20 minutes.

2. Remove the cover and raise the heat slightly. Cook until almost all liquid has evaporated. Discard the cloves. Stir in the grated ginger, the rum, and the butter. Cook, uncovered, 5 minutes.

Serves 4 to 6.

TURNIP PUREE

Don't count on having any leftovers of this eminently satisfying ginger-and-orange-scented dish.

1 pound turnips, peeled, cubed
½ pound potatoes, peeled, cubed
¼ cup orange juice
1 tablespoon dark brown sugar
⅛ teaspoon ground ginger
3½ tablespoons unsalted butter, melted
Salt and freshly ground black pepper

1. Cook the turnips with the potatoes in boiling salted water until tender, 15 to 20 minutes. Drain.

2. Place the turnips and potatoes in the container of a food processor. Process, using the on/off switch, until smooth.

3. Transfer the mixture to a medium saucepan. Stir in the orange juice, brown sugar, ginger, and melted butter. Cook over medium-low heat until warmed through, about 5 minutes. Add salt and pepper to taste.

Serves 4.

TURNIP PAPRIKASH

This dish is Hungarian, and rosy as all get-out—ablush, no doubt, at the surprising federation with cream, wine, and sweet red pepper in which it has found itself.

2 tablespoons unsalted butter
2 scallions, bulbs and green tops, minced
1 pound turnips, peeled, diced
6 tablespoons dry white wine or vermouth
2 teaspoons sugar
1½ tablespoons sweet Hungarian paprika
½ cup heavy or whipping cream
Salt and freshly ground black pepper
Chopped fresh parsley

1. Melt the butter in a medium saucepan over medium-low heat. Add the scallions and turnips; toss well.

2. Combine the wine, sugar, and paprika in a small bowl. Mix well and pour over the turnips. Cook, covered, until the turnips are tender, about 15 minutes.

3. Stir the cream into the turnips. Cook, uncovered, until slightly thickened, about 5 minutes. Add salt and pepper to taste and sprinkle with parsley.

Serves 4.

TURNIPS SICILIAN-STYLE

This devise, while Sicilian in origin, came from a waiter I knew at the Minetta Tavern in New York's Greenwich Village many years ago.

1 tablespoon unsalted butter
2 small leeks (about ½ pound), bulb and 2 inches of green stem, washed, chopped
1 clove garlic, minced
⅓ cup chopped pancetta (Italian bacon), or slab bacon
1 pound small turnips, peeled, cut into ¼-inch strips
½ cup chicken broth (see page 414)
1 teaspoon red wine vinegar
Salt and freshly ground black pepper

1. Melt the butter in a medium saucepan over medium-low heat. Add the leeks; cook 1 minute. Add the garlic; cook 1 minute. Stir in the pancetta; cook 10 minutes.

2. Stir in the turnips and chicken broth. Cook, covered, over low heat until the turnips are tender, 15 to 20 minutes. Stir in the vinegar, and salt and pepper to taste.

Serves 4 to 6.

RUTABAGA SCRATCH BACKS

One of the finest rutabaga recipes ever was found along the Tennessee-Georgia border. This vegetable fritter is best when made of leftover mashed or bashed, so put a cup aside next time around.

1½ cups water
3 tablespoons unsalted butter
½ teaspoon salt
¾ cup yellow cornmeal
Pinch of cayenne pepper
1 cup cold mashed rutabagas

1. Preheat the oven to 450°F. Place the water with 2 tablespoons of the butter and the salt in a medium saucepan. Stir, over medium heat, until the butter melts. Stir in the cornmeal; reduce the heat. Cook, stirring constantly, over low heat until the mixture is very thick. Stir in the cayenne pepper and mashed rutabagas. Cook 4 minutes longer.

2. Melt the remaining 1 tablespoon butter. Spoon the rutabaga mixture into a buttered shallow baking dish and brush with the melted butter. Bake 15 minutes. Let stand 10 minutes before serving.

Serves 4.

BEEF AND TURNIP STEW

Since they are an old vegetable, possibly the oldest, turnips come with considerable myth and malison. One of the most curious conceits stems from the fifteenth-century English botanist Theophrast Turner, who declared he could change a turnip's sex in the vegetable patch. "Turnepes sowen and sette thicke together," he wrote, "grow al into males. But if they be thynner sette, they grow into females—which are tastiest!"

The following soporific stew may be prepared unchauvinistically of either gender and still be merely marvelous.

4 ounces slab bacon (about ½ cup), diced
⅓ cup plus 1 teaspoon all-purpose flour
¼ teaspoon salt
¼ teaspoon freshly ground black pepper
⅛ teaspoon ground cinnamon
Pinch of ground cloves
2 pounds chuck steak, cut into 2-inch cubes
4 tablespoons (½ stick) unsalted butter, plus 1 tablespoon softened
1 large onion, finely chopped
1 clove garlic, minced
⅛ teaspoon freshly grated nutmeg
1 teaspoon vegetable oil
1½ cups beef broth (see page 414)
1 cup dry white wine
3 tablespoons cognac
1 pound turnips, peeled, cut into ¼-inch cubes
Chopped fresh parsley

1. Preheat the oven to 350°F. Cook the bacon in boiling water for 5 minutes. Drain; pat dry on paper towels. Reserve.

2. Combine the ⅓ cup flour, the salt, pepper, cinnamon, and cloves in a shallow bowl. Lightly coat the meat with this mixture. Reserve.

3. Melt 2 tablespoons of the butter in a Dutch oven. Add the onion; cook 1 minute. Add the garlic and nutmeg; cook 4 minutes. Remove from the heat.

4. Heat the oil in a large heavy skillet over medium heat. Add the bacon; sauté until golden, about 4 minutes. With a slotted spoon, transfer the bacon to the Dutch oven.

5. Add 2 tablespoons butter to the skillet. Sauté the beef, a few pieces at a time, until browned on all sides. Transfer to the Dutch oven.

6. When the meat has been sautéed, add the broth to the skillet. Heat to boiling, scraping the bottom and sides of the pan with a wooden spoon. Pour this over the meat in the Dutch oven. Add the wine and cognac. Bake, covered, 1½ hours.

7. Stir in the turnips; continue to bake, covered, 10 minutes. Remove the cover and bake 10 minutes longer.

8. Combine the softened butter with the remaining 1 teaspoon flour. Stir until smooth. Mix into the stew. Bake uncovered, 20 minutes. Sprinkle with parsley.

Serves 4 to 6.

ZUCCHINI

The Standout Squash

If I did not cook (or write) for a living, I suspect I would seriously till the soil, for I inherited my grandmother's solid jade thumb. To prove it I do battle with a spade and hoe every spring. But working the land, as any true gardener knows, is a full year's occupation and I simply never have the time.

When I ran The Store in Amagansett, summers took a great toll on my garden. Working from sunup to sundown, I had no alternative but to pass the care of my vegetable patch on to a red-haired neighbor boy. With no feel for agriculture whatsoever, he weeded like Attila the Hun—deflowering seedlings ruthlessly but permitting burdock and chickweed to grow waist high. Eventually a family of moles took over the territory.

During the very first season of The Store's existence, my garden did have a small respite. My appendix had just been summarily removed in a New York hospital and I came back to Amagansett to convalesce. Miserable with pain and weak with the heat, I accepted my mother's noble offer to care for me while I recuperated.

I had grown very independent over the years since I had left home, but it was remarkably pleasurable to lapse into childhood ways again. So I accepted my mother's cool hand on my brow—and her bequests of lemonade and iced tea—with good grace.

In her late sixties at the time, my mother had recently become drawn to ethical Christian Science, as she called it, and insisted that I not languish in my bed for long. So together we would walk the entire backyard as she quizzed me on the status of every plant. Never drawn to gardening before, she now watered each green clump every morning, reporting later what was about to bud and what had already burst into bloom. Visiting these vegetable rows in the late afternoon became a daily ritual, and we would sit there for hours without the need for any further conversation at all.

When I became strong enough to do the weeding myself, my parent knew that her time spent "being a mother again" was drawing to a close. The night before she left for the city, she accompanied me out to the garden one last time. As we bent over the cool, damp earth, we tried to calculate the size of the harvest but soon gave up—too many tomatoes, far too many peppers, peas, and beans on the vine for even my mother's sharp eye to keep track of. Pointing to a newly opened squash blossom, she lifted the flower and gave a small cry. There on the ground were the first zucchini of the season. Five of them, tiny as a child's fingers and still fuzzy in their green wrapping.

Without a second thought I picked one, then another, and handed them to my mother. On our knees, we ate the tender young squash raw. The taste? Forgive me, but almost twenty years later it is still impossible to describe.

"Kiddo," said my mother at last, "this makes you know there really is a God."

She had never been so right in her life.

Vegetable Roots

Zucchini's name is Italian, a derivative of the word meaning "sweetest." Most decidedly a member of the native American summer squash tribe (those ubiquitous cucurbits I wrote about earlier on) this green gourd is one local vegetable that really made it big on foreign shores—in Italy. No one seems to know for sure how (or why) zucchini went Italian in the first place, but speculation is rife. Most historians subscribe to the theory that seeds arrived there via some early Italian explorer's rucksack, for zucchini cultivation in the Po valley has been documented for over three hundred years. Italians are so proprietary about this plant that the rest of the world has come to think of zucchini as Italian Squash. In the *Zucchini Cookbook*, author Paula Simmons reported an alternative version of its ancestry:

> According to local legend, seeds were given by the gods to the peoples of Abruzzi (in eastern Italy). They were told to protect the zucchini seed from any non-Italian, which they did until Christopher Columbus brought the seeds to America.

From there on, the zucchini lore is up for grabs, but the squash certainly did bear an Italian imprint for years. When I was a child growing up in a borough of New York City, no one but second-generation Italians grew (or ate) this wonderful vegetable, for it was rumored to be highly indigestible, at least at the Greene's table. I know I never sampled a morsel until well after World War II. But I have made up for that defection. Not a week goes by that a plateful does not appear as an accompaniment at dinner or find itself sliced into translucent rounds and tossed into a luncheon salad bowl.

What to Look For

In the kitchen, the aim is to cook zucchini quickly. In the garden, to pick it early!

There is really no trick to the latter doctrine. Merely start late. I never put out a seed until the weather is truly temperate, in early June. Starting late means zucchini before you know it—but one must remember to keep the seedlings moist (not sodden) until the first green leaves form. For me that usually occurs by the Fourth of July. I celebrate Independence Day in the garden battling mildew, sunstroke (mine, not the zucchini's), and slugs. I deflect the last-named enemy with Maginot Lines rather than pesticides, building deep trenches between the plants to outmaneuver and outflank the snails. It usually works too, though I must confess it makes it hard to weed my garden.

Like a slug I can never resist a tender green squashling. The hardest part of growing zucchini is the appetite one develops waiting for each green sprout to mature to the required four inches in length so one can pick it with good conscience.

Zucchini squash is best when picked young. Look for light green or yellow-flecked vegetables that are slightly pliable to the hand. The fingernail test is always a sign of fresh produce; the scrapings will be bright green.

I have always maintained that the paler a zucchini is in color, the sweeter it will be on the tongue. However, Burpee and friends have recently come up with a rash of absolutely shocking zucchini hues ranging from bright gold to gray, blue-black, and white; and each one I have sampled is, if anything, sweeter than the last. All of which proves that the old maxim is right: you obviously cannot judge a squash by its cover!

Keep zucchini in a loose plastic bag in the refrigerator for no longer than a week. A pound will yield approximately 3½ cups sliced or 4 cups grated (before salting, of course).

Like other summer squash, zucchini is low in calories (a mere 29) and high in water (95.5 grams), potassium (296 milligrams), and vitamin A (a rousing 820 units) in a cooked cupful.

Preparation

Zucchini (like most other summer squash) needs little basic preparation. I never peel this vegetable. But then, I am addicted to young, tender, small-size squash in general and will sift through a pile at the greengrocer's for a half hour to come up with ones that are no thicker around than a good cigar. Larger, older zucchini are sometimes tough-skinned; they will need to have the skin and seeds removed. It is not hard to seed a zucchini. Merely halve the squash lengthwise and scoop out all the seeds with a small spoon, working in one direction. I rarely salt zucchini after it is cut, unless of course it has been grated. Zucchini has a particularly high water content, so salting and draining it will dissipate the excessive juices and permit faster, more even cooking. Unless I am using a special recipe, I almost always prepare zucchini in the simplest way: sautéing or braising it over moderate heat with just a dab of butter and a sprinkling of shallots and/or herbs for flavor. I prefer zucchini on the crisp (almost underdone) side, for I relish its bite.

TURKISH GOZLEME

(Sautéed Zucchini Cakes)

A Mideastern croquette, this will do wonders for a bland main course or an uninspired hors d'oeuvre tray. Make them in advance—keep 'em hot and keep 'em coming, like potato chips. Only better!

½ pound zucchini, trimmed, grated (about 2 cups)
Salt
1 teaspoon chopped canned jalapeño peppers
1 small shallot, minced
1 large clove garlic, minced
½ teaspoon curry powder
2 tablespoons olive oil
½ teaspoon baking powder
⅔ cup stone-ground whole-wheat flour
3 tablespoons vegetable oil

1. Place the zucchini in a colander and lightly sprinkle with salt. Let stand 20 minutes. Gently press the zucchini with your hands to remove the excess liquid.

2. Place the zucchini in a large bowl. Add the peppers, shallot, garlic, curry, olive oil, and salt to taste. Mix well. Stir in the baking powder and flour.

3. With floured hands, form the zucchini mixture into sixteen small rounds. Flatten them slightly.

4. Heat the vegetable oil in a 12-inch skillet over medium heat. Add the zucchini cakes and sauté until golden on the bottom, about 1 minute. Turn over and sauté 30 seconds. Reduce the heat to medium-low. Continue to cook the cakes, covered, 15 minutes, turning once.

Serves 4 to 6.

CHICKEN AND ZUCCHINI SOUP

This is one dish in which the grated zucchini needs no salting, as the juices help flavor the broth.

1 large chicken (about 3½ pounds)
2 onions, unpeeled, halved
2 cloves garlic
2 whole cloves
2 large carrots, peeled, roughly chopped
2 large ribs celery, chopped
1 medium white turnip, peeled, chopped
1 large parsnip, peeled, chopped
3 sprigs parsley, plus ¼ cup chopped fresh parsley
1 slice lemon
10 peppercorns
1 teaspoon salt
3 cups Chicken Stock (see page 410)
Water
1 pound sweet Italian sausages, cut into 1-inch pieces
1 cup pasta shells
2 medium zucchini (about ⅔ pound), trimmed, grated
Salt and freshly ground black pepper

1. Place the chicken in a 6-quart pot. Add all the ingredients through the parsnip, plus the parsley sprigs, lemon slice, peppercorns, and 1 teaspoon salt. Add the chicken stock and enough water to cover the chicken by 2 inches. Heat to boiling, skimming any residue as it gathers. Reduce the heat and simmer, partially covered, 1 hour.

2. Remove the chicken from the stock and set the stock aside. Allow the chicken to cool down enough to handle, then carefully remove the meat from the bones and cut it into bite-size pieces. Cover and reserve. Return the bones and skin to the stock. Return it to the boil; reduce the heat and simmer, uncovered, 45 minutes. Strain the stock into another pot, pressing the vegetables gently with the back of a spoon to release their juices.

3. Meanwhile, sauté the sausage pieces in a lightly oiled heavy skillet until well browned, about 8 minutes. Drain on paper towels.

4. Add the sausages to the stock. Heat to boiling; reduce the heat. Simmer, uncovered, skimming any fat that rises to the surface, for 20 minutes. Add the pasta shells; cook 10 minutes longer. Add the zucchini and the reserved chicken; cook 5 minutes. Add salt and pepper to taste, and sprinkle with the chopped parsley.

Serves 6 to 8.

MINGLE MANGLE

(Warm Zucchini Salad)

The following dish is one that can do double duty, as either a warm salad or a tonic first course. The name means "a toss." This is a prime example of raw zucchini in its finest and un-gussied-up guise. The squash is merely sliced thin, then tossed into a panful of reduced herbed and seasoned cream.

1 tablespoon unsalted butter
2 shallots, minced
2/3 cup heavy or whipping cream
1/4 cup plus 1 tablespoon chopped fresh basil
1 teaspoon lemon juice
1 teaspoon red wine vinegar
1/4 teaspoon hot pepper sauce
Salt and freshly ground black pepper
3/4 pound zucchini, trimmed, cut into 1/8-inch-thick rounds
2 medium ripe tomatoes, peeled, seeded, cubed

1. Melt the butter in a large heavy skillet over medium heat. Add the shallots; cook 1 minute. Add the cream and 1/4 cup basil. Heat to boiling; reduce the heat. Simmer, stirring occasionally, until thick, about 10 minutes.

2. Add the lemon juice, vinegar, hot pepper sauce, and salt and pepper to taste. Stir in the zucchini and toss it until well coated. Add the tomatoes; toss lightly. Sprinkle with the remaining 1 tablespoon basil. Serve immediately.

Serves 4 to 6.

ZUCCHINI AND LEMON SALAD

If you are searching for health food, have the next formula with my blessing. It comes from Italy, where it was originally dubbed a *salsa.* But it's a salad to me. Happily it's not only good for what ails you—it tastes good too!

3 tablespoons unsalted butter
1 tablespoon olive oil
3 medium zucchini (about 1 pound), trimmed, sliced thin
1 red bell pepper, seeded, cut into thin strips
1 small onion, halved, sliced thin
1 clove garlic, minced
1 large tomato, peeled, seeded, cut into thin wedges
Pinch of oregano
¼ cup chopped fresh parsley
1 small lemon, peeled, seeds removed, cut into paper-thin slices
1 tablespoon red wine vinegar
Salt and freshly ground black pepper

1. Melt 1 tablespoon of the butter in the oil in a large heavy skillet over medium heat. Add the zucchini; cook, tossing constantly, until just wilted, about 3 minutes. Transfer to a large bowl.

2. Add 1 tablespoon butter to the skillet. Add the red pepper. Cook over medium-low heat until almost tender, about 5 minutes. Add this to the zucchini.

3. Add the remaining 1 tablespoon butter to the skillet. Add the onion; cook over medium-low heat for 1 minute. Add the garlic; cook 5 minutes. Add this to the zucchini mixture.

4. Toss the tomato with the oregano in the skillet over medium-high heat for 1 minute. Add this to the zucchini mixture along with the parsley, sliced lemon, and vinegar. Let stand, covered, 1 hour. Add salt and pepper to taste before serving.

Serves 4.

ZUCCHINI FROMAGE

For me the classic zucchini prescription is the one that is simplest to whip together. The following recipe is a prime example: the squash is cooked in three minutes, tossed with two cheeses and amended with a third, and then broiled.

2 tablespoons unsalted butter
2 shallots, minced
3 medium zucchini (about 1 pound), trimmed, cut into ⅛-inch-thick rounds
2 tablespoons chopped fresh basil, or 2 teaspoons dried
½ teaspoon salt
¼ teaspoon freshly ground black pepper
¼ cup freshly grated Parmesan cheese
¼ cup freshly grated Romano cheese
¼ cup grated Doux de Montagne or Gruyère cheese

1. Preheat the broiling unit. Melt the butter in a 9- to 10-inch cast-iron skillet over medium-low heat. Add the shallots; cook 3 minutes. Raise the heat to medium-high. Add the zucchini; cook, tossing constantly, until just barely soft, about 3 minutes. Toss in the basil, and add the salt and pepper.

2. Stir the Parmesan and Romano cheeses into the zucchini. Sprinkle the Doux de Montagne or Gruyère over the top. Place the skillet under the broiler to lightly brown the top.

Serves 4.

Zucchini is consumed under various aliases in other parts of the globe. The French know it as *courgette*, while the English dub it *baby marrow*. The Spanish, who mix it into stews and soups, call it *calabacin*. Italians, who named it *zucchino* in the first place now perversely tag it *zucchine*, but they still enjoy its bounty with ardor just the same.

TOUSLED ZUCCHINI

Tousled zucchini may appear to be the latest coiffure out of Paris, but it's not. It's merely the best vegetable custard in my neighborhood! Yours too, if you have a mite of initiative. Look for small zucchini, please!

¼ cup olive oil
2 tablespoons unsalted butter
1 medium onion, chopped
2 cloves garlic, minced
2 small zucchini (about ½ pound), trimmed, sliced thin
1 small tomato, peeled, seeded, chopped
2 tablespoons chopped fresh parsley
2 tablespoons chopped fresh basil, or 2 teaspoons dried
1 teaspoon chopped fresh tarragon, or ¼ teaspoon dried
1 tablespoon red wine vinegar
Salt and freshly ground black pepper
4 eggs
¼ cup heavy or whipping cream
¼ cup grated Gruyère or Monterey jack cheese
2 tablespoons freshly grated Parmesan cheese

1. Preheat the oven to 350°F. Heat the oil and butter in a large skillet over medium heat. Add the onion; cook 1 minute. Add the garlic; cook 2 minutes. Stir in the zucchini, tomato, parsley, basil, tarragon, and vinegar. Reduce the heat to low; cook 4 minutes. Add salt and pepper to taste.

2. Transfer the zucchini mixture into a buttered 10-inch glass or ceramic quiche dish.

3. Beat the eggs with the cream in a medium bowl. Pour this over the zucchini and sprinkle with the cheeses. Bake until golden, about 25 minutes. Let stand 10 minutes before serving.

Serves 6.

ZUCCHINI PICKLES

There is obviously something for every food lover in the world. Apple aficionados gather in Kent, Michigan, every summer; garlic gobblers congregate in Gilroy, California. Zucchini zealots travel to Harrisville, New Hampshire, where the annual zucchini festival is held. In the shadow of the White Mountains, a mountain of zucchini is converted into breads, cakes, pancakes, jams, and even ice cream on occasion. But zucchini comestibles are not the only residual of this squash bacchanal: zucchinis large and small are also carved and molded into towering works of art. Speaking for myself (an acknowledged zucchini buff), I'd just as soon pass up the cultural achievements for the grub—such as the blue-ribbon zucchini pickle that follows. It's a winner!

4 medium zucchini (about 1½ pounds), trimmed, sliced thin
2 small yellow onions, halved, sliced thin
3 tablespoons salt
Cold water
2 cups distilled white vinegar
1 cup sugar
1 teaspoon celery seeds
1 teaspoon anise seeds
2 teaspoons dry mustard

1. Place the zucchini and onions in a medium bowl. Sprinkle with the salt. Cover with cold water; let stand 1 hour.

2. Combine the vinegar, sugar, celery seeds, anise seeds, and mustard in a medium saucepan. Heat to boiling; remove from the heat.

3. Drain the zucchini and onions. Place them in a large pot and pour the hot liquid over. Let stand 1 hour.

4. Heat the mixture to boiling; simmer 3 minutes. Remove from the heat and place in sterilized jars.

Makes 3 pints.

ZUCCHINI HOECAKE

Not truly a hoecake at all, it was named thusly by a gardening pal of mine who lives in Amagansett. This fellow claims that he drops his hoe the moment he detects that this dish will be on the supper table.

1 pound zucchini, trimmed, coarsely grated
Salt
6 tablespoons (¾ stick) unsalted butter
1 small onion, minced
1 teaspoon chopped fresh basil, or ½ teaspoon dried
2 tablespoons chopped fresh parsley
Pinch of ground cloves
⅛ teaspoon freshly grated nutmeg
2½ cups light cream or half-and-half
1 tablespoon sugar
1 tablespoon honey
1 cup white cornmeal
4 egg yolks
1 teaspoon baking powder
Pinch of ground white pepper
5 egg whites

1. Place the zucchini in a colander and lightly sprinkle with salt. Let stand 20 minutes. Gently press the zucchini with your hands to remove the excess liquid.

2. Preheat the oven to 375°F. Melt 2 tablespoons of the butter in a heavy skillet over medium heat. Add the onion, zucchini, basil, parsley, cloves, and nutmeg. Stir well. Cook, covered, 5 minutes. Then remove the cover and cook, tossing constantly, until the mixture is dry, about 4 minutes. Remove from the heat.

3. Combine the cream, the remaining 4 tablespoons butter, the sugar, honey, and ¼ teaspoon salt in a medium saucepan over low heat. Cook, stirring constantly, until the butter melts. Stir in the cornmeal. Cook, still stirring constantly, until thick, about 5 minutes. Do not allow to boil.

4. Transfer the cornmeal mixture to a large bowl. Beat in the egg yolks, one at a time, beating thoroughly after each addition. Stir in the baking powder and white pepper. Stir in the zucchini mixture.

5. Beat the egg whites until stiff but not dry. Fold them into the mixture and pour it into a buttered 2-quart soufflé dish or casserole. Bake until puffed and golden, 30 to 35 minutes.

Serves 6 to 8.

According to the diaries of early American settlers, zucchini was believed to anesthetize the pain of childbirth, toothache, and chilblains, not necessarily in that order. The sufferer merely chewed on the squash, it seems, and got better. If that seems bizarre, consider the next prescription from Jamestown, Virginia. Colonists there believed that this squash, when boiled and made into a hot paste, would cure the sting of runny eyes. And Indians in the Southwest had the idea (because the zucchini was similar in shape, one presumes) that eating enough squash would cure the deadly sting of snakebite. None of the reports of these "cures" come with a tally of results, which is just as well for us *and* the zucchini!

ELEANOR TOBIN'S MOTHER'S ZUCCHINI MUFFIN GEMS

The recipe for Eleanor Tobin's Mother's Zucchini Muffin Gems (and they are, they are) was passed on to me by my friend Jody Gillis, who is the director of the Something More Cooking School in La Mesa, California. Jody gave me the prescription with this note in the margin: "These are just superb! I was going to be selfish for fear Eleanor Tobin's mother's recipe would end up in the book and my recipes wouldn't, but they're just too great to hold back!"

Jody is right. Make a batch and salute Eleanor Tobin and her mother as well!

½ cup sugar
1 large egg, lightly beaten
¼ cup vegetable oil
¾ cup all-purpose flour
¼ teaspoon baking powder
¼ teaspoon baking soda
¼ teaspoon salt
¼ teaspoon freshly grated nutmeg
1 cup grated zucchini (about ¼ pound)
¼ cup raisins, finely chopped
¼ cup chopped pecans

1. Preheat the oven to 350°F. Combine the sugar, egg, and oil in a large bowl. Mix well.

2. Sift the flour with the baking powder, baking soda, salt, and nutmeg in a medium bowl. Stir this into the sugar-egg mixture.

3. Add the zucchini, raisins, and pecans, and stir only until mixed. Do not overwork. Spoon the batter into a well-buttered muffin tin, filling each cup about two-thirds full. Bake until the muffins are golden brown and a toothpick inserted in the center comes out clean, about 25 minutes. Run a knife around the edges to loosen.

Makes 9 muffins.

CRISPY FRIED ZUCCHINI AND SQUASH BLOSSOMS FILLED WITH GOAT CHEESE

I am not one of those cooks who nibble on rose petals or violets in the privacy of my kitchen. And "Please don't eat the daisies!" is an injunction that I have managed to live with for years. However, I must confess, zucchini blossoms turn me on! In fact, they are the staples of the tastiest dish I have ever eaten—fresh-picked flowers are crammed with goat cheese and dipped in frothy batter before they hit the pan.

Now, before you start imagining that one must have a small plantation in order to assuage this floral addiction, think again! Fine greengrocers (and farmer's markets) carry a huge supply of these aureate blooms from June through September in my neighborhood. Ask in yours—or if worst comes to worst, invest in a packet of zucchini seed. As I told you before, the plants grow fast!

2 eggs, separated
¼ cup dry white wine
½ cup cold water
1½ tablespoons olive oil
1 cup all-purpose flour
½ teaspoon salt
⅛ teaspoon ground mace
Dash of hot pepper sauce
24 squash blossoms (zucchini, pumpkin, or Hubbard), each about 3½ to 4 inches in length
4 ounces mild goat cheese (chèvre), cut into ¼-inch-thick strips, 2½ inches long
Oil for frying
1 large zucchini (about ½ pound), trimmed, cut into ½-inch-thick strips, about 2 inches long
Salt and freshly ground black pepper

1. Beat the egg yolks in a large bowl until light. Beat in the wine, water, and olive oil. Slowly beat in the flour. Add the ½ teaspoon salt, the mace, and the hot pepper sauce. Let stand, covered, at room temperature for 2 hours.

2. With a sharp knife, remove the long stems from the blossoms. Remove any green from around the blossoms. Using your fingers, open each blossom at one side. Place a piece of goat cheese inside and press the edges together. Refrigerate until ready to use.

3. Beat the egg whites until stiff but not dry. Fold them into the batter.

4. Heat 2 inches of oil in a medium saucepan until hot but not smoking.

5. Dip the zucchini strips into the batter and deep-fry in the oil until golden, about 2 or 3 minutes. Drain on paper towels. Keep warm in a low oven.

6. Dip the cheese-filled squash blossoms into the batter and deep-fry them until golden, about 2 minutes. Serve the zucchini and the blossoms together, sprinkled with salt and pepper to taste.

Serves 6.

CHICKEN-STUFFED ZUCCHINI

Although the American-born zucchini has been in common currency in markets for over thirty years, it is still not a very popular vegetable in its native land. In most Mediterranean households, however, it is a thrice-weekly staple; and when stuffed with a bit of ground meat or cheese and baked, it often replaces far costlier cuts of meat at the dinner table.

A totally Americanized version of such a stuffed zucchini follows. It is included here not for economy's sake but because it is simply one of the best vegetable dishes I have ever tasted. The zucchini is crammed with velvety creamed-chicken hash, flecked with nubbins of smoky ham and a dusting of redolent Parmesan cheese. Best of all, it may be prepared early in the day and baked later, perhaps between rounds of drinks. Add the sauce, brown the zucchini under the broiler, and voilà, a great meal in minutes.

2 large zucchini (about 1 pound), trimmed
2 tablespoons plus 2 teaspoons unsalted butter
1 shallot, minced
2 tablespoons plus 2 teaspoons all-purpose flour
1 cup Chicken Stock (see page 410)
1 tablespoon sherry
1 ¼ cups diced cooked chicken
¼ pound chopped smoked ham (about ½ cup)
Salt and freshly ground black pepper
½ cup heavy or whipping cream
1 egg yolk, lightly beaten
1 tablespoon freshly grated Parmesan cheese

1. Cut the zucchini in half lengthwise. Cook, covered, in boiling salted water until tender, about 5 minutes. Rinse under cold running water; drain.

2. Carefully scoop out the center of each zucchini half. Set the shells aside. Squeeze the pulp with your hands to extract the excess liquid. Chop it fine.

3. Preheat the oven to 300°F. Melt the 2 tablespoons butter in a large heavy skillet over medium-low heat. Stir in the shallot; cook 2 minutes. Stir in the 2 tablespoons flour. Cook, stirring constantly, 2 minutes. Whisk in the stock. Cook over medium heat until thick, about 4 minutes. Stir in the sherry, chopped zucchini, chicken, and ham. Add salt and pepper to taste. Spoon the mixture into the zucchini shells. Place them in a shallow baking dish; bake 15 minutes.

4. Meanwhile, melt the remaining 2 teaspoons butter in a small saucepan over medium-low heat. Stir in the remaining 2 teaspoons flour. Cook, stirring constantly, 2 minutes. Whisk in the cream. Remove from the heat and whisk in the egg yolk. Stir in the cheese, and spoon the mixture over the zucchini. Place the dish under the broiler until the tops are lightly browned.

Serves 2 to 4.

ZUCCHINI PANCAKES

One of the fatal mistakes of almost all untried gardeners is to plant too much zucchini in the spring and then neglect to harvest it—until the gourds are literally over the hill.

Every midsummer, when I write in my newspaper column about the joys of picking tiny baby-finger-size zucchini, I am inevitably bombarded with letters from readers, all demanding advice about what to do with the green torpedoes they have uncovered in the vegetable patch. The answers do not come easily. Aside from doorstops or ballast in an uneven keel, there's not a heck of a lot one can do with an overgrown zucchini. However, if you can manage to stem the growth before it passes the twelve-inch mark, consider these pancakes made of grated, salted zucchini—they will cover up a multitude of gardening sins as a nifty brunch dish or last-minute supper number.

¾ pound zucchini, trimmed, grated (about 3 cups)
Salt
1 egg, lightly beaten
¼ cup milk
¼ cup freshly grated Parmesan cheese
¼ teaspoon hot pepper sauce, or to taste
Freshly ground black pepper
½ cup all-purpose flour
1½ teaspoons baking powder

1. Place the zucchini in a colander and lightly sprinkle with salt. Let stand 20 minutes. Gently press the zucchini with your hands to remove the excess liquid.

2. Combine the zucchini with the egg, milk, cheese, and hot pepper sauce in a large bowl. Add salt and pepper to taste.

3. Sift the flour with the baking powder and stir this into the zucchini mixture. Mix well.

4. Heat a lightly greased cast-iron skillet or griddle over medium heat until hot but not smoking. Cook the pancakes, a few at a time, using about 3 tablespoons batter per pancake. When lightly browned, about 3 minutes, turn over and cook the other side for 1 minute. Transfer to a serving platter and keep warm in a low oven while cooking the remaining pancakes. Serve with plenty of butter.

Serves 4 as a side dish; 2 or 3 as an entrée.

ZUCCHINI POUND CAKE

The last zucchini devise I have up my sleeve is a pound cake (green—studded with zucchini, naturally), and it's the last bequest I can pass on. Bake it with green and Greene joy!

1 cup grated zucchini (about ¼ pound)
2 cups plus 1 tablespoon all-purpose flour
1 cup (2 sticks) unsalted butter, softened
1⅔ cups sugar
1 tablespoon vanilla extract
2 tablespoons orange liqueur
2 teaspoons finely grated orange peel
5 eggs, separated

1. Preheat the oven to 350°F. Toss the zucchini with the 1 tablespoon flour in a bowl. Set aside.

2. Beat the butter with the sugar in the large bowl of an electric mixer until light and fluffy. Beat in the vanilla, orange liqueur, and orange peel. Add the egg yolks, one at a time, beating thoroughly after each addition. Stir in the zucchini.

3. Beat the egg whites until stiff but not dry.

4. Fold the 2 cups flour into the batter in three batches, alternating with batches of the egg white. Pour the mixture into a buttered and floured 9-inch tube pan. Bake until a toothpick inserted in the center comes out clean, about 1 hour. Cool on a rack for 10 minutes before unmolding.

Serves 8 to 10.

An old English cure for warts instructs the afflicted person to touch each blemish with the cut end of a zucchini by the light of a full moon, then to bury the squash in a field that faces north. Reputedly the warts will disappear before the squash decomposes. A gardening friend, who knows nothing whatsoever of witchcraft but dotes on zucchini, adds a coda: if the time of year is late spring, she claims, the buried zucchini will yield a plant or two within the month! So even if the warts remain, the magic cannot be considered a total loss.

KITCHEN BASICS

MAYONNAISE

Mayonnaise is a culinary adjunct that many good cooks skip, out of fear of failure and the notion that it will be time-consuming. Mayonnaise will never fail *if* all the ingredients at hand, plus the bowl and whip (or blender jar or processor bowl), are at room temperature before you begin. If the eggs have been refrigerated, place them in warm (not boiling) water for five minutes prior to whisking. I must confess that I make mayonnaise the prehistoric way—using only my right arm, an earthenware bowl, and a wire whisk—and it takes less than five minutes from start to finish. One word of advice: taste the mixture as it thickens. If it is too bland, add white pepper or more lemon juice. If it is too spicy, whip in more oil. A jot of boiling water stabilizes homemade mayonnaise. Store it in a clean bowl or sterilized jar. Mayonnaise keeps for several days in a cold refrigerator.

2 egg yolks
2 teaspoons white wine vinegar
Juice of ½ lemon
½ teaspoon salt
Pinch of ground white pepper
½ teaspoon Dijon mustard
1 cup vegetable oil combined with ½ cup olive oil
Dash of hot pepper sauce
1 tablespoon boiling water

1. Whisk the egg yolks in a large bowl until light. Slowly whisk in the vinegar, lemon juice, salt, white pepper, and mustard.

2. Beat in the oil, a few drops at a time, until ½ cup has been incorporated. (The mayonnaise should be very thick at this point.) Continue to beat in the oil, 2 tablespoons at a time. Season with hot pepper sauce and, if you like, more salt or lemon juice. Thin with the boiling water.

3. Store, tightly covered, in the refrigerator. Mayonnaise will keep five to six days in the refrigerator, but bring it to room temperature before using.

Makes about 1½ cups, enough for 4 servings.

Variations

Green Mayonnaise: Add ½ cup chopped fresh herbs (mixed or individual)—such as dill, parsley, tarragon, and chives—to 1½ cups mayonnaise.

Curry Mayonnaise: Add 2 tablespoons curry powder, 1 teaspoon turmeric, and 1 tablespoon white wine vinegar to 1½ cups mayonnaise. Stir in 2 teaspoons capers.

Tomato Mayonnaise: Peel, seed, and chop 1 large tomato. Place it in a saucepan with 1 teaspoon chopped fresh basil, ¼ teaspoon sugar, and ¼ cup chicken stock, and cook over medium heat until very, very thick. Cool, and combine with 2 tablespoons sour cream and 1 cup mayonnaise.

FAIL-SAFE HOLLANDAISE

This recipe came to me a while back from a whiz of a cook named Ginnie Ward. The trick that makes the elegant golden sauce fail-safe is the increment of frozen butter, added bit by bit as the eggs and lemon juice homogenize. Hollandaise will keep in a double boiler half filled with warm (not boiling) water for about half an hour prior to serving.

3 egg yolks
Juice of ½ lemon
½ teaspoon Dijon mustard
¾ cup unsalted butter, frozen
Dash of hot pepper sauce
Pinch of ground white pepper
Salt

1. Beat the egg yolks with the lemon juice in the top of a double boiler. Place over simmering water; stir in the mustard.

2. Cut the butter into eight pieces. Using a small wire whisk, beat the butter into the egg yolk mixture, one piece at a time. Stir well after each addition. Stir in the hot pepper sauce, white pepper, and salt to taste.

Makes about 1½ cups.

Variations

Anchovy Hollandaise: Add ½ teaspoon anchovy paste to the egg yolks.

Rosy Hollandaise: Add 1 teaspoon tomato paste to the egg yolks, and omit the mustard.

Sauce Maltese: Add 1 tablespoon orange juice and ½ teaspoon finely grated orange peel to the egg yolks, and omit the lemon juice.

BEEF STOCK

4 pounds raw beef bones, including some meat
3 large onions, peeled, chopped
4 carrots, peeled, roughly chopped
4 ribs celery with leaves, chopped
2 cloves garlic
6 parsley sprigs
1 bay leaf
4 whole cloves
10 whole black peppercorns
2 teaspoons salt, or to taste
3 quarts plus 2 cups water
2 tablespoons red wine vinegar

1. Preheat the oven to 475°F. Place the bones in a large roasting pan, and bake them until brown, 15 minutes. Turn the bones over and reduce the temperature to 450°F. Continue to bake, another 15 minutes, until the second side is browned as well. This step will give color to the stock.

2. Meanwhile, combine the remaining ingredients except the 2 cups water and the vinegar in a large heavy pot. Heat to boiling; reduce the heat.

3. Add the browned meat bones to the stock. Pour off the grease in the roasting pan and stir in the 2 cups water, scraping the bottom and sides of the pan with a wooden spoon. Add this liquid to the stock. Heat stock to boiling again; reduce the heat to low. Simmer, partially covered, skimming the surface occasionally, for 3 hours. Stir in the vinegar, and continue to simmer, partially covered, until reduced to about 1½ quarts, about 2 hours longer. Strain.

Makes 1½ quarts.

FISH STOCK

2½ to 3 pounds fish bones, including heads
4 cups water
2 cups dry white wine
3 cups clam juice
2 onions, chopped
2 ribs celery with leaves, chopped
6 sprigs parsley
1 bay leaf
4 whole cloves
10 peppercorns
1 teaspoon salt
1 lemon, halved

Combine all the ingredients in a large pot. Heat to boiling; reduce the heat to medium-low. Simmer, partially covered, until reduced to about 6 cups. Strain.

Makes 1½ quarts.

CHICKEN STOCK

4 pounds chicken pieces (backs, necks, wings)
4 quarts water, approximately
2 yellow onions, unpeeled
1 leek, cleaned, chopped
2 cloves garlic
2 carrots, peeled, roughly chopped
2 ribs celery with leaves, chopped
2 turnips, peeled, roughly chopped
2 parsnips, peeled, roughly chopped
8 sprigs parsley
4 whole cloves
10 peppercorns
1 teaspoon salt, or to taste
1 small bay leaf
1 teaspoon chopped fresh thyme, or ½ teaspoon dried
2 tablespoons red wine vinegar

1. Place the chicken pieces in a large pot and add the water. The chicken should be totally covered, so add more water if necessary. Heat to boiling; boil 5 minutes, skimming the surface as the scum rises to the top.

2. Add the remaining ingredients with enough water to cover the chicken by 3 inches (about 4 quarts altogether). Return to boiling; reduce the heat to low. Simmer, partially covered, skimming the surface occasionally, until the stock is reduced to 1½ quarts, about 3 hours. Strain.

Makes 1½ quarts.

VEGETABLE STOCK

In a pinch, the following vegetable stock will do in place of chicken or beef stock in any recipe where it is used to add savor to a vegetable as it is braised. Its devise is included for those whose dietary strictures prohibit the use of meat and poultry, but nonvegetarians as well will enjoy the remarkable savor vegetable stock adds to a dish.

4 tablespoons (½ stick) unsalted butter
5 onions, chopped
2 cloves garlic
4 ribs celery with leaves, chopped
4 carrots, peeled, roughly chopped
2 leeks, cleaned, chopped
½ ounce dried mushrooms
1 bunch parsley
1 teaspoon chopped fresh thyme, or ½ teaspoon dried
1 sage leaf, or a pinch of dried, crumbled
1 bay leaf
1½ teaspoons salt
10 peppercorns, lightly crushed
10 allspice berries, lightly crushed
Pinch of freshly grated nutmeg
4 quarts water
½ teaspoon crushed dried hot red pepper
1 tablespoon red wine vinegar

Melt the butter in a large heavy pot over medium heat. Stir in the onions; cook 5 minutes. Add the remaining ingredients through the water. Heat to boiling; reduce the heat to low. Simmer, partially covered, until reduced to about 2½ quarts, about 2 hours. Add the hot pepper and vinegar. Simmer, uncovered, 30 minutes longer. Strain, gently pressing the liquid out of the vegetables with the back of a spoon.

Makes 1½ to 2 quarts.

The secret to a rich, flavorsome stock is always fresh ingredients plus a long tenure of stove time, for the taste of really good stock depends upon prolonged cooking. A general rule of thumb is to expect only half the amount of liquid you originally begin with, as the reduction gives the stock its richness. A trick I sometimes indulge in when time is short is to add half canned broth (beef, chicken, or clam juice, as the case may be) instead of all water. If you "beef up" your stock with a canned product, however, here's a cavil: make sure to appreciably reduce the amount of salt called for in the recipe, for all canned broths are sodium-high!

All of these stocks keep for three weeks when stored in the refrigerator, tightly covered. If you wish to keep the stock longer, it is best to reboil it and allow it to cool before returning it to the refrigerator. Freezing stock will keep it usable for at least six months.

HOT STEAMED RICE

The trick to the following steamed rice is its ease. It may be prepared in under a half hour's time, but then it can be kept (steaming) over minimal heat for several hours—with every grain still separate and intact whenever the rice is eventually served. A rule of thumb worth filing away is that rice triples as it cooks. One-third cup raw rice will produce one cup cooked rice—and so on.

1⅓ cups uncooked long-grain rice
4 quarts boiling salted water

1. Add the rice to the boiling water. Stir once with a wooden spoon so that the rice does not stick to the bottom of the pot. When the water returns to boiling, reduce the heat. Simmer, uncovered, until just tender, 12 to 15 minutes. Drain in a colander.

2. Place the colander over 2 inches of boiling water in another pot. Do not let the bottom of the colander touch the water. Cover the rice with a single layer of paper towels. Steam for at least 15 minutes. Rice can be held this way for several hours without harm.

Makes four 1-cup servings.

SHORT CRUST PASTRY

1 cup all-purpose flour
¼ teaspoon salt
4 tablespoons (½ stick) unsalted butter, chilled
1½ tablespoons vegetable shortening, chilled
2½ to 3 tablespoons cold water

Sift the flour with the salt in a large bowl. Cut in the butter and shortening with a pastry blender until the mixture has the texture of coarse crumbs. Add just enough water to form a soft dough. Wrap, and chill for 1 hour before using.

Makes enough for one 9- to 10-inch single-crust pie.

ORANGE CRUST PASTRY

1¼ cups all-purpose flour
¼ teaspoon salt
4 tablespoons (½ stick) unsalted butter, chilled
¼ cup vegetable shortening, chilled
½ teaspoon finely grated orange peel
2 tablespoons orange juice, approximately

1. Sift the flour with the salt in a large bowl. Cut in the butter, shortening, and orange peel with a knife. Blend the mixture with a pastry blender until it has the texture of coarse crumbs.

2. Using a fork or a knife, cut in enough orange juice to make a soft dough. Do not overwork. Refrigerate for 1 hour before using.

Makes enough for one 9- to 10-inch single crust pie.

These are two of my favorite recipes for pie and tart shells. The short crust is appropriate to all non-sweet fillings, while the orange-flavored pastry lends a delicate savor to dulcet concoctions. There is also an excellently crumbly lard-and-vinegar pastry (on page 166) that will do admirably in either instance.

NOTES ON INGREDIENTS

Broth and Bouillon

Stock is the secret to most good cooking. However, when I do not have homemade on hand, I often make do with canned broth—usually Progresso or College Inn. When a recipe requires strong broth, I double the amount called for and boil it down to half before proceeding with the recipe. On occasion I use bouillon cubes or powder. For powder, G. Washington brand is easy to find. Knorr-Swiss bouillon cubes, made in Switzerland, are now available in supermarkets around the country; they are made of real beef and real chicken. Brand-new to the retail market are Minor's Bases (beef, chicken, clam, lobster, mushroom, etc.), which until recently were sold only to restaurants. This high-quality product is available by mail order only. Write to *BY 2 Foodservice*, P.O. Box 34707, Los Angeles, CA 90034 for further information. Be advised that all these packaged bases and broths contain some MSG.

Cheese

BLEU: Some of the finest bleu cheese in the world is made right here in the U.S., by Maytag Dairy Farms. Available in two-pound wheels from *Maytag Dairy Farms*, R. R. 1, Box 806, Newton, IA 50208.

GOAT: Many kinds of imported goat cheeses are available from *Say Cheese*, 856 Cole Street, San Francisco, CA 94117; *Balducci's*, 424 Avenue of the Americas, New York, NY 10011; *Chalet Wine & Cheese*, 405 Armitage Street, Chicago, IL 60614; and from many other shops around the country. American-made Laura Çhenel's chèvre, largely responsible for the boom in American goat cheese, can be mail-ordered from *Say Cheese* or from the *Ideal Cheese Shop*, 1205 Second Ave., New York, NY 10021. One of my favorite cheeses comes from Interlaken in New York's wine-growing district. Though the Goat Folks cheese is available only in the Northeast, it can be ordered from *Balducci's* or from *Goat Folks Farm*, Tunison Road, Interlaken, NY 14847.

PARMESAN: Nothing can top Parmigiano-Reggiano, the Italian wonder of cheeses. Expensive as it is, it is worth seeking out and is available at most of the above-mentioned cheese stores. However, I often make do with Stella brand Parmesan, distributed by Universal Foods, without irreparable harm to the dish I am preparing. One might also consider the dry Jack being made by the Vella Cheese Company in Sonoma, California. Very much like Parmesan in taste and texture, Vella dry Jack is rated as one of America's great cheeses. Available from *Vella Cheese Company*, P.O. Box 191, Sonoma, CA 95476.

Chiles

The chili powder one finds on the supermarket shelf just cannot compare to the fresh and ground chiles sold at Spanish markets around the country. The assortment is tremendous. One I favor is the red Colorado variety, which is mild but still intensely flavorful. A poblano chile, while not particularly hot, gives a corncake an indispensable bite. However, when fresh chiles are not available, use a bell pepper for texture and make up the tang with a pinch or two of cayenne or Tabasco sauce. For canned chiles such as jalapeños, and "salsas," I find that Herdez and Ortega brands are generally available around the country. Four Spanish stores that will fill mail orders are: *Casa Moneo,* 210 West 14th Street, New York, NY 10011; *Casa Esteiro,* 2719 West Division, Chicago, IL 60622; *El Mercado,* First Avenue and Lorenzo, Los Angeles, CA 90063; and *Mexican Kitchen,* Box 213, Brownsville, TX 78520.

Chorizos

Spanish sausages, hot or mild, are available at most Spanish markets around the country. See Chiles for mail-order sources.

Cornmeal

Harina de maíz (finely ground cornmeal) is available from the aforementioned Hispanic grocers. I notice that Quaker Oats also markets *harina de maíz* in supermarkets these days. In a pinch, however, one can make do with any available cornmeal. Just grind it in a food processor or blender until it is fine. The extra milling makes for a lighter, smoother result in the pan.

Cream, Heavy or Whipping

Cream marketed in the East is most often sold under the cognomen of "heavy" cream and has a slightly higher milk fat content (36 percent minimum) than much of the "whipping" cream (30 to 36 percent) found elsewhere in the country. For a longer shelf life almost all supermarket varieties are ultra-pasteurized these days. The recipes in this book will work with either. If you are lucky enough to have an "old-fashioned" dairy nearby, make the effort to get your cream there. Cream so thick it literally doesn't pour (40 percent milk fat and up) is hard to come by in the 1980s, but the American Dairy Association assures me that if enough consumers make a true demand, it *can* be brought back.

Filé Powder

I have seen this seasoning—dried crushed sassafras, used in Cajun cookery—almost everywhere of late. If you can not find it locally, filé powder may be ordered from *Veron's Quality Meats,* 4303 Johnston St., Lafayette, LA 70503.

Flour

Most often I use Hecker's unbleached all-purpose flour, found in the Northeast, and in other areas where I teach I use what is generally available. With success, I might add. If you are particular about the flour you use, try White Lily Flour, an exceptional soft wheat flour from *White Lily Flour Company,* Box 871, Knoxville, TN 37901. Pillsbury bread flour makes a very admirable loaf in my kitchen, but for aficionados Great Valley Mills, one of the oldest businesses in the country (and for good reason), offers a selection of twenty different types of flour, all stone-ground: *Great Valley Mills,* Quakertown, PA 18951.

Ham

When it comes to American hams, I think that the Dubuque Fleur de Lis brand ranks among the best. I always use the smoked cooked semi-boneless ham, which usually weighs in around 10 pounds. Its distribution is very spotty, but its parent company, FDL Foods, Inc., does a limited mail-order business, especially at Christmas time: *FDL Foods, Inc.,* 16th and Sycamore, Dubuque, IA 52001. Other hams worth the effort of mail-ordering include those from *Lawrence's Smoke House,* Route 30, Newfane, VT 05345 and *Colonel Bill Newsome's Hams,* 128 N. Highland Avenue, Princeton, KY 42445.

Herbs

Fresh herbs have become a big business, and you can find almost anything you want at a local nursery. If you are searching out a hard-to-find herb plant, try *Fox Hill Farm*, 440 W. Michigan Avenue, Dept. C14, Box 7, Parma, MI 49269. I am often lucky enough to be able to keep my herbs growing year-round on my kitchen windowsill. If I lose them and am forced to use dried, I generally halve the amount of fresh herb called for and chop the dried herb in with an equal amount of fresh parsley. The parsley will take on the flavor of the dried herb, and the herb itself will taste fresher for it.

Hot Pepper Sauce

Though there are myriad brands on the market, Tabasco is my first choice.

Mayonnaise

When I do not feel like whipping up a batch of homemade, I use Hellmann's (labeled as Best Foods in most of the U.S.)

Mushrooms

Mushrooms are mushrooms until you have tasted the fresh shiitake variety. Long used in Oriental cooking and available dried, this lusty, meaty mushroom is now being grown in America and shipped fresh around the country. Mail-order from *Oakville Grocery*, 1555 Pacific Avenue, San Francisco, CA 94109 or *Balducci's* (see Cheese). Or if you prefer, you can order Golden Oak brand shiitakes via overnight Express Mail directly from the source that grows them: *Elix Corp.*, Route 1, Arvonia, VA 23004.

Mustard

I consistently use Grey Poupon Dijon mustard, made in the United States.

Oils

The Italian olive oils I use most often are Callisto Francesconi or Sasso, available at *Balducci's* (see Cheese). Olivieri olive oil and Pucci olive oil, from Tuscany, are available through *Williams-Sonoma*, P.O. Box 7456, San Francisco, CA 94120. Some very good California olive oils are available from *Sciabica & Sons*, P.O. Box 1246, Modesto, CA 95353. Kimberley California olive oil is distributed by *San Francisco Cheese Imports*, 1908 Innes Street, San Francisco, CA 94124. The vegetable oils I most often use are Wesson or Hain, a polyunsaturated variety that is largely available in health food stores. In many parts of the world, peanut oil is used for deep frying as it has the unique ability to become intensely hot without burning. I, however, use Crisco shortening. Old-fashioned perhaps, but then in my opinion, so is the art of cooking.

Onions

For a list of growers who sell the Vidalia onion by mail-order, write the *Vidalia Chamber of Commerce*, P.O. Box 306, Vidalia, GA 30474. Walla Walla onions are available from *Walla Walla Gardeners' Association*, 210 N. 11th Street, Walla Walla, WA 99362. For information on Maui onions, write *Ili Ili Farms*, P.O. Box 150-C Kula, Maui, HI 96790.

Rice

I use Carolina brand long grain (unconverted) rice, but I have used others when teaching around the country, even Uncle Ben. But never converted, or instant! Short-grain Italian Arborio rice is generally available everywhere.

Seeds

Just in case you want to grow your own vegetables, Burpee seeds, the old standby, can be ordered from *Burpee Seeds*, Warminster, PA 18991. A fairly new company that specializes in "American Heirloom" varieties, which do not lend themselves to commercial production, is Le Marché. Also available are imported seeds for radicchio, lamb's lettuce, and believe it or not, fourteen kinds of peppers including purple, yellow, and chocolate bell peppers! Write for their catalog: *Le Marché Seeds International*, P.O. Box 566, Dixon, CA 95620.

Soy Sauce

There are a lot of different varieties on the shelf, but Kikkoman is my hands-down choice.

Spices

Perhaps my favorite store in the entire country is Aphrodisia in New York. I don't know of any other shop that carries the variety of spices and dried herbs found there: *Aphrodisia Products, Inc.*, 282 Bleecker Street, New York, NY 10012. Other sources for spices include *The Complete Cook*, 405 Lake Cook Plaza, Deerfield, IL 60015; *La Cuisine*, 323 Cameron Street, Alexandria, VA 22314; and *Oakville Grocery* (see Mushrooms).

Tomatoes, Canned

The best bet is the imported Italian plum. Progresso is the brand I use most often, but San Marsano, although pricier, are highly recommended canned tomatoes.

Tomatoes, Sun-Dried

Pumate sun-dried tomatoes can be mail-ordered from *Dean & Deluca*, 121 Prince Street, New York, NY 10012 and from *Christopher Stephens Importer*, P.O. Box 114, Carversville, PA 18913.

Vinegar

I have used Dessaux Fils, imported from France, for years. Available in red wine and tarragon-flavored white wine vinegars, I am happy to see that it is now being carried in supermarkets everywhere. And no one should be without a bottle of balsamic vinegar on hand. Made only in the Modena province of Italy's Emilia-Romagna, this unique, intensely flavored wine vinegar is aged, and a little goes a long way. One of the best is Fini, carried by *Williams-Sonoma* (see Oils).

INDEX

C

T